The University
of La

2 New York Stre
Manchester
M1 4HJ

CW00660943

Lnm
(FmLy)
ScH
STo

RECEIVED

1 3 MAY 2016

The University of Law, Manchester

N08215

MARITAL AGREEMENTS AND PRIVATE AUTONOMY IN COMPARATIVE PERSPECTIVE

This book deals with a subject that has recently been the focus of debate and law reform in many jurisdictions: how much scope should spouses have to conclude agreements concerning their financial affairs—and under what circumstances should such agreements be binding and enforceable? These marital agreements include pre-nuptial, post-nuptial and separation agreements.

The book is the result of a British Academy-funded research project which investigated and compared the relevant law of England and Wales, Australia, Austria, Belgium, France, Germany, Ireland, the Netherlands, New Zealand, Scotland, Singapore, Spain, Sweden and the jurisdictions of the United States. In addition to chapters on these jurisdictions, the book includes a chapter on the 'English practitioner's view'. It also provides a comparative analysis of the different matrimonial property regimes and the rules on marital agreements that explores underlying themes and principles and makes recommendations for regulating marital agreements.

A key theme is the function and effect of marital agreements in the different jurisdictions. Thus, each chapter first explains the underlying 'default' rules for ancillary relief/matrimonial property and maintenance. It then analyses the current rules for marital agreements, and gives a brief account of the private international law rules.

The book provides a comprehensive source of reference on ancillary relief/ matrimonial property and maintenance and the rules on pre-nuptial, post-nuptial and separation agreements in 14 jurisdictions. It offers guidance for academics and practitioners dealing with international matters, and a basis for discussions on law reform.

Marital Agreements and Private Autonomy in Comparative Perspective

Edited by
Jens M Scherpe

·HART·
PUBLISHING

OXFORD AND PORTLAND, OREGON
2012

Published in the United Kingdom by Hart Publishing Ltd
16C Worcester Place, Oxford, OX1 2JW
Telephone:+44 (0)1865 517530
Fax: +44 (0)1865 510710
E-mail: mail@hartpub.co.uk
Website: http://www.hartpub.co.uk

Published in North America (US and Canada) by
Hart Publishing
c/o International Specialized Book Services
920 NE 58th Avenue, Suite 300
Portland, OR 97213-3786
USA
Tel: +1 503 287 3093 or toll-free: (1) 800 944 6190
Fax: +1 503 280 8832
E-mail: orders@isbs.com
Website: http://www.isbs.com

© The editor and contributors severally 2012

The editor and contributors have asserted their right under the Copyright, Designs and Patents Act 1988,
to be identified as the authors of this work.

All rights reserved. No part of this publication may be reproduced, stored in a retrieval
system, or transmitted, in any form or by any means, without the prior permission of Hart
Publishing, or as expressly permitted by law or under the terms agreed with the appropriate
reprographic rights organisation. Enquiries concerning reproduction which may not be
covered by the above should be addressed to Hart Publishing Ltd at the address above.

British Library Cataloguing in Publication Data
Data Available

ISBN: 978-1-84946-012-5

Typeset by Compuscript Ltd, Shannon
Printed and bound in Great Britain by
CPI Group (UK) Ltd, Croydon, CR0 4YY

In memory of

Tony Weir

who probably would not have approved

Foreword

The Rt Hon Lord Wilson of Culworth
Justice of the Supreme Court of the United Kingdom

One of my worst moments as a young English advocate was in 1969 when a judge refused to grant my client a divorce in the light of her 'collusion' with her husband: for they had reached an agreement which not only resolved their financial issues but provided that he would not oppose the divorce. Unlike the type of agreements which are the main subject of this book, theirs was simply an agreement reached following their separation and a mutual disclosure of their resources and as a prelude to immediate proceedings. It is hard to believe, but English law was then hostile to any agreement between separated spouses, particularly if it identified a non-contentious route to their divorce.

Slowly—too slowly—English law has turned almost 180 degrees. Agreements of the type which, in my inexperienced forensic hands, absurdly resulted in my client's continued marriage to her husband, are now encouraged at every turn. But what about pre-nuptial and post-nuptial agreements, ie agreements reached significantly *in advance* not only of the divorce but also often of the separation and not infrequently of the marriage itself?

Here, English law has much to learn from other jurisdictions ahead of it in this area. And it will best learn it from this book. Indeed, in that reform of this subject is currently under active discussion, led (as in her chapter Professor Cooke explains) by the English Law Commission, the timing of its publication could not be better.

The book demonstrates that a marital agreement which—as in a civil law country—replaces one defined outcome with another defined outcome is very different from one which—as in a common law country—replaces an undefined outcome, dependent on the future exercise of a court's discretion, with a defined outcome. In the latter case, however, the defined outcome for which the agreement provides is illusory unless the law clearly provides that the agreement will be upheld. More important than whether it moves as far as I personally would wish is that future English law on this subject should be clear.

But let me not remain parochial. It is clear that other jurisdictions also consider that, in relation to marital agreements, they have yet to achieve the optimum fine balance between two of the central goals of any democratic society—to promote autonomy and to protect the vulnerable. So this is a book not only of international comparisons but also—so I forecast—of international interest.

I have had high hopes of this book ever since I attended the conference in Cambridge to which in his preface Jens Scherpe refers. The quality of the contributions by all the speakers from across the world was arrestingly high. But what I did not realise is how well the contributions would convert to the written page. I find many presentations of foreign law impenetrable even when written in English.

But the clarity of each chapter of this book—and I have read each page of it out of interest rather than out of duty—confers upon it a vastly increased value.

I applaud the vision and perseverance of Jens Scherpe in having conceived this book and, with so much distinguished help, in now bringing it to birth. I will be using it for many years, and I warmly invite my fellow family lawyers across the world to do likewise.

18 August 2011
Nicholas Wilson

Preface and Acknowledgements

This book is based on (and indeed part of) a research project entitled 'Marital agreements and private autonomy in a comparative perspective', the idea for which was first conceived in 2007. It was apparent that the legal position on marital agreements in England and Wales contrasted starkly with that of the continental European jurisdictions, which seemed to merit a comparative study. I am very grateful to Stuart Bridge that he supported the project (and even paid for the coffee) when I first presented it to him. Shortly afterwards the decision in *NG v KR (Pre-nuptial contract)*[1] was handed down, and it became apparent that further academic and particularly comparative study of marital agreements not only had merit but was needed. This case was not only in part the original motivation for the project, but was also to become its biggest motor—and, in some ways, obstacle. The Law Commission of England and Wales then made marital property agreements part of its 10th Programme for Law Reform, which provided further stimulus. Walter Pintens, Josep Ferrer-Riba, Joanna Miles and Elizabeth Cooke were of invaluable help when drafting and discussing the questionnaire for the national reports.

With the generous financial assistance of Mills & Reeve LLP a conference was organised in Cambridge on 26–27 June 2009, where the drafts of the national reports and initial comparative findings were presented. In the afternoon of 27 June a workshop followed, where the reports and findings were discussed with the national reporters, Law Commissioner Prof Elizabeth Cooke and Matthew Jolley, also of the Law Commission, in a very productive session.

Lord Justice Wilson (as he then was) very kindly agreed to give concluding remarks at the conference—just days before the Court of Appeal decision in *Radmacher v Granatino*[2] was to be handed down, in which he together with Lord Justice Thorpe and Lord Justice Rix overturned the above-mentioned first instance decision. I had not realised when I invited him a long time before the conference that this would put him in the difficult position of not being able to talk about what we all would be talking about only a few days later! Needless to say, the impact of the Court of Appeal decision on the project was very significant.

When the case later was appealed to the Supreme Court, a decision had to be taken. While most of the national reports had been written already, the book was in great danger of being out of date by the time it was published, if this latest development was not taken into account. So it was decided to wait until the Supreme Court's decision[3] was handed down, which took somewhat longer than expected—namely until 20 October 2010. Then the Law Commission's Consultation Paper (on which see Law Commissioner Prof Cooke's chapter in this book) was about to be published. It was only in January 2011 that the comparative work could really

---

[1] *NG v KR (Pre-nuptial contract)* [2008] EWHC 1532 (Fam).
[2] *Radmacher v Granatino* [2009] EWCA Civ 649.
[3] *Radmacher v Granatino* [2010] UKSC 42.

be completed—and most chapters needed to be updated at this point. I am very grateful to the authors of the national reports for their patience and understanding. Likewise, Hart Publishing and particularly Rachel Turner, Melanie Hamill and Tom Adams were very supportive throughout the entire time.

There are quite a few people and organisations I would like to thank: first of all, Mills & Reeve, and particularly Roger Bamber and David Salter, for their financial support of the conference; the British Association for Comparative Law and the Centre for European Legal Studies of the University of Cambridge and the Faculty of Law generally (and Felicity Eves-Rey, Elizabeth Aitken and Rosie Šnajdr particularly) for their administrative support; Andrew Gerard and Steve Burdett who made sure that the computing side of things worked; Daniel Bates for his wonderful work on the various websites; Brian Sloan and Bevan Marten for their support during the workshop; my conference helpers, Sneha Ramakrishnan, Emily Rayner, Ella Westby and Heather Flemming for their support during very busy conference days; Roger Bamber (Mills & Reeve LLP), Stuart Bridge (University of Cambridge), Anne Barlow (University of Exeter) and Walter Pintens (University of Leuven) for chairing sessions at the conference; Lord Wilson (as he now is) for his concluding remarks at the conference and for writing the foreword of this book.

The research project and this book would not have been possible without the support of a Small Research Grant from the British Academy. The editing of the book was supported by a Newton Trust Small Research Grant and undertaken with tremendous skill and energy by Claire Nielsen (currently a PhD candidate at the University of Cambridge)—thank you very much for doing such great work.

My final thanks go to Ann-Christin Maak (who as I write this is my fiancée and hopefully will be my wife when this book is published) who—apart from the authors—is probably the one who suffered most because of this project. May we never need to rely on a marital agreement!

Jens M Scherpe, July 2011

Contents

Table of Contributors

Professor Katharina Boele-Woelki, Professor of Private International Law, Comparative Law and Family Law at the Molengraaff Institute for Private Law, Utrecht University, the Netherlands; Extraordinary Professor at the University of the Western Cape, South Africa; Chair of the Organising Committee of the Commission on European Family Law (CEFL).

Dr Bente Braat, Legal officer at the European Court of Human Rights.

Associate Professor Margaret Briggs, Faculty of Law, University of Otago, New Zealand.

Professor Elizabeth Cooke, Law Commissioner for England and Wales; Professor of Law, University of Reading, England.

Dr Louise Crowley, Faculty of Law, University College Cork, Republic of Ireland.

Dr Anatol Dutta, Senior Research Fellow at the Max Planck Institute for Comparative and International Private Law, Hamburg, Germany.

Professor Ira Mark Ellman, Professor of Law and Willard H Pedrick Distinguished Research Scholar, Sandra Day O'Connor College of Law, Arizona State University, United States of America.

Professor Susanne Ferrari, Institut für Zivilrecht, Ausländisches und Internationales Privatrecht, Karl-Franzens-Universität Graz, Austria.

Professor Josep Ferrer-Riba, Professor of Private Law, Facultat de Dret, Universitat Pompeu Fabra, Barcelona, Spain.

Brett Frankle, Solicitor, Withers LLP, London, England.

Mark Harper, Partner, Withers LLP, London, England.

Professor Maarit Jänterä-Jareborg, Professor of Private International Law and International Civil Procedure, Former Dean of the Faculty, Uppsala University; Member of the Organising Committee of the Commission on European Family Law (CEFL).

Dr Owen Jessep, Senior Visiting Fellow, Faculty of Law, University of New South Wales, Sydney, Australia.

Professor Wai Kum Leong, Faculty of Law, National University of Singapore.

Joanna Miles, Senior University Lecturer and Fellow of Trinity College, University of Cambridge, England; Academic Door Tenant, 1 Hare Court, Temple, London, England.

Professor Kenneth McK Norrie, Law School, University of Strathclyde, Glasgow, Scotland.

Professor Walter Pintens, Professor of Law, University of Leuven, Belgium; Honorary Professor, Saarland University, Germany; Secretary General of the International Commission on Civil Status (Strasbourg); Member of the Organising Committee of the Commission on European Family Law (CEFL).

Dr Jens M Scherpe, Senior University Lecturer and Fellow and Tutor of Gonville and Caius College, University of Cambridge, England; Honorary Fellow of St. John's College, University of Hong Kong; Academic Door Tenant, Queen Elizabeth Building, Temple, London, England.

Introduction

JENS M SCHERPE

CONTENTS

I. DEFAULT RULES AND AUTONOMY

This book is concerned with an area of family law which is subject to special legal provisions in all jurisdictions: the financial relations of spouses.[1] The policies underpinning those provisions unsurprisingly differ from jurisdiction to jurisdiction, but what they all have in common is the desire to support families and to protect the weaker spouse and the children in the event of separation and divorce.[2] Each jurisdiction therefore subjects the spouses to a specific set of rules that governs their financial relations. Such a set of rules in principle applies to every marriage concluded, even (and indeed particularly) if the couple give no thought to their financial relations. Hence these rules apply 'by default' and therefore the legal rules that then apply often are called the 'default system' or 'default rules'. If the couple want different rules to apply to their financial relations, they have to 'contract out' of the default rules by what this book calls a 'marital agreement' (see also the questionnaire following this introduction, on terminology). The interrelation of default system and 'contracting out' is

---

[1] It is important to point out at the outset that in many jurisdictions the rules explained and discussed here also apply to other formalised family regimes, such as civil/registered partnerships, and that of course in many jurisdictions 'spouses' can now refer not only to husband and wife but also to same-sex couples. Hence when the term 'spouse' is used in this book the term applies to all married individuals, irrespective of their gender or the gender of their partner. See also the section on 'Terminology and areas not covered' in the questionnaire below.

[2] See eg A Lüderitz and N Dethloff, *Familienrecht,* 28th edn (Munich, CH Beck, 2007) 1 ff; N Lowe and G Douglas, *Bromley's Family Law*, 10th edn (Oxford, OUP 2007) 1 ff; A Agell and M Brattström, *Äktenskap Samboende Partnerskap,* 4th edn (Uppsala, Iustus Förlag, 2008) 14 ff. In many jurisdictions, eg Germany (Art 6 of the Basic Law, the German Constitution), Spain (Art 32 of the Constitution), Ireland (Art 41 of the Constitution) and Slovenia (Art 53 of the Constitution), there even is a constitutional mandate to protect 'marriage' and/or 'the family'.

the focal point of this book, and the research agenda can be summarised in this question:

> If the spouses do not want the default rules to apply to their financial relations, should they be free to conclude an agreement to 'contract out' of the default system—and if so, to what extent?

The central question that this book addresses therefore is how much autonomy legal systems allow or should allow spouses to regulate their financial relations themselves. Private autonomy of course is a very highly valued good in most societies, a central feature of modern democracies, the backbone of our economies and often even protected by constitutions. Private autonomy is seen as the ultimate expression of the freedom of an individual, and legislatures and courts generally are very hesitant to interfere with it. But in all jurisdictions there are some areas governed by mandatory rules which cannot be derogated from by an agreement between the parties, and party autonomy on the face of it is therefore limited by law. Such limitations require strong and clear policy justifications, and typically mandatory rules cover situations where there frequently is an imbalance of power between the parties, leading to an unequal bargaining position: for example in labour law, insurance law, consumer law and, of course, family law. In these contexts, the mandatory rules are seen as a measure to ensure that both parties, to the furthest possible extent, actually are in a position to take an autonomous decision. Hence many of the mandatory rules which at first glance appear to limit the autonomy of the parties are actually in place *to protect autonomy*. But in other areas—not least family law, and the financial relations of the spouses in particular—the mandatory rules go beyond this aim: the law takes a paternalistic approach and the mandatory rules protect *from* autonomy, curtailing the freedom of the individual for his or her 'own good'. Here the rules are an expression of different policy objectives, which, in the context of the financial relations of the spouses and family law in general, are to support families and to protect the weaker spouse and the children in case of separation and divorce.[3]

II. THE APPROACH TAKEN IN THIS BOOK AND TERMINOLOGY

Obviously the answer to the question about how much autonomy the spouses should have to regulate their financial relations to a large degree depends on the nature and content of the default rules that would otherwise apply. But the answer in each jurisdiction also depends on the policy approach to marriage in general, the financial relations of the spouses in particular, and on the specific societal, cultural and economic context. This includes issues such as labour market accessibility for women and men, social welfare provisions in general, state support for or provision of child care etc. Therefore a comparative study of the autonomy of the spouses to determine their financial relations faces considerable difficulties because of the breadth of the issues involved. Thus even when the comparison is undertaken in full awareness of the broader nature of the issues at hand, it will never be able to give a

---

[3] See above n 2.

truly 'full picture', and the comparison therefore inevitably is incomplete and limited. However, this does not mean that such a comparative study is therefore futile. On the contrary, provided one is aware of the limitations of such comparisons, it can nevertheless inform and stimulate academic discussion on the topic, which is the aim of this book.

The approach taken in this book is common for comparative projects: a questionnaire by which the same set of questions is answered by expert lawyers from the several jurisdictions and a comparative analysis is then undertaken based on their answers. The questionnaire following this introduction was drafted very carefully[4] but is not as detailed as questionnaires for other comparative projects.[5] The aim was, on the one hand, to allow the national reporters to explain their national system in its full legal, social and cultural context without feeling constrained and limited by the questionnaire. On the other hand, it was important for the purposes of the comparison that all national reports address roughly the same issues, even if (and perhaps especially if) a particular issue is not relevant in all jurisdictions. Nevertheless, each national report was to be written in a way that it could be read and understood without reference to the introduction, the questionnaire or any of the other chapters in the book.

As explained above, all jurisdictions have some form of 'default system' for the financial relations of the spouses, and the extent to which the parties are allowed to derogate from this system by agreement naturally depends greatly on the nature and content of the default rules. Therefore each national reporter was asked briefly to explain the default rules in the first part of his or her report. The comparison of these default systems alone merits a greater and more extensive comparative study, such as the one undertaken by the Commission on European Family Law.[6] But a comparison of the default systems was necessary for this project too, and this comparison is found in the final chapter of this book.

Having reported on the default system, national reporters were asked next to describe the rules on agreements wishing to derogate from the default system. The terminological approach here was difficult, because such agreements are not necessarily (or with certainty) considered to be 'contracts' in all jurisdictions.[7] The neutral term 'marital agreements' was therefore used. As stated in the questionnaire, for the purpose of this comparative project 'marital agreements' were taken to include pre-nuptial agreements (sometimes also referred to as ante-nuptial agreements) and post-nuptial agreements, ie agreements concluded before and after the wedding, respectively. But the term 'separation agreements' was to be used for a

---

[4] I would like to thank Walter Pintens, Josep Ferrer-Riba, Joanna Miles and Elizabeth Cooke for their invaluable help in the drafting of the questionnaire.

[5] See for examples the questionnaires used by the Commission on European Family Law for their projects on divorce and maintenance between former spouses, parental responsibilities and property relations between spouses, all available at www.ceflonline.net/.

[6] K Boele-Woelki, B Braat and I Sumner (eds), *European Family Law in Action II: Maintenance Between Former Spouses* (Antwerp, Intersentia, 2003); K Boele-Woelki, W Pintens, F Ferrand, C Gonzalez-Beilfuss, M Jänterä-Jareborg, N Lowe and D Martiny, *Principles of European Family Law Regarding Divorce and Maintenance Between Former Spouses* (Antwerp, Intersentia, 2004); K Boele-Woelki, B Braat and I Curry-Sumner (eds), *European Family Law in Action IV: Property Relations between Spouses* (Antwerp, Intersentia, 2009).

[7] See eg the discussion in *Radmacher v Granatino* [2010] UKSC 42, especially [62 ff].

special kind of post-nuptial agreement, namely agreements concluded shortly before or during divorce proceedings, ie at a point in time where the spouses have already decided that they will separate/divorce and are merely regulating the division of assets, maintenance etc.[8] Such separation agreements differ from the other marital agreements because they are made at a point in time when the parties know (or at least are in a position to know) exactly what they are agreeing to, whereas the pre-nuptial and post-nuptial agreements otherwise are agreements that are to apply in a more or less uncertain future. For this reason, the national reporters were asked to deal with separation agreements in a distinct part of their report if/where this was appropriate.

After the description of the rules on marital agreements, the national reporters were asked to describe the private international law/conflict of laws rules concerning such agreements. While, because of the complexity of this issue, no comparison of it is undertaken in the final chapter study, it was nevertheless felt that the exposition of these rules was necessary to inform an interested reader.

Finally, readers will note that the reports, while written in English, do not quite read as typical academic texts published in an anglophone country; this is intentional. For the purpose of this comparative project it was felt that the language should only be edited where this was essential for the understanding of the text; otherwise the aim of the editing was to stick closely to the original text.[9] Hence there is no full consistency in the usage of certain words or terms (eg gift/donation; maintenance/alimony), and each chapter needs to be considered by itself. As is appropriate for comparative projects, the citations largely follow national customs, so that an interested reader can more easily identify and find the sources in the respective jurisdictions.

III. THE JURISDICTIONS CHOSEN AND STRUCTURE OF THE BOOK

The jurisdictions for this comparative project were chosen very deliberately. The idea for this project arose because of the somewhat bizarre state of the law on marital agreement in **England and Wales** at the time, and indeed long before the decisions of the Privy Council in *MacLeod v MacLeod*[10] and the Court of Appeal's decision (and later the Supreme Court's decision) in *Radmacher v Granatino*.[11] Unlike many jurisdictions, England and Wales does not have a matrimonial property regime as such, and so there is no clear distinction between property division and

---

[8] 'Separation agreements' for this project were also to include those agreements that are specifically concluded in order to be part of court proceedings or even to form the basis of a court's decision or to provide a substitute for a court order. It is to be noted that in some jurisdictions, for example Ireland, the term can have a different meaning, namely referring to agreements upon separation without the intent to actually divorce.

[9] I would once again like to thank Claire Nielsen for editing the chapters so competently and thoroughly, and the Newton Trust for its financial support in the form of a Newton Trust Small Research Grant.

[10] *MacLeod v MacLeod* [2008] UKPC 64.

[11] *Radmacher v Granatino* [2009] EWCA 649 and [2010] UKSC 42. The Supreme Court since 1 October 2009 has replaced the Appellate Committee of the House of Lords as the highest court in the United Kingdom.

maintenance. Instead, the courts are given a wide discretion as to how to determine the financial consequences of a divorce. While this allows for a great degree of flexibility and thus—at least theoretically—for a fair outcome in each particular case, it creates significant uncertainty for the spouses, despite (or maybe even because of) the recent House of Lords decisions in *White v White*[12] and *Miller v Miller; McFarlane v McFarlane*.[13] One obvious way of achieving greater certainty for spouses in their financial affairs would be to allow parties to make binding marital agreements in which the couple regulate their property and other consequences in case of divorce. Therefore it seemed quite surprising that, despite the lack of legal certainty under the default rules in England and Wales, such marital agreements were not (and indeed still are not) binding or enforceable in this jurisdiction, and that the private autonomy of the parties in this regard appears not to be respected. Contrariwise, in many other jurisdictions, including those with rigid matrimonial property regimes which provide for a high degree of legal certainty (at the expense of flexibility), marital agreements can be binding and enforceable in principle, but nevertheless to a certain extent remain subject to review by the courts. The legal status of such agreements in England and Wales at the time when the project was conceived was therefore the subject of much criticism and debate amongst academics and practitioners, and 'Marital Property Agreements' were made part of the Law Commission of England and Wales's Tenth Programme of Law Reform.[14] The research project and conference were inter alia set up to provide a comparative background for the Law Commission's work. The subsequent decisions in *MacLeod* and *Radmacher v Granatino*[15] to a certain extent changed or at least clarified the law, and the Law Commission published its consultation paper on the matter in January 2011.[16] Because of the special circumstances, to complement the English national report in this volume and to stimulate the reform discussion in England and Wales, a report on the Law Commission's consultation paper and 'a practitioner's view' are also included here.

England and Wales of course is a common law jurisdiction, and therefore it seemed logical to look at the way the issue was dealt with in other common law jurisdictions. **Australia** was chosen because it has a rather complicated (and some say, unfortunate) history of legislating on the topic, and it was hoped that much could be learned from that. **New Zealand** also legislated on marital agreements, but some time after Australia did so, and could therefore benefit from the 'Australian experience'; moreover, the default system in New Zealand is quite different (and since the 2001 and 2004 amendments, includes de facto relationships and civil unions of

---

[12] *White v White* [2001] 1 AC 596.

[13] *Miller v Miller; McFarlane v McFarlane* [2006] UKHL 24.

[14] Law Commission for England and Wales, *Tenth Programme of Law Reform* (Law Com No 311, 2008), available at www.official-documents.gov.uk/document/hc0708/hc06/0605/0605.pdf.

[15] The conference accompanying this project was actually held one day before the Court of Appeal decision was handed down. This decision, and the following appeal to the Supreme Court, caused considerable delay to this project as they of course led to a partial reassessment of the comparison and required a rewriting of some of the chapters, and I would once more like to thank the national reporters and the publisher for their patience and understanding.

[16] The Law Commission, *Marital Property Agreements—A Consultation Paper* (Consultation Paper No 198, 2011), available at www.justice.gov.uk/lawcommission/docs/cp198_Marital_Property_Agreements_Consultation.pdf.

the same or opposite sex) and therefore a comparison promised to be interesting. **Singapore** often is said to be the 'purest' of the common law jurisdictions, but while there is, of course, the heritage of the English common law, the societal and cultural background is a very different one which, it was assumed, could potentially lead to a very different view on marital agreements. The **United States** were chosen because of the sheer number of jurisdictions comprised, which promised a wealth of comparative material, but also because of the publication of the *Principles of the Law of Family Dissolution* by the American Law Institute in 2002, which contain specific provisions for marital agreements, and the Uniform Premarital Agreement Act of 1983, drafted by the National Conference of Commissioners on Uniform Sate Laws. **Ireland** was also of specific interest because Irish family law is one of the most rapidly developing in Europe; only in 1996 was divorce introduced, and before that the issue of marital agreements (with the exception of agreements regulating factual separation) did not really arise. The financial consequences of divorce are subject to very tight policy guidelines in Ireland and thus the scope for derogation by agreement appeared particularly limited. Nevertheless, in 2006 the Minister for Justice, Equality and Law Reform set up the Study Group on Pre-Nuptial Agreements, whose report was published in 2007.

Like Ireland, **Scotland** is often overlooked in comparative studies. But as a mixed jurisdiction whose approach to marriage and family law in general is quite different from the English one, it was expected that it could contribute much to the discussion.

The continental European civil law jurisdictions were chosen because their approaches to matrimonial property and financial relief on divorce are fundamentally different from that in England and Wales. **Germany** in recent years had seen a number of decisions on marital agreements which significantly changed the law, and it represents the jurisdictions operating with a community of accrued gains as the default matrimonial property system. Some features of the default system in **Austria** appear to be rather similar, but in many areas this jurisdiction takes a refreshingly different view on financial relief, particularly by (in principle) giving the courts discretion to divide the property under the default matrimonial property regime, thereby bringing Austria much closer to the approach taken in the common law world. Likewise, in **Sweden**, which in this project represents the Nordic countries and their matrimonial property system of a deferred community of property, the courts are afforded a considerable degree of discretion with regard to the division of assets, including where there is a marital agreement.

Belgium and **France** were chosen as representatives of the Romanic legal family with its community of acquest, which is also the predominant matrimonial property system in Eastern Europe. The community of acquests creates a community of property for some assets from the day of the marriage, and the high prevalence of marital agreements in these jurisdictions seems to suggest that a significant number of couples wish to regulate their financial relations differently, which merited closer study. It will be evident already that the function of marital agreements regarding property is a very different one here because they are to apply not only in the event of divorce but also during the marriage. While **Spain** belongs to the same legal family, many of the autonomous regions of Spain have their own jurisdiction in family law, leading to very diverse approaches.

Finally, the **Netherlands**, as the only country in Europe where the universal community of property is the default matrimonial property system, presumably has the highest proportion of marital agreements, as many couples and families regard this default system as inadequate for their situation, and so a significant body of jurisprudence and academic writing was to be expected as a valuable source for comparative study.

After this introduction and the questionnaire, the national reports (and in the case of England and Wales, the complementing Law Commissioner's and practitioners' chapters) follow in alphabetical order. Grouping them, for example into 'common law' and 'civil law' groups, seemed inappropriate after having undertaken the comparison, as this (and other) dividing lines are not as clear as they at first appear to be, as the final, comparative chapter explores. This last chapter also contains a comparative analysis and some conclusions regarding the law (and possible reform of the law) on marital agreements.

Questionnaire[*]

CONTENTS

Background to the Research Project

Unlike many jurisdictions, England and Wales does not have a matrimonial property regime as such. Instead the courts are given a wide discretion as to how to determine the financial consequences of a divorce. While this allows for a great degree of flexibility and thus—at least theoretically—for fair outcomes in each particular case, it creates significant uncertainty for the spouses, despite (or maybe even because of) recent House of Lords decisions like *White v White* [2001] 1 AC 596 and *Miller v Miller; McFarlane v McFarlane* [2006] UKHL 24.

One obvious way of achieving greater certainty for spouses in their financial affairs could be to allow parties to make binding marital agreements in which the couple regulate their property and other consequences in case of divorce. Therefore it seems quite surprising that despite the lack of legal certainty in England and Wales, such marital agreements currently are not enforceable in this jurisdiction, and that the private autonomy of the parties in this regard is not respected. Contrariwise, in many other jurisdictions, including those with rigid matrimonial property regimes which provide for a high degree of legal certainty (at the expense of flexibility), such marital agreements can be binding and enforceable. The current legal status of such agreements in England and Wales has been the subject of much criticism and debate amongst academics and practitioners, and many have argued for greater recognition

---

[*] This questionnaire was sent to the national reporters at the beginning of the project in 2008.

of such agreements (see eg Sir Mark Potter P. in *Charman v Charman* [2007] EWCA Civ 503 at [124]). This has led the Law Commission of England and Wales to make 'Marital Property Agreements' part of its 10th Programme of Law Reform; the Law Commission's project will commence in September 2009 and a report and draft Bill are expected in September 2012.

The proposed research project, 'Marital Agreements and Private Autonomy in a Comparative Perspective', therefore is a timely one and will contribute to the academic and political debate and indeed the work of the Law Commission from a comparative law perspective. In addition, it will also make available up-to-date information on foreign matrimonial property regimes, spousal maintenance after divorce and marital agreements in the English language.

General Points Regarding the Questionnaire

The purpose of the questionnaire approach is to ensure that the same areas and problems are covered in each national report. Some of the points might not be of relevance in some jurisdictions—that in itself can be valuable information from a comparative point of view.

The questionnaire is meant as a guideline and tool, and not a straitjacket into which the information must fit. *The main aim is that each national report, while following roughly the same structure, is self-contained and readable.* Many of the legal rules can only be understood in their full legal, social and cultural context, and this should not be prevented by rigidly following the questionnaire. Please feel free to add any information you consider relevant, and particularly an introduction giving a historical background and some statistical data concerning the use/practical relevance of agreements between spouses. In order to make the book and the comparison accessible to the readers, however, please follow the structure indicated with Roman numbers.

Terminology and Areas not Covered

For the purpose of this project, the term **marital agreements** is meant to include **pre-nuptial agreements** (sometimes also referred to as ante-nuptial agreements) and also **post-nuptial agreements**, ie agreements concluded after the marriage. Of course, some (if not most) of these agreements will provide for/apply in the case of separation and/or divorce.

However, for the purpose of this project the term **separation agreements** is to be used for a special kind of post-nuptial agreements, namely agreements concluded shortly before or during divorce proceedings, ie at a point in time where the spouses have already decided that they will divorce and are merely deliberating the division of assets, maintenance etc. 'Separation agreements' for this project should also be taken to include those agreements that are specifically concluded in order to be part of court proceedings or even to form the basis of a court's decision or to provide a substitute for a court order.

It is generally assumed that the rules apply to all marriages, irrespective of whether they are (as is possible in a number of jurisdictions now) between couples of the same or the opposite sex. Should the rules differ, please explain. Should the jurisdiction possess a legal regime solely for same-sex couples which is the functional equivalent of marriage (eg civil partnership in the United Kingdom, *registreret partnerskab* in Denmark or *Eingetragene Lebenspartnerschaft* in Germany), then please state whether the rules applying to agreements within that regime differ from those for married couples (and if so, briefly how and why). Agreements concerning other forms of formalised relationships, which are open to both same-sex and opposite-sex couples (like the French *PACS* or the Dutch *geregistreerd partnerschap*) and hence might be seen as alternative to marriage are principally not part of this project.

Further, agreements between cohabitants (ie couples living together without having formalised their relationship) are not part of the project, and neither are agreements concerning the children (eg regarding parental responsibility/custody, maintenance for children etc).

I. THE FINANCIAL CONSEQUENCES OF DIVORCE (ANCILLARY RELIEF/ MATRIMONIAL PROPERTY AND MAINTENANCE ETC)

This part

(a) is meant to provide the background against which the rules concerning marital agreements and separation agreements are to be understood, and
(b) generally to be a source of information on this area of law.

For this, a general outline should be sufficient and overly detailed discussions should be avoided unless they are necessary to understand this area of law.

Please set out briefly the **default** system (ie the one applying if there are no agreements) for the financial consequences of divorce/ancillary relief (ie matrimonial property, maintenance, pension rights adjustment and allocation of the matrimonial home following divorce) in your jurisdiction.

Please also—where appropriate—discuss the following points:

— What is the role of matrimonial property in your jurisdiction? What is the function of maintenance and pension rights?
For example, is it the purpose of matrimonial property division to make the weaker party/the children financially secure (as far as possible under the circumstances) or is that objective to be achieved through maintenance obligations/ pension rights?
— Please explain the relationship between matrimonial property and maintenance/ pension rights and how they interact.
For example will receiving a large sum in the division of the matrimonial property have an impact on the provision of maintenance and vice versa?
— What is the role of the state (if any) in post-divorce financial support? Is securing the economic well-being of a former spouse considered a duty of the state or will the other former spouse be obliged to pay (and, in case of maintenance, for how long) as part of his or her post-marital duties?

For example, it might be the case that the level of social welfare/state support/ female labour market participation etc is such that maintenance payments are unusual/uncommon?
— Is there a clean break-philosophy/legislation (ie is it a general policy aim in divorce proceedings to bring the financial ties between the spouses to an end)?

II. PRE-NUPTIAL AND POST-NUPTIAL AGREEMENTS

1. *Generally*

Do the general rules of contract law apply? Are they modified/applied differently for marital agreements? Are there special family law rules?

2. *Form and Procedure*

What are the formal/procedural requirements for concluding such agreements? Please include the following points:

— Is the state involved in any way (ie through a court/competent authority or notary or a registration of the agreement)? If so, what is the role and effect of the state's involvement? Is an approval of the content of the agreement required? If so, is there a potential liability in case the court/competent authority/notary/ registrar made a mistake etc.?
— What is the role of legal advice? Is independent legal advice mandatory? What are the consequences of inaccurate legal advice for the enforceability of the agreement? Is there a problem with the general statute of limitation concerning this (after all, legal advice may be given a very long time before the matter actually becomes relevant!)?
— What are the consequences of a failure to comply with formal/procedural requirements?

The following might be considered a formal/procedural requirement in some jurisdictions, but a matter of substantive law/content in others. Please include this where appropriate for your jurisdiction:

— Is there a duty of full and frank disclosure of assets? If so, what is the result of a failure to fulfil that duty? Does such a failure have consequences even if full disclosure would not have made any difference?

3. *Content of the Agreements and Binding Effect/Enforceability*

In jurisdictions where there is a default matrimonial property regime, the main function of a marital agreement is to alter that regime; in other words, the agreement is not necessarily centred on the dissolution of marriage as such. Therefore, in this section please discuss the effect of agreements

(a) during marriage,
(b) in case of divorce, and
(c) in case of death.

In your jurisdiction, can the couple make binding/enforceable agreements concerning **their property relations**? If not, what is the practical legal effect of such agreements?

Is the choice of the spouses regarding their matrimonial property limited to an (exhaustive) number of legal regimes provided by statute etc (perhaps including slight alterations of these regimes) or are the spouses free to 'design' their own matrimonial property regime? Can they choose a foreign matrimonial property regime?

Can the couple make binding/enforceable agreements concerning **maintenance** after divorce? If not, what is the practical legal effect of such agreements?

What are the limits of the contractual freedom/'safeguards' in your jurisdiction to ensure a) the autonomy of the parties AND/OR b) the protection of the weaker party and/or the children? Is it made clear by legislation/case law what the aim of those safeguards is? Can a court/competent authority set aside and/or modify an agreement, and if so, on what grounds and in what (changed) circumstances?

What sort of factors tend to play a role in deciding whether an agreement will be upheld?

Examples might include:

— The source and amount of the assets/debts (ie whether owned before the marriage, inherited, gift…)
— Pregnancy at the time of the conclusion of the agreement
— Whether there are (joint) children
— Job/occupation before/during marriage; whether there was an agreement that one of the spouses should give up work or whether a spouse gave up work despite the express disapproval of the other spouse
— Period of time that elapsed between the conclusion of the agreement and the wedding

What threshold test, if any, is applied by the court in deciding whether to disapply an agreement (eg 'simple unfairness', 'manifest unfairness' etc) and how difficult in practice is it to get an agreement set aside?

If the legal rules applying to pre-nuptial agreements and post-nuptial agreements (and changing existing agreements) differ, please elaborate.

III. SEPARATION AGREEMENTS

Separation agreements[1] as a special form of post-nuptial agreements are concluded at a point in time when the marriage has failed, the decision to divorce has been taken by the spouses and they merely are regulating the division of assets, maintenance etc. It is likely therefore that the spouses' factual position is very different from that of other marital agreements: they know they are divorcing and are likely to know all the facts in light of which the agreement will operate, at least

---

[1] Please see the section on 'Terminology and areas not covered' above for the exact meaning of the term 'separation agreements' for the purposes of this project.

in the short term. Hence the legal evaluation of separation agreements in many jurisdictions differs from that concerning other marital agreements.

In your jurisdiction, at which point in time can separation agreements as just described be concluded: before or only after actual divorce proceedings have been initiated?

Do the rules applicable to separation agreements differ from those set out above? Please explain in detail whether/when there are any such differences as to the:

— formalities/procedure,
— the content, and
— the binding effect or enforceability of separation agreements.

IV. CONFLICT OF LAWS

How will a foreign marital agreement be treated in a dispute in your jurisdiction, if that agreement is valid and binding according to the law of the jurisdiction in which it was concluded and/or the parties held the relevant nationality, were habitually resident or domiciled in that jurisdiction at the time?

V. CONCLUSION

Please evaluate the status quo and the development that led up to it. Is the law regarded as workable?

What do practitioners/academics/the courts/the competent authorities think about the current state of the law? Are there suggestions for reform?

National Reports on Marital Agreements and Private Autonomy

Marital Agreements and Private Autonomy in Australia

OWEN JESSEP

CONTENTS

I. INTRODUCTION

Although separation agreements have been recognised and enforced in Australia for almost 50 years, agreements dealing with financial matters entered into before marriage or while the marriage is still on foot have only been possible since the end of 2000. The main purpose of this chapter is to describe these recent developments and consider the issues arising from the greater availability of agreements to regulate division of property and adult maintenance between spouses. It will be helpful, however, to set the scene by providing some background details about the Australian legal system and the distribution of legislative powers in Australia.

Australia has a federal system of government, in which the national (or Commonwealth) government and the eight state and territory governments[1] have different powers over different aspects of family law. Under the federal Constitution, the national government has power to pass laws about marriage, and about divorce and matters connected to divorce.[2] In contrast, the eight states generally have power to pass laws about non-marital relationships. This used to mean also that the states had powers in relation to children of non-marital relationships, but by 1990 the states had agreed to give up their powers over guardianship and parental rights and custody and maintenance of those children to the national government.[3] As a result, there are now national laws which apply to all disputes over custody or mainte-nance of children in Australia, regardless of whether or not the parents were ever married to each other or ever lived together.[4] Again, recently seven states[5] referred to the national government their powers in relation to financial disputes arising on the breakdown of de facto relationships (whether between same-sex or opposite-sex partners). As a result, the national government amended the principal family law statute, the Family Law Act 1975 (Cth), so that the same principles and provisions relevant to property adjustment, maintenance and agreements as to financial mat-ters between married persons will now apply in those referring states to same-sex and opposite-sex de facto partners as well. In contrast, financial disputes arising in other family or domestic contexts (eg between relatives, or friends, or concerning non-sexual 'caring' relationships) remain to be dealt with in state courts according to the law of each state. The states also retain power over major areas of criminal and civil law, together with other areas of law affecting children, such as adoption of children, protection of abused children, juvenile delinquency, and so on. In addi-tion, the states have power in relation to inheritance for all persons, married or otherwise.

II. FINANCIAL CONSEQUENCES OF MARITAL BREAKDOWN AND DIVORCE

Marriage in Australia remains an exclusively heterosexual institution. Although at both federal and state levels, in an increasing number of legal contexts, the rights and responsibilities of same-sex couples (and of opposite-sex unmarried couples) are being assimilated to those applicable to married persons, both the former con-servative Liberal government and the current Labor government have been firmly

---

[1] There are six states and two territories, namely New South Wales, Victoria, Queensland, South Australia, Western Australia, Tasmania, Northern Territory and the Australian Capital Territory. For convenience, I will refer to them collectively as the 'eight states' of Australia.

[2] Australian Constitution, s 51(xxi) and (xxii).

[3] Australian Constitution, s 51(xxxvii) allows the Commonwealth to receive references of legislative power from the states.

[4] See especially Family Law Act 1975 (Cth) Part VII, and Child Support (Assessment) Act 1989 (Cth). A slightly different situation applies in Western Australia, but the differences are not important for pur-poses of this discussion. (Note: '(Cth)' is an abbreviation for 'Commonwealth', and indicates a statute of the national Parliament.)

[5] All except Western Australia, which is still considering the issue. The amendments take effect in the referring states from 1 March 2009, except in South Australia where the commencement date is 1 July 2010.

against the idea of making marriage available to same-sex couples. Divorce is freely available, and does not depend on any concept of 'fault' or marital misconduct. Since 1976 the only ground for divorce (without any exceptions or alternatives) has been 'irretrievable breakdown of marriage' as established by proof that the parties have in fact separated and the separation has continued for a minimum period of 12 months.[6]

As in a number of countries which share the English common law heritage, getting married in Australia does not change the property rights of husband or wife. During the marriage a system of separate property applies, in the sense that his property remains his, and her property remains hers. According to these rules, property acquired after the marriage may legally be his, or hers, or may belong to both of them (eg if a property is bought in both their names). In brief, and ignoring a number of exceptions, we can say that under the general principles of the law of property, items of property will be owned by the spouse who paid for them. This means that a spouse who stays at home and provides domestic labour rather than money is in a very vulnerable position under the general law of property. These principles of separate property may be particularly relevant if, say, one spouse is being hounded by creditors or has become bankrupt—the money or assets of the particular spouse which will become available for the creditors will be determined by application of these principles of general property law. Similarly, if one spouse dies, what goes into his or her estate and becomes subject to the law of inheritance is again determined by the general law of property relating to legal and equitable interests.

Where a married couple experience marital breakdown and divorce, however, a very different law becomes applicable. In the event of a financial dispute, unless the couple have provided otherwise for their financial affairs by a binding agreement,[7] a judge of the Family Court is given a very wide statutory discretion to divide or redistribute the property of the spouses, whether acquired before or during the marriage or after separation, in order to produce a just result.[8] As a matter of jurisdiction, then, the Family Court can consider not just property acquired due to the joint efforts of the parties during the marriage (eg house, cars, insurance policies, bank accounts), but also property owned by a spouse prior to the marriage, or acquired by one or other spouse by way of gift, inheritance, award of damages, lottery winnings, and the like. Since 2002 the court has also been able to make orders directly affecting the parties' respective superannuation rights (that is, future rights to a retirement pension or entitlement to lump sums arising from either party's employment).[9] This discretionary power to divide and redistribute property is exercised according to a list of statutory criteria.[10] Again, 'fault' or arguments about responsibility for the breakdown of the marriage are here irrelevant (although behaviour which has led to wasting or destruction of assets will certainly be considered).

---

[6] Family Law Act 1975 (Cth), ss 48–50.

[7] Family Law Act 1975 (Cth), s 87 (if the agreement was made before 27 December 2000), or Pt VIIIA (if the agreement was made on or after 27 December 2000).

[8] Family Law Act 1975 (Cth), ss 79, 75(2).

[9] Family Law Legislation Amendment (Superannuation) Act 2001 (Cth), introducing new Pt VIIIB.

[10] Family Law Act 1975 (Cth), ss 79(4), 75(2).

Of the list of statutory criteria, the two fundamental considerations to be taken into account by the court in deciding on a just and equitable division of the pool of property are:

(i) the different sorts of contributions made by each spouse during the course of the marital relationship (eg financial contributions, non-financial contributions such as home maintenance and repairs, and all sorts of domestic contributions such as housework and having and raising children);[11] and

(ii) the economic circumstances of each spouse at the time of the hearing and looking into the future (especially their age and state of health, their relative earning capacity and the continuing responsibility for care of children).[12] At this second stage, for example, the court can adjust the division of assets which might have been just and equitable on the basis of the parties' respective contributions, to take account of the fact that one spouse has lost income and earning capacity by staying home to look after the family, and may be similarly occupied with the children for some time to come.[13]

It should be clear that the discretionary system which I have sketched is anything but a statutory formula which could be simply applied to determine the appropriate result, or which would operate analogously to the rules of a matrimonial property regime. While there can be advantages in allowing the court to consider the particular history and circumstances of the couple and tailor a result which is just and fair in their situation, there are also obvious disadvantages in having such a wide judicial discretion which on occasions may lead to unpredictability and uncertainty as to the likely outcome, consequently making it difficult for parties to understand their legal position in advance, or for lawyers to give precise advice to their separated clients as to whether to settle a financial dispute rather than litigate (or bring an appeal, in the event of an unfavourable decision).

In relation to adult maintenance, the ideal is for spouses to become self-supporting where possible, and long-term maintenance awards are uncommon.[14] But the Family Court has also emphasised the importance, in the context of financial adjustment, of the body of research literature (in Australia, Canada and elsewhere) dealing with the differential economic consequences of marriage and divorce for husbands and wives.[15] This research has drawn attention to what is commonly referred to as the

---

[11] Family Law Act 1975 (Cth), s 79(4)(a)–(c). Although the court may often find that the various contributions of each party during the marriage should be regarded as equivalent, the High Court of Australia has made it clear that the court cannot apply presumptions to this effect, but must look at the evidence in each case: see *Mallet v Mallet* (1984) 156 CLR 605, and *cf Marriage of Ferraro* (1992) 16 Fam LR 1; *Marriage of Figgins* (2002) FLC 93-122.

[12] Family Law Act 1975 (Cth), s 79(4)(e), which incorporates the provisions of s 75(2) so far as they are relevant. See, eg A Dickey, *Family Law*, 5th edn (Sydney, Lawbook Co, 2007) ch 37; G Monahan and L Young, *Family Law in Australia*, 6th edn (Sydney, LexisNexis Butterworths, 2006) chs 11–13; and B Fehlberg and J Behrens, *Australian Family Law—The Contemporary Context* (Melbourne, Oxford University Press, 2008) ch 9.

[13] See, eg *Marriage of Horsley* (1991) 14 Fam LR 550; *Marriage of Waters and Jurek* (1995) 20 Fam LR 190.

[14] On spousal maintenance, see Dickey, *Family Law* above n 12, chs 24–25; Monahan and Young, *Family Law in Australia* above n 12, ch 8; and Fehlberg and Behrens, *Australian Family Law* above n 12, ch 10. Note Family Law Act 1975 (Cth), s 81, discussed in *Marriage of Bevan* (1993) 19 Fam LR 35.

[15] *Marriage of Mitchell* (1995) FLC 92-601.

'feminisation of poverty', that after separation wives and mothers more often suffer greater financial hardship and experience greater economic deprivations and loss of earning capacity and employment opportunities for longer periods of time than their male partners.[16] Following the decision of Full Family Court in *Marriage of Mitchell*, trial judges hearing applications for maintenance (or property division, for that matter) are able to take judicial notice of this research data and are expected to apply a degree of social realism in the assessment of the economic circumstances and future prospects of each of the spouses.[17]

Where spousal maintenance is awarded, the principal criteria for the order are the reasonable needs of one spouse (usually the wife), and the reasonable capacity to pay of the other spouse.[18] Since 1988 the Family Court has been statutorily forbidden to take account of whether the applicant for maintenance is in receipt of or eligible for social security (that is, any means-tested government pension) in assessing whether maintenance should be paid by the other spouse.[19] In other words, the emphasis is on private support, where this is possible, rather than public support in responding to the needs of the economically weaker spouse. If the court is hearing an application for property adjustment and spousal maintenance at the same time, it is normally appropriate to deal first with the property issues, for if there is a substantial pool of assets to be divided between the parties, the results of the property division may remove the need for any spousal maintenance, or at least reduce the quantum or duration of any maintenance award.[20]

As to the law of inheritance in the different states of Australia (the details of which are very similar in each state), there is no concept of guaranteed or reserved shares for spouses or children of the deceased person. Instead, the law starts with the idea of testamentary freedom; that a person can do what he or she wants with their property. If there is no valid will (ie a situation of intestacy), the relevant state statute will set out the people (eg spouse, children, other relatives) who will inherit the property. On the other hand, if there is a valid will, but there is a dispute about the persons to whom, or the way in which, the deceased's property has been distributed under that will, then certain persons (eg spouse, children, other dependants) may apply to the state court to receive a share of the property under what is called the law of family provision. This is a very different situation from receiving a guaranteed share, however; the court has a number of criteria according to which it will exercise its discretion as to whether to override the terms of the will or not, and the result of the court's decision may be quite difficult to predict.[21]

---

[16] As to the Australian research on this topic, see, eg the publications of researchers at the Australian Institute of Family Studies: P McDonald et al (eds), *Settling Up* (Melbourne, Prentice-Hall, 1986), and M Harrison et al, *Settling Down: Pathways of Parents after Divorce* (Melbourne, AIFS, 1993).

[17] *Marriage of Mitchell* (1995) FLC 92-601, and see R Bailey-Harris, 'The Role of Maintenance and Property Orders in Redressing Inequality: Re-opening the Debate', (1998) 12 *Australian Journal of Family Law* 3–18.

[18] Family Law Act 1975 (Cth), ss 72, 74, and 75(2).

[19] See ss 75(2)(f), 75(3), following Family Law Amendment Act 1987 (Cth).

[20] *Marriage of Clauson* (1995) FLC 92-595.

[21] See for example Succession Act 2006 (NSW) Ch 3. The criteria to be considered by the court under s 60 include the nature of the relationship between the applicant and the deceased; the nature and extent of any obligations or responsibilities owed by the deceased to the applicant; the character and conduct

III. PRE-NUPTIAL, POST-NUPTIAL AND SEPARATION AGREEMENTS

A. Recognition of Separation Agreements Prior to 2000

i. Historical Background

Prior to the 1960s, Australian courts generally applied common law doctrines based upon considerations of public policy in refusing to hold valid and enforceable agreements which provided for the financial consequences of separation or divorce, purported to take away a spouse's rights to seek financial orders from the courts, or attempted to take away or limit the courts' jurisdiction and powers to make such orders.[22] The first major development in this area came with the federal Matrimonial Causes Act 1959 (Cth), which remained in force from 1961 until 1975. Under this legislation, divorce was available on a number of grounds, most of which were based on notions of marital fault and misconduct. At the time of divorce, however, as an alternative to seeking court orders for spousal maintenance or division of property, the relevant court was empowered to sanction an agreement for the acceptance of money or property or other benefits. Where the court was persuaded to approve the terms of the agreement, the effect of the court's approval was to remove objections to the agreement based upon the traditionally applicable doctrines of public policy.[23] From the time of approval, the parties' rights then depended upon the terms of the agreement, and disputes arising from the agreement would be determined according to the law of contract and pursued in the normal courts dealing with civil claims.

ii. Agreements under ss 86 and 87 of Family Law Act 1975 (Cth)

The second stage in the history of spousal financial agreements began in 1976, when the Matrimonial Causes Act 1959 (Cth) was repealed and replaced by the Family Law Act 1975 (Cth). Two types of agreement were recognised (rather confusingly called 'maintenance agreements', although such an agreement might deal with matters of property or maintenance alone, or both together). Agreements which dealt with financial matters but did not purport to take away either party's rights to seek financial orders from the Family Court could simply be registered at the Court (s 86(1)), and theoretically enforced by either of the spouses in the event of default or breach of the agreement (s 88(1)). In practice such an agreement (known as an 's 86 agreement') conferred virtually no finality for the parties, since in the event of one spouse seeking to enforce it, the other spouse could immediately institute proceedings under Part VIII of the Family Law Act for property or maintenance orders. A section 86 agreement was therefore of little utility in most cases, and was rarely recommended by family lawyers advising their clients. Of more interest for

---

and financial position and needs of the applicant; any contributions previously made by the applicant to the deceased's property and welfare; and the size of the estate and the needs of other relevant parties.

[22] Eg *Hyman v Hyman* [1929] AC 601; *Davies v Davies* (1919) 26 CLR 348; and *Brooks v Burns Philp Trustee Co Ltd* (1969) 121 CLR 432. See Dickey above n 12, 650.

[23] Matrimonial Causes Act 1959 (Cth) s 87(1)(k). See Dickey above n 12, 651.

present purposes is the second type of agreement (known as an 's 87 agreement'), by which either party could agree to the terms of the agreement in substitution for the rights to seek court orders for property division or for spousal maintenance, or both (s 87(1)). An agreement of this type, in substitution for either party's rights under the Family Law Act, had no effect and was not enforceable in any way unless it had been approved by the Family Court (s 87(2)). It was not a statutory requirement that the parties should already be involved in proceedings for divorce, but the Court adopted the position that unless the parties had already separated and there was no prospect of reconciliation, it would not be appropriate for the judge even to consider approving the agreement.[24]

The Court was not to approve an agreement in substitution for rights unless it was satisfied that the provisions with respect to financial matters were 'proper' (s 87(3)). Relevant considerations in deciding this issue included whether there was full and frank disclosure of the parties' financial circumstances, whether the parties' interests appeared to be fairly protected, whether the parties understood the meaning and effect of the agreement and had the capacity to perform their obligations under it, and whether the agreement was one which it would be appropriate for the Court to enforce.[25] While it was not essential that each party had received legal advice, the Court's task was normally made easier where this had been done. As mentioned, if the Court refused to give its approval (or for that matter if the parties had never sought the Court's approval), the agreement had no legal effect and was not enforceable, although if either party had acted in reliance on the agreement, evidence of those matters could be considered in later proceedings for property or maintenance orders.[26]

One qualification to the finality of an approved agreement was introduced in 1988, again with the objective of protecting the public purse: if it was established that at the time of the approval a party was unable to support himself or herself without the benefit of social security pension payments, then any clause in the agreement limiting that party's rights to seek maintenance was ineffective to exclude the court's powers to award maintenance against the other party.[27] Finally, it should be noted that on application by a spouse, or an interested third party,[28] the court could subsequently revoke the approval on the grounds of fraud, or mutual consent of the parties, or where it was impracticable for part of the agreement to be carried out, or where the agreement was found to be void, voidable or unenforceable according to the common law and equitable principles of contract law (eg because of uncertainty, duress, undue influence, misrepresentation, unconscionability or mistake).[29]

iii. Proposals for Wider Use of Agreements

The provisions just outlined continued in operation from 1976 until 2000, when a new regime of private ordering of financial matters between spouses was introduced,

---

[24] *Marriage of Wright* (1977) 3 Fam LR 11,150.
[25] *Marriage of Wright* (1977) 3 Fam LR 11,150. See Monahan and Young above n 12, 539–40.
[26] See Monahan and Young above n 12, 541. Relevant authorities include *Woodcock v Woodcock* (1998) FLC 92-739; *G v G* (2000) 26 Fam LR 592; and *Woodland v Todd* (2005) FLC 93-217.
[27] Family Law Act 1975 (Cth), s 87(4A)–(4B), inserted by Family Law Amendment Act 1987 (Cth).
[28] See, eg *Chemaisse v Commissioner of Taxation (Cth)* (1988) FLC 91-915.
[29] Family Law Act 1975 (Cth), s 87(8).

allowing agreements to be made prior to marriage and during marriage, as well as after separation and divorce. Discussions concerning the greater use of marital financial agreements, however, had been circulating since the late 1980s. In 1987, the Australian Law Reform Commission considered the topic as part of its extensive review of the law of matrimonial property in Australia. Following from its consultations with members of the community and with family lawyers, the Commission believed there was increasing public support for the introduction of agreements which could be made before or during marriage, rather than only after marital breakdown.[30]

Among the advantages put forward by the Commission for such agreements were the greater degree of 'control' for spouses or intending spouses over their financial affairs and the greater 'certainty' that this would provide when compared to the discretionary system of property adjustment provided by the Family Law Act. Further, such a reform would reflect the fact that Australia was a multicultural society, with many people coming from countries where marriage contracts were customary. As well, cohabitation contracts were already being introduced by some of the Australian states for de facto partners, and to allow a similar mechanism for married couples would remove a source of discrimination against them and possibly even encourage persons to marry rather than remain in an informal relationship.[31] Lastly, given the statistics as to increasing numbers of second marriages, the Commission was of the view that marital contracts might well be an attractive option for people wishing to preserve assets for children of a first marriage, or for persons with inherited wealth and interests derived from family businesses, family farming properties and the like. [32]

In brief, the Commission recommended the introduction of marital agreements, which would be generally subject to the ordinary law of contract, but with restrictions on the parties' ability to contract out of rights to spousal maintenance, and with the Family Court being able to disregard part or all of an agreement if 'substantial injustice' would be caused by following it.[33] Where an agreement went further and sought to exclude altogether the court's jurisdiction to make property or maintenance orders, however, the Commission recommended (rather confusingly) that the then existing system which required the court's approval to give legal effect to the agreement should be continued.[34]

No immediate action was taken by the federal government in response to the Commission's report and recommendations,[35] but a few years later a Joint Parliamentary Committee was established to investigate various aspects of the operation of the Family Law Act. In its 1992 Report, the Committee recommended the wider use and enforceability of agreements on financial matters, including agreements made prior to marriage, but with the court having a discretion to disregard

---

[30] Australian Law Reform Commission, *Report No 39*, 'Matrimonial Property' (Canberra, AGPS, 1987) [438].

[31] Ibid [438], [440].

[32] Ibid [438]–[439].

[33] Ibid [445], [447]–[448].

[34] Ibid [451]–[452].

[35] See also (to similar effect) Australian Law Reform Commission, *Report No 57*, 'Multiculturalism and the Law' (Sydney, ALRC, 1992) [5.43]–[5.46].

an agreement if to enforce it in the light of changing circumstances would lead to 'serious injustice'.[36]

After draft legislation in 1995 had lapsed with the federal elections and a change of government,[37] a revised set of amendments were introduced in the Family Law Amendment Bill 1999 (Cth), subsequently enacted as the Family Law Amendment Act 2000 (Cth). According to the Attorney-General's second reading speech, the Australian community, and its attitude to marriage, had changed substantially since the Family Law Act 1975 (Cth) came into operation in 1976.[38] One objective of the new provisions therefore was 'to bring the Act into line with prevailing community attitudes and needs'.[39] The introduction of binding financial agreements[40] would especially benefit people about to enter a subsequent marriage as well as those on the land and those with family businesses.[41] More generally, the aim was to encourage people to agree on how their property should be distributed if they separated, thereby allowing people 'greater control and choice over their own affairs in the event of marital breakdown'.[42] It was also suggested that, along with other measures, the amendments would provide a more efficient and less costly means of resolving disputes than was provided by the existing legislation.[43]

Before outlining the important aspects of the new regime for financial agreements, it may be noted that some observers were sceptical or hostile about the government's stated objectives and its view as to the likely results of the reforms. The then Chief Justice of the Family Court, for example, expressed his personal scepticism in a speech to the Bar Association.[44] It would be difficult, he said, to ensure that the parties to pre-marital agreements had equal bargaining power, and given that such an agreement was 'an open ended contract that may extend for fifty years or more', it was impossible to predict what might happen in that time.[45] Further, he doubted that the proposed legislation contained sufficient protection for the parties, especially in violent or abusive marriages, and considered the proposed law more likely to increase rather than reduce the amount of litigation. In his view, the existing system requiring judicial scrutiny of separation agreements provided better safeguards and deterred unreasonable behaviour.[46] In a similar vein, having referred to the rather limited literature on the common law experience with pre-nuptial agreements, Fehlberg and

---

[36] Joint Select Committee, *The Family Law Act 1975: Aspects of its Operation and Interpretation* (Canberra, AGPS, 1992) [1224], Recommendation 97. See Monahan and Young above n 12, 542.

[37] B Fehlberg and B Smyth, 'Pre-Nuptial Agreements for Australia: Why Not?' (2000) 14 *Australian Journal of Family Law* 80–101, 85–86.

[38] Second Reading Speech, Mr Williams, House of Representatives, Hansard 22 September 1999, 10151–53, 10152.

[39] Ibid, 10152.

[40] The term 'financial agreement' in the Bill, and subsequently in Pt VIIIA of the Family Law Act 1975 (Cth) refers to agreements dealing with financial matters regardless of when the agreement is made, ie whether made prior to or during marriage, or following separation or divorce (see Family Law Act 1975 (Cth) ss 90B, 90C and 90D).

[41] Second Reading Speech n 38 above, 10152.

[42] Ibid, 10152.

[43] Ibid, 10153.

[44] Alastair Nicholson, 'Proposed Changes to Property Matters under the Family Law Act', 20 May 1999 (Bar Association of NSW, Sydney), 1–18.

[45] Ibid, 15.

[46] Ibid, 15–16.

Smyth argued that it was unlikely that any of the government's stated legislative purposes as to efficiency, cost-saving and reduction of conflict would be achieved by the introduction of the planned Part VIIIA of the Act.[47] Further, references to the so-called benefits of increased 'control' and 'choice' for parties overlooked the reality of differences in bargaining power and the advantages likely to flow to the economically more powerful spouse (usually the male, as reported by some overseas studies).[48] The authors also doubted whether the changes were in fact a response to 'prevailing community attitudes and needs',[49] and also warned against the lack of sufficient safeguards in the legislation to protect vulnerable spouses in relation to the making of agreements and in the grounds for setting aside agreements.[50]

A Senate Committee examining the Bill received submissions from members of the public, legal observers and community organisations, a good number of which were negative and pessimistic.[51] As one example, a submission from the National Network of Women's Legal Services, in addition to criticising specific sections of the Bill, was strongly opposed to the amendments as a whole. The submission argued that the changes were premature and there had been insufficient time for proper community consultation or adequate empirical research, and that the likely consequences of the changes would be to decrease women's entitlement to property after separation, leading to increased levels of poverty and greater need for government assistance for women and children. Moreover,

> The agreements favour the party with assets and in the stronger negotiating position and therefore will generally benefit men. Of particular concern is that [binding financial agreements] will provide an easy legal mechanism for rural women to be excluded from farming properties and further disadvantage women from non-English speaking backgrounds and women who have suffered domestic violence.[52]

The Senate Committee nevertheless was generally in favour of the proposed amendments,[53] and, with some minor changes recommended by the Committee, the amendment Act came into operation in December 2000.

B. Part VIIIA of Family Law Act 1975 (Cth)

i. Outline of Provisions of Part VIIIA as at 27 December 2000

As a result of the amending Act, the previously mentioned sections 86 and 87 of the Family Law Act 1975 (Cth) have no application to agreements made on or after 27

---

[47] Fehlberg and Smyth, 'Pre-Nuptial Agreements' above n 37, 96.

[48] Ibid, 96–98. Among the studies referred to by the authors are B Atwood, 'Ten Years Later: Lingering Concerns about the Uniform Premarital Agreements Act' (1993) 19 *Journal of Legislation* 127; and G Frommer Brod, 'Premarital Agreements and Gender Justice' (1994) *Yale Journal of Law and Feminism* 229. See also A Mackay, 'Who Gets a Better Deal? Women and Prenuptial Agreements in Australia and the USA' (2003) 7 *University of Western Sydney Law Review* 109–33.

[49] Fehlberg and Smyth above n 37, 100–01.

[50] Ibid, 105–06.

[51] Senate Legal and Constitutional Legislation Committee, 'Provisions of the Family Law Amendment Bill 1999' (Canberra, December 1999) 19–29.

[52] National Network of Women's Legal Services (NNWLS), *Submission to Senate Legal and Constitutional Legislation Committee* (1 November 1999).

[53] Senate Legal and Constitutional Legislation Committee above n 51, 35–36.

December 2000.[54] With effect from that date a new Part VIIIA came into operation, providing a very different system of private ordering of financial matters between spouses, allowing agreements to be made prior to marriage, while the marriage is still on foot, or after separation or divorce. Given that substantial amendments to Part VIIIA have already occurred on multiple occasions, it will suffice here to outline the main features of the new regime as originally enacted, before addressing the more recent developments.[55]

From the end of 2000, parties could make binding written agreements entered into prior to marriage (s 90B), or during marriage (whether before or after separation—s 90C), or following divorce (s 90D). The basic principles of Part VIIIA were applicable in each situation; that is, regardless of whether the agreement was made before or after separation. In each case the agreement could set out how the property or financial resources of either of the parties were to be dealt with[56] in the event of the breakdown of the marriage (or in the event of divorce, in the case of a s 90D agreement), and also deal with issues of spousal maintenance. As a result of amendments to other parts of the Family Law Act, which commenced at the end of 2002, giving the Family Court powers to deal with the parties' superannuation interests as though they were property, from that time also it became possible for superannuation interests to be dealt with in a financial agreement (s 90MH et seq).

For the agreement to be binding, and thereby exclude the court's powers to make financial orders under Part VIII (see s 71A), it was not necessary that the court should approve the contents of the agreement, or that the agreement should be registered. Rather, each party was instead required to obtain independent legal advice on the agreement, and certificates to that effect had to be signed by the lawyers concerned and attached to the agreement (s 90G). If this was done, the agreement would be binding, subject again, however, to the familiar qualifications concerning spousal maintenance if it was shown that at the time when the agreement came into effect the relevant party was unable to support himself or herself without the assistance of a means-tested social security pension (s 90F(1)).[57] Where the requirements as to legal advice and certification were not complied with (or for that matter where the parties had simply made an informal agreement for distribution of property between themselves), the agreement would not then be binding on the parties (s 90G), and thus the court's powers to make financial orders would continue to be available (s 71A).[58] In the event of a party's subsequent death, a binding agreement could continue to operate and be binding on that party's legal personal representative (s 90H).

---

[54] See Family Law Act 1975 (Cth), ss 86(1A), 87(1A).

[55] The provisions of Pt VIIIA current as at 1 March 2009, together with changes to s 90G introduced with effect from 4 January 2010, are set out at the end of this paper.

[56] By s 90F(2), the term 'dealt with' extends to a provision in an agreement that provides for property or financial resources owned by a party to continue in the ownership of that party.

[57] See now also s 90F(1A).

[58] It may be noted that anything done in reliance on the informal or non-binding agreement would nevertheless remain as part of the financial history of the parties and could subsequently be taken into account if the court was asked to make orders for property division or maintenance. Cf eg *Woodland v Todd* (2005) FLC 93-217.

According to the provisions as enacted in 2000, a binding agreement could only be set aside if the court was satisfied that:

(i) there had been fraud (including non-disclosure of a material matter) (s 90K(1) (a)); or

(ii) the agreement was void, voidable or unenforceable (s 90K(1)(b)) (which was to be determined according to general principles of law and equity applicable to contracts (s 90KA)); or

(iii) circumstances since the making of the agreement made it impracticable for the agreement to be carried out (s 90K(1)(c)); or

(iv) since the making of the agreement a material change of circumstances had occurred relating to the care and welfare of a child of the marriage such that the child or the relevant caretaking parent would suffer hardship if the agreement was not set aside (s 90K(1)(d)); or

(v) a party had engaged in unconscionable conduct in relation to the making of the agreement (s 90K(1)(e)).[59]

ii. Initial Reaction to the New Regime

Reviewing the situation after the new Part VIIIA had been in operation for one year, Fehlberg and Smyth pointed to the difficulties in obtaining data as to the attitude of lawyers and their clients to the new provisions, and the absence of any central registry of agreements (since registration is not required) prevented any analysis of agreements which had been made.[60] They nevertheless made a number of observations on the basis of interviews conducted with family lawyers and other information derived from legal professional organisations and professional papers and articles. With regard to pre-nuptial agreements, some lawyers had reported enquiries and interest on the part of certain types of client, such as persons entering second marriages, but it nevertheless appeared that 'interest in entering a pre-nuptial agreement remains a relatively rare phenomenon'.[61]

Apart from emotional resistance by clients to the idea of involving lawyers and engaging in negotiations over the financial future of their relationships, lawyers themselves appeared dissatisfied with a number of aspects of the new provisions, which made them reluctant to recommend the use of the new agreements. One issue was possibly the result of legislative oversight—unlike the position with financial orders made by the court, there were as yet no statutory exemptions from payment of stamp duty and capital gains tax on property transactions arising from financial agreements.[62] A second issue, even more worrying for lawyers, was the type of

---

[59] For discussion, see P Parkinson, 'Setting Aside Financial Agreements' (2001) 15 *Australian Journal of Family Law* 26–50, and J Campbell, 'Cutting Loose: Possible Escape Routes from Pre-Nuptial Agreements' (2005) 61(8) *Law Society Journal* 62–65.

[60] B Fehlberg and B Smyth, 'Binding Pre-Nuptial Agreements in the First Year' (2002) 16 *International Journal of Law, Policy and the Family* 127–40, 133–34.

[61] Ibid, 135.

[62] Ibid, 135. See also G Watts, 'Binding Financial Agreements—Possibilities and Pitfalls' (2001) 23(5) *Bulletin of the Law Society of South Australia* 28–30.

certificated advice which had to be provided to make the agreement binding. As originally enacted, section 90G required the lawyer's advice as to:

(i)   the effects of the agreement on the client's rights;
(ii) whether at that time it was to the client's advantage, financially or otherwise, to enter the agreement;
(iii) whether at that time it was prudent for the client to make the agreement; and
(iv) whether at that time and in the light of reasonably foreseeable circumstances, the terms of the agreement were fair and reasonable.

Some lawyers (with the support of their professional association) were in fact refusing to act for potential clients on the basis that the requirements were too onerous, that they were not qualified to give financial advice, and that they might not be covered by their professional indemnity insurance in the event of future negligence claims against them.[63] The authors concluded, on the basis of their enquiries made of 'a very small sample of family lawyers', that:

> there was a general view that the legislation is poorly drafted and contains many potential loopholes, making it hard to guarantee that a client would in the future have the 'certainty' they were hoping to achieve. The complexity and resulting legal costs of preparing a pre-nuptial agreement often appeared to be more than clients expected.[64]

These various objections by practising lawyers were not only applicable to agreements made prior to marriage (s 90B), but were equally relevant to separation agreements under section 90C (where the parties were not yet divorced) and section 90D (where divorce had already occurred). But in relation to arrangements following marital breakdown, there was also another reason for lawyers' reluctance to use the new agreements, namely the well-established practice of obtaining consent orders from the court to record financial arrangements which had been agreed between the parties. Not only were the lawyers interviewed more familiar with the procedures relating to consent orders, but (depending on the circumstances) the costs to the client might be less, lawyers were less likely to face future complaints and negligence claims, and the client also received relief from capital gains tax and stamp duties for any resulting property transfers.[65]

iii. Amendments to Part VIIIA up to 2009

Following submissions by professional associations, the federal government put in train changes to the capital gains tax legislation, and some relief from state stamp duty also became available on property transactions arising from a financial agreement.[66] As well, by amendments to Part VIIIA which were passed in 2003 with

---

[63] Fehlberg and Smyth 'Binding Pre-Nuptial Agreements' above n 60, 135–36.
[64] Ibid, 136.
[65] Ibid, 133. Note however that court approval of proposed consent orders is not automatic, but requires a degree of scrutiny by the court so that it is satisfied that the s 79 orders are just and equitable in the circumstances: see *Harris v Caladine* (1991) 172 CLR 84.
[66] See J Campbell and L Seivers, 'Financial Agreements' in *CCH Australian Master Family Law Guide*, 3rd edn (Sydney, CCH Australia Ltd, 2009) [19-140].

effect from 14 January 2004,[67] the requirements for certificated legal advice were modified, so that under section 90G(1)(b) lawyers would now only have to advise as to:

(i) the effects of the agreement on the rights of that party; and
(ii) the advantages and disadvantages, at the time the advice was provided, to the party of making the agreement.

Another difficulty with the original terms of Part VIIIA was discovered in 2001 when the founding director of a telecommunications company purported to transfer assets worth several million dollars to his wife, with whom he was still living, by way of a financial agreement purportedly made under section 90C. Two months later the company was placed into liquidation with alleged losses of many millions of dollars. In August 2002 the Australian Securities and Investments Commission (ASIC), which had been investigating the husband for suspected breaches of the Corporations law, filed an application in the Family Court asking that the financial agreement be set aside under sections 90K(1)(b) and 90KA of the Family Law Act, on the basis that the agreement had been entered into to defeat the interests of third party creditors. In October 2003, in *Australian Securities and Investments Commission v Rich*, O'Ryan J found however that the Family Court had no jurisdiction to make the orders sought by ASIC because (unlike the position where a financial order had been made under s 79 or an agreement had been approved by the court under the former s 87), there was nothing in the new Part VIIIA or elsewhere in the Act authorising the institution of proceedings under section 90K by a third party affected by the operation of a marital financial agreement. Not surprisingly, the trial judge recommended that the Act should be amended promptly to prevent financial agreements being used in ongoing marriages for dishonest motives so as to cause harm to the legitimate interests of third parties.[68]

In the instant case, faced with the prospect of other proceedings being initiated against them by ASIC in a state court, the husband and wife decided to terminate the agreement, and the assets were re-transferred as though the agreement had not been made.[69] To avoid similar cases arising in the future, however, the federal government took immediate action. In December 2003 an amending Act was passed which conferred jurisdiction on the Family Court to entertain complaints by third parties seeking to have a marital financial agreement set aside. As well, additional grounds for setting aside an agreement were added to section 90K where either party enters the agreement for the purpose (or for purposes that include the purpose) of defrauding or defeating a creditor, or with reckless disregard for the interests of a creditor. In this context, a 'creditor' includes a person who could reasonably have been foreseen by the party as reasonably likely to become a creditor (s 90K(1A)).[70]

---

[67] See Family Law Amendment Act 2003 (Cth).
[68] *Australian Securities and Investments Commission v Rich* [2003] FamCA 1114 [118]. See also D Hodson, 'How the Rich get Richer: A Case Study in Legislative Response to Lawyer Initiatives' (2004) 17(3) *Australian Family Lawyer* 19–20.
[69] Hodson, 'How the Rich get Richer' above n 68, 20.
[70] See Family Law Amendment Act 2003 (Cth).

There were additional legislative developments in 2005, no doubt to some extent a further reaction to the *ASIC v Rich* case in 2003. These amendments were part of a project to remove anomalies and promote coordination generally between the federal bankruptcy legislation and the family law legislation.[71] So far as is relevant, it is now possible for the Family Court to hear proceedings between a spouse and the bankruptcy trustee of a bankrupt spouse in relation to (i) maintenance of the first spouse (definition of 'matrimonial cause', s 4(1)(caa)), or (ii) any vested bankruptcy property, where the proceedings can be said to arise from the marital relationship or are in relation to divorce or nullity proceedings between the spouses (definition of 'matrimonial cause', s 4(1)(cb)). In such proceedings involving the trustee in bankruptcy, it is now provided in section 71A(2) that an otherwise binding financial agreement between the spouses will not have the effect of excluding the court's powers to make financial orders.

Another innovation in 2005, again directed to preventing the improper or fraudulent use of financial agreements, was an amendment to Part VIIIA introducing the requirement of a 'separation declaration'.[72] The underlying idea is that a binding financial agreement which deals with how property or financial resources of the spouses are to be dealt with in the event of marital breakdown is of no force or effect until a separation declaration is made (s 90DA).[73] A separation declaration must be in writing and signed by at least one of the spouses, and state that the parties have separated and are living separately and apart and there is no reasonable likelihood of cohabitation being resumed (s 90DA(4)). While there remain some unresolved problems regarding the interpretation of this section, in *Kostres v Kostres* it was held that, in the absence of a separation declaration, the relevant financial agreement was still valid and binding on the parties, but unable to be enforced. Further, the existence of the separation declaration was held to be merely a procedural matter, and so the declaration could be filed during the enforcement proceedings, or the court's orders for enforcement could even be expressed to be contingent on the prompt filing of the required declaration at the end of the proceedings.[74]

A further amending Act was passed in 2008, some of the amendments coming into force in November 2008 and others early in 2009.[75] As a result, it is now possible for third parties to be included as parties to financial agreements. What is more, identical provisions to those outlined earlier for spouses, ie for the making of discretionary orders for financial adjustment and the alternative availability of binding financial agreements, have now been extended in all states, except Western Australia, to heterosexual and same-sex de facto partners as well.[76]

---

[71] See Bankruptcy and Family Law Legislation Amendment Act 2005 (Cth).

[72] See s 90DA, inserted by Family Law Amendment Act 2005 (Cth).

[73] The requirement ceases to apply if the parties divorce, or if a spouse dies: s 90DA(1A).

[74] *Kostres v Kostres* [2008] FMCAfam 1124 [72]–[73], not affected on this point by the Full Court decision on appeal in *Kostres v Kostres* [2009] FamCAFC 222. Cf *Stoddard v Stoddard* [2007] FMCAfam 735 [22]–[24].

[75] See Family Law Amendment (De Facto Financial Matters and Other Measures) Act 2008 (Cth).

[76] Family Law Amendment (De Facto Financial Matters and Other Measures) Act 2008 (Cth), inserting Pt VIIIAB into the Family Law Act 1975 (Cth). As noted earlier, this amendment to the Family Law Act 1975 (Cth) was as a result of a reference of the relevant legislative powers to the Commonwealth Government from all states except Western Australia. The amendments came into force in the referring states on 1 March 2009, except for South Australia where the commencement date was 1 July 2010.

iv. Case Law Concerning Section 90G

The proper interpretation of section 90G has been the subject of a steadily increasing body of case law. While it has been observed that 's 90G does not, by its terms, place any relevance on the quality or correctness of the advice given to a party',[77] some cases have considered the circumstances in which the advice was given, whether the lawyer giving the advice had the right to practise in the relevant jurisdiction, and whether claims based on estoppel can nevertheless be relevant where section 90G has not been satisfied. Thus, in *Fitzpatrick v Griffin*, where the husband chose and paid the costs for a firm of solicitors to act for both parties to the financial agreement, the Court, in holding for several reasons that the resulting agreement was not binding, noted that 'there can be no question that there was little that resembled "independent advice"'.[78] In *Murphy v Murphy*, the husband proposed marriage to the wife when visiting her in the Philippines. He also presented her with a pre-nuptial agreement, saying that she would have to sign it or the marriage would not go ahead. Shortly afterwards she sought advice from a Filipino lawyer who completed the relevant certificate for the purposes of section 90G. After the marriage broke down and the husband sought to rely on the agreement, the wife argued that the agreement was not binding because the Filipino lawyer was not enrolled as a practitioner in Australia. The Court agreed with the wife's argument, interpreting the term 'legal practitioner' in section 90G to mean a lawyer 'qualified to practise in the Australian federal jurisdiction'.[79] A similar conclusion was reached in *Ruane v Bachmann-Ruane*, where an agreement was held not to be binding for non-compliance with section 90G because the advice given to the wife was provided by an English lawyer not admitted to practise in Australia. Cronin J stated that while the intention of section 90G was not necessarily to require a specialist family lawyer to give the advice, 'it is directed to lawyers who are subject to the controls of the state regulatory bodies as well as the courts because of the need to protect the public and ensure accountability'.[80]

Can a party ever be estopped from seeking to rely on the fact that an agreement does not comply with the requirements of section 90G? This issue arose in *Fevia v Carmel-Fevia*, where a wealthy man married a woman of modest means following the execution of what purported to be a pre-nuptial agreement. It was found by the Court in subsequent financial proceedings commenced by the wife that on basic contractual principles, in the light of the circumstances in which alterations had been made to the documents executed by the parties, there was no valid and enforceable agreement between them.[81] The Court nevertheless went on to consider, in the alternative, whether, if there was in fact an agreement, it complied with section 90G, and again found in the negative.[82] Finally, the Court also considered the husband's remaining argument that the wife should be estopped from relying on the fact of non-compliance with section 90G, on the basis that both parties

---

[77] *Kostres v Kostres* [2008] FMCAfam 1124 [25], and note the similar conclusion in *Ruane v Bachmann-Ruane* [2009] FamCA 1101 [76].

[78] *Fitzpatrick v Griffin* [2008] FMCAfam 555 [19].

[79] *Murphy v Murphy* [2009] FMCAfam 270 [75].

[80] *Ruane v Bachmann-Ruane* [2009] FamCA 1101 [78].

[81] *Fevia v Carmel-Fevia* [2009] FamCA 816 [158]–[164].

[82] Ibid [213]–[215] ff.

had assumed the 'agreement' to be valid and that certain payments had been made pursuant to the 'agreement'. In the Court's view, which emphasised the significance of the operation of section 71A as to the ousting of the court's jurisdiction to make orders under Part VIII:

> Section 90G has a purpose separate from those sections within [Part VIIIA] that have as their focus the formation, validity and effectiveness of a 'financial agreement'. Section 90G's purpose is to specify how those arrangements which are otherwise 'agreements', and otherwise 'financial agreements', attract s 71A by becoming 'binding'. The section operates separately to, and additional upon, ss 90B and 90KA; s 90G does not affect (or effect) the validity, enforceability or effectiveness of the contract or the contractual relationship; it affects (and effects) only the specific statutory function which is that provided for by s 71A. ... The [husband's] submission [as to estoppel] conflates the potential application of that doctrine to s 90G with its potential application to s 90B or Part VIIIA as a whole. ... Parties may by agreement seek to exclude the provisions of Part VIII of the Act. But the Act does not allow the parties to do so by any agreement which (though enforceable as a contract) they choose to adopt. The Act prescribes one manner alone in which that may occur and that is by compliance with s 90G. ... [E]stoppel has no operation to s 90G.[83]

In general agreement with this view, Murphy J in *Ruane v Bachmann-Ruane* discussed the approach which had been taken previously in relation to the former operation of section 87 of the Act, with particular reference to the Full Court decision in *Woodcock v Woodcock*, and concluded:

> [T]he Full Court said that the doctrine [of estoppel] did not oust the jurisdiction of the court to make orders under Part VIII of the Act but noted that equitable concepts might operate when determining the various statutory components of Part VIII. ... [F]or the purposes of Part VIIIA, estoppel as a principle cannot apply notwithstanding s 90KA. That is because in respect of Part VIII, the Full Court said that estoppel could not oust the jurisdiction of the court and the same principle must apply in respect of Part VIIIA as it is also a statutory provision which if strictly followed, would oust the jurisdiction of the court. Accordingly, the wife's argument that estoppel should deny the husband the right to rely upon the statutory imperfections of the agreement, cannot succeed.[84]

v. Compliance with Formalities of Section 90G—Strict or Substantial?

Another particularly vexed issue, now the subject of the very latest set of amendments to Part VIIIA, has been whether the requirements in section 90G as to certification of the independent legal advice received by both parties have to be followed to the letter. In *J v J*, the solicitors completed certificates based on an out-of-date precedent which did not follow the precise wording of section 90G at the time the agreement was made. The trial judge held the agreement not to be binding, stating:

> To my mind, the words that appear in section 90G(1), 'if and only if', are words of real significance. They have a meaning. They import a requirement for a level of compliance, if the agreement is to be binding, that is clearly a standard or level above and beyond what might

---

[83] Ibid [185], [285], [291], [294].
[84] *Ruane v Bachmann-Ruane* [2009] FamCA 1101 [92]–[94]. For cases to similar effect as *Woodcock v Woodcock* (1998) FLC 92-739, see also *G v G* (2000) 26 Fam LR 592 and *Woodland v Todd* (2005) FLC 93-217.

be described as substantial compliance. Those words 'if and only if' make it clear that each of the parties must ensure that that which is required to be contained and dealt with in the agreement, and the annexures to it, is in fact contained, appropriately and completely. Compliance must therefore be a full compliance, satisfying the statutory requirements.[85]

A contrasting approach was taken by the trial judge in *Black v Black*. There, the independent legal advice had been provided to each party, but there were some inaccuracies in the form of certificates used and, contrary to the precise wording of s 90G, there was no recital in the body of the agreement itself that each party had been so advised. The trial judge upheld the agreement, preferring to adopt a purposive construction of the section in deciding that substantial rather than strict compliance with the requirements of the legislation was sufficient. In his view,

> [t]he intention of Part VIIIA is to enable ordinary people to enter into financial agreements ... The explanatory memorandum observes that it is the legislative intent to encourage the use of financial agreements ... If courts require strict interpretation of the legislation then this would have the effect of making such agreements less available to the broader community. It would positively discourage the use of financial agreements and it would limit the pool of legal practitioners who are equipped and willing to draft and/or advise in relation to such agreements. Such strict and inevitably narrow construction would add to the cost of such agreements ... That is not the legislative intent. The form should not defeat the substance. The Act does not create a regime of strict compliance and there is a requirement on courts to give purpose to legislation.[86]

Prior to the hearing of an appeal in *Black v Black*, both the full compliance approach required in *J v J* and the less onerous substantial compliance test adopted by the trial judge in *Black v Black* had found support among other judges.[87] On appeal, however, the Full Court disagreed with the trial judge's 'substantial compliance' interpretation, and overturned the agreement:

> The Act permits parties to make an agreement which provides an amicable resolution to their financial matters in the event of separation. ... Care must be taken in interpreting any provision of the Act that has the effect of ousting the jurisdiction of the court. ... The compromise reached by the legislature was to permit the parties to oust the court's jurisdiction to make adjustive orders but only if certain stringent requirements were met. ... We are of the view that strict compliance with the statutory requirements is necessary to oust the court's jurisdiction to make adjustive orders under s 79.[88]

As a result of the Full Court's decision in 2008 in *Black v Black*, numerous agreements have been overturned for insufficient compliance with the requirements of section 90G concerning certification, or concerning the identification and distribution of the original and copy agreements.[89]

---

[85] *J v J* [2006] FamCA 442 [19].

[86] *Black v Black* [2006] FamCA 972 [110].

[87] As to the strict compliance test, see, eg *Millington v Millington* [2007] FamCA 687, and *Whatley v Whatley* [2007] FamCA 1671. Cases which instead followed the substantial compliance approach favoured by the trial judge in *Black v Black* include *Ruzic v Ruzic* [2007] FamCA 473, and *Stoddard v Stoddard* [2007] FMCAfam 735.

[88] *Black v Black* [2008] FamCAFC 7 [40], [42], [45].

[89] Cases where the agreements have been overturned for non-compliance with s 90G requirements include *Charney v Charney* [2009] FamCA 751, *Fevia v Carmel*-Fevia [2009] FamCA 816, *Gardiner v Baker* [2009] FMCAfam 1029, *Moreno v Moreno* [2009] FMCAfam 1109, *Balzia v Covich* [2009]

vi. Amendments to section 90G in 2010[90]

The decision in favour of strict compliance caused dismay among some members of the legal profession. One newspaper article referred to a view among lawyers as to the possibility of thousands of agreements being invalid due to technical errors.[91] Two specialist practitioners, who had already in 2006 argued in a professional journal that lawyers faced a serious risk of liability claims in preparing pre-nuptial agreements, and that they personally 'would not touch a pre-nuptial agreement without the clients acknowledging that the costs will run into thousands of dollars even without substantial negotiations or drafting',[92] described the Full Court decision as 'a very dark (and dare we say, black) day for legal practitioners and their insurers'.[93] They also stated:

> Financial agreements are here to stay. In this climate, practitioners need to come up to speed with the potential 'out' clauses to agreements, both to protect themselves from a negligence claim and to advise future clients who may seek to set agreements aside. A technical avoidance mechanism has been embodied in the law and some clients will benefit. Practitioners must be mindful that if an agreement turns sour, the most obvious litigation target is the solicitor who signed the certificate of independent legal advice.[94]

Submissions by professional associations, supported by the Family Law Council and the Family Law Section of the Law Council of Australia, were made in 2008 to the federal Attorney-General's department. It was argued that the implications of the Full Court's support of strict compliance in *Black v Black* would reduce public confidence in the binding nature of financial agreements, and would increase lawyers' potential liability to negligence claims.[95] In response, the federal government moved to introduce a new set of amendments, included in the Federal Justice System Amendment (Efficiency Measures) Bill (No 1) 2008 (Cth). These amendments, in short, were designed to simplify the technical requirements as to certification, while preserving intact the general requirement of independent legal advice. The Bill was sent to the Senate Standing Committee on Legal and Constitutional Affairs, which reported in February 2009. The report referred in rather inconclusive terms to a submission received from the Family Law Section of the Law Council of Australia,[96]

FamCA 1357, *Norton v Norton* [2009] FamCA 359, *Smart v Smart* [2008] FMCAfam 341, *Suffolk v Suffolk (No 2)* [2009] FamCA 917, and see *Tsarouhi v Tsarouhi* [2009] FMCAfam 126 (this point not finally determined). Cf also the cases of *Adamidis v Adamidis* [2009] FMCAfam 1104 and *Blackmore v Webber* [2009] FMCAfam 154.

[90] The discussion of these amendments draws on O Jessep, 'Section 90G and Pt VIIIA of the Family Law Act 1975 (Cth)' (2010) 24 *Australian Journal of Family Law* 104–14.

[91] R Nickless, 'Best-laid Plans Won't Stop Rows' *Australian Financial Review* (18 December 2009) 49.

[92] P Staindl and L Bradley, 'Binding Financial Agreements—How Safe Are They?' (2006) 12 *Current Family Law* 187–97, 194.

[93] L Bradley and P Staindl, '*Black v Black*—A Dark Day for Financial Agreements' (2008) 82(12) *Law Institute Journal* 36–39, 36. See also P Staindl and L Bradley, 'Financial Agreements: Risks, Responsibilities and Rewards' (2008) 13 *Current Family Law* 64–69; R Benjamin, 'The Practical Implications of Financial Agreements: Adopting a Strict Interpretation' (2008) 13 *Current Family Law* 185–94; and J Dowd and A Harland, 'Bound by Strict Compliance' (2008) 60(3) *Law Society Journal* 60–63.

[94] Bradley and Staindl, '*Black v Black*' above n 93, 39.

[95] Law Council of Australia, Family Law Section, Letter to Attorney-General, 7 May 2008.

[96] Law Council of Australia, Family Law Section, 'Submission on Federal Justice System Amendment (Efficiency Measures) Bill 2008' (22 January 2009).

and recommended that the proposed amendments be passed.[97] There were however further amendments made by the government during the parliamentary process, and the final version of the Bill, then entitled the Federal Justice System Amendment (Efficiency Measures) Bill (No 1) 2009 (Cth), was passed in late 2009. The new provisions dealing with financial agreements came into force on 4 January 2010. As a result of the amendments, the relevant provisions of section 90G now read as follows:

(1) Subject to subsection (1A), a financial agreement is binding on the parties to the agreement if, and only if:

    (a) the agreement is signed by all parties; and

    (b) before signing the agreement, each spouse party was provided with independent legal advice from a legal practitioner about the effect of the agreement on the rights of that party and about the advantages and disadvantages, at the time that the advice was provided, to that party of making the agreement; and

    (c) either before or after signing the agreement, each spouse party was provided with a signed statement by the legal practitioner stating that the advice referred to in paragraph (b) was provided to that party (whether or not the statement is annexed to the agreement); and

    (ca) a copy of the statement referred to in paragraph (c) that was provided to a spouse party is given to the other spouse party or to a legal practitioner for the other spouse party; and

    (d) the agreement has not been terminated and has not been set aside by a court.

(1A) A financial agreement is binding on the parties to the agreement if:

    (a) the agreement is signed by all parties; and

    (b) one or more of paragraphs (1)(b), (c) and (ca) are not satisfied in relation to the agreement; and

    (c) a court is satisfied that it would be unjust and inequitable if the agreement were not binding on the spouse parties to the agreement (disregarding any changes in circumstances from the time the agreement was made); and

    (d) the court makes an order under subsection (1B) declaring that the agreement is binding on the parties to the agreement; and

    (e) the agreement has not been terminated and has not been set aside by a court.

(1B) For the purposes of paragraph (1A)(d), a court may make an order declaring that a financial agreement is binding on the parties to the agreement, upon application (the ***enforcement application***) by a spouse party seeking to enforce the agreement.

(1C) To avoid doubt, section 90KA applies in relation to the enforcement application.

---

[97] For the Senate Committee's discussion, see Senate Standing Committee on Legal and Constitutional Affairs, *Inquiry into the Federal Justice System Amendment (Efficiency Measures) Bill (No 1) 2008* (Canberra, 23 February 2009) [3.4]–[3.21].

It is not possible here to tease out all the implications of the 2010 amendments. Attention has already been drawn by the Family Law Section of the Law Council of Australia to problems concerning the partial retrospectivity of the amendments, and ambiguity and confusion in the application of the transitional provisions.[98] Instead, it will be sufficient simply to refer to a striking difference between the first amendments in the 2008 Bill and the final government amendments introduced in October 2009. The original Explanatory Memorandum for the 2008 Bill referred to the need for a response to the Full Court decision in *Black v Black* in order to restore confidence in the binding nature of financial agreements, and consequently the amendments to section 90G(1) were intended 'to relax certain requirements that must be strictly satisfied for financial agreements and termination agreements to be binding'.[99] The same intention is evident in part of the 2009 Bill, and the provisions of sub-section (1), set out above, reflect some changes urged upon the government by the Family Law Section of the Law Council of Australia.[100] It can be seen that the current version of sub-section (1)(a) to (ca) contains some changes and simplification to the way in which the legal advice requirement is to be documented.

But sub-section (1) is now made 'subject to sub-section (1A)', and sub-section (1A) is accompanied by sub-sections (1B) and (1C). This is new material, which was not contained in the original 2008 Bill. In the Supplementary Explanatory Memorandum to the government amendments moved in October 2009, it is simply stated that the government amendments 'will address issues that have arisen in submissions to the inquiry of the Senate Standing Committee on Legal and Constitutional Affairs into the provisions of the Bill and following consultation with key stakeholders'.[101] It should be observed, however, that the material in sub-sections (1A) to (1C) was not considered by the Senate Standing Committee on Legal and Constitutional Affairs, and was not mentioned in the Law Council of Australia submission. On the contrary, the Family Law Section of the Law Council of Australia has lost no time in expressing to members its concern over these amendments, warning of the dangers of professional negligence claims, and stating its intention to liaise further with the government to address the issues.[102]

In short, these new sub-sections (1A) to (1C) provide that the court in proceedings for enforcement of a financial agreement which does not satisfy one or more of the requirements in sub-sections (1)(b), (c) and (ca) may nevertheless declare that the agreement is binding on the parties where it would be unjust and inequitable not to do so (disregarding any changes in circumstances from the time the agreement was made). Other than the 'unjust and inequitable if the agreement is not binding'

---

[98] As to the retrospective operation of and the transitional provisions for the amendments to s 90G, see Federal Justice System Amendment (Efficiency Measures) Act (No 1) 2009, Sch 5, Items 8 and 8A. See Law Council of Australia, Family Law Section, *FLS Online News 2010—No 1* (5 January 2010), 'Amendments to the Family Law Act 1975 concerning Financial Agreements', and note *Wallace v Stelzer* [2011] FamCA 54.

[99] Explanatory Memorandum to Federal Justice Amendment (Efficiency Measures) Bill (No 1) 2008, 2.

[100] See Law Council of Australia, Family Law Section, 'Submission' above n 96.

[101] Supplementary Explanatory Memorandum to the Federal Justice System Amendment (Efficiency Measures) Bill (No 1) 2008, 2.

[102] Law Council of Australia, Family Law Section, *FLS Online News* above n 98.

test, the new sub-sections give no guidance to the court as to what matters should be taken into account in deciding the issue. The court is thus left with a very wide discretion. Further, the wording of sub-section (1A)(b) ('one or more of paragraphs (1)(b), (c) and (ca)') as to the omissions or oversights which the court might excuse in the interests of justice and equity go well beyond what might be considered merely 'technical' requirements such as those debated in the *Black v Black* decision itself. That is, on the wording of sub-section (1A)(b), read in conjunction with sub-section (1)(b), for example, it will be possible to apply to have a financial agreement declared binding even where there has been no legal advice provided at all. Such a possibility represents a striking departure from the consistent emphasis in the Family Law Act ever since 1976 on safeguarding the rights of parties under Part VIII of the Act and strictly limiting the situations in which the court's jurisdiction can be excluded by agreement.

vii. Other Case Law Developments Since 2000

Other than the steady flow of cases concerning the requirements and interpretation of section 90G, a number of attempts have been made to set aside otherwise binding agreements under section 90K. The grounds upon which an agreement may be set aside pursuant to section 90K have been referred to earlier. In brief, the main grounds are those of fraud, including non-disclosure of a material matter (s 90K(1)(a)); matters which make the agreement void, voidable or unenforceable (s 90K(1)(b)); where it is impracticable to carry out the agreement as a result of subsequent circumstances (s 90K(1)(c)); a subsequent material change of circumstances affecting a child's welfare such that the child or the caretaking parent would suffer hardship if the agreement is not set aside (s 90K(1)(d)); and unconscionable conduct by a party in respect of the making of the agreement (s 90K(1)(e)). To date, cases have arisen where the court has been prepared to set aside agreements on the basis of fraud as a result of non-disclosure,[103] duress,[104] misrepresentation[105] and unconscionability,[106] while refusing an application to set aside based upon alleged mental incapacity.[107]

Some decisions have relied on several grounds for invalidating an agreement. For example, in *Blackmore v Webber*, an Australian man met and began living with a Thai woman who had come to Australia as a student. She became pregnant, and the couple planned a wedding, following which she was due to visit her relatives in Thailand. Five days before the wedding he presented her with an agreement prepared by his lawyers, and told her that the marriage could not go ahead unless she signed it. She reluctantly signed it two days later after seeing a firm of solicitors, and the wedding took place. The parties separated two and a half years later, and the

---

[103] See *Blackmore v Webber* [2009] FMCAfam 154 and *Stoddard v Stoddard* [2007] FMCAfam 735.

[104] *Blackmore v Webber* [2009] FMCAfam 154, *Tsarouhi v Tsarouhi* [2009] FMCAfam 126 and *Moreno v Moreno* [2009] FMCAfam 1109.

[105] *Stoddard v Stoddard* [2007] FMCAfam 735.

[106] *Blackmore v Webber* [2009] FMCAfam 154, *Tsarouhi v Tsarouhi* [2009] FMCAfam 126 and *Moreno v Moreno* [2009] FMCAfam 1109. Note also *Jacobs v Vaile* [2008] FMCAfam 641, where the court refused an application for summary dismissal of a claim based upon this ground.

[107] *Cole v Cole* [2008] FMCAfam 664.

wife initiated proceedings to set aside the agreement. On the evidence it appeared that the details of the husband's superannuation had been omitted from the list of the husband's assets in the agreement, and the Court thought this non-disclosure was sufficient to set aside the agreement for fraud pursuant to section 90(1)(a).[108] Further, the wife alleged that the agreement was 'void, voidable or unenforceable' under section 90(1)(b) because of duress. The Court agreed, noting:

> Producing the Agreement for signature less than five days before marriage, when she was four to five months pregnant, about to return to Thailand in circumstances where her family expected her to return as a married woman, and where she was faced with the real risk of not being able to remain in Australia, as her visa was about to expire, [and] threatening her with no marriage placed the wife in a position where she had little to no choice but to sign the agreement. In requiring her to do so in these circumstances, I find that the pressure placed on the wife by the husband was 'illegitimate' ... Accordingly, I find that the wife signed the Agreement under duress, as defined in law.[109]

Finally, the Court also agreed with the wife's argument that the agreement should be set aside under section 90(1)(e) because the husband had behaved unconscionably in relation to the making of the agreement:

> In addition to being pregnant and without family support in a foreign country, she was totally dependent upon the husband for her accommodation, food, financial support and for her very presence in the country. I am satisfied that the husband was very much aware of the wife's circumstances and that the manner in which he presented the Agreement and demanded its immediate signing so close to the wedding date is such that he took unconscionable advantage of the wife's special disadvantage.[110]

Another case involving a foreign wife is that of *Moreno v Moreno*, where the Court began its judgment with a question:

> Is it unconscionable for a husband who has sought and obtained a wife from Russia to come to Australia, where the relationship is unstable and marked by separations [often caused by the husband's violent and aggressive behaviour] and where the husband is the sole sponsor and indeed, sole basis for the wife's residence status, to require her to sign a binding Financial Agreement which is most unfavourable to her, on the understanding that if she does not sign the document the marriage is at an end?[111]

The Court concluded that the agreement should indeed be set aside on the basis of the husband's duress, which was of such a level as to amount to unconscionable conduct.[112]

viii. Future Issues

What of the future? Are further difficulties with Part VIIIA likely to be encountered, and further reforms contemplated as a result? Almost certainly. Several cases

---

[108] *Blackmore v Webber* [2009] FMCAfam 154 [57].
[109] Ibid [106].
[110] Ibid [122]–[123].
[111] *Moreno v Moreno* [2009] FMCAfam 1109 [1]. The husband's violence and aggression are referred to at [37]–[38] and [42]–[43].
[112] *Moreno v Moreno* [2009] FMCAfam 1109 [44].

concerning the application of the amendments to section 90G in 2010 have already arisen.[113] The giving of legal advice in relation to future and existing agreements will require particular care and attention, and some lawyers may again find the responsibilities and risks in giving such advice prohibitive. The government's stated objective with the latest amendments to provide greater certainty and confidence in the binding nature of financial agreements seems quite unrealistic. On the contrary, the open-ended wording of the new version of section 90G when read with the new sub-sections (1A) to (1C) is likely to open up new possibilities for litigation. One specialist practitioner has stated that:

> the amending Act [of 2010] has arguably gone too far. Financial agreements will be less stable, less attractive and less predictable as to their binding nature and enforceability.[114]

With respect to agreements made following separation or on divorce, however, the position is somewhat different. As mentioned earlier, it was possible from the early 1960s until the new regime began at the end of 2000 for a separated or divorcing spouse to seek the court's approval of an agreement in substitution for rights to bring proceedings for financial orders. In that respect, what is novel in Part VIIIA is the adoption of certificated independent legal advice for each party, instead of court approval, as the mechanism to give legal effect to the agreement and remove the court's jurisdiction (subject to various restrictions concerning spousal maintenance). In this context, however, the alternative option of obtaining consent orders dealing with financial matters from the court has always been popular.

While seeking orders by consent also by definition involves a degree of 'agreement' between the parties, in that they are of one mind as to the orders which they wish the court to make to resolve the proceedings, this is a quite different procedure to that of entering an agreement under Part VIIIA which takes away the court's jurisdiction to make financial orders. Whether making a Part VIIIA agreement after separation or on divorce (that is, under s 90C or s 90D) or applying for consent orders is the best option in a particular case will, it seems, depend on a range of factors and may change over time. Among the relevant matters variously mentioned in the literature as favouring one or other option are questions of relative cost and speed, incidence of stamp duty or other taxes, degree and type of financial disclosure required at the time by the Rules of Court, relative degree of privacy, degree of difficulty in subsequently attempting to set aside the order or agreement, as well as individual practitioner preference and expertise (including familiarity with the provisions of Part VIIIA).[115] In contrast to a consent order, a binding financial agreement under Part VIIIA does not have to be 'just and equitable', may in some

---

[113] See, eg *Senior v Anderson* [2010] FamCA 601, and *Wallace v Stelzer* [2011] FamCA 54 (where the agreements were declared to be binding), and *Parker v Parker* [2010] FamCA 664 (where the agreement was held not to be binding). Cf also *Grant v Grant-Lovett* [2009] FamCA 1357.

[114] J Campbell, 'Financial agreements—is this the end?', CCH *Australian Family Law and Practice* (Sydney, CCH, 2010) [80-040] 74, 101.

[115] See, eg A Harland, 'Financial Agreements and Consent Orders' in A Dickey and O Jessep (eds), *Family Law, The Laws of Australia*, Vol 17 (Sydney, Law Book Co, 2008) [17.16.470]–[17.16.560]; Campbell and Seivers, 'Financial Agreements' above n 66 [19-060]–[19-080]; Monahan and Young above n 12, 536–37; and Fehlberg and Behrens above n 12, 557–60.

circumstances require a lesser degree of financial disclosure,[116] and does not expose a party's financial affairs to any scrutiny on the part of the court. While there is no overall consensus on the issue of whether a consent order from the court or a binding agreement is a 'better' course of action, it seems that for separated parties consent orders are likely to remain a popular alternative.[117] The same specialist practitioner, for example, while predicting that the 2010 amendments to section 90G would bring 'a new era of uncertainty and confusion', concluded that for separated couples, 'consent orders ... look to be a much more secure option'.[118]

Returning to financial agreements in general, there are also further issues of interpretation of Part VIIIA which will require clarification, even without imagining any hypothetical situations involving the attempted inclusion of 'lifestyle' clauses in such agreements, or speculating as to the proper approach of the court when confronted with competing financial agreements (arising, say, from a person's first and second marriages, or from a person's marriage and the same person's de facto relationship). As one example, a problem may arise over the meaning of section 90H, which provides that a binding financial agreement continues to operate despite the death of a party to the agreement and operates in favour of, and is binding on, the legal personal representative of that party. This section may in some cases have relevance for the continuation of maintenance payments after a spouse's death, but it is possible as well to envisage a situation where one party to a financial agreement has died and the terms of the agreement appear to be in conflict with or inconsistent with that party's will, or with the provisions of the state inheritance laws. A problem of this sort in Australia would not simply be a question of interpretation of the relevant documents and construction of the different statutes, but might ultimately also raise constitutional questions as to the relative legislative competence of the federal and state legislatures in this context.[119]

IV. CONFLICT OF LAWS

There are no special provisions in the Family Law Act prescribing which laws apply in conflict situations involving marital financial agreements. But let us suppose that the parties to a marital agreement which is valid according to the law of the overseas country where it has been made (for example, prescribing the way in which their property is to be divided in the event of their separation) subsequently come to live in Australia. If the marriage breaks down while they are living in Australia and they have a financial dispute, then assuming requirements as to Family Law Act jurisdiction are satisfied,[120] the foreign agreement could not have the effect of taking

---

[116] Note A Dickey, 'Financial Agreements and Duty to Disclose Financial Position' (2005) 79 *Australian Law Journal* 484.

[117] See, eg Fehlberg and Smyth above n 60, 133; and Fehlberg and Behrens above n 12, 557–60.

[118] Campbell above n 114 [80-040] 74,151.

[119] Note the High Court of Australia decision of *Smith v Smith* (1986) 161 CLR 217, dealing with a related issue arising in relation to an agreement approved under s 87 of the Family Law Act 1975 (Cth), and see Dickey above n 12, 672.

[120] If divorce proceedings are contemplated, it is sufficient if one of the parties is an Australian citizen, or is domiciled in Australia, or is ordinarily resident in Australia and has been so for not less than a year: s 39(4)(a). For other proceedings such as parenting disputes, or for financial adjustment, it is sufficient

away the parties' rights to seek orders for property division under section 79 of the Family Law Act, because that can only be done by complying with section 90G and the other provisions of Part VIIIA.[121] At most, therefore, the foreign agreement would be relevant as part of the financial history of the couple, as evidence of what they agreed to when the agreement was made, and could be considered along with all the other evidence by the court in deciding how to exercise its discretion under section 79 to produce a just and equitable result.[122] If, in contrast, a hypothetical couple living in Australia were about to make a financial agreement which complied with the requirements of Part VIIIA of the Family Law Act, then given that they are more or less able to write their own agreement there is presumably no reason why they could not decide in that agreement to divide the property according to the principles of an overseas legal system. In this case, however, the principles of the overseas law would not be taking effect of their own force, or as overseas law which is recognised in Australia according to conflicts of law rules, but rather as part of the terms of a financial agreement made in Australia by the parties in accordance with Part VIIIA.

V. CONCLUSION

In contrast to the position regarding agreements dealing with financial matters after separation or divorce, the Australian experience since 2000 with financial agreements which can be entered into prior to marriage, or during marriage prior to separation, is obviously very limited. It is only a decade since such agreements became a legal possibility with the introduction of Part VIIIA of the Family Law Act 1975 (Cth). Some lawyers welcomed the new provisions which made pre-nuptial agreements possible, seeing in them an opportunity to market new legal services, with one lawyer pointing out that even for young people without assets, a binding financial agreement could provide peace of mind by protecting a spouse from the other spouse's debts and liabilities.[123] But the immediate reaction from other members of the legal profession, as from the public in general, appeared more measured and cautious.[124] More recent anecdotal evidence perhaps suggests a slow increase in public interest in the new agreements since 2005, especially among older couples or the adult children of well-to-do families.[125] Very recently, the reference by seven states to the federal government of powers in relation to financial adjustment on the breakdown of de facto relationships (same-sex and

---

if one of the parties is an Australian citizen, or ordinarily resident in Australia or is present in Australia: s 39(4)(b).

[121] See, eg *Marriage of Hannema* (1981) 7 Fam LR 542, and note L Jarvis, 'Conflicts of Law' (2006) *Australian Journal of Family Law* 79–88, 84. As to the concept of 'clearly inappropriate forum' in private international law, see eg *Marriage of Gilmore* (1992) 16 Fam LR 285, 293 and *Henry v Henry* (1996) 185 CLR 571.

[122] See, eg *Marriage of Hannema* (1981) 7 Fam LR 542 and *Marriage of Plut* (1987) 11 Fam LR 687.

[123] T Altobelli, 'Marketing Financial Agreements' (2003) 17(1) *Australian Family Lawyer* 14–15.

[124] Fehlberg and Smyth above n 60, 133–38.

[125] T Dick, 'Clause 27(a) I do, except ...' *Sydney Morning Herald* (3 May 2008) 13.

opposite-sex), and the consequent insertion in the Family Law Act, with effect from 1 March 2009 (and from 1 July 2010 in the case of South Australia), of financial provisions for unmarried partners identical to those which apply to married spouses, have been said to have increased the general interest in and demand for financial agreements.[126]

As to the legislation itself, there have been frequent criticisms and suggestions for reform of the original provisions of Part VIIIA, especially from members of the legal profession, and the government has legislated promptly and even enthusiastically in response. In turn, some of these amendments have been seen as inadequate, requiring further clarification and revision, while new problems have also been encountered. Whether the need for some of these amendments has been contributed to by a lack of clarity in government policy, insufficient time for consultation with key parties, or inadequate legislative drafting cannot be stated with any certainty. What is clear, however, is that this process of repeated modification is likely to continue, as evidenced by the response to the latest series of amendments introduced in 2010.[127]

As a final comment, a crucial question for anyone interested in financial agreements and the competing policies of protecting vulnerable family members, on the one hand, and encouraging private contractual autonomy, on the other, is in what circumstances a properly formalised agreement can be set aside. In relation to Part VIIIA and section 90K in particular, one recently published text predicted that, by analogy with the Family Court's reluctance to overturn financial orders obtained by consent,[128] and in light of the recent practice of courts in other countries such as Canada and New Zealand, parties to binding financial agreements in Australia 'are likely to be held to their bargain, even if the outcome is patently unfair'.[129] Putting to one side the decisions as to the invalidity of agreements for non-compliance with section 90G formalities, the handful of cases so far decided on Part VIIIA is naturally far from sufficient to suggest whether this prediction will prove accurate. In particular, no cases have yet come to notice on the interpretation of section 90K(1)(d) (subsequent material change of circumstances relating to care and welfare of a child of the marriage, such that the child or the caretaker parent of the child would suffer hardship if agreement not set aside). On the other hand, as outlined earlier, there has been a number of recent cases where the Court has been prepared to set aside agreements for lack of independent legal advice, insufficient financial disclosure, false representations, duress and unconscionability.[130]

---

[126] R Nickless, 'Pre-nuptial Agreements just got Easier' *Australian Financial Review* (18 December 2009) 1, 49.

[127] See, eg Campbell above n 114 [80-040].

[128] Fehlberg and Behrens above n 12, 557–62; and Dickey above n 12, ch 38.

[129] Fehlberg and Behrens above n 12, 562.

[130] See, eg *Fitzpatrick v Griffin* [2008] FMCAfam 555, *Murphy v Murphy* [2009] FMCAfam 270, *Ruane v Bachmann-Ruane* [2009] FamCA 1101, *Blackmore v Webber* [2009] FMCAfam 154, *Stoddard v Stoddard* [2007] FMCAfam 735, *Tsarouhi v Tsarouhi* [2009] FMCAfam 126 and *Moreno v Moreno* [2009] FMCAfam 1109.

VI. SELECTED PROVISIONS OF FAMILY LAW ACT 1975 (CTH)

(As at 1 March 2009, with the inclusion of s 90G as amended with effect from 4 January 2010.)

71A   This Part does not apply to certain matters covered by binding financial agreements
(1) This Part does not apply to:
  (a) financial matters to which a financial agreement that is binding on the parties to the agreement applies; or
  (b) financial resources to which a financial agreement that is binding on the parties to the agreement applies.
(2) Subsection (1) does not apply in relation to proceedings of a kind referred to in paragraph (caa) or (cb) of the definition of **matrimonial cause** in subsection 4(1).

[s 4(1) (definition of "matrimonial cause"):
(caa) proceedings between:
   (i) a party to a marriage; and
   (ii) the bankruptcy trustee of a bankrupt party to the marriage;
        with respect to the maintenance of the first-mentioned party; or
   [...]
(cb) proceedings between:
   (i) a party to a marriage; and
   (ii) the bankruptcy trustee of a bankrupt party to the marriage;
        with respect to any vested bankruptcy property in relation to the bankrupt party, being proceedings:
   (iii) arising out of the marital relationship; or
   (iv) in relation to concurrent, pending or completed divorce or validity of marriage proceedings between the parties to the marriage; ...]

PART VIIIA—FINANCIAL AGREEMENTS

90A   Definitions
In this Part:
dealt with includes the meaning given by subsection 90F(2).
marriage includes a void marriage.

90B   Financial agreements before marriage
(1) If:
  (a) people who are contemplating entering into a marriage with each other make a written agreement with respect to any of the matters mentioned in subsection (2); and
    (aa) at the time of the making of the agreement, the people are not the spouse parties to any other binding agreement (whether made under this section or section 90C or 90D) with respect to any of those matters; and
  (b) the agreement is expressed to be made under this section;
     the agreement is a **financial agreement**. The people may make the financial agreement with one or more other people.
(2) The matters referred to in paragraph (1)(a) are the following:
  (a) how, in the event of the breakdown of the marriage, all or any of the property or financial resources of either or both of the spouse parties at the time when the agreement is made, or at a later time and before divorce, is to be dealt with;
  (b) the maintenance of either of the spouse parties:
   (i) during the marriage; or
   (ii) after divorce; or
   (iii) both during the marriage and after divorce.

(3) A financial agreement made as mentioned in subsection (1) may also contain:
  (a) matters incidental or ancillary to those mentioned in subsection (2); and
  (b) other matters.
(4) A financial agreement (the **new agreement**) made as mentioned in subsection (1) may terminate a previous financial agreement (however made) if all of the parties to the previous agreement are parties to the new agreement.

90C Financial agreements during marriage

(1) If:
  (a) the parties to a marriage make a written agreement with respect to any of the matters mentioned in subsection (2); and
    (aa) at the time of the making of the agreement, the parties to the marriage are not the spouse parties to any other binding agreement (whether made under this section or section 90B or 90D) with respect to any of those matters; and
  (b) the agreement is expressed to be made under this section;
    the agreement is a **financial agreement**. The parties to the marriage may make the financial agreement with one or more other people.
(2) The matters referred to in paragraph (1)(a) are the following:
  (a) how, in the event of the breakdown of the marriage, all or any of the property or financial resources of either or both of the spouse parties at the time when the agreement is made, or at a later time and during the marriage, is to be dealt with;
  (b) the maintenance of either of the spouse parties:
    (i)   during the marriage; or
    (ii) after divorce; or
    (iii) both during the marriage and after divorce.
  (2A) For the avoidance of doubt, a financial agreement under this section may be made before or after the marriage has broken down.
(3) A financial agreement made as mentioned in subsection (1) may also contain:
  (a) matters incidental or ancillary to those mentioned in subsection (2); and
  (b) other matters.
(4) A financial agreement (the **new agreement**) made as mentioned in subsection (1) may terminate a previous financial agreement (however made) if all of the parties to the previous agreement are parties to the new agreement.

90D Financial agreements after divorce order is made

(1) If:
  (a) after a divorce order is made in relation to a marriage (whether it has taken effect or not), the parties to the former marriage make a written agreement with respect to any of the matters mentioned in subsection (2); and
    (aa) at the time of the making of the agreement, the parties to the former marriage are not the spouse parties to any other binding agreement (whether made under this section or section 90B or 90C) with respect to any of those matters; and
  (b) the agreement is expressed to be made under this section;
    the agreement is a **financial agreement**. The parties to the former marriage may make the financial agreement with one or more other people.
(2) The matters referred to in paragraph (1)(a) are the following:
  (a) how all or any of the property or financial resources that either or both of the spouse parties had or acquired during the former marriage is to be dealt with;
  (b) the maintenance of either of the spouse parties.
(3) A financial agreement made as mentioned in subsection (1) may also contain:
  (a) matters incidental or ancillary to those mentioned in subsection (2); and
  (b) other matters.

(4) A financial agreement (the **new agreement**) made as mentioned in subsection (1) may terminate a previous financial agreement (however made) if all of the parties to the previous agreement are parties to the new agreement.

90DA Need for separation declaration for certain provisions of financial agreement to take effect

(1) A financial agreement that is binding on the parties to the agreement, to the extent to which it deals with how, in the event of the breakdown of the marriage, all or any of the property or financial resources of either or both of the spouse parties:
 (a) at the time when the agreement is made; or
 (b) at a later time and before the termination of the marriage by divorce; are to be dealt with, is of no force or effect until a separation declaration is made.

Note: Before the separation declaration is made, the financial agreement will be of force and effect in relation to the other matters it deals with (except for any matters covered by section 90DB).

 (1A) Subsection (1) ceases to apply if:
  (a) the spouse parties divorce; or
  (b) either or both of them die.

Note: This means the financial agreement will be of force and effect in relation to the matters mentioned in subsection (1) from the time of the divorce or death(s).

(2) A separation declaration is a written declaration that complies with subsections (3) and (4), and may be included in the financial agreement to which it relates.
(3) The declaration must be signed by at least one of the spouse parties to the financial agreement.
(4) The declaration must state that:
 (a) the spouse parties have separated and are living separately and apart at the declaration time; and
 (b) in the opinion of the spouse parties making the declaration, there is no reasonable likelihood of cohabitation being resumed.
(5) In this section:
 declaration time means the time when the declaration was signed by a spouse party to the financial agreement.
 separated has the same meaning as in section 48 (as affected by section 49).

90DB Whether or when certain other provisions of financial agreements take effect

(1) A financial agreement that is binding on the parties to the agreement, to the extent to which it provides for a third party to contribute to the maintenance of a spouse party during the marriage, is of no force or effect.
(2) A financial agreement that is binding on the parties to the agreement, to the extent to which it provides for matters covered by paragraph 90B(3)(b) or 90C(3)(b), is of no force or effect unless and until the marriage breaks down.

90E Requirements with respect to provisions in financial agreements relating to the maintenance of a party or a child or children

A provision of a financial agreement that relates to the maintenance of a spouse party to the agreement or a child or children is void unless the provision specifies:
(a) the party, or the child or children, for whose maintenance provision is made; and
(b) the amount provided for, or the value of the portion of the relevant property attributable to, the maintenance of the party, or of the child or each child, as the case may be.

90F Certain provisions in agreements

(1) No provision of a financial agreement excludes or limits the power of a court to make an order in relation to the maintenance of a party to a marriage if subsection (1A) applies.

(1A) This subsection applies if the court is satisfied that, when the agreement came into effect, the circumstances of the party were such that, taking into account the terms and effect of the agreement, the party was unable to support himself or herself without an income tested pension, allowance or benefit.

(2) To avoid doubt, a provision in an agreement made as mentioned in subsection 90B(1), 90C(1) or 90D(1) that provides for property or financial resources owned by a spouse party to the agreement to continue in the ownership of that party is taken, for the purposes of that section, to be a provision with respect to how the property or financial resources are to be dealt with.

90G When financial agreements are binding

(1) A financial agreement is binding on the parties to the agreement if, and only if:
  (a) the agreement is signed by all parties; and
  (b) the agreement contains, in relation to each spouse party to the agreement, a statement to the effect that the party to whom the statement relates has been provided, before the agreement was signed by him or her, as certified in an annexure to the agreement, with independent legal advice from a legal practitioner as to the following matters:
    (i) the effect of the agreement on the rights of that party;
    (ii) the advantages and disadvantages, at the time that the advice was provided, to the party of making the agreement; and
  (c) the annexure to the agreement contains a certificate signed by the person providing the independent legal advice stating that the advice was provided; and
  (d) the agreement has not been terminated and has not been set aside by a court; and
  (e) after the agreement is signed, the original agreement is given to one of the spouse parties and a copy is given to each of the other parties.

Note: For the manner in which the contents of a financial agreement may be proved, see section 48 of the Evidence Act 1995.

(2) A court may make such orders for the enforcement of a financial agreement that is binding on the parties to the agreement as it thinks necessary.

[NB Section 90G was amended by the Federal Justice System Amendment (Efficiency Measures) Act (No 1) 2009 (Cth), with effect from 4 January 2010. As a result, s 90G reads as follows:

90G When financial agreements are binding

(1) Subject to subsection (1A), a financial agreement is binding on the parties to the agreement if, and only if:
  (a) the agreement is signed by all parties; and
  (b) before signing the agreement, each spouse party was provided with independent legal advice from a legal practitioner about the effect of the agreement on the rights of that party and about the advantages and disadvantages, at the time that the advice was provided, to that party of making the agreement; and
  (c) either before or after signing the agreement, each spouse party was provided with a signed statement by the legal practitioner stating that the advice referred to in paragraph (b) was provided to that party (whether or not the statement is annexed to the agreement); and
  (ca) a copy of the statement referred to in paragraph (c) that was provided to a spouse party is given to the other spouse party or to a legal practitioner for the other spouse party; and
  (d) the agreement has not been terminated and has not been set aside by a court.

(1A) A financial agreement is binding on the parties to the agreement if:
    (a) the agreement is signed by all parties; and
    (b) one or more of paragraphs (1)(b), (c) and (ca) are not satisfied in relation to the agreement; and
    (c) a court is satisfied that it would be unjust and inequitable if the agreement were not binding on the spouse parties to the agreement (disregarding any changes in circumstances from the time the agreement was made); and
    (d) the court makes an order under subsection (1B) declaring that the agreement is binding on the parties to the agreement; and
    (e) the agreement has not been terminated and has not been set aside by a court.
(1B) For the purposes of paragraph (1A)(d), a court may make an order declaring that a financial agreement is binding on the parties to the agreement, upon application (the enforcement application) by a spouse party seeking to enforce the agreement.
(1C) To avoid doubt, section 90KA applies in relation to the enforcement application.]

90H Effect of death of party to financial agreement

A financial agreement that is binding on the parties to the agreement continues to operate despite the death of a party to the agreement and operates in favour of, and is binding on, the legal personal representative of that party.

90J Termination of financial agreement

(1) The parties to a financial agreement may terminate the agreement only by:
    (a) including a provision to that effect in another financial agreement as mentioned in subsection 90B(4), 90C(4) or 90D(4); or
    (b) making a written agreement (a termination agreement) to that effect.
(2) A termination agreement is binding on the parties if, and only if:
    (a) the agreement is signed by all parties to the agreement; and
    (b) the agreement contains, in relation to each spouse party to the agreement, a statement to the effect that the party to whom the statement relates has been provided, before the agreement was signed by him or her, as certified in an annexure to the agreement, with independent legal advice from a legal practitioner as to the following matters:
        (i) the effect of the agreement on the rights of that party;
        (ii) the advantages and disadvantages, at the time that the advice was provided, to the party of making the agreement; and
    (c) the annexure to the agreement contains a certificate signed by the person providing the independent legal advice stating that the advice was provided; and
    (d) the agreement has not been set aside by a court; and
    (e) after the agreement is signed, the original agreement is given to one of the spouse parties and a copy is given to each of the other parties.
(3) A court may, on an application by a person who was a party to the financial agreement that has been terminated, or by any other interested person, make such order or orders (including an order for the transfer of property) as it considers just and equitable for the purpose of preserving or adjusting the rights of persons who were parties to that financial agreement and any other interested persons.

Note: For the manner in which the contents of a financial agreement may be proved, see section 48 of the Evidence Act 1995.

90K Circumstances in which court may set aside a financial agreement or termination agreement

(1) A court may make an order setting aside a financial agreement or a termination agreement if, and only if, the court is satisfied that:
    (a) the agreement was obtained by fraud (including non-disclosure of a material matter); or

    (aa) a party to the agreement entered into the agreement:
        (i) for the purpose, or for purposes that included the purpose, of defrauding or defeating a creditor or creditors of the party; or
        (ii) with reckless disregard of the interests of a creditor or creditors of the party; or
    (ab) a party (the **agreement party**) to the agreement entered into the agreement:
        (i) for the purpose, or for purposes that included the purpose, of defrauding another person who is a party to a de facto relationship with a spouse party; or
        (ii) for the purpose, or for purposes that included the purpose, of defeating the interests of that other person in relation to any possible or pending application for an order under section 90SM, or a declaration under section 90SL, in relation to the de facto relationship; or
        (iii) with reckless disregard of those interests of that other person; or
  (b) the agreement is void, voidable or unenforceable; or
  (c) in the circumstances that have arisen since the agreement was made it is impracticable for the agreement or a part of the agreement to be carried out; or
  (d) since the making of the agreement, a material change in circumstances has occurred (being circumstances relating to the care, welfare and development of a child of the marriage) and, as a result of the change, the child or, if the applicant has caring responsibility for the child (as defined in subsection (2)), a party to the agreement will suffer hardship if the court does not set the agreement aside; or
  (e) in respect of the making of a financial agreement—a party to the agreement engaged in conduct that was, in all the circumstances, unconscionable; or
  (f) a payment flag is operating under Part VIIIB on a superannuation interest covered by the agreement and there is no reasonable likelihood that the operation of the flag will be terminated by a flag lifting agreement under that Part; or
  (g) the agreement covers at least one superannuation interest that is an unsplittable interest for the purposes of Part VIIIB.

(1A) For the purposes of paragraph (1)(aa), creditor, in relation to a party to the agreement, includes a person who could reasonably have been foreseen by the party as being reasonably likely to become a creditor of the party.

 (2) For the purposes of paragraph (1)(d), a person has caring responsibility for a child if:
  (a) the person is a parent of the child with whom the child lives; or
  (b) a parenting order provides that:
    (i) the child is to live with the person; or
    (ii) the person has parental responsibility for the child.

 (3) A court may, on an application by a person who was a party to the financial agreement that has been set aside, or by any other interested person, make such order or orders (including an order for the transfer of property) as it considers just and equitable for the purpose of preserving or adjusting the rights of persons who were parties to that financial agreement and any other interested persons.

 (4) An order under subsection (1) or (3) may, after the death of a party to the proceedings in which the order was made, be enforced on behalf of, or against, as the case may be, the estate of the deceased party.

 (5) If a party to proceedings under this section dies before the proceedings are completed:
  (a) the proceedings may be continued by or against, as the case may be, the legal personal representative of the deceased party and the applicable Rules of Court may make provision in relation to the substitution of the legal personal representative as a party to the proceedings; and

   (b) if the court is of the opinion:
     (i) that it would have exercised its powers under this section if the deceased party had not died; and
     (ii) that it is still appropriate to exercise those powers; the court may make any order that it could have made under subsection (1) or (3); and
   (c) an order under paragraph (b) may be enforced on behalf of, or against, as the case may be, the estate of the deceased party.

(6) The court must not make an order under this section if the order would:
   (a) result in the acquisition of property from a person otherwise than on just terms; and
   (b) be invalid because of paragraph 51(xxxi) of the Constitution.

For this purpose, **acquisition of property** and **just terms** have the same meanings as in paragraph 51(xxxi) of the Constitution.

90KA Validity, enforceability and effect of financial agreements and termination agreements
The question whether a financial agreement or a termination agreement is valid, enforceable or effective is to be determined by the court according to the principles of law and equity that are applicable in determining the validity, enforceability and effect of contracts and purported contracts, and, in proceedings relating to such an agreement, the court:

(a) subject to paragraph (b), has the same powers, may grant the same remedies and must have the same regard to the rights of third parties as the High Court has, may grant and is required to have in proceedings in connection with contracts or purported contracts, being proceedings in which the High Court has original jurisdiction; and
(b) has power to make an order for the payment, by a party to the agreement to another party to the agreement, of interest on an amount payable under the agreement, from the time when the amount became or becomes due and payable, at a rate not exceeding the rate prescribed by the applicable Rules of Court; and
(c) in addition to, or instead of, making an order or orders under paragraph (a) or (b), may order that the agreement, or a specified part of the agreement, be enforced as if it were an order of the court. [...]

Marital Agreements and Private Autonomy in Austria

SUSANNE FERRARI

CONTENTS

I. THE FINANCIAL CONSEQUENCES OF DIVORCE

A. Matrimonial Property

i. General Points

Austria's statutory matrimonial property regime is a hybrid resulting from the separation of property (ss 1233, 1237 of the ABGB, the Austrian Civil Code) and the equalisation of accrued gains. The principle of the separation of property applies throughout the period of marriage: each spouse acquires goods for him/herself and is free to dispose of any such goods and rights acquired during this time as he/she alone chooses. Spouses are not liable for each other's debts.[1] The principle of the separation of property during marriage can of course result in the spouses' financial circumstances becoming very different from each other's in the course of the marriage; this is particularly true when only one spouse is in gainful employment and may, consequently, accumulate significantly more assets than the other.

It is for this reason that Austria provides for the equalisation of matrimonial property in the event of divorce.[2] The result of the Austrian approach has much in common with the equalisation of accrued gains provided for by German law,[3] although accrued gains are not automatically halved and, unlike German law, the spouse is entitled to demand the division of the matrimonial goods. However, the division of assets does not follow automatically once a marriage has been dissolved. It is either resolved by mutual agreement by the two parties (the legally preferred way) or, in the absence of a contractual agreement, the former spouses have a specified time frame[4] in which to submit an application for a decision from a dispute settlement court (s 85, EheG, the Marriage Act).[5] In practice, division by agreement is far more common than division by a court decision, with approximately 90 per cent of all divorces in Austria being settled by mutual consent;[6] a mutually agreed settlement by the spouses of all legal matters concerning assets constitutes a precondition for divorce (s 55a (2), Marriage Act).

ii. The Assets to be Divided

The assets to be divided comprise the matrimonial material assets and the matrimonial savings, as well as debts that are inextricably linked with the matrimonial material

---

[1] In relation to provisions outside the law on matrimonial proptery which take precedence over the principle of the separation of property see S Ferrari, 'Die vermögensrechtliche Situation von Ehegatten und Lebensgefährten in Österreich' in D Henrich and D Schwab (eds), *Eheliche Gemeinschaft, Partnerschaft und Vermögen im europäischen Vergleich* (Bielefeld, Gieseking, 1999) 179 et seq.

[2] There is no provision for equalisation in the event of a spouse's death. In my opinion the matrimonial property regime is thus a hybrid form of the separation of property and the equalisation of accrued gains.

[3] See Anatol Dutta's chapter on German marital law.

[4] The entitlement to division expires if it has not been asserted by court action or recognised within one year of the date on which the divorce became legally effective (s 95, Marriage Act).

[5] Unless the spouses make other arrangements, the separation of property continues to apply after the marriage is dissolved.

[6] In 2009 87.3 per cent of all divorces in Austria were settled by agreement, see www.statistik.at/web_de/statistiken/bevoelkerung/scheidungen/index.html (10 January 2011).

assets and matrimonial savings (s 81 et seq, Marriage Act). The duration of the 'intact matrimonial community' (*aufrechte eheliche Lebensgemeinschaft*) dictates the period of time an object can be said to belong to the assets to be divided (s 81 (2) and (3), Marriage Act). This means that assets which are acquired before divorce but after separation cannot be divided. The distinction between material assets and savings is, as from 2010,[7] of lesser significance (see below section II.C.ii.d.). Matrimonial material assets are physical goods which have been at the disposal of both spouses during their intact matrimonial community; this includes household equipment or goods and the matrimonial home (s 81 (2), Marriage Act). Absolutely anything the spouses have had at their disposal during their married life together is regarded as a matrimonial material asset; for example, a horse, a holiday home, or a castle.[8] Matrimonial savings are valuable investments, irrespective of their nature, which the spouses have accumulated during their intact matrimonial community and which, depending on their exact nature, are usually intended for use (s 81 (3), Marriage Act). These include, for example, cash, financial savings investments, real estate, works of art, a house that is not yet habitable, or a stamp collection. If these investments are also being used (eg jewellery, works of art) they must be declared as matrimonial material assets.[9] The goods exempted from the division of assets pursuant to section 82 of the Marriage Act are those which a spouse has brought into the marriage, which he/she has inherited or received as a gift from a third party (s 82 (1) (1), Marriage Act), which are for the exclusive personal use of one spouse or which he/she requires to carry out his/her profession (s 82 (1) (2), Marriage Act), and goods which are the property of a business enterprise or are holdings in a business enterprise, except where these are merely financial investments (s 82 (1) (3 and 4), Marriage Act). However, the following applies to the matrimonial home[10] and the household equipment or goods: where the other spouse has compelling reasons for being dependent on their continued use, these must be included in the division of property even if they have been brought into the marriage by a spouse, or inherited or received as a gift from a third party. Further, the matrimonial home brought into the marriage by a spouse or inherited or received as a gift from a third party has to be included in the division of assets, if a child from the marriage has a need for its continued use which merits consideration (s 82 (2), Marriage Act).

There is no provision in Austrian law for the statutory equalisation of pensions as it is understood in German law.

iii. Criteria for Division

This brings us to the question of what the law deems to be the most important criteria for deciding on the division of assets. The following points apply above all to court decisions on division, although they also regularly provide a point of reference for contractually agreed divisions.

---

[7] Date of the entry into force of the Family Law Amendment 2009 BGBl I 2009/75.

[8] Evidence of this is cited in H Koziol and R Welser, *Grundriss des bürgerlichen Rechts I: Allgemeiner Teil, Sachenrecht, Familienrecht* 13th edn (Vienna, Manz, 2006) 505.

[9] See ibid, 506.

[10] In relation to the declaration of a dwelling as the matrimonial home, see B A Koch in H Koziol, P Bydlinski and R Bollenberger (eds), *Kurzkommentar zum ABGB* 3rd edn (Vienna, Springer, 2010) § 81 EheG Rz 5.

Division must be undertaken in accordance with the principle of equity: the primary legal concern is that the contribution that each spouse made to the creation of the total assets is taken into account and that the children's welfare is taken into consideration. A contribution includes providing maintenance, participating in earning an income, the upkeep of the joint household, the care and education of the children of the marriage, and rendering any other matrimonial assistance (s 83, Marriage Act). Moreover, once the property has been divided, divorced spouses should not need to be in contact more than absolutely necessary if they do not wish to be (s 84, Marriage Act). Division is not, however, undertaken with a view to strengthening the position of the weaker party by means of special benefits from the division of assets, even if each party's 'ability to enjoy continued well-being' is taken into consideration in each particular case. The intention is for the former spouses to be able to maintain their standard of living as far as possible and for the start of a new chapter in life to be made as easy as possible.[11]

In court decisions, there is a very wide discretion to decide how the assets are to be divided: the judge can transfer the property of one spouse to the other, adjust the real and obligatory rights of one spouse in favour of goods belonging to the other etc. Specifically, a distinction is made between movable and immovable assets and also whether the assets in question are material assets or matrimonial savings.[12] An equalisation payment is only imposed if an equitable division of assets cannot be reached (s 94, Marriage Act).

Thus, accrued gains are not halved under Austrian law (as they are under German law); instead, the allocation of assets corresponds with the size of the contribution each spouse has made. In practice, however, a 50:50 division is quite common; the courts judge the gainful employment of one spouse as equivalent to the other spouse's responsibilities for housekeeping and the children's education, irrespective of the number of children, the size of the household, or the amount of the earnings.[13] In some cases, however, the Supreme Court (OGH) has decided on a 2:1 division if the woman has also been in employment at the same time as being responsible for the housekeeping and the children's education.[14] The issue of fault for the divorce is not taken into account in the division of assets. The division is concerned above all with the contributions made to the assets in the past. Following a decision of the OGH, however, the innocent party may select his/her preferred items from the assets to be divided.[15]

B. Maintenance

i. General Points

The post-marital legal maintenance provisions are complicated and multi-layered and are directly applied in only a small percentage of divorces. As mentioned above,

---

[11] See evidence cited in G Hopf and G Kathrein, *Eherecht* 2nd edn (Vienna, Manz, 2005) § 83 EheG Anm 16.
[12] See s 86 et seq, Marriage Act.
[13] OGH 5 Ob 736/80 JBl 1982, 321; 30.8.2007, 2 Ob 143/07d (unpublished).
[14] See evidence cited in Hopf and Kathrein above n 11, § 83 EheG Anm 17.
[15] Eg OGH 4 Ob 230/97w SZ 67/38; 27.1.1999, 3 Ob 108/97x (unpublished).

approximately 90 per cent of all divorces in Austria are settled by mutual consent and as part of the divorce proceedings; in such cases the spouses are required to reach an agreement on post-marital maintenance (s 55a (2), Marriage Act). The statutory provisions do, however, constitute important guidelines for the spouses' respective negotiating positions.

Austrian law regulates statutory post-marital maintenance entirely independently of matrimonial property rights. There is no connection by virtue of law between the division of assets and the granting of maintenance; under no circumstances is the post-marital maintenance entitlement of one party taken into consideration in the division of assets and, conversely, the proportion of the divided assets allocated to a spouse has no effect whatsoever on the assessment of the amount of maintenance to be paid. In practice, however, in mutually agreed divorces there is very often a link between maintenance and matrimonial property rights. For example, the woman can waive all rights to maintenance and receive a correspondingly larger share of the divided assets.

In general it should be noted that post-marital maintenance is closely linked with the question of divorce fault. Under Austrian law the question of whether the divorce decree has established sole or predominant fault for the breakdown of the marriage is of considerable significance in deciding post-marital maintenance (see s 66 et seq, Marriage Act). It is hence primarily a question of fault and not of strengthening the position of the financially weaker party by means of maintenance payments.[16] In addition, in contested divorce cases where no fault has been pronounced, the role played by the individual parties is important: in these cases, only the respondent is entitled to maintenance. However, there is also a maintenance entitlement that is independent of fault and the role played by the individual parties, which was introduced in 1999 and is laid down as a rule in section 68a of the Marriage Act.[17]

ii. Individual Post-Marital Maintenance Entitlements

Based on the above rules a spouse who is solely or predominantly at fault must pay the other spouse (insofar as the latter's income from assets and earnings from reasonable gainful employment is insufficient) maintenance appropriate for their living conditions (s 66, Marriage Act). The judiciary has developed a set of suggested percentage rates as guidelines for assessment criteria, according to which the spouse entitled to maintenance can receive a maximum of 33 per cent of the other spouse's net income.[18] The law does not recognise a limit to the amount ('the luxury limit') — unlike in the case of child maintenance.[19] The law takes account of the weak financial position of the party liable to pay maintenance, to the extent that the liable party must pay only as much as can be considered equitable with regard

[16] However, Austrian law also recognises the possibility of a spouse who cannot afford his/her own upkeep being granted a maintenance allowance at the other's expense if the divorce proceedings have pronounced both spouses to be equally at fault for the breakdown of the marriage (s 68, Marriage Act).

[17] See the following section.

[18] For a detailed account see M Schwimann and S Ferrari in M Schwimann and B Verschraegen (eds), *Praxiskommentar zum Allgemeinen bürgerlichen Gesetzbuch I* 3rd edn (Vienna, LexisNexis, 2005) § 94 Rz 16 et seq.

[19] OGH 1 Ob 288/98d JBl 1999, 725.

to the needs, assets and earnings of the other spouse, if the payment of maintenance is likely to jeopardise his/her own appropriate maintenance. In this event, the party entitled to receive maintenance may, in certain circumstances, have to bear the costs of his/her maintenance from the core of his/her own assets (s 67 (1) and (2), Marriage Act).

A divorced spouse is entitled to the highest level of post-marital maintenance if the petition for divorce is submitted by the spouse who is solely or predominantly at fault for the breakdown of the marriage. The earliest date at which this can take place under these circumstances is three years after the couple have ceased to live together (s 55, Marriage Act). The maintenance entitlement in this case remains essentially the same as during the marriage; if the spouse entitled to maintenance was not in gainful employment, there is no requirement for him/her to take up gainful employment. The entitlement to maintenance is for an unlimited period of time, and as a matter of principle it takes precedence over any new spouse's entitlement. The entitlement includes the reimbursement of the voluntary contributions made by the respondent to statutory health insurance (s 69 (2), Marriage Act). The full widow's/widower's pension will also be paid on certain conditions (s 264 (10), ASVG, the General Social Insurance Act). Unlike maintenance during a marriage, the divorced spouse is responsible for his/her national insurance contributions him/herself as soon as the marriage is dissolved by decree absolute; these contributions cannot be claimed in addition, but are included in the legal entitlement to maintenance.[20]

Where both spouses are at fault for the divorce but neither is pronounced as being predominantly so, a contribution may be granted towards the maintenance of the indigent spouse if, and in so far as, this can be considered equitable with regard to the needs, assets and earnings of the other spouse. It is possible to limit the period of this contribution (s 68, Marriage Act).

In contested divorce cases where no fault has been pronounced because of behaviour resulting from mental disturbance (s 50, Marriage Act) or mental disease (s 51, Marriage Act), or for reasons of a contagious or nauseating disease (s 52, Marriage Act), or because the spouses are living in separate homes (s 55, Marriage Act), the petitioner must, in certain circumstances, pay the other spouse maintenance for reasons of equity (s 69 (3), Marriage Act). The respondent cannot be obliged to pay maintenance under this provision.

Section 68a of the Marriage Act, which, as mentioned above, was incorporated into the law under an amendment in 1999, grants a divorced spouse an entitlement to maintenance independent of fault if he/she cares for the children of the marriage after the divorce (para 1). Independently of this paragraph 1 maintenance entitlement, section 68a (2) of the Marriage Act gives a maintenance entitlement (also independent of fault) if a spouse has devoted him/herself by mutual agreement during the marriage to the housekeeping and, if applicable, also to the care of the children or relatives, and cannot now be reasonably expected to provide for his/her own maintenance as a result of a lack of gainful employment opportunities, the length of time spent in matrimonial community, or because of his/her age or state of

---

[20] OGH 1 Ob 180/01d JBl 2002, 172; 7 Ob 170/06k FamZ 2007/48.

health. The amount of maintenance is determined by the entitled party's living needs and lies between 15 per cent and 33 per cent of the liable spouse's income.[21] As a matter of principle, maintenance is payable for a limited period of time only and, pursuant to section 68a(3) of the Marriage Act, it can be restricted or not granted at all, if granting it would be deemed inequitable on the grounds listed including, for example, if the indigent spouse has been guilty of an especially serious and one-sided offence against the marriage.[22]

iii. Expiry of Maintenance, Change of Circumstances Clause

Unless it is limited to a period of time, the entitlement to maintenance expires only on the death of the entitled party (s 77 (1), Marriage Act). If the liable party dies, his/her respective maintenance obligations transfer to his/her successors[23] (s 78, Marriage Act). Maintenance obligations after divorce can thus last even beyond the lifetime of the liable party. There are currently no signs that the legislative body in Austria wishes to terminate such obligations as soon as possible. The change of circumstances clause automatically applies to each maintenance settlement; any divorced spouse can demand a reassessment of maintenance by bringing an action if there is a change in the circumstances relevant to the entitlement.[24] Moreover, a post-marital entitlement to maintenance expires when the entitled spouse remarries. The revival of the entitlement is not possible (s 75, Marriage Act). If the entitled party enters into a heterosexual or homosexual long-term relationship, the courts can suspend the claim to maintenance.[25] Following the death of the liable spouse a divorced spouse is entitled, under certain conditions, to a pension for surviving dependants from the state for the same amount as his/her maintenance entitlement.[26]

iv. State Assistance

There is no specific state support for divorced persons in Austria; a divorce can therefore often become a poverty trap. Maintenance is not a general entitlement, but applies only in the cases listed above. An alternative entitlement to state social welfare benefits is available only if maintenance from the divorced spouse, or from any other relatives obliged to provide maintenance, is withheld.

---

[21] See, eg, OGH 4 Ob 278/02i JBl 2003, 526; 6 Ob 108/08p EF-Z 2008/139.

[22] If a marriage is dissolved for reasons other than fault, the respondent may be entitled, inter alia, to equity maintenance (s 69 (3), Marriage Act). Equity maintenance can also be asserted by court action if the maintenance agreement reached in the course of a mutually agreed divorce is invalid (s 69a (2), Marriage Act).

[23] Except the maintenance obligation pursuant to s 68 Marriage Act.

[24] See, eg, M Schwimann in M Schwimann (ed), *ABGB Taschenkommentar* (Vienna, Lexis Nexis, 2010) § 66 EheG Rz 2.

[25] See the summary of the case law in Hopf and Kathrein above n 11, § 66 EheG Anm 19

[26] See U Aichhorn in E Gitschthaler and J Höllwerth (eds), *Kommentar zum Ehegesetz* (Vienna, Springer, 2008) § 258 ASVG Rz 1 et seq.

II. PRE-NUPTIAL AND POST-NUPTIAL AGREEMENTS

A. General Points

As well as wanting to be able to make their own arrangements as to how their marriage is to proceed, in practice, people wishing to get married increasingly also want to draw up a contract to determine the consequences of a possible divorce at the time they enter into the marriage. People now widely use the term 'marriage contract'[27] to describe these agreements although there are no special provisions for them in Austrian law – unlike, for example, in German law – and the conclusion of such marriage contracts is as yet relatively rare in Austria. The jurisdiction has yet to have a single Supreme Court decision dealing with the validity or content of a marriage contract. A marriage contract which regulates both the (financial and non-financial) arrangements during the marriage and the consequences of the dissolution of the marriage in one document may not, per se, have become widely popular in Austria yet, but agreements between spouses concerning the period of and following the marriage are by no means unusual. Agreements between spouses and engaged couples concerning post-marital maintenance and the division of property in the event of divorce are particularly common; the following will focus mainly on such agreements.

B. Form and Procedure

Since the marriage contract as such is not regulated by Austrian law, no specific formal requirements for it exist. Certain agreements, for example the agreement that the matrimonial property regime is to be a community of property, or the anticipatory consent to an agreement on the division of the matrimonial savings or the matrimonial home,[28] must be concluded in the form of a notarial deed (s 1 (1), lit a NotaktsG, the Austrian Notary Act; s 97 (1), Marriage Act). The law does not require independent legal advice for such transactions. In the case of a notarial deed, however, the notary must advise the parties as to the meaning and consequences of the legal transaction. In the event that the notary fails to give advice or imparts inaccurate advice, he/she can be liable for damages.[29] There is no specific entitlement to disclosure of the other spouse's assets. If it emerges, once the agreement has been concluded, that assets have not been disclosed, the agreement would have to be rescinded.

---

[27] In Austrian law the term 'marriage contract' is used only for the conclusion of a marriage between two opposite-sex partners (s 44, Civil Code).

[28] The Family Law Amendment 2009 introduced new possibilities and formal requirements for anticipatory agreements concerning the matrimonial home and other matrimonial material assets: see below section II.C.ii.d.

[29] See K Wagner and G Knechtel, *Kommentar zur Notariatsordnung* 6th edn (Vienna, Manz, 2010) § 52 NO Rz 6 et seq.

C. Content of the Agreements and Binding Effect

i. Agreements on the Effects of Marriage

Spouses can arrange their entire matrimonial community by consent. Freedom of arrangement is however limited, in particular, by the essence of marriage, the children's welfare, the principle of equal participation and the obligation of respect for each other (see s 91, Civil Code). Thus, for example, a mutually agreed exclusion of the indispensable essential elements of marriage (loyalty, support, decency) would be unethical.[30]

The prevailing view is, however, that a mutually agreed arrangement of the effects of marriage outside property law is only a de facto agreement and not a binding contract. An actionable entitlement cannot, therefore, be derived from an agreement of this kind.[31] It is possible, according to the prevailing opinion, for spouses to regulate contractually any property law issues during their marriage (eg participation in earning an income, maintenance). These agreements are subject only to the general regulations for legal transactions (usury, violation of moral principles); they are binding and can be enforced during the marriage by bringing an action.[32] It is not permissible, however, to waive spousal maintenance entirely while the marriage is intact (s 94 (3), Civil Code).

Agreements on the dissolution of a marriage are possible only in a very limited number of circumstances. For example, a couple may not waive the assertion of future grounds for divorce or the entitlement to divorce per se at the time they enter into the marriage.[33] The agreement of new grounds for divorce which are not regulated by law is also not permissible.[34]

ii. Contracts Concerning Matrimonial Property

a. Community of Property

Spouses or engaged couples[35] may exclude the principle of separation of property contained in the statutory matrimonial property regime (see above); they can agree on a community of property regime. Such agreements require the form of a notarial deed (s 1 (1), lit a NotaktsG), the intention being to prevent spouses manipulating assets to the disadvantage of creditors.[36] However, these statutory formal requirements for marital agreements have been relaxed by the courts, which have held that

---

[30] See evidence in Hopf and Kathrein above n 11, § 91 Rz 8 et seq.

[31] However, a breach of the agreement can be asserted, inter alia, in a divorce suit. See S Ferrari, 'Die Bedeutung der Privatautonomie im österreichischen Recht' in S Hofer, D Schwab and D Henrich (eds), *From Status to Contract?—Die Bedeutung des Vertrages im europäischen Familienrecht* (Bielefeld, Giesking, 2005) 97, 100 et seq.

[32] J Stabentheiner in P Rummel (ed), *Kommentar zum Allgemeinen bürgerlichen Gesetzbuch I* 3rd edn (Vienna, Manz, 2000) § 91 Rz 8.

[33] OGH 2 Ob 545/58 RZ 1959, 71.

[34] See J Stabentheiner in P Rummel (ed), *Kommentar zum Allgemeinen bürgerlichen Gesetzbuch II/4* 3rd edn (Vienna, Manz, 2002) § 46 EheG Rz 2.

[35] Pre-nuptial agreements are only valid on condition of subsequent marriage.

[36] See Koziol and Welser above n 8, 480.

informally concluded transactions that would generally require a notarial deed are enforceable by virtue of 'actual implementation' (*tatsächliche Erfüllung*).[37] Parties can make very different arrangements for a community of property; that is to say, the principle of the contractual freedom of arrangement applies.

b. Community of Property in the Event of Death

The law regulates the community of property only in the event of death, although, in practice, this rarely occurs. In this form of community of property, the principle of separation of property applies during the spouses' lifetime. Only when one of the spouses dies are the two spouses' assets first combined in order that they can then be divided – in accordance with the proportions agreed in the marriage contract – between the surviving spouse and the deceased's estate (s 1234 et seq, Civil Code).[38]

c. Community of Property Inter Vivos

The law does not regulate agreements on the community of property of living persons,[39] which can be found in some rural areas and which can vary enormously in what they cover. Such an agreement may comprise the spouses' total present and future (acquired or inherited) assets, thereby constituting a general community of property. Even in this case, it is possible to agree that certain assets do not belong to the common assets (and thus are separate property). Another form of agreement is a limited community of property,[40] which can be limited, for example, to presently held assets only, future acquisitions only (joint ownership of property acquired during marriage), assets acquired and inherited in the future, or to the totality of the personal property and real property acquired. Other limitations are also conceivable; spouses are free to agree to atypical limited community of property arrangements.

In a community of property of living persons the spouses jointly own the assets included in the agreement.[41] It is the predominantly held opinion that a community of property constitutes a binding obligation only between the contracting partners; third parties are affected however in the case of real estate through the incorporation of prohibitions on transfer and on subjecting the property to charges or encumbrances, pursuant to section 364c of the Civil Code.[42]

Following the death of one of the spouses in a community of property arrangement, once all debts have been deducted, the remaining net assets are divided

---

[37] Eg OGH 7 Ob 780/79 NZ 1981, 37; 7 Ob 598/82 SZ 56/119; 1 Ob 519/90 JBl 1990, 715.

[38] The surviving spouse can also be included in the deceased's estate but must as a principle have everything that he/she receives on the basis of a property contract agreement included in his/her share of the inheritance (s 757 (2), Civil Code).

[39] For more detail on communities of property see Koziol and Welser above n 8, 480 et seq; Ferrari, above n 1, 182 et seq.

[40] Where assets are limited to present or future assets, an inventory must be drawn up (s 1178, Civil Code).

[41] Joint ownership requires an act of transfer in addition to the marital agreement as title. See Koziol and Welser above n 8, 481.

[42] For evidence of this and of a different opinion that this constitutes joint title of property see Hopf and Kathrein above n 11, § 1234 Anm 9.

between the surviving spouse and the deceased's estate.[43] In the event of divorce and, if the spouses cannot reach agreement on the division of the joint assets, the following applies: if neither spouse is at fault for the breakdown of the marriage, or if both are equally at fault, the marital agreement is deemed to be rescinded (s 1266, sentence 1, Civil Code). In this case each spouse retrieves the assets they brought to the marriage plus what they have accrued.[44] If, on the other hand, one spouse is solely or predominantly at fault for the dissolution of the marriage, the innocent party has the additional right, pursuant to section 1266 of the Civil Code, to elect for a division of the joint property as in the case of death, whereby the agreed proportion is the determining factor (in the case of doubt, this is deemed to be half the property pursuant to s 1234 of the Civil Code).[45]

d. Barriers to Matrimonial Property Agreements

Community of property agreements of this kind, and any other kinds of matrimonial property agreements, cannot, however, completely exclude the statutory provision of an entitlement to division following the dissolution of a marriage (s 81 et seq, Marriage Act).[46] This is not possible even if the community of property agreement expressly waives the entitlement to division. Up to the end of 2009, the waiving of the entitlement to division of matrimonial material assets *in advance* had no legal validity (s 97 (1), Marriage Act). The prevailing opinion was that not even the allocation of certain material items to a spouse could be agreed with legal effect.[47] On the other hand, a waiver of an entitlement to division with regard to the matrimonial savings which was declared *in advance* is deemed to be valid if it has been concluded in the form of a notarial deed. Based on the provision that a waiver of entitlement to the division of matrimonial material assets had no legal validity, an agreement in respect of a total separation of property that also had effects after a possible divorce could not bind the court.[48]

Due to the Family Law Amendment 2009, however, these statutory provisions only applied until 31 December 2009. Since 1 January 2010 spouses have been able to conclude anticipatory contracts concerning the division of all matrimonial assets (s 97 (1), Marriage Act). Agreements in advance with regard to the matrimonial savings and the matrimonial home must be concluded in the form of a notarial deed; for anticipatory agreements on the division of other matrimonial material assets the law requires a written contract (s 97 (1), Marriage Act). In the case of a divorce, each spouse can nonetheless assert his/her entitlement to division by court action. However, only in cases where the judge deems the agreement inequitable can his/her

---

[43] See, eg, Koziol and Welser above n 8, 482.

[44] For an assessment of gains and losses see, eg, OGH 6 Ob 245/01z JBl 2001, 309 (*Pfersmann*).

[45] For greater detail see A Deixler-Hübner, *Der Ehevertrag. Vereinbarungen zwischen Ehegatten und Lebenspartnern* (Vienna, Linde, 2009) 124 et seq. There is controversy over whether the community of property can be terminated for important reasons in the same way as other continuing obligations.

[46] That is to say, s 81 et seq of the Marriage Act take precedence as leges speciales over the provisions on the effect of a divorce on marital agreements (s 1265 et seq, Civil Code). For a detailed account see Koziol and Welser above n 8, 515 et seq.

[47] For evidence see Stabentheiner above n 34, § 97 EheG Rz 1.

[48] See Ferrari, above n 31, 104.

decision depart from it (s 97 (2), Marriage Act). In relation to the use of the matrimonial home, the court may, pursuant to section 97, paragraph 3, Marriage Act, deviate from an anticipatory agreement if one spouse or a child from the marriage cannot provide for his/her own maintenance or if his/her living conditions would deteriorate considerably (eg because of disability). In order to determine whether the court should deviate from a valid anticipatory agreement in advance the judge has to take into account, in particular, the matrimonial living conditions, the length of time spent in matrimonial community, to what extent legal advice has been provided and the form of the agreement (s 97 (4), Marriage Act).

Spouses are now able to use an anticipatory disposal to exclude the transfer of ownership of a matrimonial home or the creation of a right in rem to it. This makes the anticipatory disposal of the matrimonial home easier where it was brought into the marriage or was inherited or received as a present by one of the spouses from a third party ('opt-out', s 87 (1), sentence 2, Marriage Act). In relation to the use of the matrimonial home the court may, nevertheless, deviate from an anticipatory agreement (s 97 (3), Marriage Act).

e. Can the Spouses Choose a Foreign Matrimonial Property Regime?

Pursuant to section 19 of IPRG, the Austrian Act on Private International Law, matrimonial property law must be judged pursuant to the law which the parties have expressly[49] stipulated; a choice of law is therefore desirable. Two factors must, however, be observed. First, as a matter of principle, only permanent arrangements for assets resulting from marriage come under the jurisdictional ambit of 'matrimonial property law'; these include, for example, community of property agreements and, if need be, the division of matrimonial savings pursuant to section 81 of the Marriage Act.[50] The division of the matrimonial home and household equipment or goods should, however, be determined pursuant to the effects of the law applicable to the marriage or the divorce (s 18, Act on Private International Law),[51] which do not provide for a choice of law. Secondly, it is a condition of the choice of law that a relevant foreign connection exists, so that the court is not dealing with foreign law in a purely domestic case. The reason for this is to prevent the requirement for a notarial deed for matrimonial property agreements from being circumvented. The law does not however define precisely what form the requisite foreign connection must take, and this is the subject of frequent debate.[52]

---

[49] Purely logical assumption of the choice of law is not possible for marital property law: OGH 1 Ob 264/98z SZ 72/48.

[50] More recent court decisions however favour a subsumption of the entire post-marital division of assets (including therefore the division of the matrimonial savings) pursuant to s 20, IPRG (divorce statute): see, eg, OGH 1 Ob 17/05i ZfRV 2005, 158, with the effect that the spouses' choice of law in this respect would be void.

[51] More recent court decisions impute the entire post-marital division of assets to the divorce statute of s 20, IPRG: see previous footnote. Evidence of the great difficulty posed in establishing the limits of property statutes and the statutes on the effects of marriage or divorce can be found in B Verschraegen, in P Rummel (ed), *Kommentar zum Allgemeinen bürgerlichen Gesetzbuch II/6* 3rd edn (Vienna, Manz, 2004) § 19 IPRG Rz 2 with notes on different opinions.

[52] See ibid, § 19 IPRG Rz 4, § 11 IPRG Rz 8. It is her opinion that a foreign connection exists, and hence also a valid choice of law, if there is any relevant legal aspect in the facts and circumstances of the case which in Austrian opinion or in foreign opinion of a conflict of laws could constitute a point of

iii. Anticipatory Contracts Concerning Possible Divorce Maintenance

Some spouses wish to conclude an agreement on possible divorce maintenance at the time they enter into the marriage or during the course of their marriage. Such agreements are permissible under Austrian law (s 80, Marriage Act). The prevailing opinion is that an agreement on maintenance obligations for the time after marriage can be concluded prior to marriage.[53] The conclusion of the agreement is exempt from formal requirements.[54] Maintenance contracts are subject to the *clausula rebus sic stantibus* (fundamental change of circumstance clause); however the parties may agree that a subsequent change of circumstances shall be of no importance.[55]

The general principles governing contracts apply to maintenance agreements; there are no specific family law provisions in Austrian law. In the event of a breach of the general contract law principles (for example, through juridical incapacity, erroneous expression of intention, fictitious transactions, violation of moral principles) the maintenance agreement can become invalid (in whole or in part) or contestable. An agreement is contrary to morality if, for example, the livelihood of the obligated party is endangered by the performance of maintenance payments or if the agreement is concluded only with the intention of passing the maintenance on to third parties such as the public welfare system.[56]

A maintenance agreement for the time after the marriage often comprises a reciprocal waiver of any post-marital maintenance; it often also excludes the change of circumstances clause and provides for the event of poverty. A waiver of necessary maintenance even in the event of poverty could, however, be judged to be unethical, as the Supreme Court has accepted that a waiver of this kind in the course of a mutually agreed divorce is a violation of moral principles.[57] That is to say, in my opinion, it is clear that a waiver of maintenance entitlement which was concluded outside a divorce suit cannot extend beyond a waiver of maintenance entitlement within the framework of a divorce suit (see below section III.B). When concluding such a waiver the spouses or engaged couple must therefore take into account the possibility that it might not withstand a challenge at a later date.[58]

D. Limits to Contractual Freedom in Marriage Contracts

Unlike Germany, Austria does not have a court decision on the possible extent of the subject matter of comprehensive marriage contracts. This is possibly due to the fact that in practice such marriage contracts are still fairly uncommon. In the future, however, if Austrian courts have to deal with challenges to contracts of this kind,

---

reference for a foreign legal regime. According to this opinion, for example, it is possible for two married Austrians who are living in Austria to choose a foreign property regime if they intend to move abroad or already have assets there.

[53] See evidence cited in W Zankl in Schwimann and Verschraegen above n 18 § 80 EheG Rz 6 et seq.
[54] Koch, above n 10, § 80 EheG Rz 3; OGH 11.5.2005, 7 Ob 55/05x (unpubl.).
[55] See Koziol and Welser above n 8, 517; OGH 3 Ob 468/53 SZ 26/222; 8 Ob 2213/96s SZ 70/111.
[56] Further evidence can be found in Koch, above n 10, § 80 EheG Rz 4.
[57] See OGH 3 Ob 229/98t JBl 2000, 513 (*F. Bydlinski*).
[58] See also Ferrari, above n 31, 109.

they will probably align themselves with the German jurisdiction on judicial review of such contracts.

III. SEPARATION AGREEMENTS

A. Contracts Concerning Matrimonial Property in Connection with a Divorce Suit

The restrictions mentioned above[59] do not apply to agreements on the division of the matrimonial material assets and the matrimonial savings that the spouses conclude in connection with a divorce suit. They may conclude such contracts without restriction and free from formal requirements. Even if the judge deems the agreement inequitable, he/she cannot deviate from it.[60] Such contracts are (only) contestable pursuant to general contractual rules (error, fraud, juridical incapacity or violation of moral principles). It is permissible for such agreements to include a total waiver of the entitlement to division.[61]

On the crucial question of when such a connection with a divorce suit exists, the Supreme Court has made numerous decisions: the required connection is deemed to exist in any case if such an agreement was concluded immediately before a divorce suit was initiated.[62] Otherwise, it depends first and foremost on the connection of function between the agreement and the (later) divorce suit.[63] The connection thus established must not, however, be eliminated as a result of 'any intervening events' such as, for example, a temporary reconciliation.[64] There is no strict temporal rule but the temporal element is taken into account in determining whether there is a connection: Should a period of some months (four to six) elapse between the agreement and the divorce being sought, this does not as a rule damage the connection.[65] However, in the event of a longer period elapsing (such as nine months), an inner connection can scarcely be deemed to exist.[66] By contrast however, in individual cases, even where a period of about a year elapses, the required connection may possibly be still deemed to exist.[67]

B. Contracts Concerning Post-Marital Maintenance in the Course of a Divorce Suit

The maintenance due after a divorce can be settled by an agreement concluded free from formal requirements (s 80, Marriage Act). If the spouses are aiming for

---

[59] S 97 (1) to (4), Marriage Act.
[60] S 97 (5), Marriage Act.
[61] See OGH 1 Ob 685/80 SZ 53/125 concerning the legal situation before the Family Law Amendment 2009.
[62] See OGH 1 Ob 685/80 SZ 53/125; 1 Ob 596/87 SZ 60/95; 10 Ob 12/09a EFSlg 123.995.
[63] OGH 4 Ob 546/90 EvBl 1990/153; 7 Ob 47/99h EFSlg 94.040.
[64] See, eg, OGH 1 Ob 685/80 SZ 53/125; 6 Ob 37/03i NZ 2005/62.
[65] OGH 1 Ob 685/80 SZ 53/125.
[66] OGH 7 Ob 47/99h EFSlg 94.039.
[67] OGH 6 Ob 642/84 EvBl 1985/121.

a mutually agreed divorce, an agreement on post-marital maintenance is in fact a precondition (s 55a, Marriage Act). The agreement need not simply stipulate a fixed sum (which one spouse must pay to the other), it may also constitute a waiver of maintenance entitlement which can be reciprocal. Post-marital maintenance agreements are subject, in principle, to the change of circumstances clause; the clause can however be excluded. In such an event, however, it should be noted that insistence on the exclusion of the change of circumstances clause may, in individual cases, be unethical.[68]

A total waiver of post-marital maintenance is also permissible according to law; no provisions exist to limit this. However, following a highly controversial Supreme Court decision[69] it can be assumed that it is not permissible to waive essential maintenance in the event of poverty. In that case a waiver of this kind, which was concluded in a mutually agreed divorce, was regarded as unethical.[70]

IV. CONFLICT OF LAWS

The purpose of this section is to examine whether a marital agreement that was concluded and is binding and valid under a foreign law is also valid in Austria.

The following point should be noted: there is currently no overall European Union ruling on a material or procedural level with regard to the whole of marital property law between spouses; a European marriage contract is, however, already under discussion. For the time being, cases where the facts are international must still be solved using private international law.[71] When it is presented with a case whose facts have a foreign connection, provided that the condition of international jurisdiction is fulfilled,[72] the Austrian court must therefore use the rules of private international law to establish which national law actually applies. There is, however, no independent point of reference in Austrian private international law for a marriage contract which provides for the entire period of matrimonial, as well as post-matrimonial, life. It is probably for this reason that in establishing the link a distinction must be made between issues relating to property law and non-property law provisions, in the same way that a distinction must be made between agreements for the time of the marriage and those which apply to the time after divorce. On any issue of matrimonial or post nuptial maintenance the conflict of laws rules of the Hague Protocol on the Law Applicable to Maintenance Obligations 2007 must be applied.

The individual connecting factors (*Anknüpfungspunkte*), especially the issue of establishing the limits between matrimonial property law and the law on the

---

[68] See evidence in Hopf and Kathrein above n 11, § 80 EheG Anm 5 with further references.

[69] See OGH 3 Ob 229/98t JBl 2000, 513 (*F. Bydlinski*). For references to critical literature see Hopf and Kathrein above n 11, § 94 Anm 48.

[70] For deliberations on how a challenge could be successfully withstood see Ferrari, above n 31, 108 et seq.

[71] Deixler-Hübner above n 45, 173 et seq.

[72] See Art 3 et seq, Council Regulation (EC) No 4/2009 of 18 December 2008 on jurisdiction, applicable law, recognition and enforcement of decisions and cooperation in matters relating to maintenance obligations (= EC Maintenance Regulation) for issues of maintenance; s 76 (2), JN for contested matrimonial causes and s 114a, JN for uncontested matrimonial causes.

consequences of divorce, are complicated, with many exceptions.[73] The main point of reference in the Austrian family law part of the Act on Private International Law, however, is section 18. Section 18 provides that the personal legal effects of the marriage[74] are to be judged primarily according to the personal status law that the spouses have in common and, in its absence, according to the last common personal status law of the spouses,[75] if one of them has retained it (s 18 (1) (1), Act on Private International Law). The personal legal effects of the marriage must comply, secondly, with the law of the state in which both spouses have their usual place of residence (s 18 (1) (2), Act on Private International Law), and in the absence of such, the law of the state in which they both had their last usual place of residence, if one of them has retained it.[76]

Matrimonial property provisions, in the absence of an express choice of law, shall be judged according to the law governing the personal legal effects of the marriage at the time of entry into marriage (s 19, Act on Private International Law). The matrimonial property statute is thereby unchangeable.[77]

The effects of a divorce (except maintenance issues[78]) shall be judged according to the law governing the personal legal effects at the time of the divorce (s 20, Act on Private International Law).

In Austria, therefore, any judgments on marital matters must be based on agreements between foreign spouses that were concluded and are valid under a foreign law, provided that Austrian private international law points to the law according to which the agreements were concluded. If, on the other hand, Austrian law is applicable according to the rules of private international law, the validity of the foreign marital agreement would have to be judged pursuant to Austrian law; all that is required for the necessary formalities, however, is compliance with the formal requirements of the state in which the legal transaction took place (s 8, Act on Private International Law).

V. CONCLUSION

On the whole, spouses have a considerable degree of freedom under Austrian law in arranging matters of family law by mutual agreement. There are only a few limits which they need to take into consideration: for example, certain essential elements

---

[73] See, eg, Schwimann and Verschraegen, above n 18 at § 19 IPRG Rz 2 ff and H Ofner, *Internationales Ehegüterrecht. Abgrenzungsfragen zwischen Güterrechtsstatut gem § 19 IPRG und Scheidungsstatut gem § 20 IPRG*, ZfRV 2006, 84.

[74] These are the effects of the matrimonial community outside property law, the right to use the matrimonial home and the matrimonial materials assets, as well as all those property law effects of marriage which do not fall under matrimonial property law such as participation in earning an income. For maintenance during the marriage see the conflict of laws rules of the Hague Protocol on the Law Applicable to Maintenance Obligations 2007.

[75] Pursuant to s 9 (1), IPRG the personal status law (*Personalstatut*) of a natural person is the law of the state of which he/she is a citizen.

[76] For further possible points of reference see s 18 (2), IPRG.

[77] M Nademleinsky and M Neumayr, *Internationales Familienrecht* (Vienna, facultas.wuv, 2007) Rz 04.18.

[78] On maintenance issues the Hague Protocol on the Law Applicable to Maintenance Obligations 2007 has to be applied.

of matrimonial community cannot be excluded; as a point of principle, spousal maintenance during marriage cannot be waived; the legal grounds for divorce cannot be either excluded by agreement or redefined. The Family Law Amendment 2009 has enlarged the scope for agreements in advance concerning matrimonial property. Consideration must be taken, however, of the fact that specific formal requirements exist, and that the judge may deviate from an anticipatory agreement where that puts one of the spouses at an inequitable disadvantage. In this respect the Austrian legal system tries to a certain extent to protect, above all, subsistence needs such as accommodation and maintenance.

Austrians use the freedom of arrangement of matters of family law by mutual agreement in particular in the event of divorce. As noted above, approximately 90 per cent of all divorces are settled by mutual consent and divorce settlements have an obligatory contractual provision inter alia for legal maintenance and property law matters between the spouses. For agreements of this kind in connection with a divorce suit there is wide-ranging freedom of contract. It must be noted, however, that the courts take a sceptical view of a total waiver of maintenance after divorce. The legal provisions for the divisions of assets and post-marital maintenance are thus rarely applied. They are, however, an important guide for the spouses' respective negotiating positions. The legal provisions for the division of assets, in particular, have generally proven effective. A significant advantage of these provisions is almost certainly the fact that it is permissible in Austrian law to take account of the contribution each spouse has made to the marriage and the approach does not rely on a rigid halving of the assets. The legal provisions for maintenance are likewise widely accepted by the population.

By contrast, the legal situation with regard to the dissolution of a marriage as a result of the death of one of the spouses is very unsatisfactory in the case of spouses who had been bound throughout their marriage by the statutory marital property regime of the separation of property. That is to say, there is no provision in such cases for the division of assets, unlike in the event of the dissolution of the marriage of living persons (s 81 et seq, Marriage Act). Death activates only those consequences under the law of succession which are formally linked to the assets the deceased has bequeathed. A spouse's financial circumstances during an intact marriage may, however, differ greatly from the contributions he/she made to the marriage; this is the case, for example, when only one spouse had been in gainful employment and purchased all the essential material assets, but the other spouse (usually the woman) made a substantial contribution to the creation of their joint wealth by participating in earning an income, and looking after the children's education and the housekeeping.[79] Apart from that the evaluation of the current situation is a positive one.

---

[79] For further evidence see Ferrari, above n 1, 191 et seq.

Marital Agreements and Private Autonomy in France and Belgium

WALTER PINTENS

CONTENTS

I. INTRODUCTION

Both French and Belgian law belong to the Romanic legal tradition. These legal orders are interrelated, Belgian law having derived and been developed from the original French law, and thus they share a common body of ideas and maxims. The French *Code Civil*, which was introduced in what today is Belgium in 1804, serves as a common legal foundation in both countries. That commonality is still apparent today in some fields of private law, particularly the law of contract and tort. However, in other legal fields, especially family and succession law, the reforms carried out in both legal orders have resulted in a substantial diminution in commonality and, in fact, vast differences have emerged.

Nevertheless, broad similarities between both systems can still be found in matrimonial property law, although the legal orders are drifting apart in several sub-areas.

Unlike in the European common law jurisdictions, the French and Belgian legal systems, like all civil law systems, regulate the proprietary consequences of marriage by way of matrimonial property and maintenance law, rather than leaving them to be governed by rules of general property law. While both French and Belgian law contain mandatory provisions relating to property in the general law on marriage (*régime primaire*), for example rules governing the family home and liability for household debts, which are independent from the matrimonial property regime (*régime sécondaire*), it is the matrimonial property regime which lies at the core of both systems. Spouses can exercise a large degree of autonomy in their selection of a matrimonial property regime by way of a binding pre-nuptial or post-nuptial agreement. The default matrimonial property regime is therefore only a default rule. However, even if the spouses choose a separation of property regime, unlike under common law, their property relationship will still be regulated by matrimonial rather than general property law.

The default and self-selected matrimonial property regimes differ completely from regulation in the common law context. They cannot be considered as default or contractual mechanisms for the regulation of spousal separation, since they primarily deal with the financial consequences upon and during marriage, rather than being limited to regulating the distribution of assets in the event of marital dissolution by death or divorce.

Most continental legal systems draw a clear distinction between matrimonial property and maintenance, whereas common law systems in principle deal with both issues at the same time. Belgian law has no special provisions regulating the distribution of marital property by the courts, and where a community system applies, the community property is simply divided into equal parts. Maintenance is a separate issue and the interrelationship between maintenance and marital property is limited, the only interface being that the income obtained out of the marital property will reduce need and thus influence the maintenance quantum. The same rules apply in French law, but a *prestation compensatoire*, a kind of maintenance claim in cases where there is a disparity between the living conditions of the spouses, can be awarded in the form of proprietary redistribution. While this French mechanism is not comparable to the common law system of reallocation, it does combine elements of both maintenance and matrimonial property.

The legal provisions on matrimonial property law are laid down in the French and Belgian Civil Codes.[1] Articles 212 to 226 FCC and Articles 212 to 224 BCC contain the rights and duties of the spouses, while Articles 1387 to 1581 FCC and Articles 1387 to 1474 BCC contain the matrimonial property regimes.[2] Maintenance after divorce is regulated by Articles 270 to 281 FCC and by Article 301 BCC.

In Belgium, marriage has been opened up to same-sex couples, and matrimonial property law applies to both same-sex and opposite-sex marriages.[3] Outside of marriage, the French and Belgian legal systems have a legal regime for formalised relationships, which are open to opposite-sex and same-sex couples, with the regime in Belgium even extending to family members.[4] The French PACS and the Belgian legal cohabitation differ from marriage, since the rights and duties of the cohabitants are more limited.

II. FINANCIAL CONSEQUENCES OF DIVORCE

Since the financial consequences of divorce are related to the matrimonial property regime, they cannot be understood without any knowledge of the mandatory *régime primaire*, describing the rights and duties of the spouses, and the default matrimonial property regime. Some information about the different categories of assets and their composition is necessary to explain the system of liquidation and distribution of the common property.

A. Régime Primaire: Rights and Duties of the Spouses

The *régime primaire* affords private autonomy little latitude. In both Belgium and France, the provisions of the *régime primaire* are *ius cogens* and apply to each and every marriage, irrespective of the specific matrimonial property regime (Art 226 FCC; Art 212 BCC). Whereas in Belgium only some of the family law provisions have an *ordre public* (public policy) character and only the property law rules are *ius cogens*,[5] French doctrine traditionally holds the view that the whole *régime primaire* is part of the *ordre public*. Today, legal doctrine favours the *ius cogens*

---

[1] The following abbreviations are used: BCC: Belgian Civil Code, FCC: French Civil Code, CPIL: Belgian Code on private international law; NCPC: New Civil Procedure Code (France).

[2] For an overview of the Belgian system, see P De Page, *Le régime matrimonial*, 2nd edn (Brussels, Bruylant, 2008); W Pintens, CH Declerck, J Du Mongh and K Vanwinckelen, *Familiaal vermogensrecht*, 2nd edn (Antwerp, Intersentia, 2010); W Pintens, S Seyns, V Allaerts and D Pignolet, 'Belgium', in K Boele-Woelki, B Braat and I Curry-Sumner (eds), *European Family Law in Action IV: Property Relations between Spouses* (Antwerp, Intersentia, 2009). For an overview of the French system, see F Ferrand and B Braat, 'France' in K Boele-Woelki, B Braat and I Curry-Sumner (eds), *European Family Law in Action IV: Property Relations between Spouses* (Antwerp, Intersentia, 2009); P Malaurie and L Aynes, *Les régimes matrimoniaux*, 2nd edn (Paris, Cujas, 2007); F Terré and P Simler, *Les régimes matrimoniaux*, 5th edn (Paris, Dalloz, 2008). See also W Pintens, 'Privatautonomie im belgischen und französischen Familienrecht', in S Hofer, D Schwab, and D Henrich (eds), *From Status to Contract?—Die Bedeutung des Vertrags im europäischen Familienrecht* (Bielefeld, Gieseking, 2005) 125 et seq.

[3] Art 1387 et seq BCC.

[4] Art 1475 et seq BCC; Art 515-1 et seq FCC.

[5] Pintens et al, n 2 above 60 ff.

qualification.[6] In both systems, the restrictions on the autonomy of the parties are repeated in Articles 1388 FCC and BCC of the matrimonial property law, which state that the spouses may not deviate from the rules governing their mutual rights and duties.

The *régime primaire* tries to find a balance between solidarity between the spouses and autonomy.

Both spouses must contribute to the marital expenses in proportion to their respective means and in accordance with their standard of living (Art 214 FCC; Art 213 and Art 221 para 1 BCC).

Each spouse can enter into contracts concerning the householding and education of their children. The other spouse is jointly and severally liable for the debts arising from such contracts in so far as the expenses are not manifestly excessive in relation to the couple's standard of living (Art 220 FCC; Art 222 BCC). In France, joint and several liability for household debts or debts related to the education of children does not extend to instalment purchases and loans, unless they cover modest sums necessary for the needs of everyday life or were concluded by both spouses (Art 220 para 3 FCC). This restriction does not exist in Belgian law.

The most important rule of the *régime primaire* protects the family home and the household assets (Art 215 BCC, Arts 215 and 1751 FCC).[7] Even if the family home is the personal property of one of the spouses, that spouse cannot dispose of his or her rights without the consent of the other spouse. If this rule is infringed, the other spouse may apply for annulment of that disposition. If the family home is rented by one spouse, even before the marriage, the lease belongs to both spouses. One spouse alone may not dispose of the lease, and the landlord cannot terminate the lease without sending a separate letter of termination to each spouse.

B. Default Matrimonial Property Regime

In 80 to 90 per cent of all marriages, spouses do not avail themselves of the broad private autonomy options which matrimonial property law provides, and the default matrimonial property regime is therefore adopted. The default matrimonial property regimes of Belgium and France are highly comparable. In both systems, the default matrimonial property regime is a limited community of property, which can be described as a community of acquests.

Before the introduction of the *Code Napoléon*, Northern France and the Belgian provinces lived under customary law prescribing a community property regime.[8] Southern France was governed by written law with a *régime dotal* in which the husband received and administered his wife's dowry, but she could administer and dispose independently of her other assets. The *Code Napoléon* introduced the community of movables and acquests as a default regime, although the spouses could still opt for another regime. Under the default regime the community property

---

[6] Terré and Simler, n 2 above 42.
[7] Pintens et al, n 2 above 77 ff; Terré and Simler, n 2 above 50 ff.
[8] For historical developments in Belgium see Pintens et al, n 2 above Question 2; in France see Ferrand and Braat, n 2 above Question 2.

consisted of all assets acquired before and during the marriage, extending even to movables acquired by gift and inheritance. Only immovable assets acquired before the marriage or acquired during the marriage by gift, inheritance or bequest were personal property.

After the Second World War, some politicians in Belgium, as well as in France, favoured the introduction of a regime of participation of acquisitions,[9] but the community property system was so deeply rooted in popular consciousness that the French Act of 13 July 1965[10] and the Belgian Act of 14 July 1976[11] ultimately adopted a modernised form of the community property system. All assets and debts before marriage and all assets and debts acquired by gift, bequest and inheritance are personal, with no distinction between movables and immovables. All other assets, including all the gains of the spouses, belong to the community property.

i. Composition of the Categories of Property

The community of acquests is based on three separate categories of property: the personal property of the husband, the personal property of the wife, and the common or community property of both spouses (Arts 1398–1405 BCC; Arts 1401–08 FCC). Those categories are composed of assets and claims and of debts.

a. Assets and Claims

The personal property comprises all assets and claims that belong to a spouse at the moment of marriage, as well as those assets and claims that a spouse acquires during the marriage by gift, inheritance or bequest. Further assets which are part of the personal property are, for example, the accessories of personal immovable assets and personal shares, assets acquired by subrogation, and assets and rights that are closely linked with the spouse's person (Arts 1403–08 FCC; Arts 1399–1404 BCC). Professional assets such as medical instruments or books are also personal property (Art 1404 para 2 FCC; Art 1400 no 6 BCC). In Belgium all professional assets are personal property, in France only necessary assets fall within this category. Even if such assets have been acquired with community assets they are personal, but in both systems compensation will be due when the community property is dissolved and liquidated.

The community property, which has no legal personality, comprises gains from employment, inclusive of subsidiary earnings, as well as gains from personal property (eg interest payments, rental income, etc), all assets acquired by one or both spouses during the marriage using community means, and all gifts and bequests jointly allocated to both spouses. Finally, all assets which cannot be proven to be personal in nature are part of the community property (Arts 1401–02 FCC, Art 1405 BCC).

b. Debts

The rules on debts are related to the composition of the personal property and the community property (Arts 1406–14 BCC; Arts 1410–18 FCC). A distinction must

---

[9] For a description of such a regime see Art. 196 ff Swiss Civil Code.
[10] Act of 13 July 1965, *Journal Officiel* 14 July 1965.
[11] Act of 14 July 1976, *Belgisch Staatsblad* 19 September 1976.

be drawn between the nature of the debt as between the spouses *inter se* and the liability for debts against creditors.

As to the first issue, personal debts (and thus debts between the spouses *inter se*) are those which came into existence before the marriage or which result from gifts, inheritance and bequests to one spouse during the marriage (Art 1410 FCC; Art 1407 BCC), as well as those debts which were incurred in the sole interest of the personal property of one of the spouses (Art 1416 FCC; Art 1407 BCC). In Belgium only the capital of a loan is a personal debt, whereas the interest is a common debt (Art 1408 BCC). In France, both capital and interest are personal debts (Art 1410 FCC). Debts arising from providing security for a third parties' debts not incurred in the interest of the community property is personal (Art 1415 FCC). Debts incurred in disregard of the marital duties (Art 1407 BCC), as well as debts resulting from a criminal conviction or tort, are also personal (Art 1417 FCC; Art 1407 BCC).

Under Belgian law, community debts are liabilities that spouses have entered into both jointly and severally, or as co-debtors (Art 1408 BCC). Debts in the interest of the household, children's education or the community property are also common debts (Art 1408 BCC). Since professional earnings are part of the community property, professional debts are community debts (Art 1408 BCC). Under French law, maintenance due by a spouse and debts for the household and the education of the children are common by nature (Art 1409 FCC). Other debts incurred during the marriage may be common due to their purpose. This will be the case when the debt has not been incurred in the interest of the personal property of one of the spouses, but in the interest of the community property (Art 1416 FCC; Art 1408 BCC).

With regard to the second issue, that is liability for debts against creditors, under Belgian law, personal debts are payable from personal property and earnings (Art 1409 BCC). Community debts are payable from all three categories of property: the personal property of each spouse and the community property (Art 1414 para 1 BCC). There are important exceptions to these two basic rules. Personal debts may be recovered against the community property in so far as personal assets have fallen into the community property (Art 1410 BCC). In the case of debts resulting from tortious conduct, not only the personal property is liable, but the community property up to half of its net value (Art 1412 BCC). Professional debts are only payable from the debtor spouse's personal property and the community property, rather than all three categories of property.[12] French law makes no clear distinction between personal debts and community debts.[13] In principle all debts may be recovered from the personal property of the debtor spouse and the community property, except in the cases of fraud by the debtor spouse and bad faith by the creditor (Art 1413 FCC). However, personal debts incurred before the marriage and debts from successions and gifts received during the marriage can only be recovered from the personal property and income of the debtor spouse, and the community property in so far as personal assets have been merged with community assets (Arts 1410–11 FCC). In cases where only one spouse entered into a debt, the other spouse does not vouch with his or her earnings, although the latter is part of the

---

[12] Pintens et al, n 2 above Questions 32 and 33.
[13] Ferrand and Braat, n 2 above Questions 32 and 33.

community property (Art 1414 FCC). Some debts, such as a loan or a security entered into by one spouse, can only be recovered against personal property and income (Art 1415 FCC). Maintenance debts and debts for the household and the education of the children may be recovered from the personal property of both spouses and from the community property (Arts 220 and 1414 FCC).

ii. Administration

Personal property is subject to personal administration (Art 1425 BCC; Art 1429 FCC).[14]

The community property is subject to the principle of concurrent administration by both spouses (Art 1416 BCC; Art 1421 FCC).[15] On the basis of this rule, each spouse may autonomously administer the community property and must tolerate legal acts performed by the other spouse. Administration comprises all capacities relating to the actual administration *sensu stricto*, disposal and utilisation. However, the property must be administered in the family's interest.

The principle of concurrent administration is subject to exceptions. For a limited number of important dispositive legal acts, the consent of both spouses is required (Arts 1418–19 BCC; Arts 1422–25 FCC). Joint administration is applied, for example, to the sale of immovable community assets or to the gifting of community assets.

iii. Liquidation and Distribution

Under the default regime no distinction is drawn in the liquidation of the community property between dissolution as a result of death, divorce or modification of the matrimonial property regime (Art 1441 FCC; Art 1427 BCC).[16]

The composition of personal and community property can undergo important proprietary changes during marriage, for example when the community property invests in personal property, or vice versa, without obtaining any ownership rights. Should this property shift remain uncompensated, personal property would be enriched without justification at the expense of the community property. Therefore, the first step in liquidation is the calculation of any compensation.

Compensation will be due whenever personal property has benefited from the community property (eg if community assets have been used for investments in the personal property) or when the community property has benefited from personal property (eg when personal money has not been invested or reinvested and has fallen into the community property) (Art 1434 BCC).

As to compensation quantum, the general rule provides that compensation may not be less than the amount lost by the category of property which is entitled to be compensated (Art 1435 BCC; Art 1469 para 2 FCC). Article 1435 BCC and

---

[14] Pintens et al, n 2 above Question 34; Ferrand and Braat, n 2 above Question 34.

[15] Pintens et al, n 2 above Question 35; Ferrand and Braat, n 2 above Question 35.

[16] J-M De Carmo Silva and A Fouquet, *Liquidations de régimes matrimoniaux et de successions*, 2nd edn (Paris, Defrénois, 2005); A Pene, *Méthodologie des liquidations-partages en droit patrimonial de la famille* (Paris, Litec, 2005).

Article 1469 FCC do not provide for a general adjustment as a result of inflation (principle of nominal compensation). However, this is subject to an important exception: if personal assets have been used for the acquisition, maintenance or improvement of an asset of the community property, the increase in the value of that latter asset needs to be taken into account (Art 1435 BCC; Art 1469 FCC). Three situations must be distinguished:

1. At the time of dissolution, the asset still belongs to the property entitled to compensation. In order to calculate this compensation, the value of the asset at the time of dissolution must be taken into account.
2. The asset has been alienated before dissolution. The basis for the calculation of the compensation is the value of the asset at the time of alienation.
3. The alienated asset has been replaced by another asset. The compensation must be calculated on the basis of the value of the new asset at the time of dissolution.

Since nominal compensation is the general rule and the revaluation of compensation the exception, the possibilities for revaluation must be interpreted restrictively. The invested money must have really been used for the acquisition, maintenance or improvement of an asset. A causal link between the investment and the acquisition is required. A causal link is accepted, for example, when a spouse pays a community mortgage with money from an inheritance, if community assets have been bought with that loan. In that case, the compensation has to be revaluated since a causal link exists between the investment and the acquisition of the asset, which took place before the investment.

According to some academic authors, a particular exception to the general rule of nominal value also applies in respect of tools and instruments which are useful for the professional practice of a spouse (and thus which belong to his personal property). If these have been bought with common funds, compensation needs to be paid when the community property is dissolved. Although the compensation may not in principle be less than the sum of money spent by the community property, a strict application of this rule would lead to a particularly unfair outcome, since these assets are subject to a high rate of depreciation and have contributed to the acquisition of common income. It therefore seems fair that compensation is payable only for the residual value.[17]

After compensation, a balance sheet of the community property must be drawn up. Assets and debts at the time of dissolution must therefore be listed. In the event of dissolution by divorce, the relevant time is the date upon which the divorce petition was issued.

Under French law there is no rule of priority as between compensation rights and the rights of creditors, except for the preference resulting from a legal mortgage (Art 1474 FCC). This is in contrast to the preference which is given to creditors under Belgian law (Art 1430 BCC).

The law describes in detail how community debts are to be settled before and after distribution (Arts 1439–41 BCC; Arts 1482–83 FCC).

---

[17] Pintens et al, n 2 above 166 ff.

The credit balance is divided in half (Art 1445 BCC). Spouses are, however, entitled to deviate from equal division in a pre- or post-nuptial agreement or in a specific agreement after divorce. Furthermore, Article 1448 BCC and Article 1477 FCC provide that any spouse who is found guilty of concealing assets loses his or her share in the fenced assets.

Distribution principally takes place in kind. Assets which cannot be divided will be sold, if the spouses cannot agree on the distribution of those assets.

A spouse can apply for preferential allocation of specific assets. This right of preferential allocation is provided for in the case of dissolution upon death (Art 1446 BCC and Art 1476 FCC), as well as following divorce (Art 1447 BCC and Art 1476 FCC). Preferential allocation can only be claimed in relation to community assets and does not apply to the other spouse's personal assets.

According to Article 1446 BCC the surviving spouse can seek allocation of one of the immovable properties which serves as the family home, together with the present household assets of that property. The law does not require the family home to be the main family home, so that spouses may choose which home they wish to be allocated (eg a weekend residence). According to Article 1446 BCC, the court must grant the surviving spouse's request for allocation.

When the legal regime is dissolved by divorce, preferential allocation can be sought by each spouse in accordance with Article 1447 para 1 BCC. However, the request for allocation is not binding on the court, even if the allocation has been requested by only one of the spouses. If the other spouse opposes allocation, the court will have to decide the matter having regard to the social and family interests involved and the compensation rights or claims of the other spouse (Art 1447 para 3 BCC). The court has a large margin of discretion and is not obliged to grant the allocation. Domestic violence excludes the availability of preferential allocation for the guilty spouse.

According to Article 1446 BCC, spouses can also seek allocation of immovable property which serves or has served as their professional practice, together with the movable property which is present for professional purposes.

French law has comparable rules (Art 1476 FCC), but the possibilities are broader and can include the lease, annex buildings etc (Art 1475 FCC).

C. Maintenance

The Belgian Act of 27 April 2007 on divorce reform modified Article 301 BCC, which now provides that the court should determine the amount of any maintenance payment, which must at least cover the needs of the claimant spouse. Standard of living is no longer the absolute yardstick, but remains a factor which the court may take into consideration.[18] The income and potential income of the spouse in need are taken into account in the court's determination and quantification of a maintenance claim. Income encompasses professional income as well as income obtained within the scope of distributed matrimonial property. Distribution of the

---

[18] Cass. 12 October 2009, *Revue critique de jurisprudence belge* 2010, 470, note N Dandoy, *Tijdschrift voor Familierecht* 2010, 71, note C Van Roy.

community property will affect needs and can diminish them. Maintenance cannot exceed one-third of the income of the debtor spouse owing maintenance.

The same rules apply in France, but the yardstick used for attribution of a *prestation compensatoire* is the standard of living during the marriage. This standard of living will be influenced by the community property's division and distribution. If, after distribution, there is no inequity between the spouses, there will be no *prestation compensatoire*. If inequity remains, the court fixes the maintenance quantum on the basis of need and financial ability. The court must take into account the spouses' assets, as a capital sum and as an income, after the liquidation of the matrimonial property regime (Art 271 FCC). The *prestation compensatoire* is paid in community assets or capital. If this is not possible, it will be paid in instalments.

D. Pension Rights

Since in the Belgian default regime all income belongs to the community property, pensions received during the existence of the marriage, and replacing income and not eg compensatory payments for personal injury, also fall within the community property.[19] This rule applies equally when the pension is provided for by an insurance contract. The capital paid during the existence of the marriage falls into the community property.[20]

The distribution of community property does not affect spousal pension rights and claims. The entitlement to a pension and its payments still belong to the holder's personal property. Whether the community property is entitled to compensation for the payment of the premiums remains a debated issue, because the spouse who is not entitled to a pension has a pension claim derived from the pension rights of the other spouse based on social security law.[21] Insurance covering pension or savings plans and paid after the dissolution of the marriage is personal, but the community property must be reimbursed.[22]

In French law pension rights are taken into account when the *prestation compensatoire* is fixed (Art 271 FCC).

III. PRE-NUPTIAL AND POST-NUPTIAL AGREEMENTS

A. Basic Principles

If spouses do not want to fall within the scope of the default regime, they are entitled to make a pre-nuptial agreement (Art 1387 BCC and FCC). The spouses have a considerable degree of freedom in choosing and constructing their matrimonial property regime. This freedom to decide upon the content of their pre-nuptial

---

[19] Pintens et al, n 2 above 176–77.

[20] Ibid, 169 ff.

[21] See N Torfs and W Pintens, 'Pensioenverrekening bij echtscheiding', in *Opstellen De Bounge* (Antwerp, Kluwer, 1985) 156–57 and M Van Opstal and W Van Eeckhoutte, 'Het lot van sociale-zekerheidsbijdragen en prestaties', in H Casman, *Huwelijksvermogensrecht* (Antwerp, Kluwer, 2004) 8.

[22] Pintens et al, n 2 above 172 ff.

agreement is considered to be a particular application of the principle of private autonomy.

French law has allowed post-nuptial agreements since the Act of 13 July 1965. However, the regime can only be altered if it has been in force for at least two years (Art 1397 FCC). The ability to change the matrimonial property regime by mutual consent was only introduced in Belgium with the Act of 14 July 1976 (Arts 1394–96 BCC). Prior to these dates post-nuptials were forbidden.

Spouses modify their agreed or default matrimonial property regime at their own discretion. They can even adopt another matrimonial property regime (Art 1394 para 1 BCC; Art 1397 para 1). The law is very liberal: the number of successive modifications is infinite, a reason for modification is not required and spouses are free to determine the scope of the modification.

Pre- and post-nuptial agreements are subject to the general rules of the law of obligations. Consequently, a pre-nuptial agreement must satisfy the requirements of consent, capacity, lawful cause and object if it is to have legal validity.

In both France and Belgium the (relative) immutability of the matrimonial property regime renders the spouses unable to enter into contracts either with each other or with third parties which indirectly alter the matrimonial property regime. However, that does not mean that all contracts are excluded. The spouses may conclude partnership deeds or labour contracts with each other, for example. They may also grant power of attorney to each other (Art 218 FCC; Art 219 BCC). Sales agreements between spouses have always been problematic in this context. Such agreements were prohibited by the *Code Civil* save in a few exceptional situations. In Belgium, this prohibition has been maintained (Art 1595 BCC). In France, the prohibition was abolished in 1985, but exceptions still exist.[23] Purchases are only possible in cases of a separation of property regime. In cases where a community of assets has been established, it is impossible to buy an asset that belongs to the community property, because this would undermine the immutability of the matrimonial property regime. Acquisition of an asset which is part of the personal property is only allowed in cases where the requirements for reinvestment of one's own property are fulfilled. Otherwise the purchased asset would have been acquired for the community property and not for the personal property.

B. Form and Procedure

i. General Formal Requirements

Pre- and post-nuptial agreements must be drawn up in a notarial deed as prescribed by Article 1392 BCC and Article 1394 FCC. Article 1389 BCC prohibits the stipulation of conditions by means of a simple reference to repealed legislation. Such regimes must be taken *in extenso*. If the spouses opt for a regime contained in the BCC, a simple reference will be sufficient (Art 1389 *in fine*).

---

[23] Terré and Simler, n 2 above 287.

The notary must inform the parties fully and objectively and is liable for negligence. The notary's informational duty covers all possible economic and fiscal consequences of the contract which the parties intend to have drawn up. The Belgian law on notaries expressly prescribes that where unbalanced clauses or a threat of conflicting interests exist, the notary must indicate this and inform the parties that they have the right to ask for the assistance of a lawyer or another notary (Art 9 Act on notaries). The notaries' liability is not seen as a significant problem. Notaries have extensive experience with pre- and post-nuptial contracts. These are regarded as relatively simple contracts which are generally not more complicated than any other contract. Moreover the liability is covered by insurance.

Full disclosure of the spouses' assets and debts is not necessary for the making of a pre-nuptial agreement. This rule applies also to post-nuptial agreements in France, whereas in Belgium full disclosure is necessary in cases where the new regime implies the liquidation of the former regime. In such cases an inventory is necessary (Art 1397 BCC).

In France, children who have attained the age of majority have to be personally informed about a planned modification of the matrimonial property regime (Art 1397 para 2 FCC). Creditors are informed through publication of an announcement in a newspaper (Art 1397 para 3 FCC). These rules do not exist in Belgian law.

ii. Judicial Control

The pre-nuptial contract is not subject to any preceding test, because no judicial approval is prescribed.

Until recently a post-nuptial contract required ratification (*homologation*) by the court.

In France judicial control was abolished by an Act of 23 June 2006[24] as a general rule. The law does however provide exceptions.[25] Children of age of majority and creditors may oppose the agreement. In this case the court has to ratify the modification (Art 1397 paras 2–4 FCC). If a spouse has minor children, ratification is obligatory (Art 1397 para 5 FCC). The court will take into account the interests of children and creditors, but refusals to ratify are exceptional. Children's interests are not violated by a contract that the spouses could have agreed on before the marriage without any judicial control. Creditors find protection in matrimonial property law and in the law on obligations.

The Belgian Act of 18 July 2008[26] abolished judicial control.[27] During the parliamentary debates it was argued that spouses suffered discrimination because they had to tolerate judicial control during their marriage, whereas there was no judicial control when they made a pre-nuptial agreement. Third persons can find their protection in the *actio pauliana* (Art 1167 BCC).

---

[24] Act of 23 June 2006, *Journal Officiel* 24 June 2006.
[25] Terré and Simler, n 2 above 185 ff.
[26] Act of 18 July 2008, *Belgisch Staatsblad* 14 August 2008.
[27] See W Pintens, 'Wijziging van het huwelijksvermogensstelsel. Een commentaar op de Wet van 18 juli 2008', *Rechtskundig Weekblad* 2008–09, 946 ff; F Tainmont, 'La modification conventionnelle du régime matrimonial à la lumière de la loi du 18 juillet 2008', *Revue du notariat belge* 2009, 6 ff.

iii. Registration

In Belgium the marriage certificate must mention the date of the pre-nuptial agreement, the name and the duty station of the notary who has drawn up the agreement, and the matrimonial property regime (Art 76 BCC). If these elements are not mentioned, the terms which differ from the default regime cannot be invoked against third parties who have concluded contracts with one or both of the spouses, unless they were informed in an alternative way about the pre-nuptial agreement. If these third parties will not suffer loss due to the stipulated matrimonial property regime, but rather profit, they are entitled to rely on it, even if they were not initially aware of the matrimonial property regime.

A pre-nuptial agreement which contains an immediate transfer of immovable property, or immovable property rights, needs to be registered on the land and mortgage register (Art 1, Act on Land and Mortgage Register).[28]

Contractual appointments of heirs, conditions to take in advance and terms providing for an unequal division of property, also have an impact on the liquidation and distribution of the estate. Pre-nuptial agreements in which future spouses assign the whole or a part of the assets of their inheritance to one another must be registered in the central register of wills. This central register is kept by the Royal Federation of Belgian Notaries.

If one of the spouses is a merchant at the moment that the agreement has been drawn up, an extract of the pre-nuptial agreement must be sent to the chancery of the court of commerce within the jurisdiction where the trading spouse is registered on the trade register (Art 12 para 1 Belgian Commercial Code).

Post-nuptial agreements are noted in the margin of the marriage certificate (Art 76 BCC). Article 1396 BCC provides that the notary is responsible for the publication of the post-nuptial agreement in the Belgian Bulletin of Acts and Decrees. However, this publication is not required for modifications concerning matrimonial advantages and the appointment of the surviving spouse as an heir. They can be invoked against a third party as soon as they are mentioned in the margin of the marriage certificate.

Comparable regulations exist in France (Art 76, 6° and 1397 FCC).

iv. Content of the Agreement

The Belgian and French Civil Codes contain optional matrimonial property regimes ranging from an enhanced community of property to a universal community (Arts 1451–56 BCC; Arts 1497–98 and Art 1526 FCC). Furthermore, the codes provide the option of agreeing upon deviations from the rule prescribing equal division of the community property (Arts 1457–65 BCC; Arts 1511–26 FCC). Community property is predominantly assigned to the surviving spouse. The spouse's position is thus strengthened as against the children. The allocation of community property tends not to qualify as a gift, but rather as an onerous contract. Consequently, the children cannot plead their claim for a compulsory portion in cases where the allocation exceeds the available part of the estate.

---

[28] Act of 16 December 1851, *Belgisch Staatsblad* 22 december 1851 (integrated in the BCC).

Both codes include a separation of property regime (Arts 1466–69 BCC; Arts 1536–42 FCC). In addition, the French *Code Civil* contains an optional regime of participation in accrued gains (*participation aux acquêts*), which is comparable with the German community of accrued gains (*Zugewinngemeinschaft*). In Belgium, the Civil Code does not offer this matrimonial property regime. It can, however, be contractually agreed upon.

The spouses may also introduce modifications to the legal regime which are not stipulated in the law, for example the exclusion of certain assets from the community assets, although in community property regimes it is impossible to exclude earnings from labour.

The spouses can also choose a regime which differs completely from the regimes which have been proposed by the legislator. Thus, the parties have the option of choosing a foreign regime or a 'tailor-made' regime.

Marital agreements must not contain any clauses which infringe the *ordre public*, or good morals (Arts 6 and 1387 BCC and FCC). The equality and capacity of both spouses to contract is of crucial importance. Moreover, spouses cannot include terms limiting personal freedom, such as an agreement not to divorce or not to remarry after divorce, an agreement not to claim the judicial separation of property, or the exclusion of a conventional modification of the pre-nuptial agreement. However, it is possible to provide that certain advantages will cease to have effect upon a second marriage. Waiving spousal maintenance after divorce is also contrary to public policy.

Marital agreements must not deviate from the legal provisions governing the *régime primaire*, parental responsibility, guardianship and the legal order of succession (Art 1388 BCC; Arts 1388–89 FCC). Thus it is not possible to agree upon the upbringing and education of the children (eg upon their religion), or the attribution and exercise of parental responsibility after divorce.

In situations where a community of property regime is selected, Belgian law prohibits deviations from the default matrimonial property regime's rules concerning the administration of personal and community property (Art 1451 BCC). The legislator's intention is to avoid contracts which impair equal treatment of men and women. This norm is also applicable to foreign matrimonial property regimes. This means that Belgian spouses are not allowed to agree upon the German community of property regime without performing the necessary adjustments, as § 421 BGB (German Civil Code) prescribes that the spouses determine within the marriage contract whether the community property is subject to the husband's, the wife's or joint administration. If the marriage contract does not contain any rules at all pertaining to this issue, the spouses jointly administer the community property. The concurrent individual administrative powers for both spouses are excluded by this text. In France, it is also impossible to deviate from the rules on administration of personal property. These provisions are part of the *ordre public* (Art 225 FCC). With regard to the administration of the community property, Article 1503 FCC allows joint administration to be extended to all administrative and dispositive acts. This does not apply vice versa; the scope of application of joint administration cannot be abated. It is also impossible to question spousal equality by granting more administrative powers to one spouse. Equality in administration is part of the *ordre public*.[29]

---

[29] Terré and Simler, n 2 above 441 ff.

Spouses must also respect the essential characteristics of the stipulated regime as these are mandatory. The agreement has to be drawn up as one coherent whole and the regime cannot contain any contradictions. Besides the consistency of the regime, the spouses also must guarantee the stability of the matrimonial property regime. Consequently it is not possible for the spouses to choose their matrimonial property regime merely for the case of dissolution by divorce or by death. Case law and legal doctrine accept that a clause which conflicts with the essential characteristics of the regime is not contrary to public policy, but is invalid because of this contradiction. In a community of property, compensation for example cannot be totally excluded because it is an essential element of this matrimonial regime. It is however possible to exclude certain compensation or to adjust the manner of settlement.[30]

Finally, the spouses are unable to deviate from the rules of mandatory law, for example the furnishing of proof towards third parties.

v. Binding Effect and Enforceability

Pre- and post-nuptial agreements are binding and enforceable between the spouses. They cannot be set aside by the parties or by the court, except when they are contrary to public policy or morality, or when one of the spouses alleges a violation of mandatory rules.

The agreement can be declared completely or partially null and void. Complete nullity arises when, for example, a formal requirement has not been observed, or when the consent of a spouse is lacking.[31]

In cases of partial nullity the agreement remains valid in respect of the other provisions, unless the void condition is connected to the remainder of the agreement in such a way that it can only be seen as one inseparable whole. In such a case, the nullity of the condition will result in the nullity of the whole agreement, since the conditions of the pre-nuptial agreement are indivisible.

Spouses whose agreement has been declared null and void will be deemed to have been married under the default regime *ex tunc*.[32]

In French law post-nuptial agreements can be opposed by third parties up to three months after they are noted on the marriage certificate (Art 1397, para 6 FCC). In Belgium they can be opposed from the date of notification on the marriage certificate or, when prescribed, from the date of publication in the Belgian Bulletin of Acts and Decrees (see above, section III.B.iii).

IV. SEPARATION AGREEMENTS

In Belgium and France the (relative) immutability of the matrimonial property regime prevents the conclusion of contracts on property distribution before its dissolution. Such contracts are voidable; however, exceptions do exist.

---

[30] Pintens et al, n 2 above 329. Cf for French law: Terré and Simler, *matrimoniaux* n 2 above 578, where a total exclusion of compensation is considered as lawful but is strongly discouraged.

[31] Pintens et al, n 2 above 424.

[32] Ibid, 426.

In Belgium, in the case of divorce proceedings based upon mutual consent, the spouses are obliged to settle the property law consequences in their entirety (Art 1287 CCP). In those cases spouses are obliged to regulate maintenance rights on a contractual basis (Art 1288 CCP). However, they are not forced to negotiate maintenance, and may simply exclude the matter from the agreement. The court may only control validity, and a substantive review is excluded. Private autonomy applies in an unrestrained fashion. Each spouse is responsible for his or her own interests.

In the case of divorce proceedings based upon the irretrievable breakdown of the marriage, spouses may conclude agreements on the liquidation and distribution of their property. These are not binding, since their confirmation is required after divorce (Art 1257 para 3 Belgian Judicial Code).

In France exhaustive settlements including the *prestation compensatoire* are compulsory in cases of mutual consent divorce (Art 278-1 FCC). The court has significant powers of review and may substantially scrutinise the agreement. The court must approve the agreements and is required to reject them where they infringe the interests of one spouse (Art 232 para 2 FCC). Without ratification (*homologation*) of the agreement, a judge cannot dissolve the marriage.

Since 1975, agreements during divorce proceedings not based on mutual consent have been allowed (Arts 268 and 279-1 FCC). These agreements are subject to substantial judicial control (Arts 278 and 279-1 FCC).

V. CONFLICT OF LAWS

A. Jurisdiction

i. Belgian Law

Belgian courts have international jurisdiction if the defendant has his or her domicile or habitual residence in Belgium when the divorce application is introduced (Art 5 CPIL).[33] In addition to the cases provided for in the general provisions for international jurisdiction, Belgian courts have jurisdiction to hear actions regarding matrimonial property law, if:

1. in case of a joint application, either spouse was habitually resident in Belgium when the application was introduced;
2. not more than 12 months before the application was introduced, the last joint habitual residence of the spouses was in Belgium;
3. the spouse who introduces the application was habitually resident in Belgium for 12 months preceding when the application was introduced;
4. both spouses had Belgian nationality when the application was introduced (Art 42 CPIL).[34]

---

[33] The text follows the unofficial translation of the Code by C Clymans and P Torremans, available at www.ipr.be.
[34] See F Bouckaert, *Notarieel internationaal privaatrecht* (Antwerp, Kluwer, 2009) 31 ff; J Erauw and H Storme, *Internationaal Privaatrecht* (Antwerp, Kluwer, 2009) 525 ff.

ii. French Law

French courts have international jurisdiction when the defendant resides in France (Art 1070 NCPC). When there is no jurisdiction on this basis, French courts can have jurisdiction due to a *privilège de jurisdiction*, which applies when either the petitioner (Art 14 FCC) or the defendant has French nationality (Art 15 FCC).[35]

B. Applicable Law

i. Rights and Duties of the Spouses

a. Belgian Law
In Belgian law the rights and duties of the spouses under the *régime primaire* are governed:

1. by the law of the state on the territory of which both spouses have their habitual residence at the time the effects are invoked or, if the invoked effect affects a legal act, at the time the act took place; or
2. in the absence of a habitual residence on the territory of the same state, by the law of the state of which both spouses are nationals at the time the effects are invoked or, if the invoked effect affects a legal act, at the time the act took place; or
3. in other cases, by Belgian law (Art 48 CPIL).

The designated law determines, in particular, the contribution of the spouses to the expenses of the marriage, the receipt of revenues by each spouse and their disposition, the admissibility of contracts and gifts between spouses and their revocation, the specific rule under which one spouse may represent the other, and the validity of an act of one spouse that may be detrimental to the family interests vis-à-vis the other spouse and the modes of reparation for its harmful effects (Art 48 § 2 CPIL). This does not apply to the exercise of the rights of a spouse to the principal matrimonial home or the chattels furnishing it. Here the *lex rei sitae* applies (Art 48 § 3 CPIL).

b. French Law
Under French law, the law of the common nationality of the spouses is applicable. In cases of different nationality, the law of the common residence is applicable.[36] If the spouses have neither common nationality nor common residence, the *lex fori*, ie French law, applies.[37] But the applicability of the law of the common nationality or residence is limited, since many rules of the *régime primaire* are considered as *loi de police*. In this case the *lex fori* applies, for example, to the contribution to marital expenses.[38]

---

[35] Y Loussouarn, P Bourel and P de Vareilles-Sommières, *Droit international privé*, 9th edn (Paris, Dalloz, 2007) 636 ff.
[36] Cass. 17 April 1953, Revue critique de droit international privé 1953, 412, note H Batiffol; B Audit, *Droit international privé*, 5th edn (Paris, Economiva, 2008) 553.
[37] Cass. 15 May 1961, Dalloz, 1961, Jur., 437, note G Holleaux.
[38] Cass. 20 October 1987, Revue critique de droit international privé 1988, 540, note Y Lequette.

ii. Matrimonial Property Regime

a. French Law

In French law the Hague Convention of 14 March 1978 on the Law Applicable to Matrimonial Property Regimes applies to all spouses married since 1 September 1992.[39] The Convention applies even if the nationality, the habitual residence of the spouses, or the law to be applied is not that of a Contracting State (Art 2).

Spouses have a choice of law before the marriage restricted to:

1. the law of any state of which either spouse is a national at the time of designation;
2. the law of the state in which either spouse has his habitual residence at the time of designation;
3. the law of the first state in which one of the spouses establishes a new habitual residence after marriage (Art 3 paras 1 and 2).

The law thus designated applies to the whole of their property; nonetheless, the spouses, whether or not they have designated a law under the previous paragraphs, may designate with respect to all or some of the immovables the law of the place where these immovables are situated. They may also provide that any immovables which may subsequently be acquired shall be governed by the law of the place where such immovables are situated (Art 3 paras 3 and 4).[40]

If the spouses, before marriage, have not designated the applicable law, their matrimonial property regime is governed by the internal law of the state in which both spouses establish their first habitual residence after marriage (Art 4 para 1). Nonetheless, in the following cases, the matrimonial property regime is governed by the internal law of the state of the common nationality of the spouses:

1. where a declaration in accordance with Article 5 has been made by that state and its application to the spouses is not excluded by the provisions of the second paragraph of that article;[41]
2. where that state is not a party to the Convention and according to the rules of private international law of that state its internal law is applicable, and the spouses establish their first habitual residence after marriage in a state which has made a declaration in accordance with Art 5, or in a state which is not a party to

---

[39] The Convention is in force between France, Luxemburg and The Netherlands. See Lousouarn et al, (n 35) 530 ff. The Convention does not apply to spouses married before 1 September 1992. Those spouses can make a choice of law before the marriage on the basis of the non-codified French private international law. If a choice of law has not been made, the intended implicit choice has to be ascertained. In practice this means that the law of the first marital residence will be applicable. See A Devers, in P Murat, *Droit de la famille*, 4th edn (Paris, Dalloz, 2007) 1128.

[40] Comparable rules allow a choice of law during the marriage (Arts 6 to 8).

[41] Art 5 states that any State may, not later than the moment of ratification, acceptance, approval or accession, make a declaration requiring the application of its internal law according to sub-para 1 of the second para of Art 4. This declaration shall not apply to spouses who both retain their habitual residence in the State in which they have both had their habitual residence at the time of marriage for a period of not less than five years, unless that State is a Contracting State which has made the declaration provided for in the first paragraph of this Article, or is a State which is not a Party to the Convention and whose rules of private international law require the application of the national law. Only the Netherlands made such a declaration.

the Convention and whose rules of private international law also provide for the application of the law of their nationality;

3. where the spouses do not establish their first habitual residence after marriage in the same state (Art 4 para 2).

If the spouses do not have their habitual residence in the same state, nor have a common nationality, their matrimonial property regime is governed by the internal law of the state with which, taking all circumstances into account, the matrimonial property regime is most closely connected (Art 4 para 3).

Under certain circumstances a change of the habitual residence provokes a change of the applicable law (Art 7).

The effects of the matrimonial property regime on the legal relations between a spouse and a third party are governed by the law applicable to the matrimonial property regime in accordance with the Convention (Art 9 para 1). Nonetheless, the law of a contracting state may provide that the law applicable to the matrimonial property regime may not be relied upon by a spouse against a third party where either that spouse or the third party has his or her habitual residence in its territory, unless any requirements of publicity or registration specified by that law have been complied with, or the legal relations between that spouse and the third party arose at a time when the third party either knew or should have known of the law applicable to the matrimonial property regime (Art 9 para 2). The law of a Contracting State where an immovable is situated may provide an analogous rule for the legal relations between a spouse and a third party as regards that immovable (Art 9 para 3).

The application of the law determined by the Convention may be refused only if it is manifestly incompatible with public policy (Art 14).

b. Belgian Law

Although Belgium did not sign the Hague Convention, the rules of the Code on private international law are to a certain extent comparable with the Convention.[42]

The matrimonial property regime is governed by the law chosen by the spouses. This choice of law is restricted to:

1. the law of the state on the territory of which they will establish their first habitual residence after the celebration of the marriage;
2. the law of the state on the territory of which one of the spouses has his or her habitual residence at the time of the choice;
3. the law of the state of a spouse's nationality at the time of the choice (Art 49 CPIL).

The choice of law may be made before or during the marriage and may modify a previous choice (Art 50 § 1 CPIL). The choice should relate to all assets (Art 50 § 2 CPIL). In principle the choice only has effect as to the future, but the spouses may agree otherwise without affecting the rights of third parties (Art 50 § 3 CPIL).

The choice of the matrimonial property regime is valid as to its form if the requirements of the law applicable to the matrimonial regime at the time of the choice or of the *lex loci* are fulfilled (Art 52 para 1 CPIL). The rule *locus regit actum* applies to the modification of the matrimonial property regime (Art 52 para 2 CPIL).

---

[42] See Bouckaert, n 34 above 39 ff.

In the absence of a choice of law, the matrimonial property regime is governed by:

1. the law of the state on the territory of which both spouses establish their first habitual residence after the celebration of the marriage;
2. in the absence of a habitual residence on the territory of a same state, by the law of the state of which both spouses are nationals at the time of the marriage;
3. in other cases, by the law of the state on the territory of which the marriage was celebrated (Art 51 CPIL).

The designated law determines in particular:

1. the validity of the consent to the choice of law;
2. the admissibility and validity of the marital agreement;
3. whether it is possible to choose a matrimonial property regime and, if so, to what extent;
4. if and to what extent the spouses can change the matrimonial property regime, and whether the new regime has retroactive effect or whether the spouses can give it such effect;
5. the composition of the properties and the attribution of the administration powers;
6. the dissolution and the liquidation of the matrimonial property regime, as well as the distribution rules (Art 53 § 1 CPIL).

An exception exists for the manner of composition and attribution of the shares. The *lex rei sitae* at the time of the distribution applies (Art 53 § 2 CPIL).

Article 54 CPIL regulates the protection of third parties. The law applicable to the matrimonial property regime governs the question of whether or not the regime can be opposed by third parties, but with an important exception for debts.

If at the time a debt is incurred, the spouse and his or her creditor have their habitual residence on the territory of the same state, the law of that state will be applicable, unless:

1. the publicity or registration requirements under the law applicable to the matrimonial property were fulfilled; or
2. the creditor either knew of the matrimonial property regime at the time the debt was incurred, or was unaware of it solely through his own negligence; or
3. the publicity rules in relation to real property rights required under the law of the state on whose territory the immovable property is located were fulfilled (Art 54 § 1 CPIL).

The law applicable to the matrimonial property regime also determines if and to what extent a debt incurred by one of the spouses for the needs of the household or the education of the children engages the other. This rule does not apply if at the time the debt is incurred the spouse and the creditor have their habitual residence on the territory of the same state. The law of that state then applies (Art 54 § 2 CPIL).

iii. Recognition and Enforcement

If a foreign marital agreement is valid and binding according to the law of the jurisdiction in which it was concluded, it will be recognised in France provided that it does not contain any clause contrary to public policy.[43] The same rule applies in Belgium, but Belgian law further requires that the validity of the agreement is established in accordance with the law designated by Belgian private international law (*révision au fond*) (Art 27 § 1 CPIL).[44]

A judgment is necessary for enforcement of a foreign marital agreement (Art 27 § 2 CPIL).

VI. CONCLUSION

In both the French and the Belgian legal systems the default regime attaches huge importance to spousal solidarity by creating community property which is owned and administered by both spouses. During the marriage each spouse thereby participates in the other spouse's property acquired during the marriage. The default regime therefore allows a spouse who has no income, or who earns a very modest one, to enjoy certain autonomy as he or she directly acquires common property and takes part in the administration of the latter. Thus, the default regime provides particular protection for the economically dependent spouse.

Solidarity is also achieved by an equal division of the community property after dissolution. Although the courts do not enjoy discretionary powers – save in the granting of preferential allocation – and therefore cannot redistribute the property, equal division ensures that each spouse participates in the wealth which the other spouse accumulated during the marriage. The underlying idea is that each spouse should participate in the other spouse's property gained during the marriage without taking into consideration the assignment of tasks during the marriage, because the gains result from both spouses' efforts.

The present status of the law satisfies academics and practitioners. The default matrimonial property regime is regarded as workable. An acceptable balance appears to have been found between personal and common property. The small number of marriage contracts is evidence that this regime is convenient for the large majority of the population.

Spouses enjoy a large degree of autonomy to make a binding marital contract. Judicial control does not exist in Belgium and is very restricted in France. This reflects the idea that, although marriage is a community of life, the spouses should decide to what extent the marriage should also be a community of property.

---

[43] Lousouarn et al, n 35 above 735 ff.
[44] Bouckaert, n 34 above 9 ff.

Marital Agreements and Private Autonomy in England and Wales

JOANNA MILES

CONTENTS

I. THE FINANCIAL CONSEQUENCES OF DIVORCE

A. Historical Background

i. *Property Relations between Spouses and the Evolution of 'Ancillary Relief' on Divorce*

Contemporary English law[1] regarding marital property agreements can only be understood against the background of the evolution in English law's approach to the relationship of husband and wife. English law knows no concept of community of property between spouses. The property implications of the common law doctrine of unity[2] were swept away by late nineteenth-century legislation that introduced a separate property regime during marriage.[3] Henceforth, husband and wife were to be treated as separate individuals, each equally and independently capable of earning wealth and owning property (and of suing each other in tort and contract) like those who are legal strangers to each other. Neither would have any automatic rights in relation to each other's property either during marriage, on divorce or on death, freedom of testation being a valued principle of English succession law.

However, while husband and wife became separate entities for the purposes of property and contract law, the husband remained subject to his common law duty to maintain the wife, both during marriage,[4] on separation and (except, generally speaking, in case of fault by the wife) under statutory powers to order periodical payments in case of divorce.[5] Gender-specific duties to maintain were in due course replaced by gender-neutral statutory obligations,[6] and husbands ceased to be liable for debts incurred by their wives in the course of expenditure on 'necessaries', creating a total separation of debts as well as of property.[7] But, most significantly, legislation in the second half of the twentieth century (now found in the Matrimonial Causes Act 1973, Part II) conferred on the courts the power not only to order payment of maintenance on divorce, but also to transfer capital sums and, later, property.[8] Indeed, current legislation also empowers the court to share the parties' pension entitlements. These powers (largely also exercisable on petitions

---

[1] This and cognate expressions will be used to refer to the law of England and Wales.

[2] Discussed authoritatively in Cretney's magisterial *Family Law in the Twentieth Century* (Oxford, Oxford University Press, 2005) ch 3.

[3] Married Women's Property Act 1870 and 1882. See now the Law of Property Act 1925, s 37 and the Law Reform (Married Women and Tortfeasors) Act 1935, ss 1–4.

[4] This included a duty to provide the wife with accommodation, now superseded by the statutory 'home rights' regime: Family Law Act 1996, ss 30–34.

[5] See first the Matrimonial Causes Act 1857, s 32.

[6] See, eg, Matrimonial Homes Act 1963 (see now the Family Law Act 1996, ss 30–34) in relation to the right to occupy the matrimonial home; Domestic Proceedings and Magistrates' Court Act 1978 (and now Civil Partnership Act 2004, Sch 6), Matrimonial Property and Proceedings Act 1970 (now the Matrimonial Causes Act 1973, s 27 and Civil Partnership Act 2004, Sch 5 Pt 9). The husband's common law duty will be abolished if and when s 198 of the Equality Act 2010 is brought into force.

[7] Matrimonial Proceedings and Property Act 1970, s 41.

[8] See Cretney, *Family Law*, above n 2, ch 10 for an account of those developments.

for nullity and judicial separation) are generally referred to collectively as 'ancillary relief'.[9]

The important point to grasp from this is one that the great comparative lawyer Otto Kahn-Freund frequently highlighted:[10] that while it is often said that English law operates a system of 'separate property' and has rejected the option of moving to a community system,[11] the courts' extensive powers to adjust spouses' property and financial rights on divorce (together with the intestacy rules[12] and power to order family provision on death in both intestate and testate cases[13]) trump the parties' separate property rights. The property relations of husband and wife in English law, particularly following death and divorce, are therefore more closely intertwined than might at first sight be appreciated from the separate property starting point.

ii. The Introduction of Civil Partnership

One final historical point is the introduction of civil partnership. The Civil Partnership Act 2004 created for same-sex couples an institution almost entirely identical, both in the manner of its creation and termination[14] and in its legal consequences,[15] to that offered to opposite-sex couples by the law of marriage. For ease of presentation, references in the text below to 'marriage', 'spouses' and cognate expressions should be taken to include equivalent civil partnership concepts.[16]

However, one note of caution should be lodged. There is at the time of writing no reported case law dealing with the issues covered by this report in the context of civil partnership. It will therefore be assumed in the following discussion that relevant statute law and associated case law will be applied to civil partners in the same way that it is applied to spouses. However, that assumption may prove to be unsafe. For example, particular questions might arise in relation to agreements

---

[9] The notion is that the financial consequences of divorce are 'ancillary' to the main petition, which is that for the divorce itself. In practice, of course, divorces are rarely contested and proceed undefended through a fast-tracked procedure. The main matter of dispute will therefore commonly be the financial settlement. Under the Family Procedure Rules 2010 (SI 2010/2955), which came into effect in April 2011, this terminology has formally been dropped in favour of applications for a 'financial remedy' and 'financial orders'.

[10] See, eg his chapter 'Matrimonial Property Law in England', in W Friedmann (ed), *Matrimonial Property Law* (London, Stevens, 1955), pre-dating many of the reforms addressed in the text, but nevertheless noting the extent to which the law already complicated the separate property picture.

[11] See the long-running early Law Commission projects on family property which explored various options, including community of property and various joint ownership schemes, beginning with Law Com WP 42, *Family Property Law* (1971) and Law Com No 52, *First Report on Family Property: A New Approach* (1973).

[12] Administration of Estates Act 1925.

[13] See now the Inheritance (Provision for Family and Dependants) Act 1975, as amended; this Act builds substantially on more limited powers first introduced in 1938.

[14] Differences here turn on the omission of any grounds for nullity or dissolution (the term used for divorce) relating to any sexual relationship between the parties (such as non-consummation and adultery).

[15] Only a very few, practically unimportant gender-specific statutory provisions and equitable doctrines were omitted from civil partnership law; recent legislation enables civil partners and cohabiting same-sex couples to acquire legal parentage of children born with donated gametes on the same footing as opposite-sex couples: Human Fertilisation and Embryology Act 2008.

[16] References to relevant provisions of the 2004 Act are included in footnotes alongside those to identical provisions of the Matrimonial Causes Act 1973.

concluded by civil partners who had for several *decades* lived together waiting for the law to provide them with a means of formalising their relationship. Such partners might have special reason to wish to have their agreements upheld, particularly (perhaps) to protect property acquired before their relationship became one of civil partnership. More generally, the advent of civil partnership—in which concerns about gender-based inequality clearly have no place—places hitherto familiar questions in a new light and may contribute to further development of the law away from its paternalistic tradition in favour of greater party autonomy.

B. Social Context

The financial remedies provided by a given legal system on divorce can only be fully appreciated given the wider social context in which they operate. Crucial here is the existence, or otherwise, of substantial state support for those who are unemployed, ill or disabled, undertaking child-care obligations or who need child-care to facilitate paid employment. While the rates of labour market participation by women—and of mothers, in particular—have risen over the last century and lone parents (usually mothers) are actively encouraged by welfare benefit law and policy to seek paid employment, many of those women work part-time, are more likely than men to apply for flexible working hours, and are paying an increasingly high penalty in terms of downward mobility following absences from the full-time labour market to raise children.[17] Lower earnings and intermittent or longer-term absences from paid employment in turn leave many women with meagre pension savings and so facing poverty in old age.[18] The continuing problem of female poverty post-divorce is often ameliorated only by repartnering, rather than by the development of independent earning power.[19] There is limited state support to enable parents who wish to work to obtain professional child-care,[20] but for many parents the sums remain tight: the extra money brought into the household by both working may be swallowed up by child-care and travel-to-work costs, leaving them with a difficult decision balancing financial, career, parenting and lifestyle considerations. The nature of the housing market is also very important, and key here is the predominance of owner-occupied accommodation and the relative dearth (compared with many other European jurisdictions) of affordable, good quality rental accommodation in England and Wales.[21]

---

[17] See Scott and Dex, 'Paid and Unpaid Work: Can Policy Improve Gender Inequalities?', in Miles and Probert (eds) *Sharing Lives, Dividing Assets* (Oxford, Hart Publishing, 2009) and Office for National Statistics, *Social Trends* 39 (2009) ch 4.

[18] See Price, 'Pension Accumulation and Household Structures ...', in Miles and Probert, *Sharing Lives*, above n 17.

[19] See Fisher and Low, 'Who Wins, Who Loses and Who Recovers from Divorce?', in Miles and Probert, above n 17.

[20] In the form of a notoriously complicated tax credits scheme.

[21] See generally the government's *English Housing Survey* most recently, the *Headline Report 2008–9*, available at: www.communities.gov.uk/documents/statistics/pdf/1479789.pdf.

C. The Current Law of Ancillary Relief on Divorce

i. *Wide, Holistic Powers of the Court*

The first important point to appreciate about English ancillary relief law is that, by contrast with many other jurisdictions, no formal distinction is drawn between division of property and payment of maintenance. Under the Matrimonial Causes Act 1973 Part II, the courts have a comprehensive 'tool box' of orders, including periodical payments (unsecured and secured), lump sum payments, property adjustment, property settlement and pension-sharing, and can order the sale of particular assets.[22] All of those orders may be used for any legitimate purpose (pursuant to the principles explored in the next section). So, for example, periodical payments orders are not confined simply to the relief of 'need', however widely that term might be construed; they may also be used to achieve—in effect—a redistribution of capital wealth where there is no free capital immediately available for transfer. In practice, periodical payments orders are not often made,[23] the potential payor's free income being taken up in child support payments, which are governed by entirely separate legislation and fall largely beyond the courts' competence.[24] Capital provision and special periodical provision[25] for children, as opposed to general maintenance, are again a separate matter, albeit one for the courts acting under the 1973 Act (or cognate provisions of Schedule 1 to the Children Act 1989, which also apply between unmarried parents). But in most divorce cases, the children will benefit from orders made for the benefit of the primary carer and so specific orders for the children— save, for example, in respect of school fees—will rarely be made.

ii. *'Fair' Distribution*

The courts have a wide discretion as to how they should exercise their powers to make provision for a spouse following divorce. Until 1984, they were required to exercise those powers in such a way as would keep the parties, so far as it was practicable and (having regard to their conduct) just to do so, in the financial position in which they would have been had the marriage not broken down. That duty was removed by the Matrimonial and Family Proceedings Act 1984. Since then, the legislation has given the courts no guidance regarding the objective pursuant to which they should exercise their wide discretion. Sections 25–25A simply require the courts to give first consideration to the welfare of any child of the family,[26] to take all the circumstances of the case into account (providing a list of specific but non-exhaustive factors),[27] and to consider the desirability of making a set of orders that will achieve a clean break, ending any ongoing financial ties between the

---

[22] Matrimonial Causes Act 1973, ss 21–24D; Civil Partnership Act 2004, Sch 5, Pts 1–4.
[23] See Department for Constitutional Affairs, *Judicial Statistics (Revised) England and Wales for the Year 2005*, Cm 6903, table 5.7.
[24] Child Support Act 1991, as amended.
[25] See Child Support Act 1991, s 8: eg school fees, costs associated with disability.
[26] Matrimonial Causes Act 1973, s 25(1); Civil Partnership Act 2004, Sch 5, para 20.
[27] Matrimonial Causes Act 1973, s 25(2); Civil Partnership Act 2004, Sch 5, para 21.

parties.[28] In line with the shift away from fault-based divorce law to divorce based on irretrievable breakdown of the marriage, the parties' conduct—save where it is 'obvious and gross'—generally does not influence the financial outcome.[29]

The principles underpinning the exercise of the courts' section 25 discretion have evolved substantially over the years, most recently as a result of the House of Lords' decisions in *White v White*[30] and *Miller; McFarlane*,[31] which the Court of Appeal sought to elucidate in *Charman v Charman*.[32] The goal, unsurprisingly, is to attain a 'fair' outcome. In *Miller; McFarlane*, the House of Lords identified three potential rationales that might underpin a 'fair' allocation of assets: equal sharing, need and compensation. This proliferation of principles poses some difficulty from a theoretical perspective, since each rationale reflects a different model of marriage, and it is not immediately clear how the principles interrelate in practice: for example, whether, and if so when, needs should take precedence over sharing, and how compensation is brought into account.[33]

There have been debates about what property falls within the equal sharing pool. Unlike Scots law, which sets out definitively in statute what property counts as matrimonial, the characterisation of property—and the outcome of that characterisation—in English law is less clear-cut. In English law, does the equal sharing principle only apply to assets acquired as a result of the parties' joint efforts during the marriage, or does it extend to other assets acquired before,[34] during, or after[35] this period?[36] The Court of Appeal in *Charman* considered that prima facie the principle applies to all assets, but that equal sharing of those assets might be departed from on various grounds, or a combination of grounds,[37] such as the (short) duration of the marriage, the source of particular assets (regarded as being 'non-matrimonial'), one party's stellar contribution to the marriage, and (of course) pursuant to the other two principles or to separate concerns such as conduct and the clean-break objective.[38] But none of this is relevant where the award is based on need or compensation: in that case, resort may be had to any of the respondent's property in order to satisfy the claim of the applicant.[39]

---

[28] Matrimonial Causes Act 1973, s 25A; Civil Partnership Act 2004, Sch 5, para 23.

[29] *Wachtel v Wachtel (No 2)* [1973] Fam 72; *Miller; McFarlane* [2006] UKHL 24, [56]–[63], [145], [154].

[30] *White v White* [2001] 1 AC 596.

[31] *Miller; McFarlane*, above n 29.

[32] *Charman v Charman* [2007] EWCA Civ 503.

[33] See generally J Miles, '*Charman v Charman (No 4)*—Making Sense of Need, Compensation and Equal Sharing after *Miller/McFarlane*' (2008) 20 *Child and Family Law Quarterly* 378.

[34] A clear answer in the negative was given in *B v B (Ancillary Relief)* [2008] EWCA Civ 543; see also *McCartney v Mills McCartney* [2008] EWHC 401; and treatment of pre-marital property in *Jones v Jones* [2011] EWCA Civ 41.

[35] See, eg the debates regarding post-separation property in *Rossi v Rossi* [2006] EWHC 1482; *S v S* [2006] EWHC 2339; *H v H* [2007] EWHC 459.

[36] See also *Vaughan v Vaughan* [2007] EWCA Civ 1085, in which Wilson LJ distinguished between equality of *assets* and equality of *outcome*.

[37] *Charman v Charman*, above n 32, [65].

[38] See, eg *S v S (Non-Matrimonial Property: Conduct)* [2006] EWHC 2793; *NA v MA* [2006] EWHC 2900; *McCartney v Mills McCartney*, above n 34.

[39] *White v White*, above n 30, 610.

The courts' flexible approach to the exercise of their ancillary relief powers reflects their resistance to any sort of formulaic approach.[40] They constantly emphasise the discretionary nature of the exercise,[41] object to attempts to invoke the three principles from *Miller; McFarlane* like 'heads of claim' in a tort action, and have been particularly reluctant to develop the idea of compensation. While there is now a greater awareness of the long-term impact of giving up paid employment to undertake caring responsibilities in the home,[42] such sacrifices tend to be addressed by means other than including a specifically compensatory element in that party's share of the assets.[43] In lower-income cases, the ongoing effect of sacrifices made during the marriage will be dealt with as an aspect of that party's needs;[44] in higher-income cases, the sharing principle may produce more than the spouse could ever have earned from paid employment[45] and, or alternatively, the loss of earning capacity will be recognised through a 'generous assessment' of that party's needs.[46] In other cases the principle seems irrelevant, either because the spouse had no developed career prior to marriage,[47] or because giving up work was a 'lifestyle choice' rather than a necessity.[48] And even if the principle is seen as appropriate, courts may struggle to apply it in practice: one judge suggested that it was neither possible nor desirable to attempt to ascertain the career that the spouse would have had.[49] There have therefore been few cases in which 'compensation' has played a distinct role.[50]

However, whether or not the court adopts equal sharing as its starting point or has regard to compensation as a distinct element, in the vast majority of 'normal' (as opposed to 'big money') cases, the predominant concern is to cater for both parties' needs from *all* the parties' assets, which are unlikely to be sufficiently extensive to achieve even that modest objective. That will often mandate unequal sharing of capital assets, a particular concern being to house the primary carer and dependent children.[51] In many cases, the parties—or one of them—will inevitably end up relying to some extent on welfare benefits and/or social housing, though it should be noted that welfare benefit rules increasingly and strongly encourage lone parents to engage in paid employment, particularly where their children are of school age.

---

[40] See, eg *H v H*, above n 35.

[41] Note in particular the Court of Appeal decision in *B v B*, above n 34, which contrasts starkly with the earlier CA decision in *Charman*, which appeared to advocate a more structured approach.

[42] See, eg *Lauder v Lauder* [2007] EWHC 1227; *VB v JP* [2008] EWHC 112.

[43] See, eg *H v H*, above n 35.

[44] See, eg *Lauder v Lauder*, above n 42.

[45] *CR v CR* [2007] EWHC 3334.

[46] See, eg *Lauder v Lauder*, above n 42; *VB v JP*, above n 42; *McFarlane v McFarlane (No 2)* [2009] EWHC 891.

[47] *NA v MA*, above n 38.

[48] *Radmacher v Granatino* [2010] UKSC 42 [121]; *S v S*, above n 38 [59]. This issue has proved controversial in New Zealand: see the discussion prompted by *X v X* [2006] NZFLR 361, recently heard on appeal to the Court of Appeal: [2009] NZCA 399; *cf* the English attitude in *McFarlane v McFarlane (No 2)*, above n 46.

[49] *P v P* [2007] EWHC 779. See also *VB v JP*, above n 42; *CR v CR*, above n 45; *McFarlane v McFarlane (No 2)*, above n 46.

[50] Though note the recent decision of Charles J in *McFarlane v McFarlane (No 2)*, above n 46.

[51] *M v B (ancillary relief proceedings: lump sum)* [1998] 1 FCR 213.

II. PRE-NUPTIAL AND POST-NUPTIAL AGREEMENTS[52]

A. The General Law and Public Policy

i. Some Introductory Observations

The starting point, pursuant to the separate property principle of the late nineteenth century, is that husband and wife—and those intending to become husband and wife—have capacity to contract with each other like any other private individuals. The general rules of contract law therefore apply. Particularly when the marriage is on foot, the question may arise whether the parties intend by their agreements (especially oral agreements) to create legal relations, or merely domestic arrangements not intended to have any legal force.[53] But where the agreement is in signed writing, and a fortiori where legal advice has been taken, that hurdle will not be difficult to leap.[54] And English contract law's requirement for consideration may be overcome by the use of a deed. The application of the general law to marital agreements is implicit in one of the statutory provisions discussed below.[55] The law of property and trusts likewise applies to spouses in the ordinary way so that, for example, declarations of trust determining the basis on which they beneficially own the matrimonial home and other land will be binding on normal principles.[56] Indeed, most owner-occupier spouses deliberately opt to own their home in joint names.[57] Declarations of trust and contracts purporting to create or dispose of an interest in land must comply with the ordinary formality requirements applying to such agreements under the general law, though the complex law of implied trusts and proprietary estoppel will sometimes permit interests in land to arise without completion of the usual formalities.[58] Self-evidently, in the English separate property context, pre- and post-nuptial agreements have no function in terms of altering any default regime of matrimonial property that would otherwise apply. It is essential also to distinguish between pre-nuptial *agreements* and pre-nuptial *settlements*: the latter, which seek to regulate the parties' property relations on and during marriage, not on its demise, are binding on the parties but variable on divorce under section 24 of the Matrimonial Causes Act 1973.

---

[52] Readers may wish to consult the author's commentaries on the Court of Appeal and Supreme Court decisions in the leading case on marital agreements, *Radmacher v Granatino*: '*Radmacher v Granatino*: Upping the Ante-Nuptial Agreement' (2009) 21 *Child and Family Law Quarterly* 513, and 'Marriage and Divorce in the Supreme Court: For Love or Money?' (2011) 74 *Modern Law Review* 430, from which much of the account of the law provided here is drawn. See also S Harris-Short and J Miles, *Family Law: Text, Cases, and Materials*, 2nd edn (Oxford, OUP, 2011) section 7.7.

[53] *Balfour v Balfour* [1919] 2 KB 571.

[54] Especially where divorce is pending: see, eg *Merritt v Merritt* [1970] 1 WLR 1211.

[55] Matrimonial Causes Act 1973, s 34(1)(b): 'any other financial arrangements contained in the agreement shall ..., *unless they are void or unenforceable for any other reason* ..., be binding on the parties to the agreement' (emphasis added); Civil Partnership Act 2004, Sch 5, para 68.

[56] *Goodman v Gallant* [1986] Fam 106.

[57] Office of the Deputy Prime Minister, *Survey of English Housing* (2004–05), tables on 'Households: by household type by tenure' and 'Owner-occupier households: by number of owners by whether own outright or buying with a mortgage'.

[58] See Law of Property Act 1925, ss 52–53; on implied trusts law and estoppel, see most recently *Stack v Dowden* [2007] UKHL 17 and *Thorner v Majors* [2009] UKHL 18.

However, there are significant points at which the general law position is modified in the case of spouses. First, it is worth reiterating that any declaration of trust (or implied trust) allocating the beneficial ownership of the matrimonial home under the general law may be readily displaced (as may legal ownership) by the court exercising its discretion to grant ancillary relief under the Matrimonial Causes Act 1973 at the point of divorce. A declaration of trust (or pre-nuptial settlement) cannot exclude the operation of the ancillary relief jurisdiction. And the same is true for any contract made between the spouses, whether it is pre- or post-nuptial or made at the point of separation. The general principle here, long established by the case of *Hyman v Hyman*[59] (a case concerning a separation agreement), is that the courts' ancillary relief jurisdiction cannot be excluded by agreement between the parties. So the basic starting point for *any* marital agreement is that, even if it is binding as a matter of contract law (as to which, see below) such that the payment creditor can in principle sue the debtor under general contract law for non-performance, either party remains free to invoke the courts' ancillary relief jurisdiction on divorce and seek to have that agreement superseded by a court order making different (or no) provision.

ii. The Old Public Policy Objections to Pre- and Post-Nuptial Agreements

Until very recently, both pre- and post-nuptial agreements were regarded as entirely void, and so unenforceable as a matter of contract law.[60] In the case of post-nuptial agreements, this objection applied whether the agreement was made immediately following the wedding, or 20 years in. The objection was that intended spouses or current spouses who were neither separated nor in the process of separating should not make financial provision for the eventuality of a *possible future* separation. Nineteenth-century case law based this objection on the grounds that spouses had a duty to live together, in the absence of grounds for divorce *a mensa et thoro*[61] or, following the reforms of 1857, judicial divorce. This duty was not one which the parties could choose to abridge by private agreement.[62] Judicial remarks in the nineteenth-century cases[63] reveal a concern that agreements should not create any financial incentive either for one party to separate (and so to secure the payment due under the agreement) or to permit the other spouse to leave (and not seek a restitution of conjugal rights, where that party would rather pay the amount then due than enforce continued cohabitation). To nineteenth-century judicial eyes, either type of incentive damaged the institution of marriage and so such agreements were held to be void as a matter of public policy.

---

[59] *Hyman v Hyman* [1929] AC 601.

[60] See recently *X v X (Y and Z intervening)* [2002] 1 FLR 508 [79].

[61] The 'divorce', in fact an order permitting the spouses to live separate and apart, granted by ecclesiastical courts prior to the assumption of jurisdiction by the civil courts following the 1857 divorce reforms.

[62] *Duchess of Marlborough v Duke of Marlborough* [1901] 1 Ch 165, 171. See also *Brodie v Brodie* [1917] P 271.

[63] *Westmeath v Westmeath* (1830) 6 ER 619; *Cocksedge v Cocksedge* (1844) 60 ER 351; *Cartwright v Cartwright* (1853) 43 ER 385; *H v W* (1857) 69 ER 1157; and the *Marlborough* case, above n 62.

However, since the nineteenth century, the legal foundations for this public policy concern have been substantially eroded. Spouses no longer have a duty to cohabit, though desertion still provides a basis on which the abandoned spouse may petition for divorce. The husband no longer enjoys the 'self-help' remedy of reasonable confinement to control his wife's behaviour.[64] Legislation in 1970 abolished the decree for restitution of conjugal rights[65] and actions for interference by third parties with the spousal relationship.[66] It was accordingly acknowledged, first in relation to post-nuptial agreements (by the Privy Council in *MacLeod v MacLeod*[67]), and then in relation to pre-nuptial agreements (by the Supreme Court in *Radmacher v Granatino*[68]), that the old public policy objection could no longer apply. Neither type of agreement is therefore void on public policy grounds.[69] Indeed, prior to these decisions the courts had in any event been giving substantial, sometimes even decisive, weight to the terms of pre-nuptial agreements in certain types of case.[70] Rix LJ, a commercial lawyer who formed part of the Court of Appeal which heard the first appeal in *Radmacher*, may be forgiven for having wondered how an agreement that was formally void could have any relevance at all.[71] That awkwardness is now removed from the law.

However, what is substantially less clear—and currently disputed—is whether either type of agreement creates a contract which can be sued on by either party.[72] In considering that question, it is important to bear in mind that the *Hyman* principle applies to these agreements as well as to separation agreements: even if otherwise valid contractually, no agreement can oust the jurisdiction of the matrimonial court to grant ancillary relief; any clause to that effect remains void. So, in the vast majority of cases in which the issue might arise, the agreement will be subject to the matrimonial jurisdiction;[73] its impact in that context is discussed below. But it is possible to envisage situations in which the contractual enforceability of a pre- or post-nuptial agreement might matter—for example, where one party promises to make a will in favour of the other party, but dies without having done so (can the survivor sue the estate?[74]), or promises to transfer land (thus constituting an estate contract which can in certain circumstances constitute a property right binding

---

[64] *R v Jackson* [1891] 1 QB 671; *R v Reid* [1973] QB 299.

[65] Matrimonial Proceedings and Property Act 1970, s 20.

[66] Law Reform (Miscellaneous Provisions) Act 1970, s 5.

[67] *MacLeod v MacLeod* [2008] UKPC 64.

[68] *Radmacher v Granatino* (SC), above n 48.

[69] For criticism of the Privy Council's view that a distinction could be drawn between post- and pre-nuptial agreements here—the former valid, the latter still void—see Miles, above n 52 and the Supreme Court decision in *Radmacher v Granatino*, above n 48.

[70] Eg, *Crossley v Crossley* [2007] EWCA Civ 1491; *K v K (Ancillary relief: Pre-nuptial agreement)* [2003] 1 FLR 120; *M v M (Prenuptial agreement)* [2002] 1 FLR 654.

[71] *Radmacher v Granatino* [2009] EWCA Civ 649 [64].

[72] The Privy Council in *MacLeod v MacLeod,* above n 67 considered that *post*-nuptial agreements fall within Matrimonial Causes Act 1973, s 34 and so are legally valid as contracts; this decision is only of persuasive force in an English court, and the majority of the Supreme Court in *Radmacher*, obiter, disagreed with the Privy Council's view on this point. The matter therefore remains formally undecided as a matter of English law, though the weight of judicial opinion is clearly against the *MacLeod* approach.

[73] *Radmacher v Granatino* (SC), above n 48, [62].

[74] Cf *Soulsbury v Soulsbury* [2007] EWCA Civ 969.

on third parties[75]) and, say, either party then falls bankrupt.[76] A majority of the Supreme Court in *Radmacher* come close to suggesting that they are contractually binding, but the matter was not necessary for the decision in that case and so the point remains formally open. However, it is difficult to see, now that the old public policy objections have been swept away, on what basis they could be held to be anything other than contractually valid, subject only to *Hyman*.

B. Form and Procedure

i. Pre-Nuptial Agreements

Since pre-nuptial agreements are not dealt with by any legislative provisions, they are not subject to any formal or other procedural 'requirements', as such. However, case law identifies factors surrounding the making of a pre-nuptial agreement which give that agreement added weight should one party seek ancillary relief on divorce inconsistent with the terms of the agreement.

Until the Court of Appeal decision in *Radmacher v Granatino*,[77] it had been widely assumed that if parties wanted a court to pay attention to their agreement in subsequent divorce proceedings, it was more or less essential that certain procedural safeguards be observed. For example, in the first instance decisions in *Radmacher v Granatino*[78] and in *NA v MA*,[79] Baron J essentially adopted the criteria for enforceability mooted in a government consultation paper published in 1998: that the agreement be in writing;[80] that it be enforceable under the general law of contract; that the parties each had independent legal advice and full disclosure from the other side prior to entering into the agreement; that the agreement was not made within the 21 days preceding the wedding;[81] that enforcement would not cause 'significant injustice'; and (apparently regardless of whether the agreement anticipated and provided for it), that there is now a child of the family.[82] Understandably, having been concluded in Germany, the *Radmacher* agreement failed to meet these criteria fully (a fact which would not trouble a German court called upon to uphold the agreement),[83] yet Baron J regarded it as 'defective under English law'.[84]

---

[75] See Gray and Gray, *Elements of Land Law*, 5th edn (Oxford, Oxford University Press, 2008) 8.1.

[76] These examples are considered further in Miles, above n 52, 439–40.

[77] *Radmacher v Granatino* (CA), above n 71.

[78] Reported as *NG v KR* [2008] EWHC 1532.

[79] *NA v MA*, above n 38.

[80] Interestingly, this is the only formal requirement for agreements falling within Matrimonial Causes Act 1973, s 34, discussed at section III below. Other circumstances surrounding the making of the agreement will, however, be considered in deciding what weight to give the agreement in ancillary relief proceedings under *Edgar v Edgar* [1980] 1 WLR 1410.

[81] Clearly, the closer the agreement to the wedding day, the greater the likely pressure on the more vulnerable spouse to sign, and so the greater suspicion might be directed at the fairness of the agreement.

[82] Home Office, *Supporting Families: a Consultation Document* (HMSO, 1998) para 4.23. Contrast the checklist adopted by Rodger Hayward Smith QC, sitting as a deputy High Court judge, in *K v K (Ancillary Relief: Prenuptial Agreement)*, above n 70.

[83] See chapter by Dutta, in this volume.

[84] *NG v KR*, above n 78, [137].

However, the Court of Appeal took a rather different approach, adopting what may be called a de facto rather than de jure approach to formalities,[85] exemplified by Wilson LJ's discussion of independent legal advice:

[137] In most cases it is necessary and in every case it is desirable that the party against whose claim a pre-nuptial contract is raised should have received independent legal advice prior to entry into it. Why so? Because proof of receipt of independent legal advice is often the only, and always the simplest, way of demonstrating that that party entered into it knowingly…

[140] It may be that, even if only in the interests of simplicity, any legislative reform of the law's treatment of nuptial contracts will include, for example as a condition of their presumptive dispositiveness, a requirement that independent legal advice should—in *every* case, irrespective of its surrounding circumstances – have been received in relation to them by both parties prior to execution. But the fluidity of the present law perhaps at any rate enables the court to apply common sense to a situation in which, as here, a husband well understands the effect of the contract,[86] has ample opportunity to take independent legal advice and decides not to do so;[87] and thus to reject his argument that the absence of such advice enables him to escape its effect.

The Court of Appeal was also influenced by several other features of the case: Mr Granatino had not suggested that he would have been influenced either not to sign the agreement or to try to renegotiate its terms had he received independent advice against signing it; the parties' use of a single notary is standard practice in Germany for pre-nuptial agreements, which are themselves commonplace; and Mr Granatino was a well-established international banker and as such was clearly able to judge and protect his own interests.[88] The Court was not concerned that there had been no disclosure of assets between the parties: Mr Granatino knew that Ms Radmacher was from an extremely wealthy family;[89] there was no suggestion that disclosure would or even might have dissuaded Mr Granatino from going ahead with the agreement, and he had had plenty of opportunity to request disclosure.[90] Nor was the lack of any negotiation over the terms of the agreement thought to be problematic, since the husband chose not to negotiate and the type of agreement the parties were reaching was commonplace in Germany.[91] The common theme underpinning this

---

[85] See further Miles, above n 52, 524–28.

[86] Despite the fact that it had not been formally translated for him in full, as the notary had wished.

[87] The Court differed here from Baron J. She was concerned that there was only a week between the date on which the husband was given the final draft and the date fixed for executing the contract, *NG v KR*, above n 78, [33]. The Court instead noted that the wedding date was four months off, and so there was ample opportunity to postpone the trip to Germany to execute the agreement until the husband had obtained a translation and independent advice: see *Radmacher v Granatino* (CA), above n 71, [138] (Wilson LJ). Opportunity is the test adopted in some US states and by the American Law Institute recommendations—see chapter by Ellman, this volume.

[88] *Radmacher v Granatino* (CA), above n 71, [33] (Thorpe LJ), [81] (Rix LJ), [137] (Wilson LJ). Contrast the views of Baron J at *NG v KR*, above n 78, [38c] and, perhaps less than consistently, [139]: see criticism by Rix LJ, *Radmacher v Granatino* (CA), above n 71, [78].

[89] *Radmacher v Granatino* (CA), above n 71, [33] (Thorpe LJ). See also the flexibility exhibited in *K v K (Ancillary Relief: Prenuptial Agreement)*, above n 70 regarding the lack of full disclosure (there having been no abuse of position by the husband) and the timetable (agreement signed day before wedding but parties had had ample time to consider it before then).

[90] *Radmacher v Granatino* (CA), above n 71, [141] (Wilson LJ); see also Rix LJ, [78].

[91] Ibid, [33] (Thorpe LJ) and [142] (Wilson LJ).

analysis of the facts of *Radmacher v Granatino* is that the parties knew what they were doing, with a sufficient—if not complete—grasp of the details, such that the 'necessary basis of consent'[92] was present.[93] Provided that this can be shown, in fact, to be the case, the court will not insist upon compliance with any particular formal steps in order for a pre-nuptial agreement to be relevant to the court's discretionary decision about what is a 'fair' financial outcome between the parties.

This approach was endorsed by the Supreme Court.[94] While noting that it was 'obviously desirable' that each should have legal advice and full disclosure,[95] the majority were not prescriptive about any particular formal requirements, saying that:

> 69. ... What is important is that each party should have all the information that is material to his or her decision, and that each party should intend that the agreement should govern the financial consequences of the marriage coming to an end.

On the latter issue of intention, the majority suggested that it would be easier to find the requisite intention in relation to agreements made after the date of its judgment in *Radmacher*. This presumably reflects the view that any lawyer giving advice on an English agreement[96] made before this date would have had to say that, on the state of the case law at the time, the agreement would probably be held to be void and would only be a relevant factor for the court to take into account in exercising its wide discretion to grant ancillary relief, though (depending on the circumstances) a factor that might carry significant weight. As discussed above, such agreements are no longer void and, as indicated below, the advice on the relevance of the agreement in ancillary relief proceedings will now be different. Another factor relevant to the question of party intention is that the presence of vitiating factors may 'negate any effect the agreement might otherwise have', or at least reduce the weight that it should attract.[97] Self-evidently, this covers grounds that would vitiate the agreement as a matter of contract law, such as duress, fraud and misrepresentation. But the family courts will be alert to other problems which might properly deprive the agreement of weight: undue pressure falling short of duress;[98] exploitation of a dominant bargaining position to secure an unfair advantage; and the existence of an emotional state which propelled one or other party into an agreement that he or she would not otherwise have made.[99] Regard would be had to the parties' age, maturity and relationship history as part of the background in which they reached their agreement.[100]

---

[92] Ibid, [78] (Rix LJ).

[93] Cf the US test of 'voluntariness', discussed in *Marriage of Bonds* 24 Cal. 4th 1, 5 P.3d 815, 99 Cal. Rptr. 2d 252 (Cal. 2000): see chapter by Ellman, this volume.

[94] *Radmacher v Granatino* (SC), above n 48.

[95] For an examination of practitioners' attitudes towards formalities prior to the decision in *Radmacher*, see E Hitchings, 'From Pre-nups to Post-nups: Dealing with Marital Property Agreements' (2009) 39 *Family Law* 1056.

[96] For agreements concluded abroad, see section IV below.

[97] *Radmacher v Granatino* (SC), above n 48, [71].

[98] Cf *NA v MA*, above n 38.

[99] *Radmacher v Granatino* (SC), above n 48, [71]–[72].

[100] Ibid, [72].

An agreement which passes muster against these criteria will not thereby be prima facie binding on the matrimonial court because of *Hyman*, but it will fall within the scope of the Supreme Court's principal proposition or 'starting point':[101]

> 75. ... The court should give effect to a nuptial agreement that is freely entered into by each party with a full appreciation of its implications unless in the circumstances prevailing it would not be fair to hold the parties to their agreement.

We explore the 'unless...' clause of that test below.

ii. Post-Nuptial Agreements

The better view is very probably that the formal aspects of post-nuptial agreements are regulated on the same basis as pre-nuptial agreements, as just discussed. The majority of the Supreme Court in *Radmacher* clearly treated the two classes of agreement identically for these purposes.[102] However, the treatment of post-nuptial agreements was not relevant to the decision in that case, and the Privy Council decision in *MacLeod v MacLeod*[103] therefore still needs to be considered. The Privy Council is the final appellate court for a number of Commonwealth countries and UK overseas territories and Crown dependencies, generally composed of Justices of the Supreme Court and other senior UK or other Commonwealth judges. Decisions of the Privy Council have only persuasive force in the English courts, though where the foreign law in question is identical to the equivalent point of English law, the decision enjoys added weight. *MacLeod* concerned a point of Manx (Isle of Man) law identical to the English legislation, and the unanimous judgment of the five-strong Board was delivered by Baroness Hale, with Lords Scott and Walker two of the concurring judges. The Board effectively held (in English terms) that post-nuptial agreements should be understood to fall within section 34 of the Matrimonial Causes Act, previously thought only to apply to separation agreements. Section 34 is discussed below in relation to that type of agreement. Suffice it to note here that the only formal requirement prescribed by section 34 for the agreement to be valid and binding is that it be in writing. By the time of *Radmacher*, Lady Hale (as she is now called) found herself the lone dissenting voice seeking to maintain any difference in the legal regulation of pre- and post-nuptial agreements, Lord Walker having joined the majority of eight on this issue (Lord Scott has retired from the Court). While *MacLeod* therefore remains a persuasive authority in English courts on post-nuptial agreements, sheer weight of numbers in the Supreme Court mean that it is very unlikely that the Privy Council's approach would be taken in any future case in that Court on post-nuptial agreements, and lower courts may be expected to follow the dicta of the Supreme Court on this issue. Clarifying legislation would, of course, be welcome, an issue discussed in the Conclusion below.

---

[101] As Lord Mance calls it, ibid, [129]; cf criticism by Lady Hale, from [165].
[102] Ibid, [63].
[103] *MacLeod v MacLeod*, above n 67.

C. Content and Binding Effect/Enforceability

i. Introductory Remarks

This section focuses on the enforceability of pre- and post-nuptial agreements at the point of divorce, but for completeness begins with a few observations concerning the position during marriage and on death.

As discussed above, it is open to parties to regulate their financial and property relationship during marriage however they see fit, subject to potential liability to the State should one spouse seek a means-tested benefit whilst living separately from the other spouse during marriage.[104] Spouses living apart during marriage may make maintenance agreements for the support of one by the other (which fall within s 34 of the Matrimonial Causes Act 1973). But just as agreements making provision in the event of divorce may be superseded by orders made in ancillary relief proceedings, so too may they be superseded by applications to court for maintenance during marriage under various statutory provisions.[105]

It is also open to spouses and former spouses to make contracts concerning provision in the event of death. For example, in *Soulsbury v Soulsbury,* the former husband had agreed that he would leave his ex-wife £100,000 in his will, subject to the condition that she did not seek to enforce the order made in her favour on divorce for periodical payments. The husband made a will in those terms, but it was revoked by operation of law when he remarried,[106] and the ex-wife in due course successfully sued his estate for specific performance of the contract.[107] That aside, English law having no regime of fixed shares for particular family members, the position on death is governed initially by the deceased's will or the intestacy rules, subject to applications from various categories of person for family provision under the Inheritance (Provision for Family and Dependants) Act 1975, from which there is no facility for potential claimants to opt out by agreement.

ii. Pre- and Post-Nuptial Agreements after Radmacher

As noted in the previous section, the legal regulation of post-nuptial agreements as a matter of English law was not, strictly speaking, decided by the Supreme Court in *Radmacher*. On this issue, as on the question of formalities, the decision in *MacLeod* that post-nuptial agreements should be treated in the same way as separation agreements offers a different approach from that advocated by the Supreme Court in *Radmacher*. Readers should refer to the section on separation agreements for discussion of the law applied by the Privy Council to post-nuptial agreements. This section examines the law expounded by the Supreme Court, which should, again, very probably be taken now to apply to post-nuptial agreements as well as pre-nuptial agreements, pending any statutory reform. However, it is probably fair

---

[104] Social Security Administration Act 1992, ss 105–08.
[105] See n 6 above. Similarly, no provision is made on the face of the Act for parties to opt out of their statutory home rights in relation to the matrimonial home.
[106] Wills Act 1837, s 18.
[107] *Soulsbury v Soulsbury*, above n 74.

to say that the same outcome is likely to be achieved in practice in a post-nuptial agreement case, whichever formal route to that outcome is taken, for reasons which will become clear below.

Before *Radmacher* decided that public policy objections to pre-nuptial agreements no longer rendered them void, the courts had nevertheless given such agreements significant weight in the exercise of their wide discretion to grant ancillary relief on divorce.[108] Some of those cases, like *Radmacher*, involved couples connected with another jurisdiction in which pre-nuptial agreements are more common and enjoy greater legal force.[109] Agreements were taken into account within the courts' discretion as part of 'all the circumstances of the case' to which the courts are required by statute to have regard in seeking a fair outcome.[110] Needless to say, the longer the marriage, the greater the likelihood that circumstances would have changed dramatically since the agreement was made (birth of children, acquisition of particular wealth or assets, career developments or sacrifices, etc), such that the agreement might be considered unfair and so be given negligible weight.[111] But the birth of children since the agreement, or even unplanned pregnancy which precipitated the marriage and so the agreement, did not invariably mean that the agreement was dismissed as irrelevant. Much depended on the terms of the agreement itself. An agreement that expressly contemplated and made provision for the birth of children might be found to offer an amply fair settlement to the applicant for ancillary relief.[112]

The hesitancy and incoherence of this approach was cast aside by the Supreme Court in *Radmacher v Granatino*. Agreements no longer being void on grounds of public policy, the interests of party autonomy are now held to require that the court give effect to agreements untainted by the circumstances in which they were made, unless... (The quotation cited above is repeated here for convenience):

> 75. ... The court should give effect to a nuptial agreement that is freely entered into by each party with a full appreciation of its implications unless in the circumstances prevailing it would not be fair to hold the parties to their agreement.[113]

What matters, then, are the circumstances in which it will be found that fairness requires departure from what was at the outset a proper agreement (in the sense discussed in the previous section). While emphasising that this is a very fact-dependent question, the Supreme Court laid down some guidance. First, the agreement cannot 'prejudice the reasonable requirements of any children of the family', whose welfare is by statute the 'first consideration' for the court on granting ancillary relief.[114]

---

[108] Cf the observation of Thorpe J, as he then was and then thought, in *F v F (Ancillary Relief: Substantial Assets)* [1995] 2 FCR 397, 419, that pre-nuptial agreements 'must be of very limited significance'.

[109] The conflict of laws issues that arise here are explored in section IV below.

[110] Matrimonial Causes Act 1973, s 25(1).

[111] Cf the circumstances in *Crossley v Crossley,* above n 70.

[112] Contrast *K v K (Ancillary Relief: Prenuptial agreement)*, above n 70 and *M v M (Prenuptial agreement)*, above n 70.

[113] Baroness Hale, dissenting, objected to the question being framed in this way, preferring instead to ask whether it would be fair to hold the parties to their agreement: *Radmacher v Granatino* (SC), above n 48, [169]. Lord Mance (at [129]) suggested that it does not much matter which question is asked, and it is notable that much of Baroness Hale's analysis is similar to that of the majority.

[114] *Radmacher v Granatino* (SC), above n 48, [77].

Otherwise, the court should respect the parties' autonomy in regulating their financial affairs: 'It would be paternalistic and patronising to override their agreement simply on the basis that the court knows best'.[115] This consideration carries particular weight where the agreement deals with known circumstances[116]—so agreements made near or at the point of divorce will presumably have greater force than those made earlier. But the Court also suggests that agreements wishing to preserve a particular item of 'non-matrimonial property', such as an inheritance, may also be afforded greater respect.[117] However, different considerations will apply where the agreement attempts to provide for 'the contingencies of an uncertain future',[118] as in these cases the passage of time and changes of circumstance may have rendered the agreement unfair.[119] Self-evidently, pre-nuptial agreements and post-nuptial agreements made early on in the marriage are more likely than post-nuptial agreements made shortly before the breakdown of the marriage to suffer from this problem.

The most significant part of the Court's decision, and the most interesting from a comparative law perspective, is that if one party is left in a 'predicament of real need, while the other enjoys a sufficiency or more' at the end of the marriage, the court may readily find an agreement making no provision for that party to be unfair. Similarly, where one spouse's devotion to home-making and child-care freed the other to accumulate wealth, an agreement allowing the breadwinner to 'retain all that he or she has earned' is likely to be viewed as unfair.[120] In those types of case, it is likely that—despite the agreement—provision based on the *Miller; McFarlane* principles of need and/or compensation will be ordered. But provision based on the principle of equal sharing is far less likely to be ordered. Indeed, it may further be said that where neither party is experiencing 'real need'[121] at the point of divorce or in the foreseeable future, needs-based provision would not be warranted anyway and so it may be entirely fair to make no order for financial relief between the spouses.[122]

At this point, it is worth considering the facts of *Radmacher* itself. The German wife and French husband were married for eight years and had two children. The wife, Ms Radmacher, was extremely wealthy with family money, and the parties therefore had a pre-nuptial agreement—concluded in Germany, subject to German law,[123] and which would have been enforced by both German and French courts—which barred Mr Granatino from bringing any claim for financial provision in the event of divorce; the agreement made no alternative provision for him. When the parties married, the husband was working as a merchant banker, but during the marriage he ended that career to take a considerably less lucrative path in academia, first by obtaining a PhD in biotechnology. When the marriage broke down, the wife

---

[115] Ibid, [78].
[116] Ibid.
[117] Ibid, [79].
[118] Ibid, [78].
[119] Ibid, [80].
[120] Ibid, [81].
[121] Ibid, [118]: it seems that this is a narrower concept than the normal standard of 'need' applied by the family courts, which is conditioned by reference to the standard of living enjoyed during marriage, certainly following a long relationship.
[122] Ibid, [81]–[82] and [178].
[123] Though as discussed at section IV below, English courts must apply the lex fori.

petitioned for divorce in London,[124] and—despite the pre-nuptial agreement—the husband sought ancillary relief. In recognition of the agreement and the fact that English law would regard the wife's wealth as 'non-matrimonial property' (having been acquired prior to the marriage and/or from family sources), he formulated his claim in terms of needs only. However, the Supreme Court, like the Court of Appeal before it, found no reason to make provision for the husband's own needs. Instead, the order focused on his role as father of the parties' two children, whose residence was to be shared between the parents following divorce, and the provision necessary to enable him to care for them until they reached independence. After that point, however, no provision would be made to cater for his ongoing needs: he had earning capacity (albeit not one that would necessarily enable him to sustain the standard of living enjoyed during the marriage) and the diminution of that earning capacity during the marriage was held to be the result of his pursuing a personal preference.[125] Had his change of direction been demanded by the needs of the family (as in the common case where one spouse gives up or reduces his or her hours of paid employment in order to care for the children), further provision to enable him to enjoy a better standard of living in the longer term might well have been ordered.[126]

Testing the facts of earlier pre-nuptial agreement cases under the *Radmacher* approach readily leads to the conclusion that the Supreme Court's approach may not in practice mark a radical departure from the evolving practice of English courts giving substantial, even decisive, weight to pre-nuptial agreements in certain types of case.[127] For example, in *Crossley v Crossley*, the parties were independently wealthy, middle-aged divorcees. They were married to each other only briefly and the marriage had no impact on the economic position of either. In such circumstances, it is easy to conclude that there is no unfairness in holding the parties to the agreement and in making no provision at all, neither having any 'need', real or otherwise, which required satisfaction. It would certainly be appropriate, as the Court of Appeal decided in that case, to curtail the evidence-gathering procedures that would be otherwise be required on ancillary relief cases.[128] By way of comparison, *M v M (Prenuptial Agreement)*[129] and *K v K (Ancillary Relief: Prenuptial Agreement)*[130] also both involved quite short marriages, but marriages which had produced a child, leaving the mother's long-term economic position impaired by child-care responsibilities. The courts in both cases ordered what may essentially be viewed as

---

[124] She submitted to the jurisdiction of the English court rather than petitioning in Germany since to do the latter she would have needed to have been habitually resident in Germany for six months, but she wanted to return to Germany with the children and required the English court's permission to remove them from the UK.

[125] This is not dissimilar to the outcome in *MacLeod v MacLeod*, above n 67, where the capital provision already made to the wife by the husband was considered sufficient to meet her long-term requirements, leaving the court simply to make additional provision for her in the role of mother for the period while the children were still dependent.

[126] *Radmacher v Granatino* (SC), above n 48, [118]–[123].

[127] See also the similar outcome achieved in the post-nuptial context in *MacLeod v MacLeod*, above n 67.

[128] *Crossley v Crossley*, above n 70.

[129] *M v M (Prenuptial agreement)*, above n 70.

[130] *K v K (Ancillary Relief: Prenuptial Agreement)*, above n 70. Both cases were discussed in Harris-Short and Miles, *Family Law: Text, Cases, and Materials*, 1st edn (Oxford, Oxford University Press, 2007) 553–54.

needs-based provision, against the terms of less generous pre-nuptial agreements (which in *M v M* was tainted by improper pressure on the wife to sign the agreement). A similar outcome would be expected applying the *Radmacher* approach.

To summarise: while a pre- or post-nuptial agreement may readily displace the equal sharing principle, provision for needs (and compensation) on divorce appears to constitute an irreducible minimum obligation of marriage. Parties should therefore ensure that their agreement makes suitable provision for each other's needs in the event of divorce in order for it to be regarded as fair. This conclusion places significant weight on an issue which English law arguably has yet satisfactorily to address: when does a former spouse come under an obligation to meet the other's needs, and how extensive (in terms of quantum and duration) is that obligation? And is 'real need' a narrower concept than the concept of need commonly deployed on divorce, a standard of 'reasonable requirements' reflecting the standard of living enjoyed during marriage?[131] But what is most striking about this conclusion from a comparative perspective is its broad similarity to the position in a number of other European jurisdictions, such as Germany,[132] where it is considerably easier to make an agreement departing from the default matrimonial property regime (which may rather loosely be regarded as akin to English law's equal sharing principle) than it is to exclude or restrict the maintenance obligation (which may, again only rather loosely, be regarded as akin to needs-based relief in England and Wales).[133]

III. SEPARATION AGREEMENTS

A. Introduction

i. The Settlement Culture

Private ordering of issues relating to parenting and finances at the point of separation and divorce is a key policy goal in England and Wales. As in many other jurisdictions, a strong settlement culture actively encourages parties and their advisors to settle their disputes on divorce by agreement, rather than litigating. Separation agreements—that is to say, agreements made by spouses who are in the process of separating, or who have separated and are now negotiating the financial and property implications of (usually) their pending divorce—and consent orders (considered below) are important tools for achieving this.

ii. A Note on the Legal Regulation of Post-Nuptial Agreements

It should be borne in mind in reading this section that the Privy Council decision in *MacLeod v MacLeod*[134] aligned post-nuptial agreements not with pre-nuptial

---

[131] This issue is explored further in Miles, above n 52, 441–44.

[132] See Dutta, this volume.

[133] On the looseness of this analogy, note Scherpe and Dutta's discussion of a German court's treatment of an English order: 'Cross-Border Enforcement of English Ancillary Relief Orders: Fog in the Channel—Europe Cut Off?' (2010) 40 *Family Law* 385.

[134] *MacLeod v MacLeod*, above n 67.

agreements (as the Supreme Court in *Radmacher v Granatino*[135]did) but rather with separation agreements. The discussion in this section therefore relates to the law which the Privy Council applied to post-nuptial agreements. But, as noted above, that approach is very probably superseded by the decision in *Radmacher,* which rejected the reasoning in *MacLeod*, albeit that the discussion of post-nuptial agreements in that case was only obiter, not being necessary for the decision in that case.

B. Form and Procedure

Agreements concerning financial arrangements made at the point of separation are partially subject to statutory regulation via section 34 of the Matrimonial Causes Act 1973:[136]

34 Validity of maintenance agreements
(1) If a maintenance agreement includes a provision purporting to restrict any right to apply to a court for an order containing financial arrangements, then—
    (a) that provision shall be void; but
    (b) any other financial arrangements contained in the agreement shall not thereby be rendered void or unenforceable and shall, unless they are void or unenforceable for any other reason (and subject to sections 35 and 36 below), be binding on the parties to the agreement.
(2) In this section and in section 35 below—
    'maintenance agreement' means any agreement *in writing* made ... between the parties to a marriage, being—
    (a) an agreement containing financial arrangements, whether made during the continuance or after the dissolution or annulment of the marriage; or
    (b) a separation agreement which contains no financial arrangements in a case where no other agreement in writing between the same parties contains such arrangements;
    'financial arrangements' means provisions governing the rights and liabilities towards one another when living separately of the parties to a marriage (including a marriage which has been dissolved or annulled) in respect of the making or securing of payments or the disposition or use of any property, including such rights and liabilities with respect to the maintenance or education of any child, whether or not a child of the family.

[Emphasis added.]

As highlighted by the added emphasis above, the only formal requirement prescribed by section 34 for such agreements to be valid is that they be made in writing. That aside, provided they are not void or unenforceable on grounds under the general law of property or contract, such agreements are 'binding on the parties'. Notably, there is no requirement of legal or other expert advice (whether delivered independently or jointly), no requirement of notarial or judicial endorsement or other mode of state registration, and no requirement of financial disclosure. However, when a court comes to exercise its discretion to order provision in terms different from those agreed (discussed in the next section), whether the parties

---

[135] *Radmacher v Granatino* (SC), above n 48.
[136] See also Civil Partnership Act 2004, Sch 5, paras 67–68.

obtained independent advice and provided full disclosure, etc. prior to concluding their agreement may affect the weight ascribed to the agreement by the court. An agreement that fails to pass muster for want of writing (assuming the terms of the agreement can still be proved) or on some general law ground might still be taken into account by the court in its discretion, though—depending on the nature of the defect—with concomitantly less weight.

C. Content and Binding Effect/Enforceability

Separation agreements that comply with the requirements of section 34 are valid and legally binding (and so can in theory be sued on and enforced as a matter of contract law) by virtue of that section under section 34 of the Matrimonial Causes Act. However, sections 34(1)(a) and 35(6) preserve the common law position stated in *Hyman* that it is not possible by agreement to oust the jurisdiction of the court to make orders for ancillary relief on divorce. There are in fact two procedural routes for attacking an agreement that is valid and binding under section 34: (i) the statutory power to apply to court under section 35 for variation of the agreement; and (ii) the court's *Hyman* power simply to hear an application for ancillary relief despite the existence of the agreement.

The statutory grounds on which a court might vary an agreement inter vivos[137] are set out in section 35(2):

> (2) If the court to which the application is made is satisfied either—
>
> (a) that by reason of a change in the circumstances in the light of which any financial arrangements contained in the agreement were made or, as the case may be, financial arrangements were omitted from it (including a change foreseen by the parties when making the agreement), the agreement should be altered so as to make different, or, as the case may be, so as to contain, financial arrangements, or
>
> (b) that the agreement does not contain proper financial arrangements with respect to any child of the family.[138]

Should the alternative procedural route be taken, the agreement simply forms part of all the circumstances of the case to be considered by the court in the exercise of its broad discretion on applications for ancillary relief under section 25 of the Matrimonial Causes Act. The courts' attitude towards the agreement in exercising that discretion remains guided largely by the Court of Appeal decision in *Edgar v Edgar*.[139] The judgment of Ormrod LJ is frequently cited, this passage in particular:

> To decide what weight should be given, in order to reach a just result, to a prior agreement not to claim a lump sum, regard must be had to the conduct of both parties, leading up to the prior agreement, and to their subsequent conduct, in consequence of it. It is not necessary in this connection to think in formal legal terms, such as misrepresentation or estoppel; *all* the circumstances as they affect each of two human beings must be considered

---

[137] s 36 deals with the event of a supervening death.
[138] For consideration of the equivalent provision in Sch 1 to the Children Act 1989, in relation to agreed provision for children, see *Morgan v Hill* [2006] EWCA Civ 1602.
[139] *Edgar v Edgar*, above n 80.

in the complex relationship of marriage. So, the circumstances surrounding the making of the agreement are relevant. Und[ue] pressure by one side, exploitation of a dominant position to secure an unreasonable advantage, inadequate knowledge, possibly bad legal advice,[140] an important change of circumstances, unforeseen or overlooked at the time of making the agreement, are all relevant to the question of justice between the parties. *Important too is the general proposition that formal agreements, properly and fairly arrived at with competent legal advice, should not be displaced unless there are good and substantial grounds for concluding that an injustice will be done by holding the parties to the terms of their agreement.* There may well be other considerations which affect the justice of this case; the above list is not intended to be an exclusive catalogue.

[Emphasis added.]

In considering this passage, it is important to bear in mind that the 1973 Act has been amended since *Edgar* was decided, so that first consideration must now be given to the welfare of minor children of the family. Where there are such children, therefore, the agreement is not entitled to primary status. But, as in *Radmacher*, the court may uphold the agreement in so far as it applies to the adults, making separate provision for the benefit of the children (including housing and a carer allowance for the residential parent while the children are dependent). However, the italicised passage obviously invites comparison with the test set out by the Supreme Court in *Radmacher v Granatino* for pre- and post-nuptial agreements. Just like the Supreme Court's test, the starting point is one of upholding the agreement unless there is good reason to do otherwise, given the injustice/unfairness that would arise. This similarity makes it unlikely that different outcomes would be achieved on the same facts under the two tests, and so reduces the significance of the lingering uncertainty that arguably remains over the proper treatment of post-nuptial agreements.

The relationship between the courts' power to vary agreements under section 35 and their normal ancillary relief jurisdiction, exercised pursuant to the *Edgar* approach, has not been well understood, the section 35 route having been rather forgotten.[141] It is notable, for instance, that the *Edgar* grounds for departing from the agreement are somewhat wider than those set out in section 35. This issue was addressed by the Privy Council in *MacLeod* (in the context of a post-nuptial agreement). Baroness Hale held that if the spouse applied for ancillary relief, instead of applying for variation of an agreement under section 35, nevertheless 'the same principles should be the starting point'.[142] So the court exercising its discretion on the ancillary relief application may decide to depart from the agreement given a change of circumstance—in a gloss added by Baroness Hale which does not appear in section 35, 'the sort of change which would make those arrangements manifestly unjust'[143]—or where inadequate provision is made for a child. But (going beyond the scope of s 35), applying *Edgar* principles, the court may also order provision different from what the parties had agreed because of the circumstances in which the agreement

---

[140] *Camm v Camm* (1983) 4 FLR 577, 580: 'bad' does not connote 'negligent' (Sir Roger Ormrod).

[141] Indeed, Wilson LJ in *Radmacher* claims never to have encountered a s 34 case throughout his practice at the Bar and years on the bench: (CA), above n 71, [134].

[142] *MacLeod v MacLeod*, above n 67, [41].

[143] In *Radmacher*, Baroness Hale resiled from the use of the word 'manifestly' as imposing too high a hurdle: (SC), above n 48, [168].

was made. Baroness Hale also observed as a matter of public policy that, regardless of whether there had been any change of circumstance, if a family member had a duty to support another, that duty should be met, even if the needy party would otherwise be entitled to support from the State.[144] However, the mere fact that a court would have made different provision will not of itself justify departure from the agreement.[145]

As with pre- and post-nuptial agreements, it is a truism that more weight will be given to agreements concluded with the benefit of independent, good quality legal advice and full disclosure than those that were not. But what goes for pre-nuptial agreements (and very probably post-nuptial agreements) after *Radmacher* should apply a fortiori to separation agreements, so observance of such formal steps is not a precondition for these agreements being followed by the court. Indeed, *Radmacher*-style flexibility has been exhibited in cases where the parties have not had independent advice or full disclosure, but can nevertheless be regarded as having reached a knowing and free agreement.[146]

Varying descriptions of the courts' approach to separation agreements under the *Edgar* criteria can be found in the reported cases. However, the differences may merely be differences of emphasis, given the particular facts of each case.[147] At times, the courts appear to approach cases on the basis that it will give effect to the agreement in the exercise of its discretion, unless the party seeking to depart from the agreement can show that the case satisfies one of the *Edgar* criteria.[148] In other cases, the courts have said that separation agreements are just one factor to be considered as part of the global section 25 analysis.[149] Thus, for example, in *Smith v Smith*[150] where the wife had had no legal advice or disclosure before agreeing to terms which were very unwise, the separation agreement—described as just one factor for the court to consider—was departed from to provide more generously for the wife.[151] More usually, however, reported decisions have followed the agreement, particularly—but by no means only—where the parties had had independent legal advice, and the courts' account of their approach to agreements has been more

---

[144] *MacLeod v MacLeod*, above n 67, [41].

[145] Ibid, [42].

[146] Eg, *X v X (Y and Z intervening)*, above n 60 where there was no full disclosure but that the wife's family were exceedingly wealthy was well-understood and good legal advice had been received on both sides; *A v B (Financial Relief: Agreement)* [2005] EWHC 314, where the parties had had oral advice from a conveyancing rather than matrimonial solicitor without full disclosure having taken place, but where the parties knew in substance what each other's position was, there was no pressure, and the agreement had in substance been fair at the time; *G v G* [2001] 2 FLR 18, where there was no independent advice, but the parties—both previously divorced—were described as mature adults who understood what they were agreeing to and had observed their agreement for three years.

[147] As in *Crossley*, the existence of a separation agreement may also justify a truncated procedure: see *S v S* [2008] EWHC 2038.

[148] *Smith v McInerney* [1994] 2 FLR 1077; *X v X (Y and Z intervening)*, above n 60, especially [103].

[149] *Xydhias v Xydhias* [1999] 1 FLR 683, 691 (Thorpe LJ); *Smith v Smith* [2000] 3 FCR 374: Black J has held that *Smith* did not indicate a change of approach: *A v B (Financial Relief: Agreements)*, above n 146, [15].

[150] *Smith v Smith*, above n 149.

[151] Another, relatively rare, case of a separation agreement being departed from is *Camm v Camm*, above n 140, where the wife was found to have been under extreme pressure to sign the agreement; cf the recent post-nuptial agreement case, *NA v MA*, above n 38.

robust.[152] In *Edgar* itself, the wife had reached an agreement with her husband contrary to her legal advice. There was no evidence of exploitation or pressure from the husband and there was no reason to justify allowing the wife, in effect, to change her mind about what she had agreed.[153] Sometimes, the court expressly remarks that the agreement which it is choosing to uphold was in substance fair, but there are plenty of examples in the case law on all types of marital agreement—not least *Edgar* itself—of courts holding parties to agreements which make provision different from that which a court might have been expected to order had it had a free rein. This approach respects the fact that parties to a private agreement may be motivated by factors that would (or could) not ordinarily be taken into account by a court.[154] Separation agreements are the least vulnerable to attack on the basis of changed circumstances, simply because they are generally made in light of known circumstances surrounding the parties' actual separation, rather than providing more or less hypothetically for that future event. In *X v X (Y and Z intervening)*,[155] it was said that regard should be had to the circumstances surrounding the making of the agreement and the extent to which the parties themselves had attached importance to the agreement and acted upon it.

The uncertain status of separation agreements, as being neither straightforwardly binding nor irrelevant to the determination of the case, has frequently been criticised, most famously from Hoffmann LJ in *Pounds v Pounds*:[156]

> The result of ... *Edgar v Edgar* ... is that we have, as it seems to me, the worst of both worlds. The agreement may be held to be binding, but whether it will be can be determined only after litigation and may involve ... examining the quality of the advice which was given to the party who wishes to resile. It is then understandably a matter for surprise and resentment on the part of the other party that one should be able to repudiate an agreement on account of the inadequacy of one's own legal advisers, over whom the other party and of whose advice he had no knowledge. The appellant's counsel who has considerable experience of these matters, told us that he reckoned that in Northampton an agreement has an 80% chance of being upheld but that attitudes varied from district judge to district judge. In our attempt to achieve finely ground justice by attributing weight but not too much weight to the agreement of the parties, we have created uncertainty and ... added to the cost and pain of litigation.

D. Consent Orders Contrasted

No account of marital agreements in English law would be complete without referring to the one mechanism whereby parties may secure finality for their financial agreements on divorce: the consent order. The consent order mechanism enables parties to enshrine their agreement in a court order, whether or not they reached their agreement with the assistance of lawyers. The vast majority of ancillary relief

---

[152] Though note that the statement in *Smith v McInerney*, above n 148 to the effect that 'overwhelmingly strong considerations' were required to interfere with an agreement was regarded by Munby J as too strong: *X v X (Y and Z intervening)*, above n 60.

[153] *Edgar v Edgar*, above n 80.

[154] See also *X v X (Y and Z intervening)*, above n 60.

[155] Ibid.

[156] *Pounds v Pounds* [1994] 1 FLR 1535, 1550–51.

orders are made by consent, rather than contested.[157] Parties wishing to obtain a consent order must present prescribed information to the court; all material that would be relevant to the section 25 discretion.[158] Given that information, the court determines whether it should make an order corresponding with the terms of the parties' agreement, or whether some further inquiry should first be undertaken. Self-evidently, an agreement reached with legal advice is more likely to pass muster than one that was not, as parties who have had legal advice are more likely to reach an agreement which the court will view as fair. Once the content of the parties' agreement is enshrined in an order, their rights and duties flow from the court order,[159] and the order is binding, just like orders made following contested litigation. It can therefore only be varied,[160] or appealed against outside the normal time limits, or set aside, on relatively limited grounds.[161] Pursuant to the policy of encouraging private settlement, some reported cases indicate that because consent orders are based on the parties' agreement, the court considering an application for a consent order to be varied or for leave to appeal against such an order beyond the normal time limit should be particularly slow to allow any such challenge to proceed.[162] A consent order therefore provides parties with the certainty that a separation agreement cannot reliably secure.

The court's role in making a consent order in ancillary relief cases has been said to lie somewhere between 'rudimentary rubber stamp' and 'forensic ferret'.[163] Pursuant to the paternalistic policy of *Hyman v Hyman*, parties must submit to the court in order for their agreement to attract fully binding force. However, given the limited information available to the court when asked to make the order, it is doubtful whether it can offer much in the way of substantial oversight.[164] On the other hand, it may be undesirable for the court to make significant inquiry: that may simply undermine carefully negotiated settlements, rather than uncover any real injustice, thereby inducing the very litigation which the parties' agreement was originally intended to avoid.[165] Since the court has only limited ability to review the fairness of the agreement, the onus is on the parties' lawyers to secure a fair outcome through the agreement and to minimise the scope for either party to try to challenge the deal.[166] However, in the interests of securing finality in the resolution of disputes regarding financial and property issues on divorce, a consent order cannot be set

---

[157] Department for Constitutional Affairs, *Judicial Statistics (Revised) England and Wales for the Year 2005* (2006), table 5.7; G Davis et al, 'Research: Ancillary Relief Outcomes' (2000) 12 *Child and Family Law Quarterly* 43 found that only 4.6% of cases went to a contested final hearing.

[158] Matrimonial Causes Act 1973, s 33A; Civil Partnership Act 2004, Sch 5, Pt 13; Family Proceedings Rules 1991, SI 1991/1247, r 2.61, as amended.

[159] *De Lasala v De Lasala* [1980] AC 546, 560; *Thwaite v Thwaite* (1981) 2 FLR 280.

[160] See Matrimonial Causes Act 1973, s 31.

[161] *Barder v Calouri* [1988] AC 20; *Livesey v Jenkins* [1985] AC 424.

[162] *Richardson v Richardson (No 2)* [1996] 2 FLR 617.

[163] *B-T v B-T (Divorce: Procedure)* [1990] 2 FLR 1, 17 (Ward J).

[164] S Cretney, 'From Status to Contract' in F Rose (ed), *Consensus ad Idem* (London, Sweet and Maxwell, 1999).

[165] *Harris v Manahan* [1997] 1 FLR 205, 213 (Ward LJ).

[166] *Dinch v Dinch* [1987] 1 WLR 252, 255 (Lord Oliver of Aylmerton).

aside on the ground that it was obtained pursuant to bad legal advice,[167] however exceptional the circumstances may appear.[168]

A final note should be added regarding the compromise of ancillary relief proceedings, an issue which seems to occupy a curious twilight zone. In *Xydhias v Xydhias*,[169] the Court of Appeal held that ordinary contractual principles do not apply in this context. The parties had been negotiating with a view to obtaining a consent order and had apparently reached agreement, when the husband suddenly withdrew all offers. The wife successfully sought a consent order on the basis that an agreement had been reached. The parties argued the case as if it were a commercial dispute: had a contract been concluded or not? However, despite dismissing the husband's appeal, Thorpe LJ (giving the judgment of the Court of Appeal) rejected that approach, holding instead that whether agreement had been reached (at all) and, if so, in what terms, was a matter for the court to determine in the exercise of its discretion.[170] The purpose of parties' negotiations was, in his view, not to reach a binding agreement, but simply to reduce the length and expense of the process.[171]

That decision has been criticised,[172] and appears inconsistent both with earlier cases in which the courts dealt with agreements between separating spouses on a contractual footing,[173] and with section 34, discussed above. As examined above, liability can only be conclusively fixed by a court in the sense that the jurisdiction of the matrimonial court cannot be excluded by agreement and, once made, the order (even if made by consent) becomes the source of the parties' obligations. But it is not a necessary corollary of either of those propositions that, until the court's ancillary relief jurisdiction is invoked, the parties cannot have a binding contract enforceable as such—it is just that it will remain open to either party to 'trump' the contractual claim with an application for ancillary relief. The *Xydhias* position was doubted by Ward LJ in *Soulsbury v Soulsbury*,[174] but has since been referred to approvingly by the Privy Council in *MacLeod*.[175]

IV. CONFLICT OF LAWS

One aspect of English family law which has long confounded those from many other jurisdictions, especially in Europe, is what might unflatteringly be called its parochial attitude towards the resolution of financial and property disputes following divorce that have a foreign connection.[176] Where an English court is seised of the

---

[167] *Harris v Manahan*, above n 165, where the order was not set aside, despite the disastrous consequences for the wife in that case. Contrast the position applying to separation agreements, above. It might be possible to sue the lawyers in negligence: *Hall and Co v Simms et al* [2002] 1 AC 615.

[168] *L v L* [2006] EWHC 956.

[169] *Xydhias v Xydhias*, above n 149.

[170] Ibid. See also *Hill v Haines* [2007] EWCA Civ 1284 [55] (Thorpe LJ).

[171] Ibid, 691–92.

[172] Cretney, above n 164.

[173] Eg, *Gould v Gould* [1970] 1 QB 275; *Merritt v Merritt*, above n 54; *Amey v Amey* [1992] 2 FLR 89; see also *Peacock v Peacock* [1991] 1 FLR 324 (a judgment of Thorpe J).

[174] *Soulsbury v Soulsbury*, above n 74, [40], [44]–[45].

[175] *MacLeod v MacLeod*, above n 67, [26].

[176] The material in this section is drawn from an unpublished paper by the author delivered to the Judicial Commonwealth and Common Law Conference at Cumberland Lodge, August 2009, and

matter, family law disputes are governed by English law, the lex fori. This is the case regardless of the nationality or domicile of the parties, their habitual residence at the time of marriage and/or of making a marital property agreement, or any choice of law clause in that agreement.[177] So English law applies, and one feature of English family law that has grated with many foreign (and domestic) litigants—certainly prior to the Supreme Court decision in *Radmcher v Granatino*[178]—is its continued refusal to afford prima facie binding effect to pre-nuptial agreements.

But the source of the grievance of those who object to being subjected to English family law is arguably not purely English. The other potential obstacle to what might be regarded as an appropriate resolution of such cases derives from the pan-European adoption of wide, alternative, unranked grounds for jurisdiction to hear divorce petitions, combined with Europe's general refusal[179] to adopt the concept of forum conveniens in that supranational private international law.[180] The Brussels Regulations and related instruments instead adopt a simple, but blunt, first-seised rule.[181] Now that jurisdiction in relation to divorce is governed by Brussels II bis,[182] it is no longer possible—once the jurisdiction of the English court has been seised first on one of the grounds set out in Art 3 of the Regulation[183]—to avoid the application of English divorce law by arguing that divorce proceedings before the English court should be stayed in favour of some other, more convenient forum more closely connected with the dispute.

This is certainly true where the competition is between the courts of two Member States of the EU. However, a recent ECJ decision pertaining to the Brussels Convention on jurisdiction and the recognition and enforcement of judgments in relation to civil and commercial matters (now the Brussels I Regulation),[184]

published in abridged form in Miles, above n 52. The author is indebted to Dr Anatol Dutta (Max Planck Institute for Comparative and International Private Law, Hamburg) and Louise Merrett (Trinity College, Cambridge) for discussion of these issues.

[177] See *Chesire, North and Fawcett on Private International Law*, 14th edn (Oxford, Oxford University Press, 2008) 966 ff. The UK continues to be firmly committed to this approach: it has not opted into the Rome III proposals for a new Regulation on jurisdiction and choice of law in matrimonial matters, and is not a party to the new optional protocol to the Hague Convention on maintenance which includes applicable law rules, in turn (for those states party to that Convention) adopted by the new EC Regulation on maintenance: EC Reg 4/2009.

[178] *Radmcher v Granatino* (SC), above n 48.

[179] Cf Art 15 of EC Reg 2201/2003 in relation to child law proceedings.

[180] See the private international (common) law doctrine of forum non conveniens, effectively enshrined (even anticipated: see *de Dampierre v de Dampierre* [1988] AC 92, 106H (Lord Goff)) in the Domicile and Matrimonial Proceedings Act 1973, Sch 1, para 9; authoritatively considered in *de Dampierre v de Dampierre* [1988] AC 92. As Thorpe LJ recently remarked in *Radmacher*, forum conveniens was the English way of securing uniformity of outcome, while continental Europe did so by importing the applicable foreign law: *Radmacher v Granatino* (CA), above n 71, [10]. The EU-dictated abandonment of forum conveniens and English retention of lex fori has undermined the English courts' ability to do this.

[181] In relation to divorce, see Art 19 of Council Regulation (EC) No 2201/2003 concerning jurisdiction and the recognition and enforcement of judgments in matrimonial matters and matters of parental responsibility.

[182] EC Reg 2201/2003.

[183] Cf the situation where jurisdiction is founded under national law, pursuant to Art 7, and the other jurisdiction is not a member state: see *Chesire, North and Fawcett on Private International Law*, above n 177, 963–64.

[184] Brussels Convention on jurisdiction and the enforcement and recognition of judgments in civil and commercial matters of 1968; see now Council Regulation (EC) No 44/2001 on the same subject.

Owusu v Jackson, makes clear that this is also the position—under that Regulation—where the contest is between the English court and the court of a non-EU country.[185] Does *Owusu* apply to Brussels II bis? Notwithstanding the view of the first instance English judge in *JKN v JCN*,[186] quite probably yes, given the similarity in the wording of the relevant Articles of the two Conventions,[187] and the somewhat uncompromising reasoning of the European Court of Justice.[188] While we have yet to receive a definitive ruling from the European Court of Justice, this should mean (contrary to the conclusion reached in *JKN v JCN*) that Sch 1, para 9 of the Domicile and Matrimonial Proceedings Act 1973—under which the English court has a discretion to stay its own divorce proceedings on forum non conveniens grounds—is now inapplicable wherever the English court is first seised.[189]

But what about the proceedings for financial relief ancillary to a divorce petition? The basic position in English law is that wherever it has jurisdiction to grant the divorce, it also has jurisdiction to deal with those ancillary matters, and the conventional view is that this will happen wherever the English court has jurisdiction in the divorce under Brussels II. And that court will, of course, then apply English law in relation to those issues. Where one party does not want English law to apply to the money matters—in particular, perhaps, where the parties have a foreign pre-nuptial agreement which would be upheld in another forum but not by the English court—the practice, adopted in *JKN v JCN*, had been to seek a stay of the *divorce* proceedings, thus removing the whole package of issues (divorce and ancillary matters) from the English forum.[190] Take the example of the Israeli pre-nuptial agreement in *Ella v Ella*.[191] The parties both had dual British and Israeli nationality, and had strong connections with Israel. They lived as husband and wife in London, but they had married in Israel, where they concluded a pre-nuptial agreement which clearly provided that Israeli law should apply to any property issue whenever arising between them. Following the breakdown of the marriage, the wife issued her petition for divorce and ancillary relief in London; the husband riposted with divorce proceedings in Israel and an application to stay the London proceedings. The English court did not have *Owusu* drawn to its attention, and so decided the husband's stay application by reference to the 1973 Act discretion, concluding that the Tel Aviv court was the more convenient forum.

However, if *Owusu* applies to Brussels II bis, then an English court first seised with jurisdiction under Article 3 of that Regulation should not have been able to stay its divorce proceedings as the *Ella* court did.[192] And so, the wife having won the race to court, those proceedings would have had to be heard in London. But would

---

[185] *Owusu v Jackson* (C-281/02) [2005] QB 801.

[186] *JKN v JCN* [2010] EWHC 843 (Fam).

[187] Reg 44/2001, Art 2; and Reg 2201/2003, Art 3. See *Chesire, North and Fawcett on Private International Law,* above n 177, 962 ff.

[188] The decision has attracted a huge critical literature, even in its own sphere of operation.

[189] Though there is clearly little English enthusiasm for this outcome: see *JKN v JCN,* above n 186 and remarks in *Cook v Plummer* [2008] EWCA Civ 484.

[190] See classically *de Dampierre v de Dampierre,* above n 180.

[191] *Ella v Ella* [2007] EWCA Civ 99; [2007] 2 FLR 35.

[192] If the London court is seised *after* a non-member state court, the English court may still be able to cede jurisdiction in favour of the first court by giving the Regulation 'reflexive' effect, here by applying the spirit of the first seised rule in Art 19 to a conflict with the jurisdiction of a non-member state to

there be anything that the husband could do to secure a stay of the *ancillary relief* proceedings? These issues are not directly affected by Brussels II bis.[193] The Brussels I Regulation (and very soon the new Maintenance Regulation) covers jurisdiction in relation to maintenance, providing that (in the absence of an agreement between the parties conferring exclusive jurisdiction on a particular forum[194]) maintenance may be decided, inter alia, in the same court that has jurisdiction over the divorce.[195] If the English court hearing the divorce was also first seised in relation to maintenance under Brussels I/the Maintenance Regulation, it would not be able to stay its ancillary relief proceedings in favour of another court.[196] However, a full application for ancillary relief in the English context may be regarded as going beyond maintenance, certainly in cases where the assets to be divided exceed the needs of both parties, and so—to that extent—take the case outside the scope of Brussels I/the Maintenance Regulation.[197]

So in cases where no EU regulation determines jurisdiction over the money matters to the extent that they go beyond a question of maintenance,[198] where next? Three first instance decisions reached prior to the adoption of Brussels I[199] and II suggest that, even where the English court has granted the divorce, it has the power under its inherent jurisdiction to stay the associated proceedings for financial relief on grounds of forum non conveniens.[200] These decisions are not addressed by the leading private international law textbook writers and are far from universally accepted.[201] They have been little discussed since Brussels II bis or in the wake of *Owusu*.[202] English courts and practitioners may need to revisit this line of cases, should they wish to remove from the English forum ancillary relief proceedings that

which Art 19 does not in terms apply: see generally R. Fentiman, 'English Domicile and the Staying of Actions' (2005) *Cambridge Law Journal* 303, 304–05.

[193] Recitals 8 and 11 to Brussels II bis respectively exclude from its scope the property consequences of marriage and other ancillary matters (at least in relation to the recognition of judgments, to which recital 8 appears to be directed; cf the issue of jurisdiction) and jurisdiction in relation to maintenance obligations (which is governed by Brussels I).

[194] EC Reg 44/2001, Art 23; agreements made under this Article have, to the author's knowledge, not been tested before the English courts—the disputed clause in *Radmacher v Granatino* was conceded during the first instance hearing to be a choice of law clause, not a jurisdiction agreement: above n 78, [43]. It is also not clear whether Art 23 trumps Art 5(2).

[195] EC Reg 44/2001, Art 5(2); see also the new EC Reg 4/2009, Arts 3–4 et seq.

[196] EC Reg 44/2001, Art 27, and *Owusu v Jackson*, above n 185.

[197] *Moore v Moore* [2007] EWCA Civ 361; cf *Van den Boogaard v Laumen* [1997] QB 759; *Radmacher v Granatino* (CA), above n 71 was argued as a needs case, and so would fall within Brussels I.

[198] Cf the new draft Regulation regarding matrimonial property disputes—it is not yet known whether the UK will opt in to this instrument: Proposals for Council Regulations on jurisdiction, applicable law and the recognition and enforcement of decisions in matters of matrimonial property regimes, COM(2011) 126/2 and regarding the property consequences of registered partnerships, COM(2011) 127/2.

[199] Though after the passing of the 1968 Convention considered in *Owusu v Jackson*, above n 185.

[200] *W v W (financial relief: appropriate forum)* [1997] 1 FLR 257; *D v P (Forum Conveniens)* [1998] 2 FLR 25; *Krenge v Krenge* [1999] 1 FLR 969.

[201] The current editors of *Rayden and Jackson on Divorce and Family Matters*, 18th edn (London, LexisNexis, 2005 and updated) suggest that this suggested 'bifurcation' of divorce and ancillary relief proceedings for the purposes of stay applications may need to be tested on appeal: para 12.29.

[202] Though see in particular lengthy treatment by A Woelke, in his chapter in *International Aspects of Family Law 2009* (London, Resolution, 2009). The point appears not to have been argued in *JKN v JCN*, above n 186.

should—from a common lawyer's forum conveniens perspective—be heard in a foreign court applying foreign law.

However, Andrea Woelke argues that seeking to stay the ancillary relief proceedings may not provide a fail-safe method of circumventing the effect of Brussels II bis, whether within Europe or (after *Owusu*) in conflicts with a non-EU forum.[203] He gives two examples of situations in which English law might end up applying to the money proceedings. First, where the competing forum has no freestanding jurisdiction to deal with property and financial matters following an overseas divorce, in which case the English court, in the exercise of its discretion to stay, might not regard that forum as being more convenient, or even available as a forum. This problem would only be averted if the English court had the power to stay the original *divorce* proceedings, allowing the other jurisdiction to deal with the entire package. Second, where the competing forum would, as a result of the English divorce, treat English law as the applicable law for dealing with the property and financial matters.[204]

At the very least, clients in international divorce cases who wish to ensure the application of a foreign law to the money issues, and so the enforcement of a pre-nuptial agreement, might—if the other spouse races to London first—be put to the inconvenience and cost of having to proceed in two jurisdictions: England for the divorce and, if successful in seeking a stay (in itself likely to be a costly application), the other forum for the financial matters. But Woelke's arguments alert us to the possibility of: first, situations in which a discretionary stay of the financial proceedings might be unlikely, leaving the parties in England; and, secondly, other situations in which the English divorce might lead the foreign court to apply English law in any event. As ever, practitioners must give the private international law and key aspects of the other jurisdiction's substantive family law and procedural rules close attention in divorce planning for their clients. Some of these cases may be suitable for international mediation, offering a way of cutting through these potentially difficult jurisdictional questions and so reducing costs.[205]

In sum: given the reach of Brussels I and (it may be assumed) the Maintenance Regulation and Woelke's concerns about reliance on the (in any event disputed) inherent jurisdiction to stay financial proceedings, English courts will regularly find themselves dealing with the financial aspects of cases in which they would—pre-Brussels and pre-*Owusu*—have stayed their divorce proceedings entirely in favour of another forum which might simply have upheld a pre-nuptial or other marital agreement made by the parties. Moreover, whatever the scope of the Brussels regime may be, the conventional English view seems to be that ancillary relief applications ought not to be stayed where the court has jurisdiction in the divorce.

How might an English court respond to that situation? A foreign pre-nuptial or other marital agreement that would be upheld by the foreign court cannot straightforwardly be given effect by the English court which finds itself, however 'inconveniently', with jurisdiction and which has to apply English law. The question then

---

[203] *International Aspects of Family Law 2009*, above n 202, ch 4, 69–73.
[204] See, eg *Moore v Moore*, above n 197.
[205] See the observations of Thorpe LJ in *Ella v Ella*, above n 191, [28].

is what weight English law will attach to the fact that the parties had concluded a foreign agreement which would be binding in that other jurisdiction.

This was, of course, a key issue in *Radmacher v Granatino*, where the parties' German pre-nuptial agreement would have been binding in Germany (and in the husband's national jurisdiction, France). The Court of Appeal decision[206] attached rather more weight to the foreign aspects of the case than the Supreme Court did. English courts have in recent years recognised that it is desirable in cases with a foreign aspect to have a 'sideways look' at the outcome that would be achieved were the relevant foreign law to be applied.[207] The Court of Appeal in *Radmacher* might be regarded as not so much glancing sideways at as 'eyeballing' the foreign law.[208] Thorpe LJ justified this approach explicitly on the basis that it enables the English court 'to alleviate injustice that would otherwise result from the jurisdictional rules introduced by Brussels II and the widely divergent legal and social traditions of the civil and common law states of Europe'.[209] So, for the Court of Appeal, the agreement rightly attracted 'decisive weight', the foreign element not being decisive of itself, but rather a factor that 'fortified' the conclusion (reached on other grounds) to give the agreement determinative weight.[210] The Supreme Court offered no direct commentary on this aspect of the Court of Appeal's reasoning or on the 'sideways look' case law, though it emphasised that English law alone governed the issues to be decided. The fact that the agreement would have been binding in German law was simply a factor which 'clearly demonstrate[d] the intention of the parties that the ante-nuptial agreement should, if possible, be binding on them'.[211] This fact, combined with the new starting point for deciding applications for ancillary relief in cases where there is a pre-nuptial agreement and the different responses to agreements ousting equal sharing and those attempting to oust provision for need— discussed earlier—may make English family courts less of lottery for European and other foreign litigants from jurisdictions where marital agreements attract prima facie binding force.

V. CONCLUSION

As the Court of Appeal has observed,[212] increasing globalisation brings with it free movement of spouses and their family law disputes across borders. It may be thought scarcely satisfactory that one party should be able to avoid contractual obligations freely undertaken in a jurisdiction where those obligations would be enforced, by the simple expedient of racing to the English forum.[213] Indeed, whatever we may

---

[206] *Radmacher v Granatino* (CA), above n 71.
[207] See exposition by Wilson LJ, *Radmacher v Granatino* (CA), above n 71, [147].
[208] For critical comment, see Miles, above n 52, 530–31.
[209] *Radmacher v Granatino* (CA), above n 71, [51].
[210] Ibid, [146].
[211] *Radmacher v Granatino* (SC), above n 48, [108] and [76].
[212] *Charman v Charman*, above n 32.
[213] Thorpe LJ in *Wermuth v Wermuth* [2003] EWCA Civ 50, [3] reported the findings of early research into the operation of Brussels II and its 'first seised' rule, which suggested that forum shopping had not noticeably increased; but compare the more recent observations of the European Policy Evaluation Consortium, 'Study to Inform a Subsequent Impact Assessment on the Commisison Proposal

think of the Brussels jurisdictional rules and their rejection of a forum conveniens principle, this problem has also been a source of pressure on English law to revise its attitude towards the enforcement of marital agreements.[214] As just discussed, *Radmacher* may now offer some degree of comfort to foreign litigants.

However, private international law issues are not the only driver for reform in England and Wales. Prior to *Radmacher,* a groundswell of opinion had developed (not least from within the Court of Appeal,[215] from family solicitors' organisation *Resolution*[216] and the Centre for Social Justice[217]) in favour of radical revision of English law's approach to pre-nuptial agreements, in particular. One of the most significant pressures on the law in this area is commonly felt to be[218] the judicial development of the courts' Matrimonial Causes Act discretion in the grant of ancillary relief, which now exposes affluent respondents to substantially greater liability than they would previously have experienced.[219] Following *Miller; McFarlane*'s endorsement of equal sharing, wealthy individuals contemplating marriage are said to have become more anxious to protect existing and future assets via pre-nuptial agreements. It was even suggested that if they cannot rely on a pre-nuptial agreement, some individuals might not marry at all.[220] It is notable that all European jurisdictions with any form of community of property on divorce (very loosely equivalent to the English equal sharing principle) permit the parties to displace that community in favour of some other arrangement (including full separation of property) by prima facie binding agreement. Pre-nuptial agreements may also be popular amongst those who have experienced divorce and wish only to remarry if their assets are protected, perhaps for the benefit of children from the earlier

on Jurisdiction and Applicable Law in Divorce Matters' (2006) 48–49; available at: http://ec.europa.eu/justice_home/news/consulting_public/divorce_matters/study.pdf. It has also been observed that the race to issue proceedings may discourage good family law practice, endorsed by Resolution and the Law Society Family Law Protocol: providing the opportunity for calm negotiation or mediation leading to settlement without resort to litigation, or even for reconciliation to occur. See Centre for Social Justice, 'Every Family Matters: A Policy Report by the Family Law Review', www.centreforsocialjustice.org.uk/default.asp?pageRef=266.

[214] *Charman v Charman (No 4),* above n 32, from [106] to the end; *Radmacher v Granatino* (CA), above n 71, [29] (Thorpe LJ), [70] (Rix LJ). Attempts to invoke the European Convention on Human Rights in this sphere have been unsuccessful: see an argument made by the wife at first instance proceedings in *Radmacher v Granatino* but not pursued on appeal: *NG v KR,* above n 78, [96]–[132].

[215] See *Charman v Charman,* above n 32 and *Crossley v Crossley,* above n 70, [17].

[216] Most recently, Resolution, *Family Agreements: Seeking Certainty to Reduce Disputes* (2010).

[217] An independent think tank advising the Conservative Party: see *Every Family Matters: A Policy Report by the Family Law Review,* www.centreforsocialjustice.org.uk/default.asp?pageRef=266.

[218] Cf Baroness Hale in *MacLeod v MacLeod,* above n 67, [33], who responds that if that is the source of concern, then ancillary relief law itself should be examined and reformed.

[219] Prior to *White v White,* above n 30 and the advent of equal sharing, husbands could be fairly confident that the wife's claim would be capped by the somewhat nebulous concept of her 'reasonable requirements'.

[220] Cf Home Office, *Supporting Families* (1998), para 4.22. Again, Baroness Hale is sceptical: she remarks in *MacLeod* that, 'It certainly cannot be demonstrated that the lack of enforceable ante-nuptial agreements in this country is depressing the marriage rate here as compared with other countries where such agreements can be made': *MacLeod v MacLeod,* above n 67, [33]. The matter may be difficult to prove empirically one way or another, but anecdotal evidence indicates that a number of wealthy individuals, concerned to protect their wealth, are not marrying, rather than relying on an unenforceable pre-nuptial agreement—and that that is the best advice that may be given to clients.

relationship.[221] The experience of a previous, hostile divorce may also make parties keen to minimise potential conflict by reaching prior agreement.[222]

Radmacher v Granatino may alleviate these concerns to some degree, particularly in its endorsement of the notion that the equal sharing principle may be more readily displaced by agreement than needs-based provision. However, the case for reform remains, not least given the many points of uncertainty that arise from the complex interrelationship of the decisions in *Radmacher* and *MacLeod*, and the points they leave undecided. While *Radmacher* doubtless goes too far for some, for others it does not go far enough: a future Mr Crossley[223] would ideally want to have his wife's claim for ancillary relief struck out *in limine* on the basis that, given their valid pre-nuptial agreement and the other circumstances, there was no arguable case for provision different from that agreed to be made. Whatever view one takes of the merits of the debate about marital agreements, as Baroness Hale compellingly argued,[224] the potency of the policy arguments on both sides of the debate concerning the enforcement of pre-nuptial agreements (in particular) are such that the matter ought to be dealt with by a more democratic and transparent mechanism than Supreme Court litigation. And so it is that the Law Commission for England and Wales is charged with publishing consultation proposals in this area, with a view to publishing a draft Bill for consideration by government and, perhaps in due course, Parliament. That consultation paper was published early in 2011. While legal advisors and courts will have to spend the immediate future grappling with the implications of *Radmacher*, it may be hoped that legislation will in due course create a clear framework within which the legal status and regulation of all categories of marital agreements may be determined. As Baroness Hale's judgment in *Radmacher* indicates, a jurisdiction's approach to marital agreements, the regime or remedies that it applies without such agreements, and spouses' ability to displace that default position say much about that jurisdiction's attitude towards and understanding of marriage itself. This is clearly a large and fundamental matter of social policy which demands careful attention.

---

[221] There is some evidence of this caseload in recent research into the use of marital agreements in England by Emma Hitchings: 'From Pre-nups to Post-nups: Dealing with Marital Property Agreements' (2009) 39 *Family Law* 1056.

[222] For further evaluation of the arguments both for and against increased status for pre-nuptial agreements, see Harris-Short and Miles, above n 52, section 7.7.5.

[223] *Crossley v Crossley*, above n 70.

[224] *Radmacher v Granatino* (SC), above n 48, [132]–[137].

An English Practitioner's View on Pre-Nuptial, Post-Nuptial and Separation Agreements

MARK HARPER AND BRETT FRANKLE

CONTENTS

A Court when considering the grant of ancillary relief is not obliged to give effect to nuptial agreements—whether they are ante-nuptial or post-nuptial. The parties cannot, by agreement, oust the jurisdiction of the Court. The Court must, however, give appropriate weight to such an agreement.

The above comment by Lord Phillips for the majority in the Supreme Court decision in *Radmacher*[1] encapsulates the English law approach to pre- and post-nuptial agreements. They are not binding per se, but in the right circumstances the court might decide that there is no reason to depart from the agreed terms.

The Radmacher decision was greeted with huge media interest in England and abroad. On its face the decision paves the way for pre-nuptial agreements to be

---

[1] *Radmacher (formerly Granatino) v Granatino* [2010] UKSC 42.

binding. However, from a practitioner's perspective, when we come to look at how pre-nuptial agreements work in practice, one might query whether anything has really changed.

Back in 2006, in the case of *NA v MA*,[2] Baron J held that:

> It may well be that Parliament will provide legislation but, until that occurs, current authority makes it clear that the provisions are not enforceable per se although they can be persuasive (or definitive) depending upon the precise circumstances that lead to their completion.

Is this inconsistent with what the Supreme Court decided?

There remains an inconsistency in the Court's approach, in that whilst divorcing parties are generally encouraged to come to an amicable settlement between themselves, for example by the use of judicially assisted conciliation or negotiation hearings (albeit agreements between spouses are still subject to the Court's overriding discretion), pre-nuptial agreements entered into between parties prior to a marriage and designed to regulate their financial affairs on divorce, are neither binding nor enforceable as of right.

I. WHAT HAS CHANGED?

The practical impact of the *Radmacher* decision has been to change the burden of proof; the presumption now being that pre-nuptial agreements are to be upheld unless good reason to the contrary can be shown.

Despite the comments of Baron J in *NA v MA*, in practice in the past (pre-*Radmacher*) an unfair agreement would almost be automatically discounted. That will now no longer be the case. As the Supreme Court has made clear, 'in future it will be natural to infer that parties who enter into an ante-nuptial agreement to which English law is likely to be applied intend that effect should be given to it'.[3] Even if an agreement is unfair, that may not of itself prevent a court from attaching weight to the document or even upholding it in part, but an agreement that is unfair may not be applied in its entirety.

As Lord Phillips said in *Radmacher*: 'Had the husband been incapacitated in the course of the marriage, so that he was incapable of earning his living, this might well have justified, in the interests of fairness, not holding him to the *full rigours* of the ante-nuptial agreement'[4] (emphasis added). This obviously leaves the door open for arguments as to the extent to which an agreement could, in such circumstances, still be applied. However, to avoid uncertainty, practitioners would be well advised to advise their clients to propose fair terms, even if these terms are 'mean'.

In practice, whilst practitioners have for some time erred on the side of caution and advised any client signing up to a pre-nuptial agreement that they should assume they will be bound by it, we now have judicial authority for the proposition that there should be respect for 'individual autonomy'.[5] As Lord Philips made clear: 'It

---

[2] *NA v MA* [2006] EWHC 2900.
[3] *Radmacher v Granatino*, above n 1, [70].
[4] Ibid, [119].
[5] Ibid, [178].

would be paternalistic and patronising to override their agreement simply on the basis that the Court knows best.'[6] Instead, '[t]he Court should give effect to a nuptial agreement that is freely entered into by each party with a full appreciation of its implications unless in the circumstances prevailing it would not be fair to hold the parties to their agreement.'[7] This is the critical test and summarises the current state of the law.

A practitioner's task will now (at least when acting for the financially stronger party) be to do the best that he or she can to ensure that the terms of any agreement are such as will stand the best possible chance of being upheld and in so doing, despite the dictum of Lord Phillips, most practitioners will still advise clients to 'dot all Is and cross all Ts', which, in practice, means ensuring that the agreement is both procedurally and substantively fair, as everybody tried to do before the Supreme Court decision.

Of course, in so doing, practitioners ought also to take heed of the emotional health warning that comes with a pre-nuptial agreement. At a time when couples should be focusing on what will likely be (one of) the happiest and most important days of their lives, at the start of what they hope will be a long and prosperous marriage, it is rather strange for parties to be asked to consider what ought to happen to them in the event of a divorce.

II. CONFLICT BETWEEN THE COURT'S VIEW OF FAIRNESS AND THOSE OF THE PARTIES?

If a pre-nuptial agreement is to stand the greatest chance of being upheld by the courts, full consideration needs to be given to all the relevant issues. A pre-nuptial agreement should still address these issues by reference to the way in which the courts of England and Wales would determine the case in accordance with section 25 Matrimonial Causes Act 1973. This is where one of the problems lies.

The motivation of the couple (or at least the financially stronger party to a marriage) for entering into a pre-nuptial agreement may well be precisely to avoid submitting to the court's determination of 'fairness' and whilst parties may, between themselves, consider the terms of their pre-nuptial agreement to be fair, this may not necessarily accord with how the courts consider fairness. Even in *Radmacher* the Court did not hold Mr Granatino to the full rigours of the pre-nuptial agreement which would, if applied, have seen him walk away from the marriage with only debts.

One need only look on the internet or in the national press to see how public opinion differs from that of many a family law judge. Even lawyers themselves have publicly berated the current system, with one experienced solicitor declaring to *The Times* newspaper that the current law represents a 'gold-digger's charter'.[8] 'Any attractive woman will now say, "Why should I work, when I can go down to

---

[6] Ibid, [78].
[7] Ibid, [75].
[8] Cover story, *Sunday Times Magazine* 9 October 2005.

Tramp, find a likely candidate, and seduce him?" She'll annoy him sufficiently that he'll probably go off with someone else. But then she'll obtain enough to live the rest of her life in luxury.'[9] If practitioners feel this way, what hope for our clients?

However, despite, or possibly as a result of, the perceived 'unfairness' of the current law, England has harboured a reputation as the divorce capital of the world and it is fair to say that many more couples, particularly where there is a relatively significant level of assets or a foreign aspect to the case, enter into a pre-nuptial agreement as a way of seeking to regulate what should happen in the event of divorce. This will no doubt become more so the case following the *Radmacher* decision, as parties seek to minimise their financial exposure on divorce.

Generally speaking, it is not in the interests of the financially weaker party to enter into a pre-nuptial agreement. However, in certain jurisdictions, including England, the rights of unmarried spouses are (extremely) limited and to that extent it would be better to be married with a potentially non-binding and/or 'mean' pre-nuptial agreement, than remain unmarried with little, if any, rights at all.

Practitioners also need to consider liability issues and whether attempts should be made to limit their potential liability as financially weaker parties entering into a pre-nuptial agreement may well be agreeing to terms far less advantageous than those they could receive on a divorce. It is not surprising that in some US states, where it is not possible to limit liability, or at least not to an extent with which practitioners would feel comfortable, practitioners simply will not advise on pre-nuptial agreements, because of the risks.

In addition to issues of fairness, one must also consider formalities, albeit that as the law currently stands, the ultimate downfall of any pre-nuptial agreement will more likely be the perceived unfairness of the agreement, rather than whether the parties have jumped through the requisite hoops in preparing and executing the agreement.

The current English law approach to pre-nuptial agreements is beyond the scope of this chapter, and instead the purpose of this overview is to set out some of the factors that practitioners in this field might like to consider when drafting pre-nuptial agreements, and to consider the interplay often faced by practitioners in cases involving international clients where they may have signed pre-nuptial agreements/marriage contracts in other jurisdictions but then file for divorce in England or indeed Wales.

III. FORMALITIES

In England[10] there is some basis in fact for the perception that pre-nuptial agreements tend to be the preserve of the wealthy or those who aspire to be wealthy (ie parties who might inherit monies in the future). It is equally fair to say that pre-nuptial agreements are more commonplace outside of England, regardless of a party's financial status.

---

[9] Ibid.
[10] 'England' includes Wales; Scotland is a separate legal jurisdiction.

The advantages of entering into a pre-nuptial agreement prior to marriage are many. The intentions of the parties during their married lives are disclosed at the outset, for example, if one party wishes to pass assets to their children from a prior marriage. The manner in which the parties will live during their married lives may also be detailed, at least to some degree. This can provide a useful window into each other's expectations of the marriage. A pre-nuptial agreement can also provide useful protection for pre-acquired or future inherited wealth from the ravages of divorce. It is axiomatic that if parties sign up to a pre-nuptial agreement with good intentions, it is more likely than not that they will adhere to its terms in the event of a divorce which in turn reduces the risk of litigation should a marriage subsequently break down.

That said, pre-nuptial agreements are still seen as unromantic and can cause conflict before the marriage has even commenced. The horror stories that are told about parties breaking off an engagement as a result of not being able to agree the terms of a pre-nuptial agreement are all too often true (albeit rare), but one has to question whether a marriage was ever destined to work, in circumstances where even during their engagement the parties could not agree upon what should happen in the event of divorce.

There is also the argument, sometimes founded upon religious beliefs, that to seek to determine what should happen in the event of the breakdown of a marriage undermines the institution of marriage itself. Nonetheless, pre-nuptial agreements, or marriage contracts, are commonplace in many continental European countries with strong religious ideologies in the same way that pre-nuptial agreements are commonplace in much of North America.

In a 1998 Green Paper, *Supporting Families: a Consultation Document*, the British Government suggested guidance for legislation the effect of which would be to render pre-nuptial agreements binding.[11]

The Green Paper was met with scepticism by a majority of the judiciary, and the judges of the Family Division expressed their 'unanimous lack of enthusiasm for the pre-nuptial agreement', pointing out that there would have to be full financial disclosure and separate legal advice for each side, and that the advent of a child 'should deprive the nuptial agreement of much if not all of its effect.'[12] A minority of judges however argued that 'where there is an agreement, whether pre- or post-nuptial, which satisfies the elementary requirements, the shape of the law should be that it be enforced'.[13]

In *Radmacher* the Supreme Court suggested that, in considering the extent to which a pre-nup should be upheld, '[t]he first question will be whether any of the standard vitiating factors: duress, fraud or misrepresentation, is present ... If the terms of the agreement are unfair from the start, this will reduce its weight.'[14] To avoid unfairness from the start, most practitioners still try to follow the approach

---

[11] Home Office, *Supporting Families: a Consultation Document* (Norwich, Stationery Office Books, 1998).

[12] Response of the Judges of the Family Division to the Government Proposals (made by way of submission to the Lord Chancellor's Ancillary Relief Advisory Group) [1999] *Family Law* 159.

[13] Report of Lord Justice Wilson dated 13 June 1998 [1999] *Family Law* 159.

[14] *Radmacher v Granatino*, above n 1, [71].

of the Green Paper and, in particular, its suggestions as to when a pre-nuptial agreement would not be legally binding. These include:[15]

— where there is a child of the family, whether that child was alive at the time the agreement was made;
— where under the general rule of contract the agreement was enforceable;
— when one or both of the couples did not receive independent legal advice before entering into the agreement;
— where the court considers that the enforcement of the agreement would cause significant injustice;
— where one or both of the couple have failed to give disclosure of assets and property before the agreement was made; or
— where the agreement was made fewer than 21 days before marriage.

Although the Green Paper has not found its way into legislation, these 'safeguards' are still often adhered to and were considered by many as non-negotiable formalities with which parties must comply if a pre-nuptial agreement is to have any chance of being upheld. *K v K (Ancillary Relief: Pre-Nuptial Agreement)*[16] is one such example. In that case, Roger Hayward Smith QC, sitting as deputy High Court judge, was faced with a 14-month marriage in which the parties had entered into a pre-nuptial agreement prior to their wedding (with the assistance of independent legal advice). That agreement provided that if the marriage was dissolved within five years, the wife would receive £100,000 and the husband would make reasonable provision for any children. The facts of the case are somewhat strange in that the wife, or at least her family, had actually pushed for a pre-nuptial agreement because the wife had unexpectedly fallen pregnant and, not wishing to be a single mother, had wanted to get married. She told the husband that if he did not marry her, she would have an abortion. The husband was wholly against the idea of termination but did not feel that he and the wife were ready for marriage. The wife's family sought to intervene and discussions regarding a pre-nuptial agreement ensued.

In analysing the pre-nuptial agreement, the judge addressed a list of pertinent questions, following the above-mentioned 'safeguards', including whether the wife was properly advised as to the terms of the agreement, whether she was put under any pressure by the husband to sign the agreement, whether there was any other pressure which was placed on the wife, whether there had been full financial disclosure, and whether the husband had exploited a dominant position, either financially or otherwise.

It was held in this particular case that the wife ought to receive a lump sum in accordance with the pre-nuptial agreement, and the husband's offer. The case demonstrates the importance placed on the above-mentioned 'safeguards'/questions in practice. A practitioner, therefore, must have these questions at the forefront of their mind when advising upon and drafting a pre-nuptial agreement, and these questions often form the blueprint for drafting pre-nuptial agreements themselves.

Has the position changed post-Radmacher, though? Certainly it is interesting to note that had the 1998 Green Paper been implemented, the agreement in

---

[15] Home Office, above n 11, [4.23].
[16] *K v K (Ancillary Relief: Pre-Nuptial Agreement)* [2003] 1 FLR 120.

Radmacher would not have been effective. The husband did not receive independent legal advice in the form envisaged by the Green Paper. Moreover, as Baroness Hale said in *Radmacher*, 'He [the husband] did not have an English translation and he did not have independent legal advice. He was presented with a "take it or leave it" agreement.'

It is, therefore, true that the fact that the Green Paper's suggested requirements are not complied with will not mean that a pre-nuptial agreement will be viewed as unenforceable, but the suggestions do form a sensible and coherent list which parties to a pre-nuptial agreement would be well-advised to comply with. Going forwards, practitioners will still likely advise their clients to follow the suggestions, if only to try to nip in the bud any suggestion of undue influence or irregularities that could be used at a future date by a party seeking to resile from the agreement.

IV. INDEPENDENT LEGAL ADVICE

Unlike in many continental European states, in England parties to a pre-nuptial agreement cannot use a single adviser (such as a notary). Instead it is advantageous, albeit, following *Radmacher,* not necessarily essential, to ensure that both parties receive independent legal advice. The independence of a lawyer will not be compromised because one party pays for the other's legal advice. Indeed, a financially stronger party is often advised to pay the legal fees of the financially weaker party to ensure that they receive satisfactory advice. The independence of a lawyer may/will be compromised if one party has/had a personal or professional relationship with the lawyer advising the other.

It goes without saying that ideally, advisers should have specialist experience of finances on divorce. This is a point that was considered by Ormrod LJ in *Camm v Camm*.[17] In that case, Ormrod LJ said that bad legal advice meant just that, and does not necessarily involve negligence. It is not necessarily negligent advice to take a course of action, or permit a client to do so, which a more experienced, or stronger-minded legal adviser would have discouraged. However, in comparing and contrasting that case with the case of *Edgar v Edgar*[18] Ormrod LJ held that in *Camm* there was:

> very much less clear legal advice by her solicitor and the whole matter was dealt with, obviously, on a quite different level. In Edgar the whole thing was formally negotiated between solicitors for a period of months, and there could have been no possible misunderstanding or shadow of a doubt in the mind of the wife when she elected to ignore the legal advice that she had been given. In this case there was no question, I think, of the wife ignoring any legal advice. It is said that she was told, somehow, that the effect of entering into this agreement, might deprive her of her whole future maintenance, but, like Mr Thorpe, I would have expected that at least she would have been required by her solicitor to sign a document which would make it absolutely clear that she knew what she was doing. I think

---

[17] *Camm v Camm* [1983] 4 FLR 577.
[18] *Edgar v Edgar* [1981] 2 FLR 19.

the quality of legal advice is relevant on the issue of justice but not in terms of negligence actions.[19]

In *Harris v Manahan*[20] Ward LJ stated that:

the effect of these authorities seems to me to amount to this: because the Court is under a duty imposed by s 25 of the 1973 [Matrimonial Causes] Act, to have regard to all the circumstances, and they are under a duty itself to decide whether it would exercise any of its powers and if so how they will be exercised, 'bad legal advice' must be taken into account whether as a good justification or as a weak excuse for a party not being held to his or her bargain. The quality of advice clearly has a part to play.[21]

Whilst bad legal advice does not justify setting aside a financial consent order[22] and, as Mr Granatino found out in *Radmacher*, the fact that no legal advice is taken may not discredit a pre-nuptial agreement if legal advice could have been taken, a party may be able to resile from a pre-nuptial agreement because of bad legal advice, even if that legal advice is not negligent.

V. INDEPENDENT LEGAL ADVICE AND INTERNATIONAL ASPECTS

Consideration should be given to the need to take foreign law advice in cases involving international spouses or where the parties indicate that they may live abroad during their marriage. Even if parties do not wish to take foreign law advice, often for fear of the costs or delay, practitioners should at least recommend to clients that advice be taken abroad.

Depending on where spouses were previously/are habitually resident/domiciled at the time of their divorce, the English courts may or may not have jurisdiction to deal with their case.

In EU cases where the potential exists for parties to a divorce being able to petition for divorce in one or more EU state, practitioners should be aware of Council Regulation (EC) No 2201/2003 (Brussels II (bis)) which essentially provides that first in time wins, ie the first EU state (other than Denmark) in which divorce proceedings are initiated shall hear the divorce.

A court is deemed to be seised of jurisdiction for Brussels II (bis) purposes when the document initiating the proceedings, or an equivalent document, is lodged with the court, provided that the applicant has not subsequently failed to take the steps he or she was required to take to have service effected on the respondent. In *Wermuth v Wermuth (No 1)*,[23] a German husband and Russian wife issued divorce proceedings, the husband first in Germany, then the wife in England. The wife's divorce was however served first by substituted service. Bracewell J granted a stay of the wife's divorce pending final determination of the husband's divorce in Germany, as the German court was the first seised.

---

[19] *Camm v Camm* [1983] 4 FLR 577 at 580.
[20] *Harris v Manahan* [1996] 4 All ER 454.
[21] Ibid, [222].
[22] *Tibbs v Dick* [1999] 2 FCR 322.
[23] *Wermuth v Wermuth (No 1)* [2002] EWHC 3049 (Fam).

If the second country in the dispute is not within the EU, or one country is Denmark, then the forum of the divorce will be determined by reference to which is the more appropriate or convenient country (forum non conveniens), and an election of a country in a pre-nuptial agreement can be very important in resolving that dispute, although it cannot override the 'first in time' rule between EU countries referred to above. An example of this can be seen in the case of *Ella v Ella*.[24] In this case, the husband and wife had dual Israeli and British nationality, and prior to the marriage had entered into a pre-nuptial agreement which stated that the provisions of Israeli law should apply on any question affecting property. Upon the breakdown of the marriage, the wife petitioned for divorce in England and the husband issued a competing petition in Israel (Tel Aviv). The English Court of Appeal held that the right weight had been given to the pre-nuptial agreement in sending the case to Israel. Although at first sight, this looked like an English case because of the family's principal base being in London, it was also equally correct that the family's relationship with Israel was a profound one that extended far beyond holiday periods, particularly in light of the pre-nuptial agreement.

Practitioners in the family law field involved in forum disputes should bear in mind the Court of Justice of the European Union decision *in Owusu v Jackson*.[25] In that case, Mr Owusu, the claimant, a British national domiciled in England, suffered serious injuries in Mammee Bay, Jamaica, when he struck his head when swimming against a submerged sandbank. Mr Jackson, the first defendant, who was also domiciled in England, had let the holiday villa to Mr Owusu.

Mr Owusu sued the first defendant in the English courts for breach of an implied term that the private beach where the accident occurred would be reasonably safe or free from hidden dangers. Mr Owusu also sued in the same action several Jamaican companies who owned, occupied or licensed the use of the beach. The action alleged a failure to warn swimmers of the hazard constituted by the submerged sandbank, and also that the defendants had failed to heed a similar earlier accident.

The Court of Justice of the European Union held that Article 2 of Council Regulation 44/2001 ('Brussels I') was not subject to a condition that there should be a legal relationship involving a number of states, although for Brussels I to apply at all, the existence of an international element was required.

Whilst the Court accepted that there would be a greater expense in English proceedings and that there would be difficulties for the defendants in recovering costs if Mr Owusu's claim was dismissed, together with the logistical difficulties resulting from the geographical distance etc, the Court of Justice of the European Union determined that Article 2 of Brussels I is mandatory in nature and can only be derogated from in ways expressly provided for in Brussels I.

Whilst on the facts the *Owusu* decision has no relevance to family law practitioners, the judgment of the Court of Justice of the European Union will have a significant impact on the determination of jurisdiction questions where both parties are able to apply for maintenance in England/a contracting EU state, even if it is also the case that a court outside of the EU also has jurisdiction. The judgment

---

[24] *Ella v Ella* [2007] EWCA Civ 99.
[25] *Owusu v Jackson* ECJ Case C-281/02.

appears to lead to the conclusion that where the English courts, or a court of any EU contracting state for that matter, has jurisdiction, they will not stay proceedings relating to maintenance even if the natural forum is in a non-contracting state.

The position is different for divorce (Brussels II (bis)[26]) purposes. In *JKN v JCN*[27] Lucy Theis QC sitting as a deputy High Court judge held that it was neither necessary nor desirable to hold that *Owusu* prevents the English courts from exercising the stay of jurisdiction conferred by the Domicile and Matrimonial Proceedings Act 1973.

In that case, the parties, both from New York, moved to London immediately after their marriage. By 2008 the marriage was in difficulties and in the summer of that year the wife moved back to New York with the children. The husband followed in June 2009, by which time the wife had initiated divorce proceedings in England. The husband then filed for divorce in New York and applied to stay the wife's suit.

The wife argued, amongst other things, that because of the *Owusu* decision the English court had no power to grant a stay, and her divorce should proceed in England accordingly. This was rejected by the Court. Unlike Brussels I, Brussels II (bis) was held not to prescribe a single jurisdiction in which a person must be sued, such that the principle of legal certainty which lies at the heart of *Owusu* is therefore less significant in Brussels II (bis) cases. The Court also held that, unlike in *Owusu*, Brussels II (bis) is not concerned with the common law doctrine of forum conveniens, but with statute, the Domicile and Matrimonial Proceedings Act 1973, which provides that the court can stay proceedings other than those where there are competing proceedings in another Member State and where the first in time provisions of Article 19 of Brussels II (bis) are engaged.

Many commentators believe that the *JKN v JCN* decision is wrong and would not stand on appeal, certainly to the Court of Justice of the European Union.

VI. MARRIAGE CONTRACTS/PRE-NUPTIAL AGREEMENTS

The need for foreign law advice is essential in cases involving international parties where two or more countries might have jurisdiction at the time of divorce. The laws in different jurisdictions differ significantly, and that which is deemed to be 'fair' in one country may not be deemed to be 'fair' in another.

In many continental European countries prior to their marriage, parties enter into an election of matrimonial property regime which governs how assets are held both during the marriage, as well as after, whether by divorce or death.

Generally, such elections are made a few days before a marriage, or even on the day of the marriage itself, without full financial disclosure and without independent legal advice. At most, each party attends before a notary who explains the agreement to them prior to their signing.

Such agreements were often seen by the English courts as a circumstance of the case, at best, and were often discounted by the courts. For example, in *F v F*

---

[26] Council Regulation (EC) No 2201/2003.
[27] *JKN v JCN* [2010] EWHC 843.

(Ancillary Relief: Substantial Assets)[28] a wife had entered into a German agreement (regulated in accordance with German and Swiss law, together with a second agreement governed by US law) which made little provision for her on divorce.

Mr Justice Thorpe (as he then was) held that whilst:

> these contracts would be strictly enforced against the wife in Germany. I have declined to enlarge the arena to allow evidence from German experts in that field. I cannot think that even in Germany the wife would not have the right to deploy a case either that there was some inequality of bargaining power, alternatively undue influence, or that they are inconsistent with social policy in Germany. For the purposes of my determination I do not attach any significant weight to those contracts.[29]

This position can be contrasted with the position of the Supreme Court in *Radmacher*.

In *Radmacher*, the parties were described as having 'all the hallmarks of internationality'.[30] The German wife (a wealthy heiress) married her French husband, having entered into a German law marriage contract which provided for a separation of assets and no financial provision to be made for either spouse in the event of a divorce. At the time of the marriage the husband was working for an investment bank in London, earning approximately £300,000 per annum, but by the time of the divorce he was studying for a PhD at Oxford University and his earning capacity as a long-term researcher was put at around £20,000 net per year.

In contrast, the wife had significant wealth in the form of shares in a family company (worth around £50m) and further assets outside of the company of around £55m. Her net annual income was around £2.6m.

Whilst the Supreme Court endorsed the Court of Appeal's approach that the validity and effect of pre-nuptial agreements 'is more appropriate to legislative rather than judicial development' they considered that the 'old rule that agreements providing for future separation are contrary to public policy is obsolete and should be swept away'.[31]

Although English courts will only apply English law, the Supreme Court made clear in *Radmacher* that the relevance of foreign law and foreign choice of law clauses may be 'that they clearly demonstrate the intention of the parties that the ante-nuptial agreement should, if possible, be binding on them'.[32]

In *Radmacher*, Mr Granatino, whilst not receiving independent legal advice had 'well understood the effect of the agreement, had had the opportunity to take independent advice [and] in these circumstances he could not pray in aid the fact that he had not taken independent legal advice'.[33]

At first instance in *Radmacher* Mrs Justice Baron considered that Mr Granatino's award should be 'circumscribed to a degree' to reflect the fact that he had signed a marriage contract.[34] Mr Granatino was awarded £2.5m for a home, £700,000 to

---

[28] *F v F (Ancillary Relief: Substantial Assets)* [1995] 2 FLR 45.
[29] Ibid, [66].
[30] *Radmacher (formerly Granatino) v Granatino* [2009] EWCA Civ 649 [2].
[31] *Radmacher v Granatino*, above n 1, [38].
[32] Ibid, [108].
[33] Ibid, [69].
[34] *NG v KR (Pre-nuptial contract)* [2008] EWHC 1532 (Fam) [139].

pay off his debts and £2.335m which he could draw on for the rest of his life to provide him with an income. Ms Radmacher was also ordered to pay Mr Granatino £25,000 for a new car and fund the costs of a furnished house in Germany for her former husband, to enable him to visit their children at the weekends.

The Court of Appeal and subsequently the Supreme Court reduced Mr Granatino's award by holding that his £2.5m home, which Ms Radmacher should provide for him as father to their children, should revert to her once their youngest daughter turns 22 (ie in 15 years' time) and that the £2.335m lump sum he had been given to provide him with an income for life should be reduced to £911,000, an amount that would provide him with an income for 15 years, when his financial responsibilities in providing for his daughters as a home-maker would come to an end. This is the same approach as the English courts adopt for unmarried parents.

Questions will be asked as to whether the outcome of this case would have been different had the parties not had 'all the hallmarks of internationality' (or if it had involved a poor wife marrying a wealthy man), but this case does go some way to show the current English courts' approach in dealing with the realities of parties being able to agree on the terms of a pre-nuptial agreement which would bind them in some European states but not others. Indeed, in the Court of Appeal judgment in *Radmacher* Lord Justice Thorpe suggested, in respect of *F v F*, that he 'would not be so dismissive if such a case were now to come before this Court on appeal.'[35]

That said, pre-nuptial agreements remain unenforceable per se. It is ultimately for the court to decide the weight to be attached to them. Whilst the Supreme Court have endorsed the view that 'the old rule that agreements providing for the future separation are contrary to public policy is obsolete and should be swept away',[36] it remains the case that pre-nuptial agreements are at one and the same time both unenforceable per se and matters which the Court is prepared to take into account (and possibly decisively) for the purposes of its section 25 jurisdiction. As Lord Justice Hoffmann described in *Pounds v Pounds*,[37] *this is to some degree the 'worst of both worlds'*.

Ultimately, from a practitioner's perspective the English courts have shown that in the right circumstances they will follow the terms of a pre-nuptial agreement, or at least parts of it, but until legislative change, the courts remain somewhat paternalistic in protecting divorcing spouses from themselves. Such agreements cannot leave a spouse in a predicament of 'real need'. Indeed the Supreme Court said that no person could intend to leave their spouse in such a situation, even if that is what is expressly provided for in the agreement and what a foreign court would enforce. What a foreign court may or may not do will not impact on how the English courts will decide a case though. English courts will apply only English law, but this illustrates the importance of ensuring that in cases including international clients, foreign law advice is taken to ensure that a fully informed decision is taken as to the terms of an agreement and whether choices of law and jurisdiction clauses should be included.

---

[35] *Radmacher (formerly Granatino) v Granatino* [2009] EWCA Civ 649 [13].
[36] Ibid, [52].
[37] *Pounds v Pounds* [1994] 1 WLR 1535, 1550–51.

Of course to involve another lawyer or lawyers comes at a cost, which often puts clients off taking foreign advice. However, if a client's objective is to try to ensure at the outset of a marriage that what will happen in the event of a divorce is known to all concerned and binding, to the extent that it can be, then it is better to be certain and there is no excuse for not at least recommending to a client that foreign law advice be taken.

From a practical perspective, given the difference between the divorce laws of states/countries around the world, clients need to understand that it is not always an easy process. Questions arise as to whether there should be only one agreement, so as to avoid inconsistency or arguments as to which document should be signed first and which has priority in the event of inconsistency. It is often the case that the requirements for a pre-nuptial agreement in one country differ from those of another.

Questions also arise as to the interplay between pre-nuptial agreements which govern how assets should be dealt with on divorce, and continental-style elections of matrimonial property regimes which determine how assets are held between parties during their marriage. Would the electing of a matrimonial property regime in one EU Member State impact on a pre-nuptial agreement executed in another; for example, if parties elected a separate property regime in France but also executed a pre-nuptial agreement in England that made provision for the financially weaker party on divorce, which takes precedence, and why? In some countries, the second in time agreement is the effective one.

From an English perspective, the simple fact remains that many English judges (and lawyers) regard a separate property regime, preventing any claims for capital on divorce, as fundamentally unfair. Even in *Radmacher* the Supreme Court could not help but make some provision for Mr Granatino. Yet Anglo/US-style pre-nuptial agreements which provide as to what payments should be made regarding maintenance on divorce, may be in whole or in part contrary to public policy in continental Europe. This obviously causes drafting problems, but solutions can, usually, be found. For example, in Monaco even though parties cannot enter binding pre-nuptial contracts per se, they may be able to execute private contracts after marriage fixing the level of maintenance that a financially stronger party should pay the weaker party during each year of marriage, albeit for that payment to be deferred until divorce.

Consideration should also be given to choice of law/choice of jurisdiction provisions in pre-nuptial agreements. Whilst it is true that a choice of jurisdiction and governing law clause may help to prevent a divorce in England (see *Ella* above) there is paradox in that pre-nuptial agreements themselves are not binding in England or Wales, and it is unclear as to whether a choice of law/jurisdiction clause can be made in an agreement which is of itself not binding in law, ie a pre-nuptial agreement, under English law.

That said, Article 23 of Brussels I (now replaced by Art 4 of Council Regulation 4/2009[38]) provides for the prorogation of jurisdiction for maintenance claims and,

---

[38] On jurisdiction, applicable law, recognition and enforcement of decisions and cooperation in matters relating to maintenance obligations.

to this extent, careful consideration needs to be given as to the choice of law/choice of jurisdiction, with specialist advice being taken in each foreign state as appropriate. Further consideration should be given to how to make such an election and whether a separate agreement will be needed from a marriage contract. Unfortunately, the law in this area is particularly unclear and untested.

VII. FINANCIAL DISCLOSURE

Whilst the Supreme Court in *Radmacher* did not consider the failure of both parties to provide financial disclosure to be determinative, it is best practice to ensure that full and certainly frank disclosure of all assets and liabilities is included in a pre-nuptial agreement. In *K v K* there was not full financial disclosure, but the decision not to press for detailed valuation of assets came from the wife (the financially weaker party). Assets belonging to the husband of up to £150m were acknowledged by the wife's father to be in existence, but the judge found that notwithstanding the absence of financial disclosure the husband had not exploited his dominant position either financially or otherwise.

That said, it is safe to assume that financial non-disclosure will leave a pre-nuptial agreement more vulnerable if a divorce ensues and parties should be advised to make financial disclosure to each other in as full and frank a manner as possible. At the very least there should be a schedule setting out assets held and in some cases, documentation to support the figures. Any reasonable requests for financial information received from the other side should be answered, also, so as to avoid any arguments that there has been anything less than open and honest disclosure of financial means.

VIII. IMPROPER/UNDUE PRESSURE

The parties should have the opportunity for proper negotiations and they should clearly sign the agreement willingly. *Supporting Families* suggested that no pre-nuptial agreement should be signed less than 21 days prior to a marriage,[39] although in the decision of Mrs Justice Baron in *NA v MA*, the judge recommended that agreements should provide for a 'proper period of reflection' being at least 28 days prior to the marriage.[40] In *Radmacher,* although the parties married on 28 November 1998, they had signed their marriage contract on 1 August 1998. In practice, the greater the length of time between the signing of the pre-nuptial agreement and the wedding the better, but the Supreme Court made clear that the existence of duress 'will lead to the agreement carrying no, or less, weight',[41] which seems to suggest that in future a pre-nuptial agreement will not be ignored even if there is some duress, albeit less weight might be placed on it.

What amounts to duress though? The emphasis really is on there being 'improper' pressure, rather than simply mere pressure, as was emphasised by Roger Hayward

---

[39] Home Office, above n 11, [4.23].
[40] Ibid.
[41] *Radmacher v Granatino*, above n 1, [60].

Smith QC, sitting as a deputy High Court judge, in the case of *K v K*. In that case, the judge found that the circumstances in which the wife found herself amounted to pressure, particularly from her own family. However, the judge could not find that the wife was under pressure to sign the agreement itself. Indeed, the judge also found that the husband in the case was also under pressure; he was being pressed by the wife's family to enter into a marriage about which he had serious misgivings. The wife said in one affidavit that she signed the agreement in a hurry the day before the marriage, but the terms of the agreement had been discussed and agreed before then and she had had plenty of time to consider it.

The fact that one party might adopt a position that they will not marry the other unless a pre-nuptial agreement is signed does not of itself usually amount to improper pressure, although it may become improper if accompanied by threats. Presenting an ultimatum too close to the wedding day may well constitute improper pressure, and potentially the fact that the soon-to-be wife is pregnant at the time of entering into an agreement could amount to improper pressure, depending on the circumstances.

In *M v M (pre-nuptial agreement)*[42] the wife had fallen pregnant, claiming it was accidental, and the husband claimed it was deliberate. Whilst the wife considered an abortion, the husband was adamantly opposed. The wife insisted on a marriage, because she was not prepared to contemplate bringing up a child as a single mother, and the husband told the wife that he would only consider marrying her if she agreed to sign a pre-nuptial agreement. The first two lawyers the wife approached refused to represent her after the husband refused to provide financial disclosure. The wife eventually found a lawyer who was willing to act, but who was only able to make superficial changes to a pre-nuptial agreement which effectively provided that after a marriage of five years the wife would be entitled to a capital payment of £275,000 by way of a clean break.

When the parties divorced, the husband contended that the wife should be held to the terms, while the wife contended that the agreement was, at most, a material circumstance, and she claimed £1.3m by way of a lump sum.

Connell J said that:

> on the one hand this husband would not have married the wife unless she signed the agreement. On the other hand this wife signed the agreement because she was pregnant and did not relish single parenthood either herself or for her child and because she wanted to marry the husband. In my view it would be as unjust to the husband to ignore the existence of the agreement and its terms as it would be to the wife to hold her strictly to those terms.[43]

The wife was therefore awarded a lump sum of £875,000.

Practitioners do, however, need to be wary of less direct forms of undue pressure exerted by the financially stronger party to an agreement to ensure that a pre-nuptial agreement is signed. These are not always clear and straightforward, but they can be compelling.

Furthermore, some may also question whether financial inequality between spouses, together with social factors, could ever result in anything but improper

---

[42] *M v M (pre-nuptial agreement)* [2002] 1 FLR 654.
[43] Ibid, [26].

pressure, or indeed the need for careful consideration of any agreement by the court. For example, in *Miglin v Miglin*,[44] LeBel J, in his dissenting judgment, argued that:

> Separation agreements are often negotiated in situations that are emotionally charged. Their negotiation may be further complicated by what are typically gender-based inequalities in bargaining positions between the parties. In addition, separation agreements are inherently prospective in nature and, as family law experts stress, the parties may have difficulty accurately forecasting how the economic consequences of their marriage and its breakdown will play out over time ... In my view, one does not need to entertain a heavy-handed or paternalistic view of the propriety of judicial intervention to 'save people from themselves' in order to express scepticism about the background negotiating conditions for separation agreements and about whether, in light of these conditions, waivers of support can always be taken at face value ... many people ... do very unwise things, things that are anything but mature and sensible, even when they consult legal counsel.[45]

Presumably these arguments would also hold weight in cases involving pre-nuptial agreements as well as separation agreements and one must question whether the customary safeguards set out by the Law Commission are mere window dressing. Can receipt of independent legal advice truly be said to counter-balance what LeBel J stated were the 'economic disparities between the parties and the parties' respective familial roles, both of which continue to be gender-based, [which] may play into the negotiating process and significantly influence its outcome'?[46]

IX. FAIRNESS

Even if the formalities with which parties must comply in order to optimise the chances that their pre-nuptial agreement will be upheld are undertaken, as English law currently stands, the court will nevertheless look to consider whether the enforcement of the agreement would cause significant injustice, ie whether the agreement itself is fair.

The fact that one party might have done better by going to court than by signing the pre-nuptial agreement is not of itself a ground for permitting that party to resile from what has been agreed. However, given what has already been stated, a draftsman's task is to do his or her best to ensure that the terms of the agreement are such that will stand the best possible chance of being upheld by the court in the event that one party chooses to renege on the agreed deal. Fairness is ultimately the yardstick by which pre-nuptial agreements will be measured.

Fairness, like beauty, is in the eye of the beholder, but in considering the terms of a pre-nuptial agreement the practitioner's starting point will be to consider the section 25[47] factors and in particular the three strands of need, compensation and

---

[44] *Miglin v Miglin* [2003] 1 SCR 303 (a decision of the Supreme Court of Canada involving a separation, rather than a pre-nuptial, agreement).
[45] Ibid, [209].
[46] Ibid, [216].
[47] Matrimonial Causes Act 1973.

sharing, as highlighted by the House of Lords in *Miller v Miller* and *McFarlane v McFarlane*.[48]

First priority must be given to the needs of any children or potential children of the family. Where there are children of the family, a pre-nuptial agreement must make proper provision for them if it is to have any chance of being upheld. Such provision should incorporate housing and other financial needs. That said, couples need to be made aware that the court will retain jurisdiction to make orders for financial provision for any children of the family.[49] Any child of the family will not be party to the pre-nuptial agreement, and as a result nothing in the terms of the agreement can or should affect the claims which can be brought by or on behalf of a child.

Whilst there is much that can be done within the terms of the agreement and recitals to highlight the fact that the parties considered the terms fair, the court will want to look at the substance of the agreement. The court will compare and contrast with what provision would have been made without the agreement, albeit the starting point will be that by signing up to a pre-nuptial agreement the parties will be treated as having intended to be bound by its terms. As a result, the longer the marriage, the more likely it is that there will be unforeseen changes of circumstances which affect the likelihood of a pre-nuptial agreement being upheld. If significant changes occur, for example, if one party loses a job or is unable to work, or if there is an unforeseen uplift in lifestyle not provided for by the terms of the agreement, then it is possible that despite having agreed on what was considered to be a fair agreement at the time of the marriage, that agreement will no longer be considered fair in the event of a divorce. One way around this issue might be to make provision for a review of the terms on the happening of a certain event, ie on the birth of a child, a party's incapacity through disability or illness, or a party's loss of employment. However, questions then arise as to what happens in circumstances where the parties cannot agree upon revised terms, as discussed below.

One must also remember that the law is likely to change, and indeed the Law Commission of England and Wales intend to produce a draft Bill on the law relating to marital agreements in 2012. Until that time, other than ensuring that the above formalities are complied with and relevant circumstances taken into account, practitioners can only advise their clients to ensure that the terms of any pre-nuptial agreement are fair by reference to the law at the time, albeit if meanly so.

This requires family law practitioners to be up-to-date with court decisions and, as necessary, appropriate advice should be obtained from a specialist family law barrister, in respect of the terms of the pre-nuptial agreement and indeed the drafting of the agreement. From an insurance perspective, practitioners may consider it prudent to involve barristers with pre-nuptial agreements, particularly in bigger money cases.[50]

---

[48]   *Miller v Miller; McFarlane v McFarlane* [2006] UKHL 24.
[49]   s 23(1)(d)(e) and (f) Matrimonial Causes Act 1973 and s 15 and Sch 1 Children Act 1989.
[50]   An example of the responsibilities of solicitors and barristers can be found in the case of *Williams v Thompson Leatherdale* [2008] EWHC 2574 which, albeit not a case involving a pre-nuptial agreement, found that the solicitors acting in financial remedy proceedings were entitled to rely on counsel to advise them of an impending House of Lords decision which could affect the position of their client.

X. DRAFTING

Each pre-nuptial agreement needs to reflect the circumstances of the particular case. That said, pre-nuptial agreements tend to fall into one of three separate camps, being tariff-based agreements (where a set amount is paid depending on duration of marriage), accrual-type agreements (which can include a guaranteed sum), or agreements where no provision is made, somewhat like continental European elections of separate property.

The latter types of agreements are rare, but best fit those cases in which each party to a marriage is independently wealthy, particularly if such wealth has been accumulated by previous divorce settlements, such as in the case of *Crossley v Crossley*.[51] Mrs Crossley, who had been married three times before (resulting in her having assets of £18m) married Mr Crossley, who had assets worth £45m. The parties entered into a pre-nuptial agreement which essentially provided for each of them, on divorce, to walk away with their pre-existing assets with no claims against the other. Lord Justice Thorpe commented that:

> This is a quite exceptional case on its facts. If ever there is to be a paradigm case in which the Courts will look to the prenuptial agreement as not simply one of the peripheral factors of the case but a factor of magnetic importance, then it seems to me that this is such a case.[52]

A tariff-based pre-nuptial agreement is often favoured by parties who have significant resources at the outset of their marriage and who do not necessarily need to rely on future earnings to fund a divorce settlement. These agreements are seen by some to be the least romantic, being akin to a taxi meter or performance-related pay (if based on number of children produced), with additional sums payable for each defined period of time, ie for each month or year of marriage the financially weaker party will receive a set sum of money.

Alternatively, parties can include an accrual provision in their pre-nuptial agreements, such that whatever is built up during the marriage will be divided between the spouses on divorce. This begs the question as to what should happen if nothing is accumulated during the marriage, ie if the parties spend what they earn. It is for this reason that financially stronger parties often provide for the financially weaker by guaranteeing a minimum amount, so as to safeguard against a situation where the accrual during the marriage is insufficient to meet the financially weaker party's needs. This can however be tempered by limiting the financial provision by reference to the value of the financially stronger party's assets, for example by saying that the guaranteed sum shall not exceed 33 per cent of the total assets of the financially stronger party.

The duration of a pre-nuptial agreement is also an issue which causes debate amongst practitioners. A lawyer for a financially weaker party will want the duration of the pre-nuptial agreement to be as short as possible, but parties often agree that the agreement shall be subject to review after a specified period of time. This gives rise to an issue as to what will happen if the parties cannot agree upon a

---

[51] *Crossley v Crossley* [2008] 1 FLR 1467.
[52] Ibid, [15].

revision of the terms at the point of review? Does the original pre-nuptial agreement remain in place, or is it undermined by the disagreement as to its revision? If there will be doubt, should the pre-nuptial agreement have a limited duration at all? In any event, review of a pre-nuptial agreement can trigger a divorce.

XI. ENFORCING A PRE-NUPTIAL AGREEMENT

In the case of *Crossley v Crossley*, the Court of Appeal ruled that it is possible to short-circuit normal court procedures when a financial claim in a divorce appears to be weak or hopeless and there is a pre-nuptial agreement in place. Lord Justice Thorpe's judgment outlined the view that pre-nuptial agreements are growing in importance in a fraught area of law.

The unanimous decision of the Court of Appeal dismissed Mrs Crossley's appeal against a High Court decision which ruled that the facts of the case could be heard in a single one-day hearing, rather than following the usual procedures which entail three court hearings and a delay of up to 18 months.

Stuart Crossley had requested that the Court 'short-circuit' the normal procedures, given it was a short, childless marriage, both parties had independent wealth, and a pre-nuptial agreement was in place.

There is much to commend in the Court of Appeal's pragmatic approach, which paves the way for parties to avoid the time, money and emotional distress associated with protracted legal proceedings, by placing the onus on the party seeking to resile from the agreement to show why they should not be held to the terms. 'Notice to show cause' applications will not work in all cases, and each case will turn on its own facts, but with the right circumstances the Court of Appeal have provided a useful tool for practitioners in this field.

XII. POST-NUPTIAL AGREEMENTS

Although this overview has focused on pre-nuptial agreements, it is worth spending a little time talking about agreements entered into after marriage, known as post-nuptial agreements, particularly following the Privy Council decision in *McLeod v McLeod*.[53]

The case of *McLeod* involved an American couple, based in Florida, who subsequently moved to the Isle of Man. On the day of their wedding the parties entered into a pre-nuptial agreement which would have been binding in Florida, and during the course of the marriage they entered into two post-nuptial agreements which varied the terms of the pre-nuptial agreement. The final post-nuptial agreement was entered into after 14 months of negotiations (with the benefit of legal advisers) when the marriage was already 'on the rocks' and the wife was in an extra-marital relationship. The agreement set out the financial provision that would be made for the wife, in the event of divorce, including capital totalling £1.8m.

---

[53] *McLeod v McLeod* [2008] UKPC 64.

Upon divorce, the wife argued that all three documents (the pre-nuptial agreement and the two post-nuptial agreements) should be torn up and disregarded and, in contrast to the provision made for any agreement, she sought 30 per cent of the husband's pre-marital wealth and 10 per cent of the increase in his assets during the marriage; a total of £5.6m. The husband argued that the provision for the wife as set out in the post-nuptial agreement should be upheld.

The Privy Council, in considering all of the circumstances of the case, found there was nothing to stop a couple entering into a contractual financial arrangement after their marriage governing their life together or the terms of any future separation. Such contracts would have full legal efficacy if entered into by deed following legal advice in the absence of undue influence. The 'old rule' providing that post-nuptial agreements were contrary to public policy was abandoned as contrary to modern legal thinking. The Supreme Court echoed this approach for pre-nuptial agreements in the decision in *Radmacher*. The Privy Council were keen to stress that courts should be careful to make sure that there was no change in a couple's circumstances in light of which any financial agreement reached between the parties would be seen to be manifestly unjust, but the decision itself sets a precedent as, if the wife had not entered into the post-nuptial agreement, it is likely that she would have been awarded more money by the court than she was.

Whilst this case does not mean that all post-nuptial agreements will automatically be binding, it is certainly the case that such agreements are potentially binding, and provided certain criteria are met and the terms are not manifestly unfair, they can be upheld as valid contracts. As a result of this, whilst practitioners may feel that a post-nuptial agreement can be seen as a useful tool in cases where parties, for whatever reason, wish to try to agree what should happen in the event of a divorce without actually divorcing, others may wish to consider whether a pre-nuptial agreement signed before the Supreme Court decision in *Radmacher* should be followed up by a post-nuptial agreement in light of the Supreme Court's comments that it is only 'in future' that it will be natural to infer that parties who enter into a pre-nuptial agreement intended to be bound by it.[54] Whilst the general consensus is that to have a post-nuptial agreement after a pre-nuptial agreement is now unnecessary, careful consideration should be given to whether a belt-and-braces approach should be adopted.

XIII. THE LAW COMMISSION

The recent Consultation Paper on marital agreements for which responses were to have been submitted by 11 April 2011 did not presuppose that reform is needed. After reviewing the way in which the current law resolves financial disputes in divorce and treats marital property agreements, the Law Commission instead set out the main arguments for and against reform, confirming that whether the law should permit some agreements to exclude the jurisdiction of the court to grant ancillary relief is a step that cannot be taken by the courts; new legislation would be required.

---

[54] *Radmacher v Granatino*, above n 1, [70].

The Law Commission posed a series of questions focusing on whether and to what extent a couple should be able to enter into a binding agreement not to seek ancillary relief in the event of divorce or dissolution, and the safeguards that should apply if the law is to be changed.

Personal opinion on the merits and demerits of the existing law and on the options for reform vary hugely, and the wide spectrum of opinion was well represented amongst the members of our firm and no doubt in the responses received by the Law Commission.

From our experience, broadly, the views of our practitioners can be categorised in one of three ways:

1. Following the decision in *Radmacher*,[55] the current law now provides appropriate treatment of pre-nuptial agreements. As such, couples now have sufficient opportunity to set out at the beginning of their marriage what they agree will be a fair division of their assets in the event that they separate, with the expectation that they will be held to that agreement in the event of their divorce. Of course with the overview of the court's discretionary powers to check the fairness of that agreement in the circumstances of the parties at the date, possibly many years down the line, when they separate.

2. The current law requires reform to ensure that pre-nuptial agreements, entered into between adults who have had legal advice, the benefit of full financial disclosure, sufficient time for contemplation and who have not been put under unfair pressure, are fully binding on the parties.

3. The current law in relation to financial remedies on divorce as a whole requires reform and full codification with a view to providing parties who marry with greater certainty as to what might happen in the event of a divorce and, on that basis, there should not be piecemeal reform at this stage on marital agreements.

Such broad generalisations carry the risk of ignoring some of the refinements emphasised by those who adopt the above positions, but it is beyond the scope of this chapter to consider the potential responses in detail.

Instead, dealing with the practical issues, should the Law Commission adopt qualifying nuptial agreements in the manner in which they were raised in the Consultation Paper, then one might question whether the black and white approach, for either an 'unlimited' version (at paragraph 5.56 of the Paper) or a 'narrow model' (encompassing situations concerning pre-acquired property, inherited property or gifts), is an unnecessarily restrictive stance. Perhaps there is scope for ensuring that the specific statutory factors such as needs and standard of living are instead enshrined as the foundation of any statutory model? In this respect, could needs be addressed by reference to the equivalent Schedule 1 to the Children Act 1989 provision (effectively the result of *Radmacher*)?

In any event, should a qualifying nuptial agreement be found to be enforceable, it would make sense for certain formalities to be required, such as both parties having independent legal advice (or at least the opportunity to take such advice), and for there to be financial disclosure, with the more information and documentation

---

[55] *Radmacher v Granatino*, above n 1.

made available in support, the better. As a minimum, it should probably be enough for the stronger party to provide disclosure in a schedule of assets and income, provided that approach is agreed on the face of the agreement and there has been appropriate legal advice as to the extent of that disclosure.

As to timing, although the Consultation Paper proposes the removal of any time limit, on the basis that there is unlikely to be any less pressure to sign an agreement if it is signed 22 days before a wedding rather than 21 days before, in practice a timing requirement does provide useful protection to both parties. It is particularly important to the extent that it addresses the 'duress' point (ie if the agreement is signed in the week before the wedding, it is far easier for the weaker party to say that they were under duress to sign the agreement before the wedding day) and those drafting agreements will be aware of the stresses and strains parties show closer to their wedding. It would be far better to have pre-nuptial agreements signed and already gathering dust well before a wedding date, so some reasonable time frame including time for reflection would not be unreasonable.

Another bug-bear for practitioners is how does one identify property over time? It is all well and good for parties to want to ring-fence assets at the time of their marriage, but, in practice, many people simply cannot afford to leave assets in an untouched state, and the ensuing tracing exercise is often costly and time-consuming. Perhaps rules could be introduced to set out the consequences of investment in property by the non-owning other party, or of the mixing of that property with property of the other party. The development of this concept with the recognition of a right of reimbursement for any such investment may be appropriate, depending on the circumstances, and perhaps an approach akin to equity calculation in co-owned property is an option.

XIV. CONCLUSION

Whilst many within the family law field consider that the Supreme Court decision in *Radmacher* might be one step too far without a fundamental change to statute, it is clear that pre-nuptial agreements are becoming ever more common, and the courts in turn are becoming ever more willing to consider whether the existence of such agreements should impact on the ultimate financial award following divorce.

It is frustrating for clients who are considering pre-nuptial agreements to be told that the agreement they sign, which will likely cost a not insignificant sum to prepare, might be binding, but at the same time might not. Clarity and certainty are needed. The *Radmacher* case is a welcome clarification as to the judiciary's approach, until reform of the law takes place. However, lawyers will still not be able to say to clients that their pre-nuptial agreements will be binding; only that if the right hoops are jumped through in terms of signing up to the agreement, and the agreement is not unfair in the future, it should be upheld by the courts.

There is much to be said for upholding pre-nuptial agreements in the right circumstances, to avoid the stress, anxieties and expense of contested financial proceedings further down the line. At the same time, these factors should not have the effect of binding parties to agreements which do not make fair provision for the financially weaker party on divorce, even if meanly so. We will have to wait to see how the Law Commission propose to move matters forward.

The Law Commission's Consultation on Marital Property Agreements

PROFESSOR ELIZABETH COOKE

CONTENTS

I write this chapter in March 2011, long after the research project, funded by the British Academy, and the wonderful conference that this book celebrates. In doing so I mark a significant point in a journey that was barely begun when the conference took place, and for which the research project and conference provided some valuable signposts. The journey is the Law Commission's project on marital property agreements. The significant point I can mark now is the publication in January 2011 of the Commission's Consultation Paper.[1]

---

[1] Law Commission for England and Wales, *Marital Property Agreements* (Law Com CP No 198, 2011).

In what follows I explain, first, what is the Law Commission; then I look at the background to our current project, including the relationship between our work and the research project and conference of June 2009. Finally, I outline our Consultation Paper. I take as read Joanna Miles' excellent account of the current law in the chapter preceding this one, on which I could not improve and which is essential reading for an understanding of the Law Commission's project.

I. THE LAW COMMISSION FOR ENGLAND AND WALES

The Law Commission, along with the Scottish Law Commission, was established by the Law Commissions Act 1965 as an independent statutory body whose task is to keep the law under review and to recommend reform to the government of the day. The Law Commission for England and Wales has four commissioners and a chairman—the latter is a Lord Justice of Appeal (currently Lord Justice Munby, a distinguished family lawyer). The statute requires that the commissioners each be either a judge, a barrister, a solicitor or a teacher of law in a university.

Our virtues are, therefore, independence from government, and expertise. We derive our statutory mission from the vision of Gerald Gardiner, who became Lord Chancellor in 1965; his book *Law Reform Now*, published in 1963 and co-authored with Andrew Martin, set out that vision in a series of chapters written by experts of the day in various different areas of the law. The chapter on family law, written by Olive M Stone and Antonia Gerard, makes fascinating reading; it identified pressing need for reform of the law relating to marriage, divorce and separation, children, and succession to property on death. Marital property agreements were not among the issues identified as candidates for reform.

But a project on marital property agreements is consistent with the Law Commission vision. Our focus has always been on projects that are of some technical difficulty; our projects have not always been uncontroversial, but we have steered clear of party political issues. The Children Act 1989 derived from the Law Commission's family law work steered at that date by Brenda Hoggett—now Baroness Hale of Richmond, a justice of our Supreme Court. It remains the foundation of the law relating to children in England and Wales. The Family Law Act 1996 also derived from our work, and consolidated the law relating to domestic violence; its provisions for no-fault divorce have, sadly, not been brought into force.

A. The Background to a Project on Marital Property Agreements

The Law Commission has organised its work in programmes, consulting every few years—currently every three years—so as to gather views about the projects that it should take on. In 2008 we consulted on the contents of the Commission's 10th programme.

One of the projects urged upon us at that date was the reform of the law of ancillary relief.[2] However, we did not take that up; we recognised the importance of the issue, but concluded that:

> There are strong arguments against the Commission conducting such a project. Issues concerning marriage and civil partnership are becoming increasingly politicised. A project conducted in the current climate would, no matter how closely it was focused on legal issues, inevitably have to engage with highly controversial socio-political debate. Government has indicated that it has no enthusiasm for the Commission carrying out this work (in contrast to our recent cohabitation project which was requested and funded by the Ministry of Justice). These considerations, together with the significant resource implications of such a major undertaking, have persuaded the Commission that it should not include this project in the Tenth Programme.[3]

Instead, therefore, we undertook to look at marital property agreements. We use that term to mean:

— Pre-nuptial agreements, made before marriage or civil partnership that seek (sometimes among other things) to make provision for the financial consequences of divorce or dissolution.
— Post-nuptial agreements to that effect made after marriage or civil partnership.
— Separation agreements, made on or after separation and usually in anticipation of an imminent divorce or dissolution.

Work was to start formally at the point when we were going to be able to make a legal team available, in the autumn of 2009. Thinking about the project commenced far sooner; that was inevitable, given the Law Commission's existing work on cohabitation contracts[4] and my own research.[5] And so it was that a research project and conference on marital agreements and private autonomy in comparative perspective, specifically intended to inform the Law Commission, was a most timely and helpful prelude to the project.

II. THE LAW COMMISSION'S PROJECT AND CONSULTATION PAPER

We had planned to publish a Consultation Paper in the early summer of 2010. But then came the Supreme Court hearing in March 2010 of *Radmacher v Granatino*,[6] and we decided to await the outcome of that before publishing.

---

[2] That is, the law relating to financial provision on divorce and on dissolution of civil partnership; see the chapter on England and Wales in this volume. References to marriage in this chapter are to be read as including civil partnership, and I use the term 'spouse' to mean husbands, wives and civil partners; for conciseness I have referred to the provision of the Matrimonial Causes Act 1973, which relates to marriage and divorce, but the same provisions can be found in the Civil Partnership Act 2004 and are to be taken equally to be referred to.

[3] Law Commission for England and Wales *Tenth Programme of Law Reform* (Law Com No 311, 2008) para 5.6.

[4] Law Commission for England and Wales *Cohabitation: the Financial Consequences of Relationship Breakdown* (Law Com No 307, 2007), Pt 5.

[5] E Cooke, A Barlow and T Callus, Community of Property: A Regime for England and Wales? Nuffield Foundation Report (2006).

[6] *Radmacher v Granatino* [2010] UKSC 42.

The wait for the decision—it was handed down in October 2010—was rather longer than we had anticipated. The key point of the decision was of course Lord Philips' statement of principle, on behalf of the majority:

> The court should give effect to a nuptial agreement that is freely entered into by each party with a full appreciation of its implications unless in the circumstances prevailing it would not be fair to hold the parties to their agreement.[7]

The decision and its implications are discussed in Joanna Miles' chapter; as she explains, it leaves open the question whether there should be further reform. Whilst under the current law there is nothing to prevent couples making any agreement they like, an agreement will not be effective to exclude the court's powers to grant ancillary relief. The agreement will be treated as one of the circumstances that the court takes into account in deciding what orders to make (if any) and, following *Radmacher v Granatino*, it will be given decisive weight unless other circumstances make it unfair to do so.

Our consultation, therefore, addresses the question that follows from that position. Should it be possible for a couple to enter into a binding agreement not to seek ancillary relief in the event of divorce or dissolution, thus excluding the discretionary jurisdiction of the court? For many, the current law goes far enough, leaving the court's ultimate decision-making power as a safety-net and a filter for fairness. Others argue that this is inappropriate; adults should be able to decide for themselves what is fair for them, and it should be possible to rule out, by agreement, the expense and uncertainty of ancillary relief.

The Law Commission has taken a neutral stance on that central issue in our Consultation Paper. We do not propose reform. I now go on to summarise the Paper;[8] at its heart is an open question as to whether reform is desirable. Following on from that, and making no assumptions, we ask what might be the features of a new scheme of 'qualifying nuptial agreements', making some provisional proposals so as to put flesh on the bones of possibility, while remaining neutral on the central question.

In summarising the Paper I pass swiftly over the opening chapters which relate to the current law. In summarising the later chapters I have simply adapted, and in places reproduced, the text of the Commission's Executive Summary,[9] and then added some further comments about contracts relating to inheritance and about international issues.

III. PARTS 1–3 OF THE CONSULTATION PAPER: THE CURRENT LAW

Traditionally, a Law Commission publication starts from the current law and aims to build a consultation upon the foundation of a clear account of where we start from. The difficulty in writing this Consultation Paper, in the early months of 2010,

---

[7] Ibid, [75].
[8] This can be downloaded from www.lawcom.gov.uk/docs/cp198.pdf.
[9] See at www.lawcom.gov.uk/docs/cp198_summary_web.pdf.

was that it became apparent that the current law might well change, as a result of the pending Supreme Court hearing in *Radmacher v Granatino*.

And so it did; for example, whereas we had planned to discuss, and consult upon, the distinction between pre- and post-nuptial agreements established in *MacLeod v MacLeod*,[10] that became unnecessary when that distinction was swept away by the Supreme Court. We agreed with that reform; we noted that in some jurisdictions post-nuptial agreements are regarded with greater suspicion that pre-nuptial ones. A pre-nuptial agreement may indeed be the price of a wedding; but a post-nuptial agreement may be the price of peace with a dearly loved spouse from whom one does not wish to divorce. The reality must be that both types of agreement may be attended by more or less pressure, depending upon the circumstances.[11]

So the opening parts of the Consultation Paper looked at the current law and at the implications of the decision in *Radmacher*; readers of this volume will find an excellent discussion of both in Joanna Miles' chapter.

IV. PART 4: THE COMPARATIVE PERSPECTIVE

In Part 4 of the Consultation Paper we looked at the position in other jurisdictions[12] in the common law world and, closer to home, in continental Europe. In doing so, of course, we drew extensively upon what we had learnt from the research project and at the 2009 conference[13] in Cambridge. We were concerned not only to give a balanced picture of the range of legal structures and approaches to marital property agreements, but also to warn the reader away from misleading analogies. It will be readily apparent to readers of this volume that it is too simplistic to say that marital property agreements are enforceable throughout Europe and that they should therefore be enforceable in England and Wales; the comparison is useful, but should not be taken too far because of the absence of a rule-based marital property regime in this jurisdiction.

V. PART 5: THE ARGUMENTS FOR AND AGAINST REFORM

The Paper then moves back home, examining in Part 5 the arguments for and against the introduction of what we have called 'qualifying nuptial agreements'. By that we mean agreements that satisfy a prescribed level of formality and can then prevent an application for ancillary relief. The objective—if such agreements were to be adopted—would be for them to be enforced as contracts, without risk of adjustment at the discretion of the court under the Matrimonial Causes Act 1973.[14]

We found it useful to go through some of the more commonly encountered arguments for and against the making of enforceable marital property agreements.

---

[10] *MacLeod v MacLeod* [2008] UKPC 64; [2010] 1 AC 298
[11] Law Commission, *Marital Property Agreements* above n 1, para 3.79.
[12] Ibid, Pt 4.
[13] Ibid, para 1.50.
[14] Subject to what we say later about Pt 7 of the Consultation Paper.

A. Supporting Marriage

Both those who advocate reform and those who oppose it argue that their position supports the institution of marriage.[15] There is anecdotal evidence that the prospect of sharing their wealth on divorce, particularly if it was acquired before the marriage, or inherited, is for some a disincentive to marry (because under current law it is more financially advantageous to cohabit without marrying). Others argue that the ability to contract out of the consequences of divorce even before the wedding itself devalues marriage. These arguments simply cannot be tested, but we doubt that reform of the law would have the dramatic effects suggested by some on both sides of the debate.

B. Autonomy

A common argument in favour of reform is that the current law is paternalistic and even patronising in refusing to enforce agreements freely entered into by adults. The law fails, it is said, to recognise their autonomy.[16]

We can see force in this argument, but there are reasons to be cautious. In particular, the circumstances in which marital property agreements are entered into mean that an act that appears to be autonomous may in fact be tainted by pressure—from a fiancé(e) or spouse, from the wider family and community, or simply from the fact that a wedding has been planned and would now be very difficult to cancel. Moreover, autonomous adults may fail to foresee the events of many years of marriage; an agreement that was entered into freely, but in ignorance of the future, may not be one that they would have entered into had they known how life would unfold.

To some extent, the imposition of the sort of formality requirements we discuss later in the Consultation Paper, in particular a requirement to take legal advice, may protect vulnerable parties from the effects of pressure. But autonomy is still limited by the invisibility of the future. We take the view that respect for the autonomy of capable adults does not, by itself, make the case for reform of the law of marital property agreements overwhelming.

C. Certainty

It is well recognised that there are significant unresolved issues of principle within the law of ancillary relief. There is continuing uncertainty over how the three strands of fairness set out above (needs, compensation and sharing) interrelate, and over the definition and treatment of non-matrimonial property. It is not straightforward for lawyers to advise clients what the likely outcome of ancillary relief proceedings will be. Would enforceable marital property agreements enable couples to avoid the uncertainties in the law, with the attendant financial and emotional costs?[17]

---

[15] Law Commission, *Marital Property Agreements* above n 1, paras 5.18 to 5.23.
[16] Ibid, paras 5.24 to 5.32.
[17] Ibid, paras 5.33 to 5.36.

To some extent that may be possible. On the other hand, it has to be added that for the majority of couples who do not have significant surplus resources, the law applicable to ancillary relief proceedings is not uncertain: the court will apportion what limited resources there are in order to meet the parties' needs, with priority given to housing any children and the parent they will live with. Uncertainty arises only in the practical difficulty of sorting out how to achieve this with limited resources. Any agreement would be futile, as the courts would not enforce it if it did not provide for the needs of both parties and their children.

Reform would therefore bring welcome certainty for some, and we do not discount that benefit, but we do not anticipate that agreements could or should be used by everyone. In many cases they will remain inappropriate.

D. Special Property

In many cases, those who would like to be able to enter into a binding marital property agreement are not motivated by a desire to prevent their partner getting any of their assets on divorce or dissolution. Instead, they would like to protect only certain types of property.[18] For example, they may feel that they should not have to share wealth built up or assets acquired before the marriage, or they may be concerned to protect the integrity of a family farm or business that might not survive if it was partitioned on divorce. In other cases, there may be a desire to retain assets inherited from family or from a previous partner, or property recovered from an earlier divorce, particularly if they have children from a previous relationship whom they would like to benefit.

There is uncertainty in the current law of ancillary relief over what property will be considered to be 'non-matrimonial' and what the consequences of such a designation will be.[19] The ability to agree in advance what property is non-matrimonial and to 'ring fence' it in a binding marital property agreement may be attractive to some people.

We noted that in effect such an agreement might create a 'community of acquests' matrimonial property regime, whereby pre-acquired, inherited and gifted property is not shared on divorce (unless the couple have agreed to opt into a 'total community of property')—a concept that will be familiar to readers of this volume.

E. Our Questions for Consultees

Part 5 therefore closed with two questions:[20] first, whether couples should be able to enter into a binding agreement not to seek ancillary relief (a 'qualifying nuptial agreement') in the event of divorce or dissolution and, second (building on the

---

[18]   Ibid, paras 5.49 to 5.61.

[19]   See the chapter on England and Wales in this volume, especially the text at nn 33 et seq. The position of inherited property remains ambiguous; a clear answer was given in *B v B (Ancillary Relief)* [2008] EWCA Civ 543, but on very clear-cut and unusual facts.

[20]   Law Commission, *Marital Property Agreements* above n 1, paras 5.69 to 5.72.

community of acquests comparison), whether such agreements should be able to encompass all of a couple's property, or to contain only terms relating to pre-acquired, gifted or inherited property.

The Law Commission makes no assumption about the answers to those questions. The Consultation Paper goes on to look at some of the detail of the law that would have to be framed if such reform were to take place.

VI. PART 6: THE PREREQUISITES TO A QUALIFYING NUPTIAL AGREEMENT

Part 6 examines the formalities that might be required for a qualifying nuptial agreement. The issues raised will be familiar in any jurisdiction that recognises marital property agreements.

At the very least, there must be contractual safeguards. If a qualifying nuptial agreement is to be enforceable as a contract, it must meet certain requirements derived from the law of contract and not from family law. There must be an agreement, each party to that agreement must intend to be legally bound by it, and each party must get something from the bargain. Where the agreement is one-sided, that last requirement may be met by having the terms set out in a deed.[21]

Even if all of these features are present, the contract may be invalidated if one of the parties was mistaken about the fundamental nature of the agreement, or was compelled to enter into it under duress or the undue influence of another party, or if one party misrepresented key information (though there is no general duty to disclose all facts relevant to the transaction).

These contractual safeguards ensure that the courts only enforce contracts which are entered into freely. They are, however, developed largely in the context of commercial transactions.[22] By their nature, marital property agreements are entered into in a very different context. The potential for one party to feel pressured, whether by the overt acts of a partner or the pressure of the situation, is great. The risks are also greater, relatively, than in many commercial contracts; a marital property agreement potentially governs a couple's entire assets, which would be unusual in a business agreement. In the Consultation Paper we set out a number of additional safeguards that might be appropriate if qualifying nuptial agreements were to be permitted.

One such would be signed writing; we take the view that a qualifying nuptial agreement must be in writing and signed by both parties, and the Consultation Paper makes a provisional proposal to that effect.[23]

Financial disclosure is a contentious issue. Detailed disclosure of assets is a routine aspect of ancillary relief proceedings. Should a similar exercise be required when entering into a qualifying nuptial agreement? It has been suggested to us that making an agreement without a reasonable understanding of what the other party is worth would amount to 'operating blindfolded'. We can see the force in

---

[21] Law Commission, *Marital Property Agreements*, above n 1, para 6.13.

[22] But note that their development has been heavily influences by the cases involving one spouse guaranteeing the other's debt; see *Royal Bank of Scotland v Etridge (No 2)* [2001] UKHL 44; [2002] 2 AC 773, and the discussion at para 6.37 in Law Commission, *Marital Property Agreements*, above n 1.

[23] Law Commission, *Marital Property Agreements*, above n 1, para 6.56.

that argument, although we appreciate that some couples might regard a disclosure requirement as intrusive, unnecessary or unnecessarily expensive.

Practice in other jurisdictions where it is possible to enter into binding marital property agreements varies; in particular, whether the requirement for one party to disclose assets can be waived (that is, dispensed with) by the other party.

We set out in the Consultation Paper our provisional proposal that a marital property agreement would not be enforceable against a party as a qualifying nuptial agreement unless that party had received material full and frank disclosure of the other party's financial situation.[24] The emphasis on disclosure of material financial information means that, for example, failure to disclose a particular asset would mean that the agreement would not be binding in relation to that asset. The court would therefore still be able to award ancillary relief from that asset. We also ask consultees whether parties should be able to waive the need for disclosure.

Another possibility is legal advice. English law does not normally insist on a party being legally advised or represented when entering into a contract; but the consequence of entering into a qualifying nuptial agreement is to forgo the financial protection of the law on divorce or dissolution. Legal advice is a prerequisite to the enforceability of marital property agreements in a number of common law jurisdictions, and other organisations that have made proposals for the introduction of binding marital property agreements in England and Wales have required legal advice, or at least the opportunity to obtain legal advice.[25]

We agree that legal advice should be required (and not just an opportunity to obtain advice), and we make a provisional proposal in the Consultation Paper to that effect. Where a party has not received legal advice, the agreement would not be treated as a qualifying nuptial agreement against that party. As a minimum, we provisionally propose that the advice should include an explanation of the effect of the agreement on the legal rights of the party being advised and the advantages and disadvantages of the agreement.

Finally, a number of existing law reform proposals include a requirement that a pre-nuptial agreement must not be entered into too soon before the wedding or civil partnership ceremony itself (the suggested time limits range from 21 to 42 days). The courts have not commented directly on this question, but have shown reluctance to enforce agreements entered into on the eve of a wedding.

The rationale for a timing requirement of this sort is to reduce the pressure on parties to sign a pre-nuptial agreement simply because the wedding or civil partnership ceremony is imminent. But where there is a timing requirement, pressure is simply transferred to the deadline that that requirement creates. Where an agreement is invalid if it is signed more than 21 days, say, before a wedding, the pressure to sign an agreement presented 22 days beforehand may be considerable. So we provisionally propose that there should be no such time limits that would automatically invalidate a qualifying nuptial agreement.

---

[24] Ibid, para 6.74.
[25] Resolution, *Family Agreements—Seeking Certainty to Reduce Disputes: the Recognition and Enforcement of pre-nuptial and post-nuptial agreements in England and Wales* (2009) para 5.9.

VII. PART 7: THE EFFECT OF A QUALIFYING NUPTIAL AGREEMENT

Part 7 of the Consultation Paper looks at the effect these agreements would have when they come to be enforced at the end of the relationship. The Consultation Paper explains that, if introduced, a qualifying nuptial agreement would be enforceable as a contract and would exclude the court's discretion to make an order in response to an application for ancillary relief. We nevertheless take the view that certain outcomes should be unacceptable. We ask consultees for their views on possible restrictions to the enforceability of qualifying nuptial agreements.

First, the Law Commission takes the view that a marital property agreement, even if it met the formal requirements for validity as a qualifying nuptial agreement, should not be enforceable to the extent that it failed to provide for the needs of any children of the family. This echoes the concerns expressed by Lord Phillips in *Radmacher v Granatino*, who said: 'A nuptial agreement cannot be allowed to prejudice the reasonable requirements of any children of the family.'[26]

We also take the view that the same approach should be adopted towards agreements which leave one spouse reliant on state benefits, at least where that could be avoided by distributing the couple's resources in a different way on divorce or dissolution. It would be wrong, we think, for the public to be required to support those whose basic need for support could be met by their former spouse (and would have been, had they not entered into a qualifying nuptial agreement). The Consultation Paper, therefore, makes provisional proposals to this effect.[27]

Beyond these two clear provisos, the Paper asks consultees to consider what other outcomes should be restricted.

A. A 'Cast-Iron' Agreement

It would be possible to go no further than what has already been said. An agreement which met the formal requirements for a qualifying nuptial agreement, which made proper provision for any children and did not leave either party on state benefits would therefore be enforceable. This would be the case no matter how disastrous the effect upon the parties, either because the agreement was so one-sided from the outset or as a result of unforeseen subsequent events.[28]

The Consultation Paper suggests that this stark approach would not be appropriate in English law unless the model of reform ultimately adopted was restricted to the type of 'community of acquests' model seen elsewhere in Europe and discussed above. If agreements were limited to pre-acquired, inherited and gifted property only—leaving the rest of a couple's property to be divided according to conventional ancillary relief principles—then we can see some force in the argument that further restrictions may be unnecessary. We ask consultees for their views on this.

---

[26] *Radmacher v Granatino*, above n 6, [77].
[27] Law Commission, *Marital Property Agreements*, above n 1, para 7.16.
[28] Ibid, paras 7.23 to 7.28.

B. Safeguards Based on Time and Events

One criticism of marital property agreements—particularly those entered into early in the relationship—is that the parties may not contemplate at the outset of a marriage or civil partnership the consequences of the passage of time or significant events. An agreement that may be appropriate for a young couple at the start of their relationship may be far less appropriate after the birth of a child, or if one of the parties suffers serious illness, unemployment or a business failure. Recent research indicates a common public attitude that pre-nuptial agreements should be accorded less significance the longer a marriage lasts.

The Consultation Paper explores the idea that it would be possible for a qualifying nuptial agreement to cease to have effect after a certain period of time (what might be termed an automatic 'sunset clause'), or on the happening of a specified event (the birth of a child of the marriage or civil partnership being the obvious example). But we also point out some of the difficulties in formulating such a restriction. Few events are so easily and objectively verifiable as the birth of a child. It would also need to be decided whether such an event should make the agreement unenforceable, even if the event was in fact anticipated in the agreement. We therefore seek consultees' views.

C. Fairness as a Safeguard[29]

For many, it is intuitively attractive to provide that an agreement should be enforced unless the outcome would be 'unfair' or 'unjust', and indeed this has featured in previous reform proposals by other organisations. Reform to this effect would, we think, be unnecessary, as it would closely match the decision of the Supreme Court in *Radmacher v Granatino*. But it might be possible to formulate a restriction based on some more stringent test of fairness: 'manifest unfairness' or 'serious injustice' perhaps.

The Consultation Paper explores this question in more detail, looking at the law in other jurisdictions and reform proposals made by other organisations. On balance, we doubt whether any such test would give any more certainty than does the current law. We nevertheless ask consultees for their views.

D. Compensation and the Protection of Needs[30]

An alternative approach would be to allow qualifying nuptial agreements to be enforced except to the extent that the needs of either spouse were not met. Provision for a partner's needs can be seen as the bedrock of ancillary relief: by entering into a marriage or civil partnership, spouses become responsible for one another's needs, and that responsibility continues after the termination of the relationship.

---

[29] Ibid, paras 7.37 to 7.47.
[30] Ibid, paras 7.48 to 7.57.

Clearly, there is room for debate over how needs should be assessed. In the Consultation Paper we explain that needs, in the context of ancillary relief, means more than simply ensuring that a former spouse is not left reliant on state benefits (at least where there are sufficient resources to avoid that).

In recent years, the concept of compensating a partner for financial disadvantage suffered as a result of the relationship (typically, giving up employment to look after children) has become detached from the definition of needs and has acquired its own status as a separate strand of 'fairness' in ancillary relief awards. In the Consultation Paper we consider whether reform based on the concept of needs should incorporate this compensation element, or should use a narrower concept of needs. Clearly, adopting a narrow definition of needs would lead to less generous outcomes for the financially weaker spouse. We are therefore cautious about this approach, but we ask consultees for their views.

The risk that an agreement will fail to meet the needs of one of the parties is obviously greater where it encompasses all of a couple's assets. One advantage of a 'community of acquests' model of reform (discussed above and in Part 5 of the Consultation Paper) is that only pre-acquired, inherited and gifted property is excluded from the reach of the court's powers to award ancillary relief. If there is sufficient matrimonial property to meet the needs of both parties (however needs are assessed), then there would be no need to have recourse to property governed by the terms of the qualifying nuptial agreement.

E. Weighing Up the Options

Those are the options that the Law Commission sets out in the Consultation Paper, and we ask consultees to weigh them up and to tell us what, if any, should be the safeguards imposed on the outcome of a marital property agreement.

VIII. CONTRACTS RELATING TO INHERITANCE

The law of England and Wales allows freedom of testation: it is open to us to leave property by will in whatsoever way we choose, and there is no fixed inheritance entitlement for family members. But that freedom is subject to the provisions of the Inheritance (Provision for Family and Dependants) Act 1975, often referred to simply as the 'Inheritance Act'.

The Inheritance Act enables a limited range of family members to apply for financial provision from the estate of a deceased person, on the basis that his or her will—or the rules of intestacy, if no will has been made—do not make proper provision for them. Among those entitled to claim under the Inheritance Act are surviving spouses. And while most claimants are entitled only to provision for their 'maintenance', which is quite a limited entitlement, surviving spouses are entitled to a much more generous level of provision, which would normally be at least as much as he or she would have recovered on divorce.[31] The question therefore

---

[31] Inheritance (Provision for Family and Dependants) Act 1975, s 3(2).

arises: should it be possible for a marital property agreement to contract out of the court's discretionary jurisdiction under the Inheritance Act?

It is possible that some couples, perhaps marrying later in life, might be concerned not about divorce but about what will happen to their property when they die. They might, therefore, wish not only to make wills leaving their property to, for example, their children from an earlier union, but also to make a contract preventing each other from applying for provision under the Inheritance Act. It is hard to see why such agreements should not be possible if it becomes permissible to contract out of ancillary relief. We ask for consultees' views on this, but we suggest that it should not be possible to contract out of provision for a surviving spouse's 'maintenance', within the meaning of that term in the context of the 1975 Act. The Act plays a public role in preventing hardship, and we suggest that it should not be possible to contract out of that restrictive, but essential, level of provision.[32]

IX. INTERNATIONAL ISSUES

Finally, the Consultation Paper addresses some international issues. We consider the difficulties encountered by couples from overseas who seek to marry here but find that they cannot make an enforceable marital property agreement in the way that they would be able to in another jurisdiction. Their expectations may be disappointed, and they may have difficulty in marrying here.

Others may have married elsewhere with an enforceable agreement, and may be perplexed to find that it carries rather less weight in the English courts.[33] The circumstances in which such an agreement may have been made vary so widely that it is not possible to reach a single conclusion as to the weight that should be given to them by the English courts, save to say that they are inevitably governed by the principle in *Radmacher*. The introduction of qualifying nuptial agreements, if that takes place, would not mean that overseas agreements automatically took on that status.

We also note that whilst the English courts will regard a marital property agreement made in another jurisdiction as one of the circumstances of the case, it would be inconsistent with that approach for the court not also to take into account the effect of the marital property regime under which the couple married, in cases where there is no contract. For example, where a French couple divorces here, one of the circumstances of the case which the statute requires the court to consider in the exercise of its discretion in ancillary relief must be the fact that the couple married under the French regime of community of acquests.

By the time this volume is published, the European Commission will have produced its draft regulation on Marital Property Regimes. We do not know whether the UK will opt in to that instrument, nor indeed whether it will be drafted in a way that is compatible with the law of a common law country. It is indeed a development to be awaited with interest.

---

[32] Law Commission, *Marital Property Agreements*, above n 1, para 7.16.
[33] Such were the facts of *Radmacher v Granatino*, above n 6.

We make no provisional proposals about international issues in the Consultation Paper, but we observe that there will in the coming years be an increasing number of divorces involving what the European Commission calls 'international couples', and whilst the English courts are likely to continue to apply the lex fori,[34] it will be unrealistic for them not to be aware of and take into account the property law of other jurisdictions.[35]

X. CONCLUSION

At the time of writing, no conclusion is possible; consultation continued until 11 April 2011 and it is unlikely that we shall have produced a final Report by the time that this book is published. Whatever our recommendations—whether we recommend reform or not and, if we do, what form it takes—they are likely to be the subject of some controversy. The value of opportunities to look overseas for wisdom should not be under-estimated; the benefits of the research project and the 2009 conference will be felt for many a year.

---

[34] See the chapter on England and Wales in this volume, text at n 167.
[35] Law Commission, *Marital Property Agreements* above n 1 at para 7.103.

Marital Agreements and Private Autonomy in Germany

ANATOL DUTTA[*]

CONTENTS

---

[*] This report was drafted in summer 2009. Later developments could only be considered occasionally. In the following footnotes, the abbreviation 'FamRZ' stands for the leading German family law journal 'Zeitschrift für das gesamte Familienrecht', 'NJW' denotes the weekly law journal 'Neue Juristische Wochenschrift'.

I. INTRODUCTION

In Germany, the term *Ehevertrag*, marital agreement, has both a narrow and a wide meaning. It is understood in its narrow sense by the *Bürgerliche Gesetzbuch* (BGB),[1] the German Civil Code; according to section 1408(1) of the BGB, only agreements on matrimonial property issues are *Eheverträge*. In legal theory and practice, however, the term *Ehevertrag* is used in a much wider sense, encompassing all kinds of agreements which address the financial consequences of divorce: matrimonial property, the adjustment of pension rights, post-divorce maintenance and the allocation of the marital home and household chattels. This second—wide—meaning is the one the term marital agreement shall carry in the following report. As to terminology, two further points should be noted. First, in principle, there is no legal distinction in German family law between pre- or post-nuptial agreements and separation agreements. Some authors do not even distinguish terminologically between marital agreements which are concluded before and after the marriage has failed,[2] and, as will be shown, most of the differentiations between pre- or post-nuptial agreements and separation agreements have been given up (see below section III.B; see also, however, section IV.A). This might be surprising, bearing in mind that separation agreements are, in most cases, concluded under completely different circumstances than pre- and post-nuptial agreements;[3] however, a distinction between pre- or post-nuptial agreements and separation agreements always causes problems in the delimitation of those agreements.[4] The second terminological aspect to be

---

[1] *Bürgerliches Gesetzbuch* of 18 August 1896, Bundesgesetzblatt [= Official Journal] 2002 I 42, 2909; 2003 I 38—an English translation of the BGB can be found at www.gesetze-im-internet.de/englisch_bgb/index.html.

[2] See eg J Gernhuber and D Coester-Waltjen, *Familienrecht*, 6th edn (Munich, CH Beck, 2010) 237.

[3] See D Henrich, 'Die Privatautonomie im Eherecht und ihre Grenzen im europäischen Vergleich' in S Hofer, D Schwab and D Henrich (eds), *From Status to Contract?* (Bielefeld, Gieseking, 2005) 323, 323 et seq.

[4] See Federal Government, *Draft for a Reform of the Rules on Pension Rights Adjustment*, BT-Drucks. 16/10144 (2008) 50 et seq.

borne in mind when exploring the German rules on marital agreements relates to agreements between partners of a registered partnership, the German functional equivalent of marriage for homosexual couples. The principles on marital agreements between spouses outlined in this report apply mutatis mutandis to agreements between registered partners. As to the financial consequences of a cancellation of the partnership, the *Lebenspartnerschaftsgesetz* (LPartG),[5] the Act on registered partnerships, refers to a large extent to the default rules and provisions on marital agreements for marriages.[6]

Although private autonomy in matrimonial matters is one of the cornerstones of German family law (see below section III) and is even constitutionally protected (see below section V.A), marital agreements are apparently not very common in practice. Although exact statistical data on the proliferation of marital agreements is not available, it is estimated that less than 10 per cent of couples are parties to marital agreements.[7] The small number of marital agreements is surprising on first sight, especially as the financial consequences of divorce are very important practically: more than a third of the marriages in Germany end in divorce.[8] A possible explanation might be that the default rules, which are outlined below (section II) and which have undergone considerable legislative reform in the last few years, are sensible for the majority of couples, and derogation is necessary only in exceptional cases. According to recent statistics the common family model is still represented by the couple, with one of the spouses predominantly working and the other predominantly caring for family and home.[9] It, thus, appears that the default rules are still tailored to, or at least based upon, that model.[10]

Marital agreements are, in principle, ordinary contracts which are, as to their existence, validity and interpretation, subject to the general rules on contracts contained especially in the first book of the BGB, in the general part. As a consequence, for example, the general rules on rescission due to mistake, wilful deceit and undue influence (s 119 et seq BGB) apply.[11] Furthermore, the German courts have used two general provisions of German private law—section 138(1) BGB and

---

[5] *Gesetz über die Eingetragene Lebenspartnerschaft* of 16 February 2001, BGBl 2001 I 266.

[6] See as to matrimonial property s 6 et seq LPartG, as to the adjustment of pension rights s 20 LPartG, as to maintenance s 16 LPartG and as to the attribution of the commonly used home and household s 17 LPartG. See, however, the differences in the conflict of laws which will be addressed below in section VI.B.

[7] BVerfG 6 February 2001, FamRZ 2001, 343, 344; I Schwenzer, 'Vertragsfreiheit im Ehevermögens- und Scheidungsfolgenrecht' (1996) 196 *Archiv für die civilistische Praxis* 88, 91 et seq; N Dethloff, 'Unterhalt, Zugewinn, Versorgungsausgleich—Sind unsere familienrechtlichen Ausgleichssysteme noch zeitgemäß?' in Ständige Deputation des Deutschen Juristentages (ed), *Verhandlungen des 67. Deutschen Juristentages* (Munich, CH Beck, 2008) A 1, 20—all with further references to empirical studies.

[8] Federal Government, *Draft for a Reform, inter alia, of the Statutory Matrimonial Property Regime*, BT-Drucks. 16/10798 (2008) 10.

[9] See eg Dethloff, above n 7, 16 et seq.

[10] As to the question whether the default rules are still premised on a certain family model, see eg T Helms, 'Wandel der Geschlechterrollenbilder und vermögensrechtliche Scheidungsfolgen' in J Bernreuther, R Freitag, S Leible et al (eds), *Festschrift für Ulrich Spellenberg* (Munich, Sellier European Law Publishers, 2010) 27; A Röthel, 'Institution und Intimität: Die Ehe, ihre Leitbilder und ihr Recht' in A Röthel, M Löhnig and T Helms (eds), *Ehe, Familie, Abstammung—Blicke in die Zukunft* (Frankfurt am Main, Wolfgang Metzner Verlag, 2010) 9, 14 et seq.

[11] See BGH 25 February 1987, FamRZ 1987, 934, 935; BGH 1 April 1998, FamRZ 1998, 902, 905; BGH 22 November 1995, FamRZ 1996, 605, 606; BGH 28 February 2007, FamRZ 2007, 974, 976.

section 242 BGB—to develop a system of judicial review for marital agreements, which will be addressed later in detail (see below V). Those general rules, however, apply only if there are no special rules for marital agreements, especially in the fourth book of the BGB, the book dealing with family law. This relates notably to special formal requirements for marital agreements (see below IV) and the capacity of spouses to contract.[12]

II. THE DEFAULT RULES ON THE FINANCIAL CONSEQUENCES OF DIVORCE: A MULTI-PILLAR SYSTEM IN A NUTSHELL

According to the default rules in Germany, the financial relations between spouses after divorce rest on several pillars, all of which are independent of each other: matrimonial property, the adjustment of pension rights, post-divorce maintenance and the allocation of the marital home and household chattels. Those pillars aim, in particular, to compensate marriage-related disadvantages suffered by one of the spouses, especially those resulting from a spouse's abandoning his or her career during the marriage in order to care for the family.[13]

A. Matrimonial Property (section 1363 et seq BGB)

The default matrimonial property rules determine that spouses, failing a marital agreement on their matrimonial property regime, live in a *Zugewinngemeinschaft*[14]—a regime which is based on a separation of property combined with an equal participation in the future economic gains of the couple. The increase of the value of the assets of both spouses during the marriage is regarded as earned by both spouses equally. This egalitarian notion is, however, not implemented by joint ownership of property during marriage.[15] Rather, both spouses remain owner of their property and, in principle, administer their property individually.[16] Only when the default matrimonial property regime of the *Zugewinngemeinschaft* is dissolved, for example, by death or divorce, both spouses mutually participate in the gain obtained during marriage.[17] This so-called *Zugewinnausgleich*, the compensation for the gain, is processed either, in the event of death, by increasing the statutory share of the surviving spouse in the estate[18] or, if the *Zugewinngemeinschaft* is terminated not

---

[12] See, as to agreements on matrimonial property, s 1411 BGB which deviates from the general rules contained in s 104 et seq BGB.

[13] See BGH 25 May 2005, FamRZ 2005, 1444, 1447.

[14] Section 1363(1) BGB.

[15] As s 1363(2) sentence 1 BGB expressly clarifies.

[16] Section 1364 BGB. See, however, the restrictions for dispositions on their whole estate (ss 1365–68 BGB) and on household chattels (s 1369 BGB) which is intended, inter alia, to ensure that spouses do not dissipate their assets, thereby endangering the participation of the other spouse in the gain realised during marriage. The courts have, therefore, extended those restrictions to dispositions on major assets which form the predominant part of the property of each spouse, see BGH 28 April 1961, NJW 1961, 1301.

[17] Section 1363(2) sentence 2 BGB.

[18] Section 1371(1) BGB: The statutory share of the surviving spouse, which is determined by the general rules on intestacy in s 1924 et seq BGB and, in particular, in s 1931 BGB, is increased by 25 per cent. See s 1371(2) and (3) BGB for cases in which the surviving spouse does not become heir, eg because

by death but inter vivos, notably by divorce, by a compensation claim of the spouse whose property, in terms of value, increased to a lesser extent against the spouse who realised a higher gain.[19] The spouse who has acquired the higher gain in value during marriage has to pay a sum which equals half of the difference between the gains of both couples (the surplus).[20] The gain of each spouse is calculated by deducting from the value of his or her property at the end of the *Zugewinngemeinschaft*, the value of his or her property at the beginning of the *Zugewinngemeinschaft*.[21] Hence, if the wife was able to achieve a gain during the marriage of 100,000 euros, whereas the husband had increased the value of his property only by 50,000 euros, after divorce the husband can claim from his wife half of the difference between both gains, which would amount to a surplus of 50,000 euros (100,000 euros minus 50,000 euros), which in turn has to be divided in half; hence, 25,000 euros. This overly simplistic example should, however, not hide the fact that the calculation of the gains and, hence, the compensation claim, in practice, can entail considerable difficulties in evaluating the property, especially so far as participation in businesses, intellectual property rights or immovables are concerned. Furthermore, it might be difficult to establish the facts of the case; information on the relevant property and its value may be totally within the sphere of each spouse. These difficulties are, to a certain degree, balanced by mutual duties of disclosure.[22] According to a recent reform of the default matrimonial property rules,[23] debts of the spouses must be included in the calculation of the gain;[24] thus, a surplus is also considered to have been achieved where a spouse has only managed to reduce his or her debts during marriage. Furthermore, in order to avoid manipulation, the compensation for a gain is, according to the new rules, calculated at the point in time when the application for divorce is served[25]—and not at the, often considerably later, point in time when the divorce has become legally binding.[26]

B. Adjustment of Pension Rights (section 1587 BGB and section 1 et seq VersAusglG)

The principle of the *Zugewinngemeinschaft*, which warrants an equal participation of spouses in the gain achieved during marriage, would be incomplete if the spouses did not participate in future assets, especially in future pension rights.

---

he or she was disinherited or waived his or her succession rights; in that case the *Zugewinnausgleich* is processed by a compensation claim of the surviving spouse against the heirs.

[19] Section 1372 et seq BGB and, in particular, s 1378 BGB.
[20] Section 1378(1) BGB.
[21] Section 1373 BGB. For the evaluation of the assets see ss 1374, 1376 BGB (as to the value of the property at the beginning of the matrimonial property regime) and ss 1375, 1376 BGB (as to the value at the dissolution of the regime).
[22] Section 1379 BGB. See also s 1377(2) BGB which obliges the spouses to draw up an account of the assets at the beginning of the marriage.
[23] *Gesetz zur Änderung des Zugewinnausgleichs- und Vormundschaftsrechts* of 6 July 2009, BGBl 2009 I 1696, which entered into force on 1 September 2009.
[24] See the new ss 1374(3) and 1375(1) sentence 2 BGB.
[25] See the new ss 1378(2) and 1384 BGB.
[26] See the old ss 1378(2) and 1384 BGB.

Therefore, section 1587 BGB provides that in the event of a divorce the pension rights of spouses have to be adjusted. That pension rights adjustment, which is called *Versorgungsausgleich*, has to be conducted according to the new *Versorgungsausgleichsgesetz* (VersAusglG),[27] the new Act on pension rights adjustment. The pension rights adjustment is carried out by the court ex officio;[28] an application of one of the spouses is only needed if the marriage lasted for three years or less.[29] The scope of the pension rights to be adjusted after divorce is very broad: it covers any public or private right which (1) was established by work or capital, which (2) secures against the risks of retirement or disability, and which (3) grants an annuity.[30] The value of the pension rights is determined by the pension provider against which the pension right is directed,[31] be it—in case of public pension rights—the social security body, or be it—in the case of private (occupational or individual) pension rights—employers, pension funds or insurers.

According to section 1(2) sentence 2 VersAusglG, spouses have to mutually compensate each other for pension rights gained during the marriage.[32] Compensation for pension rights is implemented, in ordinary cases, by a so-called *internal* division of the pension rights at the pension provider where the pension right was acquired:[33] the court transfers half of the pension right to the other spouse.[34] If both spouses have pension rights against the same pension provider, or the pension providers involved have agreed on a mutual clearing system, only a surplus of one of the spouses is compensated.[35] Upon request of one of the spouses the pension rights can be adjusted by a so-called *external* division, outside the pension provider involved:[36] the court establishes a new pension right with a different pension provider by debiting the pension account of the other spouse.[37] Apart from an internal or external division of pension rights, each spouse can alternatively claim that the other spouse who already benefits from a non-adjusted pension right pays an annuity[38] or partly assigns his or her pension right against the pension provider.[39] In any case, however, an adjustment of minor pension rights is excluded.[40] Finally, pension rights will not be adjusted if the adjustment would, in the specific case, be manifestly unfair.[41]

---

[27] *Gesetz über den Versorgungsausgleich* of 3 April 2009, BGBl 2009 I 700, which entered into force on 1 September 2009.

[28] Section 137(2) sentence 2 of the *Gesetz über das Verfahren in Familiensachen und in den Angelegenheiten der freiwilligen Gerichtsbarkeit* (FamFG), BGBl 2008 I 2586 (Act on Family and Non-Contentious Proceedings), which entered into force on 1 September 2009.

[29] Section 3(3) VersAusglG. The draft of the Federal Government had proposed that in such brief marriages an adjustment of pension rights should be excluded altogether, see Federal Government above n 4, 51, 48.

[30] Section 2(1) and (2) VersAusglG.

[31] See s 5 VersAusglG.

[32] The exact period is defined in s 3(1) VersAusglG.

[33] Section 9(2) VersAusglG.

[34] Section 10(1) VersAusglG.

[35] Section 10(2) sentence 1 VersAusglG.

[36] Section 9(3) VersAusglG.

[37] Section 14 VersAusglG.

[38] Section 20(1) sentence 1 VersAusglG.

[39] Section 21(1) VersAusglG.

[40] Section 18(1) and (2), s 20(1) sentence 3 VersAusglG. See the definition of minor pension rights in s 18(3).

[41] Section 27 VersAusglG.

C. Post-divorce Maintenance (section 1569 et seq BGB)

With regard to post-divorce maintenance, German law assumes, at first glance, a clean break between spouses by following a principle of individual responsibility— a decision which was stressed by the latest maintenance law reform in 2007.[42] Section 1569 sentence 1 BGB expressly states that, after the divorce, spouses are responsible for their own maintenance. The principle of individual responsibility is, however, riddled with a number of statutory exceptions which show that the mutual responsibility of spouses during marriage[43]—which includes the mutual duty to provide maintenance[44]—does not completely cease after divorce.[45] Those exceptions aim to provide a complete system of protection for the economically weaker spouse.[46] If—and only if—maintenance is not provided by a spouse's existing assets or future income[47] and the other spouse is economically capable of providing maintenance,[48] the spouse in need can claim post-divorce maintenance in one of the cases defined in sections 1570–76 BGB. The common theme of those typified cases is the fact that reasonable work of one of the spouses cannot provide that spouse with adequate maintenance.[49] Following that theme, a spouse can claim maintenance if he or she cares for joint children (s 1570 BGB)[50] or if sufficient income cannot be expected due to the age of the spouse (s 1571 BGB), due to illness (s 1572 BGB), due to unemployment (s 1573(1), (3) and (4) BGB), or due to current education or re-education measures (s 1575 BGB). If the income of the spouse does not suffice for maintenance, he or she can claim supplementary maintenance (s 1573(2) BGB). Apart from those more or less clearly defined situations, section 1576 contains a general rule providing that post-divorce maintenance can also be claimed if due to serious reasons it cannot be expected that the claiming spouse will be able to care for his or her own maintenance and if a denial of maintenance would be, considering the mutual interests of the divorced spouses, manifestly unfair. Such equitable maintenance can be granted, for instance, if a spouse cares for children stemming not from the marriage,[51] but from a former relationship.[52] Taking these exceptions together, little remains of the legislative principle of individual responsibility.[53]

---

[42] *Gesetz zur Änderung des Unterhaltsrechts* of 21 December 2007, BGBl 2007 I 3189, which entered into force on 1 January 2008.

[43] Enunciated in s 1353(1) sentence 2 BGB.

[44] See s 1360 et seq BGB and after separation but before divorce s 1361 BGB.

[45] BGH 15 December 2004, FamRZ 2005, 442, 443.

[46] BGH 11 February 2004, FamRZ 2004, 601, 604.

[47] Section 1577(1) BGB.

[48] See s 1581 BGB

[49] As defined in s 1574 BGB.

[50] Section 1570 BGB provides that the caring spouse can claim maintenance in any case until the child has reached the age of three (s 1570(1) sentence 1 BGB). This maintenance phase can be prolonged especially keeping in mind the interests of the child and the possibilities of childcare (s 1570(1) sentences 2 and 3 BGB) or considering the division of vocational work and childcare between the spouses during marriage and the duration of the marriage (s 1570(2) BGB).

[51] In which case s 1570 BGB already would apply.

[52] See eg BGH 11 May 1983, FamRZ 1983, 800.

[53] Dethloff, above n 7, 47 and 49.

The maintenance to be granted shall cover all the necessities of life[54] and is calculated on the basis of the living conditions of the couple during marriage;[55] the divorced spouses should, in principle, be able to maintain the standard of living which they enjoyed during marriage. The living conditions are mainly reflected by the family income,[56] however, those parts of the income used for capital formation are not to be considered because they do not serve maintenance purposes and, thus, do not reflect the living standard of the spouses.[57] In practice, the maintenance to be granted is calculated on the basis of maintenance tables and formulas that have been developed by some regional courts of appeal[58] and which estimate the living conditions of the spouses and their needs based on the income of the maintenance debtor.

The maintenance reform of 2007 granted the courts some discretion in limiting post-divorce maintenance. According to section 1578b BGB, a maintenance claim can be reduced to the reasonable needs of the claiming spouse, or limited to a certain period of time if a calculation on the basis of the marital standard of living, or maintenance for an unlimited period of time, would be unjustified. Furthermore, section 1579 numbers 1–8 BGB lists a number of cases in which maintenance claims would generally be manifestly unfair and have to be denied, reduced or limited in time; for example, because the marriage lasted for only a short period of time (no 1), because upon divorce the claiming spouse takes up a permanent relationship with a new partner (no 2), because the claiming spouse has committed a crime against the respondent spouse or one of his or her close dependants (no 3), or because the claiming spouse has caused his or her need for maintenance wilfully (no 4), for example by dissipating his or her assets during the separation period in order to be able to claim post-divorce maintenance. In assessing the unfairness of granting maintenance under section 1578b BGB, or the manifest unfairness under section 1579 BGB, the care for joint children[59] and marriage-related disadvantages suffered by the claiming spouse have to be considered.[60]

D. Allocation of the Marital Home and Household Chattels (sections 1568a, 1568b BGB)

Finally, in case of divorce, the marital home and household have to be distributed between the spouses. Household chattels (*Hausrat*) refers to those movables which are used by spouses in their daily life. The allocation of the marital home and household has to be distinguished from the matrimonial property consequences of divorce. Unlike matrimonial property the allocation does not compensate property interests in the marital home and household, but rather ensures that the use of

---

[54] Section 1578(1) sentence 2 BGB including, inter alia, reasonable insurance against illness (s 1578(2) BGB) and retirement (s 1578(3) BGB).

[55] Section 1578(1) sentence 1 BGB.

[56] See eg BGH 23 April 1986, FamRZ 1986, 783, 785; BGH 4 July 2007, FamRZ 2007, 1532, 1534.

[57] BGH 4 July 2007, above n 56, 1534.

[58] See eg the so-called *Düsseldorfer Tabelle*, the maintenance table developed by the Regional Court of Appeal in Düsseldorf, published eg in its 2011 version in FamRZ 2010, 1960 et seq.

[59] See s 1578b(1) sentence 1 and s 1579 BGB.

[60] See s 1578b(1) sentence 2 and 3 BGB.

certain objects necessary for daily life is equitably distributed. Until recently, the allocation of the marital home and household after divorce was regulated in the *Hausratsverordnung*,[61] which provided for a judicial division and allocation procedure. The recent matrimonial property reform[62] integrates the allocation of the marital home and household into the BGB, as was already the case for the provisional allocation after separation.[63]

As to the allocation of the marital *home*, the new section 1568a(1) BGB obliges a spouse to leave the marital home if the best interests of children and the circumstances of the spouses are such that the claiming spouse is more dependent on the marital home or if yielding the marital home is, for other reasons, considered equitable. The latter might be the case if the couple has no children but the claiming spouse has strong emotional connections with the marital home, for example because he or she was brought up in the house.[64] If the home is owned by a spouse, that spouse is only obliged to leave the home if this is necessary to avoid manifest unfairness.[65] In cases in which the court orders a spouse to leave a rented marital home the claiming spouse enters the rental agreement as a party and becomes the sole tenant.[66] If the marital home is not rented, the claiming spouse and the person entitled to let the home (in most cases the owner but not necessarily the other spouse) can mutually claim the conclusion of a rental agreement which is based on conditions customary in the region where the home is situated.[67]

Furthermore, the new section 1568b(1) BGB obliges a spouse not only to hand over, but also to transfer the property of those parts of the household which are owned by both spouses or have been acquired during the marriage.[68] Here, again, it is necessary that the best interests of children and the circumstances of the spouses should be such that the claiming spouse is more dependent on the household, or that the transfer of the household is, for other reasons, considered equitable.[69] However, the respondent spouse can claim reasonable compensation for any transfer of property.[70] The compensation shall be assessed at the current market value.[71]

III. FREEDOM OF CONTRACT IN MARITAL MATTERS

Spouses can, to a significant extent, derogate from the outlined default rules on the financial consequences of divorce through marital agreements. They enjoy freedom of contract in marital matters.

---

[61] *Verordnung über die Behandlung der Ehewohnung und des Hausrats* of 21 October 1944, Reichsgesetzblatt [= former Official Journal] 1944 I 256.

[62] See *Gesetz zur Änderung des Zugewinnausgleichs- und Vormundschaftsrechts*, above n 23.

[63] See ss 1361a, 1361b BGB.

[64] See Federal Government, above n 8, 33.

[65] See s 1568a(2) BGB.

[66] See s 1568a(3) BGB.

[67] See s 1568a(5) BGB.

[68] See s 1568b(2) BGB, which assumes that household which was acquired during the marriage is owned by both spouses commonly, unless the sole ownership of one of the spouses can be established.

[69] Section 1568b(1) BGB.

[70] Section 1568b(3) BGB.

[71] Federal Government, above n 8, 37 et seq.

A. Matrimonial Property

The freedom of spouses to autonomously agree on the financial consequences of divorce relates especially to the matrimonial property relations of the spouses and was recently confirmed by the legislator.[72] The historical legislator of the BGB had already recognised that the principle of freedom of contract in matrimonial property was, in the past, generally accepted in German law and that spouses should be free to determine their financial relations within the borders formed by the nature of marriage.[73] It is assumed that in 90 per cent of marital agreements today, the parties address their matrimonial property relations.[74]

With regard to the default rules on the *Zugewinngemeinschaft*, section 1408(1) BGB allows spouses—under the official heading 'freedom of contract' ('*Vertragsfreiheit*')—to define their matrimonial property regime by agreement. The private autonomy of spouses does not cease with the conclusion of the marriage; section 1408(1) BGB also allows spouses to alter their matrimonial property regime at a later stage until the end of the marriage.[75] Notably, according to section 1408(1) BGB, spouses can, by marital agreement, choose instead of the *Zugewinngemeinschaft* between two optional marital property regimes offered by the BGB: separation of property (*Gütertrennung*)[76] or community of property (*Gütergemeinschaft*).[77] In the case of a separate property regime, the marriage does not, in principle,[78] affect the property relations of spouses: each spouse remains owner of his or her property which is administrated individually, and after divorce no compensation for any change in the value of the property during marriage takes place. In the case of a community property regime the pre- and post-marriage property of the spouses merges to form a so-called *Gesamtgut*, commonly held property.[79] The common property is administered by both spouses jointly if the spouses do not provide differently in their marital agreement,[80] which makes the matrimonial property regime of the *Gütergemeinschaft* very cumbersome as the spouses can only dispose of their common property together.[81] If the community of property regime is terminated, for example, by divorce, the spouses have to distribute the commonly held property equally between themselves.[82]

---

[72] Federal Government, above n 8, 13.

[73] See B Mugdan, *Die gesamten Materialien zum bürgerlichen Gesetzbuch für das Deutsche Reich*, vol IV (Berlin, Decker, 1899) 142.

[74] BVerfG 6 February 2001, above n 7, 344.

[75] See OLG Köln 20 May 1999, FamRZ 2000, 832, 832 et seq.

[76] See s 1414 BGB.

[77] See s 1415 BGB.

[78] The separation of property does not suspend property-related duties of the spouses following from the general rules on the marital relationship, notably from ss 1356–62 BGB or from the general rule in s 1353(1) sentence 2 BGB which entitles the spouses, eg, to use the marital home and household even if it is held exclusively by one of the spouses (see BGH 7 April 1978, FamRZ 1978, 496) or which obliges the spouses to file a common tax return (see BGH 12 June 2002, FamRZ 2002, 1024).

[79] Section 1416(1) BGB. See also, however, the exceptions for certain assets which do not become common property (*Sondergut* and *Vorbehaltsgut*) in ss 1417, 1418 BGB.

[80] Section 1421 BGB.

[81] See ss 1419(1), 1450(1), 1451 BGB.

[82] Section 1471 et seq BGB.

Furthermore, according to section 1408(1) BGB spouses can simply exclude, or later suspend, the default matrimonial property regime of the *Zugewinngemeinschaft*. Such an exclusion or suspension—failing a different stipulation in the marital agreement—has to be interpreted as an agreement in favour of a separation of property regime, as section 1414 sentence 1 BGB provides.[83] The parties can also exclude the *Zugewinnausgleich*, the compensation for a gain achieved during marriage. In such a case, little is left of the default matrimonial property regime of the *Zugewinngemeinschaft*, as compensation for the gain is the most important element of that regime. Consequently, therefore, section 1414 sentence 2 BGB stipulates that such exclusion has to be understood as an agreement in favour of a separate property regime if the marital agreement does not provide otherwise. The same applies if the parties have originally agreed on a community property regime and later give up that matrimonial property regime.[84] The legislator has, in the course of the reform of the pension rights adjustment, which was already mentioned,[85] abandoned the old—and often criticised[86]—rule of interpretation[87] that an exclusion of pension rights adjustment is to be interpreted as an agreement for a separation of property regime.[88]

In addition, through a marital agreement spouses can modify the default rules on the *Zugewinngemeinschaft*, although generally keeping the *Zugewinngemeinschaft* as the matrimonial property regime. Spouses can, for example, limit the compensation for a gain to a certain amount[89] or define the value of their assets at the beginning of the marriage, in order to avoid uncertainty and to ease the calculation of compensation claims in case of divorce. The same applies for modifications of the statutory rules on a community property regime if the spouses have opted for that matrimonial property regime; the spouses can, for example, stipulate in their agreement that only property which is acquired by the spouses during marriage, and not pre-marriage property, becomes common property.[90]

Some[91] argue that, apart from the options outlined so far, the private autonomy of spouses is limited by a numerus clausus of possible matrimonial property regimes in order to protect third parties: spouses should only be able to agree on one of the three regimes mentioned in the BGB (*Zugewinngemeinschaft*, *Gütertrennung*

---

[83] Some however, do not characterise s 1414 sentence 1 BGB as a rule of interpretation but rather as an expression that separation of property is the substitute matrimonial property regime, see R Kanzleiter in *Münchener Kommentar zum Bürgerlichen Gesetzbuch*, vol VII, 5th edn (Munich, CH Beck, 2010) § 1414 BGB para 3; D Schwab, *Familienrecht*, 17th edn (Munich, CH Beck, 2009) 108. For a characterisation as a rule of interpretation now apparently also the legislator, see Federal Government, above n 4, 99.

[84] Section 1414 sentence 2 BGB.

[85] See *Gesetz über den Versorgungsausgleich*, above n 27.

[86] See eg Kanzleiter in *Münchener Kommentar zum Bürgerlichen Gesetzbuch*, above n 83, § 1414 BGB para 1; Schwab, above n 83, 108.

[87] In the old version of s 1414 sentence 2 BGB.

[88] See Federal Government, above n 4, 99 for separation agreements.

[89] See also s 1378(3) sentence 2 BGB.

[90] See eg Schwab, above n 83, 108.

[91] E Körner, *Die Grenzen der Vertragsfreiheit im neuen Ehegüterrecht* (Tübingen, Präzis, 1961) 127 et seq; F Gaul in Soergel (ed), *Bürgerliches Gesetzbuch*, vol VII, 12th edn (Stuttgart, W Kohlhammer, 1988) Vor § 1408 BGB para 12 et seq; W Schlüter, *BGB—Familienrecht*, 12th edn (Heidelberg, CF Müller, 2006) 72.

or *Gütergemeinschaft*) and to use the leeway granted within those regimes. In particular, spouses should not be able to create new matrimonial property regimes, mix the existing regimes or deviate from the essence of all three regimes. This view is, however, not uncontested. Notably, it can be argued that third parties are sufficiently protected by the mandatory property law rules and the fact that the parties cannot affect the rights of third parties not privy to their contract and, therefore, spouses should be free to determine their matrimonial property relations within those general limits.[92]

One express limitation of private autonomy in matrimonial property should, however, not be overlooked. According to section 1409 BGB spouses cannot incorporate by marital agreement a foreign matrimonial property regime by reference to the foreign regime (see, however, as to a possible choice of foreign law by spouses in favour of foreign law below section VI.B.i) or agree on a former matrimonial property regime which has been abandoned by the legislator. Such an agreement would be void.[93]

B. Adjustment of Pension Rights

With regard to the division of pension rights, German law allows spouses to derogate by agreement from the default rules. Apparently, about 50 per cent of marital agreements contain provisions on the adjustment of pension rights.[94] Private autonomy has, thus far, been granted by section 1408(2) sentence 1 BGB for pre- or post-nuptial agreements and by section 1587o(1) sentence 1 BGB for separation agreements, each containing different requirements depending on whether the agreement was contained in a pre- or post-nuptial agreements or a separation agreement. This distinction caused serious practical problems in delimiting pre- or post-nuptial agreements and separation agreements and has, therefore, been abandoned by the legislator.[95] Now, agreements on the adjustment of pension rights are generally regulated in section 6 et seq of the new VersAusglG,[96] which, by virtue of the new section 1408(2) BGB, apply also to agreements contained in marital agreements addressing matrimonial property issues.

By the new VersAusglG the legislator aims to encourage spouses to use their private autonomy and to conclude agreements on the division of their pension rights.[97] By marital agreements spouses can, in general, derogate from the statutory

---

[92] See eg H Dölle, *Familienrecht*, vol I (Karlsruhe, CF Müller, 1964) 670 et seq; Kanzleiter in *Münchener Kommentar zum Bürgerlichen Gesetzbuch*, above n 83, § 1408 BGB para 13 et seq; Gernhuber and Coester-Waltjen, above n 2, 358; B Thiele in Staudinger, *Kommentar zum Bürgerlichen Gesetzbuch* (Berlin, Sellier and de Gruyter, 2007) Vor §§ 1408 ff para 19 et seq; T Rauscher, *Familienrecht*, 2nd edn (Heidelberg, CF Müller, 2008) 252 et seq; Schwab, above n 83, 109; B Brudermüller in Palandt, *Bürgerliches Gesetzbuch*, 70th edn (Munich, CH Beck, 2011) § 1408 BGB para 15. See also the decision of the Federal Court of Justice in BGH 26 March 1997, FamRZ 1997, 800 where the court denied a violation of a *numerus clausus* principle—leaving open whether such a principle exists at all.
[93] According to s 134 BGB.
[94] BVerfG 6 February 2001, above n 7, 344.
[95] Federal Government, above n 4, 50 et seq.
[96] See *Gesetz über den Versorgungsausgleich*, above n 27.
[97] Federal Government, above n 4, 51.

default rules.[98] The VersAusglG contains in section 6 a short (non-exhaustive) list of examples which can be the object of an agreement. In particular:

— Spouses shall be able to integrate, partly or completely, the pension rights adjustment into their general arrangements on the financial consequences of divorce (no 1). Hence, the pension rights adjustment must not be separated from matrimonial property issues.[99] In order to save the costs of the adjustment,[100] a spouse can, for example, waive an adjustment if the value of the pension rights to be adjusted equals his or her gain achieved during marriage and the compensation claim is—in turn—waived by the other spouse.[101] Thus, by marital agreement spouses can embrace the pillars of the financial consequences of divorce.
— Furthermore, spouses can, partly or completely, exclude a pension rights adjustment (no 2). Spouses can limit the pension rights adjustment to certain pension rights and exclude the adjustment of other pension rights.[102] This applies even if the spouse whose pension right is adjusted loses pension rights without receiving in turn, due to the partial adjustment, pension rights from the other spouse[103]—a so-called 'super splitting', which was not admissible under the old rules.[104]
— The marital agreement might, additionally, reserve—partly or completely— compensation claims in cases where a spouse already benefits from his or her pension rights which have not yet been adjusted (no 3). Hence, marital agreements are not limited to default rules for the pension rights adjustment in the stricter sense (s 9 et seq VersAusglG), but can also encompass the already mentioned (see above section II.B) optional compensation for non-adjusted pension rights (s 20 et seq VersAusglG).

As a matter of course, agreements on the adjustment of pension rights cannot affect third parties, especially not pension providers. Therefore, section 8(2) VersAusglG stipulates that pension rights can only be transferred or established by agreement between the spouses if allowed by the relevant provisions for the particular pension rights or agreed to by the pension provider. Only the court should be able to alter the pension rights in relation to the pension providers,[105] which are in any event parties to the adjustment proceedings.[106]

The old rule that an exclusion of the pension rights adjustment becomes invalid if one of the spouses applies for a divorce within one year of such an agreement's

---

[98] Section 6(1) sentence 1 VersAusglG.

[99] Federal Government, above n 4, 51.

[100] See s 13 VersAusglG.

[101] F Ruland, 'Der neue Versorgungsausgleich—Strategien und Beratung durch den Anwalt' (2009) *NJW* 1697, 1701.

[102] See Federal Government, above n 4, 51. For further examples see A Schmucker, 'Vereinbarungen zum Versorgungsausgleich nach der Strukturreform des Versorgungsausgleichs' in P Limmer (ed), *Scheidung, Trennung—Scheidungs- und Trennungsvereinbarungen* (Würzburg, Deutsche Notarrechtliche Vereinigung, 2008) 102, 110.

[103] Federal Government, above n 4, 51.

[104] See BGH 7 October 1987, FamRZ 1988, 153 to which the Federal Government, above n 4, 51, refers.

[105] Federal Government, above n 4, 53.

[106] See s 219 nos 2 and 3 FamFG.

conclusion[107] was abandoned by the legislator in the new VersAusglG.[108] In addition, the requirement that separation agreements on the adjustment of pension rights have to be authorised by the court[109] has not been adopted by the new VersAusglG.[110]

C. Post-divorce Maintenance

Only limited private autonomy is granted regarding maintenance *during* marriage. German law does not allow spouses to prospectively waive their maintenance rights,[111] only retrospective agreements which concern maintenance claims for the past are admissible.[112] However, according to section 1585c sentence 1 BGB spouses are free to modify the default rules with regard to *post-divorce* maintenance, and even to exclude post-divorce maintenance in its entirety[113]—a freedom which is surprising, especially with regard to post-divorce maintenance for the care of joint children (see s 1570 BGB and above section II.C), keeping in mind that between unmarried parents, such maintenance cannot be excluded.[114] Apparently, about 25 per cent of the marital agreements in Germany derogate from the default rules on post-divorce maintenance.[115]

It is a matter of course, that spouses, apart from their own maintenance claims, cannot modify the maintenance claims of third parties, in particular those of joint children against one of the spouses. However, a spouse can undertake to fulfil a maintenance obligation of the other spouse towards a third party.[116]

D. Allocation of the Marital Home and Household Chattels

Finally, spouses can agree on the allocation of the marital home and household,[117] as is also assumed by the legislator.[118] Such private autonomy is, however, as a matter of course, limited by rights of third parties, for example, those of the landlord of the marital home.[119]

---

[107] See the old s 1408(2) sentence 2 BGB.
[108] Federal Government, above n 4, 51.
[109] See the old s 1587o(2) sentences 3 and 4 BGB.
[110] Federal Government, above n 4, 51
[111] See ss 1360a(3), 1614(1) BGB (as to maintenance during the marriage) and ss 1361(4) sentence 4, 1360a(3), 1614(1) BGB (as to post-separation maintenance).
[112] See eg Brudermüller in Palandt, above n 92, § 1361 BGB para 71.
[113] See BGH 11 February 2004, above n 46, 604 where the court held that s 1585c BGB does not contain any limitation to the freedom of contract.
[114] Section 1615l(3) sentence 1, s 1614(1) BGB.
[115] See BVerfG 6 February 2001, above n 7, 344.
[116] BGH 25 February 1987, above n 11, 935. See, however, also BVerfG 6 February 2001, above n 7, 347 et seq.
[117] See eg Schwenzer, above n 7, 90 et seq; Gernhuber and Coester-Waltjen, above n 2, 240; Schlüter, above n 91, 66; N Dethloff, *Familienrecht*, 29th edn (Munich, CH Beck, 2009) 213; L Bergschneider, *Richterliche Inhaltskontrolle von Eheverträgen und Scheidungsvereinbarungen* (Munich, CH Beck, 2008) 76 et seq; Rauscher, above n 92, 591 et seq; Schwab, above n 83, 229.
[118] See Federal Government, above n 8, 21.
[119] Schwab, *Familienrecht*, above n 83, 229.

IV. FORMAL REQUIREMENTS FOR MARITAL AGREEMENTS

Marital agreements are subject to special formal requirements in order to protect spouses against unconsidered and premature agreements. However, with regard to the required form of the marital agreement, German law distinguishes rather unconvincingly between the different pillars of financial consequences of divorce which are touched upon by the agreement. This patchwork of formal requirements often leads to the necessity of meeting the highest formal requirement if an agreement contained in one document covers more than one pillar. If spouses do not meet the formal requirements, their marital agreement is void.[120] As far as a notarised form is necessary, the participation of the notary ensures that the legal background of the agreement is explained to the spouses and that the validity of the agreement is checked.[121] According to German law, notaries—who are, in the regular case, among the most highly qualified and educated lawyers—have to explore the intentions of the parties and the facts of the case and have, accordingly, to instruct the parties about their rights and duties.[122]

A. Matrimonial Property

As to agreements regulating matrimonial property, section 1410 BGB stipulates that the marital agreement must not only be certified by a notary, but must also be concluded in the presence of both spouses before a notary. The same applies for a later change of the agreement[123] or a binding letter of intent.[124] The requirement of simultaneous presence does not mean that the agreement must be concluded by the spouses personally. Unlike the celebration of the marriage, where representation is excluded,[125] the spouses can be represented at the conclusion of the marital agreement. The certificate authorising representation does not itself need to meet the formal requirements for the marital agreement to be concluded,[126] as long as the certificate of authority is revocable and does not bind the represented spouse legally or factually.[127] It has, though, to be noted that separation agreements on compensation for the surplus (see above section II.A), which are concluded on the occasion of the divorce, are privileged by section 1378(3) sentence 2 BGB; here, notarial certification suffices, but can be substituted by a recording of the agreement in a court minute according to section 1378(3) sentence 2 and section 127a BGB.[128]

---

[120] Section 125 sentence 1 BGB. If only parts of the agreement are void, it is assumed that the agreement is void in total unless it can be established that the parties would have concluded the agreement without the void part, see s 139 BGB and BGH 5 July 2006, FamRZ 2006, 1359, 1362.

[121] BGH 18 September 1996, FamRZ 1996, 1536.

[122] See s 17 of the *Beurkundungsgesetz* (BeurkG) of 28 August 1969, BGBl 1969 I 1513 (Act on authentication).

[123] OLG Frankfurt am Main 19 September 2000, FamRZ 2001, 1523, 1524.

[124] BGH 25 May 1966, FamRZ 1966, 492, 495 (as to the predecessor of s 1410 BGB).

[125] Section 1311 BGB.

[126] Section 167(2) BGB.

[127] See BGH 1 April 1998, above n 11, 903 et seq.

[128] As to the intricate delineation of s 1410 and s 1378(3) sentence 2 BGB, see eg Brudermüller in Palandt, above n 92, § 1408 BGB para 14.

Marital agreements on matrimonial property do not have to be registered. However, spouses can register their agreement at the matrimonial property registers maintained by the local courts.[129] A registration of the agreement has the advantage that spouses can assert their contractually agreed matrimonial property regime against third parties.[130]

B. Adjustment of Pension Rights

Formal requirements are especially important in connection with the adjustment of pension rights in order to inform the spouses of the importance of the agreement.[131] Spouses often do not know that the pensions acquired by their counterpart form the bulk of his or her assets; furthermore, unlike maintenance, the adjustment of pension rights might, for some spouses, impact the distant future and the consequences of an agreement are, thus, often underestimated. However, at first glance the formal requirements for agreements on the adjustment of pension rights are rather puzzling. Insofar as the agreement only deals with the adjustment of pension rights, section 7(1) VersAusglG only requires notarial certification.[132] If, however, the agreement on the pension rights is part of an agreement which also addresses the matrimonial property relations of the parties, the stricter formal requirements of section 1410 BGB (notarial certification plus the presence of both spouses) apply; section 7(3) VersAusglG refers such agreements to section 1410 BGB. The notarial form required by section 7(1) VersAusglG can be substituted by a court's recording of the agreement in a court minute, as sections 7(2) VersAusglG, 124a BGB stipulate. Yet the formal requirements of section 7(1) VersAusglG apply only to marital agreements which are concluded *before* a valid decision on the pension rights adjustment, which often coincides with the decree of divorce.[133] Agreements concluded after that point in time do not require any special form because the legislator assumes that the parties do not need any protection, as they—after the divorce proceedings—know their rights and duties.[134]

C. Post-divorce Maintenance

According to section 1585c sentence 2 BGB, agreements on post-divorce maintenance which are concluded before the divorce is absolute also require notarial certification.[135] Again the notarial certification can be substituted according to section 1585c sentence 3 and section 127a BGB, if the agreement is recorded by the court

---

[129] Section 1558 et seq BGB.
[130] Section 1412 BGB.
[131] Schmucker, above n 102, 111.
[132] As defined in s 128 BGB.
[133] Federal Government, above n 4, 52.
[134] Ibid.
[135] As defined in s 128 BGB.

in its minutes. However agreements concluded after the validity of the divorce[136] are not subject to any formal requirements.

D. Allocation of the Marital Home and Household Chattels

No formal requirements exist regarding agreements which allocate the marital home and household chattels between the spouses, to the extent that the general rules on contracts do not contain special formal requirements.[137]

V. JUDICIAL REVIEW OF MARITAL AGREEMENTS

If one takes together the legal principles on marital agreements outlined so far, one could form the impression that German family law follows the motto 'anything goes': the very broad scope of private autonomy vested in spouses by statutory provisions appears only to be balanced by formal requirements warning spouses that they are entering legally sensitive areas when concluding marital agreements. The default rules are only an offer to the spouses, and reflect one of many possibilities for regulating post-divorce financial relations—a liberal view that has been taken by the German courts for decades. In particular, Germany's highest ordinary court, inter alia, in family matters, the *Bundesgerichtshof* (BGH), the Federal Court of Justice, was in the past very reluctant to restrict the private autonomy of spouses: marital agreements were, in principle, enforced even if they totally derogated from the default rules.[138]

A. The Materialisation of Private Autonomy by Fundamental Rights

The laissez-faire attitude of the German courts was brought to an end in 2001 by the *Bundesverfassungsgericht* (BVerfG), the German Federal Constitutional Court, in two decisions,[139] which held that for constitutional reasons marital agreements have, in certain circumstances, to be reviewed and, if necessary, revised. The Constitutional Court stressed that private autonomy is constitutionally protected as an expression of individual self-determination,[140] not only in general with regard to contracts,[141] but also in particular with regard to marital agreements.[142] As contracts are based on the self-determination of the parties it can be assumed that contracts, in general, fairly balance the self-determined interests of the parties

---

[136] Brudermüller in Palandt, above n 92, § 1585c BGB para 4; Schwab, above n 83, 214.
[137] See eg section 311b(1) BGB for contracts on immovables.
[138] See notably BGH 24 April 1985, FamRZ 1985, 788; BGH 28 November 1990, FamRZ 1991, 306; BGH 9 July 1992, FamRZ 1992, 1403; BGH 18 September 1996, above n 121; BGH 2 October 1996, FamRZ 1997, 156.
[139] BVerfG 6 February 2001, above n 7, and BVerfG 29 March 2001, FamRZ 2001, 985.
[140] BVerfG 6 February 2001, above n 7, 345 et seq; BVerfG 29 March 2001, above n 139, 985. See also BGH 22 November 2006, FamRZ 2007, 450, 451.
[141] By article 2(1) of the *Grundgesetz* (GG) (German Constitution).
[142] By article 6(1) GG.

and, therefore, have to be respected—and enforced—by the State.[143] Such private autonomy presupposes, however, that, at the conclusion of the contract, the factual conditions for individual self-determination exist. According to the Court, individual self-determination would not be warranted if, due to an unequal bargaining position, one of the parties alone could, in fact, determine the terms of the contract or agreement; self-determination would be perverted into external determination.[144] Thus, in order to protect the constitutionally guaranteed right of self-determination, contracts that are not an expression of individual self-determination must not be enforced by the State. This 'materialisation' of private autonomy,[145] which can be traced in other areas of German private law as well,[146] conceptualises private autonomy to a lesser extent in a *formal* sense as expressed by mutual legal declarations, but, more notably, in a *material* sense as an exercise of factual self-determination by the parties.

Applying those principles to marital agreements, the Federal Constitutional Court held that marital agreements have to be judicially reviewed and, if necessary, revised, if (1) the agreement, against the background of the default rules, considerably disadvantages one of the spouses by *unilaterally imposing* financial burdens, and if (2) the agreement is not based on a relationship between equals but rather reflects a dominant position of one of the spouses as a result of an *unequal bargaining position*.[147] According to the Constitutional Court, an unequal bargaining position between wife and husband can, in ordinary cases, be assumed if the agreement disadvantages the wife and was concluded before marriage in connection with a pregnancy.[148] This assumption flows not only from the constitutional duty of the State to protect mothers,[149] but also from empirical studies which show that unmarried mothers are still under heavy social and, in particular, economic pressure; unmarried pregnant women may face the alternative of caring for the child alone or including the father in the parental responsibility by marriage—but at the price of a disadvantageous marital agreement. As to the unilateral imposition of financial burdens on one of the spouses, the Constitutional Court demanded an analysis of the family arrangement pursued by the spouses.[150] An exclusion of the default rules might not impose the financial burdens unilaterally on one of the spouses if both spouses are working and are sharing their house and family work equally. The decision must, however, be different if one spouse alone cares for home and children.

---

[143] BVerfG 6 February 2001, above n 7, 345.
[144] Ibid.
[145] As to the materialisation of private autonomy in general see C Canaris, 'Wandlungen des Schuldvertragsrechts—Tendenzen zu einer »Materialisierung«' (2000) 200 *Archiv für die civilistische Praxis* 273.
[146] See especially the jurisprudence of the German Constitutional Court as to the validity of guarantees or other loan securities given by close dependants of the creditor which grossly overburden their financial means in BVerfG 19 October 1993, BVerfGE 89, 214; BGH 13 November 2001, NJW 2002, 746; BGH 4 December 2001, NJW 2002, 744.
[147] BVerfG 6 February 2001, above n 7, 346.
[148] Ibid, 346 et seq; BVerfG 29 March 2001, above n 139, 985.
[149] Article 6(4) GG.
[150] BVerfG 6 February 2001, above n 7, 347; BVerfG 29 March 2001, above n 139, 985.

The decision of the Federal Constitutional Court was surprising but overdue. Prior to the decisions, Ingeborg Schwenzer[151] and other authors[152] had demanded the judicial review of marital agreements based, in particular, on empirical studies which showed a frequent gender imbalance at the conclusion of marital agreements and which documented the weaker bargaining position of women.[153]

B. The Materialisation of Contractual Justice: The Unilateral Imposition of Financial Burdens as the Decisive Criterion

The 2001 decision of the Federal Constitutional Court obliged the German courts to rethink their liberal position. Since 2004, the Federal Court of Justice, in numerous decisions,[154] has developed a system of judicial review for marital agreements.[155] Notwithstanding the broad scope of private autonomy in matrimonial matters and the lack of an indispensable minimum standard for the financial consequences of divorce,[156] the Court of Justice now recognises that the protection intended by the default rules—notably the compensation of marriage-related disadvantages—cannot arbitrarily be circumvented by agreement.[157] The Court of Justice assumes an undue circumvention of the default rules and, hence, the need for a judicial revision, if a marital agreement evidently unilaterally imposes financial burdens on one

---

[151] Schwenzer, above n 7, 111 et seq. The role of Ingeborg Schwenzer is assessed eg by B Dauner-Lieb, 'Reichweite und Grenzen der Privatautonomie im Ehevertragsrecht' (2001) 201 *Archiv für die civilistische Praxis* 295, 304 et seq.

[152] N Dethloff, 'Case note on BGH 18 September 1996' (1997) *Juristenzeitung* 414, 414 et seq; H Büttner, 'Grenzen ehevertraglicher Gestaltungsmöglichkeiten' (1998) *FamRZ* 1, 4 et seq. See also T Ramm, 'Eheführung und Eherecht' in H Lange, KW Nörr and HP Westermann (eds), *Festschrift für Joachim Gernhuber zum 70. Geburtstag* (Tübingen, Mohr Siebeck, 1993) 793, 797 and 798.

[153] Schwenzer, above n 7, 108 et seq, referring to the socio-economic and psychological situation at the conclusion of the agreement, even speaks of a 'struktureller Unterlegenheit der Frau', a structural inferiority of the wife.

[154] The system was developed in BGH 11 February 2004, above n 46; it was further refined notably in BGH 6 October 2004, FamRZ 2005, 26; BGH 6 October 2004, FamRZ 2005, 185; BGH 12 January 2005, FamRZ 2005, 691; BGH 25 May 2005, above n 13; BGH 25 May 2005, FamRZ 2005, 1449; BGH 17 May 2006, FamRZ 2006, 1097; BGH 5 July 2006, above n 120; BGH 25 October 2006, FamRZ 2007, 197; BGH 22 November 2006, above n 140; BGH 28 February 2007, above n 11; BGH 28 March 2007, FamRZ 2007, 1157; BGH 28 March 2007, FamRZ 2007, 1310; BGH 17 October 2007, FamRZ 2008, 386; BGH 28 November 2007, FamRZ 2008, 582; BGH 9 July 2008, FamRZ 2008, 2011; BGH 5 November 2008, FamRZ 2009, 198; BGH 18 March 2009, FamRZ 2009, 1041; BGH 2 February 2011, FamRZ 2011, 1377.

[155] A comprehensive compilation of the relevant decisions through 2008 by the chief justice of the twelfth senate of the Federal Court of Justice, the family law senate, can be found in M Hahne, 'Grundsätze der Inhaltskontrolle von Eheverträgen' in P Limmer (ed), *Scheidung, Trennung— Scheidungs- und Trennungsvereinbarungen* (Würzburg, Deutsche Notarrechtliche Vereinigung, 2008). See also the overviews provided by Bergschneider, above n 117, 14 et seq; A Sanders, *Statischer Vertrag und dynamische Vertragsbeziehung* (Bielefeld, Gieseking, 2008) 166 et seq.

[156] BGH 25 May 2005, above n 13, 1447; BGH 28 March 2007, above n 154, 1311; BGH 17 October 2007, above n 154, 387.

[157] BGH 11 February 2004, above n 46, 605; BGH 6 October 2004, above n 154, 26; BGH 6 October 2004, above n 154, 186; BGH 12 January 2005, above n 154, 691 et seq; BGH 25 May 2005, above n 13, 1446; BGH 17 May 2006, above n 154, 1097; BGH 5 July 2006, above n 120, 1360; BGH 22 November 2006, above n 140, 451; BGH 28 February 2007, above n 11, 976; BGH 28 March 2007, above n 154, 1311; BGH 17 October 2007, above n 154, 387; BGH 28 November 2007, above n 154, 584; BGH 9 July 2008, above n 154, 2012; BGH 18 March 2009, above n 154, 1042.

of the spouses, and if that unilateral imposition is unacceptable for the burdened spouse against the background of the individual circumstances, keeping in mind, on the one hand, the reliance of the other spouse on the agreement and, on the other hand, the nature of marriage.[158] Thus, the Court of Justice stresses to a lesser extent than the Constitutional Court the potentially weaker bargaining position of one of the spouses and the factual conditions at the conclusion of the marital agreement, rather focusing on a review of the content of the agreement.[159] This shift in focus shows that the Court of Justice, as the Constitutional Court, not only strives for true self-determination for spouses at the conclusion of the agreement, but, notably, tries to balance the interests of spouses in substance and to ensure the fairness of the contract.[160] The Court of Justice does emphasise, however, that in cases of an unequal bargaining position the content of the agreement has to be scrutinised more carefully.[161] Apart from the already mentioned agreements in connection with pregnancy[162] this relates especially to agreements with foreign spouses who are dependent on a marriage, for example, for immigration or residence reasons.[163] The formal requirements and the participation of a notary are no adequate substitute for the judicial review.[164]

But when does a marital agreement unilaterally impose financial burdens on one of the spouses? First, it is not entirely clear to which *financial burdens* the Court of Justice is referring. The Court appears notably to have in mind the consequences of divorce for one spouse as far as they are caused by marriage-related

---

[158] BGH 11 February 2004, above n 46, 605; BGH 6 October 2004, above n 154, 26; BGH 6 October 2004, above n 154, 186; BGH 12 January 2005, above n 154, 692; BGH 25 May 2005, above n 13, 1446; BGH 17 May 2006, above n 154, 1097; BGH 5 July 2006, above n 120, 1360; BGH 22 November 2006, above n 140, 451; BGH 28 February 2007, above n 11, 976; BGH 28 March 2007, above n 154, 1311; BGH 17 October 2007, above n 154, 387; BGH 28 November 2007, above n 154, 584; BGH 9 July 2008, above n 154, 2012; BGH 18 March 2009, above n 154, 1042.

[159] See eg BGH 11 February 2004, above n 46, 606 et seq; BGH 12 January 2005, above n 154, 692; BGH 25 May 2005, above n 154, 1450; BGH 17 October 2007, above n 154, 388 et seq; BGH 28 November 2007, above n 154, 584, where the court reviewed the content of the agreement although an unequal bargaining position was denied.

[160] See B Dauner-Lieb, 'Richterliche Überprüfung von Eheverträgen nach dem Urteil des BGH v 11.2.2004—XII ZR 265/02' (2004) *Forum Familienrecht* 65, 66; G Langenfeld, 'Die Ehevertragsgestaltung auf dem Prüfstand der richterlichen Inhaltskontrolle' (2004) *Zeitschrift für Erbrecht und Vermögensnachfolge* 311, 312; J Mayer, 'Zur Inhaltskontrolle von Eheverträgen' (2004) *Familie, Partnerschaft und Recht* 363, 368; S Hofer, 'Privatautonomie als Prinzip für Vereinbarungen zwischen Ehegatten' in S Hofer, D Schwab and D Henrich (eds), *From Status to Contract?* (Bielefeld, Gieseking, 2005) 1, 15 et seq; D Schwab, 'Zur neuen gerichtlichen Kontrolle von Eheverträgen und Scheidungsvereinbarungen' in SC Saar und AHC Roth (eds), *Recht als Erbe und Aufgabe* (Berlin, Schmidt, 2005) 410, 416; D Schwab, 'Trennungs- und Scheidungsvereinbarungen vor dem Hintegrund der Unterhaltsrechtsreform' in P Limmer (ed), *Scheidung, Trennung—Scheidungs- und Trennungsvereinbarungen* (Würzburg, Deutsche Notarrechtliche Vereinigung, 2008) 68, 74; Rauscher, above n 92, 260 et seq.

[161] BGH 25 May 2005, above n 13, 1447; BGH 5 July 2006, above n 120, 1361; BGH 28 March 2007, above n 154, 1311; BGH 17 October 2007, above n 154, 387; BGH 9 July 2008, above n 154, 2014. See also BGH 17 May 2006, above n 154, 1098; BGH 18 March 2009, above n 154, 1042.

[162] See BGH 25 May 2005, above n 13, 1447; BGH 5 July 2006 , above n 120, 1360; BGH 28 March 2007, above n 154, 1311; BGH 17 October 2007, above n 154, 387; BGH 9 July 2008, above n 154, 2014; BGH 18 March 2009, above n 154, 1042 et seq, and the references, above in n 148.

[163] See BGH 17 May 2006, above n 154, 1098; BGH 22 November 2006, above n 140, 451; BGH 28 March 2007, above n 154, 1157.

[164] BGH 11 February 2004, above n 46, 606.

disadvantages.[165] The Court in a later decision expressly confirmed that the judicial review of marital agreements should aim to compensate marriage-related disadvantages.[166] The marriage-related disadvantages concern, especially, forgone income, capital and pension rights for the time after divorce because a spouse has—with the acceptance of the other spouse—abandoned his or her career in order to care for the family.[167] *Indirect* disadvantages of the marriage which have resulted, for example, from the fact that one of the spouses, on the occasion of marriage, moved from a foreign country to Germany and after the divorce will not be able to maintain him- or herself due to a lack of German language skills, his or her education background or state of health are apparently also covered.[168] An extraordinary increase in the income of one of the spouses, however, does not necessarily result in a marriage-related disadvantage for the other spouse.[169]

More intricate is the question of the situations in which financial burdens are imposed unilaterally on one of the spouses. The Court substantiates the rather blurred criterion of unilateral imposition by defining a core area of the default rules which are regarded as essential for the compensation of marriage-related disadvantages: the more an agreement—taken as a whole[170]—enters that core area without compensation, the stricter the review of it will be, and the greater the justification must be for the unilateral imposition on one spouse, especially by the legitimate interests of the other spouse[171]—a core area theory which was already proposed by Barbara Dauner-Lieb in 2001.[172] The core area of the default rules cannot be generally fixed but has floating borders.[173] It is defined by ranking the default rules according to their importance for spouses and their individual situation[174]—which makes drafting sound marital agreements a challenging task. By linking the ranking to the facts of the individual case, the Court of Justice is probably once again referring to marriage-related disadvantages: the more a disadvantage for one of the spouses is marriage-related, the higher the preconditions for derogating by agreement from default rules which are meant to compensate such marriage-related

---

[165] Cf BGH 11 February 2004, above n 46, 608; BGH 6 October 2004, above n 154, 187; BGH 25 May 2005, above n 13, 1447; BGH 25 May 2005, above n 154, 1451; BGH 17 May 2006, above n 154, 1098; BGH 25 October 2006, above n 154, 199; BGH 28 November 2007, above n 154, 586; BGH 9 July 2008, above n 154, 2013; BGH 18 March 2009, above n 154, 1043.

[166] BGH 28 February 2007, above n 11, 977.

[167] Ibid.

[168] BGH 22 November 2006, above n 140, 451.

[169] Cf BGH 28 February 2007, above n 11, 976.

[170] BGH 12 January 2005, above n 154, 693; BGH 25 May 2005, above n 13, 1446; BGH 25 May 2005, above n 154, 1450.

[171] BGH 11 February 2004, above n 46, 605 et seq; BGH 6 October 2004, above n 154, 26; BGH 6 October 2004, above n 154, 187; BGH 12 January 2005, above n 154, 692; BGH 25 May 2005, above n 13, 1446; BGH 25 May 2005, above n 154, 1451; BGH 17 May 2006, above n 154, 1097 et seq; BGH 5 July 2006, above n 120, 1360; BGH 22 November 2006, above n 140, 451; BGH 28 March 2007, above n 154, 1311; BGH 17 October 2007, above n 154, 387; BGH 28 November 2007, above n 154, 584; BGH 9 July 2008, above n 154, 2012; BGH 18 March 2009, above n 154, 1042.

[172] Dauner-Lieb, above n 151, 319 et seq.

[173] Schwab, above n 160, 76.

[174] BGH 6 October 2004, above n 154, 26; BGH 25 May 2005, above n 154, 1450; BGH 5 July 2006, above n 120, 1360; BGH 28 March 2007, above n 154, 1311; BGH 17 October 2007, above n 154, 387; BGH 28 November 2007, above n 154, 584.

disadvantages.[175] To take an extreme example, even an agreement which excludes the default rules in total and is, therefore, at first glance, prone to be revised by the courts,[176] can be upheld in special circumstances, for example, because the spouses concerned never possessed sufficient income, capital or pension rights and, thus, neither spouse suffered marriage-related disadvantages which could be compensated by the default rules.[177]

i. Post-divorce Maintenance

The core area of the default rules, for most couples, primarily consists of the rules on post-divorce maintenance—rules which are regarded as being more important than the rules on matrimonial property or the adjustment of pension rights.[178] However, the implications of the maintenance law reform of 2007 on the judicial review of maintenance agreements are not entirely clear.[179]

In the centre of the core area is maintenance for childcare (see s 1570 BGB and above, section II.C),[180] including those parts of the maintenance that secure the caring spouse against health and retirement risks according to section 1578(2) and (3) BGB.[181] This is not at all surprising, since maintenance for childcare aims directly to compensate the marriage-related disadvantage of a care-giving spouse not being able to provide for his or her own maintenance because of the care of the joint children. According to the Federal Court of Justice, the default rules on maintenance for childcare can only be modified if, in the individual case, caring for joint children and working is compatible,[182] the duration of the maintenance is limited to a reasonable period of time by the agreement, for example, up to a certain age of the child at which personal care by the parents is no longer necessary,[183] or the sum of maintenance granted by the agreement is reasonable against the background of the default rules.[184] The latter might, however, not be the case if a sum was already fixed in the agreement without a 'stable value clause' compensating for depreciation or inflation.[185]

---

[175] Schwab, above n 160, 76.

[176] See for such an agreement the decision in BGH 17 May 2006, above n 154.

[177] Cf See BGH 25 October 2006, above n 154, 198.

[178] BGH 11 February 2004, above n 46, 605; BGH 25 May 2005, above n 13, 1446.

[179] Cf BGH 2 February 2011, above n 154. See, eg, Schwab, above n 160, 79, 80 et seq, 86 et seq, 89 et seq; C Münch, 'Unterhaltsvereinbarungen nach der Reform' (2009) *FamRZ* 171; B Dauner-Lieb, 'Gütertrennung zwischen Privatautonomie und Inhaltskontrolle—Ein Zwischenruf' (2010) 210 *Archiv für die civilistische Praxis* 580, 589.

[180] BGH 11 February 2004, above n 46, 605; BGH 12 January 2005, above n 154, 692; BGH 25 May 2005, above n 13, 1446 and 1447; BGH 25 May 2005, above n 154, 1450 and 1451; BGH 5 July 2006, above n 120, 1360 and 1361; BGH 28 March 2007, above n 154, 1311; BGH 17 October 2007, above n 154, 387; BGH 28 November 2007, above n 154, 584.

[181] BGH 25 May 2005, above n 13, 1446; BGH 25 May 2005, above n 154, 1451 et seq. More reluctant, however, BGH 11 February 2004, above n 46, 605.

[182] BGH 11 February 2004, above n 46, 605.

[183] In general, see BGH 11 February 2004, above n 46, 605, and in particular BGH 28 March 2007, above n 154, 1312, where the court regarded full maintenance for the care of a joint child up to the age of six to be reasonable (which is more than now—after the 2007 maintenance reform—regularly granted by the default rules, see section 1570(1) BGB). See also BGH 25 May 2005, above n 13, 1447.

[184] BGH 25 May 2005, above n 13, 1447. See also BGH 28 November 2007, above n 154, 584.

[185] BGH 5 July 2006, above n 120, 1361 et seq. See also BGH 28 March 2007, above n 154, 1312.

Still within the core area, although ranking below maintenance for childcare, one finds maintenance due to age (see s 1571 BGB and above section II.C)[186] and due to illness (see s 1572 BGB and above section II.C).[187] Maintenance due to age, however, can be excluded in cases where both spouses have already provided for their retirement—and, hence, marriage-related disadvantages are not apparent, for example, because the spouses already have, or will have, acquired sufficient pension rights due to their age, work history or present income,[188] or one of the spouses has undertaken to compensate the exclusion of maintenance by paying pension contributions.[189] Maintenance due to illness can be excluded if, at the time of the celebration of the marriage, one of the spouses is not able to maintain him- or herself due to health problems.[190] In that case the need for maintenance does not result from marriage-related disadvantages. Supplementary maintenance (see s 1573(2) BGB and above section II.C) can also be within the core area if the need for maintenance is caused by marriage-related disadvantages, for example, because the spouses had agreed that one of them would permanently abandon work in the interest of the family.[191]

Agreements on post-divorce maintenance due to unemployment are, however, permissible (see s 1573(1), (3) and (4) BGB and above section II.C), as the risk of unemployment has to be borne by each spouse individually.[192] The same applies to post-divorce maintenance due to current education or re-education measures (see s 1575 BGB and above section II.C).[193] The decision might, though, be different if one of the spouses totally abandons his or her career for a long period of time due to family work.[194] The Court of Justice also has no objection to de minimis clauses, which only grant post-divorce maintenance if the marriage lasted for a certain period of time, as this notion can also be found in the default rules (see 1579 no 1

---

[186] BGH 11 February 2004, above n 46, 605; BGH 6 October 2004, above n 154, 27; BGH 6 October 2004, above n 154, 187; BGH 12 January 2005, above n 154, 692; BGH 25 May 2005, above n 13, 1446 and 1447; BGH 25 May 2005, above n 154, 1450; BGH 28 March 2007, above n 154, 1312; BGH 28 November 2007, above n 154, 584; BGH 9 July 2008, above n 154, 2013; BGH 18 March 2009, above n 154, 1043.

[187] BGH 11 February 2004, above n 46, 605; BGH 12 January 2005, above n 154, 692; BGH 25 May 2005, above n 13, 1446 and 1447; BGH 25 May 2005, above n 154, 1450; BGH 28 November 2007, above n 154, 584.

[188] See BGH 11 February 2004, above n 46, 605; BGH 12 January 2005, above n 154, 692; BGH 25 May 2005, above n 154, 1450; BGH 28 November 2007, above n 154, 584 et seq; BGH 9 July 2008, above n 154, 2013.

[189] BGH 12 January 2005, above n 154, 692; BGH 25 May 2005, above n 13, 1448.

[190] BGH 11 February 2004, above n 46, 605; BGH 25 October 2006, above n 154, 198; BGH 28 March 2007, above n 154, 1312; BGH 5 November 2008, above n 154, 200. Note, however, the decision in BGH 22 November 2006, above n 140, 451 et seq, where the court invalidated an exclusion of maintenance claims although the spouses knew of the illness of the wife. See as to the apparent inconsistencies between those decisions L Bergschneider, 'Note on BGH 22 November 2006' (2007) *FamRZ* 452, 452 et seq; L Bergschneider, 'Note on BGH 28 March 2007' (2007) *FamRZ* 1312, 1313; Schwab, above n 160, 86.

[191] See BGH 11 February 2004, above n 46, 608.

[192] BGH 11 February 2004, above n 46, 605; BGH 12 January 2005, above n 154, 692; BGH 25 May 2005, above n 13, 1446 and 1448; BGH 25 May 2005, above n 154, 1450; BGH 28 November 2007, above n 154, 585.

[193] BGH 11 February 2004, above n 46, 605.

[194] Schwab, above n 160, 88.

BGB and above section II.C).[195] Neither can objections be raised to a limitation of post-divorce maintenance to the hypothetical earnings the claiming spouse would have obtained had he or she continued a career instead of caring for the family;[196] by such a clause all marriage-related disadvantages are compensated.

In that context, it should be noted that not only may agreements that negatively derogate from the default rules be judicially revised, but also those that positively modify the default rules, for example, by granting more post-divorce maintenance than provided by the default rules.[197] Such agreements can also unilaterally impose financial burdens on one of the spouses if the obliged spouse will—due to exorbitant maintenance claims agreed upon—not be able to maintain him- or herself and if the marriage-related disadvantages are overly compensated.

ii. Matrimonial Property

Unlike post-divorce maintenance, the default rules on matrimonial property—and, hence, the compensation for a gain obtained during the marriage (see above section II.A)—are not regarded by the Federal Court of Justice as belonging to the core area of the default rules on the financial consequences of divorce.[198] Notably, the compensation for a gain is—unlike post-divorce maintenance—not regarded as forming part of a persisting marital solidarity between the spouses outliving divorce, especially because it is not aimed at compensating marriage-related disadvantages, but rather at distributing marriage-related advantages.[199] Furthermore, according to the Court of Justice, there are good reasons to exclude the default rules on the *Zugewinngemeinschaft* in specific cases, especially if one of the spouses holds a share in a business the substance of which should not be endangered by later compensation claims by the other spouse.[200] According to the Court of Justice, an exclusion of the default rules on matrimonial property may not even be disputed if the spouses have only acquired minimal pension rights which can be adjusted after divorce, but one of the spouses has realised a considerable gain in the value of his or her assets during marriage[201]—a rather formalistic decision which appears hardly justifiable if the acquired assets mainly serve retirement procurement,[202] and a decision that raises doubts as to whether the liberal approach of the Court

---

[195] BGH 9 July 2008, above n 154, 2012.

[196] Ibid, 2012 et seq.

[197] BGH 5 November 2008, above n 154, 200 et seq.

[198] BGH 11 February 2004, above n 46, 605 et seq and 608; BGH 12 January 2005, above n 154, 692; BGH 25 May 2005, above n 13, 1446 and 1448; BGH 25 May 2005, above n 154, 1450; BGH 28 March 2007, above n 154, 1311 et seq BGH 17 October 2007, above n 154, 388 und 389; BGH 28 November 2007, above n 154, 585; BGH 9 July 2008, above n 154, 2013.

[199] BGH 11 February 2004, above n 46, 604.

[200] BGH 28 March 2007, above n 154, 1311; BGH 17 October 2007, above n 154, 388.

[201] BGH 17 October 2007, above n 154, 388.

[202] More convincing though OLG Celle 8 February 2008, FamRZ 2008, 2115, 2116 where the Regional Court of Appeal reviewed in a comparable case for that reason the separation of property agreement. See also BGH 11 February 2004, above n 46, 605 et seq where the court recognised that in some cases the default matrimonial property rules could have the purpose of retirement procurement.

of Justice towards contractual derogations of the default rules on matrimonial property is fully justified.[203]

iii. Adjustment of Pension Rights

In the ranking of the default rules, the adjustment of pension rights lies somewhere between post-divorce maintenance and matrimonial property, which follows from its hybrid nature: on the one hand, the adjustment of pension rights is nothing less than anticipated maintenance for age and compensates marriage-related disadvantages; on the other hand, it warrants a partaking in assets (in the form of pension rights) gained during marriage and distributes marriage-related advantages.[204] Due to the maintenance function, the Court of Justice assigns the adjustment of pension rights to the same level as maintenance due to age (s 1571 BGB) and subjects agreements limiting an adjustment to the same restrictions.[205] Thus, an exclusion of a pension rights adjustment will not be upheld if, due to the individual circumstances, a spouse will have insufficient pension rights at his or her disposal, for example, because the spouses agreed that one of them should care for the children and, as a result, was unable to acquire sufficient pension rights.[206] The duty of one of the spouses to pay maintenance on account of age does not, however, justify the exclusion of a pension rights adjustment, as both instruments compensate different consequences of marriage-related disadvantages: maintenance is directed to the future, whereas the adjustment of pension rights compensates a lack of retirement procurement in the past due to marriage-related disadvantages.[207] The maintenance function of the adjustment can be achieved if the spouse whose pensions are not to be adjusted has set up endowment insurance in favour of the other spouse,[208] or provides in some other form for his or her retirement.[209] However, this is only the case if the spouse has actually fulfilled his or her obligations under the agreement.[210] According to the Court of Justice, there is more leeway for agreement if the pensions of the spouses

---

[203] See also the general criticism of Dauner-Lieb, above n 160, 66 et seq, 67 and 69; B Dauner-Lieb, 'Note on BGH 11 February 2004' (2004) *Juristenzeitung* 1027, 1027 et seq; B Dauner-Lieb and A Sanders, 'Abdingbare Teilhabe—unabdingbare Verantwortung?' (2005) *Familie, Partnerschaft und Recht* 2005, 141, 146; Dauner-Lieb, above n 179, 591 et seq; L Bergschneider, 'Note on BGH 6 October 2004' (2005) *FamRZ* 28, 28; A Sanders, 'Teilweise sittenwidrig?—Zur Teilnichtigkeit von Eheverträgen, insbesondere von Güterstandsvereinbarungen' (2007) *Familie, Partnerschaft und Recht* 205, 207. See also H Grziwotz, 'Note on BGH 25 October 2006' (2007) *Deutsche Notar-Zeitschrift* 130, 131.

[204] BGH 6 October 2004, above n 154, 26 et seq; BGH 6 October 2004, above n 154, 187; BGH 12 January 2005, above n 154, 693; BGH 25 May 2005, above n 13, 1446 and 1448; BGH 28 November 2007, above n 154, 585; BGH 9 July 2008, above n 154, 2013; BGH 18 March 2009, above n 154, 1043.

[205] BGH 11 February 2004, above n 46, 605; BGH 6 October 2004, above n 154, 27; BGH 6 October 2004, above n 154, 187; BGH 12 January 2005, above n 154, 693; BGH 28 November 2007, above n 154, 585; BGH 9 July 2008, above n 154, 2013; BGH 18 March 2009, above n 154, 1043.

[206] BGH 6 October 2004, above n 154, 27; BGH 6 October 2004, above n 154, 187; BGH 9 July 2008, above n 154, 2013; BGH 18 March 2009, above n 154, 1043. See also BGH 17 May 2006, above n 154, 1098.

[207] BGH 17 May 2006, above n 154, 1098.

[208] BGH 11 February 2004, above n 46, 607. See also BGH 12 January 2005, above n 154, 693.

[209] See the references above in n 186 as to post-divorce maintenance.

[210] BGH 25 May 2005, above n 13, 1448 et seq.

are at a high level and, hence, a pension rights adjustment would fulfil more a matrimonial property function rather than a maintenance function.[211]

iv. Allocation of the Marital Home and Household Chattels

As to the allocation of the marital home and household chattels, so far the courts have not decided whether the default rules are within the core area of the default rules. However, it can be argued that—as with agreements on maintenance for childcare—prior agreements on the attribution of the marital home and household might, in individual cases, impose unilateral financial burdens on the caring spouse.[212]

C. The Legal Implementation

The question, however, remains how the judicial revision of marital agreements is implemented by means of private law. The Federal Court of Justice employs two very flexible general provisions which allow, in particular, the integration of constitutional notions and other overall principles into private law relations: on the one hand, section 138(1) BGB which provides that legal transactions are void if they violate public policy ('*die guten Sitten*'), and, on the other hand, section 242 BGB which enunciates that duties have to be performed in good faith ('*Treu und Glauben*').[213] These two provisions have different legal consequences: Whereas section 138(1) BGB renders an agreement void, section 242 BGB maintains the agreement's validity but limits the execution of obligations effectuated by the agreement.

By using both provisions, the Court of Justice establishes a two-tier review. Drawing on section 138(1) BGB, marital agreements are considered void which would, according to the plans of the couple, already at the time of their conclusion impose financial burdens unilaterally on one of the spouses—irrespective of the future development of the couple and its lifestyle. As a consequence, the default rules on the financial consequences of divorce apply.[214] If only parts of the marital agreement lead to a unilateral imposition on one of the spouses and, hence, technically only parts of the agreement violate section 138(1) BGB, the agreement as a whole is void, according to section 139 BGB dealing with partial invalidity, unless it can be established that the parties would have concluded the agreement without the void part.[215] However, the Court of Justice appears to be reluctant to assume a partial invalidity within section 138(1) BGB; a unilateral imposition of financial

---

[211] BGH 11 February 2004, above n 46, 605.

[212] See also Bergschneider, above n 117, 76 et seq.

[213] BGH 11 February 2004, above n 46, 606; BGH 6 October 2004, above n 154, 27; BGH 6 October 2004, above n 154, 186 et seq; BGH 12 January 2005, above n 154, 692 and 693; BGH 25 May 2005, above n 13, 1446 and 1448; BGH 25 May 2005, above n 154, 1450 et seq; BGH 17 May 2006, above n 154, 1098; BGH 5 July 2006, above n 120, 1360 et seq; BGH 25 October 2006, above n 154, 198; BGH 22 November 2006, above n 140, 41 et seq; BGH 28 February 2007, above n 11, 976; BGH 17 October 2007, above n 154, 387 and 389; BGH 28 November 2007, above n 154, 584 and 585 et seq; BGH 9 July 2008, above n 154, 2012; BGH 18 March 2009, above n 154, 1042.

[214] See eg BGH 5 July 2006, above n 120, 1362; BGH 18 March 2009, above n 154, 1043.

[215] See BGH 25 May 2005, above n 13, 1447; BGH 17 May 2006, above n 154, 1098.

burdens on one of the spouses by parts of the agreement shall in the regular case affect the agreement as a whole[216] and, thus, the question of whether the remaining agreement can be upheld pursuant to section 139 BGB does not arise.[217]

If the agreement passes the test of section 138(1) BGB, enforcement of the agreement can be declined pursuant to section 242 BGB. Invoking the agreement can be contrary to good faith because at the point in time when the marriage has failed, the agreement would impose financial burdens unilaterally on one of the spouses. This can notably be the case if the subsequent lifestyle of the spouses deviates considerably from the perceptions of the spouses at the conclusion of the marital agreement,[218] and the spouses did not, at the time the agreement was concluded, envisage that one of them would incur certain marriage-related disadvantages—thus, such disadvantages were not considered when concluding the terms of the agreement.[219] The spouses might, for example, not have anticipated the birth of children,[220] or at least not the fact that one of the spouses would later abandon his or her career in order to care for family and children.[221] The same applies if the marriage-related disadvantage was foreseeable at the conclusion of the agreement, but not its later realisation. This is, for example, the case where a spouse later becomes ill and, therefore, will not after divorce be able to maintain him- or herself due to a lack of income or capital caused by a marriage-related disadvantage.[222] This subsequent judicial review is, in particular, important: marital agreements—as one author succinctly puts it—are static contracts, however, regulating dynamic relations.[223] In cases of review under section 242 BGB, the default rules do not necessarily apply; rather, the agreement has to be adjusted to the subsequent changes and interests of the spouses,[224] especially by ascertaining their hypothetical intentions.[225] According to the Court of Justice, in ordinary cases, this requires only

---

[216] BGH 9 July 2008, above n 154, 2013 et seq.

[217] Critically Rauscher, above n 92, 264.

[218] BGH 11 February 2004, above n 46, 606; BGH 6 October 2004, above n 154, 187; BGH 25 May 2005, above n 13, 1448; BGH 25 May 2005, above n 154, 1451; BGH 28 February 2007, above n 11, 976; BGH 28 November 2007, above n 154, 586.

[219] A situation which is strongly reminiscent of the hardship rules in s 313 BGB, which are also applicable to marital agreements, see BGH 25 May 2005, above n 13, 1448; BGH 17 October 2007, above n 154, 389 et seq. However, the relationship between s 313 BGB and the jurisprudence of the Federal Court of Justice on the revision of marital agreements based on s 242 BGB is by no means clear, see Dauner-Lieb, above n 151, 326 et seq.; Dauner-Lieb, above n 160, 68; M Bengel, 'Die gerichtliche Kontrolle von Pflichtteilsverzichten' (2006) *Zeitschrift für Erbrecht und Vermögensnachfolge* 192, 195; Gernhuber and Coester-Waltjen, above n 2, 244; Thiele in Staudinger, above n 92, Vor §§ 1408 ff para 16; Sanders, above n 155, 179 et seq; Schwab, above n 160, 75.

[220] BGH 25 May 2005, above n 154, 1451; BGH 28 November 2007, above n 154, 584. However, it is difficult to conceive how spouses can, as the Court of Justices assumes, exclude in a marital agreement maintenance claims for child care (s 1570 BGB) without anticipating the later birth of a child, see Schwab, above n 160, 79.

[221] BGH 11 February 2004, above n 46, 608; BGH 28 February 2007, above n 11, 976 et seq; BGH 28 March 2007, above n 154, 1312.

[222] BGH 28 November 2007, above n 154, 586. See also BGH 12 January 2005, above n 154, 692.

[223] See the title of the monograph by Sanders, above n 155.

[224] BGH 11 February 2004, above n 46, 606; BGH 25 May 2005, above n 13, 1446; BGH 25 May 2005, above n 154, 1452; BGH 28 February 2007, above n 11, 977.

[225] BGH 6 October 2004, above n 154, 187; BGH 25 May 2005, above n 154, 1452.

a compensation of marriage-related disadvantages.[226] Not surprisingly, the Federal Court of Justice apparently tends to favour section 242 BGB, with its greater flexibility as to the consequences of review, over declaring the agreement void by way of section 138(1) BGB.[227]

The preconditions for a judicial revision have to be established by the party seeking revision of the agreement;[228] it is only as far as the agreement concerns the adjustment of pension rights that the review is carried out ex officio, as provided by section 6(2) VersAusglG.[229]

It should be noted that the system of judicial review developed by the Federal Court of Justice has been expressly approved by the German legislator. Section 8(1) of the new VersAusglG explicitly confirms that marital agreements on the adjustment of pension rights have to be reviewed by the courts—a statutory provision which might be redundant,[230] but nonetheless shows that the views of the courts towards the judicial review of marital agreements are shared by the legislator. The legislator assumes that the review will be carried out in accordance with the principles elaborated by the courts so far.[231]

D. The Role of Third Party Interests

The judicial revision described so far only focuses on the interests of the spouses the realisation of which should not unilaterally impose financial burdens on one another. As a matter of course a marital agreement cannot affect the *rights* of third parties. However, marital agreements can in certain cases touch upon the *interests* of third parties—a fact recognised by the courts long before the present system of judicial review was developed. In the past, the courts declined to enforce agreements that excluded post-divorce maintenance to the detriment of third parties, notably public welfare authorities or dependants of the spouse who would have to care for maintenance instead of the other spouse. Such agreements have been regarded as being a violation of public policy in the sense of s 138(1) BGB and, thus, void.[232] That jurisprudence remains, in principle, good law following the introduction of the new system of judicial review. However, the Court of Justice has restricted it to agreements that exclude maintenance claims resulting from marriage-related financial disadvantages.[233] Thus, if a spouse is dependent on public welfare irrespective

---

[226] See eg BGH 6 October 2004, above n 154, 187; BGH 25 May 2005, above n 154, 1452; BGH 28 February 2007, above n 11, 977; BGH 28 November 2007, above n 154, 586.

[227] G Brambring, 'Die Ehevertragsfreiheit und ihre Grenzen' in S Hofer, D Schwab and D Henrich (eds), *From Status to Contract?* (Bielefeld, Gieseking, 2005) 17, 21; Schwab, above n 160, 75.

[228] See BGH 5 November 2008, above n 154, 201 (as to s 138(1) BGB).

[229] See also Federal Government, above n 4, 52.

[230] Schmucker, above n 102, 117.

[231] See Federal Government, above n 4, 39, 51 and 52 et seq, where the government refers to the case law developed by the German Federal Constitutional Court and the Federal Court of Justice.

[232] See BGH 8 December 1982, BGHZ 86, 82, 88; BGH 24 April 1985, FamRZ 1985, 788, 790; BGH 17 September 1986, FamRZ 1987, 40, 42; BGH 17 September 1986, FamRZ 1987, 152, 154; BGH 28 November 1990, above n 138, 307; BGH 9 July 1992, above n 138, 1403 et seq.

[233] BGH 25 October 2006, above n 154, 198 et seq. See also BGH 22 November 2006, above n 140, 452.

of the marriage, an exclusion of maintenance rights does not violate public policy as there is no duty to favour the public welfare authorities. The same applies to agreements which establish exorbitant maintenance claims against one of the spouses and leave that spouse dependent on public welfare,[234] and to agreements which exclude an adjustment of pension rights,[235] at least as far as the maintenance function of the adjustment is concerned (see above section V.B.iii).

Furthermore, the Federal Court of Justice has, in the past, adjusted marital agreements that exclude maintenance for childcare (see s 1570 BGB and above section II.C) insofar as the exclusion endangered the best interests of the child as a third party on the basis of section 242 BGB.[236] This jurisprudence has probably been superseded by the new system of judicial review as maintenance for childcare belongs to the core area of the default rules, not only because it compensates marriage-related disadvantages (see above section V.B.i), but also because the best interests of the child can be affected by an exclusion of maintenance for childcare.[237]

VI. MARITAL AGREEMENTS IN PRIVATE INTERNATIONAL LAW

Particularly challenging are questions of private international law with regard to marital agreements. Problems arise not only from the fact that the pertinent provisions stem from different legal sources: rules of private international law relevant for marital agreements can be found, to a certain extent, in European Union law and in international conventions, but mainly still in national law. Also on the level of private international law, the different pillars of the financial consequences of divorce touched upon by the marital agreement have to be distinguished.

A. Jurisdiction

On the level of jurisdiction, a general tendency to concentrate disputes on the financial consequences of divorce—and on marital agreements addressing those consequences—at the court where the divorce proceedings are pending can be observed. One court should decide on all issues following a divorce in order to avoid friction between different court decisions.

i. European Union Law

Jurisdiction over disputes concerning marital agreements is addressed to only a very limited extent by European Union law. It is only as to post-divorce maintenance that jurisdiction within the Member States in the area of the financial consequences of

---

[234] BGH 5 November 2008, above n 154, 202.
[235] Federal Government, above n 4, 53.
[236] BGH 9 July 1992, above n 138, 1405; BGH 30 November 1994, FamRZ 1995, 291, 291 et seq. An exclusion of a pension rights adjustment to the detriment of the wife was, however, not regarded as affecting the best interests of the child, see BGH 18 September 1996, above n 121, 1537 et seq.
[237] BGH 11 February 2004, above n 46, 605.

divorce is harmonised by European rules. Article 5(2) of the Brussels I Regulation[238] (and of the Brussels[239] and Lugano[240] Conventions) already contains rather rudimentary jurisdictional provisions for maintenance matters. Those provisions are, however, superseded by the new Maintenance Regulation[241] according to articles 68(1), 75(2) of that Regulation.[242] The new Maintenance Regulation by its article 1(1) expressly includes within its scope matters relating to 'maintenance obligations arising from … marriage'—a notion that should also encompass proceedings on marital agreements which modify or exclude the default rules on post-divorce maintenance.[243] The Maintenance Regulation is applicable in all Member States except Denmark; the United Kingdom also takes part in the Maintenance Regulation, as it has notified the European Council and the Commission of its intention to adopt the Maintenance Regulation and this opting-in was accepted by the Commission.[244]

The term 'maintenance obligation' in article 1(1) is, however, not defined in the Maintenance Regulation. As a result, especially with regard to single-pillar systems, the problem of whether a certain financial consequence of divorce forms a matter relating to a maintenance obligation subject to the Maintenance Regulation will arise. For example, it is unclear whether—and to what extent—obligations of spouses created by measures available under sections 21 et seq of the Matrimonial Causes Act can be characterised as 'maintenance obligations'. The Maintenance Regulation has to be interpreted autonomously, not only in general,[245] but, in particular, regarding the term 'maintenance obligation'.[246] Concerning the provisions of the Brussels I regime, which are now superseded by the Maintenance Regulation, the

---

[238] Council Regulation (EC) No 44/2001 of 22 December 2000 on jurisdiction and the recognition and enforcement of judgments in civil and commercial matters, [2001] OJ L 12/1 (Brussels I Regulation).

[239] Brussels Convention on jurisdiction and enforcement of judgments in civil and commercial matters of 27 September 1968, [1998] OJ C 27/1.

[240] Convention on jurisdiction and the recognition and enforcement of judgments in civil and commercial matters of 30 October 2007, [2009] OJ L 147/5.

[241] Council Regulation No 4/2009 of 18 December 2008 on jurisdiction, applicable law, recognition and enforcement of decisions and cooperation in matters relating to maintenance obligations, [2009] OJ L 7/1 (Maintenance Regulation), which has entered into force on 18 June 2011, see as to the—rather complicated—details article 76 and the transitional provisions in article 75. See on the Regulation and its interplay with the new Hague maintenance regime in general P Beaumont, 'International Family Law in Europe—the Maintenance Project, the Hague Conference and the EC: A Triumph of Reverse Subsidiarity', (2009) 73 *Rabels Zeitschrift für ausländisches und internationales Privatrecht* 509. See as to the necessary changes of the Brussels I Regulation, above n 238, the European Commission Proposal for a Regulation of the European Parliament and of the Council on jurisdiction and the recognition and enforcement of judgments in civil and commercial matters, COM(2010) 748 final of 14 December 2010, pp 14, 21, 24 and 53.

[242] At first glance, however, the relationship between the Maintenance Regulation, above n 241, and the Lugano Convention, above n 240, does not appear to be entirely clear. As the Maintenance Regulation amends the Brussels I Regulation, above n 238, the conflict is probably solved by article 64 of the Lugano Convention. In that case, before a Member State court the Maintenance Regulation would apply (article 64[1]) as long as the defendant is not domiciled in a Contracting State to the Lugano Convention which is not at the same time a Member State (article 64[2][a]).

[243] Cf BGH 12 August 2009, FamRZ 2009, 1659, 1660.

[244] See Commission Decision of 8 June 2009 on the intention of the United Kingdom to accept Council Regulation (EC) No 4/2009 on jurisdiction, applicable law, recognition and enforcement of decisions and cooperation in matters relating to maintenance obligations, [2009] OJ L 149/73.

[245] Cf, in general, for all European instruments now based on article 81 of the Treaty on the Functioning of the European Union, [2008] OJ C 115/47: ECJ 8 November 2005—Case C-443/03 *(Leffler)* [2005] ECR I-9611, para 22 et seq.

[246] Recital 11 sentence 2 of the Maintenance Regulation, above n 241.

European Court of Justice followed a rather teleological approach, referring to the aim of the obligation to be characterised. Thus, obligations flowing from the Matrimonial Causes Act can be regarded as maintenance matters as far as the order aims to maintain one of the spouses; that is the case if the measures ordered are dependent, on the one hand, on the need of that spouse and, on the other hand, on the capability of the other spouse to provide maintenance.[247] The same criteria have to be employed in relation to the Maintenance Regulation which replaced the Brussels I Regulation.

The second chapter of the Maintenance Regulation contains elaborate rules on jurisdiction in maintenance matters which adopt the general approach taken by Brussels I.[248] With regard to post-divorce maintenance, the Maintenance Regulation vests the courts of the Member States with jurisdiction in which the defendant (article 3(a)) or the creditor (article 3(b)) is habitually resident. Furthermore, article 3(c) of the Regulation allows spouses to concentrate divorce proceedings and proceedings on post-divorce maintenance in a single forum: spouses can also sue before a court which enjoys, according to its own law, 'jurisdiction to entertain proceedings concerning the status of a person if the matter relating to maintenance is ancillary to those proceedings, unless that jurisdiction is based solely on the nationality of one of the parties'. For post-divorce maintenance, the phrase 'jurisdiction to entertain proceedings concerning the status of a person' in article 3(c) of the Maintenance Regulation refers to the jurisdiction for divorce proceedings, now widely regulated within the European Union by articles 3 et seq of the Brussels IIbis Regulation.[249] Additionally, in order to increase legal certainty, predictability of jurisdiction and party autonomy,[250] article 4 of the Maintenance Regulation recognises choice-of-court agreements; it should, however, be noted that spouses can only choose from a set menu of possible fora, cf article 4(1). Jurisdiction in maintenance matters can also be established by appearance, article 5 of the Regulation. Also noteworthy are two ancillary heads of jurisdiction: on the one hand, the subsidiary jurisdiction of the courts of the Member State whose nationality is shared by the parties (article 6) if there is no jurisdiction in a Member State according to articles 3–5 and, on the other hand, the *forum necessitatis* (article 7) if no court has jurisdiction according to the Regulation and proceedings on the asserted maintenance claim 'cannot reasonably be brought or conducted or would be impossible in a third State with which the dispute is closely connected', for example, because justice in the third

---

[247] ECJ 27 February 1997—Case C-220/95 *(van den Boogaard)* [1997] ECR I-1147, para 22 et seq: 'if ... a provision awarded is designed to enable one spouse to provide for himself or herself or if the needs and resources of each of the spouses are taken into consideration in the determination of its amount, the decision will be concerned with maintenance. On the other hand, where the provision awarded is solely concerned with dividing property between the spouses, the decision will be concerned with rights in property arising out of a matrimonial relationship and will not therefore be enforceable under the Brussels Convention ... It makes no difference in this regard that payment of maintenance is provided for in the form of a lump sum. This form of payment may also be in the nature of maintenance where the capital sum set is designed to ensure a predetermined level of income.' See also BGH 12 August 2009, above n 243, 1661 and JM Scherpe and A Dutta, 'Cross-Border Enforcement of English Ancillary Relief Orders—Fog in the Channel, Europe cut off?' (2010) *Family Law* 385.

[248] Recital 15 sentence 1 of the Maintenance Regulation, above n 241.

[249] Council Regulation (EC) No. 2201/2003 of 27 November 2003 concerning jurisdiction and the recognition and enforcement of judgments in matrimonial matters and the matters of parental responsibility, [2003] OJ L 338/1 (Brussels IIbis Regulation).

[250] Recital 19 sentence 1 of the Maintenance Regulation, above n 241.

State is affected by a civil war.[251] However, a court shall only assume jurisdiction as a *forum necessitatis* if it has sufficient links to the dispute (article 7 sub-para 2), for example, if one of the parties is a national of the relevant Member State.[252] Also very important is the limit article 8 of the Maintenance Regulation places on the power of the courts of one Member State to modify prior maintenance decisions which have been obtained in another Member State or a Contracting State to the 2007 Hague Maintenance Convention[253] or on the power to give a new maintenance decision. Article 8(1) provides in such situations for a kind of perpetuatio fori; new proceedings cannot be entertained by a court of another Member State as long as the creditor retains his or her habitual residence in the State in which the first decision was given[254] and which remains competent to modify the prior decision or to render a new decision.[255] Taking those jurisdictional rules for maintenance matters together—and especially considering the subsidiary jurisdiction under article 6—no space is left for national law, especially as the Maintenance Regulation also applies if the defendant habitually resides outside the European Union. Thus, the recitals to the Regulation rightly state that the 'circumstance that the defendant is habitually resident in a third State should no longer entail the non-application of European Union rules on jurisdiction, and there should no longer be any referral to national law'.[256]

Proceedings on the *other* financial consequences of divorce—and respective marital agreements addressing those consequences—are not covered by the European rules. The Brussels IIbis Regulation[257] is, according to its article 1(1)(a), only applicable to divorce proceedings, but does not apply to ancillary proceedings regarding the financial consequences of divorce even if, according to the lex fori, those ancillary proceedings are jointly heard together with the divorce proceedings. Maintenance obligations are explicitly excluded from the scope of the Brussels IIbis Regulation by article 1(3)(e). The other financial consequences of divorce are also not covered by the Regulation: Recital 8 states that the Brussels IIbis Regulation 'should apply only to the dissolution of matrimonial ties and should not deal with issues such as ... property consequences of the marriage or any other ancillary measures'. The same view was taken in the planned, but failed European Convention on Jurisdiction and the Recognition and Enforcement of Judgments in Matrimonial Matters,[258] which was later superseded by the Brussels II and Brussels IIbis Regulations: the official *Borrás* report explains that the European Convention was meant to be 'confined to proceedings relating to the marriage bond as such, i.e. annulment, divorce and legal separation. ... Despite the fact that they may be interrelated, the Convention does

---

[251] Recital 16 sentence 2 of the Maintenance Regulation, above n 241.

[252] Recital 16 sentence 3 of the Maintenance Regulation, above n 241.

[253] Convention of 23 November 2007 on the International Recovery of Child Support and Other Forms of Family Maintenance [2011] OJ 192/51. The Convention has been approved by the European Union (Council Decision of June 2011 [2011] OJ 192/39), but not yet entered into force.

[254] See, however, also the exceptions to that rule provided by article 8(2) of the Maintenance Regulation, above n 241.

[255] See Recital 17 sentence 1 of the Maintenance Regulation, above n 241.

[256] Recital 15 sentence 2 of the Maintenance Regulation, above n 241.

[257] Brussels IIbis Regulation, above n 249.

[258] European Convention on Jurisdiction and the Recognition and Enforcement of Judgments in Matrimonial Matters [1998] OJ C 221/1.

not affect issues such as, for example, ... property consequences of the marriage, the maintenance obligation or other possible accessory measures' (para 22). In addition, the Brussels I Regulation—after the entering into force of the Maintenance Regulation[259]—does not encompass disputes on marital agreements. In particular, the special rule in article 5(1) of the Brussels I Regulation for contractual claims does not apply to marital agreements on the financial consequences of divorce, as article 1(2)(a) excludes 'rights in property arising out of matrimonial relationship' from the scope of the Regulation.

However, it should not be overlooked that jurisdiction in matters dealing with the other financial consequences of divorce is on the European political agenda. In the future, there might be, for example, harmonised jurisdictional rules for matrimonial property matters for spouses and registered partners. So far, the European Commission has issued a Green Paper on matrimonial property which was recently followed by comprehensive proposals for two Matrimonial Property Regulations, containing, inter alia, jurisdictional rules.[260]

ii. National Law

Hence, with the exception of post-divorce maintenance, jurisdiction in cases concerning marital agreements jurisdiction is determined by national law and in the case of Germany notably by the new *Gesetz über das Verfahren in Familiensachen und in den Angelegenheiten der freiwilligen Gerichtsbarkeit* (FamFG),[261] the Act on Family and Non-Contentious Proceedings, which contains provisions on jurisdiction in family matters. Similar to the European Maintenance Regulation, the FamFG also strives for a concentration of the proceedings on the financial consequences of divorce at the divorce court. According to section 98(2) FamFG, the courts that are competent to determine the divorce proceedings also have jurisdiction to decide on ancillary proceedings regarding the financial consequences of divorce in so far as those proceedings are joined with the divorce proceedings. Proceedings are regarded, according to section 137(2) FamFG, as ancillary if they presuppose a divorce and have been instituted by a spouse two weeks before the court hearing of the divorce. However, the different financial consequences of divorce can also be enforced by separate proceedings subject to their own jurisdiction rules: according to section 102 FamFG the German courts are competent to adjust pension rights if the applicant or the respondent has his or her habitual residence in Germany, pension rights acquired in Germany are to be adjusted, or a German court has divorced the spouses concerned. As to separate matrimonial property proceedings, the court where the divorce proceedings are currently pending has jurisdiction

---

[259] Maintenance Regulation, above n 241.

[260] See Green Paper on conflict of laws in matters concerning matrimonial property regimes, including the question of jurisdiction and mutual recognition, COM(2006) 400 final of 17 July 2006; Proposal for a Council Regulation on jurisdiction, applicable law and the recognition and enforcement of decisions in matters of matrimonial property regimes, COM(2011) 126 final of 17 July 2011; Proposal for a Council Regulation on jurisdiction, applicable law and the recognition and enforcement of decisions regarding the property consequences of registered partnerships, COM(2011) 127 final of 17 July 2011.

[261] Reference above in n 28.

exclusively, sections 262(1), 105 FamFG. After the divorce has become res iudicata, the general rules on jurisdiction of the German *Zivilprozessordnung* (ZPO),[262] the Civil Procedural Code, apply to matrimonial property claims, with the modification that for purposes of general jurisdiction in the domicile of the defendant according to section 12 et seq ZPO the connecting factor of domicile ('*Wohnsitz*') has to be replaced by habitual residence, sections 262(2), 105 FamFG. As to the attribution of the marital home and household chattels by separate procedure, according to sections 201, 105 FamFG the following courts are exclusively competent: during divorce proceedings the court where the divorce is pending, afterwards the court where the common home of the spouses is situated, or, failing a common home of the spouses, the court where the respondent spouse habitually resides, and otherwise (for example, if the habitual residence of the respondent spouse is unknown) the court where the applicant spouse is habitually resident.

B. Choice of Law: Existence, Material Validity, Effects and Interpretation of the Agreement

Choice of law in relation to marital agreements is governed in Germany mainly by national law, which is partly based on international conventions. European private international law remains, so far, almost silent in this area (see, however, below section VI.B.i), with the exception of post-divorce maintenance (see below section VI.B.iii). Notably the Rome I Regulation on the law applicable to contractual obligations[263] is not applicable to contracts in the area of family law, as article 1(2)(b) excludes contracts on 'obligations arising out of family relationships and relationships deemed by the law applicable to such relationships to have comparable effects, including maintenance obligations'.[264] In addition the Divorce Regulation on the law applicable to divorce and legal separation[265] does not apply to the financial consequences of the divorce, article 1(2)(e) and (g), and, hence, not to agreements dealing with those consequences. The German *Einführungsgesetz zum Bürgerlichen Gesetzbuche* (EGBGB),[266] the Introductory Act to the BGB, sets out different conflict rules for matrimonial property, the adjustment of pension rights, maintenance and the attribution of the marital home and household chattels, and by that approach continues the multi-pillar system in the conflict of laws area. With regard to the existence, material validity, effects and interpretation of the marital agreement, on the choice of law level, that multi-pillar system causes problems of *characterisation* and *coordination*. First, agreements that have been concluded under foreign law have to be characterised in order to subject them to the pertinent conflict rules.

---

[262] *Zivilprozeßordnung* of 30 January 1877, Reichsgesetzblatt 1877, 83; Bundesgesetzblatt 2005 I 3202; 2006 I 431; 2007 I 1781.

[263] Regulation (EC) No 593/2008 of the European Parliament and of the Council of 17 June 2008 on the law applicable to contractual obligations (Rome I), [2008] OJ L 177/6.

[264] Cf also BGH 9 December 2009, BGHZ 183, 287, 293.

[265] Council Regulation (EU) No 1259/2010 of 20 December 2010 implementing enhanced cooperation in the area of the law applicable to divorce and legal separation, [2010] OJ L 343/10.

[266] *Einführungsgesetz zum Bürgerlichen Gesetzbuche* of 18 August 1896, Bundesgesetzblatt 1994 I 2494; 1997 I 1061—an English translation of the EGBGB can be found at www.gesetze-im-internet.de/englisch_bgbeg/index.html.

That characterisation can be especially difficult if the marital agreement was drafted against the background of a single-pillar system and a German court has to explore, from a German perspective, which of the pillars the agreement relates to in order to determine the law governing the agreement. Furthermore, different laws can be applicable to a single agreement that touches on more than one of the pillars. Those laws have to be coordinated, especially if the parties have combined the different pillars in their agreement (see as to the adjustment of pension rights, above section III.B).

It should not be overlooked, though, that these problems of characterisation and coordination can be balanced, at least to a certain extent. The private autonomy granted by German substantive law to spouses is complemented by limited party autonomy for spouses on the choice of law level. Thus, at least in some cases, spouses might be able to synchronise the potentially different applicable laws by a choice of law.

So far, registered partnerships and marriages have been treated equally. That harmony ends in the conflict of laws. The conflict rules for partners of a registered partnership partly deviate from the conflict rules for married spouses. This follows notably from the fact that the special conflict rules for registered partnerships in article 17b EGBGB subject those partnerships predominantly to the law of the State where the partnership is registered. Furthermore, a special public policy clause in article 17b(4) EGBGB states that the effects of a partnership registered abroad cannot go any further than is provided for German registered partnerships in the BGB and the LPartG. For purposes of the conflict of laws, same-sex marriages concluded under foreign law—within Europe eg under Belgian, Dutch, Portuguese or Spanish law—are characterised as registered partnerships by German courts.[267]

Finally, as a last general point, it should be noted that the German system of judicial review of marital agreements might be regarded as a part of the German public policy—and, hence, might be applicable, according to article 6 EGBGB, to a marital agreement although its material validity and effects are governed by foreign law pursuant to the conflict rules outlined below.

i. Matrimonial Property

As already seen, section 1409 BGB does not allow spouses to choose a foreign matrimonial property regime (see above section III.A). However, that rule only applies if German law is the governing matrimonial property law. The relevant conflict rules for matrimonial property can be found in the EGBGB. On the European level, the harmonisation of the conflict rules for matrimonial property is still in statu nascendi.[268] In addition, the 1978 Hague Convention on the law applicable to matrimonial property regimes[269] is not in force for Germany. According to article 15(2) EGBGB, spouses can choose in their marital agreement the law of one of their

---

[267] OLG Zweibrücken 21 March 2011, Das Standesamt 2011, 184.
[268] See the references above in n 260.
[269] Hague Convention of 14 March 1978 on the law applicable to matrimonial property regimes, 16 ILM 14.

nationalities or habitual residences and—as far as immovables are concerned—the lex rei sitae as the law governing their matrimonial property relations.[270] In the absence of a choice of law, pursuant to article 15(1) EGBGB the law that governed the general effects of the marriage at the time the marriage was celebrated applies. The general effects of the marriage are governed, according to the flow chart in article 14(1) EGBGB, by:

— the law of the country of the nationality which is shared by both spouses or the law of the country of the last nationality shared during the marriage, but only if one of the spouses is still a national of that country; otherwise
— the law of the country in which both spouses have their habitual residence or had their habitual residence during the marriage, if one of them still has his or her habitual residence in that country; otherwise
— the law of the country to which both spouses are jointly most closely connected.

However, article 14(2)–(4) allows spouses, to a limited extent, to choose the law governing the effects of their marriage—a choice which would indirectly be relevant for article 15(1) EGBGB and the law governing matrimonial property as well. If one of the spouses has more than one nationality, the spouses can, pursuant to article 14(2) EGBGB, choose from the laws of those nationalities insofar as the other spouse is also a national of the country whose law has been chosen. Furthermore, according to article 14(3) EGBGB, spouses can choose the law of the nationality of one spouse for the general effects of their marriage if they do not—and never did—share the same nationality *and* neither spouse is a national of the country in which both spouses have their habitual residence *or* the spouses do not habitually reside in the same country.

The law governing matrimonial property applies also to marital agreements on the matrimonial property relations of spouses.[271] It has, though, to be noted that third parties are protected by article 16(1) EGBGB; as long as the applicability of foreign matrimonial property law is not registered in the matrimonial property registers, spouses cannot assert foreign law against third parties if one of the spouses has his or her habitual residence in Germany or conducts trade there.

Marital agreements between partners of a registered partnership are, according to article 17b(1) sentence 1 EGBGB, subject to the law of the State where the partnership is registered without any party autonomy being granted.[272]

ii. Adjustment of Pension Rights

A special conflict rule exists for the adjustment of pension rights in article 17(3) EGBGB. In principle, the adjustment is governed by the law applicable to the divorce according to article 17(1) sentence 1 EGBGB, which is the law governing the general effects of the marriage pursuant to article 14(1) EGBGB (see above section

---

[270] As to the form of the choice of law agreement see articles 15(3), 14(4) EGBGB.
[271] See eg K Thorn in Palandt, above n 92, Art 15 EGBGB para 30.
[272] An analogous application of article 15(2)–(4) EGBGB is considered eg by P Mankowski in Staudinger, *Kommentar zum Bürgerlichen Gesetzbuch* (Berlin, Sellier and de Gruyter, 2003) Art 17b EGBGB para 41.

VI.B.i) at the point in time at which the divorce application is served. That law also applies to an agreement on a pension rights adjustment.[273] However, it is sufficient if the agreement is valid according to the law which would have hypothetically governed the divorce at the time the agreement was concluded.[274] This exception is necessary; otherwise the spouses would not know at the time of the conclusion of the marital agreement which law will apply to the pension rights adjustment and whether their agreement is valid.

Article 17(3) sentence 1 EGBGB contains the additional condition that an adjustment of pension rights shall only be carried out if such an adjustment is recognised by the law of one of the countries of which the spouses are nationals at the time when the divorce application is served. That exception is, however, in turn restricted by article 17(3) sentence 2 EGBGB, which allows in certain circumstances that at the request of a spouse the pension rights adjustment shall be carried out under German law.

An analogous set of conflict rules for partners of a registered partnership is contained in article 17b(1) sentences 3 and 4 EGBGB, however, with the difference that—instead of the law governing the general effects of the marriage at the point of the divorce application—the law of the State where the partnership is registered applies.

iii. Post-divorce Maintenance

To the extent that a marital agreement concerns post-divorce maintenance, the agreement is subject to the law governing maintenance. The new European Maintenance Regulation[275] does not contain conflict rules but simply refers in article 15 to the 2007 Hague Protocol on the law applicable to maintenance obligations[276] which has been signed and approved by the European Union for the Member States and has—based on European Union law— to be applied by the Member States (except Denmark and the United Kingdom) since summer 2011.[277]

Prior to the Hague Protocol, the law governing maintenance was to be determined according to article 18 EGBGB which incorporated the 1973 Hague Convention on the law applicable to maintenance obligations.[278] According to those conflict rules, which—at least according to the prevailing opinion in Germany—did not only apply to statutory maintenance claims but also to agreements modifying those statutory maintenance obligations,[279] the law of the place where the person

---

[273] Cf OLG München 12 December 2006, FamRZ 2007, 1244, 1245.

[274] Against an application of the hypothetically applicable law K Schurig in Soergel, *Bürgerliches Gesetzbuch*, vol X, 12th edn (Stuttgart, W Kohlhammer, 1996) Art 17 EGBGB para 131. Cf also Thorn in Palandt, above n 92, Art 17 EGBGB para 19.

[275] Maintenance Regulation, above n 241.

[276] See the reference above in n 241.

[277] See Council Decision of 30 November 2009 on the conclusion by the European Community of the Hague Protocol of 23 November 2007 on the law applicable to maintenance obligations, [2009] OJ L 331/17. See also Recital 20 to the Maintenance Regulation, above n 241.

[278] Hague Convention on the law applicable to maintenance obligations of 2 October 1973, [1973] 209 UNTS 1021 (1973 Hague Convention).

[279] BGH 25 October 2006, above n 154, 198; BGH 5 November 2008, above n 154, 200. See, as to purely contractual maintenance obligations, Mankowski in Staudinger above, n 272, Anh I zu Art 18 EGBGB para 119.

entitled to maintenance, the creditor, had his or her habitual residence applied.[280] If the claiming spouse could not obtain maintenance from the maintenance debtor according to that law, the law of the country of common nationality was applied.[281] If the claiming spouse was unable to obtain maintenance from the debtor under either of these laws, German law was applicable.[282] A remarkable exception for post-divorce maintenance was contained in article 18(4) EGBGB.[283] In the case of a decreed divorce, the law applied to the divorce was applicable to maintenance issues between spouses. Finally, German law was applicable if both spouses were German nationals and the debtor had his or her habitual residence in Germany.[284] As with the adjustment of pension rights (above section VI.B.ii), it was also argued here, as to marital agreement on post-divorce maintenance, that the law hypothetically governing the maintenance obligations at the point in time when the agreement was concluded should apply to the existence and validity of the agreement.[285] However, the Court of Justice appears to have rejected that argument.[286] According to article 17b(1) sentence 2 EGBGB, the conflict rules on post-divorce maintenance for spouses also applied to partners of a registered partnership. However, it was disputed whether this also relates to the special conflict rule for post-divorce maintenance contained in article 18(4) EGBGB or whether that provision presupposes a marriage.[287]

According to the general conflict rule of the new Hague Protocol regime contained in article 3(1), maintenance obligations are governed by the law of the creditor's habitual residence. Article 3(2) clarifies that a change of the creditor's habitual residence triggers a change of the applicable law. Important for post-divorce maintenance is article 5 of the Protocol which creates a special escape clause for maintenance obligations between spouses and former spouses: the general conflict rule shall not apply if—upon the request of one of the spouses—the law of another State, in particular the State of the spouses' last common habitual residence, has a closer connection with the marriage, in which case that law shall apply. However, the debtor can defend a claim according to article 6 if 'there is no such obligation under both the law of the State of the habitual residence of the debtor and the law of the State of the common nationality of the parties, if there is one'. Article 7 and article 8 allow the creditor and debtor to choose—under certain circumstances—the law applicable to their maintenance obligations. As the 1973 Hague Convention on the Law Aapplicable to Maintenance Obligations, the Protocol does not explicitly

---

[280] Article 18(1) sentence 1 EGBGB = article 4 of the 1973 Hague Convention, above n 278.
[281] Article 18(1) sentence 2 EGBGB = article 5 of the 1973 Hague Convention, above n 278.
[282] Article 18(2) EGBGB = article 6 of the 1973 Hague Convention, above n 278.
[283] Article 18(4) EGBGB = article 8 of the 1973 Hague Convention, above n 278.
[284] Article 18(5) EGBGB = article 15 of the 1973 Hague Convention, above n 278.
[285] D Henrich, 'Unterhaltsvereinbarungen und Unterhaltsverzicht in Fällen mit Auslandsberührung' in K Schnitzler und I Groß (eds), *Festschrift für Rechtsanwältin Dr. Ingrid Groß* (Bonn, Deutscher Anwaltverlag, 2004) 109, 119; UP Gruber, 'Unterhaltsvereinbarung und Statutenwechsel' (2011) *Praxis des Internationalen Privat- und Verfahrensrechts* 559, 561.
[286] At least it was not considered in BGH 5 November 2008, above n 154, 200. See also OLG Karlsruhe 2 October 1991, FamRZ 1992, 316; OLG Hamm 27 August 1997, FamRZ 1998, 1532; OLG Jena 17 February 2010, FamRZ 2010, 1364; Thorn in Palandt, above n 92, Art 18 EGBGB para 12.
[287] Against the application of article 18(4) EGBGB eg Mankowski in Staudinger, above n 272, Art 17b EGBGB para 54, for the application eg Thorn in Palandt, above n 92, Art 17b EGBGB para 9.

clarify its application to contractually modified maintenance obligations. However, one has to assume that the Protocol applies at least to agreements affecting the default maintenance regime—a view which is also shared by the explanatory *Bonomi* report (para 32).

iv. Attribution of the Marital Home and Household Chattels

As far as a marital agreement addresses the attribution of a marital home and household situated in Germany, the agreement is governed by German law, as provided by the special conflict rule in article 17a EGBGB, which applies between partners of a registered partnership as well.[288] If the marital home or household to be attributed is situated abroad, article 17a EGBGB does not apply.[289] It is disputed whether in that case the law applicable to the general effects of marriage (article 14 EGBGB, see above section VI.B.i)[290] or the law applicable to maintenance (article 18 EGBGB, see above section VI.B.iii) applies.[291]

C. Choice of Law: Formal Validity of the Agreement

The conflict rules mentioned so far do not, however, designate the law applicable to the formal requirements for a marital agreement. Rather, that law is determined by article 11 EGBGB[292] which, in an expression of the favor-negotii principle, supports the formal validity of an agreement by subjecting it to several alternatively applicable laws. According to article 11(1) EGBGB a marital agreement is formally valid if its form complies either with the formal requirements of the law applicable to the legal relationship forming the subject matter of the agreement (see above section VI.B.i–iv) or the law of the country in which the agreement was concluded. Article 11(2)–(5) EGBGB contains some special conflict rules for certain agreements. Article 11(4) and (5) EGBGB could be of particular interest in relation to marital agreements dealing with immovables and rights in rem.

D. Recognition and Enforcement of Foreign Decisions

Foreign decisions on marital agreements must be recognised by German courts according to the general European, international and national rules on recognition and enforcement. As far as decisions of a Member State court on maintenance

---

[288] Article 17b(2) EGBGB.

[289] Especially article 17a EGBGB cannot be extended to objects situated abroad by analogy, see Mankowski in Staudinger, above n 272, Art 17a EGBGB para 10.

[290] For that solution cf eg OLG Düsseldorf 2 May 1990, NJW 1990, 3091, 3092; OLG Koblenz 26 November 1990, NJW-RR 1991, 522.

[291] For that solution cf eg OLG Frankfurt am Main 11 March 1988, FamRZ 1989, 84, 85; KG 5 April 1991, FamRZ 1991, 1190, 1190 et seq.

[292] See eg Thorn in Palandt, above n 92, Art 15 EGBGB para 30.

obligations are concerned, the provisions of the Maintenance Regulation in article 16 et seq apply, rather than the provisions of the Brussels I Regulations which are—for maintenance obligations—superseded by the Maintenance Regulation (see above section VI.A.i). Those provisions distinguish between decisions rendered by courts of Member States being bound by the 2007 Hague Protocol—in which case the need for exequatur (declaration of enforceability) is abolished—and of other Member States. In addition, Germany is party to the 1973 Convention on the Recognition and Enforcement of Decisions Relating to Maintenance Obligations Decisions. Thus decisions on post-divorce maintenance by courts of a Contracting State, which is not at the same time a Member State,[293] will be recognised and enforced according to article 4 et seq of that Convention. The 1973 Hague Convention will be replaced by the new 2007 Hague Maintenance Convention (notably articles 19 et seq, article 48), which is about to be adopted by the European Union (see above section VI.A.i in n 253). As neither the Brussels IIbis nor the Brussels I Regulation is applicable to decisions on marital agreements (see above section VI.A.i), all other foreign decisions on the financial consequences of divorce—and respective marital agreements—are recognised and enforced according to the general internal rules in section 107 et seq FamFG, especially in section 108 FamFG.

VII. CONCLUSIONS

The German approach to marital agreements regulating the financial consequences of divorce can be summed up by the following principles:

(1) The default rules on the financial consequences of divorce follow a multi-pillar system and distinguish between matrimonial property, the adjustment of pension rights, post-divorce maintenance and the attribution of the marital home and household chattels (above section II). They aim, in particular, to provide post-divorce compensation for marriage-related disadvantages suffered by one of the spouses, for example, by abandoning one's own career in order to care for the family and children.

(2) Within all pillars spouses are, in principle, free to determine their relations by marital agreements—be it by pre-nuptial or post-nuptial agreements or by separation agreements (above sections I and III).

(3) In order to avoid inadequately considered and premature agreements, marital agreements are subject to certain formal requirements and presuppose, in most cases, the participation of a notary (above section IV).

(4) The private autonomy granted to spouses is, however, considerably limited by a system of judicial review which strives to avoid marriage-related disadvantages being borne by one of the spouses alone—a system which has been developed by the Federal Court of Justice since 2004 as a consequence of constitutional

---

[293] Cf article 69(2) of the Maintenance Regulation, above n 241. See for the relationship between the Brussels I Regulation, above n 238, and the 1973 Hague Convention, above n 278, before the entering into force of the Maintenance Regulation, BGH 12 August 2009, above n 243, 1660.

concerns expressed by the Federal Constitutional Court in respect of unlimited private autonomy in matrimonial matters (above section V):

(a) According to that system spouses are free, in principle, to determine their financial relations after divorce.

(b) The party autonomy of spouses shall, however, not be used to arbitrarily circumvent the protection aimed for by the default rules, notably the compensation of marriage-related disadvantages.

(c) An undue circumvention of the default rules can be assumed if a marital agreement evidently imposes financial burdens unilaterally on one of the spouses—burdens which mainly relate to the financial consequences incurred by a spouse as a result of the marriage.

(d) Financial burdens are, in particular, imposed unilaterally on one of the spouses if the agreement touches upon a core area of the default rules without providing sufficient compensation.

(e) The core area consists especially of the rules on post-divorce maintenance for childcare and maintenance due to age and illness of a spouse, but also to the adjustment of pension rights.

(f) If the unilateral imposition of financial burdens was foreseeable at the time the agreement was concluded, the agreement is void as a violation of public policy (s 138(1) BGB) and the default rules apply. If the unilateral imposition of financial burdens only occurs later, invoking the agreement would be contrary to good faith (s 242 BGB) and the court has to adjust the agreement with a particular eye to the subsequent changes and to the interests of the spouses.

(g) This system of judicial review has caused considerable uncertainty among spouses and their legal advisors. However, after almost 20 decisions of the Court of Justice since 2004, the system of review is becoming more and more workable. One of the last decisions of the Court of Justice reviewing a marital agreement[294] was celebrated by a commentator not only for its reasoning, but also for the fact that all three instances—the Family Court, the Court of Appeal and the Federal Court of Justice—reached the same conclusion.[295]

(5) The European and German internal jurisdictional rules allow spouses to concentrate their disputes as to the financial consequences of divorce—and marital agreements addressing those consequences—at the court where the divorce is pending (above section VI.A), although spouses might be able to start separate proceedings on certain financial consequences.

(6) In the conflict of laws marital agreements are not subject to a single conflict rule. Rather, depending on the areas affected by the agreement, the conflict rules for matrimonial property, the adjustment of pension rights, maintenance and the attribution of the marital home and household apply in respect of the existence, material validity, effects and interpretation of the agreement (above section VI.B). Problems of characterisation and coordination of potentially

---

[294] BGH 18 March 2009, above n 154.
[295] L Bergschneider, 'Note on BGH 18 March 2009' (2009) *FamRZ* 1044.

different applicable laws are balanced by a moderate freedom of spouses to choose the applicable law. As to formal validity, it suffices that the agreement is formally valid according to the law of the place where the agreement was concluded (above section VI.C).

(7) Decisions of foreign courts on marital agreements must be recognised and enforced by German courts according to the European Maintenance Regulation, the 1973 Hague Convention on the Recognition and Enforcement of Maintenance Decisions, and the general internal rules on recognition and enforcement contained in the FamFG (above section VI.D).

Marital Agreements and Private Autonomy in Ireland

LOUISE CROWLEY

CONTENTS

I. THE FINANCIAL CONSEQUENCES OF DIVORCE

A. Historical Background

i. Social and Religious Context

The notion of social and family life in Ireland was historically premised upon strict Catholic teaching, reflecting the views of most Irish citizens in the 1930s and in particular the identity for Ireland and its citizens favoured by Eamon de Valera, founder of Fianna Fail and the person largely responsible for the drafting of Ireland's 1937 Constitution. For many years Catholic Church involvement in the State's approach to the legal regulation of personal choice was not only prevalent, but expected by the people and lawmakers of Ireland. The influence of Catholicism is particularly reflected in Article 41's limitation of the constitutional family to one based on marriage, and the identification of the woman's role within the family as one preferably confined to the domestic duties of a mother and a wife.[1] In 1950/51 the collapse of the proposed Mother and Child scheme, intended to provide medical support for mothers and children irrespective of their marital or personal circumstances, came about directly as a result of strenuous objections from the Bishops of Ireland, and served as a reminder of the extent of the Church's influence on state policy.[2] This influence was difficult to defeat, given the almost absolute affiliation to Catholicism amongst Irish citizens, and perhaps even more importantly, the manner and extent to which the Articles of the Irish Constitution are premised upon the ultimate authority of the Holy Trinity.[3] Such deference to the Catholic Church influenced in particular the State's capacity to regulate the family, which was regarded as autonomous and expressly regarded as 'superior to all positive law'. Consequently the prohibition on divorce was an expected aspect of the vision of Ireland as a Catholic state, with the State unwilling to challenge the supremacy of the marital union and thus adamantly refusing to permit the dissolution of a marriage.

ii. Constitutional Reform and the Introduction of Divorce

In more recent years the influence of the Catholic Church has waned and Catholic teachings in respect of the family and personal autonomy are far less relevant to individual and state decisions regarding the regulation of the family and, in particular, to the development of legal remedies for marital breakdown. Kennedy in her Economic and Social Research Institute (ESRI) research paper, published prior to the introduction

---

[1] Art 41.3.1 provides that 'The State pledges itself to guard with special care the institution of Marriage, on which the Family is founded, and to protect it against attack.' In addition, Art 41.2.1 recognises that 'In particular, the State recognises that by her life within the home, woman gives to the State a support without which the common good cannot be achieved.'

[2] The scheme, proposed by the then Minister for Health Noel Browne, proposed to provide medical care for mothers and newborn children, irrespective of the marital status of the mother. The Bishops of Ireland objected to the State's failure to distinguish between mothers and children born within a marital family unit and mothers whose children were born outside wedlock.

[3] The Preamble to the Constitution commences as follows: 'In the Name of the Most Holy Trinity, from whom all authority and to Whom, as our final end, all actions both of men and States must be referred ...'.

of the legislative remedies of judicial separation and divorce, noted the undeniable changes in 'social and economic conditions, and [how the]... accompanying changes in values and policies have raised fundamental questions about the nature, role and limits of the family.'[4] This diminution of societal deference towards the marital family and the growth in the development and acceptance of alternate family formations[5] forced the state to provide practical support and remedies for those affected by marital breakdown and focused attention upon the very real need for legal capacity to dissolve the union in appropriate circumstances. Kennedy noted the significant developments with regard to the family in Irish society in the 50 years since the publication of the Irish Constitution and the manner in which the changing family has contributed to 'great change in Irish society and the Irish economy'.[6] The cultural, societal and moral norms that existed in 1937, and thus influenced both the drafting and interpretation of the Constitution, had undoubtedly shifted by 1989 when the state first enacted the remedy of judicial separation for marital breakdown.[7] Such changes were necessitated by changing societal circumstances in which marital breakdown was more openly admitted and socially accepted.

The first referendum of the people required to delete the constitutional prohibition on divorce was held on 26 June 1986[8] and was strongly defeated.[9] It has been suggested that the lack of consideration and clarification of the economic consequences of divorce and the consequential uncertainty served to fortify the cautious conservative views of Irish citizens and ultimately dissuaded voters on the basis that such a change was fraught with danger, particularly for the economically more vulnerable spouse.[10] Kennedy suggests that the uncertainty regarding the viability

---

[4] F Kennedy, *Family, Economy and Government in Ireland* (ESRI General Research Series Paper no 143, January 1989) 9. Kennedy cites Goode's observations regarding the impact of the expansion of an economic system through industrialisation and the consequential change to family patterns.

[5] Legal protection and recognition of the rights of cohabitees and legal facilitation and regulation of the registration of civil partnership is now permitted and regulated by the terms of the Civil Partnership and Certain Rights and Obligations of Cohabitants Act 2010, which became effective on 4 January 2011.

[6] Kennedy, above n 4, 8.

[7] Judicial Separation and Family Law Reform Act 1989 (the 1989 Act). Beale noted 'the social and economic changes of recent years, during which significant changes in the status of women have taken place': J Beale, *Women in Ireland; Voices of Change* (Dublin, Gill and Macmillan, 1986) 6.

[8] The Tenth Amendment of the Constitution Bill 1986 proposed that the prohibition on divorce be deleted from the Constitution and be replaced by the following wording in Art 41.3.2:

Where, and only where, such court established under this Constitution as may be prescribed by law is satisfied that:

i a marriage has failed,

ii the failure has continued for a period of, or periods amounting to, at least five years,

iii that there is no reasonable possibility of reconciliation between the parties to the marriage, and

iv any other condition prescribed by law has been complied with,

the court may in accordance with law grant a dissolution of the marriage provided that the court is satisfied that adequate and proper provision having regard to the circumstances will be made for any dependent spouse and for any child who is dependent on either spouse.

[9] The referendum to remove the constitutional prohibition on divorce was defeated by 63% to 37%.

[10] See further CP James, 'Céad Míle Fáilte? Ireland Welcomes Divorce: The 1995 Irish Divorce Referendum and the Family (Divorce) Act of 1996' 8 *Duke Journal of Comparative & International Law* 175, 195 f. James notes that many of the essential financial issues, including pension and succession rights, were 'not worked out until the very eve of the Referendum'. See also W Binchy, *Is Divorce the Answer? An Examination of No-Fault Divorce Against the Background of the Irish Debate* (Dublin, Irish Academic Press, 1984); and P Ward, *Divorce in Ireland: Who Should Bear the Cost?* (Cork, Cork University Press, 1993).

of a claim by a dependent spouse for a share in the family home as compensation for her indirect contribution to their joint wealth, or for loss suffered from forgoing her career, needed further consideration, the lack of which had led to confusion in the run-up to the referendum.[11] The existence of such significant, yet unanswered, policy questions in respect of divorce and its potential consequences merely served to bolster the position of the anti-amendment lobby, and ultimately contributed to the defeat of the 1986 referendum.

A more pro-active government approach was apparent in the lead-up to the second referendum on divorce, held in 1995. As part of its pro-change campaign the Government commissioned a study which resulted in the publication and distribution of an outline of the procedures attaching to the proposed remedy of divorce for public consideration and debate.[12] The study, entitled *The Right to Remarry: A Government Information Paper on the Divorce Referendum*, was published two months before the referendum and did not attempt to disguise the Government's very pro-change stance. In its introduction, the Paper was declared to be 'a guide to members of the public who wished to inform themselves about the legislative and other provisions which would apply if divorce was introduced'.[13] This contrasts sharply with the information vacuum within which the 1986 referendum took place.[14] However, as the debate progressed, it became apparent that the economic issues attaching to a decree of divorce were quite a secondary issue for the electorate. It is evident from the information paper and contemporary commentary that the emphasis was centred on the impact of divorce on the institution of marriage and Irish society generally, the implication being that to focus the debate on the financial consequences was to belittle marriage and the marital union, and was thus inappropriate, if not offensive, in the eyes of Irish society. Similarly with reference to the 1986 referendum, Dillon notes that economic issues never formed a central part of the Irish divorce debate, and for them to have done so 'would have been perceived as trivialising marriage'.[15] She expresses the view that for the Government to have 'initiated arguments for divorce grounded in the context of its practical and economic consequences would have been to exacerbate the radical nature of their proposals and to de-legitimate further their agenda.'[16]

---

[11] Kennedy, above n 4, 86.

[12] It had previously been suggested in the course of the debates surrounding the enactment of the 1989 Act that its speedy passage through the Oireachtas and general cross-party support was greatly aided by the detailed nature of the draft legislation. Deputy McCartan suggested that the defeated 1986 referendum might well have succeeded if the Government at that time had published 'simple legislation similar to [the 1987 Bill] ... which would have helped people to find an answer to ... questions.' Deputy McCartan was critical of the Government's failure in 1986 to 'have the political courage ... to see the matter through and to couple it with effective legislation.' Dail Debates Vol 377 9 Feb 1989—Second Stage (Resumed) of the Judicial Separation and Family Law Reform Bill 1987, 1632.

[13] *The Right to Remarry: A Government Information Paper on the Divorce Referendum* (1995) Pl 1932; introduction at 5.

[14] Ward, in advance of the 1995 referendum, noted that the Minister for Justice, with responsibility for tabling the draft legislation, was taking the steps necessary 'to avoid the absence of a comprehensive legislative framework for the introduction of divorce which was so apparent during the debate in 1986.' P Ward, 'The Path to Divorce' (1994) 12 *Irish Law Times* 29.

[15] M Dillon, *Debating Divorce: Moral Conflict in Ireland* (Kentucky, University Press of Kentucky, 1993) 46.

[16] Ibid.

The draft Family Law (Divorce) Bill, included as an appendix to the information paper, outlined the proposed process for the grant of a decree of divorce and, where appropriate, ancillary financial relief. It was proposed that such orders would be determined on the basis of unfettered judicial discretion and applications for financial relief could be validly made on the granting of the decree or at any time thereafter.[17] Why the proposed Irish divorce laws ensured that inter-spousal financial responsibilities would need to survive every marriage dissolution is unclear, as is the infinite right of a spouse to make claims for ancillary relief orders in respect of earnings and assets of the former spouse, secured well after the marriage has ended. The lack of a statutory right to apply for a clean break or any judicial right to impose a clean break reflects a conservative approach on the part of the drafters, who sought to ensure that financial ties would remain and be enforceable wherever necessary. It appears that in recognising the need to properly inform the public, the Government was forced to take a premature stance on the process to be enacted, arguably causing the adoption of a conservative statutory approach to avoid the alienation of undecided voters or those who might disapprove of a limited approach to the availability of financial relief.

The referendum was held on 24 November 1995 and was carried by a mere 9,114 votes: 50.28 per cent of the people voting supported the proposed amendment. Thus, although the pro-amendment groups were successful in their campaign, it was immediately apparent that this was not a popular mandate, especially as only two-thirds of the people had voted, meaning only one-third of the Irish electorate had voted in favour of the introduction of divorce.

B. Introduction of the Remedy of Divorce to Ireland

i. Current Regulatory Provisions for Ancillary Relief on Divorce

One of the main bases upon which the Irish Government succeeded in convincing the Irish electorate in 1995 to vote positively in respect of the proposed deletion of the constitutional ban on divorce, was to convince them that the vulnerable spouse would not be left destitute should the remedy become available to the Irish people. In order to prove its commitment to the financially dependent spouse, the Government ensured that both the proposed amendment to the Constitution and the Divorce Bill contained the requirement that prior to the granting of a decree of divorce, the court would need to be satisfied that 'such provision as the court considers proper having regard to the circumstances exists or will be made for the spouses and any dependent members of the family'.[18] Failure to secure this standard of provision for the parties serves to prevent the ordering of the decree of divorce.

Part III of the Family Law (Divorce) Act 1996 (the Divorce Act) grants wide-ranging powers to the courts to make one or more of an extensive array of orders

---

[17] This infinite right to apply arises in respect of all orders for ancillary relief as outlined in ss 13–18 of the Family Law (Divorce) Act 1996.

[18] This quote represents part of the wording of the proposed amendment to the Constitution, now contained in Art 41.3.2 of the Constitution, also included in s 5(1) of the Family Law (Divorce) Act 1996.

to provide for the financial needs of the applicant, respondent and any dependent members of the family.[19] Immediately the breadth of the powers of the judiciary in divorce proceedings is apparent; it is open to either spouse to apply for any or every form of ancillary relief provided for by the Divorce Act[20] at the time of making the initial application or defence and counterclaim to the court, or at any time into the future, save where the proposed applicant has remarried. Once any such application is before the court, the judiciary is entitled to make whatever order it considers appropriate, once it is satisfied that 'it would be in the interest of justice to do so.'[21] It is for the courts to decide if this is the case and any directions in the Divorce Act simply serve as guidelines for the judiciary.

The judiciary can make an order in respect of any assets held legally or equitably by the parties, jointly, individually or otherwise.[22] However, notwithstanding these broad powers to make whatever order is necessary, there is no requirement that ancillary relief orders be made in every case.[23] Rather, the legislature is distinctly silent on the over-riding aims of the legislation, preferring to identify basic pre-requisites, financial and otherwise, for the granting of the decree, and to set out a series of issues and factors which might particularly, but not exhaustively, influence the deliberations of the presiding judge. The detailed contents, in particular of section 20(2)(a)-(l) setting out the 12 factors to which the courts must have regard to, merely serve to confirm the power, if not duty, of the courts to decide each case with primary and almost absolute reference to the individual circumstances before them. For the most part the Irish judiciary have welcomed this delegation of power, which, in not identifying strict principles and policies, has encouraged the judiciary to decide each case on its own merits. This has been strengthened by the suggestion from the Supreme Court that judges should avoid the creation of judicially developed principles and guidelines, preferring that the courts retain their freedom to decide each case in its own right:

> It is only with the greatest care, therefore, that one should formulate any general propositions. The judge must always, and in every case, have regard to the particular circumstances of the case.[24]

---

[19] For a detailed consideration of the remedy of divorce under Irish law, see further L Crowley, 'Divorce Law in Ireland—facilitating or frustrating the resolution process?' [2004] 16(1) *Child and Family Law Quarterly* 49.

[20] s 13—periodical payments and lump sum orders; s 14—property adjustment orders; s 15—miscellaneous ancillary orders; s 16—financial compensation orders; s 17—pension adjustment orders; s 18—provision from estate of deceased spouse; s 19—orders for the sale of property.

[21] s 20(5).

[22] The only attempt to identify what might be available for distribution is found in the Rules of the Court and relates to the content of the mandatory affidavit of means which must be signed and sworn by both parties to the proceedings. The affidavit of means must accompany the Family Law Civil Bill when filed with the court to commence proceedings, or equally the defence and counterclaim where the proceedings are being defended. Ord 70A as enacted by the Rules of the Superior Courts (No 3) 1997 SI 343/1997, requires the deponent of the affidavit to declare all the assets to which he or she is 'legally or beneficially entitled'.

[23] O'Higgins J has emphasised in *MP v AP* [2005] IEHC 326, at p 25 of the transcript, that the law 'does not mandate any particular ancillary form of order in divorce cases.'

[24] *T v T* [2002] 3 IR 321, 418 per Fennelly J. Similarly Murray J in the same case emphasised at 409 that 'Each case will necessarily depend on its own particular circumstances.'

ii. Proper Provision

As a regulatory standard of provision to be achieved on marital breakdown, the concept of proper provision when introduced in 1996 was a novel benchmark under Irish matrimonial law. When first enacted, the Family Law Act 1995 (the 1995 Act), which governs ancillary relief on judicial separation, included, in section 16, a reference to the making of 'adequate' and 'reasonable' provision for the spouses and dependent members of the family on separation. When defending the proper provision requirement on divorce, Minister Taylor emphasised that it 'is similar to the situation that pertains at present with regard to separation applications', noting that this requirement 'would be the position on divorce as it is now on separation'.[25] Of course, this is not strictly correct, given that the statutory requirement on separation up to the enactment of the Divorce Act was the making of 'adequate' and 'reasonable' provision. However, subsequent to the passing of the referendum and the enactment of the Divorce Act, proper provision was substituted as the new test for judicial separation by section 52(h).[26] Thus, whatever differences between the remedies of judicial separation and divorce, the statutory approach in respect of ancillary financial relief has been to avoid such distinctions, giving rise to almost identical governing statutory regimes.[27]

It is arguable that the only identifiable policy aim of the Irish divorce process immediately upon the passing of the 1995 referendum was the overriding obligation to ensure that proper provision is made for the spouses and dependent children of the marriage. This prerequisite has since been regarded as the central focus when securing the remedy, such provision being determined with reference to other aspects of the Divorce Act:

> The scheme established under the Act of 1996 is not a division of property. The scheme established under the Act of 1996 provides for proper provision, not division. It is not a question of dividing the assets at the trial on a percentage or equal basis. However, all circumstances of the family, including the particular factors referred to in s. 20(2) of the Act of 1996, are relevant in assessing the matter of provision from the assets.[28]

Pursuant to its constitutional and legislative obligations, the court must be so satisfied and the parties cannot contract out of this inter-parte obligation.[29]

Despite varying judicial statements on the matter, it appears that the time for assessing whether proper provision has been made for the parties is at the date of the

---

[25] Seanad Eireann Debates Vol 144 18 10 1995, 1678.

[26] The constitutional imperative of proper provision is confined to divorce, as distinct from judicial separation. However, the mirroring of the statutory regulation of judicial separation to include the same test of proper provision is again evident in this context.

[27] In *AK v JK* [2008] IEHC 341 [14], in the context of an application to vary existing ancillary relief orders made on foot of a decree of judicial separation, Abbott J noted that the test of proper provision for separating parties 'is to be informed by the test of justice'.

[28] *T v T* above n 24, 383 (Denham J). Buckley has suggested, with reference to this Supreme Court judgment, that 'the emphasis of the Supreme Court on "proper provision" rather than the "division" of assets was designed to rule out any strict rules or principles on division and to ensure that the prescribed statutory factors were fully considered in each case': LA Buckley, '"Proper Provision" and "Property Division": Partnership in Irish Matrimonial Property Law in the Wake of *T v T*' [2004] 7(3) *Irish Journal of Family Law* 8, 13.

[29] See section III C below, which considers the relevance of pre-existing separation agreements.

divorce hearing.[30] More typically perhaps, proper provision is often secured over a period of time, thereby allowing a decree to be granted in limited resources cases. Although the parties may not be able to afford to finalise matters immediately, the decree is not necessarily denied by the courts. To meet the precondition of proper provision, such circumstances often require the ordering of ongoing maintenance and other arrangements to allow proper provision to be made over an extended period of time, as necessary. In *JC v MC*[31] Abbott J considered the proper provision requirement in light of economic realities and emphasised that the making of proper provision at the time of the decree or into the future is a 'condition precedent' of the granting of a divorce, creating a situation:

> where a court is obliged as a preliminary to a divorce to assess the capacity in the future for provision but leaving the actual delivery of such provision to the future as in the case of maintenance or other executory possibilities including the frequently occurring pension provisions the effects of which may only 'kick in' in certain cases well into the future.[32]

An alternative interpretation of the proper provision standard was delivered by Hardiman J, where, in the context of an application for divorce with ancillary relief where the parties had executed a separation agreement 13 years earlier, he defined the concept of 'proper' provision by relying upon the notion of what might be 'fit, apt or suitable'.[33] It appears that Hardiman J focused on what he regarded as just for all the parties and proper in the circumstances, as distinct from what might be regarded as proper *financial* provision for the parties, thereby presenting a distinctly alternative interpretation of the statutory requirement.[34]

The term 'proper provision' has not been defined in any part of the Divorce Act and thus must be determined judicially in the circumstances of each case. In the course of the passage of the Divorce Bill, Deputy Gallagher recognised this constitutional prerequisite as a 'general statement which is open to wide interpretation.'[35] Consequently he welcomed the inclusion of statutory factors to which the court is obliged to have regard, and emphasised the importance of the 'specific criteria that must be taken into account by the court' as set out by the legislature.[36]

As a starting point it has been emphasised by the courts that proper provision does not mean that the dependent spouse should receive financial support to provide merely for his or her basic needs. It has been judicially asserted that any surplus

---

[30] See the views of the Supreme Court in *T v T* above n 24 and those of Finlay Geoghegan J in *RG v CG* [2005] 2 IR 418, as discussed in section III C below. Similarly in *AB v RB* [2005] IEHC 456, O'Higgins J at p 11 of the transcript confirmed that it is the duty of the court in the context of divorce proceedings to 'assess whether proper provision exists for the parties at the date of the hearing'. Conversely, and somewhat controversially, Hardiman J appears to suggest in *WA v MA* [2005] 1 IR 1 that a 13-year-old separation settlement satisfied the proper provision test on a subsequent application for divorce, given that it was deemed sufficient by the parties when executed.

[31] *JC v MC* (High Court, 22 January 2007) (Abbott J).

[32] Ibid, p 23 of the transcript. Notwithstanding the doubts expressed by some members of the court in the earlier case of *T v T* above n 24, Abbott J, again at p 23 of the transcript, referred to the yardstick of equal contributions and one-third/two-third division of assets between the breadwinner and homemaker as being 'the authority of the Supreme Court'.

[33] *WA v MA* above n 30, 20.

[34] See below at section III C in the context of a consideration of the impact and relevance of existing separation agreements.

[35] Dail Eireann Debates Vol 467 27 June 1996 Second Stage, 1802.

[36] Ibid.

wealth remaining after the needs of both parties are satisfied should be available for distribution by the courts, and not retained by the earning spouse:

> But the Oireachtas did not limit the 'proper provision' for a spouse solely to his or her financial needs and responsibilities ... Proper provision should seek to reflect the equal partnership of the spouses. Proper provision for a spouse who falls into the category of a financially dependent spouse ... should seek, so far as the circumstances of the case permit, to ensure that the spouse is not only in a position to meet her financial liabilities and obligations and continue with a standard of living commensurate with her standard of living during marriage but to enjoy what may reasonably be regarded as the fruits of the marriage so that she can live an independent life and have security in the control of her own affairs, with a personal dignity that such autonomy confers, without necessarily being dependent on receiving periodic payments for the rest of her life from her former husband.[37]

This Supreme Court explanation of the concept and impact of the proper provision requirement represents a helpful judicial statement of the overriding aims of the precondition, and allows it to form the basis of the 'marriage as partnership' approach which is evident in other jurisdictions.[38] In *T v T* the five-judge Supreme Court made effective use of this ample resources case to expound on the parameters of proper provision. Keane CJ preferred a formulaic approach, suggesting a starting point of one-third of the assets for the dependent spouse[39] and received some support for this view from Denham J.[40] However, a more typical view is that proper provision is more rightly a matter that should be determined with reference to the individual circumstances of each case, in the context of recognised legal principles:

> Each case must be decided on its own circumstances. However, there are relevant fundamental legal principles—such as to recognition of spouses' work in the home—as to spouses' rights under the Succession Act—as to the place of the family in our society.[41]

---

[37] *T v T* above n 24, 408 (Murray J). Similarly in the more recent Supreme Court appeal hearing in *MF v EF* [2005] IESC 45 [29], McGuinness J affirmed as 'entirely correct' the view of the lower court regarding the extent of the applicant's entitlements. Quoting from p 12 of the lower court judgment, McGuinness J at para 22 cited the views of O'Sullivan J: 'I approach the issue of asset share on the basis that the court should provide not only for the needs of the applicant (where there is provision to do so) but also should assess a fair lump sum to reflect her interest in the family assets (not necessarily 50%) even if this is greater than her specific needs'.

[38] Buckley, above n 28, 8 regards sharing principles and partnership as being of 'fundamental concern to the issue of marriage and our resulting attitude to property regulation.' She regards marriage as 'more than simply a legal bond between individuals ... hence it is appropriate to think of needs and objectives, including financial needs, in joint rather than individualistic terms.'

[39] *T v T* above n 24, 368–69.

[40] Ibid, 384, 385. Denham J acknowledged that a figure of one-third of the assets may be a useful benchmark to fairness against which could be aligned, 'both positively and negatively, the specific circumstances of a case, and in particular the factors set out in s 20(2)(a)-(l) of the Act of 1996.' However, she noted (ibid, 384), that such a formulaic approach 'may have no application in many cases', in particular it would be an unsuitable benchmark for a family with inadequate assets or one of adequate means, where such a sum could only be achieved by a sale of assets which might ultimately destroy a previously viable business.

[41] Ibid (Denham J), although unfortunately she offered no further clarification on the nature or make-up of these 'recognised legal principles'. It was later suggested by O'Neill J in *MK v JK* [2003] 1 IR 326 that the one-third starting point, although far from appropriate in every case, has evolved from the historical approach of the Irish courts to spousal entitlement on death, which has influenced applications for spousal maintenance.

Irrespective of the varying views of the five presiding judges regarding the judicial creation of yardsticks or formulaic approaches in *T v T*, general agreement was evident amongst them as to the fact of the trial judge's overriding broad discretion in determining what constitutes proper provision in the circumstances of a particular case. Even Keane CJ, who favoured a formula-based division of assets where the wealth of the parties so permitted, ultimately recognised that notwithstanding the section 20(2) factors:

> the circumstances of individual cases will vary so widely that ultimately, where the parties are unable to agree, the trial judge must be regarded as having a relatively broad discretion in reaching what he or she considers a just resolution in all the circumstances.[42]

Thus, whilst the efforts of the legislature to guide the decision-making process were acknowledged, ultimately it was declared that the 'discretion given by the legislature to the trial judge under this scheme is ample.'[43]

More recently in the aforementioned case of *JC v MC*[44] O'Higgins J rejected the suitability of relying upon percentages as the best approach for adjudicating upon the merits of an application for ancillary relief, stating:

> In the present case the property assets of the parties were inherited and brought to the marriage by the applicant. The concept of one third as a check on fairness is not in my view useful.[45]

By way of contrast he regarded 'the purchase of a suitable home and a suitable and proper level of maintenance' as his priority and quite simply as 'the basis that proper provision' can be achieved as distinct from the blind application of a percentage or fraction of the available assets.[46] In *MS v PS*[47] Sheehan J made no reference to percentage-based spousal entitlements; rather, having considered the section 20 statutory factors with reference to the circumstances of the case, he made six orders for financial and property relief, the combination of which he deemed necessary to make 'proper provision for the applicant and the children of the marriage'.[48] Interestingly, O'Neill J identified a role for the spouses in the calculation of what might constitute proper provision in the circumstances, commending 'the approach adopted by the parties in setting out at the start of the trial what they considered to be a proper provision' and regarded their views as being 'of great assistance to the court'.[49]

---

[42] *T v T* above n 24, 365. It was emphasised subsequently by O'Higgins J in *CD v PD* [2006] IEHC 100 that where there is significant wealth, this must be taken into account in determining what constitutes proper provision. Citing Thorpe LJ in *Parlour v Parlour* [2004] EWCA Civ 872, O'Higgins J stated at p 10 of the transcript that 'it is of course correct that the proper provision must be assessed on the basis of the assets and that the concept of proper provision cannot be assessed without taking into account the assets.'

[43] *T v T* above n 24, 389 (Denham J).

[44] *JC v MC* [2005] IEHC 276.

[45] Ibid, p 28 of the transcript.

[46] Ibid.

[47] *MS v PS* (High Court, 21 November 2008).

[48] Ibid, 10. McKechnie J in *BD v JD* [2003] IEHC 106, in deciding what constituted proper provision for the parties in the circumstances, had recognised his obligation to 'be guided by section 16' and his duty to 'utilise the facts of this case within the provisions of that section so that the resulting orders are fair, just and equitable.'

[49] *MK v JK* above n 41, 344. This view was echoed by O'Higgins J in *CD v PD* above n 42.

In October 2011, the Irish Supreme Court was again presented with the opportunity to consider the concept of proper provision in this context, and to assess its impact upon the key issue of asset distribution on divorce. In *YG v NG*[50] Denham CJ, on behalf of a five-judge Supreme Court, emphasised that the requirement arising from the governing provisions is to make proper provision and not to effect a redistribution of wealth.[51]

iii. Absence of Principles and Yardsticks

The judiciary has recognised the lack of statutorily stated principles of division and, in particular, the absence of rules or preference for equal division. Fennelly J in *T v T* emphasised the absence of 'any automatic or mechanical rule of equality'.[52] He was supported in this view by Murray J, who rejected the suggestion that 'in making financial provision for spouses…their assets should be divided between them. Neither the Constitution nor the 1996 Act requires that, expressly or implicitly.'[53] Thus in rejecting a principle favouring equal division, the Supreme Court has also refused to regard the Divorce Act as mandating any approach which might focus judicial attention upon the division of the assets of the spouses:

> The Act of 1996 and the constitutional provision pursuant to which it was enacted makes no reference to division. In any divorce proceedings the court in making an order approving or imposing financial dispositions in favour of a spouse is concerned with provision and not division.[54]

Although not expressly stated, this view lends itself more towards the reasonable needs of the dependent spouse, rather than an entitlement to a share in the wealth of the financially stronger spouse. Thus it appears that the fact of a wealthy spouse is unlikely in itself to convince the courts to award the dependent spouse an equal share in that wealth, howsoever accumulated. With reference to the Irish constitutional and statutory prerequisites, Keane CJ recognised the distinguishing aspect of the Irish approach, when compared to that in England and Wales, noting that under Irish divorce law, 'the appropriate criterion is the making of proper provision for the parties concerned', as distinct from the English approach which seeks to divide the assets fairly.[55] Thus, whilst proper provision cannot be achieved without some division of the available assets, the latter is simply the means to achieve the former, and once proper provision is secured it appears that the courts may not be willing to act beyond this.

iv. Second-Bite Applications

A more novel issue for the courts to consider is an application to vary the terms of an existing divorce decree. The High Court has recently had a number of opportunities

---

[50] Supreme Court 19 October 2011.
[51] Ibid at para 22(vi). This case is considered in more detail below.
[52] *T v T* above n 24, 417.
[53] Ibid, 407.
[54] Ibid, 398 (Murphy J).
[55] Ibid, 368.

to consider its powers to vary existing ancillary relief orders made pursuant to a decree of divorce. In particular, given the dramatic economic downturn in Ireland since 2008, former spouses have occasionally become unable to realise their assets at the values upon which the original orders were based, and have returned to the courts for assistance through variation or vacation of existing orders.[56]

The fact and extent of the court's jurisdiction to vary previous orders for ancillary relief made on divorce was considered at length by Abbott J in *JC v MC*.[57] The wife brought an application seeking an increase in maintenance and a lump sum order in circumstances where two weeks after the decree of divorce was granted, the husband sold for a significant profit what had been viewed as an unrealisable asset. Having identified the right to vary under section 22 of the Divorce Act as simply a right to 'fine-tune' the orders previously made, Abbott J regarded the court as incapable of making fresh orders, not originally made at the time of the decree. However, this did not prevent the court from making alternative relief orders following the conclusion of the proceedings 'in the event of the tables having turned between the spouses as regards their earning capacity, wealth and fortune, whether by way of windfall or misfortune, legislative interference or change of career or increased dependence by another marriage.'[58] In support of his open-ended view of the spousal right to return to court, Abbott J placed the governing divorce legislation within its constitutional and social context:

> To my mind, it is entirely inconsistent with the relieving nature of the legislation and the constitutional imperative underlying same that for proper provision to be made that the parties in such a situation would not be able to relieve a catastrophe by granting an application or a lump sum even when the original divorce decree or settlement did not contain an order for such relief.[59]

More recently in *AK v JK*,[60] 12 years after the original ancillary relief was granted, the husband re-entered the proceedings and sought an increase in his financial payout from the sale of the family home. Abbott J used the opportunity to further develop his interpretation of the governing provisions and the general right of the court to review existing orders made in earlier proceedings. Whilst he recognised that section 22 of the Divorce Act only permits the variation of a property adjustment order that establishes, varies, extinguishes or reduces a settlement, Abbott J asserted that in addition to the legislative framework on both separation and divorce,[61] the court can also exercise its *inherent* jurisdiction to vary existing property adjustment orders.[62] This assertion of a fundamental common law right to vary, notwithstanding or, perhaps in conjunction with, the statutorily created rights, demonstrates a willingness on the part of Abbott J to create and direct policy in this area. To this

---

[56] See R Aylward, 'Dissolved Marriages and the Recession: The Variation of Orders for Ancillary Relief' [2009] 12(1) *Irish Journal of Family Law* 9.
[57] *JC v MC*, above n 31.
[58] Ibid, 25.
[59] Ibid.
[60] *AK v JK*, above n 27.
[61] s 18 of the 1995 Act and s 22 of the Divorce Act.
[62] *AK v JK*, above n 27 [14].

end, in the course of his judgment in *AK v JK*, he enunciated the following test to determine a party's entitlement to additional relief:

> Hence, I conclude that the test as to whether a change, or changes, in circumstances ought to ground a strategic application going outside the limited circumstances envisaged by s. 18 should be that, ('other things' being equal) if they were of such a fundamental nature that it would be unfair and unjust to ignore such change or changes. The 'other things' to be considered before this necessary condition for a further strategic order to be made after a separation order may be made sufficient, must, I conclude, be guided by the statutory framework set out in the provisions of s. 16(1) and (2), with the final overriding test of fairness and justice contained in subsection 5.[63]

Applying the test to the case before him, Abbott J concluded that it was 'manifestly in the interest of justice' to refuse the application brought by the husband. Fitzgerald has welcomed this approach, regarding the judgment as being 'of considerable importance in the context of changed circumstances. ... the ultimate objective is to do justice between the parties under other sections of the legislation by way of a fresh application even where a variation application simpliciter could not be entertained.'[64] This case demonstrates a welcome judicial enthusiasm to direct the governance of this important area, and to identify the parameters required for the consistent implementation of the incomplete legislative provisions.

Abbott J got a third opportunity to pronounce on the issue in *F v F*[65] and once more used the determination of an ongoing dispute to develop the governing law and principles. The application concerned a request to the court to vary the terms of an existing Order of the Court which was still executory, that is not yet completed. Aylward has identified three principles enunciated by Abbott J in this most recent case, which he suggests should be considered in similar future applications before the courts:[66]

1. Where parts of the provision made in a divorce decree become impossible to give effect to, the court is obliged to consider alternatives so as to ensure proper provision under the Divorce Act.
2. The court has jurisdiction to vary the terms of an executory order where the circumstances have 'fundamentally changed'; however, such variation must strike a 'balance and symmetry' with the original order. The court noted the test in *Thwaite v Thwaite*, which is premised upon enforcement of the original order being 'inequitable'. Rather than adopting such a test, Abbott J preferred the test he had previously set out in *AK v JK*, where varying the earlier orders will ensure fairness and justice in the circumstances.
3. The court will only exercise this jurisdiction provided that the alternative provision is appropriate in accordance with the Constitution and the Divorce Act.[67]

---

[63] Ibid.

[64] A Fitzgerald, 'Divorce in a Cold Climate' (Family Lawyers Association conference, Cork, January 2011) 13. Fitzgerald regards this approach as constituting a much wider interpretation of the courts' power to vary an order than in neighbouring jurisdictions, and regards it as tying in with the discretionary basis of the Irish divorce legislation.

[65] *F v F* (High Court, 19 December 2008).

[66] Above n 56, 14.

[67] Ibid, paraphrasing the judgment of Abbott J.

However, on the issue of the weight to be attached to the terms of an existing divorce settlement, Abbott J has refused to take a definite stance. In *JC v AC*,[68] in refusing to grant the supplemental financial compensation order sought by the wife, he declined to make any over-arching statements of policy, preferring that the 'weight to be given to the divorce settlement would…depend upon the justice of the case'.[69]

In an approach similar to that of Abbott J in *AK v JK*, Dunne J more recently regarded justice as demanding the making of a new property adjustment order even where the legislative structure prevents her from varying the existing order.[70] She was of the view that this limitation did not prevent the court from making a property adjustment order in relation to the same property on more than one occasion. The couple had executed a judicial separation consent, which was then made an Order of Court. Whilst the applicant wife had fulfilled her obligations pursuant to the agreement, the husband had failed to do so, claiming his depressed financial circumstances prevented this. In the instant proceedings he sought an Order of the Court under section 18 of the 1995 Act discharging him of his obligations. Relying upon a number of decided English cases, Dunne J approved in particular the dicta of Bracewell J in *Benson v Benson (deceased)*[71] when identifying the criteria to determine if an application to vary or set aside consent orders should be entertained, concluding as follows:

> Leave to appeal out of time could be granted where new events had occurred since the making of the order, which invalidated the basis of the order so that the appeal would be likely to succeed. The new events should have occurred within a relatively short time of the making of the order and the application for leave should in the circumstances be made reasonably promptly. The grant of leave should not prejudice any third party with an interest in the property.[72]

Ultimately, Dunne J favoured securing the accommodation needs of the applicant wife and four children of the union, and ordered that the entire interest in the family home be transferred to the wife. Dunne J, agreeing with the approach of the courts in England and Wales, surmised that Irish courts were likely to follow the approach referred to in *Benson v Benson* 'that the courts would uphold agreements freely entered into at arm's length by parties who were properly advised.'[73]

A similarly robust defence of an existing separation agreement was evident in the very recent Supreme Court case of *YG v NG* where on an application for a divorce the respondent wife sought significant supplemental financial relief, notwithstanding the existence of the agreement which included a full and final settlement clause. The Supreme Court ruling was an appeal by the husband of the judgment and orders of Abbott J in the High Court which were ultimately regarded by the Supreme Court as both excessive and in error.[74]

---

[68] *JC v AC* (High Court, 14 November 2007).
[69] Ibid.
[70] *O'C v O'C* [2009] IEHC 248.
[71] *Benson v Benson (deceased)* [1996] 1 FLR 692.
[72] *O'C v O'C* above n 67 at p 8 of the transcript.
[73] Ibid, 9.
[74] Above n 50, paras 28–36.

Despite the early reluctance to create judicial policy in these matters, it appears that the Irish courts have of late, within the context of existing arrangements, become more prepared to challenge the legislative framework, and react to the circumstances of each case. They have quite legitimately defended such policy-making with reference to the overriding obligation to ensure that justice and fairness are secured. This legislative safety-net contained in section 20(5) provides the judiciary with the scope to tackle challenging issues or legislative restrictions within the existing framework.

II. PRE-NUPTIAL AND POST-NUPTIAL AGREEMENTS

A. General Law and Policy

i. Historical View

The Irish courts have rarely been called upon to consider the role and impact of either pre-nuptial or post-nuptial agreements, other than in the guise of separation agreements. One of the few instances where a pre-nuptial agreement has been considered by the courts was in *Re Tilson (Infants)*,[75] where the Supreme Court had to measure the validity of an agreement which sought to regulate the future religious upbringing of any children of the union. The case concerned the marriage of a Protestant husband and a Roman Catholic wife. Prior to the marriage taking place, the parties signed an agreement which provided that in the course of the marriage all children of the marriage would be brought up in the Roman Catholic faith. No other issue was dealt with by the terms of the agreement. In considering the enforceability of the agreement, the Supreme Court ultimately held that a pre-nuptial agreement made by parties to a marriage, dealing with matters which might arise during the marriage, was effective and binding in law once the marriage was validly solemnised. In respect of the agreement at issue, the court further noted that it could not be revoked by one party alone; a valid revocation required the consent of both parties. The court directed that the children be returned to the mother to be educated by her in the Roman Catholic faith, as per the terms of the agreement. Thus, whilst the *Tilson* case did recognise as valid and binding a pre-nuptial agreement signed by the parties, the specific focus of the agreement limits greatly its scope as a precedent. Post-nuptial agreements, other than those presented as separation agreements have also rarely been considered by the Irish courts. It is suggested that inter-spousal agreements are not typically executed except in order to deal with an actual rather than possible future breakdown of a marriage.

ii. Pre- and Post-Nuptial Agreements—Contrary to Public Policy?

Prior to the introduction of divorce in Ireland there was a strong line of authority to the effect that any agreement which envisaged or provided for the breakdown of a marital union was void at common law on the grounds that it was contrary to

---

[75] *Re Tilson (Infants) (No 3)* (1951) 1 IR 1.

public policy. The philosophical basis for this was that such agreements undermined the institution of marriage as a lifelong union. This was evidenced in the old Irish case of *Marquess of Westmeath v Marquess of Salisbury*,[76] ultimately determined by the House of Lords, on appeal from the Court of Chancery in Ireland. The case concerned two deeds executed by the parties with a view to regulating their antici-pated separation. As the parties recommenced cohabitation after the first deed was executed, it was deemed to be null and void. However, the second deed was also declared unenforceable as a matter of public policy, as it anticipated the break-down of the union. Following independence and the drafting of the Constitution of Ireland, the express prohibition on divorce further enhanced the view that an agreement which provided for the future breakdown of a union could not attract the force of law.

Given the removal of the constitutional prohibition of divorce in Ireland in 1995 and the subsequent enactment of the Family Law (Divorce) Act 1996, the public policy grounds for declaring agreements which regulate the future (possible) break-down as void ab initio were greatly weakened. However, whilst both pre-nuptial and post-nuptial agreements envisaging the future breakdown of a marital union may now be regarded as likely to have legal standing, they have not as yet been positively validated by the Irish courts.

iii. Current Status of Pre-Nuptial and Post-Nuptial Agreements

Whilst parties entering into a marital union are not in any way prevented from exe-cuting a pre-nuptial agreement, at present it appears that the courts are not obliged to enforce or even recognise as valid the fact or content of such an agreement on separation or divorce. The fact of their existence is certainly recognised by virtue of section 9 of the 1995 Act and section 14 of the Divorce Act, which expressly empower the courts on granting a decree of judicial separation or divorce or at any time thereafter, to make an order providing for the variation of any ante-nuptial or post-nuptial settlement made by the spouses and/or to extinguish or reduce the interest of either of the spouses under any such settlement. The wide discretionary judicial powers created by both Acts prevent the parties from contracting out of their statutory obligations, thereby preventing the powers of the courts from being usurped by private arrangement. In addition, as noted above, even where the parties negotiate a settlement upon divorce, the court must be satisfied that such arrange-ments constitute proper provision for the parties, prior to granting the decree of divorce. Although a pre-nuptial agreement has yet to be presented to the courts for enforcement in the context of divorce proceedings, given the broad discretion-ary judicial powers upon which the divorce regime is operated, it is probable that more people will seek to protect their property interests in the event of marital breakdown.

Whilst both the 1995 Act and the Divorce Act may permit the courts to vary the terms of any pre-nuptial or post-nuptial settlement of the parties, section 113 of the Succession Act 1965 had already recognised the right of spouses to regulate, prior

---

[76] *Marquess of Westmeath v Marquess of Salisbury* (1830) 5 BL1 339.

to entering into a marital union, one aspect of future inter-spousal financial and property affairs. It permits the execution of an agreement prior to, or during the course of the marriage, which would have the effect of renouncing the legal right share to which each spouse would otherwise be entitled on the death of the other spouse.[77] Well before the introduction of judicial separation or divorce, this long-standing legislative provision, although limited to the renunciation of the spousal legal right share, was permitted so long as it was not executed in contemplation of a future separation, as to do so would have offended against public policy. It has thus been recognised as a statutory acknowledgment of the fact that prior to marriage the parties could decide to enter into an agreement which would regulate the distribution of certain assets at some time in the future.[78]

iv. Variation of Ante-Nuptial and Post-Nuptial Settlements

As mentioned above, section 9(1)(c) of the 1995 Act, which is repeated in section 14(1)(c) of the Divorce Act, provides that the court may make an order providing for the variation for the benefit of either of the spouses and of any dependent member of the family, and of any or all of those persons, of any ante-nuptial or post-nuptial settlement (including such a settlement made by will or codicil) made on the spouse. This judicial capacity to vary such a settlement was considered by the Irish High Court, which had to determine if a family discretionary trust could be regarded as a post-nuptial settlement for the purposes of section 9 of the 1995 Act. In *FJWT v CNRT and by Order Trust Corps Services Ltd*,[79] the applicant wife sought a decree of judicial separation with ancillary relief. In so doing the applicant requested that the court vary, for her benefit and the benefit of the dependent members of the family, a discretionary trust known as the 'Repus' Trust. It was accepted by the court that the trust had been entered into on foot of property and taxation advice and was not regarded as a tool created to allow the husband avoid any spousal or familial financial responsibilities. McKechnie J referring to this fact, declared himself satisfied that the husband had:

> acted genuinely and in a *bona fide* manner and was simply endeavouring to achieve the most tax efficient manner of succeeding to this estate. At no stage, nor is there any question of this, was the aforesaid scheme devised so as to diminish the assets of the family or otherwise to disadvantage his wife or children.[80]

Thus the court was satisfied that it was never the intention of the parties that this major asset would be excluded from consideration in the event of the marriage not succeeding.

---

[77] s 113 Succession Act 1965 provides as follows: 'The legal right of a spouse may be renounced in an ante-nuptial contract made in writing between the parties to an intended marriage, or may be renounced in writing by the spouse after marriage and during the lifetime of the testator.'

[78] Study Group on Pre-Nuptial Agreements, *Report of the Study Group on Pre-Nuptial Agreements*, presented to the Tánaiste and Minister for Justice Equality and Law Reform, April 2007, 24.

[79] *FJWT v CNRT and by Order Trust Corps Services Ltd* [2005] 1 IR 321.

[80] Ibid, 328. The husband was the settlor and the original beneficiaries were the children of the marriage, their spouses, their issue and the spouses of such issue. In addition, any widow of the settlor was included in the definition of settlor. The trustees, who were joined as a notice party to the proceedings, had a power to vary the category of beneficiary and to exclude any of the persons named in the deed.

Notwithstanding this view, the Court spent some time considering the specific categorisation of the trust, with counsel on behalf of the applicant wife arguing that the trust was a 'post-nuptial' settlement which was governed by section 9(1)(c). Conversely, counsel on behalf of the respondent husband asserted that the trust did not come within the remit of section 9 of the 1995 Act, as it had not been 'made on the spouses' as required by the statutory power to vary, and further that as the trust was a discretionary trust, none of the individual nominated beneficiaries had any absolute entitlement to receive a benefit. Ultimately, in interpreting the scope of the statutory power, the Court was not willing to give such a narrow meaning to the term 'settlement', and in particular refused to limit it to the traditionally strict meaning used in a conveyancing instrument. What the Court required was evidence that the settlement at issue simply had the effect of conferring some financial benefit on one or both of the spouses, with reference to the fact of their marital status.

Although the scope and precedent value of this case is relatively limited, it did reflect a willingness on the part of the courts to recognise the fact of the agreement and to utilise the existing statutory powers to take those assets regulated by the agreement into account when determining the division of assets and the securing of proper provision for the parties.

v. 2007 Report of the Study Group on Pre-Nuptial Agreements

The validity and enforceability of pre-nuptial agreements has received significant recent attention in Ireland. In December 2006, the then Minister for Justice Equality and Law Reform established the Study Group on Pre-Nuptial Agreements whose terms of reference were:

> To study and report on the operation of the law since the introduction of divorce in 1996 with respect to pre-nuptial agreements taking into account constitutional requirements.[81]

Given the special protection afforded to the family based on marriage by the Irish Constitution, one of the fundamental considerations for the Study Group was whether pre-nuptial agreements, if given recognition under Irish law, could withstand the constitutional protection afforded to the institution of marriage. Given the significance of proper provision as a determinant of the entitlement to a decree of divorce, it is difficult to envisage that a pre-nuptial agreement could displace entirely, the judicial discretion exercisable in calculating what constitutes such proper provision in the circumstances.

The following is an overview of the Executive Summary of the report published by the Study Group in April 2007.[82]

a. Constitutional Considerations

Pre-nuptial agreements do not offend against the constitutional protection accorded to the institution of marriage and the right to marry. Nonetheless, the constitutional requirement of proper provision will serve to prevent pre-nuptial agreements from

---

[81] www.justice.ie/en/JELR/Pages/Membership_of_pre-nuptial_study_group_announced.
[82] Above n 78, 5–6.

being automatically enforceable. Rather the Group recommended that a degree of recognition should be afforded to such agreements, to be considered in light of various other relevant factors in divorce and ancillary relief proceedings.[83]

b. The Current Legal Status of Pre-Nuptial Agreements in Ireland

The Group was of the view that pre-nuptial agreements are both enforceable and capable of variation under existing Irish statute law. It was suggested that the weight to be attached to an agreement should be determined by the courts in light of the requirement for proper provision and the relevant statutory criteria.[84]

c. Public Policy Considerations

Long-standing public policy objections to pre-nuptial agreements as an attack on the institution of marriage have been diminished through the introduction of divorce in Ireland and in principle may no longer be valid.[85]

d. The 'Common Good'

It was considered by the Group that a legislative rule of universal application seeking to prohibit pre-nuptial agreements on the basis that they offend the common good would probably be deemed unconstitutional. Instead, the common good would be better served if the validity and effect of a pre-nuptial agreement be determined by the courts in each case.[86]

e. Private Ordering of Financial Affairs

In considering the case in favour of the enforceability of pre-nuptial agreements, the initial view adopted by the Group was that clarity in the law was most likely to result in increased predictability and reduced costs. However, it was also recognised that invariably couples may embark on litigation on the preliminary issue of contesting the enforceability of a pre-nuptial agreement in advance of seeking ancillary relief orders. In fact, it was ultimately concluded that in certain instances there could be an increase in costs overall.[87]

f. Arguments Against Pre-Nuptial Agreements

The Group considered the arguments against enforcing pre-nuptial agreements, noting that they may not always provide a fair solution to marital break-up, they may prompt litigation and drain marital resources, and they may be viewed as offending

---

[83] Ibid, see further ch 2.
[84] Ibid, see further ch 3.
[85] Ibid, ch 5.
[86] Ibid, ch 6.
[87] Ibid, ch 7.

public policy to a degree. However, on balance it was concluded that it would be both difficult and inappropriate to universally exclude them from consideration.[88]

g. Recommendations

The Report of the Study Group was published in 2007. Minister for Justice, Equaltiy and Law Reform McDowell regarded it as:

> a comprehensive analysis of the law in this area and the recommendations it makes are well considered and deserve implementation. This report will now form the basis for the formulation of legislative proposals that will be developed in consultation with the Attorney General.[89]

Ultimately the Study Group made a series of recommendations to the Minister as to how the proposed role for pre-nuptial agreements should be regulated under Irish law, incorporating recommendations for legislative reform.[90] It now appears likely that these recommendations will be included in a draft Family Law Bill, due to be published in early 2012. The recommendations are as follows:

1. The Study Group recommended that express statutory provision be made for pre-nuptial agreements. In this regard, pre-nuptial agreements should be capable of being scrutinised by the court in separation and divorce proceedings in much the same way as separation agreements are currently dealt with under section 20(3) of the Family Law (Divorce) Act 1996. However given the Group's view that pre-nuptial agreements are subject to different considerations when compared to separation agreements, it was suggested that a discrete provision be enacted to require a court to *have regard* to these agreements.
2. The Group did not regard it as appropriate to include the execution of a pre-nuptial agreement as one of the statutory factors (currently comprised of section 20(2)(a)-(l)) to be considered, as to do so would fail to create a sufficiently transparent means of identifying what weight, if any, had been attached to the agreement.
3. The Study Group recommended that pre-nuptial agreements should be reviewable on death, regarding it as highly probable that a pre-nuptial agreement which came to be enforced upon the death of one of the parties to the marriage would need to be reviewed due to the passage of time. Therefore, it recommended the introduction of a statutory basis for review in a manner somewhat similar to the existing legislative position in England and Wales.
4. Finally, the Group considered the procedural requirements surrounding a valid pre-nuptial agreement and recommended that procedural safeguards be imposed as a matter of law. It was recommended that the governing legislation (Family Law Act 1995 and the Family Law (Divorce) Act 1996) should be amended to include a definition of a pre-nuptial agreement such that an enforceable agreement must be executed in writing, signed and witnessed; made after each party

---

[88] Ibid, see further ch 8.
[89] Press release 25/04/2007, available at www.justice.ie/en/JELR/Pages/Report_of_study_group_on_pre_nuptial_agreements_published.
[90] *Report of the Study Group on Pre-Nuptial Agreements*, above n 78, the recommendations of the Group are contained in chs 9–12.

has received separate legal advice; made with disclosure of financial information; and made not less than 28 days before the intended marriage.

B. Form and Procedure

i. Pre-Nuptial Agreements

Given that pre-nuptial agreements are not as yet statutorily governed under Irish law, nor has one been presented for adjudication by the courts, it is difficult to present a statement of the form and procedures to be followed. However, the matter did receive significant attention from the Study Group on Pre-Nuptial Agreements.[91] Whilst it was recognised that the common law had established detailed and comprehensive jurisprudence on the formation of a binding contract, the Group regarded it as prudent to identify certain fundamental requirements for a validly executed pre-nuptial agreement. In this context the Group referred to the 'heightened emotional atmosphere that surrounds both the marriage contract and the months leading up to the ceremony itself'.[92]

Following an examination and brief statement of the approach adopted by other jurisdictions,[93] the Group proposed the creation of a regulatory system which mandated certain compulsory requirements, but would also retain sufficient scope for subjective judicial review and adjudication in the particular circumstances. Thus the Group proposed that the following conditions be regarded as 'conditions precedent' to the valid execution of a pre-nuptial agreement:

(a) The agreement should be in written form, signed by both parties and witnessed, but not necessarily by a solicitor.
(b) The parties should each have received separate legal advice as to the effect and meaning of the agreement.
(c) Each of the parties should have made disclosure of all relevant financial information.
(d) The agreement should be executed not less than 28 days before the marriage.[94]

Failure to satisfy one or more of these requirements would render the agreement void ab initio. In addition to these basic statutory requirements, the Group also expressly noted that such an agreement would also have to comply with general contractual principles, and thus a court would have to be satisfied that it was not entered into as a result of duress or undue influence, and that it was not an unconscionable bargain.[95] As regards the entitlement of a spouse to rely upon the terms of a pre-nuptial agreement in circumstances where these procedural requirements have been met, the Group did not endorse the Australian approach which regards such an agreement to be binding once the statutory prerequisites have been fulfilled. The

---

[91] Ibid, see generally ch 12 of the Report.
[92] Ibid, 81.
[93] The Study Group considered the procedural requirements existing under the domestic regimes of Australia, the United States and England and Wales.
[94] *Report of the Study Group on Pre-Nuptial Agreements*, above n 78, 84.
[95] Ibid, 85.

Report regarded this model as having 'unduly restricted the scope for judicial review or variation of a pre-nuptial agreement and believes that this approach is neither proper nor appropriate in the Irish context'.[96]

Although the Study Group, given a mere 12 weeks to consider and report on the validity and potential regulation of pre-nuptial agreements under Irish law, issued its report in April 2007, no further developments have occurred. Repeated assurances have been given by the Department of Justice, Equality and Law Reform that the recommendations of the Study Group will be incorporated in the long-promised Family Law Bill. As of December 2011, the position remained the same.[97]

ii. Post-Nuptial Agreements

Post-nuptial agreements, other than separation agreements, typically address the issue of the payment of maintenance in respect of the spouse and/or children of the union. Section 8 of the Family Law (Maintenance of Spouses and Children) Act 1976 sets out the court's capacity to review and/or make orders in respect of marital agreements which concern the making of periodical payments by one spouse towards the maintenance of the other spouse or any dependent children of the family. The court is permitted to make such an agreement an order of court 'if it is satisfied that the agreement is a fair and reasonable one which in all the circumstances adequately protects the interests of both spouses and the dependent children'. Thus, whilst the legislature has recognised the capacity of parties to enter into post-nuptial arrangements regarding financial support, the court retains a residual power to declare such an arrangement unfair and/or unreasonable and to refuse to make it an order of the court. This reflects the practice in respect of both judicial separation and divorce where inter parte consents come before the courts for ruling. In such instances the courts are mandated to ensure that proper provision is achieved by the terms of the financial settlement reached and thus retain the residual power to vary the terms of the arrangement as presented.

In relation to the issue of maintenance, it has long been settled law that a spouse cannot contract out of his/her maintenance obligations, and he/she retains the right to return to court at any future time to seek further maintenance or to amend the existing position, despite any covenants to the contrary. In *HD v PD*[98] the petitioner wife had previously issued proceedings and these had been settled by way of agreement in 1973. The agreement provided, inter alia, that the respondent husband would pay to the wife the sum of £10,000 in 'full satisfaction of all the claims in the petition'. The wife sought further periodical payments for the support of herself and two of her children. The husband claimed that she was estopped from succeeding with this claim by virtue of the consent signed in 1973. With reference to inter-spousal obligations to maintain arising under the 1976 Act, Walsh J confirmed that 'it is not possible to contract out of the Act by an agreement made after the Act came into force or by an agreement entered into before the legislation was enacted' and

---

[96] Ibid.
[97] The author, as a member of the Study Group, has been privy to the progress, however limited, of these proposed legislative developments.
[98] *HD v PD* (Supreme Court, 8 May 1978) (Walsh J).

ordered the payment of maintenance by the respondent.[99] More recently, this was followed by Barr J in the High Court case of *JH v RH*[100] where he stated that the petitioning wife was entitled to ignore the provisions of the separation agreement, which had provided that it was:

> a full and final settlement of all matters outstanding between them including any claim which the wife might have under the Judicial Separation and Family Law Reform Act 1989 or any amending legislation.[101]

These cases affirmed the special treatment accorded to the issue of maintenance and the inability of a post-nuptial settlement, in the guise of a separation agreement or otherwise, to eliminate the inter-spousal entitlement to be maintained.[102]

III. SEPARATION AGREEMENTS

A. Historical Significance of Separation Agreements

Given the absence of the remedy of judicial separation in Ireland until 1989, and of divorce until 1996, separation agreements were the long-standing legal means of regulating the breakdown of a marital relationship under Irish law. Such an agreement would traditionally have included clauses dealing with the parties' agreement to live apart, a non-molestation clause, an agreement as to the custody and access arrangements for children of the marriage, the division and distribution of the assets of the parties, and often a clause providing for the ongoing maintenance of the dependent spouse.

B. Status of Separation Agreements

The limitations of a separation agreement as a means of determining and enforcing the terms to govern the resolution of a marital dispute are well documented. Given that it is in essence a private arrangement between two persons, it has always suffered from the lack of force of a court order. Where a default occurs in relation to any aspect of the agreement, the parties do not have recourse to the courts for contempt; rather the remedy lies in the more difficult breach of contract proceedings. The issue of maintenance can never be definitively agreed upon and is always subject to change, even where a spouse covenants in the separation agreement that the issue of maintenance is settled in full and final agreement of the parties. A pension adjustment arrangement requires a court order to have effect, as the trustees of a pension scheme are not party to the separation agreement and thus are not bound

---

[99] Ibid, p 7 of the transcript.
[100] *JH v RH* [1995] 3 Fam LJ 96.
[101] Ibid.
[102] Equally in *MC v JC* [1982] 2 ILRM 562 Costello J held that an alimony agreement between spouses could, even in the absence of an express clause permitting review or variation, be varied so as to reduce the husband's liability. Costello J rejected the argument that the court had no power to vary the husband's contractual obligations; although he did decline to vary it in light of the financial evidence before him.

by its contents.[103] Finally it was confirmed in *PO'D v AO'D*[104] that executing a separation agreement also acts as a bar to the issuing of judicial separation proceedings and thus access to the associated ancillary relief orders. In delivering the decision of the Supreme Court, Keane J (as he then was), declared a decree of judicial separation unnecessary as the existing separation agreement had already removed the obligation to cohabit. Essentially, the motivation for this decision was to prevent an injustice where one party could unilaterally repudiate the agreement by instituting proceedings under the 1989 Act.

C. Impact of Pre-Existing Separation Agreement upon Divorce Process

Prior to the introduction of divorce, the Irish courts had developed a strict view regarding attempts to reopen separation agreements, and had effectively prohibited such claims for further financial relief. Section 20(3) of the Divorce Act obliges the court to take account of any separation agreement that may exist between the parties to the marriage, in considering whether to make financial relief orders on divorce. However, although the parties to the agreement may be contractually bound by its terms, given the underlying obligation to ensure that proper provision is made for the parties, on divorce the court is ultimately empowered under section 14 to disregard or even set aside any or all aspects of the agreement. The general approach of the courts to date has been a willingness to reopen matters, particularly where the separation agreement has been in place for some time. However the difficulties arising from the generality of section 20(3) are evident in the case law since the enactment of the Divorce Act, which illustrates radically different judicial approaches to the relevance and impact of a separation agreement on a subsequent application for ancillary relief on divorce.

In *MK v JK*[105] at first instance, notwithstanding the execution of a separation agreement by the parties in 1982 which purported to finalise matters between them, Lavan J ordered that the respondent pay an additional lump sum of £1.5 million to the applicant on divorce. This order was appealed to the Supreme Court on the basis of Lavan J's failure to have any due or sufficient regard for the existing agreement as mandated by section 20(3). Without conducting a substantive hearing of the issues, McGuinness J recognised the shortcomings of the approach of the trial judge and ordered that the matter be returned to the High Court 'so that the question of proper provision for the parties to the divorce may be considered in the light of the mandatory provisions of the statute'.[106] At the eventual rehearing[107] O'Neill J ultimately ordered a significant reduction of the £1.5 million award, although equally recognising that the separation agreement had failed to make proper provision for the applicant. O'Neill J regarded it as still necessary to vary the terms of the original

---

[103] The benefits payable pursuant to a pension scheme are determined by the terms of the pension scheme and cannot be interfered with by agreement between the members and the trustees of the pension scheme.

[104] *PO'D v AO'D* [1998] 1 ILRM 543.

[105] *MK v JK* (High Court, 20 November 2000).

[106] *MK v JK* [2001] 3 IR 371, 384.

[107] *MK v JK* [2003] 1 IR 326.

inter parte settlement in circumstances where the applicant had not been adequately catered for by the terms of the agreement. Thus, notwithstanding the existence of a written, negotiated agreement, on divorce the court was willing to vary what was previously regarded as a binding full and final settlement:

> Section 20(3) of the Act places upon the court an obligation to have regard to the terms of any separation agreement which is still in force. Section 20 (1) places upon the court an obligation to ensure that … such provision as the courts thinks proper either exists or will be made for dependent spouses or members of the family concerned. Thus, the court has two unavoidable mandatory obligations.[108]

In discussing how these mandatory obligations should be fulfilled, O'Neill J regarded the order in which they should be applied as best left to the discretion of the courts in each case, but placed emphasis on the 'length of disconnection' between the parties, ie the extent of the lapse of time between the execution of the original agreement and the current application before the courts. He suggested that the greater the 'antiquity of the agreement', the more likely that the court will have to intervene to ensure that proper provision exists on divorce.[109]

More recently, O'Higgins J in *MP v AP*[110] noted that the weight to be attached to a prior settlement between the parties would vary from case to case, depending on many factors, but specifically highlighted the importance of the length of time since the matters had previously been compromised, the existing financial background when compared with current financial circumstances, and the reasonable expectations of the parties at that time.[111] Given that the intention of the parties was that the judicial separation order would be 'long term and lasting', that the bulk of the family assets were transferred to the applicant, and that the circumstances had not changed from those anticipated at the time of the judicial separation settlement, O'Higgins J ultimately decided that the terms of the prior separation order were of 'very great importance', and that it was not necessary to make any property orders, notwithstanding a significant economic disparity between the parties.[112] He did, however, vary maintenance upwards in favour of the applicant. The sufficiency of the separation order and the 13-year period before divorce proceedings were issued undoubtedly limited greatly the success of the claims of the applicant wife, who was regarded as having been effectively provided for the terms of the original settlement.

More recently in *WA v MA*[113] Hardiman J took a radically different view, in delivering a judgment which accorded great weight to the pre-existing separation agreement between the parties. With reference to both section 20(3) and the overarching requirement of section 20(5) that justice be achieved, Hardiman J refused to make any award in favour of the applicant wife. In adopting this view, Hardiman J referred expressly to the length of time that had passed since the signing of the agreement, the length of disconnection between the spouses and the fact that the

---

[108] Ibid, 344, 345.
[109] Ibid, 345, 346.
[110] *MP v AP*, above n 23.
[111] Ibid, p 15 of the transcript.
[112] Ibid.
[113] *WA v MA*, above n 30.

agreement had been executed after the enactment of the Judicial Separation and Family Law Reform Act 1989. In addition, he recognised the need to 'factor' into the consideration, the various matters set out in section 20(2).[114] He carried out this exercise, albeit briefly, concluding that justice required him to make no further orders for ancillary relief. Interestingly, Hardiman J was ultimately of the view that he was statutorily prevented from doing so by virtue of the terms of section 20(5).[115]

It is arguable that in *SJN v PCO'D*,[116] notwithstanding the making of additional orders in favour of the less wealthy husband, Abbott J appeared quite limited by the terms of the five-year-old judicial separation order. Had it not existed, it is reasonable to presume that the husband would have received a far greater share of the wife's substantial assets in the circumstances. In light of the existing judicial separation order, however, he was awarded a lump sum of €2.15 million. On the same day, in *SMcM v MMcM*,[117] again before Abbott J, the applicant wife sought further ancillary relief, notwithstanding the existence of a 15-year-old separation agreement which included a full and final settlement clause. Although he regarded the separation agreement as reasonable in the circumstances, Abbott J was of the view that it would be unfair to rely upon the agreement in order to prevent the wife from enjoying a better standard of living and lifestyle, akin to that experienced throughout the country generally, and more specifically by the husband.[118] Similarly in *RG v CG*[119] the court considered the weight to be attached to the pre-existing judicial separation consent order secured by the parties, such order including a declaration that its terms constituted a full and final settlement of all matters arising at that time *and* in the event of proceedings being issued under the Divorce Act. In concluding her judgment, Finlay Geoghegan J stated that the content of section 20 and all the circumstances of the family in question were each to be regarded as influencing factors in determining the issue of ancillary relief.[120] Given the court's obligations under both Article 41.3.2 of the Constitution and section 5(1) of the Divorce Act, Finlay Geoghegan J rejected the suggestion that parties could effectively enter into an agreement to relieve the court of its future obligation to be satisfied as to the making of proper provision on divorce:

> These provisions require the Court to exercise its judgment as to what constitutes proper provision. The obligation on the court to make such determination cannot be removed either by an acknowledgement or agreement, such as that contained in ... the consent between the parties herein.[121]

Finlay Geoghegan J was particularly influenced by the argument that when drafting the agreement, even if it could be said that divorce proceedings were contemplated, they could not be regarded as imminent, and thus she refused to determine the issue of proper provision with reference to the existing agreement. Rather she

---

[114] Ibid, 16.
[115] s 20(5) prohibits the court from making any ancillary relief order that is not in the interests of justice.
[116] *SJN v PCO'D* (High Court, 29 November 2006).
[117] *SMcM v MMcM* [2006] IEHC 451.
[118] Ibid, pp 3, 4 of the transcript.
[119] *RG v CG*, above n 30.
[120] Ibid, 428.
[121] Ibid, 424.

stated that this standard had to be assessed at the date of the hearing of the decree of divorce.[122] Adopting this position in respect of the relevance of the agreement, it was inevitable that the court would prove itself willing to reopen the financial arrangements between the parties. This judicial willingness to order significant supplemental relief, notwithstanding an existing separation agreement was again evident in *YG v NG* where the generous orders of the High Court, contrary to the provisions and apparent intentions of the 15-year old separation agreement, resulted in substantial financial and property orders in respect of the applicant wife. However these orders were admonished by the Supreme Court as excessive and were an error in law in light of the existing agreement and the statutory obligation to take its terms into account. In emphasising the significant weight to be attached to an existing separation agreement, Denham CJ very helpfully set out a series of general principles which may be applied where there has been a prior separation agreement followed by a subsequent application by a party to court. Set out below is an abbreviated overview of the principles identified by the court:

(i) Given that a separation agreement is a legal document entered into with consent by both parties, it should be given significant weight. This is particularly so where the agreement is intended to be in full and final settlement of all matters arising between the parties. In addition it was noted that where a court order is subsequently sought, the terms of any such agreement should be incorporated into the court order.

(ii) Referring to the earlier decision of the Supreme Court in *T v T*, whilst it was acknowledged that Irish divorce law does not establish a right to a clean break; it must be regarded as a 'legitimate aspiration'.

(iii) The existence of a separation agreement, stated to be in full and final settlement, is a significant factor in determining proper provision in all the circumstances.

(iv) If the circumstances are the same as at the time of executing the agreement, and the provision made at that time is regarded as proper, then the provision made by the court on a subsequent application should be the same.

(v) Where the circumstances of one or both parties have changed since the execution of the agreement, the court must consider all the circumstances carefully, but must not seek to effect a redistribution of wealth.

(vi) The acquisition of wealth post separation by one spouse is not to be regarded as a factor of itself to vest in the other spouse a right to further monies or assets.

(vii) The length of time since the separation agreement was executed is a relevant factor; the greater the length of time that has passed, barring catastrophic circumstances, the less likely a court will be to alter the existing arrangements.

(viii) Assets inherited by one party will not be treated as assets acquired by both parties in the course of the marriage.[123]

Ultimately, when considering the impact of an existing separation agreement, the Supreme Court emphasised that any application for additional financial relief can only be considered if such an application addresses the needs of a party. No entitlement

---

[122] Ibid, 428.
[123] Above n 50 at para 22.

arises simply because one party obtains a windfall post separation and the concept of proper provision on divorce should not be dominated by the favourable change in financial circumstances of one spouse.

Although it remains impossible to predict the outcome of a divorce application where a separation agreement or order exists, the Irish courts are beginning to show an increased willingness to bind the parties to their agreed terms. Whilst there remains both scope and willingness to supplement the agreement made, the courts do not appear willing to allow one party to entirely repudiate an existing arrangement on a unilateral basis. On balance, although the courts have acknowledged the fact and significance of pre-existing separation agreements, particularly where they include a full and final settlement clause, this has typically, however, not prevented the courts from making significant additional orders for financial relief, in light of the circumstances at the time of granting the decree of divorce. However the recent ruling of the Supreme Court is likely to have a significant bearing on future cases involving existing agreements and it is very likely that the Irish courts may give much more weight to such agreements in such cases.

IV. CONFLICT OF LAWS

The Irish Study Group on Pre-Nuptial Agreements considered the legal status of pre-nuptial agreements that have been executed in another jurisdiction in circumstances where that agreement might come before an Irish court for enforcement in divorce proceedings.[124] The legality and enforceability of pre-nuptial agreements in many other jurisdictions was acknowledged by the Group. The enforceability of such a validly executed agreement before the Irish courts would most likely turn on the facts of the individual case, and it was concluded that, whilst few jurisdictions were likely to rigidly enforce an agreement where to do so would cause grave injustice, the validity would more typically turn on compliance with the formalities of the jurisdiction of origin.[125] In this context the Group recognised the multiple and varying approaches to the issues of formalities and fairness.[126] Any reform of the law regulating the enforceability of pre-nuptial agreements in Ireland would thus require the legislature and/or judiciary to give detailed consideration to the formalities to govern a valid and/or enforceable agreement. Ultimately however, where an applicant seeks a decree of divorce from the Irish courts, Irish law dictates that the court must be satisfied that the fundamental proper provision requirement is satisfied.

V. CONCLUSION

Irish lawmakers, both legislative and judicial, have long asserted the importance of the State's capacity to retain ultimate control over the resolution of familial disputes. The genesis of this need for control is perhaps easily identified, given the

---

[124] *Report of the Study Group on Pre-Nuptial Agreements*, above n 78, 39–41.
[125] Ibid, 40.
[126] Ibid.

State's responsibilities towards the family as expressed in Article 41 of Ireland's Constitution. Although this conflicts with the notion and practice of private contract law and the capacity of individuals to enter into a binding contract, such intervention by the State is permitted and even encouraged in family law, given the underlying and inescapable issues of public policy that arise. In particular, the Irish courts have regarded themselves as responsible for the protection of vulnerable family members, recognising the imbalance of power that might often exist within a family unit.

Notwithstanding this overriding supervisory role of the State, there is now an indisputable right for spouses to control to some extent the terms of the dissolution of their marriage. The capacity of married parties to negotiate and be bound by a pre-nuptial or post-nuptial agreement reflects the more non-interventionist approach adopted by many jurisdictions in the private sphere of the family, preferring to allow parties to self-determine their respective roles and responsibilities. In practice, separation agreements and inter parte consents negotiated by the parties and drawn up in lieu of a full court hearing typically receive significant support from the Irish courts, and are often made orders of the court in the form in which they are presented. Spousal agreements executed prior to, or in the course of, the marriage arguably represent an extension of this currently accepted practice. However, such agreements are unlikely to be enforced by the Irish courts without consideration of the roles of the parties both during the marriage and upon its breakdown, as well as the sufficiency of the provision made for them by the terms of the agreement. In line with their current legislative and constitutional obligations, the Irish courts are obliged to retain a residual supervisory role in respect of the resolution of financial issues between married parties. Certainly the views expressed by Finlay Geoghegan J confirm the judicial intention to maintain and exercise this supervisory role.[127] However the recent Supreme Court ruling in *YG v NG* signals a greater willingness on the part of the Irish judiciary to hold the parties to the terms of their previous arrangements, particularly where such agreement(s) were expressly executed in full and final settlement of all matters arsing into the future. If the proposals of the Irish Study Group on Pre-Nuptial Agreements are enacted as part of the proposed Family Law Bill 2012, the courts will be obliged to have regard to the fact and content of any pre-nuptial or post-nuptial agreement, but will retain the discretion to determine asset distribution on the more over-arching requirement of securing proper provision in the circumstances. Any future movement to bind parties to the terms of a pre-nuptial agreement would most likely depend upon a judicial willingness to develop such policy.

---

[127] See *RG v CG*, above n 30; considered in section IIIC above.

Marital Agreements and Private Autonomy in the Netherlands

KATHARINA BOELE-WOELKI AND BENTE BRAAT

CONTENTS

I. INTRODUCTION

The Netherlands has a number of peculiarities: windmills, clogs, and a universal community of property regime regulating property relations between spouses. This 'universal' character may be surprising and even of concern, but it seems that Dutch lawyers and several legal scholars are very attached to it, with all attempts to reduce the extent of the community thus far ending in failure. According to its apologists, it is a Dutch national monument. Its adversaries, however, would like to see it dead and buried as soon as possible.[1] However, thanks to private autonomy, married couples are not forced to be subjected to this regime: spouses' freedom to enter into marital agreements is extremely broad, though not unlimited. Indeed, just as it has determined that the general rules of the law of obligations are not adequate to regulate the property relations between spouses and between spouses and third persons (thus creating special matrimonial property law[2]), so Dutch law also considers that all spouses should have some rights and duties that are mandatory and, as a result, cannot be contracted out of.

II. THE FINANCIAL CONSEQUENCES OF DIVORCE

A. Mandatory Rights and Duties of Spouses

The rules laid down in Title 1.6 Dutch Civil Code, 'Rights and Duties of the Spouses', apply regardless of the specific property relationship of the spouses. They are to be applied when the spouses are married under the statutory community of

---

[1] M Antokolskaia, and K Boele-Woelki, 'Dutch Family Law in the 21st Century: Trend-Setting and Straggling Behind at the Same Time' (2002) *Electronic Journal of Comparative Law* www.ejcl.org/64/art64-5.html.

[2] The notion of 'matrimonial property law' covers:
Title 1.6 ('Rights and Duties of the Spouses', Arts 1:81–1:92a Dutch Civil Code) which regulates rights and duties;
Title 1.7 ('The Statutory Community of Property', Arts 1:93–1:113 Dutch Civil Code) which provides for rules on the community of property; and
Title 1.8 ('Marriage Contracts', Arts 1:114–1:143 Dutch Civil Code) containing provisions on marital agreements, which mostly relate to the possibilities of entering into contractual agreements.

property regime, but also when they have agreed to exclude the statutory regime by entering into a pre-nuptial or post-nuptial marital agreement. In other words, most of these rules are mandatory and deal with contributions to the costs of the household, joint liability for household debts, protection of the matrimonial home and household assets and, finally, protection against other important acts.

i. Contributions to the Costs of the Household

According to Art 1:84 paras 1 and 2 Dutch Civil Code, both spouses are required to contribute to the costs of the household. Generally, all expenses which serve the physical and mental well-being of the spouses and their children are considered to be the costs of maintaining the household.[3] The extent of the duty of each spouse to contribute to the costs of maintaining the household is regulated by statute according to a four-step system. First, the costs are chargeable to the common income of the spouses; second, insofar as this is insufficient, to their own income on a pro rata basis; third, insofar as their income is insufficient, such costs are chargeable to the common capital; and fourth and finally, insofar as this is also insufficient, to their own capital on a pro rata basis (Art 1:84 para 1 Dutch Civil Code). These rules do not concern the spouses' liability in respect of third parties, but exclusively deal with the relationship as between the spouses. Although spouses may deviate from these rules of contribution through a written contract (Art 1:84 para 3 Dutch Civil Code), this rarely occurs in practice.

The spouses have reciprocal duties to contribute correspondingly to covering the expenditure for the property insofar as special circumstances do not preclude this (Art 1:84 para 2 Dutch Civil Code).

ii. Joint Liability for Household Debts

Each spouse is, together with the other spouse, liable for obligations entered into by the other for the benefit of the ordinary running of the household, including obligations arising from employment contracts entered into by the spouse as an employer on behalf of the household (Art 1:85 Dutch Civil Code). From the creditor's point of view, both spouses are debtors. The non-acting spouse does not, however, become a party to the contract and does not derive the power to exercise creditors' rights from Art 1:85 Dutch Civil Code. What the 'ordinary running of the household' includes depends on the circumstances of each particular case, whereby the nature of the expenses as well as the family's financial circumstances and lifestyle as they appear to the outside world are considered to be decisive factors. Those expenses that fall within the 'ordinary running of the household' are less wide-ranging than the 'costs of the household'.[4] There is hardly any recent case law concerning the definition of the term 'ordinary running of the household' used in Art 1:85 Dutch

---

[3] ALGA Stille, *Personen- en familierecht* (loose-leaf edition) title 6 *Rechten en verplichtingen van echtgenoten*, Artikel 84, Nos 1–7 (Deventer, Kluwer) 84-1–84-22.

[4] EAA Luijten and WR Meijer, *Huwelijksgoederen- en erfrecht, Huwelijksgoederenrecht* (Deventer, Kluwer, 2005) 59–67.

Civil Code. Furthermore, in the past, consideration has been given to whether to abolish the provision altogether.[5]

iii. Protection of the Matrimonial Home and Household Assets

A spouse requires the written consent of the other spouse (with some exceptions[6]) for:

— contracts for the disposal (sale or barter), encumbrance (in particular mortgaging), or usufruct (personal rights of use), and
— legal transactions for the discontinuation of the usufruct (notice to terminate a tenancy agreement)

of a dwelling in which the spouses live jointly or in which the other spouse is living alone or of things pertaining to such a dwelling or to the household effects (Art 1:88 para 1(a) Dutch Civil Code). This protection also applies to household assets as, generally, contracts for the disposal, encumbrance or usufruct, and legal transactions for the discontinuation of the usufruct, of household assets require the written consent of the non-acting spouse (Art 1:88 para 1(a) Dutch Civil Code).

iv. Protection against other Important Acts

In addition, a spouse requires the written consent of the other spouse (a few exceptions are contained in Art 1:88 para 4 and 5 Dutch Civil Code) regardless of the matrimonial property regime in force between them, for the following legal transactions:[7]

— Gifts,[8] with the exception of normal, non-excessive gifts and those for which nothing is drawn from a spouse's own capital during his or her life (Art 1:88 para 1(b) Dutch Civil Code). These gifts comprise legacies and the revocable and irrevocable benefit of a third-party from life insurance for which (single) premiums have been paid.
— Contracts in which a spouse, other than in the normal conduct of his or her profession or business, commits him or herself as a surety or as a joint and several co-obligor, or will answer for a third party or bind him or herself on behalf of a third person (Art 1:88 para 1(c) Dutch Civil Code). The simple fact that the conclusion of a contract can result in solidary debtorship (for example, entering into a general partnership) does not give rise to the requirement of consent.

---

[5] An amendment by the Second Chamber prevented the repeal of Art 1:85 Dutch Civil Code which the government considered to be outdated during the revision of Title 6 of Book 1 (Rights and Duties of the Spouses) in 2001. See Asser-De Boer, *Handleiding tot de beoefening van het Nederlands Burgerlijk recht, eerste deel—Personenrecht, eerste stuk—Natuurlijke personen en familierecht* (Deventer, Kluwer, 2006) 228.

[6] Art 1:88 para 2 Dutch Civil Code determines that a spouse does not need consent where the legal transaction must be performed on the grounds of a rule of law or of a preceding legal transaction for which consent was granted or was not required.

[7] ALGA Stille, 'Beperking van de handelingsbevoegdheid van echtgenoten' in F Schonewille (ed), *Relatievermogensrecht geschetst* (Nijmegen, Ars Aequi, 2007) 9–26.

[8] A gift is any material favour which is also a legal act.

— Hire-purchase contracts (payment in instalments),[9] except for things which only or mainly serve the normal conduct of his or her profession or business (Art 1:88 para 1(d) Dutch Civil Code).

A legal transaction performed by a spouse in breach of Article 1:88 Dutch Civil Code is voidable. Only the other spouse may claim lack of consent as grounds for avoiding the legal transaction (Art 1:89 para 2). This will not apply, however, in respect of any transaction other than a gift where the other party acted in good faith. The end of the marriage and a judicial separation do not affect the right to claim breach of this article as grounds for avoiding a legal transaction which arose prior to this.

B. The Default Community of Property Regime

i. Origin and Legal Nature of the Community of Property

As soon as the spouses are married, a general community of property exists by operation of law. The community property comprises, in principle, all of the assets and all of the debts of both spouses.

   The community property is the joint property of both spouses, and has a rather specific nature. The general rules of contract and property law on joint property/community in title 7 of Book 3 Dutch Civil Code are not applicable according to Art 3:189 para 1 Dutch Civil Code. This means that it is not possible to apply for an order to divide the community property while the relationship remains intact.[10]

ii. Categories of Assets

a. The Principle: The Community Property Comprises all Present and Future
   Property of Both Spouses
In principle the community property comprises all the present and future property of both spouses. And thus, as a general point of departure, it may be presumed that all assets are community assets (Art 1:94 para 1 and para 3 Dutch Civil Code). If a spouse claims that an asset is personal property (see below), this has to be proven by him or her. Thus, there may be three different categories of assets: 1) the community property containing both assets and debts; 2) personal property and personal debts of spouse A; 3) personal property and personal debts of spouse B. How the spouse may prove his or her personal property depends on the nature of the asset.[11] If it concerns assets which a testator has determined will personally belong to a spouse,

---

   [9] In this context an important decision was taken by the Dutch Supreme Court on 28 March 2008, RvdW, 2008, 362 (*Dexia-zaak*). Here the Court held that a contract for a share lease is to be considered as a sale on deferred terms which according to Art 1:88 para 1(d) Dutch Civil Code requires the consent of the other spouse. Again it has been confirmed that this provision protects the other spouse and if follows from Art 1:80b Dutch Civil Code that this protection also includes registered partners. Unmarried partners, however, do not fall within the scope of Art 1:88 para 1(d) Dutch Civil Code.
   [10] Luijten and Meijer, *Huwelijksgoederen- en erfrecht, Huwelijksgoederenrecht*, above n 4, 160.
   [11] Dutch Supreme Court 03.11.2006, NJ, 2008, 258.

the last will drawn up by a notary will provide this evidence (Art 157 Dutch Code of Civil Procedure). If it concerns assets which are closely related to a spouse, the spouse who claims this 'affinity' (*verknochtheid*) has to assert this in order to prevent the asset from falling within the community property.

b. The Exceptions: Some Assets are Personal

Some assets may be personal property. Article 1:94 Dutch Civil Code provides a list:

— Assets which have been obtained from the will of a testator or by means of a gift and where the testator/donor has provided that these assets will not fall within the community of property by means of an exclusion clause (*uitsluitingsclausule*) (Art 1:94 para 1 Dutch Civil Code).[12]

— Assets which have a close affinity with one of the spouses in any particular manner (*verknochte goederen*). These assets will only fall within the community property insofar as this would not be contrary to such affinity (Art 1:94 para 3 Dutch Civil Code).

— The right of usufruct in Article 4:29 and Article 4:30 Dutch Civil Code is excluded. This type of asset falls outside the community property (Art 1:94 para 1 Dutch Civil Code).[13]

— Pension rights covered by the Pension Rights Equalisation (Separation) Act and rights to a pension for dependants connected with such pension rights (Art 1:94 para 4 Dutch Civil Code).

Each of these will be discussed in turn below.

1. Exclusion Clause   Article 1:94 para 1 Dutch Civil Code provides for the use of an exclusion clause, to the extent that if the third party stipulates that the assets will personally belong to spouse A, these assets will be the personal property of A.[14] In practice many testators do include such an 'exclusion clause', which is one of the reasons the government has proposed changes to the community of property system. The spouses themselves cannot subsequently contract otherwise.[15]

2. Assets which are Specifically Attached or which Have a Close Affinity with one of the Spouses   These are assets which are specifically attached to or which have a close affinity with one of the spouses (Art 1:94 para 3 Dutch Civil Code). These assets will only fall within the community property insofar as this would not be contrary to such an affinity. As this is an exception to the general rule, it

---

[12] A testator may, eg, include the following clause in his or her will: 'I stipulate that no acquisitions from my estate may become part of any community of property to which the acquirer is entitled by marriage or a registered partnership, nor be involved in a settlement on the basis of any stipulation agreed in an ante-nuptial or post-nuptial agreement or registration agreement.'

[13] Luijten and Meijer, *Huwelijksgoederen- en erfrecht, Huwelijksgoederenrecht*, above n 4, 183.

[14] B Breederveld, *De huwelijksgemeenschap bij echtscheiding, De omvang, ontbinding en verdeling door de rechter* (The Hague, Boom Juridische Uitgevers, 2008) 61–86.

[15] Asser-De Boer, *Nederlands Burgerlijk recht—Natuurlijke personen en familierecht*, above n 5; Luijten and Meijer, *Huwelijksgoederen- en erfrecht, Huwelijksgoederenrecht*, above n 4, 169.

should be interpreted narrowly.[16] There is a gradual classification of affinity and its implication for the status of the assets.[17] As a last resort, the Dutch Supreme Court will determine which assets belong to which category and what the consequences of that type of close relationship between one spouse and the asset are. For instance, the right of spouse A to obtain maintenance from a former spouse is his or her personal property, and any subsequent spouse of spouse A does not have to be compensated for its value upon the dissolution of the community of property.[18] The other spouse is therefore not entitled to any economic ownership of the right to maintenance. On the other hand, damages relating to an accident suffered by spouse A and received before the marriage do fall within the community property and will, upon the dissolution of the community of property, be conferred upon spouse A, but with spouse B having a right to be compensated for the value.[19]

Intellectual property rights fall within the community property and the spouse who originally acquired these rights has no right to claim that they be assigned to him or her. However, principles of good faith may indicate that such a distribution is appropriate. When these types of rights are used in the profession of one of the spouses, there might be a right to have these rights assigned to that particular spouse on the basis of Article 1:101 Dutch Civil Code.[20] There is a lack of relevant case law from the Dutch Supreme Court with respect to some types of assets, and there is consequent debate among legal scholars as to which category certain assets belong.[21]

Another provision provides that after the dissolution of the community of property, each spouse may claim the value of his or her clothing and other small personal belongings against their estimated value (Art 1:101 Dutch Civil Code). However, these are not the personal assets of one of the spouses as such; the provision only confers a right to make a claim against the estimated value of these objects.

3. Right of Usufruct   On the basis of inheritance law a spouse has a number of statutory rights which are of a mandatory nature. If necessary for the support of the surviving spouse, the heirs are required to cooperate in establishing a usufruct with respect to a number of goods, including the dwelling and household effects (Arts 4:29 and 4:30 Dutch Civil Code). If these rights to establish a usufruct and the usufruct itself were to fall within the community property, the surviving spouse would be unable to enjoy the protection deemed necessary by the legislature.

---

[16] Asser-De Boer, *Nederlands Burgerlijk recht—Natuurlijke personen en familierecht*, above n 5, 301.

[17] Ibid; Luijten and Meijer *Huwelijksgoederen- en erfrecht, Huwelijksgoederenrecht*, above n 4 184–88; EAA Luijten, 'De algehele gemeenschap van goederen' in Schonewille (ed), *Relatievermogensrecht*, above n 7, 30–31 with a typology of different categories of closely related assets and the consequences thereof.

[18] Dutch Supreme Court 26.1.1933, NJ, 1933, 797.

[19] Dutch Supreme Court 3.11.2006, LJN AX8843 and Dutch Supreme Court 3.11.2006 LJN AX7805.

[20] Luijten and Meijer, *Huwelijksgoederen- en erfrecht, Huwelijksgoederenrecht*, above n 4, 200.

[21] G Van der Burght, 'Relativiteit in het huwelijksvermogensrecht' (2008) *Financieel Tijdschrift Vermogen*, 22–31.

4. Pension Rights   The exception relating to pension rights has to be understood in the context of the Dutch Pension Rights Equalisation (Separation) Act, which is a *lex specialis*. On the basis of this act, old age pension rights accrued during the marriage which fall under the scope of the Act have to be divided, in principle equally, between the ex-spouses after divorce. This is independent from the marital property regime of the spouses and thus applies to all spouses, unless the spouses have explicitly agreed otherwise. This implies that during the marriage the pension rights are the personal property of the spouse who is entitled to these rights. So if a spouse as an employee has accrued old age pension rights, these rights are his or her personal property.

After a divorce, the old age pension rights accrued during the marriage which fall under the scope of the Pension Rights Equalisation (Separation) Act have to be divided, in principle equally, between the ex-spouses. This is independent of the marital property regime of the spouses, and thus applies to both spouses, unless they have explicitly agreed otherwise in their marital contract or in a divorce covenant (*echtscheidingsconvenant*, Art 1:155 Dutch Civil Code). The ex-spouses may have a direct claim against the insurance company.[22]

When spouses have agreed to opt out of the Pension Rights Equalisation (Separation) Act, the old-age pension rights are personal property on the basis of Article 1:94 paragraph 4 Dutch Civil Code. There is no right after a divorce to a division of pension rights acquired after the divorce.

Other pension rights which do not fall within the scope of the Dutch Pension Rights Equalisation (Separation) Act may fall within the community property. In that case the general rules on the division of the community property will apply. On the other hand, some types of pension rights might be personal property by reason of their close relationship with just one of the spouses. An example is a disability insurance or benefit (*invaliditeitsuitkering*). Upon divorce the other spouse is not entitled to half of the accrued value of such a pension right.[23]

In relation to other pension rights such as private pension rights which are independent from employment conditions and annuity, the case law of the Dutch Supreme Court applies. This means that after a divorce, spouses who have been married under a community of property regime have to set off the value of the pension rights accrued during the marriage.[24]

In respect of life insurance a distinction is made between the right under the policy (the right to designate a beneficiary) and the right from the policy (the right to payment arising from the revocable or irrevocable designation as the beneficiary and from the death of the policyholder/insured). The right under the policy falls within the community property. The right to payment will only fall within the community property when it arises from an irrevocable designation as a beneficiary.[25]

---

[22] Asser-De Boer, *Nederlands Burgerlijk recht—Natuurlijke personen en familierecht*, above n 5, 615a.

[23] Dutch Supreme Court 23.12.1988, NJ, 1989, 700.

[24] Dutch Supreme Court 27.11.2001, NJ, 1982, 503 (*Boon/Van Loon*). Asser-De Boer, *Nederlands Burgerlijk recht—Natuurlijke personen en familierecht*, above n 5, 308; CA Kraan, *Huwelijksvermogensrecht* (Deventer, Kluwer, 2008) 85–87; Luijten and Meijer, *Huwelijksgoederen- en erfrecht, Huwelijksgoederenrecht*, above n 4, 229 and 233.

[25] Kraan, *Huwelijksvermogensrecht*, above n 24, 91–92; M de Rooij, G Schmidt, and BJ Van het Kaar, 'National Report, The Netherlands' (TMC Asser Institute/ULC, *Study on Matrimonial Property Regimes*

c. Community and Personal Debts

1. The Principle: All Debts Fall within the Community Property   All debts fall within the community property, regardless of whether the debt has been incurred before or during the marriage.

2. Exception   There is one exception to the above rule, for debts which have a close connection with one spouse.[26] A debt contracted in relation to a personal asset is a personal debt (Art 1:94 para 3 Dutch Civil Code). An example is a debt contracted by spouse A for the renovation of a house which is his or her personal property. A debt relating to an inheritance acquired under an exclusion clause (*uitsluitingsclausule*), such as succession tax, is also a personal debt.

   This question concerning the characterisation of personal and community debts should not be confused with the issue of the recovery of debts. Suppose only spouse A is liable for a debt, then the creditor may recover the debt from the community property as well as from the personal assets of spouse A (Art 1:96 para 1 Dutch Civil Code), but not from spouse's B personal property. However, if the debtor recovers the debt from the community property, spouse A is under a legal duty to compensate the community property (Art 1:96 para 2 Dutch Civil Code). Spouse B may, however, designate property owned by spouse A that will constitute sufficient recourse (Art 1:96 Dutch Civil Code). If both spouses are liable for the debt, it may be recovered from the personal assets of spouse B as well (Art 1:95 para 1 Dutch Civil Code).

iii. Administration of Community Property and Personal Assets

a. Main Rule

Each spouse administers his or her personal assets (Art 1:90 Dutch Civil Code).[27] The administration by a spouse of any property includes, to the exclusion of the other spouse, the exercise of the powers connected therewith, including the power to dispose of the property and the competence to perform and permit non-legal acts with respect to such property. This is subject to the powers of enjoyment and use belonging to the other spouse in accordance with the marital relationship (Art 1:90 para 2 Dutch Civil Code). The other spouse is not allowed to perform such acts. However, spouse B has a right to contract (*obligatoire rechtshandelingen verrichten*) with respect to goods under the administration of spouse A. This implies that spouse B may agree with a third party to sell a car that is under the administration of spouse A. However, this does not bind spouse A. Ultimately, this could result in a breach of contract by spouse B in relation to the third party.

---

and the Property of Unmarrried Couples in Private International Law and Internal Law, 2003) <http://ec.europa.eu/civiljustice/publications/docs/regimes/dutch_report_en.pdf> under no 1.2.2.2.

[26] Asser-De Boer, *Nederlands Burgerlijk recht—Natuurlijke personen en familierecht*, above n 5, 325-26; Luijten and Meijer, *Huwelijksgoederen- en erfrecht, Huwelijksgoederenrecht*, above n 4, 239–41.

[27] Asser-De Boer, *Nederlands Burgerlijk recht—Natuurlijke personen en familierecht*, above n 5, 327, 330–35; Luijten and Meijer, *Huwelijksgoederen- en erfrecht, Huwelijksgoederenrecht*, above n 4, 256–60.

Community property is subject to the administration of the spouse from whom it originated, insofar as the spouses have not agreed otherwise in a marriage contract. A court order may also alter the general administration of property (Art 1:97 Dutch Civil Code). When spouse A has acquired a car, only he/she is entitled to acts of administration in relation to that car.

If the proposed government reforms (discussed below) are enacted by Parliament, the provisions on administration will be amended. Both spouses will then each independently be entitled to administer community property which is not registered in the name of one spouse (Art 1:97 proposed Dutch Civil Code).

b. Exceptions

The most important exception to the general rule of administration concerns transactions which require the consent of both spouses. These transactions were explained in this chapter. Another kind of exception may have its origin in a mandate. Indeed a spouse can request the other spouse to administer any property (community assets or personal assets). In this case, their internal relationship is governed by the rules concerning mandates (Art 7:400 Dutch Civil Code) whereby both the marital relationship and the nature of the administered property are to be taken into account (Art 1:90 para 3 Dutch Civil Code). Second, if, as a result of absence or another cause, a spouse cannot administer his or her own property the district court may, at the request of the other spouse, order him or her to administer such property or a part thereof while excluding the incapable spouse from the administration (Art 1:91 Dutch Civil Code).[28]

A third type of exception concerns a special kind of asset: professional assets. Where community property is used by spouse B, with the consent of spouse A who administered it, in the normal pursuit of the former's profession, the administration is vested in the former spouse, and that of the property not used for professional purposes in the spouses jointly (Art 1:97 para 2 Dutch Civil Code).[29]

c. Maladministration

As the community of property has a special rule concerning administration, one should be aware of what happens when these rules are not observed. Two aspects have to be distinguished: on the one hand, the relationship between a third party and the spouse and, on the other, the relationship between the spouses themselves. Further, a distinction has to be made between registered property and movables and other non-registered property.

When a third party cannot ascertain which spouse has the power of administration over a movable asset which is not registered property or a right to bearer,[30] the third party may consider the spouse who holds the asset or the right to bearer as having such power (Art 1:92 para 1 Dutch Civil Code). The third party is then acting in good faith and this will generally result in the acquisition of the asset by the third party unless it concerns a gift (Art 3:86 Dutch Civil Code). The condition

---

[28] Kraan, *Huwelijksvermogensrecht*, above n 24, 109–10.
[29] CA Kraan, 'Bestuur', in Schonewille (ed), *Relatievermogensrecht*, above n 7, 59–60.
[30] The holder of a negotiable instrument.

of good faith is a less stringent standard than normal, when it is also necessary that a third party could not know whether the contracting party has the power of administration.

If it is registered property, a third party is generally not acting in good faith, since the third party should have consulted the relevant registers, which would have shown that the spouse with whom he was acting had no right of administration (Arts 3:88 and 3:24 Dutch Civil Code).[31]

In the relationship between the third party and the spouse who has the right of administration, Article 1:92 para 2 Dutch Civil Code determines that the spouse who is hindered by a third party in good faith in the administration of any property has a right to terminate such a hindrance within a reasonable period after having become aware of this hindrance. The third party may also give the spouse a reasonable period to exercise such a right; if the spouse does not exercise this right within the given period, the right to terminate the hindrance lapses.

If the third party cannot claim protection, the spouse who has the right of administration is still the owner of the assets. This spouse has the right to reclaim the assets. However, this would result in liability on the part of the non-competent spouse who contracted with the third party, since he or she cannot meet the obligation to transfer the property rights. This liability may result in a duty to compensate the third party for the damage, which would in the end be a debt falling within the community property. To prevent such a result, the spouse who has the right to administer may be a party to a legal transaction (Art 1:90 para 4 Dutch Civil Code).

To prevent problems recurring, the other spouse may ask the courts to terminate the community of property (Art 1:109 Dutch Civil Code). This is possible if one spouse appears to act in a way that is contrary to the other spouse's administration of community assets, or when he/she does not fulfil his or her duty to provide the information requested. The community property regime is then replaced by a separation of property regime.

iv. Dissolution of the Community

a. Grounds for Dissolution and the Date of Dissolution
The community of property will be dissolved, by operation of law, in the case of (Art 1:99 para 1 Dutch Civil Code):

— the death of a spouse;
— divorce;
— legal separation;
— termination of a registered partnership by mutual consent;
— dissolution of a registered partnership;
— where a spouse's existence is uncertain (Arts 1:412–1:425 Dutch Civil Code) and the other spouse remarries or enters into a registered partnership;
— a court order terminating the community;
— dissolution as a result of a subsequent marital agreement.

---

[31] Asser-De Boer, *Nederlands Burgerlijk recht—Natuurlijke personen en familierecht,* above n 5, 340–41; Luijten and Meijer, *Huwelijksgoederen- en erfrecht, Huwelijksgoederenrecht,* above n 4, 282.

The insolvency of a spouse is not a ground for the dissolution of the community of property.

b. Division of the Community Property

Each spouse is entitled to half of the dissolved community of property, unless it has been determined otherwise in a marital contract or written divorce agreement (Art 1:100 para 1 Dutch Civil Code). Exceptions to the equal sharing of property are possible on the basis of reasonableness and fairness, but only in extreme situations.[32] Title 3.7.2 Dutch Civil Code concerning a number of specific communities (*bijzondere gemeenschappen*) is applicable.

The provisions on the administration of property (Art 1:97 and Art 1:98 Dutch Civil Code) are no longer applicable. In addition, court orders or agreements relating to the administration of property no longer have effect. Article 3:170 Dutch Civil Code determines that both ex-spouses have to act together. There is an exception concerning urgent acts which cannot be postponed and acts which are necessary for the normal use of an asset. Each spouse is allowed to perform these two types of acts independently of the other spouse (Art 3:170 para 1 Dutch Civil Code). Apart from that, acts of administration must be performed jointly, unless otherwise determined by the spouses.

Each spouse has the right to claim clothing and small objects which serve for his or her personal use, the capital assets used in a profession or business, and family papers and mementoes against their estimated value (Art 1:101 Dutch Civil Code). This is a right in relation to the other (ex-) spouse and does not have effect in relation to third parties.

Assets which are closely related to one of the spouses may, after the dissolution of the community, be distributed to this spouse. This follows from Article 1:94 para 3 Dutch Civil Code and the principle of good faith.[33] This is a preferential right in relation to the distribution of these assets after dissolution. It has effect only in relation to the other spouse and not to third parties. An example is a collection that fell within the community property. After the dissolution, the collecting spouse is entitled to claim these assets against their estimated value.[34]

c. Settlement of Community Debts

After the dissolution of the community of property, Article 1:102 Dutch Civil Code determines exclusively in relation to community debts that each spouse will be fully liable for the community debts for which he or she was already liable before the dissolution. In relation to community debts for which the spouse was not liable, he or she will become liable for half of the debt after the dissolution of the community of property (Art 3:192 Dutch Civil Code). For instance, when spouse A contracted a community debt before the dissolution, but the creditor has not yet been paid after the dissolution of the community, the creditor may seek to recover the debt fully

---

[32] Dutch Supreme Court 07.12.1990, NJ, 1991, 593; Asser-De Boer, *Nederlands Burgerlijk recht—Natuurlijke personen en familierecht*, above n 5, 357; Luijten and Meijer, *Huwelijksgoederen- en erfrecht, Huwelijksgoederenrecht*, above n 4, 305.

[33] Luijten and Meijer, *Huwelijksgoederen- en erfrecht, Huwelijksgoederenrecht*, above n 4, 187 and 351.

[34] Ibid, 190.

from the community property and spouse A's personal property, and if necessary half of the value of the debt from spouse B's personal property.[35]

A community debt creditor may ask the courts to appoint a liquidator when the community property will be divided before the due and payable debts have been paid (Art 3:193 para 1 Dutch Civil Code). The creditor has this right also in the situation in which there is a risk that he or she will not be fully or partially paid within a reasonable time (Art 3:193 para 1 Dutch Civil Code).

d. Renunciation of the Community of Property

Each spouse has the right to renounce the community of property (Art 1:103 para 2 Dutch Civil Code). The part of the community property which is renounced will then be added to the share of the other spouse (Art 1:103 para 2 Dutch Civil Code), and the spouse who has made such a renunciation may no longer lay any claim to anything from the community property other than his or her bed, the bedding pertaining thereto, and clothing needed for personal use (Art 1:103 para 3 Dutch Civil Code). In turn, he or she is also released from liability and the obligation to contribute to the debts of the community of property for which he or she was not liable prior to the dissolution of the community property (Art 1:103 para 4 Dutch Civil Code). The spouse shall however remain liable for the debts of the community of property for which he or she was liable prior to dissolution of the community of property. A spouse who has paid more than one-half of a debt for which both spouses were fully liable prior to dissolution of the community of property may have recourse against the other spouse for the part exceeding this half (Art 1:103 para 5 Dutch Civil Code).

If the other spouse has paid a community debt, in full or in part, for which he or she was not liable prior to the dissolution of the community of property, such a spouse shall have recourse on account thereof against the spouse who has made a renunciation. A spouse who has paid more than one-half of a debt for which both spouses were wholly liable prior to the dissolution of the community of property may have recourse for such excess against the spouse who made a renunciation (Art 1:103 para 6 Dutch Civil Code).

e. Link between the Division of the Community Property and other Patrimonial Rights and Duties

1. Division of the Community Property and the Attribution of Maintenance   In theory there is no relation between the division of property, on the one hand, and the attribution of maintenance, on the other. Ex-spouses may come to an agreement on maintenance, but if they do not, the court may, upon request, determine the amount of maintenance on the basis of the needs of the maintenance creditor and the financial capacity of the maintenance debtor to pay. However, ex-spouses are allowed to enter into a contract on the division of property and spousal maintenance, which in practice will not be checked by the court. Thus it is possible, for instance, to award a lump-sum payment in lieu of periodical maintenance payments.

---

[35] Asser-De Boer, *Nederlands Burgerlijk recht—Natuurlijke personen en familierecht,* above n 5, 364–65; Luijten and Meijer, *Huwelijksgoederen- en erfrecht, Huwelijksgoederenrecht,* above n 4, 310.

2. Division of Community Property and Pension Rights and Claims by one or both Spouses   The community of property does not include pension rights which fall within the scope of the Dutch Pension Rights Equalisation (Separation) Act. Old age pension rights accrued during the marriage which fall under the scope of the Dutch Pension Rights Equalisation (Separation) Act have to be divided, in principle equally, between the ex-spouses after a divorce. This is independent of the marital property regime of the spouses and thus applies to all spouses, unless the spouses have explicitly agreed otherwise in their marital contract or in a divorce agreement (Art 1:155 Dutch Civil Code). The ex-spouse may have a direct claim against the insurance company. Other pension rights such as private pension rights which are independent of employment conditions and annuity are included in the community and have to be divided upon divorce. As it is possible to make an agreement on the exact division, pension claims could be relevant in the negotiating process.

3. Clean Break   There is no special clean break philosophy/legislation in the Netherlands, since there is still the possibility of claiming maintenance after the dissolution of a marriage. Furthermore, maintenance obligations are generally fulfilled in the form of periodical payments.

4. Role of the State in Post-Divorce Financial Support   Securing the economic well-being of a former spouse is in principle not considered a duty of the State, and the other former spouse may be obliged to pay maintenance as part of his or her post-marital duties. However, if the former spouse does not have the ability to pay, the State will take over.

According to Article 1:157 paragraph 1 Dutch Civil Code, in the decision granting a divorce or in a subsequent decision the court may award maintenance to a former spouse, at his or her request, if he or she has insufficient income to maintain himself or herself and cannot reasonably be expected to be able to gain such an income. It should be pointed out that under this provision the judge 'may' grant maintenance. He is authorised, but is not obliged to do so and, as a consequence, has wide discretion in this respect,[36] which is furthermore extended by the separation of the maintenance question and the question of fault. The judge, to a large extent, can thus be guided by fairness, but, nevertheless, is not absolutely free in reaching a decision. In awarding maintenance, two principles are of great importance, namely the principle of the lack of means, on the one hand, and, on the other, the ability to pay principle.[37]

According to Article 1:397(1) of the Dutch Civil Code, when establishing the amount of maintenance due on the part of blood relatives and relatives in law, the lack of means of a person who is entitled to maintenance, on the one hand, and the ability to pay on the part of a person who is obliged to pay maintenance, on the other, will be taken into account. Although only blood relatives and relatives in

---

[36] This discretion goes hand in hand with a strict duty to provide a reasoned decision. See, eg, Dutch Supreme Court, 06.2001, RvdW 2001, 122. In addition, the judge must remain within the limits of the legal dispute; Dutch Supreme Court, 30.10.1998, NJ 1999, 102.

[37] P Vlaardingerbroek et al, *Het hedendaagse personen- en familierecht* (Deventer, Kluwer, 2002) 129.

law are mentioned in this article, the financial conditions outlined by it are also of importance for maintenance after divorce.[38] The purpose of the limitation expressed in the text of this article is to provide for the possibility of taking other conditions into account when awarding maintenance.[39]

Under Article 1:157 (1) of the Dutch Civil Code the judge enjoys wide discretion as regards questions relating to the granting of maintenance. This freedom manifests itself, in particular, in the fact that the judge, when awarding (or modifying) maintenance after divorce, has the freedom to take all the circumstances of the case into account.[40] This means that, apart from financial circumstances, other factors can also be taken into consideration.

Among these pertinent factors of a non-financial nature, the duration of the marriage and the behaviour of the person who is entitled to maintenance may be taken into account. Depending on the duration of the marriage, its consequences for the earning capacity of the wife can be more drastic. The duration, as well as the amount of maintenance, are influenced by this factor.[41]

Shakespeare, sonnet cxvi.Until 1994 the Dutch Civil Code contained no time limits for the duration of maintenance. The courts could grant maintenance for a certain specific period of time.[42] The Law of 28 April 1994[43] and the Law of 7 July 1994[44] provided a statutory basis for limiting the duration of maintenance and signalled the end of 'a lifelong' duty to provide maintenance.

The new provisions are to be found in Articles 1:157 (3–6) and 1:158 (second sentence) of the Dutch Civil Code. The starting point is that the duration of the maintenance established by the court at the request of one of the spouses ends no later than 12 years after the date of divorce (Art 1:157 (3) of the Dutch Civil Code). The duty to provide maintenance is thus limited, in principle, to 12 years. If no period has been established by the court,[45] the maintenance duty ends after the expiry of the 12-year period, which starts to run from the date of the registration of the court decision in the civil status register (Art 1:157 (4) of the Dutch Civil Code). This also means that the first request for maintenance should be submitted within 12 years after registration. After the lapsing of this period such a request will no longer be admissible.[46] The period of 12 years is accordingly an expiry date which may not be set aside. If the judge, pursuant to Article 1:157 (3) of the Dutch Civil Code, has determined a specific period, he is not allowed to state that this period

---

[38] Dutch Supreme Court, 10.05.1974, NJ 1975, 183 (EAAL); SFM Wortmann and J Van Duijvendijk-Brand, *Compendium van het Personen- en Familierecht* (Deventer, Kluwer, 2002) 136.

[39] Wortmann and Van Duijvendijk-Brand, *Compendium van het Personen- en Familierecht,* above n 38, 136.

[40] Dutch Supreme Court, 20.12.1991, NJ 1992, 180. See also Dutch Supreme Court, 12.12.1975, NJ 1976, 573 (EAAL).

[41] Dutch Supreme Court, 19.04.1996, NJ 1997, 57.

[42] Dutch Supreme Court, 11.06.1982, NJ 1983, 595 and 596; Dutch Supreme Court, 22.01.1993, NJ 1993, 233.

[43] *Staatsblad* 1994, 324 and 325.

[44] *Staatsblad* 1994, 570.

[45] According to Asser-De Boer, *Nederlands Burgerlijk recht—Natuurlijke personen en familierecht,* above n 5, 449 it fits within the statutory system that the judge establishes the period of maintenance in all cases.

[46] Dutch Supreme Court, 08.05.1998, NJ 1998, 889.

is not subject to any prolongation.[47] At the same time the judge is authorised to reduce maintenance during the period when it continues to be due.

For those who have divorced after 1 July 1994[48] and are obliged to pay maintenance, this duty ends, in principle, after the 12-year period. It does not matter whether the parties have themselves agreed on maintenance or that the maintenance has been judicially determined. However, the 12-year period is not an absolute maximum. The parties are free to agree to a longer period in their agreement. If they have not included such a period in the agreement, the period of 12 years automatically applies.

In addition, Article 1:157 of the Dutch Civil Code concerning the termination of maintenance contains a hardship clause. According to this provision, if the end of maintenance as a result of the expiry of the period established under Article 1:157 para 4 of the Dutch Civil Code is of such a drastic nature that a non-modified adherence to this period cannot be reconciled with the requirements of fairness and reasonableness concerning a person who is entitled to maintenance, upon the request of the latter, the judge may establish an additional period of maintenance. Thus, a person who is entitled to maintenance can request the judge to prolong the period of maintenance if its termination is in conflict with the principles of fairness and reasonableness. Such a request should be submitted within three months after the end of the period of maintenance. The judge will consider whether prolonging the period is possible (Art 1:157 para 5 of the Dutch Civil Code).

The 12-year period has been chosen taking into account the most undesirable situation when the youngest child of a marriage has been born after the divorce of his or her parents. The 12-year period provides an opportunity to a person who is entitled to maintenance to care for the child and, after the children have become more independent, to take the necessary steps to make their own way in life.[49]

Finally, Article 1:157 para 6 contains a rule that does away with the lifelong enjoyment of maintenance after a marriage of a short duration without any children. If the duration of the marriage has not exceeded five years and no children have been born out of it, the duty to maintain ends after the expiry of the period equivalent to the duration of the marriage, and which starts to run from the date when the court decision is registered in the civil status register. The maintenance period set by the judge in such cases cannot, however, be longer than five years. However, its prolongation by setting an additional period according to Article 1:157 para 5 of the Dutch Civil Code is possible.

Cases where maintenance has been established or agreed upon before 1 July 1994 (the so-called old cases) and those where it has been established or agreed upon on 1 July 1994 or later must be distinguished. If the duty to maintain dates from 1 July 1994, then the transitional provisions under Article II (2–4) of the Law on the Limitation of Maintenance will apply (and thus not the provisions of Article 1:157 paragraphs 4–6 of the Dutch Civil Code). This implies, in principle, an obligation to pay for a maximum of 15 years. A person under an obligation to maintain his or

---

[47] Dutch Supreme Court, 30.01.1998, RvdW 1998, 31.

[48] The Act of 28.04.1994 entered into force on this date.

[49] Wortmann and Van Duijvendijk-Brand, *Compendium van het Personen- en Familierecht*, above n 38, 138.

her former spouse, who has paid maintenance for 15 years or longer, can request the judge to terminate the maintenance duty. The judge will grant such a request unless the termination is particularly unfair to the person who is entitled to maintenance. In such a case the judge, upon the request of a person who is entitled to maintenance, may establish an additional period. At present, Dutch law envisages three limitation periods for maintenance payments:

— 12 years for divorces granted after 1 July 1994;
— 15 years for divorces in 'old cases';
— five years for divorces after brief marriages without children.

C. Revision of the Default Regime

As a result of discussions in 1995 relating to the introduction of the registered partnership in 1998, the question of whether the current marital property regime remains adequate in light of changing social conditions was raised. Since then, Dutch matrimonial property law has been the subject of intense debate and reform. The Committee on Rights and Duties reported on this issue in 1997, and in 2000 a comprehensive comparative law research project was conducted by the Molengraaff Institute for Private Law.[50] Finally, in 2003, a Bill was sent to the Second Chamber of Parliament,[51] after consultations with many experts in the field.[52] The proposals to reform the statutory community of property regime dealt with a number of pressing problems.[53] The most far-reaching proposal in the Bill would have excluded assets acquired and debts incurred before the celebration of the marriage from the community property, as well as assets acquired by succession or gift during the marriage.[54] Under the current system, parents and other persons who wish to bequeath or to gift certain property to a spouse, must draw up a will in which they determine that the assets will not fall into the community property. Further, a new system of compensation for different types of investment in the other spouse's assets was envisaged, based on the 'rule of investment' or 'participation rule' (*beleggingsleer*), rather than on the currently used system of a nominal right of compensation.[55]

---

[50] K Boele-Woelki et al, *Huwelijksvermogensrecht in rechtsvergelijkend perspectief*, Ars Notariatus CIII (Deventer, Kluwer, 2000). See further K Boele-Woelki (ed), *Algehele gemeenschap van goederen: afschaffen!?* Ars Notariatus CVII (Deventer, Kluwer, 2000); B Braat, *Indépendance et interdépendance des époux dans le régime matrimonial légal des droits français, néerlandais et suisse* European Family Law series No 6 (Antwerp, Intersentia, 2004).

[51] Kamerstukken II, 28 867. CLM Smeets, 'Het wetsvoorstel tot aanpassing van de wettelijke gemeenschap van goederen', 2ᵉ UCERF Symposium 18 April 2008, www.arsaequi.nl/pdf/Carla%20Smeets.pdf.

[52] Asser-De Boer, *Nederlands Burgerlijk recht—Natuurlijke personen en familierecht*, above n 5, 289–91; Luijten and Meijer, *Huwelijksgoederen- en erfrecht, Huwelijksgoederenrecht*, above n 4, 12–15 and 823–48.

[53] B Braat, 'Wetsvoorstel 268 867 in rechtsvergelijkend perspectief' (2005) 6617 *Weekblad voor Privaatrecht, Notariaat en Registratie*, 290–300; Breederveld, *De huwelijksgemeenschap bij echtscheiding*, above n 14, 27–34.

[54] See Art 94(3) of the Bill of May 2003 Kamerstukken II, 28 867 No 2.

[55] Dutch Supreme Court 15.1.2008, NJ, 2008, 110. See AJM Nuytink, 'De onder uitsluitingsclausule verkregen grond en de daarop gebouwde nieuwe woning: nominaliteitsleer of beleggingsleer?' (2008) *Ars Aequi*, 628–31.

In addition, the provisions on the administration of community property were to be subject to a number of changes, thereby introducing in the proposed Article 1:97 Dutch Civil Code an independent right on the part of each spouse to administer community goods that are not registered in the name of the other spouse. Further, the proposed Article 1:95 Dutch Civil Code contains a new rule on the substitution of property in the situation where spouse A has acquired an asset using his or her personal property which constitutes more than 50 per cent of the value of the asset. The asset would then be his or her personal property, and spouse B or the community of property would then have the right to be compensated for the part provided by the personal property of B or the community property.

Although the government has consulted practitioners and scholars alike, there has been much criticism of the proposed reform.[56] As a result, the total revision of Dutch matrimonial property law took a long time . In the spring of 2008, 14 professors of notarial law and family law sent an open letter to the Second Chamber requesting speedy consideration and approval of the Bill.[57]

D. From a Limited Community of Property Regime Back to the Universal Community of Property Regime?

In the very last stage of consideration of this important Bill in the Second Chamber, three far-reaching amendments have been suggested by Members of Parliament. The first, and most significant one, aims to introduce a right to compensation to be assessed by the courts in the situation where the spouses have agreed in a marital contract to deviate from the marital property regime and where spouse A has worked for spouse B's company or profession or in the household without receiving fair compensation. This proposal specifically redresses the harsh effects of marital agreements containing a complete separation of property.[58] The idea of tailor-made decisions by the courts on fair and just compensation is completely new to the Dutch system.

The second amendment would undo an important feature of the Bill, namely the exclusion of assets acquired as a result of a gift or succession from the community

---

[56] Luijten and Meijer, *Huwelijksgoederen- en erfrecht, Huwelijksgoederenrecht,* above n 4, 824–26; see in particular CG Breedveld-De Voogd and WG Huijgen, 'Naar een beperkte gemeenschap: Niet doen!' (2004) 6562 Weekblad voor Privaatrecht, Notariaat en Registratie 43–49; HFC Schoordijk, 'Het huwelijk als partnership, vanuit rechtsvergelijkend perspectief (verdient een vierde tranche vernieuwing huwelijksvermogensrecht aanbeveling?)' (2003) 6525 Weekblad voor Privaatrecht, Notariaat en Registratie 272–78; ALPG Verbeke, 'Beperkte gemeenschap. Evenwicht en eenvoud' (2004) 6568 Weekblad voor Privaatrecht, Notariaat en Registratie, 168–73; Gr Van der Burght, EAA Luijten, and WR Meijer 'De ingreep in de wettelijke gemeenschap, een mission impossible?' (2003) 6545 Weekblad voor Privaatrecht, Notariaat en Registratie 649–57; WG Huijgen, 'Wie zit er op de nieuwe huwelijksgemeenschap te wachten?' (2005) Nederlands Juristenblad 2317; F Schonewille, 'Rechtspolitieke rede aan de open groeve(?) van wetsvoorstel 28.867' (2006) Echtscheidingsbulletin 19–24; CA Kraan 'Een drastisch gereviseerd wetsvoorstel tot aanpassing van de wettelijke gemeenschap van goederen', (2006) Fiscaal Tijdschrift Vermogen 14–19; Gr Van der Burght, 'Kanttekeningen bij de Tweede Nota van Wijziging derde tranche', (2005) Fiscaal Tijdschrift Vermogen 9–14; Gr Van der Burght, 'The Netherlands, Overview of Matrimonial Developments' in Gr Adkin (ed), The International Survey of Family Law (Bristol, Jordan Publishing, 2007) 207–15.

[57] Letter to the Minister of Justice, *NRC Handelsblad,* 3 January 2008.

[58] Kamerstukken II, 28 867, No 15.

property.[59] The amendment proposes to retain the current system, which requires parents and other persons who wish to bequeath or to gift certain property to a spouse to draw up a will in which they determine that the assets will not fall into the community property.

A third amendment proposes not to introduce Article 1:95 Dutch Civil Code concerning the substitution of property, as a result of which spouse A would become exclusively entitled to the assets acquired by him or her with more than 50 per cent of his or her personal property. The argument for not introducing this rule is that it would create uncertainty for the spouses and that it is difficult to implement in practice.[60]

It was concluded that the complex subject of the first amendment required more detailed consideration than was possible at this stage of the parliamentary process. The Minister of Justice agreed to investigate the options for mitigating the harsh results of a complete separation of property regime, and the first amendment was withdrawn.[61] The second amendment has been accepted, which means that nothing changes in this respect: unless the testator or donor determines otherwise, the assets being given or bequeathed will fall into the community property. The third amendment was also withdrawn at a later stage, thus the proposed Article 1:95 Dutch Civil Code remains part of the Bill.[62]

The Second Chamber has accepted the Bill and the First Chamber has completed its final reading.[63] Surprisingly, at the very end of the legislation process—on 22 December 2009—a resolution was adopted asking for additional information to be provided by the Minister of Justice.[64] According to the members of the First Chamber the final version of the Bill creates confusion, since the first version of the Bill was aimed at introducing a limited community of property regime whereas the later amendments re-established the universal community of property regime. The initial Bill changed several articles of Titles 6–8 of Book 1 of the Dutch Civil Code and these changes—during the legislative process the respective changes were not altered—no longer fit within the universal community of property system.[65] The Ministry of Justice took notice of these discrepancies and amended the Bill. It will enter into force on 1 January 2012. This contribution has been drafted earlier. It deals with the law as it stands in December 2009 with, where necessary, references to the rules proposed by the Bill to be enacted.

---

[59] Kamerstukken II, 28 867, No 14.

[60] Kamerstukken II 28 867, No 16, 1.

[61] The Minister of Justice has authorised comparative research on the effects of a complete separation of property based upon agreements by spouses and cohabitants. This research is currently being carried out by researchers of the universities of Groningen and Amsterdam (Free University).

[62] Handelingen II, 09.04.2008, No 68, 4741–63; Handelingen II, 11.09.2008, No 111, 8078–84; Handelingen II, 18.09.2008, No 3, 179. B Braat, 'Matrimonial property law: diversity of forms, equivalence in substance' in MV Antokolskaia (ed), *Convergence and Divergence in European Family Law, European Family Law Series No 18* (Antwerp, Intersentia, 2007) 237–50.

[63] Kamerstukken I, 28 867, A, B, C and D.

[64] Kamerstukken I, 28 867, G.

[65] In particular the following articles are to be scrutinised: 80f, 87, 88, 94–97, 102, 110, 111, 133, 139, 164 and 174.

III. PRE-NUPTIAL AND POST-NUPTIAL AGREEMENTS

In the Netherlands, the universal community of property regime comes into existence at the moment when the spouses enter into a marriage. It goes without saying that this system is both rather overwhelming, as well as being unique in the world. Fortunately, this goes hand in hand with a broad contractual freedom for the spouses to agree otherwise. Title 1.8 'Marriage Contracts', Articles 1:114–1:143 Dutch Civil Code is dedicated to marital agreements. When spouses choose not to exercise their contractual freedom, their property relations will be subject to the rules of the statutory community of property regime. But even when they choose to depart from those rules, their private autonomy is not unlimited, and certain rights and duties are mandatory.

A. Form and Procedure

i. Notarial Instrument

Both pre-nuptial and post-nuptial agreements must be entered into by means of a notarial instrument in order to be valid (Art. 1:115 para 1 Dutch Civil Code). If this is not done they are void. In addition, the approval of the district court is required for making or amending marriage contracts *during* a marriage (Art 1:119 para 1 Dutch Civil Code). The rationale behind this is the protection of creditors: the court may only refuse to give its approval where there is a risk that creditors may be prejudiced, or if one or more terms of the marital contract are in breach of the rules of mandatory law, *bonos mores* or Dutch public policy (Art 1:119 para 2 Dutch Civil Code). The pending Bill proposes abandoning the court approval requirement.[66]

ii. Full Disclosure

For the making of a pre-nuptial agreement the full disclose of the future spouses' assets and debts is not necessary. The marital contract may be drafted in general terms. The making of a post-nuptial agreement, however, requires the district court's approval (Art 1:119 para 1 Dutch Civil Code). In order to scrutinise the draft notarial deed along with the petition the court usually requests the full disclosure of the spouses' debts and assets.

iii. Validity against Third Parties

Both pre-nuptial and post-nuptial agreements must be entered into by means of a notarial instrument in order to be valid against third parties (Art 1:115 Dutch Civil Code). Marital contracts containing agreements on the property relationship between the spouses may only be used against third persons if the marital contract has been registered in the public Matrimonial Property Register kept at the clerk's

---

[66] Kamerstukken II, 28 867, No 9.

office in the district court within whose jurisdiction the marriage has been entered into (Art 1:116 para 1 Dutch Civil Code).

iv. Legal Advice

The civil notary is *qualitate qua* obliged to inform (future) spouses as to the content and consequences of the marital contract. This follows directly from notarial regulations and has recently been confirmed by two Dutch Supreme Court decisions.[67] If a notary neglects this duty he or she may be held liable according to the disciplinary rules governing notaries and for compensation in the form of damages.

B. Content of the Agreements and Binding Effect/Enforceability

i. General

Matrimonial property law will play the most important role when a marriage breaks down and the same applies to marital contracts.[68] Of course, the marital contract will already have an effect during the marriage (for example, the administration of or contributions to the costs of the household[69]), but most of the time this will go unnoticed as far as the spouses are concerned.

ii. Contractual Freedom

The general rule in Article 1:121 para 1 Dutch Civil Code applies: in their marriage contracts the spouses may derogate from the provisions of the statutory community property regime, provided that the stipulations therein do not conflict with the provisions of mandatory law, *bonos mores* or Dutch public policy. In pre- and post-nuptial agreements the spouses may re-regulate all aspects of their property relationship, provided that a spouse will not be made responsible for a larger share of the liabilities than that spouse shares in the community property (Art 1:121 para 2 Dutch Civil Code). Such a clause is void.

The contractual freedom of the spouses is almost unlimited. Only the restrictions provided in Article 1:121 para 2 Dutch Civil Code are to be taken into account. Spouses may, for instance, choose a statutory regime. The alternative matrimonial property regimes regulated by the Dutch Civil Code are the following: first, the community of benefits and income (*gemeenschap van vruchten en inkomsten*, Articles 1:123–1:127 Dutch Civil Code) and, secondly, the community of profits and losses

---

[67] Dutch Supreme Court 27.06.2003, NJ 2003, 524 (*Zweedse vrouw*) and Dutch Supreme Court 09.09.2005, NJ, 2006, 99 (*Zeeuwse notaris*).

[68] MJA Mourik and LCA Verstappen, *Handboek voor het Nederlands vermogensrecht bij scheiding* No 14-1 (Deventer, Kluwer, 2006).

[69] Art 1:84 paras 1 and 2 Dutch Civil Code concerning contributions to the costs of the household belong to the rules of Title 1.6 ('Rights and Duties of the Spouses') Dutch Civil Code and apply regardless of the specific property relationships of the spouses, being mostly mandatory. However, spouses are allowed to deviate from the provision of Art 1:84 paras 1 and 2 Dutch Civil Code concerning the contribution to the costs of the household. A written agreement (not necessarily a marriage contract) is required.

(*gemeenschap van winst en verlies*, Arts 1:128–1:130 Dutch Civil Code). Thirdly, rules are provided for netting covenants (setting-off agreements) which result in a participation in acquisitions, which are also referred to as matrimonial property set-off clauses (*verrekenbedingen*, Arts 1:132–1:143 Dutch Civil Code). Since 1 September 2002 the statutory community of property (*wettelijk deelgenootschap*) is no longer an alternative matrimonial property regime.[70] Marriage contracts which provide for one or more obligations in respect of netting income or capital are examples of how spouses may create their own 'regime'.

iii. Discretion of the Court

Generally, the courts only have a very limited competence to override, modify or set aside a marital contract if the effects thereof are unacceptable in view of the principle of reasonableness and fairness. There is no general good faith provision in Book 1 of the Civil Code on family law and the competence to interpret the marital contract is not laid down in any statutory rule which applies to marital contracts. However, there are legal provisions in which good faith is explicitly the relevant criterion for the court (for instance Art 1:157 para 5 Dutch Civil Code). Case law shows that good faith is used in order to correct unreasonable results. Take for instance the case of a couple who changed their marital property regime from a community property system into a regime of a strict separation of property and exclusion of any financial adjustment (*koude uitsluiting*). After the divorce the husband claimed financial adjustment on the basis of his spouse's behaviour. His claim was based on good faith. His spouse had not lived up to what had been agreed upon in their marital contract. The Supreme Court decided that on the basis of good faith it is, in this case, possible to deviate from a provision in a marital contract.[71]

IV. SEPARATION AGREEMENTS

A. Form and Procedure

i. Point in Time

In the Netherlands, separation agreements, called 'divorce covenants', may be concluded before or after the actual divorce proceedings have been initiated.[72]

ii. Formalities/Procedure

Divorce covenants are not subject to any formal requirements.[73] However, according to Article 1:100 para 1 Dutch Civil Code they must be in writing if the spouses

---

[70] Act of 14.03.2002, Staatsblad 2002, 152.
[71] Dutch Supreme Court 18.06.2004, NJ, 2004, 399.
[72] Compare: Asser-De Boer, *Nederlands Burgerlijk recht—Natuurlijke personen en familierecht*, above n 5, 598: even before the wedding.
[73] Dutch Supreme Court 26.01.1979, NJ 1980, 19.

agree therein to derogate from the equal share distribution of the community property upon divorce.

Divorce covenants will mostly be drawn up by a lawyer, mainly because the claim which initiates the divorce procedure must be signed and delivered by a lawyer to the court registry of the competent district court (Art 278, § 3 Dutch Civil Procedural Code). Nowadays, however, notaries are increasingly involved in the drafting of divorce covenants.[74]

iii. Full Disclosure

A full disclosure of the spouses' debts and assets is not required for a divorce covenant; however, practice has shown that it is essential for the drafting of a balanced agreement which cannot easily be altered.[75]

B. Content of the Agreement and Binding Effect/Enforceability

i. Content: General

The contractual freedom of spouses is almost unlimited (Art 1:100 para 1 Dutch Civil Code). The spouses may regulate a whole combination of things in their divorce covenant, ranging from matters relating to the spouses themselves to questions related to their children. One may distinguish between matters which are of a purely family law nature and matters which concern family property law. To the second category belong, for instance, questions relative to spousal maintenance, the costs of the education and upbringing of the children, the administration of the children's property, pensions and comparable claims, the attribution of the family home and the household assets, and the division of the community property.[76] Practice has also shown that tax-related matters (income tax) are regularly taken into account when spouses conclude a divorce covenant.[77]

ii. Content: Maintenance Agreements

The divorce covenant will thus often comprise a maintenance agreement. The possibility of concluding a maintenance agreement is expressly stipulated in Article 1:158 Dutch Civil Code: before as well as after the decision of the court, the spouses may determine whether and, if so, to what extent one will provide for the maintenance of the other after divorce. Accordingly, in their agreement the spouses can deviate

---

[74] In the spring of 2008, the Minister of Justice sent a Bill for approval by the Council of State, aimed at granting competence to civil notaries to file divorce requests under certain circumstances. See in this context www.justitie.nl/onderwerpen/wetgeving/wetgevingsprogramma/privaatrecht/wetsvoorstel-bevoegdheid-notaris-terzake-van-verzoeken-tot-echtscheiding.aspx. See also, B Breederveld, 'Huwelijkse voorwaarden: exclusief domein notaris?' (2009) *Tijdschrift voor Familie- en Jeugdrecht*, 49.

[75] District Court Breda, 24.01.2007, LJN AZ7006. See also rule III.18 which should be taken into account by advocate-mediators who belong to the Family Lawyers/Mediators Association: www.vfas.nl.

[76] Mourik and Verstappen, *Handboek*, above n 68, 14.1.1.

[77] Ibid, 5.1.1–5.1.7.

from the statutory criteria for the granting of maintenance (the ability to pay and a lack of means) as well as from the duration of the maintenance established by law. This means, and this is an exception to the main rule under Article 1:400(2),[78] that spouses can agree that no maintenance will become due (the so-called zero provision). Such an agreement, however, can only be reached during the marriage with a view to an intended divorce.[79] Accordingly, this exception to the rule under Article 1:400(2) does not cover a stipulation which was already agreed upon before the marriage according to which the right to maintenance in the case of divorce is renounced. Such a stipulation is invalid. The same applies to agreements in which the right to maintenance is renounced during the divorce proceedings.[80]

iii. Discretion of the Court

Provided that certain conditions are met, it can be stipulated in the agreement that the court cannot change or modify the agreement by invoking a change of circumstances (Art 1:401 para 1 of the Dutch Civil Code). Nevertheless, despite such a provision in the agreement, the latter can be modified by the court at the request of one of the parties in a decision on divorce or subsequently, on the ground that there has been such a radical change of circumstances that the applicant can no longer adhere to the agreement due to considerations of fairness and reasonableness (Art 1:159 para 3 of the Dutch Civil Code). Strict requirements are laid down concerning the obligation to furnish evidence by the spouse who is seeking a modification; the same is true for justifying the decision concerning modification.[81] In addition, a modification is also possible under Article 1:401 para 5, according to which an agreement concerning maintenance can also be modified or set aside if it has been concluded with a serious underestimation of the statutory standards. Such a possibility is rather restricted, however.[82]

The period stipulated in the agreement during which the maintenance obligation remains in force cannot be modified on the ground of a single change of circumstances unless this is explicitly agreed upon in writing (Art 1:401(1)(3) of the Dutch Civil Code).

iv. Interpretation

The interpretation of divorce covenants is governed by the so-called Haviltex formula, which determines that courts should pay attention to what the parties could reasonably expect of one another, and to the meaning they could reasonably attribute to a certain part of the agreement.[83]

---

[78] Art 1:400 (2): Agreements renouncing the maintenance due under the law are null and void.

[79] Dutch Supreme Court, 07.03.1980, NJ 1980, 363.

[80] Dutch Supreme Court, 19.04.1974, NJ 1975, 237.

[81] Dutch Supreme Court, 15.06.1985, NJ 1986, 489; Dutch Supreme Court, 23.12.1988, NJ 1989, 263.

[82] Wortmann and Van Duijvendijk-Brand, *Compendium van het Personen- en Familierecht*, above n 38, 140.

[83] See Dutch Supreme Court, 05.032004, NJ 2005, 494; and Dutch Supreme Court, 20.02.2004, RvdW 2004, 34; Dutch Supreme Court, 23.03.2007, NJ 2007, 175.

v. Binding Effect or Enforceability

Spouses are in principle bound by their agreement, as is the case with any other kind of agreement. Regularly, but often without success, the binding effect of such an agreement is contested. Different grounds are advanced, such as mental illness, a violation of the law, a breach of morals and public order, changed circumstances, good faith, error, deceit, threat, misuse of circumstances and, finally, so-called detriment to one of the spouses. Case law has shown, however, that only the last-mentioned ground has any real possibility of success.[84] According to Article 3:196 Dutch Civil Code a spouse can request an annulment of the division of property if he or she has erred as to the value of the assets and debts belonging to the community property. It is presumed that the spouse has erred if his or her loss is more than one quarter of the value.[85]

According to Article 819 Dutch Code of Civil Procedure the judge may include the divorce covenant in his or her decision granting the divorce. As a consequence the covenant will be enforceable.

When spouses do not exercise their private autonomy, their property relations will be subject to the general rules of the statutory regime of community of property.

V. CONFLICT OF LAWS

A. Foreign Marital Agreements

Regarding the freedom of the parties to regulate their property relationship, a distinction is to be made between the choice of the applicable law and the conclusion of a marital agreement. The one is not dependent on the other. If a marital agreement is made, the law applicable to the spouses' matrimonial property regime is to be consulted as to whether and to what extent the spouses may deviate from the statutory system.[86] The question of whether the spouses may designate another law to govern their matrimonial property regime is also regulated by the applicable law. Often a marital agreement between spouses who have different nationalities contains a choice of law clause.

B. The Law Applicable to Matrimonial Property Relationships

The Netherlands is one of the three contracting states to the 1978 Hague Convention on the law applicable to matrimonial property regimes. According to Article 2 the Convention has uniform application; the Convention's rules are applicable to marriages concluded after 1 September 1992. Three provisions refer to marriage contracts. Article 11 states that the designation of the applicable law shall be by

---

[84] See M Groenleer, 'De aantastbaarheid van een echtscheidingsconvenant' (2009) Echtscheidingsbulletin, Tijdschrift voor scheidingsrecht 18.

[85] See ibid.

[86] L Strikwerda, *Inleiding tot het Nederlandse Internationaal Privaatrecht* (Deventer, Kluwer, 2008) 141.

express stipulation, or will arise by necessary implication from the provisions of a marriage contract. Article 12 refers to the form of a marriage contract. It is valid if it complies either with the internal law which is applicable to the matrimonial property regime or with the internal law of the place where it was entered into. The law governing the property relationship of the spouses is generally the law of their first domicile after the marriage (Art 4 para 1). Exceptionally, the law of the spouses' common nationality is applicable if the conditions laid down in Article 4 paragraph 2 are met. In any event, the marriage contract shall be in writing, dated and signed by both spouses. Finally, according to Article 13 the designation of the applicable law by express stipulation shall comply with the form prescribed for marriage contracts, either by the internal law designated by the spouses, or by the internal law of the place where it is entered into. The designation of the applicable law shall also be in writing, dated and signed by both spouses. The choice of Dutch law during a divorce procedure in the Netherlands does not meet the prescriptions of the Convention as to form. A notarial act is required.[87]

A foreign marital agreement should be in accordance with these conflict of law rules.

C. Registration

Spouses with a marital contract containing a choice for a law other than Dutch law are advised to register their contract in the matrimonial property register of the district court in The Hague if they move to the Netherlands. The register is accessible to everybody who wants to obtain information about the property regime of spouses.

VI. CONCLUSION

According to the most recent empirical research, a marital agreement was drawn up in 25 per cent of marriages and registered partnerships concluded in 2003.[88] In other words, one quarter of all married couples were, in 2003, in one way or another choosing to depart from the statutory regime of universal community. This is substantial when compared to what is happening in other European countries.[89] But it seems that this number is not large enough to convince the Dutch legislator to take the plunge and to decide, after all, to amend the statutory regime. Fortunately, the spouses' freedom to regulate their property relations is almost unrestricted. The question arises, however, whether it is enough to rely on the spouses' ability to foresee and regulate their property relationship. Should a couple always be advised

---

[87] District Court of The Hague 09.10.1196, NIPR 1197 no 81 and District Court of The Hague 13.08.2001, NIPR 2001 no 251.

[88] MJM Van Mourik and W Burgerhart 'De ontwikkeling in de praktijk der huwelijks- en partnerschapsvoorwaarden in de periode 1997–2003' (2005) 6648 *Weekblad voor Privaatrecht, Notariaat en Registratie*, 1027–39.

[89] K Boele-Woelki, B Braat, and I Curry-Sumner, *European Family Law in Action, Volume IV: Property Relations Between Spouses*, European Family Law Series No 24 (Antwerp, Intersentia, 2009) 295–302.

to contract out of the default regime? In this respect, in particular, the lapsing of time might be of importance. Once a couple have decided to draw up a marital agreement, what should happen when their agreement turns out to be highly disadvantageous for one of them? Should they be bound by their contract in all circumstances? Should unforeseen situations not be further specified in order to provide the courts with guidance when they consider correcting unreasonable results? A marital agreement drawn up some 10–15 years ago might no longer reflect the spouses' current financial situation. Should the courts not be given additional powers to set marital agreements aside? It is *not* to be expected that the legislator will answer these questions in due time. Instead, the judiciary must solve any problems. In the meantime, marital agreements will certainly continue to play an important role and what is needed is new socio-legal research.[90] Why, when and how often do spouses agree to deviate from the statutory system? Most importantly, what exactly do they agree upon?

---

[90] See WM Schrama, 'Een vierde trede in het familierecht?, Een blik op het verleden en op de toekomst van het Nederlandse familierecht' (2009) *Actuele ontwikkelingen van het familierecht, UCERF bundel*, 69–91 (79).

Marital Agreements and Private Autonomy in New Zealand

MARGARET BRIGGS*

CONTENTS

* I gratefully acknowledge Professor Mark Henaghan, Faculty of Law, University of Otago, for his invaluable comments on earlier drafts.

I. THE FINANCIAL CONSEQUENCES OF RELATIONSHIP BREAKDOWN

A. Introduction

In New Zealand, the property consequences of relationship breakdown are regulated by the Property (Relationships) Act 1976 (PRA).[1] The Act is a code[2] that imposes a default property-sharing regime on married spouses, civil union partners and de facto partners[3] who do not contract out of the Act by entering into a marital agreement. The main purpose of this chapter is to discuss the key elements of marital agreements as provided for in Part 6 of the Property (Relationships) Act 1976. Before doing that, however, it is helpful to consider some preliminary points necessary for a better understanding of New Zealand's family property laws. First, a brief sketch of the history of the laws bearing on relationship breakdown will illustrate how far New Zealand has moved away from the discretionary approach that has been preferred in England. This will be followed by an overview of the relationship property laws currently in force (including the ancillary issue of spousal maintenance), which set the legislative context in which couples enter marital agreements.

B. Historical Overview

i. Early Developments

Prior to 1860, New Zealand's early colonial matrimonial property rules were founded on the common law's unitary system, the effects of which are documented elsewhere and need not be repeated in the present context.[4] Between 1860 and 1884, New Zealand began dismantling some of the common law disabilities encountered by married women, providing them with a degree of financial protection against profligate husbands.[5] These laws heralded the first signs of a move towards what would become a system of separation of property under the Married Women's Property Act 1884. That Act radically reformed the existing law, giving married women the right to acquire, hold and dispose of property in the same manner as a feme sole.[6]

Maintenance laws began to take shape around the turn of the twentieth century. A spouse's property concerns, particularly those of the wife, were not co-existent

---

[1] Ancillary matters relating to spousal maintenance are contained in a separate scheme in the Family Proceedings Act 1980. See main text, below at I.C.ii and iii.

[2] PRA, s 4. The Act is a code that 'applies instead of the rules and presumptions of the common law and of equity to the extent that they apply—(a) to transactions between spouses or partners in respect of property.'

[3] The PRA does not normally apply to de facto relationships of less than three years' duration: s 14A.

[4] See generally, M Briggs, 'Historical Analysis' in N Peart, M Briggs and M Henaghan (eds), *Relationship Property on Death* (Wellington, Thomson Brookers, 2004) 1 ff.

[5] The Married Women's Property Act 1880 consolidated the Married Women's Property Protection Acts of 1860 and 1870.

[6] Married Women's Property Act 1884, s 3.

and co-terminus with the life of the other spouse.[7] New Zealand was the first country to introduce controls on the freedom of testation in an attempt to prevent men, in particular, from bequeathing their estates to strangers, leaving their wives and children destitute.[8] The Testator's Family Maintenance Act 1900 made a deceased's estate liable for the maintenance of the surviving spouse or children, and gave the court the discretion to make 'adequate provision for the proper maintenance and support of [the deceased's] wife, husband, or children' where the deceased had failed to do so in his or her will.[9] The wording of this provision has remained largely unchanged following the introduction of the Family Protection Act 1955, which is in operation today.[10]

At a time when there were no state benefits, the Destitute Persons Act 1910 also emphasised the responsibility of family members to contribute to the support of deserted wives, as well as unmarried mothers, invalids and the unemployed.

ii. Legislative Implementation of Judicial Discretion

The Matrimonial Property Act 1963 marked another turning point in the development of family property law in New Zealand. It applied both to matrimonial property disputes during the lives of the spouses and to claims by or against the estate of the deceased spouse. Although still essentially a separate property system, judicial discretion played a central role in the Matrimonial Property Act 1963, empowering the court to make such orders as it thought fit with respect to the property in dispute,[11] having regard to the respective contributions of the husband and wife to the property.[12] The 1963 Act gave equal status to monetary and non-monetary contributions to the property, but direct monetary contributions tended to influence the courts more than non-monetary ones.[13] Moreover, there was no presumption of equal sharing under the 1963 Act, and both wives and widows regularly left a marriage with less than half of the matrimonial property. After a long marriage, the non-owner spouse might only expect to receive a quarter to one-third of the value of the other spouse's assets.[14]

The continued piecemeal development of the different facets of the property and financial consequences of divorce was reflected in the enactment of a separate system for claims for maintenance. The Domestic Proceedings Act 1968 replaced the Destitute Persons Act 1910 and, except for parents and spouses, removed liability

---

[7] Briggs, *Relationship Property on Death*, above n 4, 7.

[8] N Peart, 'The Direction of the Family Protection Act 1955' [1994] *New Zealand Recent Law Review* 193, 194. The Testator's Family Maintenance Act 1900 replaced the Destitute Persons Act 1894. See also R Atherton, 'New Zealand's Testator's Family Maintenance Act of 1900' (1990) 7 *Otago Law Review* 202.

[9] Testator's Family Maintenance Act 1900, s 2.

[10] Family Protection Act 1955, s 4. See generally, Peart, 'The Direction of the Family Protection Act 1955', above n 8.

[11] Matrimonial Property Act 1963, s 5(2).

[12] Matrimonial Property Act 1963, s 6(1).

[13] See M Henaghan and N Peart, 'Relationship Property Appeals in the New Zealand Court of Appeal 1958–2008: The Elusiveness of Equality', in R Bigwood (ed), *The Permanent New Zealand Court of Appeal, Essays on the First 50 Years* (Oxford, Hart Publishing, 2009) 99, 108–13.

[14] See *Trapski's Family Law*, vol VI (Wellington, Brookers, 1995) MA 6.15, for a discussion of the size of awards made to widows.

of relatives. Claims for spousal maintenance were needs-based, and a spouse could be held responsible for the support of a former spouse until that person's death. The concept of a 'clean break' was thus yet to emerge in any principled manner.

iii. Legislative Implementation of Equal Sharing

The Matrimonial Property Act 1976 swept away the broad judicial discretions of the earlier Matrimonial Property Act 1963 and implemented a new default regime based on deferred community property.[15] The 1976 Act treated marriage as a partnership of equals, and recognised a presumption of equal sharing of the matrimonial property at marriage breakdown.[16] The quid pro quo was that spouses could now, for the first time, opt out ('contract out') of the Act by making a marital agreement.[17] Couples did not have a completely free hand, however. Rather, they had to comply with certain procedural requirements designed to ensure that they both understood the implications of their alternative property arrangements, and that a failure to comply generally made the contract invalid. Procedurally valid contracts could be substantively challenged on the basis that it would be 'unjust' to give effect to the agreement.[18] Moreover, ordinary principles of common law and equity still applied, with the effect that a contract could be void on the grounds of duress, undue influence or unconscionable bargain.[19]

When first introduced, the Matrimonial Property Act 1976 was hailed as landmark social legislation.[20] It did not take long, however, before rapid increases in divorce rates,[21] single-parent families,[22] women in paid employment[23] and unmarried couples[24] challenged the scope of the Matrimonial Property Act 1976. The Act

---

[15] See Matrimonial Property Act 1976, s 25(1). The court's jurisdiction to make orders began once an application was made under the Act in terms of s 23.

[16] Property classified as 'matrimonial' was shared equally. The owner retained their 'separate' property: ss 8, 9. Section 15 distinguished between domestic (the home and chattels) and non-domestic matrimonial property (eg, farms and businesses). It was easier to rebut the presumption of equal sharing of the non-domestic property by showing that one spouse's contribution to the marriage partnership was 'clearly greater' than that of the other.

[17] Matrimonial Property Act 1976, s 21.

[18] Matrimonial Property Act 1976, s 21(8)(b).

[19] See eg *Moffat v Moffat* [1984] 1 NZLR 600 (CA), where the Court set aside a separation agreement as an unconscionable bargain. There, the wife had given up her interest in the family home because she was unaware that she had an enforceable claim.

[20] *Reid v Reid* [1979] 1 NZLR 572 (CA) described the Act as 'social legislation of the widest general application': 580, 605, 610 (Woodhouse and Richardson JJ).

[21] Marriage rates have fallen significantly, while divorce rates have risen. In the year ended December 2009, 21,600 marriages were registered to New Zealand residents, and 8,700 orders for dissolution were granted. That compares to 29,390 marriages and 8,590 divorces in 1981. It is estimated that around one-third of all marriages in New Zealand now end in divorce. These figures must be read in perspective with the near doubling of New Zealand's population since the 1950s. (The population of New Zealand was estimated at 4,362,000 as at 31 March 2010: http://search.stats.govt.)

[22] In 1991, when census data was first collected, there were 151,755 single-parent families. By the 2006 census, that had risen to 193,635: *Statistics New Zealand*, Census 2006, Families, All Households, Table 8.

[23] In 1986, when data was first collected, 683,300 women were in paid employment. By 2008, that had risen to 1,043,900. 'Paid employment' includes employees, employers, and the self-employed: http://search.stats.govt.nz/nav/ct2/workincomespending_employment/ct1/workincomespending/.

[24] The numbers living in de facto relationships have risen markedly since the 1980s. In 1981, 87,960 people lived in de facto relationships. By 1991, that figure had almost doubled to 161,856, and in 2001

applied only on separation or divorce, and did not extend to couples in de facto (cohabiting) relationships, whether opposite- or same-sex. Unmarried couples had to rely on common law and equity, in particular the constructive trust, to acquire a share of the assets accumulated during the relationship.[25] Even for married couples covered by the Act, equal sharing of the matrimonial property did not necessarily mean they would be placed on an equal footing after divorce.[26] The 1976 Act did not contemplate the potential future needs of the parties and did not extend to income or intangible assets, such as the earning capacities of the parties.[27] To some extent, however, maintenance might be used to fill the gap in this regard. Spousal maintenance was by now dealt with in the Family Proceedings Act 1980, which had replaced the Domestic Proceedings Act 1968. But the rationale for spousal maintenance was merely to give the recipient a temporary breathing space during which time a new life could be constructed.[28]

C. The Current Regime

i. Property (Relationships) Act 1976

The Property (Relationships) Amendment Act 2001 came into force on 1 February 2002.[29] It substantially amended the Matrimonial Property Act 1976 and was renamed the Property (Relationships) Act 1976 (PRA) to recognise the wide range of relationships now covered by the legislation.[30] Like the Matrimonial Property Act, the PRA is a default deferred property-sharing regime that applies in the absence of a valid contracting-out agreement between the couple. The PRA also continues to promote a 'clean-break' approach, rationalised on the basis of enabling former partners to achieve certainty and finality in their financial affairs to allow them to get on with their lives.[31]

---

it had more than doubled again to 336,594. By 2006, 428,130 New Zealanders were living in de facto relationships: www.stats.govt.nz/methods_and_services/information-releases/marriages-civil-unions-and-divorces.aspx.

[25] Eg, *Gillies v Keogh* [1989] 2 NZLR 327 (CA) 333. See generally, W Atkin, 'Matrimonial and De Facto Property Law Reform—Some Preliminary Reflections' (2001) *Butterworths Family Law Journal* 221, 222.

[26] See Henaghan and Peart, 'Relationship Property Appeals', above n 13, 113–25.

[27] See *Z v Z (No 2)* [1997] 2 NZLR 258 (CA).

[28] W Atkin, 'Financial Support—Who Supports Whom?' in M Henaghan and W Atkin (eds), *Family Law and Policy in New Zealand*, 3rd edn (Wellington, LexisNexis, 2007) 167, 168; W Atkin, 'Spousal Maintenance: A New Philosophy?' (1981) 9 *New Zealand Universities Law Review* 336. Spousal maintenance is considered in more detail following the analysis of the Property (Relationships) Act 1976.

[29] The contracting-out provisions took effect from the earlier date of 1 August 2001.

[30] Property (Relationships) Amendment Act 2001, s 5(1).

[31] The central philosophy of the PRA is articulated in the purpose and principles sections of the legislation: ss 1M, 1N. The purpose (s 1M) of the PRA is to: (a) reform the law relating to the property of married couples, civil union couples and de facto couples; (b) recognise the equal contributions of spouses or partners to their partnership; and (c) provide for a just division of relationship property between the spouses or partners when their relationship ends by separation or death, and in certain other circumstances, while taking account of the interests of any children of the marriage, civil union or de facto relationship. The four principles (s 1N) to guide the achievement of the purpose of the PRA are that: (a) men and women have equal status, and their equality should be maintained and enhanced;

The most far-reaching amendments apply to the range of relationships now covered by the PRA. Following the 2001 amendments, the PRA applied to married couples[32] as well as to heterosexual and same-sex de facto couples living in informal, unregistered relationships of three or more years' duration.[33] After the enactment of the Civil Union Act 2004, the PRA was amended to include registered heterosexual and same-sex civil unions.[34]

The PRA extends to marriages, civil unions and de facto relationships ending on death,[35] as well as on separation. The 2001 amendments finally repealed the Matrimonial Property Act 1963, which had continued to apply to marriages ending on death after the enactment of the Matrimonial Property Act 1976. The PRA provides a separate set of rules where the relationship ends on the death of a spouse or partner.[36] Survivors have two choices: they may either share the relationship property on the same basis as if the relationship had ended during their lifetime, or they may elect to inherit from their deceased partner under the will or on intestacy.[37]

The PRA retains much of the property classification and division system put in place under the Matrimonial Property Act 1976. All the relationship property is shared equally between the parties, but the owner partner retains his or her separate property. Property acquired during the relationship, or before the relationship in contemplation of it and for the common benefit or use of the parties, is relationship property. The family home and chattels have the added protection of being defined as relationship property *whenever* acquired.[38] Property not acquired during the relationship or in contemplation of it, or acquired during the relationship from a third

(b) all forms of contributions to the partnership are treated as equal; (c) a just division of relationship property has regard to the economic advantages or disadvantages to the spouses or partners arising from their marriage, civil union or de facto relationship or its ending; and that (d) questions arising under the PRA about relationship property should be resolved as inexpensively, simply, and speedily as is consistent with justice.

[32] Curiously, the Marriage Act 1955 does not expressly state that marriage is a heterosexual institution. However, *Quilter v Attorney General* [1998] 1 NZLR 523 (CA) held that marriage must be between a man and a woman. In New Zealand, dissolution of a marriage or civil union is 'no fault': Family Proceedings Act 1980, s 39. Dissolution is granted automatically after the couple has lived apart for two years. It is granted on the basis of irreconcilable differences, which covers all reasons for ending a marriage or civil union.

[33] De facto partners must live together for at least three years to qualify under the PRA: s 14A. To be covered by the PRA, the relationship must also have ended after 1 February 2002: s 4C.

[34] Civil Union Act 2004, s 4. The take-up rate of civil unions has been extremely low. In 2008, a mere 405 civil unions were registered. Since 2005, a total of 1506 civil unions have been registered.

[35] For an explanation of the scheme of the death provisions see generally, Peart, Briggs and Henaghan, *Relationship Property on Death,* above n 4.

[36] PRA, Pt 8.

[37] There are two exceptions to the general rule that the survivor must choose either to apply for a division of their relationship property under the Act, or to accept the inheritance from their deceased spouse or partner: (i) if the deceased's will expresses an intention that in the event that the survivor elects division under the Act s/he may *also* inherit under the will (PRA, s 76); (ii) if the Court is satisfied that it is necessary to avoid injustice, it may order that a survivor who has elected division under the Act may *also* inherit under the will (PRA, s 77).

[38] PRA, s 8(1)(a) and (b). Where the family home has been sold, the proceeds are shared equally: s 11A. Where there is no family home, the court must award each partner an equal share in such part of the relationship property as it thinks just in order to compensate for the absence of a family home: s 11B. The court may also grant an occupation order in respect of the family home (s 27), or an ancillary furniture order (s 28B).

party by gift or inheritance but not intermingled with relationship property, remains the separate property of the owner partner.[39]

Superannuation schemes (pension entitlements) are relationship property insofar as the funds have accumulated during the relationship.[40] The proportion of the value of any superannuation scheme entitlement that is 'attributable to the relationship' is included within the relationship property pool.[41] The courts have given a wide reading to the words 'attributable to the relationship'. [42] The calculation is made on the basis of the duration of the scheme as against the duration of the relationship. For example, if A entered a superannuation scheme in 1995, married B in 2000 and then divorced in 2005, 50 per cent of the superannuation would be 'attributable to the marriage', because the contributions were made during the marriage.[43]

During the relationship, the property regime does not affect the parties' common law and equitable interests. The PRA takes effect in the event of a court order or a separation agreement.[44] If the parties do not mutually agree on a distribution of the property, the equal-sharing regime dictates that the relationship property will be divided equally between the parties, unless one of the narrow exceptions recognised by the PRA applies.[45]

The PRA strengthens the presumption of equal sharing by removing the distinction drawn in the Matrimonial Property Act 1976 between domestic matrimonial property (the home and chattels) and non-domestic matrimonial property (eg, farms and businesses etc). That distinction had made it easier to rebut the presumption of equal sharing in respect of the non-domestic property, by showing that the contribution of one spouse to the marriage partnership was clearly greater than that of the other spouse.[46] As a result of the removal of that distinction, it is now much harder to challenge equal division of the relationship property.[47]

The PRA recognises that a partner's share of the relationship property may not be sufficient to meet that person's needs once the relationship is over. This came about partly in response to the 1996 landmark decision of the Court of Appeal in *Z v Z*,[48] which held that enhanced earning capacity as a result of professional qualifications and job promotions acquired during the marriage was not 'property' within the Matrimonial Property Act 1976 and could not be shared on divorce. Section 15 of

[39] PRA, ss 8, 9, 9A and 10.

[40] PRA, s 8(1)(i). See also s 31, which specifies the orders the court may make in relation to superannuation rights. Life insurance policies and other insurance policies are also relationship property: PRA, ss 8(1)(g) and (h), s 30.

[41] A 'superannuation scheme entitlement' is any pension, benefit, or right to which either party is entitled or may become entitled under any superannuation scheme, if the entitlement is derived, wholly or in part, from contributions made to the scheme after the relationship began or from employment or office held since the relationship began: PRA, s 2.

[42] *De Malmanche v De Malmanche* [2002] 2 NZLR 838.

[43] See Judge P Mahony (consulting ed), *Brookers Family Law—Family Property* (Wellington, Brookers Ltd, 2008) PR8.22–8.25.

[44] PRA, s 25.

[45] The equal-sharing provisions do not apply to a marriage or civil union of short duration in certain circumstances: PRA, ss 14, 14AA. The court has a discretion to depart from equal sharing if there are extraordinary circumstances which would render equal sharing repugnant to justice: PRA, s 13.

[46] Matrimonial Property Act 1976, s 15.

[47] PRA, s 11.

[48] *Z v Z (No 2)*, above n 27.

the PRA now allows an award of compensation to be made from the advantaged party's relationship property where, on the division of the relationship property, the income and living standards of one partner are likely to be significantly higher than those of the other partner because of the division of functions within the relationship.[49] It is designed to achieve equality of result, and contemplates situations where one partner has, for instance, given up career advancement during the relationship to look after dependent children, and is subsequently left at a disadvantage in terms of earning potential when the relationship ends.

The focus in section 15 on equality of result has parallels with the view taken by the House of Lords in *Miller v Miller; McFarlane v McFarlane*[50] that an equal partnership will not always dictate an equal sharing of the assets, and that too strict an adherence to equal sharing and a clean break can lead to a decrease in the primary carer's standard of living and an increase in the breadwinner's. Baroness Hale identified the breadwinner's unimpaired and unimpeded earning capacity as a powerful resource with which to repair loss of capital after an unequal distribution, and noted that recognition of this was one reason why English law had been so successful in retaining a home for the children:[51] 'The ultimate objective is to give each party an equal start on the road to independent living.'[52]

The New Zealand judicial experience of section 15 of the PRA has thus far been that the provision is difficult to apply in a principled manner, due in part to its highly speculative nature.[53] Compensation payments have been modest, reflecting the courts' cautious approach to section 15. There is some irony in this outcome. Since the introduction of the Matrimonial Property Act 1976, New Zealand's relationship property laws have generally been seen as very progressive, but, in practice, the creation of the inflexible regime has come at a cost. Where the courts do have judicial discretion, such as in section 15, they are guarded in its application. It might be said that England has now moved ahead of New Zealand in the pursuit of true equality, at least for marriages,[54] in cases such as *Miller v Miller; McFarlane v McFarlane*.[55]

The courts' reluctance to make generous awards under section 15 may be due in part to the uncertain relationship between section 15 and the spousal maintenance provisions in the Family Proceedings Act 1980. This issue is considered below.

ii. Post-Separation Spousal Maintenance

New Zealand lacks a cohesive approach to the different financial and property aspects of relationship breakdown. Liability for spousal maintenance is regulated

---

[49] PRA, s 15.

[50] *Miller v Miller; McFarlane v McFarlane* [2006] UKHL 24; *Miller v Miller;* [2006] 2 WLR 1283.

[51] Ibid [142] (Baroness Hale).

[52] Ibid [144] (Baroness Hale).

[53] Eg, *X v X* [2009] NZCA 399; [2009] NZFLR 985. For an analysis of s 15 and the early case law, see J Miles, 'Dealing with Economic Disparity: An Analysis of Section 15 Property (Relationships) Act 1976' [2003] *NZ Law Review* 535.

[54] Cf *Stack v Dowden* [2007] UKHL 17, which demonstrates that in de facto relationships, monetary contributions continue to be more influential than non-monetary contributions.

[55] See Henaghan and Peart, above n 13 at 99, 148.

by the Family Proceedings Act 1980,[56] a scheme that is only partially linked to the PRA.[57]

The Family Proceedings Act 1980 replaced the Domestic Proceedings Act 1968 and radically altered the approach to spousal maintenance, removing the assumption that a marriage involves a lifelong obligation. More people are now eligible for maintenance than previously, though. Amendments in 2001 (at the same time the PRA was enacted) extended the maintenance laws to de facto relationships. Civil unions were also included with the enactment of the Civil Union Act 2004.

There is no liability to pay maintenance except as provided by the Act. After a marriage or civil union is dissolved, or a de facto relationship has ended, one party is liable to maintain the other to the extent necessary to meet the reasonable needs of the other party.[58] 'Reasonable needs' is not defined, but the emphasis is on the ability to become self-supporting, having regard to the effects of the division of functions within the relationship and the likely earning capacity of each party.[59] Maintenance is not, however, intended to redress imbalances in the relative earning capacities of the former partners. The clean-break principle applies to spousal maintenance, which is not an indefinite obligation attaching automatically to a relationship.[60] The parties must assume responsibility for their own needs within a period of time that is reasonable in the circumstances of the particular case.[61] Although no time limit is specified for the duration of liability, maintenance obligations are usually a short-term measure.[62]

Cases are necessarily determined on their particular facts, a point demonstrated by the recent decision of the Court of Appeal in *C v G*.[63] This case concerned the duration of C's liability to maintain G, who was responsible for the full-time care of the parties' young daughter. The parties had entered into maintenance and property arrangements under Australian law that provided that G would be maintained

---

[56] Family Proceedings Act 1980, ss 60–70B.

[57] Financial support for children, despite its obvious link with the needs of the child's care giver, is contained in yet more separate legislation, the Child Support Act 1991. However, that scheme is very different, in that it is designed to avoid involvement with lawyers where possible, and is administered by the Inland Revenue Department. See, www.ird.govt.nz/childsupport. For a discussion of the Child Support Act 1991, see Atkin, *Family Law and Policy in New Zealand*, above n 28, 167 ff.

[58] Family Proceedings Act 1980, s 64. For liability to pay maintenance during a marriage or civil union, see s 63. There is no liability to pay maintenance during a de facto relationship.

[59] Family Proceedings Act 1980, s 64(2). The Family Proceedings Amendment Act 2001 made several changes to s 64. For an analysis of the background to the purposes and provisions of post-separation maintenance, see *Slater v Slater* [1983] NZLR 166 (CA).

[60] P Webb et al, *Family Law in New Zealand*, 14th edn (Wellington, LexisNexis, 2009) 18.

[61] Family Proceedings Act 1980, s 64A, as amended by the Family Proceedings Amendment Act 2001.

[62] For a discussion of these matters, see *Brookers Family Law—Family Property*, above n 43, FA64A.01; Webb, *Family Law in New Zealand*, above n 60, 16ff. S 82 Family Proceedings Act 1980 enables the court to make an order for interim maintenance. Such an order can remain in force for up to six months. In *DCK v RK* 20 November 2009, CIV 2009-404-4421 (HC Auckland, Heath J), the High Court upheld the lower court's interim award which was designed to maintain the high standard of living that had existed before separation. The husband, who left his wife a note in the letter box saying their three-year marriage was over, was ordered to pay interim maintenance of $10,000 a month. The Family Court judge had said that the wife had enjoyed a 'luxurious lifestyle' from which she should not be deprived 'overnight'. In the High Court, Heath J said that in the context of the couple's previous expenditure, an interim award of $60,000 over a six-month period was 'not disproportionate or unreasonable.'

[63] *C v G* [2010] NZFLR 497 (CA).

until the child was three years old. The High Court had held that G was entitled to further maintenance while she retrained as a lawyer until the child was seven years old. The Court of Appeal overturned that decision and reinstated the Family Court decision to extend the agreement until the child turned five. The Court was of the opinion that it should not lightly depart from arrangements entered into by parties, since it was in the public interest to encourage parties to reach agreements without resort to the courts. On the facts, extending the agreement until the child turned five properly recognised that G's earlier expectation of becoming self-supporting by the time the child was three was not fulfilled because she had difficulties in gaining part-time employment in her field of work in human resources. It was therefore reasonable to allow her some time to adjust to her altered circumstances until the child began school at age five. But there was no justification for extending the agreement while G retrained as a lawyer, because she had a greater capacity to support herself by continuing to work in human resources where her potential income would be two or three times more than her potential income as a lawyer.

However, the amendments made in 2001 have blurred the clean-break principle in some situations. Since 2001, the circumstances in which a party may seek maintenance on a longer-term basis have been widened to include consideration of the ages of the parties and the duration of the relationship.[64] These amendments address concerns that were raised earlier in *Z v Z*,[65] where the Court of Appeal warned against applying the clean-break principle in such a way that the Act would operate unfairly or harshly on one or other party. This is especially so in cases where the marriage or relationship has been a long one, and the disadvantaged party is now of an age where it may be impracticable to expect them to become fully self-supporting.

As noted earlier, the PRA and the Family Proceedings Act are linked, although not in a comprehensive way. The PRA recognises that maintenance may be dealt with as part of the division of property. In the course of determining property proceedings under the PRA, the court may also make an order for the maintenance of a spouse or partner, which, if capitalised, may be paid for from the available relationship property.[66] Nonetheless, the absence of a unified approach between the different elements of relationship breakdown may be observed in the overlap between spousal maintenance to meet 'reasonable needs' and compensation for economic disparity under section 15 of the PRA.[67] In each case, consideration must be given to the effect of the division of functions in relation to the capacity of the parties to earn an income after the relationship ends.[68] It is currently unclear how, and in what order, claims for spousal maintenance and economic disparity should be determined;[69]

---

[64] Family Proceedings Act 1980, s 64A. See *Brookers Family Law—Family Property,* above n 43, FA64A.01.

[65] *Z v Z (No 2),* above n 27.

[66] PRA, s 32(2)(a). See Atkin, *Family Law and Policy in New Zealand,* above n 28, 168.

[67] See the discussion in BD Inglis, *New Zealand Family Law in the 21st Century* (Wellington, Thomson Brookers, 2007) 961–63. But note that a maintenance order has the advantage of being adjusted to meet a change in circumstances, which is unavailable when lump sum compensation is awarded for economic disparity under the PRA.

[68] See also *M v B (economic disparity)* [2006] 3 NZLR 660 (CA) for a discussion of the relevance of *Miller v Miller; McFarlane v McFarlane,* above n 50, in the New Zealand context.

[69] See *de Malmanche v de Malmanche,* above n 42; *P v P* [2005] NZFLR 689 (HC).

in *M v B (economic disparity)*[70] the Court of Appeal had differing views on this issue. One writer has argued that, logically, maintenance should be favoured where possible because its periodic nature enables amendment to take account of future changes. That would leave economic disparity for those situations where the party deserves to be recognised for their contribution to the other party's career prospects.[71] On the other hand, one of the judges in *M v B (economic disparity)* argued that the section 15 economic disparity issue should be clarified first because, once that was done, an assessment could then be made as to whether one of the partners was liable to pay spousal maintenance.[72]

The role of spousal maintenance must also be viewed in the context of the wide range of welfare benefits available in New Zealand to financially support the unemployed, the sick and disabled, single parents, widows and women alone.[73] The availability of state support may be one reason why private spousal maintenance tends to play a secondary role to property division under the PRA.[74]

iii. Maintenance Agreements

It was noted in the preceding discussion that there is no liability to pay maintenance except as provided by the Family Proceedings Act 1980. That does not prevent the parties reaching a voluntary agreement regarding maintenance, however. Voluntary agreements are enforceable under general contractual principles.[75]

A voluntary agreement for 'domestic maintenance'[76] may qualify for acceptance by the Commissioner of Inland Revenue and be administered in accordance with the powers contained in the Child Support Act 1991.[77] It is the Child Support Act 1991 rather than the Family Proceedings Act 1980 that contains the requirements relating to voluntary maintenance agreements for spouses as well as children.[78] An agreement may qualify for acceptance whether it is entered into in or outside of New Zealand.[79]

In order for a voluntary agreement to be accepted by the Commissioner, certain conditions must be satisfied.[80] The agreement must be made by a husband and

---

[70] *M v B*, above n 68. See *Brookers Family Law—Family Property*, above n 43, FA63.02.

[71] Atkin, *Family Law and Policy in New Zealand*, above n 28, 192.

[72] *M v B (economic disparity)*, above n 68 [121]–[129] (Robertson J).

[73] For information on the range of welfare benefits and related state entitlements available in New Zealand, see generally www.workandincome.govt.nz and www.ird.govt.nz.

[74] Note, however, that the liability to maintain one's former spouse or partner is not extinguished by reason of the applicant's reasonable needs being met by a domestic (state) benefit: Family Proceedings Act 1980, s 62. 'Domestic benefit' is defined in s 2 as a benefit granted under the Social Security Act 1964.

[75] Child Support Act 1991, s 62(2). See *Townshend v Bellamy* 3 June 2005, CIV-2004-483-393 (HC Wanganui) [8]–[10]; *KLS v GL* 11 August 2009, FAM-2006-044-002418 (FC North Shore) [8]–[9].

[76] 'Domestic maintenance' is the term used to describe spousal maintenance. It means any payment required to be made under the Child Support Act 1991 by any person towards the support of another person under s 58(2) or s 68(2) of the Act: Child Support Act 1991, s 2.

[77] See the discussion in Webb above n 60, 49–51.

[78] The requirements for voluntary agreements are contained in the Child Support Act 1991, Pt 3, ss 47–66A.

[79] Child Support Act 1991, s 48(2).

[80] Child Support Act 1991, s 48(1). If the agreement also includes provisions of a kind not falling within s 48(1), those provisions do not have effect for the purposes of the application of this Act to the voluntary agreement: s 48(3).

wife or civil union partners, or the parties to a marriage, civil union or de facto relationship that has ended, or persons who are the parents of a child who have never been in a marriage or civil union with each other.[81] There must also be the payment by one party of a periodical sum of money to the other party towards the maintenance of the other party.[82]

An application for acceptance of a voluntary agreement is properly made if it is signed by either party to the agreement, is made to the Commissioner in the appropriate approved form and is accompanied by the necessary documents.[83] The person by whom any money is to be paid and the person to whom that money is to be paid must both either be New Zealand citizens or persons who are ordinarily resident in New Zealand.[84] If the application is properly made, the Commissioner must accept the agreement.[85] Parties may also vary a voluntary agreement. However, in order to be effective for the purposes of the Child Support Act 1991, the variation must be made by application to the Commissioner in the manner specified by the Act.[86] In addition, where proceedings are brought under the PRA the Court may cancel, vary, extend or suspend a voluntary agreement if it considers it just.[87] For example, a change to a maintenance arrangement may be appropriate where a relationship property order is made.[88]

A voluntary agreement does not qualify for acceptance by the Commissioner if a court order is already in force requiring one party to the agreement to make payments towards the maintenance of the other party to the agreement.[89] Nor does the existence of a voluntary agreement prevent a party from applying under the Family Proceedings Act 1980 for a maintenance order.[90] Where a maintenance order under the Family Proceedings Act is made against a party to the voluntary maintenance agreement, the order replaces the voluntary agreement.[91]

Section 182 of the Family Proceedings Act 1980 may also apply in certain circumstances where there is no accepted agreement in terms of the Child Support Act 1991. That provision allows the Court to inquire into the existence of any agreement between the parties to a marriage or civil union for the payment of maintenance and to make such orders as it thinks fit. On the application of either party to a maintenance agreement, the Court may cancel or vary the agreement or remit any arrears due under the agreement.[92] In order for the provision to apply, however, the marriage or the civil union of the parties to the maintenance agreement must have been dissolved.[93] It should also be noted that section 182 does not apply to de facto relationships.

---

[81] Child Support Act 1991, s 47(3).

[82] The periodic payments are required to be in the form of weekly, fortnightly, or monthly instalments and each weekly instalment must be not less than the minimum amount required by the Act (currently set at a rate of NZ$10): Child Support Act 1991, ss 48(1), 49(2).

[83] Child Support Act 1991, s 55(1).

[84] Child Support Act 1991, s 55(1)(c).

[85] Child Support Act 1991, s 57.

[86] Child Support Act 1991, s 63. For a discussion see Webb above n 60, 49ff.

[87] Property (Relationships) Act 1976, s 32(2).

[88] See Webb above n 60, 54ff.

[89] Child Support Act 1991, s 52.

[90] *KLS v GL,* above n 75, [11].

[91] Child Support Act 1991, s 66.

[92] Family Proceedings Act 1980, s 182(2).

[93] Family Proceedings Act 1980, s 182(1).

II. PRE-NUPTIAL AND POST-NUPTIAL AGREEMENTS

A. General

The raft of amendments introduced by the PRA in 2001 has resulted in more relationships and more property now being caught by the equal-sharing default provisions. For couples wanting to arrange their property affairs differently, the contracting-out option therefore assumes central importance.[94] Indeed, public acceptance of the expanded reach of the PRA, especially the inclusion of de facto relationships, was partly based on the fact that couples could choose to opt-out of the default regime and make their own alternative property arrangements.[95]

There is very little statistical data in New Zealand on the number of couples with contracting-out agreements,[96] although at present the majority of couples do not contract out of the PRA. It is foreseeable, however, that numbers will rise as more people enter second marriages or other relationships, and as public awareness about the wide reach and effects of the PRA's default regime grows.

The reasons for couples making contracting-out agreements are varied, but common motivations include the desire to protect pre-relationship separate property and anticipated gifts or inheritances. Some couples are motivated by the economic benefits to be gained by splitting income or superannuation (pensions) for tax purposes.[97] It is also common for people entering second marriages, civil unions or de facto relationships to guard separate assets for their children from the former relationship. As well, agreements may be made for other estate planning purposes, such as where an agreement classifies property as separate property before it is put into a trust or a company.[98]

The PRA broadly contemplates three different agreements. The first, dealt with in section 21, applies to spouses, civil union partners, or de facto partners, or any two persons in contemplation of entering into a marriage, civil union or de facto relationship. A couple may thus make an agreement when they are contemplating marriage or a civil union or entering a de facto relationship (a 'pre-nuptial agreement'), or during the relationship (a 'post-nuptial agreement').

Such persons may make any agreement they think fit with respect to the status, ownership, and division of their property (including future property) during their joint lives and/or when one of them dies.

The second and third types of agreement covered by the PRA are agreements made to settle existing property differences between spouses or partners. 'Separation agreements' (often referred to in New Zealand as 'compromise agreements' or 'settlement

---

[94] Most of the amendments made by the PRA came into force on 1 February 2002, but the contracting-out provisions in Pt 6 of the PRA came into force on 1 August 2001, to give couples time to organise their affairs. Transitional provisions are provided in ss 21P–21T of the PRA.

[95] N Peart, 'The Property (Relationships) Amendment Act 2001: A Conceptual Change' (2008) 39 *Victoria University of Wellington Law Review* 813, 825. See *Wells v Wells* [2006] NZFLR 870 (HC) [38].

[96] Statistics New Zealand does not gather or hold data on contracting-out agreements.

[97] Some couples use contracting-out agreements in an effort to protect property against creditors. But note that s 21 agreements are subject to s 47 and can be void against creditors and the Official Assignee in certain situations.

[98] That would prevent a subsequent claim to break the trust (s 44C) or the company (s 44F). See further, *Brookers Family Law—Family Property*, above n 43, PR21.04.

agreements') are normally made on or after separation (s 21A). They may also be made after the death of a spouse or partner, in which case the agreement will be between the survivor and the personal representative of the deceased (s 21B). Both forms of separation agreement are considered in section III (below).

B. Procedural Requirements

The PRA provides an optional model form agreement for couples to use in order to minimise their legal expenses,[99] but couples generally make their own agreements because the model agreement is somewhat rudimentary and fails to address the complicated property issues experienced by many people. Most agreements are prepared by lawyers and are tailored to meet the individual needs and requirements of the couple.

There is no registration procedure for either pre-nuptial agreements or post-nuptial agreements in New Zealand. The state plays no role in the agreement-making or agreement certification process, with the limited exception of agreements made by minors under the age of 18 years and who are not married or in a civil union (s 21I). Such agreements are not valid without the approval of the court.[100]

The PRA requires that agreements comply with a number of strictly enforced formalities designed to ensure that both parties are fully aware of the rights they are gaining and losing by entering into the agreement. If the agreement does not comply with those requirements, the agreement is void. Section 21F provides:

(1) Subject to section 21H, an agreement entered into under section 21 or section 21A or section 21B is void unless the requirements set out in subsections (2) to (5) are complied with.
(2) The agreement must be in writing and signed by both parties.
(3) Each party to the agreement must have independent legal advice before signing the agreement.
(4) The signature of each party to the agreement must be witnessed by a lawyer.
(5) The lawyer who witnesses the signature of a party must certify that, before that party signed the agreement, the lawyer explained to that party the effect and implications of the agreement.

In the absence of state involvement in the contracting-out process, the role of legal[101] advice is key. Each party must have independent legal advice before signing the agreement. Questions have arisen as to whether this requires that the lawyers must be from separate law firms, whether advice is independent if the lawyer has acted for the parties in the past, and the effect of the presence of the other party when the advice is given.[102] Unsurprisingly, cases on these issues are highly fact-sensitive. It has been argued that to safeguard the validity of the agreement, it is preferable to use

---

[99] PRA, s 21E; Property (Relationships) Model Form of Agreement Regulations 2001.

[100] It is unclear how this provision would apply to de facto partners under the age of 18, given that the PRA imposes a minimum age requirement of 18 years on de facto relationships: PRA, s 2D.

[101] A 'lawyer' is a person who holds a current practising certificate as a barrister or as a barrister and solicitor: Lawyers and Conveyancers Act 2006, s 6.

[102] *Brookers Family Law—Family Property*, above n 43, PR21F.06 and the cases discussed therein.

lawyers who have not previously acted for either or both parties and that the lawyers are from separate firms.[103]

The adequacy of the legal advice is another critical factor. The lawyer who witnesses the signature of a party must certify that, before that party signed the agreement, he explained to that party the effect and implications of the agreement (s 21F(5)). The obligation on the lawyer goes beyond merely explaining what the agreement means on a clause-by-clause basis.[104] In the *locus classicus* decision in *Coxhead v Coxhead*[105] the Court of Appeal emphasised that what is required of the certifying lawyer is no mere formalism:

> Each party must receive professional opinion as to the fairness and appropriateness of the agreement at least as it affects the party's interests. The touchstone will be the entitlement that the Act gives, and the requisite advice will involve an assessment of that entitlement, and a weighing of it against any other considerations that are said to justify a departure from it. Advice is thus more than an explanation of the meaning of the terms of the agreement. Their implications must be explained as well. In other words the party concerned is entitled to an informed professional opinion as to the wisdom of entering into an agreement in those terms. This does not mean however that the adviser must always be in possession of all the facts. It may not be possible to obtain them. There may be constraints of time or other circumstances, or the other spouse may be unable or unwilling to give the necessary information. The party being advised may be content with known inadequate terms. He or she may insist on signing irrespective of advice to the contrary. In such circumstances, provided that the advice is that the information is incomplete, and that the document should not be signed until further information is available, or should not be signed at all, the requirements of [s 21F] have been satisfied. [Section 21F] does not protect one who ignores or disregards advice.[106]

The level of disclosure required for pre-nuptial agreements and post-nuptial agreements is lower than that for separation agreements (see below). For pre-nuptial and post-nuptial agreements, the lawyer must ascertain:

> at least in a general way, the property of the parties, so that he or she can advise the person who is being advised of the consequences for that party of the provisions of the Act in respect of that property and in respect of other property which would come within the Act and of the consequences of the agreement, both in respect of that property and in respect of the provisions of the Act.[107]

It is important that the party understands what property is to be shared and what is not to be shared, and that an agreement lists all the property that is to be covered by the agreement so that the assets can be identified and valued.[108]

---

[103] Ibid.

[104] Ibid PR21F.07.

[105] *Coxhead v Coxhead* [1993] 2 NZLR 397 (CA).

[106] Ibid 404 (Hardie Boys J).

[107] *Odlum v Odlum* (1989) 5 FRNZ 41, 46.

[108] *Brookers Family Law—Family Property*, above n 43, PR21F.10. However a premium has not been placed on obtaining the value of assets in the context of pre-nuptial agreements: eg, *Wilton v Crimmons* (2003) 23 FRNZ 357.

C. Serious Injustice: section 21J

An agreement that complies with the procedural formalities of section 21F may still be set aside if the court finds that enforcing the agreement would cause 'serious injustice'. Under the Matrimonial Property Act 1976 the standard for setting aside an agreement was 'injustice' simpliciter.[109] Concerns grew that the threshold at which agreements were being set aside under the 'injustice' test was too low, thus undermining the opt-out nature of the Matrimonial Property Act 1976. In 1998 in *Wood v Wood*, the High Court observed that contracting-out agreements were being set aside too readily and:

> [t]hose who criticise the Matrimonial Property Act for the readiness with which it captures property sourced from outside the marriage partnership ... are invariably met with the same answer: if people do not like the statutory regime they can contract out from it ... but if effective contracting out were as difficult to achieve as these Family Court decisions suggest, the answer would be a hollow one.[110]

In 2001 the PRA raised the threshold for setting aside agreements to that of 'serious injustice' to provide more certainty to couples that their arrangements would be upheld. Section 21J provides:

(1) Even though an agreement satisfies the requirements of section 21F, the Court may set the agreement aside if, having regard to all the circumstances, it is satisfied that giving effect to the agreement would cause serious injustice.

(2) The Court may exercise the power in subsection (1) in the course of any proceedings under this Act, or on application made for the purpose.

(3) This section does not limit or affect any enactment or rule of law or of equity that makes a contract void, voidable, or unenforceable on any other ground.

(4) In deciding, under this section, whether giving effect to an agreement made under section 21 or section 21A or section 21B would cause serious injustice, the Court must have regard to—

    (a) the provisions of the agreement;

    (b) the length of time since the agreement was made;

    (c) whether the agreement was unfair or unreasonable in the light of all the circumstances at the time it was made;

    (d) whether the agreement has become unfair or unreasonable in the light of any changes in circumstances since it was made (whether or not those changes were foreseen by the parties);

    (e) the fact that the parties wished to achieve certainty as to the status, ownership, and division of property by entering into the agreement;

    (f) any other matters that the Court considers relevant.

(5) In deciding, under this section, whether giving effect to an agreement made under section 21B would cause serious injustice, the Court must also have regard to whether the estate of the deceased spouse or partner has been wholly or partly distributed.

The Court of Appeal has recognised and given effect to the stricter test in section 21J. In the leading case of *Harrison v Harrison*[111] the Court of Appeal held that

---

[109] Matrimonial Property Act 1976, s 21(8).
[110] *Wood v Wood* [1998] 3 NZLR 234, 235.
[111] *Harrison v Harrison* [2005] 2 NZLR 349 (CA).

in a contracting-out agreement (as opposed to a separation agreement—see below) substantial economic disparity between the applicant's statutory entitlement under the PRA and her contractual entitlement under the terms of the agreement was not sufficient in itself to set aside the agreement. *Harrison* involved a post-nuptial agreement. After two periods of separation, the husband was not prepared to reconcile again unless the wife signed a matrimonial property agreement that protected his pre-marital property as his separate property. The agreement was not completely one-sided but, rather, entitled the wife to increasing entitlements over time, based on how long the spouses stayed together. The husband's lawyer prepared the agreement and the wife had a copy of it for more than a month, during which time two lawyers advised her not to sign. When the reconciliation did not last, she applied to have the agreement set aside.

The Court of Appeal held there was no serious injustice in enforcing the agreement. The fact that, as was the case here, the contracting-out process is often negotiated under pressure in circumstances where one party may threaten to vary or end the relationship if the agreement is not signed, is not evidence of serious injustice. Indeed, the Court thought that the type of pressure the wife was under was the kind that the legislature must have seen as acceptable. Rather:

> [A]t least for contracting out agreements [as opposed to separation agreements], '*serious injustice' is likely to be demonstrated more often by an unsatisfactory process resulting in inequality of outcome rather than mere inequality of outcome itself.* Parties are in general free to agree to quite different arrangements to those otherwise imposed upon them by the Act. It may be different for settlement [separation] agreements, as such agreements are entered into in respect of entitlements already accrued and should usually reflect the reality of those entitlements.[112]

As a consequence of *Harrison*, a disparity in entitlement, even a significant one, will not generally be enough to set aside an agreement, unless accompanied by an unsatisfactory process.[113] The Court in *Harrison* did not expand upon what it meant by 'unsatisfactory process', however. It might have been assumed that this referred to procedural irregularities, but *Wells v Wells*[114] subsequently cast doubt on that analysis, suggesting that it may need to be something more than failure to comply with the procedural requirements of section 21F. In *Wells*, the agreement was void for non-compliance with the formalities in section 21F, but the High Court took the opportunity to comment on the appropriate policy approach to 'serious injustice' in section 21J. The Court identified seven principles:

(a) Serious injustice is a broad discretion which must be exercised in light of the policy underlying the legislation;

(b) An important component of the statutory scheme is the capacity of parties to contract out of its provisions so long as certain procedural requirements are met;

(c) Resultant disparity of outcome at the time of separation is relevant, but not generally as important a factor in contracting out cases as it might be in compromise cases [separation agreements]. In any particular case it might of course require considerable weight, but generally it is not to be seen as a determinative or necessarily dominant consideration;

---

[112] Ibid [112] (emphasis added).

[113] N Peart, 'Contracting out of the PRA' [2005] *New Zealand Law Journal* 142, 145.

[114] *Wells v Wells*, above n 95.

(d) Consistent with (c), a comparison to the outcomes that would be ordered if the Act were applied is relevant but not as significant as it might be in compromise cases [separation agreements];

(e) Contracting out will usually occur in circumstances where one party has the assets and is pushing for an agreement. The circumstances will often involve pressure, and may involve an issue of whether the relationship will continue in the absence of an agreement. Accordingly the presence of such circumstances is not generally relevant to the issue of serious injustice;

(f) More than disparity of outcome per se will often be present before serious injustice arises. Concern with procedure will often provide that extra factor. Case law will no doubt develop on the issue of what procedural concerns the Court is referring to. *I assume that they are something other than a breach of the s 21F requirement*;

(g) A discretion exercised in accordance with these circumstances will be difficult to disturb on appeal.[115]

The assumption in *Wells* that an 'unsatisfactory process' is 'something other than a breach of the section 21F requirement' creates some uncertainty over the meaning of serious injustice, although it is to be noted that *Wells* is of lower authority than *Harrison*.[116] Further clarification of the point must await future judicial determination.

While setting a high benchmark for 'serious injustice', the precedent value of *Harrison* is potentially constrained by the particular factual circumstances of the case. *Harrison* concerned a relatively short marriage of five years' duration; the post-nuptial agreement sought to protect pre-marital assets only, and also allowed the wife a progressively larger share of the property, dependent on the length of the marriage.[117] But not all cases are that straightforward. Procedurally valid agreements could continue to be at risk of being set aside for serious injustice where, for instance, there is no sharing of the property whatsoever, even when one party has made substantial contributions during the relationship to the other's separate assets. Equally, a major change in circumstances might effectively overtake an earlier agreement. Disparities might also become more pronounced if the marriage lasted for many years, where, but for the existence of the contracting-out agreement made many years earlier and in very different circumstances, all the property would have been regarded as relationship property and would have been divided equally.

Section 21J(4) requires regard to be had to matters such as those noted in the preceding paragraph in deciding whether giving effect to a section 21 agreement would cause serious injustice. The court must consider, inter alia, the length of time since the agreement was made[118] and whether the agreement was unfair or

---

[115] Ibid [37] (emphasis added).

[116] The term 'serious injustice' is also the threshold test in s 88(2) of the PRA, but it is arguable whether the test formulated there (see *Public Trustee v Whyman* [2005] NZFLR 433 (CA)) should be imported into s 21J. See *Brookers Family Law—Family Property*, above n 43, PR88.07.

[117] The Court of Appeal commented that the agreement was in fact broadly consistent with the accrued rights the wife had at the time she entered into it. She was not significantly worse off under the agreement than if her rights had been subject to judicial determination at the start of the relationship: *Harrison v Harrison*, above n 111, [114].

[118] PRA, s 21J(4)(b). Eg, *KDR v JAR* 6 July 2005, FAM 2003-006-000229 (FC Blenheim, Judge Grace), where 25 years had elapsed since the agreement was made: 'The longer the agreement has been in place it is arguable the less relevant it becomes ... In the normal course of events people's circumstances change. Property is bought and sold. Chattels are replaced. The longer the relationship has lasted

unreasonable in the light of all the circumstances at the time it was made,[119] including any changes in circumstances since it was made, regardless of whether those changes were foreseen by the parties.[120] But against those criteria, the 2001 amendments also expressly inserted a new factor—namely that the court must have regard to the fact that the parties wished to achieve certainty as to the status, ownership, and division of property by entering into the agreement (s 21J(4)(e)). Together with the higher threshold of 'serious injustice', this inclusion signals a clear legislative intention to boost the certainty and validity of contracting-out agreements. It has been observed that the insertion of section 21J(4)(e) 'makes it plain that the sanctity of contract is an important issue and the fact that one party may do better than another is not ... sufficient to make the agreement unfair or unreasonable in light of the circumstances at the time.'[121]

The law is currently in a bedding-down phase. While *Harrison* has found that 'serious injustice' is a hard test, further guidance from the appellate courts on a wider range of factual situations is required in order to achieve a comprehensive interpretation of section 21J.[122]

D. Protecting Children's Interests

Section 21 makes no express reference to the relevance or otherwise of children's interests in contracting-out agreements. Nonetheless, the issue might be raised in the context of assessing serious injustice within the terms of section 21J. Section 21J(4)(f) is an umbrella provision that requires the court to have regard to 'any other matters ... [it] considers relevant'. Another way that the interests of the children of the relationship can be taken into account is via section 26, which requires the court, in any proceedings under the PRA, to have regard to the interests of any minor or dependent children of the marriage, civil union or de facto relationship. If it considers it just, the court may make an order settling relationship property for the benefit of the children.[123] Moreover, an order can be made regardless of any contracting-out agreement between the couple.[124] Section 26 therefore provides the

---

the greater chance there is of intermingling and diversification of the asset base', para [65]. The judge concluded that on the facts, '[t]o enforce the agreement would deprive the applicant of the fruits of her labours over the years yet leave the respondent to have substantially improved his position through those labours', para [79]. *Cf MRWS v AHWS* 10 July 2008, FAM 2006-009-2131 (FC Christchurch, Judge CP Somerville), where the Court upheld an agreement on which the parties had relied for 17 years.

[119] PRA, s 21J(4)(c). *Cf* (i) 'contracting-out' agreements, where the purpose is to divide property differently from the statutory regime, and (ii) 'separation agreements', where the agreement should broadly reflect each party's entitlement under the PRA.

[120] PRA, s 21J(4)(d). Note, however, that the passage of time does not, of itself, make an agreement unfair: *Lowry v Lowry* [1994] NZFLR 529. One possible way to avoid the risk of an agreement being struck down for serious injustice years later, is to include a 'review clause' whereby the parties can regularly review the terms of the agreement to take into consideration major changes in circumstances: *AT v RH* [2005] NZFLR 1129.

[121] *Clark v Sims* [2004] 2 NZLR 501, [62].

[122] The lower courts have considered a number of cases where the issue of serious injustice has arisen. See *Brookers Family Law—Family Property*, above n 43, PR21J.

[123] PRA, s 26(1).

[124] PRA, s 26(3).

opportunity to bring proceedings for a further share of property that would not pass the serious injustice test.[125]

E. Survivor may Challenge an Agreement

Where the relationship ends on the death of one of the parties, section 87 of the PRA provides that the survivor[126] can challenge the validity or enforceability of an existing section 21 agreement. The purpose of this is to allow challenges under section 21F and section 21J of the PRA. A challenge can be made irrespective of the option (ie, either the share of the relationship property, or the inheritance under the will or intestacy) that the survivor intends to elect.[127] However, section 87 only applies to agreements that define 'the share of the relationship property or any part of it that each is entitled to on the death of 1 of them.'[128] It will not apply where the agreement fails to specify how the property is to be shared.

F. Contents of Agreements

The parties may make any agreement they think fit with respect to the status, ownership, and division of their property (including future property).[129] Although agreements take a wide variety of different forms, there are three common types of agreement: (i) agreements that deal only with a specific asset or assets such as the acquisition of the family home in unequal shares (in which case any relationship property not caught by the terms of the agreement is subject to the general provisions of the PRA[130]); (ii) agreements that specify that each partner's property remains their separate property; and (iii) agreements where both partners' assets are valued and then used as part of the common pool. Each partner will then take the value of their property and a prescribed proportion of any increase in value.[131]

Section 21D provides a non-exhaustive list of matters that may be covered by an agreement.[132] An agreement may classify any property as relationship property or separate property, define the share of the relationship property or any part of it, to which each partner is entitled when the relationship ends (including where the relationship ends when one partner dies), provide for the calculation of the shares, and prescribe the method by which the relationship property is to be divided.

The apparent lack of constraints on the contents of agreements is limited in practice by the PRA's imposition of several controls on the notion of unfettered

---

[125] *Brookers Family Law—Family Property,* above n 43, PR21J.08.
[126] This arguably also includes the personal representative of the deceased. See ibid, PR87.01 ff.
[127] Ibid, PR87.04. See generally, Pt 8, PRA.
[128] PRA, s 87(1).
[129] PRA, ss 21, 21A and 21B. 'Property' is broadly defined in the PRA to include real and personal property, any estate or interest in any real or personal property, any debt or thing in action, and any other right or interest: PRA, s 2.
[130] PRA, s 21O.
[131] *Brookers Family Law—Family Property,* above n 43, PR21.06.
[132] Section 21D applies to pre-nuptial and post-nuptial agreements (s 21), separation agreements (s 21A) and agreements made after the death of one partner (s 21B).

contractual freedom. As already noted, agreements must comply with certain formalities (s 21F) and cannot be seriously unjust (s 21J). In addition, and as a matter of statutory construction, section 21 is self-limiting in the sense that matters not relating to the 'status, ownership, and division' of the property should be excluded from the agreement. Spousal maintenance agreements do not fall within the subject matter of contracting-out agreements[133] and should be made separately.[134]

G. Enforcement and Non-Compliance

There are two main means of enforcing valid agreements. Agreements may be enforced through the 'order' provisions of the PRA.[135] Alternatively, ordinary contractual remedies can be used to enforce agreements. Section 21L provides that remedies which, under any enactment or rule of law or of equity, are available for the enforcement of contracts may be used for the enforcement of section 21 agreements. If ordinary contractual remedies are relied upon, then any questions relating to relationship property between the couple must be decided as if they had been raised in proceedings under the PRA.[136]

Section 21M provides that if an agreement is void or is avoided or is invalid or unenforceable, the provisions of the PRA have effect as if the agreement had never been made. However, section 21H further provides that even though an agreement is void for non-compliance with a requirement of section 21F, the Court may declare that the agreement has effect, wholly or in part or for any particular purpose, if it is satisfied that the non-compliance has not materially prejudiced the interests of any party to the agreement.[137]

Section 21 agreements are subject to other restrictions. Agreements cannot be used to defeat the rights of creditors and in some cases may be voided by creditors.[138] Agreements must also comply with the rules of common law and equity. Section 21G provides that the procedural requirements listed in section 21F do not limit or affect any enactment or rule of law or of equity that makes a contract void, voidable, or unenforceable on any other ground. Section 21J(3) repeats this in the context of serious injustice. Consequently, a section 21 agreement may be set aside on the basis of any of the usual civil law grounds including duress, undue influence, unconscionable bargain, mistake and misrepresentation.[139]

---

[133] *Brookers Family Law—Family Property*, above n 43, PR21.08. For a discussion of maintenance agreements see Webb, above n 60 at 237–38. Nor should the agreement prevent a partner from making a claim for economic disparity under s 15 of the PRA.

[134] See section I.C. iii above for a discussion of maintenance agreements.

[135] PRA, ss 25–33.

[136] PRA, s 4(4).

[137] For a discussion of s 21H, see *Brookers Family Law—Family Property*, above n 43, PR21H.

[138] Section 21 agreements are subject to s 47 of the PRA. See *Felton v Johnson* [2006] 3 NZLR 475 (SC); *Official Assignee v Johnson* [2007] NZCA 348.

[139] '[Section] 21 superimposes on a conventional contract special provisions as to form, procedure consideration and avoidance, but these are additional to, and not a substitution for, the contractual principles which also apply': R Fisher (ed), *Fisher on Matrimonial and Relationship Property* (Wellington, LexisNexis, 2002) ch 5.38. For further discussion see *Brookers Family Law—Family Property*, above n 43, PR21G.04ff.

An agreement cannot be partially validated or invalidated if it is void or invalid on grounds other than those relating to the formalities of the agreement in section 21F. Thus, if the agreement is void on general contractual grounds, or if it is set aside because it would cause serious injustice (s 21J), the default provisions of the PRA will be applied as if the agreement had not been made and the couple's relationship property will be divided according to the general provisions of the Act.

III. SEPARATION AGREEMENTS

A. Inter Vivos Separation Agreements: section 21A

Separation agreements (referred to in New Zealand as 'compromise agreements' or 'settlement agreements'[140]) are binding on the parties in the same way as pre-nuptial and post-nuptial agreements. Section 21A provides that spouses, civil union partners and de facto couples may, 'for the purpose of settling any differences that have arisen between them concerning property owned by either or both of them, make any agreement they think fit with respect to the status, ownership, and division of that property'.

Separation agreements are generally made on or after the end of the relationship, either on separation or divorce.[141] However, there is not always a bright line between the different types of agreement.[142] This was demonstrated in *Boyd v van Houten*.[143] The agreement, which financially benefited the male partner, was made when the couple had been in a de facto relationship for more than four years, although the relationship had become unstable. The relationship finally ended shortly after the agreement was made. The couple had two separate and quite inconsistent objectives and understandings as to the function of the agreement.[144] When the female partner signed the agreement and accepted less than her accrued entitlements,[145] she believed that the relationship was an ongoing one. By contrast, the male partner took the view that the relationship was at an end, and that the agreement was by way of settlement of their differences. However, he did not disabuse his partner of her belief that the relationship continued. The High Court upheld the

---

[140] *Harrison v Harrison*, above n 111 uses the terms 'compromise agreement' ([79] and [81]) and 'separation agreement' ([112]) interchangeably. See further, the discussion of the distinction between compromise/settlement agreements and contracting-out agreements in *Boyd v van Houten* 24 March 2009, CIV 2008-409-2478 (HC Christchurch, Fogarty J).

[141] Fisher, *Matrimonial and Relationship Property*, above n 139, ch 5.11. The breakdown of the relationship is likely to have been the sole or principal contingency for which the agreement was designed. That is not necessarily the case with all pre-nuptial and post-nuptial agreements concerning the couple's rights at common law and equity. The circumstances in which those agreements are made may suggest that the breakdown of the relationship was not within the intended scope of the agreement.

[142] In *Harrison v Harrison*, above n 111, the Court of Appeal took an objective approach when drawing the distinction between contracting-out agreements (pre-nuptial and post-nuptial agreements) and settlement agreements (separation agreements), based upon whether one party was foregoing accrued benefits under the Act or benefits which would accrue: See the observations in *Boyd v van Houten*, above n 140, [55].

[143] Above n 140.

[144] Ibid, [80].

[145] The agreement converted a joint asset (a business) to the separate property of the male partner.

decision of the lower court to set aside the agreement because to uphold it would be seriously unjust and would take advantage of the female partner's misunderstanding that the relationship existed and would continue.[146]

Separation agreements are often expressed to be binding regardless of whether the couple later reconcile.[147] Although there is usually no contradiction between the continuance of a separation agreement and the resumption of cohabitation,[148] in the event of reconciliation, it is in the best interests of the parties to review their position with respect to the agreement and possibly to agree to nullify it or enter into another one.[149]

Separation agreements are subject to many of the same qualifications as pre-nuptial and post-nuptial agreements. In line with agreements under section 21, separation agreements under section 21A are made with respect to the status, ownership and division of property owned by either or both of the partners (see the discussion of the contents of s 21 agreements, above). Agreements regarding spousal maintenance should therefore be made separately because they do not relate to the status, ownership or division of property.[150] Moreover, any obligations secured in the agreement could be lost if the agreement is later set aside.[151] Nor may separation agreements be made with the intention of defeating creditors.[152]

The procedural requirements for separation agreements are also the same as for pre-nuptial and post-nuptial agreements.[153] But whereas section 21J makes no distinction between the different types of agreements for the purposes of determining serious injustice, the courts have made a distinction. Unlike section 21 pre-nuptial and post-nuptial agreements, the courts have required that separation agreements made under section 21A should broadly reflect what each party would be entitled to under the PRA. This generally means an equal division of the property.[154] In *Harrison v Harrison*[155] the New Zealand Court of Appeal distinguished between contracting-out agreements and separation agreements, stating that in most separation agreements:[156]

> [T]he parties will presumably set out to provide for a division of property which accords, at least broadly, to what would be ordered under the statutory regime. So where there is a significant discrepancy between what the agreement provides and the way in which the relevant statutory regime would have operated, this in itself may well suggest that the agreement is unfair or unreasonable [in respect of matters to which the Court must have regard in s 21J(4) when determining serious injustice] and, as well, may well require explanation. In the case of a contracting-out agreement, of course, the very purpose of the parties is to make provision which differs from the statutory regime.

---

[146] *Boyd v van Houten*, above n 140, [80].
[147] Fisher, above n 139 at ch 5.10.
[148] Ibid.
[149] *Brookers Family Law—Family Property*, above n 43, PR21A.10(4).
[150] Agreements regarding child-care arrangements or child support should also be made separately.
[151] *Brookers Family Law—Family Property*, above n 43, PR21A.06.
[152] PRA, s 47.
[153] PRA, s 21F.
[154] *Brookers Family Law—Family Property*, above n 43, PR21A.02.
[155] *Harrison v Harrison*, above n 111.
[156] Ibid, [81].

That pitches the threshold for setting aside a separation agreement by reason of serious injustice at a lower level than for other contracting-out agreements under the PRA. That is not to say, however, that an unequal division will necessarily be found to be 'unjust' in all separation agreement cases. The PRA recognises the need for, and allows, unequal division in certain situations, such as in section 15 where the court may award compensation to the disadvantaged party for economic disparity.[157]

Turning to the contents of separation agreements, since they are generally intended to permanently resolve all the parties' relationship property issues,[158] they should contain a complete list of all the relationship assets and debts and how the parties have divided/will divide the assets.[159] It is also common to include the values and methods of valuation of assets so that it is clear how the property was divided/is to be divided. A disclosure clause is standard, confirming that each party has disclosed all the property to the other party. While such a clause may not make a difference to a later request for a review because of non-disclosure, it emphasises that the agreement is based on the information available to the parties at the time.[160] The disclosure requirements for separation agreements are thus higher than for contracting-out agreements. In the case of a separation agreement, the lawyer ought to have full disclosure of all the assets and the value of those assets.[161]

B. Separation Agreements Following the Death of a Party: section 21B

Section 21B allows a surviving spouse or partner to settle differences with the personal representative of the deceased. The provision applies in two different situations. If proceedings were commenced while both partners were alive and one partner then dies, the survivor and the deceased's personal representative may make an agreement in respect of the status, ownership and division of the property. Alternatively, if one partner dies and the survivor intends to commence proceedings after the death, the survivor and the deceased's personal representative may reach an agreement, instead.[162]

In line with the other agreements already considered, there is no registration procedure for this type of separation agreement. However, the personal representative must obtain independent legal advice and have the agreement certified by a lawyer in accordance with the formalities required by section 21F. Parties may take the voluntary step of submitting a draft agreement to the court for approval prior to execution.[163] Importantly, if the survivor is the sole executor or administrator of

---

[157] Eg, where one partner is entitled to compensation for economic disparity (s 15); where the relationship was of short duration and the division of property is based on contributions (ss 14, 14A, 14AA, 85); where there are extraordinary circumstances that would make equal sharing repugnant to justice (s 13); and where a valid s 21 contracting-out agreement exists.

[158] Fisher, above n 139 at ch 5.9.

[159] For a discussion on the division of the assets, see *Brookers Family Law—Family Property*, above n 43, PR21A.08.

[160] Ibid, PR21A.10.

[161] Ibid, PR21F.10.

[162] For a discussion of the potential conflict between the second situation in s 21B and the general death provisions in Pt 8 of the PRA, see ibid, PR21B.03.

[163] PRA, s 21C.

the deceased's estate, the draft agreement *must* be approved by the court, in which case it need not be signed and certified in accordance with section 21F.[164] Where the survivor is the sole executor of the estate, failure to obtain the court's approval will make the agreement invalid.[165] The PRA does not specify how the court is to make a decision to give its approval to the agreement, but it has been argued that the court is not there merely to 'rubber stamp' agreements. Rather, it would approve a proposed settlement, bearing in mind the equal-sharing principles of the PRA.[166]

In respect of serious injustice, in deciding whether giving effect to an agreement made under section 21B would cause serious injustice, the court must also have regard to whether the deceased estate has been wholly or partly distributed.[167]

IV. CONFLICT OF LAWS

A. Application of PRA to Movable and Immovable Property

The PRA applies to both movable and immovable property situated in New Zealand. It also extends jurisdiction to foreign movable property, provided that one of the parties is domiciled[168] in New Zealand at the date of the application made under the PRA, or at the date of any agreement between the parties regarding the division of property, or at the date of the death of one of the partners.[169] However, the PRA's jurisdiction does not extend to foreign immovable property.[170] Neither movable nor immovable property is defined, the law of the country where the property is situated determining whether it is movable or immovable for the purposes of the PRA.[171]

B. Choice of Law Where Parties Agree

The PRA enables parties from foreign jurisdictions to elect to have their property rights regulated by the PRA, rather than the foreign legal system that would otherwise apply.[172] The agreement must be in writing, but the formalities of section 21F need not be complied with if the agreement is valid according to the designated law.[173]

Alternatively, if the parties agreed before or at the time when their marriage or relationship began that the law of a foreign country would apply to their property,

---

[164] *Brookers Family Law—Family Property,* above n 43, PR21B.02.

[165] Fisher, above n 139 at ch 5.59A.

[166] Ibid, 5.59B. Fisher further notes that in cases where the parties have taken the voluntary step of seeking and obtaining the Court's approval under s 21C, that 'seal of approval' must make the agreement largely immune from later review on the grounds of serious injustice (s 21J).

[167] PRA, s 21J(5).

[168] Domicile Act 1976.

[169] PRA, s 7.

[170] *Walker v Walker* [1983] NZLR 560 (CA); *Samarawickrema v Samarawickrema* [1995] 1 NZLR 14; *Shepherd v Shepherd* [2009] NZFLR 226.

[171] *Smaal v Boersma* (1992) 9 FRNZ 187. A chose in action in relation to immovable property (eg, a mortgage debt) has been held to be subject to the PRA: *Bergner v Nelis* 19 December 2005, CIV 2004-404-149 (HC Auckland, Heath J), [121]–[122].

[172] PRA, s 7A(1).

[173] *Brookers Family Law—Family Property,* above n 43, PR7A.01.

the agreement will govern their property rights in place of the PRA.[174] That agreement must be in writing or otherwise valid according to the law of that foreign country.[175] A foreign agreement that complies with the necessary formalities of that system might still not be upheld if the New Zealand court determines that it would be contrary to 'justice or public policy'.[176] For instance, South African and Dutch ante-nuptial agreements that exclude all sharing of assets acquired before and during the marriage have generally not been enforced, on the basis that they are contrary to justice or public policy. This is because they substantially disadvantage one of the parties and lead to a materially different outcome to that which would be achieved under the PRA.[177]

There are recent signs, though, that the courts may be relaxing their attitude to foreign agreements. In 2004 in *H v H*[178] the Family Court recognised a South African pre-nuptial agreement in circumstances where all income obtained during the relationship was derived from assets that were one party's separate property and there was no significant contribution to those assets, either directly or indirectly, by the other party. The Court found that the failure of an agreement to provide for the growth of any joint property (by excluding an accrual regime) did not make the agreement contrary to justice or public policy. Further evidence of the judicial change in direction is to be found in the 2005 case of *Bergner v Nelis*.[179] There, the High Court observed in obiter dicta that it was seriously arguable that Parliament intended agreements entered into in another jurisdiction to be given effect, irrespective of the result of the application of the chosen law, unless (for example) the parties had insufficient connection to the chosen law to justify its use. The Court commented that, were it otherwise, there would be little point in the parties choosing the law of another jurisdiction to govern their property arrangements.[180]

C. Forum Non Conveniens

The courts do not approve of 'forum shopping' in order to obtain a more favourable decision than would otherwise be available in another jurisdiction.[181] In *F v H*,[182] although the respondent was domiciled in New Zealand, therefore giving New Zealand jurisdiction, the foreign forum was held to be the more appropriate one.

---

[174] PRA, s 7A(2); ibid, PR7A.01. See also D McLay, 'Pre-nuptial agreements: international problems' [2001] *New Zealand Law Journal* 265.

[175] Eg, in *H v H* [2004] NZFLR 1096, a South African ante-nuptial agreement was valid, notwithstanding that the parties had not received independent legal advice, because independent advice was not required in South Africa.

[176] PRA, s 7A(3). For a discussion of the meaning of the phrase, see *Brookers Family Law—Family Property*, above n 43, PR7A.02.

[177] Ibid, PR7A.01; *Koops v Den Blanken* (1999) 18 FRNZ 343 (CA); *Pretorius v Pretorius* [2000] NZFLR 72; *Bishop v Bishop* [2001] NZFLR 57.

[178] In *H v H*, above n 175.

[179] *Bergner v Nelis*, above n 171.

[180] Ibid, [27].

[181] For the principles of forum non conveniens, see *Spiliada Maritime Corp v Cansulex Ltd* [1987] AC 460. For application in the family property context in New Zealand, see *Gilmore v Gilmore* [1993] NZFLR 561; *MVD v CCD* [2005] NZFLR 83.

[182] *F v H* 10 November 2006, CIV 2006-409-849 (HC Christchurch, Hansen J).

In this case, the parties had made a separation agreement under Californian law, which made reference to assets in New Zealand. Several indicia persuaded the High Court to decline jurisdiction: the couple had lived all their married life in California; the husband was willing to abide by an order of the United States court; the witnesses (some elderly) resided in the United States; and the lawyers in the United States disagreed over the interpretation of the agreement. The Court concluded that it was odd that the wife, who did not live in New Zealand, would want the proceedings to be determined under the PRA, and drew the conclusion that it implied 'forum shopping' so that she would get a more favourable outcome.[183]

V. THE RELEVANCE OF TRUSTS

A. Trusts and the PRA

No discussion of the PRA's contracting-out provisions would be complete without reference to the role played by the family trust. In New Zealand, trusts are a very popular means of property disposition.[184] The reliance on discretionary family trusts is particularly widespread and they are often used instead of, or in addition to, contracting-out agreements, with the result that the PRA's equal-sharing regime is avoided.

As discussed earlier, the procedural requirements necessary for all forms of contracting-out agreement are designed to safeguard the parties from going into agreements with their eyes closed. Trusts, however, do not have the same formality requirements as contracting-out agreements. For a trust to be valid, there is no requirement that one party ensure their partner gets independent legal advice. Of course, depending on one's point of view, this can be either an advantage or a disadvantage. Either way, the by-product of the absence of any formality requirements is that couples (or, often just one partner) may not grasp the implications of the decision to put the property into trust. If they receive inadequate advice when the trust is set up, they may not understand that they have effectively relinquished rights they would otherwise have had under the PRA's default regime. Often, there is little or no relationship property remaining outside the trust, so that if a dispute subsequently arises, the PRA is of very limited assistance.

The PRA contains certain powers designed to counteract the equal-sharing regime being undermined by the disposition of large amounts of relationship property to trust.[185] The court may order that compensation be paid to a partner whose rights under the PRA have been defeated by a disposition of relationship property to trust

---

[183] See *Brookers Family Law—Family Property*, above n 43, PR7A.04. See also *Kane v Ethell* (Forum non conveniens) [2006] NZFLR 421.

[184] It has been estimated that there are approximately 400,000 trusts in New Zealand: 'Please sir, can we have some more?' *Sunday Star Times* (24 August 2008) Business D1. For a discussion, see N Peart, 'Can Your Trust be Trusted?' (2009) 12 *Otago Law Review* 59, 60. The abolition of gift duty in New Zealand, effective from October 2011, may see a further increase in trusts.

[185] *Brookers Family Law—Family Property*, above n 43, FA182.03.

since the relationship began (s 44C).[186] However, the court's power to compensate the affected party is relatively circumscribed. The court may order compensation to be paid to the disadvantaged partner out of the other partner's relationship or separate property or, as a last resort, it may divert trust income. However, there is no power to make an order in respect of the capital of the trust. The trust is thus upheld, but the protection for the disadvantaged party is accordingly reduced, especially if the couple has more assets inside the trust than outside it.

B. Section 182 Family Proceedings Act 1980

One further avenue of redress is available to break a trust, albeit in limited circumstances. Section 182 of the Family Proceedings Act 1980 allows the court, after an order dissolving a marriage or civil union has been made, to inquire into the existence of any agreement between the parties for the payment of maintenance or relating to the property of the parties or either of them, or any ante-nuptial or post-nuptial settlement made on the parties, and make such orders as the court thinks fit.[187] The court can alter the terms of an agreement or settlement if the financial provision that was appropriate during the marriage or civil union has ceased to be appropriate.[188] It should be noted that the application of section 182 is somewhat limited in its reach, in that it does not apply on separation or death, or to de facto relationships.

Section 182 empowers the court to remove capital from the trust for the benefit of one or both parties to a marriage or civil union. Those powers are much greater than what is available to the courts under section 44C of the PRA. Section 182 is therefore increasingly pleaded by divorcing spouses and civil union partners to get at trust assets where the PRA cannot help.[189] Importantly in the present context, however, the court's power to vary or invalidate contracting-out agreements made under Part 6 of the PRA is subject to certain constraints. Section 182(6) provides that the court must not exercise its powers so as to defeat or vary any agreement entered into under the PRA between parties to the marriage or civil union, unless it is of the opinion that the interests of any child of the relationship so require.

New Zealand's highest appellate authority, the Supreme Court, has recently considered the scope of section 182. *Ward v Ward*[190] concerned the settlement of

---

[186] PRA, s 44C. Section 44C supplements s 44, whereby the court can set aside a disposition of property made with the intention of defeating any party's interest.

[187] Family Proceedings Act 1980, s 182(1). The reference to 'any ante-nuptial or post-nuptial settlement made on the parties' has been held to include a trust for the parties to the marriage or civil union, provided that either or both spouses or partners have a beneficial interest in the settlement: *Chrystall v Chrystall* [1993] NZFLR 772; *A v A* [1998] 2 NZLR 199. See *Brookers Family Law—Family Property*, above n 43, FA182.06 for a full analysis of the requirements of s 182. See also *Ward v Ward* [2009] NZSC 125, [2010] 2 NZLR 31 (SC) and *Kidd v Van den Brink* [2010] NZCA 169, on the meaning of 'nuptial settlement'.

[188] Family Proceedings Act 1980, s 182(3). For similar powers under the PRA, see ss 21, 25 and 33(3)(m).

[189] *Brookers Family Law—Family Property*, above n 43, FA182.03.

[190] *Ward v Ward*, above n 187. See also *Ward v Ward* [2009] 3 NZLR 336 (CA). See also *X v X* [2008] NZCA 20, where the Court of Appeal warned that s 182 should not be used to avoid the boundaries set

shares in a family farming business on trust for the benefit of the spouses and their children. The spouses made a contracting-out agreement under section 21 of the PRA vesting half the shares in the wife, and then created a trust into which the shares were transferred.[191] When they divorced, the wife brought a claim under section 182 of the Family Proceedings Act 1980.

The Supreme Court confirmed the finding at first instance that the trust constituted a 'post-nuptial settlement' in terms of section 182, and upheld the order dividing the trust into two separate trusts: one for the benefit of the wife and children, the other for the husband and children, both trusts equally owning the shares in the land-owning company.[192] The Court considered that the test for whether an order should be made under section 182 should be neither formulaic nor presumptive.[193] Instead, section 182 will apply 'if the applicant's expectations of the ante or post-nuptial settlement have been wholly or partially defeated by the dissolution of the marriage', in which case '[t]he parties should be restored in an appropriate way to the position they were in, as regards the settlement, immediately after it was made, not immediately before it was made'.[194] When the couple made the post-nuptial settlement they envisaged their marriage would continue and expected to benefit equally from the settlement. The subsequent breakdown of the marriage triggered a fundamental change of circumstances because the settlement was not providing any benefit for Mrs Ward, who was no longer living on the farm. Moreover, the only remaining relationship property was the balance of the debt owed to each spouse by the trust.

The Court further found that the order dividing the trust into two separate trusts was a permissible variation of the matrimonial property agreement the parties had entered into directly before the trust was established since, on the facts, the trust was a separate transaction. For section 182(6) to apply, the trust would need to have been a term of the matrimonial property agreement or otherwise incorporated by reference into the agreement.[195] As there was no reference to the trust in the agreement, section 182(6) was not relevant. In the Court's opinion, there were good reasons for insisting on such a degree of formality and connection before a nuptial settlement external to the property relationship agreement could be treated as forming a part of it for the purposes of section 182(6):[196]

> First, if a settlement trust were too easily regarded as being part of a relationship property agreement, the remedial scope of s 182(1) would be significantly narrowed. The criteria for setting aside a relationship property agreement are more onerous than those that apply to the variation of a settlement trust when s 182 is engaged. Secondly, whereas relationship property agreements must, in order to be binding, be executed after receipt by each party of independent legal advice, deeds of trust are binding without that protection. If a deed of

---

by the PRA. Rather, s 182 'must be read within the total legislative context and in light of the clear Parliamentary intention not to insert a trust-busting route into PRA', at [45].

[191] This was done to enable the debt back to be forgiven as quickly as possible.

[192] Although the Supreme Court noted that there was no automatic entitlement or presumption in favour of a 50/50 or any other fractional division under s 182: *Ward v Ward*, above n 187, [20].

[193] Ibid, [26].

[194] Ibid, [27].

[195] Ibid, [34].

[196] Ibid, [35].

trust is incorporated into a relationship property agreement as a term of that agreement, the parties will have the benefit of independent legal advice before becoming bound to the terms of the trust. That will not be so if the deed of trust, as here, was executed separately and without there being any reference to it in the relationship property agreement. Mrs Ward, on that account, did not have the benefit of independent legal advice as to its terms and implications. The Trust was accordingly not rendered presumptively invalid by the absence of such advice, as would have been the case if it were treated as part of the matrimonial property agreement.

The Court was thus minded to preserve the general jurisdiction under section 182(1), by limiting the circumstances in which section 182(6) will apply. The Court further observed that Parliament had not removed or amended the courts' powers under section 182 when it enacted section 44C of the PRA, but thought that there was 'no necessary inconsistency in allowing the courts to exercise a trust varying power in these particular circumstances, while providing that, in the wider and distinct relationship property context, trusts will prevail, subject to ss 44 and 44C, over relationship property rights.'[197] In summary, *Ward* confirms that there remains a place for orders under section 182, notwithstanding the enactment of the PRA. Rather than seeing Parliament's failure to repeal section 182 upon the enactment of the PRA as an instance of legislative oversight, *Ward* prefers to treat the two Acts as coexisting in a workable, if not symbiotic, relationship.

VI. CONCLUDING OBSERVATIONS

'Let me not to the marriage of true minds admit impediments.'[198] That sentiment may have resonated with the masses four hundred years ago, but in the modern social, economic and legal climate, it is widely acknowledged that marriage and other intimate relationships are not necessarily lifelong institutions. That, added to the fact that more people have more property to protect than ever before, has increased the relevance of marital agreements in recent times.

In New Zealand, marital agreements have enjoyed statutory recognition and protection since the enactment of the Matrimonial Property Act 1976 heralded a new era in relationship property law. The introduction of the deferred equal sharing regime was balanced by recognition that spouses could now elect to contract out of the default regime if they so chose. Rather than retreating from that position, the latest round of reforms in the Property (Relationships) Amendment Act 2001 has strengthened many of the foundation values of the Matrimonial Property Act 1976.

The 2001 amendments have made it harder to get out of pre-nuptial and post-nuptial agreements by raising the threshold for setting aside agreements from injustice to serious injustice. Thus far at least, it appears that the courts are giving effect to the more stringent test,[199] with the result that lawyers can now have more confidence that their clients' marital agreements will be upheld than was previously

---

[197] Ibid, [19].
[198] Shakespeare, sonnet cxvi.
[199] *Harrison v Harrison*, above n 111.

the case under the Matrimonial Property Act 1976. Indeed, New Zealand might now be thought to have a system approaching a true opt-out regime.[200]

Some legal practitioners regard the contracting-out process with a measure of caution, however, due to the fact that they can be subject to negligence claims. A lawyer who advises a party under section 21F(5) owes a duty of care to the other party in certifying that he or she has explained the effect and implications of the agreement.[201] The result is that a party to an agreement, besides suing their own lawyer for inadequate advice, can also sue their ex-partner's lawyer in negligence. Lawyers who dispense negligent advice may be liable to pay compensation to their own client or the other party, including general damages and legal costs.[202] Anecdotal evidence suggests that some lawyers choose not to act as the certifying lawyer in terms of section 21F(5), in order to avoid the potential for future liability.[203]

A limitation on section 21 agreements is that they are confined to matters regarding the status, ownership and division of the *property*. Ancillary arrangements regarding spousal maintenance, child-care and child support cannot be included, but must be dealt with in separate agreements. This demonstrates the fragmented nature of New Zealand's system of dealing with the property and financial consequences of relationship breakdown, and can lead to questions over the order in which the various claims should be considered. The confusion has been compounded by the PRA's inclusion of the section 15 judicial discretion to award compensation for economic disparity.

There are differing opinions as to whether the partitioning of the individual financial elements of relationship breakdown is a good or a bad thing. One writer has argued that the statutory separation of relationship property and spousal maintenance has resulted in a systemic failure 'to come to grips with the reality that when a family unit separates ongoing financial responsibilities require not only a division of property but also a division of income, and that the two cannot sensibly be considered otherwise than in terms of a global financial package'.[204] Others are more ambivalent, however, and it has been observed that whereas the advantage of a global evaluation is that each case can be fairly decided according to its individual circumstances, the downside is that the outcome of any case is hard to predict, and the ensuing delay can be costly in terms of time and legal advice.[205] The same writer has argued that:

> [w]hile we may have qualms about treating adult maintenance as an issue isolated from property division, it probably makes sense to do so if we want reasonably clear rules to

---

[200] That conclusion is subject to the rider that the hypersensitive nature of factual circumstances in the field of contracting out means that more appellate decisions are required for a definitive answer on the real effectiveness of the serious injustice test.

[201] *Connell v Odlum* [1993] 2 NZLR 257 (CA). For a discussion of the negligence issue, see *Brookers Family Law—Family Property*, above n 43, PR21F.12–PR21F.15.

[202] *Brookers Family Law—Family Property*, above n 43, PR21F.13. Note that s 4 of the Limitation Act 1950 prevents a claim in negligence being brought more than six years from the date on which the cause of action accrued: *Thom v Davys Burton* [2009] 1 NZLR 437 (SC).

[203] This information is derived solely from the writer's conversations with a small number of family law practitioners. It should not be taken as an accurate reflection of the issue across all New Zealand practitioners.

[204] Inglis, *New Zealand Family Law in the 21st Century*, above n 67, 933.

[205] Atkin, *Family Law and Policy in New Zealand*, above n 28, 188.

guide decision making. This can help lawyers and counsellors giving advice, the parties themselves as they strive to reach agreements without resort to formal Court hearing, and Judges when cases do reach the Court.[206]

That argument neatly distils one of the central themes of this project: whether a system of relationship property is flexible or rigid, global or fragmented, it necessarily comes at a price, and individual jurisdictions must inevitably decide where that 'price' will fall.

A further potential problem with the current law is the interaction between section 21 contracting-out agreements and the use of family trusts. Both mechanisms may be used to avoid the equal sharing provisions of the PRA. Trusts are not subject to the same protective criteria as section 21 contracting-out agreements, however. As discussed above, courts have powers in certain circumstances to break into trusts. While it is unclear whether, and if so to what degree, trusts may be destabilising section 21 agreements, they are clearly becoming more popular in the general community.

At a wider level, there are also concerns associated with the PRA's inclusion of de facto relationships within a regime arguably better suited to spouses and civil union partners. Parliament recognised the right of de facto couples to contract out of the PRA before it came into force if they did not want it to apply to them. The contracting-out provisions came into force on 1 August 2001—six months before the rest of the Act took effect—to enable de facto partners to contract out in advance.[207] But despite the measures taken to ensure de facto couples had fair warning of the impending changes to the law, there are some difficulties with incorporating de facto relationships into the legislation. In the first place, the PRA operates retrospectively and, although it is an opt-out rather than an opt-in regime, the inclusion of de facto couples disregards the reality that it was not a genuine option for all those couples already in relationships before the Act came into force.

The inclusion of de facto partners in the PRA is meant to protect people coming out of long-term relationships (often involving children), where there is little to distinguish the relationship from a marriage or a civil union. But the paternalistic function of the PRA can have unexpected—and occasionally undesired—consequences. There is some uncertainty surrounding the definition and interpretation of 'de facto relationship' in the PRA, with the result that some 'couples' may not even be aware they are in a qualifying de facto relationship.[208] By the time they become aware of their 'de facto' status, it may be too late to reach a mutually satisfactory contracting-out arrangement. To apply an opt-out sharing regime to de facto relationships is problematic in

---

[206] Ibid.

[207] The PRA was adopted on 29 March 2001, but the Act did not come into force until 1 February 2002. One reason for the lengthy delay was to provide the time to educate the public about the new law and to allow de facto partners to arrange their property affairs accordingly: see the commentary to the Matrimonial Property Amendment Bill and SOP No 25 (109-3) 13. While it is not known how many couples responded to that opportunity, it is clear from the growing number of cases that many couples did nothing or, at least, their efforts in this regard came to nothing. Anecdotal evidence obtained from family law practitioners suggests that many de facto relationships broke down during this time when couples were unable to agree on contracting-out terms.

[208] PRA, s 2D. The issue is beyond the scope of this paper. See *Brookers Family Law—Family Property,* above n 43, PR2D. See *Scragg v Scott* [2006] NZFLR 1076 (HC) for an analysis of s 2D.

the sense that individuals need to be aware they are in the sort of qualifying relationship that will result in them being caught by the PRA. Only then will they be aware that there is a set of default rules from which they may opt out.

The same criticisms do not apply in respect of marriages or civil unions. Unlike de facto relationships, marriages have always carried some proprietary consequences—even if only to impose maintenance obligations on separation. Spouses know, or at least ought to know, that the change of marital status will also affect property status. Similarly, a civil union is a registered relationship and the parties will usually have considered the property-sharing consequences of entering the union. Whereas people formally opt in to marriages and civil unions, they tend to drift in to de facto relationships. This can have a significant effect on an individual's awareness and understanding of their property rights and obligations. Countries contemplating increasing the property law protections for de facto partners would do well to consider the New Zealand system, before reaching any final decisions.

To return to the central issue, the New Zealand relationship property system, like any other, has its strengths and weaknesses. Subject to the observations and criticisms noted above, the contracting-out provisions of the PRA work tolerably well in practice. The procedural requirements have changed little since 1976. The major substantive change has been to elevate the threshold for setting aside agreements from injustice to serious injustice. While that change so far seems to be having the desired effect of upholding more agreements and thereby preserving the autonomy of private individuals, only time will tell whether further reform is required.

Marital Agreements and Private Autonomy in Scotland

KENNETH MCK NORRIE

CONTENTS

I. HISTORICAL INTRODUCTION

A. Property during Marriage

The common law of Scotland originally imposed what looked like a community of property regime on married couples, analogous to the systems well-known throughout the *ius commune* of western Europe,[1] though in a form that in the modern period has been described as 'extremely crude'.[2] This regime was based neither on any partnership between the spouses, nor on a relationship involving equal shares and equal responsibilities—nor even on a division of shares and a division of responsibilities. Rather it was a much more primitive system based on the husband's absolute rights that he acquired on marriage, and a woman's economic subservence, both elements of which were perceived as being part of the natural law (ie divinely ordained).[3] Together with the primogeniture rules of succession, the form of community of property pertaining in Scotland was an effective means of ensuring that control of property remained, as far as possible, within the male domain.

The husband had two major rights. First and most important was the *ius mariti*, by which all the movable property held by a woman at the date of her marriage passed, at its constitution, to her husband; likewise all movable property acquired by the woman during the subsistence of her marriage fell to the husband.[4] In return, the husband took on liability for his wife's ante-nuptial debts, as well as an ongoing obligation of maintenance (called aliment in Scotland). Secondly, the husband had a *ius administrationis*, which was his right to administer all the property owned by his spouse that did not fall to him by dint of the *ius mariti*, most importantly of course her heritable property.[5] So even if the married woman was technically owner, she lacked legal control over her own property. A woman's autonomy was very severely compromised on marriage; her husband's was unaffected.

By the middle of the nineteenth century the unquestioned acceptance of this state of affairs was being increasingly challenged, though it took a full 60 years of legislative development for the effects of the *ius mariti* and the *ius administrationis* to be removed in their entirety. The first amelioration of the wife's position came with the Conjugal Rights (Scotland) Amendment Act 1861, which allowed a woman who had obtained a decree of judicial separation to retain such property as she acquired subsequent to

---

[1] Stair, *Institutions of the Law of Scotland* (Edinburgh, 1681) I, iv, 9 expressed it as 'a community of goods betwixt the married persons'. See also Erskine's *Institute of the Law of Scotland* (Edinburgh, 1773) I, vi, 12 and Bell's *Principles of the Law of Scotland* (Edinburgh, 1829) para 1549.

[2] A Anton, 'The Effects of Marriage Upon Property in Scots Law' (1956) 19 *Modern Law Review* 653.

[3] See Stair, *Institutions* above n 1, I, iv, 9. As early as 1683 it was being argued before the Court of Session that it was error to compare the Scottish husband's rights with a *societas* or *communion bonorum* in the European sense: *Earl of Leven v Montgomery* (1683) Mor 5803. Bell's *Lectures on Conveyancing* vol II, 3rd edn (Edinburgh, Bell and Bradfoot, 1882) 855 gets to the heart of the matter when he writes: 'A communion of goods arises by marriage, in which the husband and wife, and their children, if any, are jointly interested ... [but] during the marriage [the husband] is, to all intents and purposes, proprietor of the whole goods in communion, as regards transactions *inter vivos*.'

[4] A limited exception to this was the wife's 'paraphernalia', being her clothes, jewellery and their receptacles. She remained absolute owner of these: see F Walton, *Husband and Wife*, 3rd edn (Edinburgh, W Green & Son, 1951) 219–21.

[5] Any income generated, by means of rent and the like, from a married woman's heritable property, being movable, fell automatically to the husband.

the decree, and also entitled a deserted wife to seek an order from the court which would protect her property from the claims of her deserting husband.[6] The Married Women's Property (Scotland) Act 1877 allowed married women to retain their own earned income (though judicial interpretation of the Act tended to limit its application[7]). The most important legislation was, however, the Married Women's Property (Scotland) Acts of 1881 and 1920, the former abolishing the husband's *ius mariti* and the latter abolishing his *ius administrationis*.[8] The 1920 Act also removed the existing common law rule that donations (ie gifts) between husband and wife were always revocable by the donor.[9] In effect, from that point a separate property regime probably applied in Scotland to married couples.[10] For the avoidance of all doubt in the matter, section 24 of the Family Law (Scotland) Act 1985 ('the 1985 Act') now provides that, subject to the provisions of that or any other enactment, marriage or civil partnership[11] shall not of itself affect the respective rights of the parties in relation to their property. So during a marriage/civil partnership the ownership of property is (generally speaking) unaffected by any domestic relationship the property owner or claimant happens to be a party to. Each party separately remains owner of his or her existing property and, subject to minor qualifications,[12] it is general property law rather than family law that determines ownership of property acquired subsequent to entering into a marriage/civil partnership. Each spouse/civil partner is an autonomous individual, owner of their own property and liable for their own debts.

B. Financial Claims on Divorce

Judicial divorce has been available in Scotland since the Reformation in 1560.[13] It was originally limited to the matrimonial offences of adultery and desertion.[14] From then

---

[6] See *Turnbull, Petitioner* (1864) 2 M 402, where the word 'desertion' in this context was held to bear its natural meaning, wider than that required to give a ground for divorce.

[7] See E Clive, *The Law of Husband and Wife in Scotland*, 4th edn (Edinburgh, W Green/SULI, 1997) 14.010.

[8] An exception to this abolition of the *ius administrationis* was that the husband remained entitled to administer his wife's property for so long as she was in minority. This last vestige of the rule was abolished by s 3 of the Law Reform (Husband and Wife) (Scotland) Act 1984.

[9] Married Women's Property (Scotland) Act 1920, s 5. This allowed property to be transferred from one spouse to the other and so (subject to the normal bankruptcy rules) protect the property from the creditors of the former.

[10] The Married Women's Property (Scotland) Act 1881 simply removed the husband's *ius mariti* without explicitly putting in place a separate property regime, though in the absence of the husband's right this was almost certainly a necessary implication. But there remained room for doubt and the likelihood of unfairness in certain areas such as savings from housekeeping allowances: see Anton, 'The Effects of Marriage', above n 2.

[11] Of course, civil partnership, a purely statutory creation, never was subject to common law rules. The addition of civil partnership to the rule in s 24 is designed to ensure that there is no possibility of an argument being made that civil partnership and marriage are to be treated differently in respect of property ownership.

[12] Family Law (Scotland) Act 1985, ss 25 and 26: presumption of equal shares in, respectively, household goods and savings from housekeeping allowances.

[13] The authority of the Pope in Scotland was abolished by Act of Parliament on 24 August 1560: APS II, 534, c 2.

[14] Divorce for adultery, mandated in Matthew 19:9 which itself founds on Deuteronomy 24:1–4 and Jeremiah 3:8, was accepted immediately, while divorce for desertion was introduced by statute in

until 1964 divorce was treated as akin to death: the innocent spouse received from the estate of the guilty spouse (divorce being fault-based throughout that period[15]) such property as she or he would have inherited had the guilty spouse died.[16] As such the court had no power to award aliment or a periodical allowance, with the result that the wife of a property owner was likely to leave her marriage very significantly better provided for than the wife of a wage-earner, however high the wage. The Succession (Scotland) Act 1964 separated the rules on death from the rules on divorce, and gave the divorce court the power to make such order as it thought fit to grant to the pursuer a capital sum or (for the first time) a periodical allowance, or both. The Divorce (Scotland) Act 1976, which introduced no-fault divorce into Scots law,[17] extended the 1964 reforms to allow either pursuer or defender to apply for financial provision on divorce, irrespective of fault. This highly discretionary system, usually exercised in favour of granting an indefinite periodical allowance, and usually in practice requiring an ex-husband to pay that periodical allowance to an ex-wife, was swept away by the Family Law (Scotland) Act 1985, and this Act remains the basis of the law today.

There have been other developments. Civil partnership (an institution for same-sex couples, functionally identical to the institution of marriage for opposite-sex couples) was introduced into Scots law by Part III of the Civil Partnership Act 2004 (UK), and the 1985 Act was amended so that the financial provisions on divorce sections apply equally to dissolution of a civil partnership.[18] The Family Law (Scotland) Act 2006 introduced a regime of financial provision for separating cohabitants (same-sex and opposite-sex), but it is much more limited, and deliberately less valuable, than the regime (discussed in the next section) for spouses/civil partners.[19] So the choice to marry or enter a civil partnership is regarded by the law as a voluntarily made choice to subject one's patrimony to a higher level of control than it would be subjected to through a choice to cohabit with another person in an unregistered (though conjugal) relationship. As we will see, however, the parties' personal autonomy is not significantly restricted by either of the choices, and parties in either form of relationship are free, if they wish, to contract with each other in order to avoid the application of the 'default rules'.

1573: APS III, 81, c 1 (12mo c 55). The main intellectual force of the Reformation was a demand to return to the Primary Texts as opposed to secondary materials such as the Church of Rome's interpretations thereof. Since the Primary Texts allowed divorce, so too did the reformed Scots law, irrespective of whether the doctrines of the Church of Rome (or the Church of England) did so or not.

[15] Except that in 1938 incurable insanity was added as a ground, in which case divorce had no effect on the parties' property: Divorce (Scotland) Act 1938, s 2(1).

[16] Terce and courtesy from heritable property and *ius relictae/relicti* from movable property. A wife's terce was a liferent of one-third of the husband's heritable property; a husband's courtesy was a liferent of the whole of the wife's heritable property but was claimable only if there was a living child of the marriage who had been heard to cry: Stair, above n 1, II, vi, 19. *Ius relictae* and *ius relicti* are claims (which may still be made today on the death of a spouse or civil partner) for one-third or one-half (depending upon whether there are surviving issue) of the movable property.

[17] Retaining as alternative grounds for divorce, the fault-based grounds of adultery, unreasonable behaviour and desertion. Desertion was abolished as a ground for divorce by the Family Law (Scotland) Act 2006, but divorce today retains both fault grounds (adultery and unreasonable behaviour) and non-fault grounds (non-cohabitation, for one year with consent or two years without consent): Divorce (Scotland) Act 1976, s 1.

[18] See Civil Partnership Act 2004, Sch 28, pt II.

[19] The details of cohabitants' claims are outside the scope of this chapter. For a discussion, see K Norrie, *Family Law (Scotland) Act 2006: Text and Commentary* (Dundee, Dundee University Press, 2006) 68–72.

II. THE FINANCIAL CONSEQUENCES OF DIVORCE/DISSOLUTION: THE DEFAULT RULES FOR SPOUSES/CIVIL PARTNERS

A. The s 9 Principles

Structurally, as we have seen, Scotland does not have a community property regime for married/civilly empartnered couples, though functionally it has something very close to what might be described as deferred community property (for acquests). On divorce/dissolution[20] the effect of the financial orders that a Scottish court can make is, by and large, the same as the effect achieved by a community property regime.[21] The available orders are listed in section 8 of the 1985 Act, and include orders for the payment of a capital sum, for the transfer of property, for the payment of a periodical allowance[22] and for the sharing of interests in a pension scheme. It is competent for the court to make any of these orders only when the order is both (i) justified by one or more of five principles laid down in section 9 of the 1985 Act and (ii) reasonable having regard to the resources of the parties. Section 9 is the very heart of the 1985 Act: an order cannot be made unless justified, and it cannot be justified except by one or more of the principles listed there. There is no direct structural link between the types of order listed in section 8 and the justifications for making an order in section 9 though, as we will see, only some of the section 9 principles can be used to justify a periodical allowance.

Section 9 provides as follows:

(1) The principles which the court shall apply in deciding what order for financial provision, if any, to make are that—
  (a) the net value of the matrimonial property should be shared fairly between the parties to the marriage or as the case may be the net value of the partnership property should be so shared between the partners in the civil partnership;
  (b) fair account should be taken of any economic advantage derived by either person from contributions by the other, and of any economic disadvantage suffered by either person in the interests of the other person or of the family;
  (c) any economic burden of caring, should be shared fairly between the persons—
    (i) after divorce, for a child of the marriage under the age of 16 years;
    (ii) after dissolution of the civil partnership, for a child under that age who has been accepted by both partners as a child of the family or in respect of whom they are, by virtue of sections 33 and 42 of the Human Fertilisation and Embryology Act 2008, the parents;
  (d) a person who has been dependent to a substantial degree on the financial support of the other person should be awarded such financial provision as is reasonable to enable him to adjust, over a period of not more than three years from—
    (i) the date of the decree of divorce, to the loss of that support on divorce;

---

[20] 'Divorce' being the legal process by which a valid marriage is brought to an end; 'dissolution' being the process by which either a voidable marriage or a civil partnership is brought to an end.

[21] This similarly is explored rather more fully by K Norrie, 'The Legal Regulation of Adult Domestic Relationships' in V Palmer and E Reid (eds), *Mixed Jurisdictions Compared: Private Law in Louisiana and Scotland* (Edinburgh, Edinburgh University Press, 2009) 146–72, esp 155–56.

[22] It is important to note immediately that 'periodical allowance' is not to be regarded as precisely analogous to aliment or maintenance. Maintenance is an award of living expenses, but a periodical allowance under the 1985 Act will often have a quite different purpose.

(ii) the date of the decree of dissolution of the civil partnership, to the loss of that
support on dissolution;

(e) a person who at the time of the divorce or of the dissolution of the civil partnership, seems likely to suffer serious financial hardship as a result of the divorce or
dissolution should be awarded such financial provision as is reasonable to relieve
him of hardship over a reasonable period.

i. Fair Sharing of Matrimonial/Partnership Property

The first principle that justifies the court making an order for financial provision on
divorce/dissolution is that the net value of the 'matrimonial/partnership property'
should be shared fairly between the parties to the marriage/civil partnership.[23] This
is by far the most important, and most widely used, of the section 9 principles.

The central concept of this principle is the artificial and statutorily delineated
'matrimonial/partnership property'. This is given a precise definition in section
10(4) of the 1985 Act and is not subject to judicial discretion.[24] Property in Scotland
either is or is not 'matrimonial/partnership property' ('acquests', in the terminology
of some other legal systems) and if it is not, then it is not available for sharing under
this first, and most powerful, of the section 9 principles. 'Matrimonial/partnership
property' means all the property belonging to the parties or either of them at the
relevant date which was acquired by them or him or her (otherwise than by gift or
succession from a third party) (i) before the marriage/civil partnership for use by
them as a family home or as furnishings and plenishings for such home or (ii) during the marriage/civil partnership but before the 'relevant date'.[25] In other words,
those assets[26] that accrue to the parties or either of them between the date of the
marriage/civil partnership and (basically) the date of separation fall within the
concept of 'matrimonial/partnership property'—unless gifted by or inherited from
a third party—and their value (but not necessarily the assets themselves) is likely to
be shared 50–50. Conversely, property that either party owned before the marriage/
civil partnership is not available for such sharing, unless it was acquired before the
marriage/civil partnership for use by the parties as a family home, or furnishings and
plenishings thereof.[27] 'Property' for this purpose might include any right or interest
in benefits under a pension arrangement.[28] A periodical allowance is never justified
by this principle, which justifies only the making of an order for the payment of a
capital sum, or for the transfer of property, or for pension-splitting.

---

[23] 1985 Act, s 9(1)(a).

[24] Attempts by judges in the early years of the Act's operation to claim a discretion to include or
exclude particular types of asset from the definition have not thrived.

[25] Defined in s 10(3) and (3A).

[26] An increase in the value of an asset during the marriage/civil partnership is not itself matrimonial/
partnership property: the concept refers to the asset itself and not its value.

[27] Compare *Ranaldi v Ranaldi* 1994 SLT (Sh Ct) 25 where a house was not matrimonial property, having been purchased as a family home in contemplation of a previous marriage, with *Mitchell v Mitchell*
1995 SLT 426 where a house was matrimonial property, having been purchased in contemplation of a
previous marriage between the same parties now divorcing (again). In *Corbett v Corbett* 2009 GWD
27-437 a house purchased as an investment (from the local authority) while it was already in use as a
family home was held not to be matrimonial property.

[28] 1985 Act, s 10(5).

Fair sharing under this principle is presumed to be equal sharing.[29] So if party A owns £100,000 worth of 'matrimonial/partnership property' and party B owns £20,000 thereof, this principle will justify an order the effect of which is to require the transfer from A to B of cash or assets worth £40,000: that way each takes £60,000, which is one half of the total 'matrimonial/partnership property'. However, the presumption of equal sharing may be departed from if the court is persuaded that special circumstances exist that justify sharing in different proportions than 50-50. Examples are given in section 10(6) of the sorts of circumstances that might justify a departure from equal sharing and include the terms of any agreement between the parties, the sources of the funds used to acquire the property, the nature of the property and the use to which it is put.[30]

Valuation of the property has proved a contentious issue in practice, though it is now settled that 'net value' refers to the price paid and not the value received.[31] The date of valuation is, in most cases, the date of separation (the so-called 'relevant date'), but this was amended[32] in relation to property transfer orders to be, generally speaking, the date of the order. That amendment resolved one of the most controversial aspects of the operation of the 1985 Act, arising from the case of *Wallis v Wallis*:[33] when valuation is made at the relevant date, an order for the transfer of property which had increased in value between the relevant date and the date of the court decree would result in the party in whose favour the order was made receiving the full increase without having to share that increase with the other. This was perceived to be particularly pernicious when the property was originally jointly owned.

The underlying assumption in section 9(1)(a) is that it is in the very nature of marriage/civil partnership that the benefit of acquests must fall to both parties. During the effective life of the marriage/civil partnership ownership is not really relevant to the enjoyment of the property, but on divorce/dissolution a division is needed to guarantee that the benefit continues to accrue to both. The claim for a fair share of 'matrimonial/partnership property' is a claim almost as of right, and it will be applicable in virtually every case. As Lord McClusky put it:

> Junior counsel ... suggested that the principles listed in s 9(1) as (a), (b), (c), (d) and (e) are 'cumulative'. I should prefer to say that it is the duty of the court to apply (a) and also to apply whichever of the other specified principles are relevant in the light of the facts of the case.[34]

ii. Balancing Economic Advantages and Economic Disadvantages

The second principle that can justify the making of an award of financial provision on divorce/dissolution is that fair account should be taken of any economic advantage

---

[29] 1985 Act, s 10(1).

[30] For a full discussion of s 10(6), see K Norrie, *Stair Memorial Encyclopaedia of the Laws of Scotland: Child and Family Law* Reissue (Edinburgh, Law Society of Scotland/LexisNexis/Butterworths, 2004) para 662.

[31] *Sweeney v Sweeney (No 2)* 2005 SLT 1141.

[32] Family Law (Scotland) Act 2006, s 16.

[33] 1993 SC(HL) 49. See also *Jacques v Jacques* 1997 SC(HL) 20.

[34] *Cunniff v Cunniff* 1999 SC 537, 539F–G.

derived by either party from contributions, whether financial or otherwise, of the other, and of any economic disadvantages suffered by either party in the interests of the other party or of the family.[35] This is designed to compensate, for example, for the loss of job opportunities, which had been given up for the sake of the family, and to share the economic benefits that one spouse/civil partner received, such as enhanced career opportunities, because the other spouse/civil partner relieved him or her of a share of the family burdens. The aims of this principle are (i) to even out the advantages and disadvantages gained or suffered by one in the interests of, or for the benefit of, the other or the family, and (ii) to recognise the palpable value to families of the non-financial contributions made in the form, typically, of housekeeping and childminding. The underlying assumptions of this principle have much in common with, but are wider than, those that underpin the law of unjusti-fied enrichment. A periodical allowance is never justified by this principle, which justifies only the making of an order for the payment of a capital sum, or for the transfer of property, or for pension-splitting.

iii. Sharing the Economic Burden of Bringing up Children

The third principle is that any economic burden of caring for a child of the family under 16 should be shared fairly between the parties.[36] This allows the court to make an order that will share the actual costs of bringing up the child. It is fre-quently used to justify the transfer to the parent who has residence of the child the half share of the family home that belonged, before divorce/dissolution, to the non-resident parent. A periodical allowance might be justified by this principle, but it would terminate on the youngest child's 16th birthday. The underlying assumption is obvious—that both parents have an obligation to share the financial responsibili-ties of bringing up their children even in cases where, because of parental separa-tion, the emotional and practical responsibilities are very unevenly distributed.

iv. Affording Dependants Time to Adjust

The fourth principle is that a party who has been dependent to a substantial degree on the financial support of the other party should be awarded such financial provi-sion as is reasonable to enable him or her to adjust, over a period of no more than three years from the date of the decree, to the loss of that support resulting from the divorce/dissolution.[37] This is primarily designed to provide a short-term cushion to persons who have long been out of the job market and would therefore require a period of readjustment before being able to become fully independent. This principle will frequently be used to justify the awarding of a periodical allowance. However, it is a fundamental error to see this principle as one that is designed to provide ongoing maintenance or one that focuses on needs. It has the short-term aim of providing time for readjustment, not the long-term provision of a source of income. It would miss the whole point of the self-contained 'justifications' in section 9 to regard as

---

[35] 1985 Act, s 9(1)(b).
[36] Ibid, s 9(1)(c).
[37] Ibid, s 9(1)(d).

ungenerous the three-year limitation to the periodical allowance that can be made under this principle.

v. Relieving Serious Financial Hardship

The fifth principle is a safety net provision for a party who at the time of the divorce/dissolution seems likely to suffer serious financial hardship as a result of the divorce/dissolution. It allows the court to make such financial provision as is reasonable to relieve the party of that hardship over a reasonable period of time.[38] Originally this principle was designed for parties who might lose out on shares of pensions and the like referable to marriage but, though pensions are now more readily accessible through the application of section 9(1)(a), this principle remains relevant in cases where there is little in the way of 'matrimonial/partnership property' but one spouse/partner is a high earner and the other is not, and the differences in lifestyle before and after the divorce/dissolution are stark.[39]

vi. Overview

These principles need to be looked at together, and an award under one may satisfy the requirements of another; for example, a generous award under section 9(1)(a) may obviate the need for an award under section 9(1)(b) or (e). The court is looking to make an overall award that is 'coherent', rather than one that is 'holistic'—one, that is to say, that is based on statutorily prescribed principles rather than protean and judicially assessed concepts like 'fairness'. It will be noticed that fault (in the sense of responsibility for the breakdown of the marriage/civil partnership) plays no part in these principles. It is explicitly provided[40] that in applying the section 9 principles the court shall not take account of the conduct of the parties, unless the conduct has adversely affected the financial resources available for distribution or, in relation only to the fourth and fifth principles, it would be manifestly inequitable to leave the conduct out of account.

B. The Family Home

The family home is often the single most valuable item of 'matrimonial/partnership property' available for sharing under section 9(1)(a), and is usually the most emotionally significant. However, other than the extension of the definition of 'matrimonial/partnership property' to include property acquired before the marriage/civil partnership if acquired for the purpose of being a family home for the parties,[41] there are no special rules governing the distribution of the family home on divorce/dissolution. It follows that, if the home is part of the 'matrimonial/partnership property', its net value will be shared (presumptively equally) between the parties.

---

[38] Ibid, s 9(1)(e).
[39] See eg *Haughan v Haughan* 1996 SLT 321 (OH); 2002 SLT 1349 (IH).
[40] 1985 Act, s 11(7).
[41] Ibid, s 10(4)(a).

However, it is very common (particularly if there are still children living in the home) for the court to order the transfer of one party's half share to the other, either in satisfaction of an entitlement to receive something or, if no net transfer between the parties is justified by the section 9 principles, with a compensating transfer of an equivalent amount of cash or other property.

C. Pensions

It very frequently happens that after the family home, and often even before that, the largest single asset of a party whose marriage/civil partnership is being brought to an end is the interest he or she has in an occupational pension scheme. Such interests were always within the contemplation of the Family Law (Scotland) Act 1985,[42] and from the start pension funds were considered resources from which a party could be ordered to pay a capital sum. Problems in accessing these funds before the pension-holder's retirement, however, meant that such payment of capital sums as were ordered were frequently required to be postponed until the date of retirement, or paid in instalments. And even after retirement, the contributor's entitlement will often be a monthly income rather than a lump sum, making an order to pay a capital sum to an ex-spouse unfeasible other than by instalments.

The Pensions Act 1995 introduced new provisions into the 1985 Act,[43] relevant only to orders for financial provision justified by the principle in section 9(1)(a): that the matrimonial property should be shared fairly between the parties. If the interest in a pension scheme includes a lump sum, payable either on retirement or death of the contributor, the court may make a variety of orders requiring the trustees or managers of the scheme to pay over the whole or part of this lump sum, when it becomes due, to the non-contributor spouse. These are known as 'earmarking orders', for they earmark a portion of the lump sum which will go to the non-contributor ex-spouse at the time the lump sum becomes due in the normal course of events.

That provision does not apply to the part of the pension from which the contributor takes an income. That is clearly a valuable 'resource'. Part III of the Welfare Reform and Pensions Act 1999 introduced into the 1985 Act the power to make a 'pension sharing order'[44] under which the whole or part of the value of a pension (including that portion which generates income) can be transferred to the non-contributor partner, effectively creating two pensions out of the single scheme. The order must be made at or before the date of the decree of divorce/dissolution or declarator of nullity.[45] The order may be justified by any of the principles in s 9(1) and not just that in s 9(1)(a) of the 1985 Act.[46] Pension-sharing may also feature as an element in a separation agreement, though to be enforceable, any such agreement must be registered in the Books of Council and Session.[47]

---

[42] See ibid, s 10(5), as originally enacted.
[43] Ibid, s 8(1)(ba) and s 12A.
[44] Ibid, s 8(1)(baa).
[45] Welfare Reform and Pensions Act 1999, s 28(7), (8).
[46] *Galloway v Galloway* 2003 Fam LB 10.
[47] Welfare Reform and Pensions Act 1999, s 28(3)(b).

D. Maintenance

It is not and never has been in Scotland one of the underlying assumptions of marriage (and now civil partnership) that the parties thereto undertake a life-long obligation to maintain the other and maintenance, in the sense of providing for ongoing alimentary needs, has never been one of the goals of the financial provision that the Scottish courts make on the termination of a marriage.[48] In a system that has had judicial divorce for 450 years, it has long been accepted that consent to marriage is the undertaking of an obligation to maintain for so long as the marriage lasts, but no longer. Scots law reflects this understanding, and the obligation of aliment, now governed by the first seven sections of the Family Law (Scotland) Act 1985, lasts only as long as the marriage/civil partnership lasts. Even then, the obligation is not absolute and the parties can agree between themselves as to the terms under which that obligation is to be met. However, section 7(1) provides that any provision in an agreement that purports to exclude future liability for aliment or to restrict the right to bring an action for aliment shall have no effect unless the provision was fair and reasonable in all the circumstances of the agreement at the time it was entered into. So the agreement can be challenged on the basis that it was not fair and reasonable. These terms are discussed further below. Additionally, under section 7(2), an application may be made to the court for variation of the amount payable under an agreement, or for the termination of the agreement whenever there has been a material change in the circumstances.[49]

This statutory obligation of aliment, and the rules for variation of agreements concerning the payment of aliment, do not survive the marriage/civil partnership that gives rise to the obligation, and there is no ongoing obligation of maintenance after divorce/dissolution. A periodical allowance ordered by the court as part of the financial provision it makes is based on the justifications listed in section 9, as discussed above, and not on any obligation to maintain or right to be maintained, for none exists except between spouses/civil partners and from parents to children. However, there is nothing to prevent the parties undertaking an obligation to pay and receive a periodical sum for the purposes of maintaining the payee, either by contract or by unilateral promise (fully enforceable in Scots law). Such an agreement may be set aside or varied by the court at any time after granting a decree of divorce/dissolution if the agreement expressly provides for the court doing so,[50] or on the payer's sequestration,[51] or on the making of a maintenance calculation by virtue of which child support maintenance becomes payable by either party with respect to a child to whom or for whose benefit periodical allowance is paid under the agreement.[52] A mere change of circumstances, such as justifies the court varying an agreement relating to spousal aliment, is not sufficient to allow the court to vary

---

[48] Except, in practical terms, for the short historical period between 1964 and 1985.

[49] The making of a maintenance calculation within the meaning of s 54 of the Child Support Act 1991 in respect of a child to whom or for whose benefit aliment is payable under such an agreement is a material change of circumstances for these purposes: Family Law (Scotland) Act 1985, s 7(2A).

[50] 1985 Act, s 16(1)(a) and (2)(a).

[51] Ibid, s 16(3)(a)–(c).

[52] Ibid, s 16(3)(d), as inserted by the Child Support (Amendments to Primary Legislation) (Scotland) Order 1993, SI 1993/660.

a contract, freely undertaken, to pay non-spousal (or post-spousal) maintenance.[53] However, if the agreement is contained in a separation agreement between the parties to the marriage/civil partnership to take effect on divorce/dissolution, it may be set aside or varied if not fair and reasonable under section 16 of the 1985 Act, as discussed below.

E. Purpose of the Rules

The Family Law (Scotland) Act 1985 aims to provide a detailed structure within which the courts must operate in determining what financial provision to make when spouses or civil partners dissolve their legal relationship and have been unable to agree themselves as to the division of their property. Though designed to be far less discretionary than the pre-1985 law, a certain level of discretion clearly still rests with the court—for example, in determining a 'fair' sharing of 'matrimonial/partnership property' under section 9(1)(a), in assessing contributions and disadvantages under section 9(1)(b) and taking 'fair account' of them, and in making a 'reasonable' provision either for adjusting to loss of support under section 9(1)(d) or for ameliorating serious financial hardship under section 9(1)(e). But the Act does provide a structure within which all courts can operate to produce a result that is (to some extent at least) predictable. Predictability of judicial outcome is believed to encourage extra-judicial settlement, an important social aim of the law. Another major aim of the Scottish legislation on financial provision on divorce/dissolution is to encourage the court to design a settlement that ensures a 'clean break' between the parties. The primary order that the court can make is one for the payment of a lump sum or for the transfer of property from one ex-spouse to the other: in other words, a once-and-for-all financial settlement, after which the parties are to be free of obligation towards—and free from dependency on—each other. The two most valuable assets (the family home and pensions) are normally dealt with through a one-off payment, for the principles contained in section 9(1)(a) and (b), which are the primary means of dealing with these assets, allow for the making only of an order for the payment of a capital sum or for the transfer of property or for a pension-sharing order. Principles 9(1)(c) and (d), which tend to be supplementary to the primary claim under principle 9(1)(a), envisage the making of an order for a periodical allowance, but in both cases only for limited periods of time. Only principle 9(1)(e) ever justifies an open-ended periodical allowance, and that principle, as a safety net, has limited application and indeed has been seen less and less in the law reports as the years have gone by. The 1985 Act itself steers the court in the direction of satisfying all the principles by means of a clean-break payment: s 13(2) provides that an order for a periodical allowance, even where the making of such an order is competent, may not be made unless the court is satisfied that an order for the payment of a capital sum or for the transfer of property or a pension-sharing order would be inappropriate or insufficient to satisfy the requirements of being reasonable and being justified.

---

[53] *Drummond v Drummond* 1995 SC 321.

III. PRE-NUPTIAL AND POST-NUPTIAL AGREEMENTS

A. General Enforceability of Marriage Contracts

Marital agreements, usually referred to in Scotland as 'marriage contracts', are enforceable under Scots law in the way that other contracts are,[54] and are no less so because they have been entered into by spouses (or prospective spouses[55]), or because they tend to regulate matters that, absent the agreement, the court would be empowered to regulate. They have never been regarded as being contrary to public policy, for they far more commonly regulated property arrangements during marriage than on its termination and were not, therefore, seen as deeds that encouraged divorce, or that undermined the essential nature of marriage. Nor did their often one-sided nature pose any difficulties, for Scots law, in sharp distinction to the English common law and following a European tradition whereby unilateral promises are legally enforceable,[56] has never worried about the validity of contracts made in the absence of consideration. Autonomy of the parties, in other words, trumps both the property rules on marriage/civil partnership and the property distribution rules on divorce/dissolution. The general position was set out by Lord Kincraig in *Milne v Milne*:[57]

> In my opinion parties may by agreement oust the jurisdiction of the court to pronounce upon the pursuer's entitlement to payment of a capital sum, where such is applied for in an action for divorce, and if they do so, the court must give effect to any such agreement. It has always been the law that notwithstanding statutory provisions regulating the rights of parties, they may agree to certain terms, and if they do so they must receive effect. It is different where the court has a duty in relation to the interests of other parties affected by a decree of divorce, such as children of the marriage ... No agreement between the parties on these matters can relieve the court of its obligation. Further there may be statutes which expressly provide that no parties may contract out of the provisions of the statute.

So marital agreements in Scotland are more than simply one of the circumstances to be taken into account on divorce in terms of section 10(6) of the 1985 Act: they are contracts enforceable in a court of law[58] and will be given effect to subject to the court's power (discussed later) to vary or set aside its terms. In Scotland the courts have jurisdiction to determine financial provision on divorce/dissolution only when the parties, in the exercise of their own autonomy, either do not or cannot reach agreement themselves and so one or other of them asks the court to make an order which he or she seeks to show is justified by one or more of the s 9 principles. However, terms that purport to restrict the parties' right to seek a divorce[59] or a

---

[54] Marriage settlements may also take the form of trusts and, if so, are subject to the general Scots law of trusts and in particular the rules in the Trusts (Scotland) Act 1921 and the Trusts (Scotland) Act 1961.

[55] *Kibble v Kibble* 2010 SLT (Sh Ct) 5.

[56] So long, now, as they are in writing: Requirements of Writing (Scotland) Act 1995, s 1(2)(a)(ii).

[57] *Milne v Milne* 1987 SLT 45 at 47. See also *Thomson v Thomson* 1982 SLT 521; *Elder v Elder* 1985 SLT 471; *Horton v Horton* 1992 SLT (Sh Ct) 37.

[58] Indeed, an agreement may be enforceable even after the death of one of the parties: see *Redfern's Executor v Redfern* 1996 SLT 900; *Lavery v Lavery* 2008 Fam LR 46.

[59] *Lawson v Macculloch* (1797) Mor 6157.

term whereby one party agrees to consent to a divorce based on non-cohabitation for one year[60] are unenforcable.

B. Decreased Popularity of Marital Contracts in Scotland

Before the enactment of the Married Women's Property (Scotland) Acts, as described above, marriage contracts were 'widely used amongst the propertied classes'[61] (a relatively small proportion, it should be remembered, of the marrying population) as a means of altering or avoiding completely the rules then existing that governed the property relationship between the spouses, in particular, the rules that a married woman's movable property fell into the ownership of her husband and that her heritable property fell under his administration. As the right was the husband's, the ante-nuptial contract normally took the form of a deed granted in his name, renouncing his rights. If the husband was unwilling to grant such a deed, the wife could achieve some protection for herself by establishing an ante-nuptial trust in her own favour.[62] Marriage contracts were also a means by which a more sophisticated distribution of assets on divorce could be achieved than was provided for by the common law.

But the need to avoid these rules simply evaporated when the rules themselves changed, and the popularity of marriage contracts has waned. The Married Women's Property (Scotland) Acts, by creating a system of separate property amongst spouses, removed the major incentive for parties contemplating marriage to enter into marital agreements, and today such agreements, though generally enforceable, are not commonly met with. Even when spouses/civil partners wish to modify the separation of property provided for by the law, there is simply no culture in contemporary Scotland of doing so by means of formal agreement. Rather, when individual couples seek a closer combination of their resources than is provided by the law, or find the law's separation of property inconvenient or inappropriate, they can achieve their aims far more easily by means such as joint bank accounts, taking title to heritage in joint names, and specifying each other as beneficiaries in pension schemes, insurance policies and wills. On divorce too, the default rules for financial provision on divorce/dissolution discussed above provide much of the protection that prenuptial agreements are primarily designed to ensure. The general law to a large extent shields the capital assets that the parties owned before entering a marriage/civil partnership from claims on divorce/dissolution, as the definition of 'matrimonial/partnership property' excludes virtually all of these capital assets. The author of one practitioner textbook[63] positively advises against recommending to

---

[60] That consent is valid only if given at the time the decree is pronounced and any previously given consent may be withdrawn up until that time: *Boyle v Boyle* 1977 SLT (Notes) 69. Without such consent the non-cohabitation must be for at least two years: Divorce (Scotland) Act 1976, s 1(2)(e), as amended by the Family Law (Scotland) Act 2006.

[61] Clive, *Husband and Wife*, above n 7, 17.001.

[62] In *Beith's Trustees v Beith* 1950 SC 66 the Court of Session finally abandoned the rule that a wife was incapable of subsequently varying or renouncing her own ante-nuptial trust. This rule was designed for her own protection, for renunciation would result in the trust property falling under the control of her husband, but the need for that protection disappeared with the Married Women's Property (Scotland) Acts.

[63] G Jamieson, *Family Law Agreements* (Haywards Heath, Tottel Publishing, 2005) 35.

clients that they enter into marital agreements because (i) the Family Law (Scotland) Act 1985 creates 'a fair and sensible system', any departure from which may, in due course, become outdated and inappropriate, (ii) spouses can provide for each other by other straightforward means (such as those mentioned above), (iii) household goods are presumed to be owned equally in any case, and (iv) 'it is generally inadvisable to discuss the arrangements for the breakdown of a marriage before it has begun or at regular intervals during the marriage: this may damage or destroy the trust between the parties to the contemplated marriage, or become a recurring source of trouble after marriage'.[64]

Marital agreements are not, however, completely unknown in Scottish practice. They may be entered into where individual couples have particular reasons to do so. It is not uncommon, for example, for parties to a second or subsequent marriage/ civil partnership to wish to avoid court involvement in their financial affairs after a previous experience in the divorce/dissolution court that they perceived as unfair. And with reconstituted families—increasingly common in Scotland as elsewhere—a property-owner may seek by marriage contract to give preference to the issue of his first family over any potential claims of his new spouse. Jamieson suggests that a marital agreement might be appropriate if one of the spouses/civil partners is very wealthy and giving a generous, but less than 50 per cent share, of his or her property would be more than ample for the needs and comforts of the other.[65] Clive points out that where there is doubt as to which legal system will govern, and the parties fear being subjected to 'an uncongenial matrimonial property regime', an agreement as to which legal system is to govern the relationship will resolve that doubt and would be given effect in Scotland.[66]

C. Setting Aside or Varying Marriage Contracts

The normal rules of contract apply to marital agreements where they are entered into, except that on divorce/dissolution a court may make an 'incidental order' in relation to financial provision setting aside or varying any term in an ante-nuptial or post-nuptial marriage settlement or in any corresponding settlement in respect of a civil partnership.[67] Such an order needs to satisfy the normal requirements set out in ss 8 and 9 of the 1985 Act for the making of any order for financial provision, as discussed above, and it must not prejudice the existing rights of any third party.[68] Requesting such an incidental order is rare. The court also has the power to set aside or vary any of the terms of an agreement as to the financial provision to be made on divorce/dissolution.[69] This particular issue arises (and has been

---

[64] Ibid.

[65] Ibid.

[66] Clive, above n 7, 17.016. See also J. Kerrigan, 'Separation Agreements, Survivorship Destinations and Succession' 2010 SLT (News) 25 who suggests that separation agreements might also be used to evacuate special destinations in title deeds, not otherwise achieved under s 19 of the 1985 Act.

[67] 1985 Act, s 14(2)(h). See, for example, *Kibble v Kibble* Case No F352.08 (Falkirk Sheriff Court, February 2011).

[68] Ibid, s 15(3).

[69] Ibid, s 16.

judicially discussed) much more commonly in relation to separation agreements (which are also covered by the rule in section 16 of the 1985 Act) and will be discussed in detail in the next section.

IV. SEPARATION AGREEMENTS

A. The General Enforceability of Separation Agreements

Unlike pre- and post-nuptial agreements, separation agreements entered into by spouses who have decided that their marriage/civil partnership should be brought to an end are commonly met with, in Scotland.[70] The motivation for entering such agreements is likely to have less to do with dissatisfaction with the default rules for financial provision in the Family Law (Scotland) Act 1985, and more to do with the desire to avoid lengthy and expensive court proceedings, which invariably add an unhelpfully adversarial tone to what is already a tense and unpleasant experience. Most family law practitioners will seek to persuade their separating clients to reach agreement with their spouse/civil partner, and it is only when agreement cannot be reached that the divorce/dissolution court will be asked by one or other of the parties to make orders for financial provision, as well as an order terminating the legal relationship. Since separation agreements in Scotland, like pre- and post-nuptial agreements, are governed by the general Scots law of contract (or of unilateral promise), there is no special legal definition, nor any particular requirements as to form beyond the normal rules of contract, that such an agreement must satisfy before being validly constituted. Though a verbal agreement is valid, certain matters commonly dealt with in separation agreements are required to be writing.[71] In any case, for evidential reasons an agreement in written form is far preferable and, if executed in terms of the Requirements of Writing (Scotland) Act 1995, will be self-evidencing.[72] Most separation agreements are registered in the Books of Council and Session[73] for preservation and execution, as any deed registered there has the force of a decree of the Court of Session.[74] This is not a form of judicial scrutiny of agreements, and far less one of judicial endorsement. Rather, the parties are free to enter whatever agreement they wish, one of the terms of which will normally be consent to registration in the Books of Council and Session—and consent, therefore,

---

[70] For the purposes of this discussion, 'separation agreement' means an agreement between parties who have concluded that their relationship should be terminated by divorce/dissolution and who wish to regulate the financial consequences of that conclusion themselves, rather than leaving it to the divorce/dissolution court. 'Separation agreement' may also refer to the private regulation of a couple who have decided to separate but not to divorce: it is agreements with this latter meaning that Clive discusses in his chapter on 'Separation' in *Husband and Wife*, above n 7, 19.003–19.041.

[71] See Requirements of Writing (Scotland) Act 1995, s 1(2).

[72] s 2 of the Requirements of Writing (Scotland) Act 1995 provides that a deed is formally valid if it has been subscribed by the granter or the parties; s 3 provides that it is self-evidencing if the signature has been attested by a single witness.

[73] That is to say the Register of Deeds maintained by the Keeper of the Registers of Scotland on behalf of the Court of Session.

[74] See *Stair Memorial Encyclopaedia of the Laws of Scotland* 'Public Registers and Records' (Reissue), above n 28, para 41.

to enforceability of the agreement. The parties' autonomy is not qualified, except as described in the next section, by judicial paternalism.

The term 'separation agreement' is a factual one, referring to any agreement concluded by the parties to a marriage/civil partnership (existing or prospective) governing, inter alia, the financial arrangements in the event of their separation. This might involve an agreement for the transfer of assets, the undertaking of an obligation of maintenance, or the sharing of a pension in terms of the Welfare Reform and Pensions Act 1999. Separation agreements of this sort tend in practice to be negotiated after, rather than before, the parties have decided to split up. They are, again like pre- and post-nuptial agreements, enforceable in the normal way,[75] at least insofar as they deal with financial matters,[76] and subject only to special rules for their variation or setting aside contained in section 16 of the Family Law (Scotland) Act 1985. Insofar as they deal with maintenance, these rules have already been described.

B. Setting Aside Agreements on Financial Provision

There is, of course, an inconvenient truth in all of this, which a strict adherence to party autonomy fails to confront: that within domestic relationships, opposite-sex certainly and same-sex probably, the parties are seldom of equivalent economic strengths. Even when they are, there may be disparities in social or psychological strengths that create opportunities for exploitation of the weaker and more vulnerable party. It is this high likelihood of a disparity in bargaining power that justifies a difference of treatment between separation agreements and normal commercial contracts. The law's continuing preference for marriage/civil partnership over cohabitation is revealed by its treating agreements between the latter as if they were commercial rather than domestic contracts, notwithstanding a likelihood of bargaining power disparity that is at least as great as with couples who have formalised their relationship.

Prior to the 1985 Act, an agreement on the financial provision to be made on divorce could not be set aside unless there was evidence of a vitiating factor such as error, fraud, undue influence or misrepresentation—in other words the normal contractual rules were applied without qualification due to the fact that the agreement had been made between spouses.[77] In addition, an agreement might be rescinded by one party due to the material breach of the other.[78] These remain the only means

---

[75] This has been the case at least since Stair's *Institutions,* above n 1. At I, iv, 9 he wrote: 'By private pactions the interest in, and division of, the goods of married persons after the dissolution of their marriage, may be according to their pleasure, as they agree'.

[76] Separation agreements are not in practice limited to financial matters and if, for example, there are children involved, they will frequently set out the arrangements for the future care of and contact with the children. Such terms are not enforceable in the normal way and it is open to either party to go to court to seek an order under s 11 of the Children (Scotland) Act 1995. The terms of the agreement have no bearing on the court's assessment of the welfare of the child.

[77] Other than that the agreement could be held to be frustrated by the later reconciliation of the parties: see *Davidson v Davidson* 1989 SLT 466. Resumption of cohabitation is strong, but not necessarily conclusive, evidence of reconciliation and mutual revocation of the agreement: *Methven v Methven* 1999 SLT (Sh Ct) 117 (Sheriff Scott).

[78] See *Morrison v Morrison* 1999 *Green's Family Law Bulletin* 43/6.

of setting aside cohabitation contracts. Section 16 of the Family Law (Scotland) Act 1985, however, gives the court a limited additional[79] power to set aside or vary agreements made between spouses/civil partners on the financial provision to be made on their divorce/dissolution. Section 16 applies to agreements made either before or after the commencement of the 1985 Act,[80] and it cannot itself, by a term in the agreement, be excluded.[81]

The test by which the court may set aside or vary an agreement or any term of such an agreement (including those relating to transfer of property, capital sums and pension sharing) is that the agreement is shown to be not fair and reasonable at the time it was made.[82] This is not to be interpreted identically to the test in the Unfair Contract Terms Act 1977.[83] 'Unfairness' and 'unreasonableness' are two separate bases upon which the agreement can be set aside, and it is not necessary for the party seeking reduction of the agreement to show that it was both unfair and unreasonable.[84] 'Reasonableness', as always, implies a range of acceptable outcomes and so an agreement is not challengeable solely on the ground that the parties might have reached a different, more reasonable, agreement.[85] The focus of enquiry in most cases has not been on the fairness of the outcome (in the way that the English courts seek 'fairness' in determining an appropriate financial provision on divorce/dissolution, or 'ancillary relief', in their recondite terminology) but rather on the fairness of the agreement itself and in particular on the process that led to the agreement being reached. So, for example, all the circumstances pertaining to the parties at the time the agreement was made are to be taken into account including in particular the nature and quality of any legal advice obtained by either party.[86] A failure to seek legal advice is unlikely on its own to justify the court setting aside an agreement.[87] Putting pressure on a spouse/partner to agree may, if severe, render the agreement unfair,[88] but giving up a valuable future claim in order to achieve an immediate, short-term, goal such as the departure of an unwanted spouse from the matrimonial home is not a reaction to unwarrantable pressure sufficient to satisfy the test.[89] Whether advantage

---

[79] The normal contractual grounds for reduction or rescission continue to exist and, sometimes, may prove useful: see G Junor, 'Separation Agreements and Common Law Remedies' 1998 *Green's Family Law Bulletin* 36/2.

[80] 1985 Act, s 16(5).

[81] Ibid, s 16(4).

[82] Ibid, s 16(1)(b).

[83] *Gillon v Gillon (No 1)* 1994 SLT 978 (Lord Penrose).

[84] *Gillon v Gillon (No 3)* 1995 SLT 678. This is the leading case on s 16. See also *Clarkson v Clarkson* 2008 SLT (Sh Ct) 2. But see *Hanif v Hanif* 2011 *Green's Family Law Bulletin* 112/5.

[85] In *Turner v Turner* 2009 *Green's Family Law Bulletin* 102/7 the sheriff held that a reasonable agreement would have given the husband less than the actual agreement did, but that this was insufficient to make the actual agreement unreasonable.

[86] *Young v Young (No 2)* 1991 SLT 869; *Anderson v Anderson* 1991 SLT (Sh Ct) 11; *Short v Short* 1994 *Green's Family Law Bulletin* 10/5; *Inglis v Inglis* 1999 SLT (Sh Ct) 59.

[87] *Inglis v Inglis* 1999 SLT (Sh Ct) 59.

[88] In *MacDonald v MacDonald* 2009 *Green's Family Law Bulletin* 99/5 (Sheriff Principal Lockhart) the agreement was set aside after the wife signed it against the advice of her solicitor, because there was ample evidence to show that she had been so bullied by her husband that she was afraid not to sign it. And in *Kibble v Kibble* Case No. F352.08 (Falkirk Sheriff Court, February 2011), Sheriff McCartney held that undue pressure had been brought to bear on a bride presented with an ante-nuptial agreement the evening before her wedding, in a language that she did not fully understand, and while she knew that if the marriage did not go ahead the next day she would be required, by the terms of her visa, to return home to Russia.

[89] *Inglis v Inglis* 1999 SLT (Sh Ct) 59, 62E (Sheriff Farrell).

has been taken by one party of the other is relevant,[90] but unequal division of assets, even with a great disparity, is not per se evidence of unfairness or unreasonableness.[91] The omission from the agreement, whether through oversight or otherwise, of a significant asset might be sufficient to justify the court overturning the agreement,[92] as might the failure of one party to give full and frank disclosure of his or her financial position.[93] Inadvertent misevaluation, if substantial, is likely to render any agreement made on the basis of such valuation unreasonable.[94] But making a bargain that turns out to be bad is not unreasonable: the agreement needs to be unfair or unreasonable at the time it was made. So events, for example a drop in the value of property, subsequent to the agreement are irrelevant to an application to vary or set aside the agreement on the ground of unfairness or unreasonableness.[95]

The onus is on the party seeking to escape the agreement and, generally speaking, the courts in Scotland have been slow to set aside or vary agreements on financial provision. But this reluctance must not be allowed to inhibit the effectiveness of section 16. In *Clarkson v Clarkson*[96] Sheriff MacNair said this:

> Whilst I accept that the courts should not be unduly ready to overturn agreements reached between parties, equally they should not construe s 16 so narrowly so as to deny a party the right given to him or her by Parliament to have an unfair or unreasonable agreement set aside.

C. The Time for Setting Aside

An order setting aside or varying an agreement relating to pension-sharing may be made only on granting the decree of divorce/dissolution, and not thereafter.[97] If the agreement does not contain a term relating to pension-sharing, it may be set aside or varied on the granting of the decree of divorce/dissolution or within such time thereafter as the court granting such decree may specify.[98] If the matter is not raised at that point the agreement becomes unchallengeable thereafter on the statutory basis, though it will remain challengeable on the more difficult common law grounds of error, fraud, undue influence and misrepresentation. The court is entitled to make a finding that the agreement is unfair or unreasonable at an earlier point in the process, but it may not act upon that finding by actually setting aside or varying the agreement until the decree of divorce/dissolution is pronounced.[99]

---

[90] See *McAfee v McAfee* 1990 SCLR 805; *Gillon v Gillon (No 3)* 1995 SLT 678.

[91] *Gillon v Gillon (No 3)* 1995 SLT 678. Here Lord Weir (at 682) concluded that 'the intangible value in terms of peace of mind and a sense of security' had to be balanced with the disparity in the division agreed.

[92] See *Worth v Worth* 1994 SLT (Sh Ct) 54; *McKay v McKay* 2006 SLT (Sh Ct) 149; *Clarkson v Clarkson* 2008 SLT (Sh Ct) 2.

[93] Ibid.

[94] *Clarkson v Clarkson* 2008 SLT (Sh Ct) 2.

[95] *Anderson v Anderson* 1989 SCLR 475.

[96] *Clarkson v Clarkson* 2008 SLT (Sh Ct) 2 [13].

[97] 1985 Act, s 16(2)(c)(i).

[98] Ibid, s 16(2)(b).

[99] *Gillon v Gillon (No 2)* 1994 SC 162; *MacDonald v MacDonald* 2009 *Green's Family Law Bulletin* 99/5 (Sheriff Principal Lockhart).

V. CONFLICT OF LAWS

In a provision that is not in its terms applicable to civil partnership, Scottish legislation sets out rules for the determination of which legal system is to apply to questions in relation to the rights of spouses to each other's property, movable and immovable,[100] but these rules are explicitly disapplied 'to the extent that the spouses agree otherwise'.[101] It follows that spouses (and there is no reason not to suppose civil partners also) can agree between themselves which legal system is to govern their property relationship. At present, 'rights in property arising out of a matrimonial relationship' are excluded from the terms of the Rome Convention on the law applicable to contractual obligations.[102] So the validity of marital agreements contracted abroad (which presumably for this purpose include such agreements entered into by civil partners) is governed by the common law. That provides that foreign agreements will be enforceable in Scotland if (i) formally valid either by the law of the place of execution or by the proper law of the contract,[103] that is to say the legal system chosen by the parties to govern the agreement[104] or, failing such choice, the system with the closest connection to the agreement,[105] and (ii) the parties had capacity to enter the contract (though there is some doubt as to how that capacity is determined).[106] It follows that 'the important question of the effect which a marriage contract has in the event of divorce is governed by its proper law and not by the law of the country in which the divorce is obtained'.[107] It is thought that, even where a marital agreement is governed by foreign law, the Scottish court retains the power to vary or revoke the agreement under section 16 of the Family Law (Scotland) Act 1985.[108]

VI. CONCLUSION

Autonomy of the parties in regulating their own financial affairs is the starting point in Scots law and is not significantly affected by the fact that the parties to an agreement marry or enter a civil partnership with each other.[109] During the relationship

---

[100] Family Law (Scotland) Act 2006, s 39(1)–(3).

[101] Ibid, s 39(6)(b).

[102] Brought into UK law by the Contracts (Applicable Law) Act 1990.

[103] See P Beaumont and P McEleavy, *Anton's Private International Law*, 3rd edn (Edinburgh, W Green/SULI, 2011) para 20.12.

[104] Though no such choice will affect the court in making orders for financial provision under s 8 of the Family Law (Scotland) Act 1985.

[105] See, eg *Goold Stuart's Trs v McPhail* 1947 SLT 221.

[106] See Beaumont and McEleavy, *Private International Law*, above n 103, para 20.13. Clive, above n 7, at 17.033 expresses the unqualified opinion that capacity to enter into a marriage contract depends on the law of the party's domicile at the time it is made.

[107] Clive, above n 7, 17.032, citing *Montgomery v Zarifi* 1918 SC(HL) 128.

[108] s 16(4) of the 1985 Act does not permit the s 16 power to be contracted out of. This must include not only explicit but implicit contracting out, such as by choosing a system of law to govern that has no analogous power, and it would be anomalous to adopt any different rule for agreements governed by a legal system not chosen, but imposed as having the closest connection to the agreement.

[109] It is as well to note here that this is true only during life. On death, Scots law eschews autonomy of the testator in favour of protected inheritance rights for spouses/civil partners and for issue. As we have already seen, before 1964 the distribution of a person's estate was more or less the same whether a conjugal relationship ended by death or by divorce, and though there are sometimes calls to restore the link (see D Reid, 'From the Cradle to the Grave: Politics, Family and Inheritance Law' (2008) 12

they remain autonomous individuals, with the power of course to limit their own freedom of action by contract or unilateral promise. On divorce/dissolution the rules governing financial provision are truly default rules because they apply only when the parties themselves do not or cannot agree as to the financial settlement that is to be made. The primary aims of the default rules for financial provision on divorce/dissolution are interconnected: clean break, predictability and the encouragement of extra-judicial settlement. It is assumed that a predictable system with limited room for judicial discretion will enable parties to negotiate what is mutually considered a more suitable result with full knowledge of what the courts are likely to do if agreement cannot be reached. Predictability is for this reason regarded as more important than the uncertainties of 'fairness in the individual case', being more likely to avoid fraught and contentious disputes. Inevitably this means that the law is rather less flexible than, say, English law when faced with an unusual scenario: this is most noticeable in 'big money' cases. Nevertheless the law is widely regarded by the legal profession in Scotland as being satisfactory and eminently workable. After a quarter of a century of operation, and substantial judicial discussion, the Family Law (Scotland) Act 1985 is familiar and its principles well-embedded into legal practice. There has been little scope for judicial development such as has been seen in the higher courts in England, though there is an extensive interpretative jurisprudence.[110] There have of course been statutory amendments, in particular in 1999 bringing in pension-sharing,[111] and in 2006 qualifying the 'relevant date' in order to resolve the '*Wallis* conundrum'.[112] But the basic principles themselves are generally regarded as robust and sensible.

Sometimes there are calls to make Scots law more discretionary or to change the balance between flexibility and predictability,[113] but the most recent substantial reform of Scottish family law[114] dealt only with the 'relevant date' issue and the various consultations that preceded that reform did not identify either serious practical problems or professional discontent with the operation of the 1985 Act.

All the more surprising, then, that when the House of Lords handed down its judgment in the English case of *Miller v Miller; McFarlane v McFarlane*,[115] the Scottish judge sitting on the Appellate Committee in that case, Lord Hope of Craighead, used his speech to call for a review of the Scottish law, believing that the fair result achieved by the application of English law in these cases could not have been reached in Scotland. This caused no little consternation in Scotland, where there has been no equivalent expression of judicial disquiet.[116] He based this conclusion,

---

Edinburgh Law Review 391), the approach of the Scottish Law Commission in their 2009 *Report on Succession* (Scot Law Com No 215, May 2009) is to keep the two systems well apart.

[110] See Norrie, *Stair Memorial Encyclopaedia*, above n 28, paras 646–75.
[111] Welfare Reform and Pensions Act 1999.
[112] Family Law (Scotland) Act 2006, s 16.
[113] See, eg C Barton and A Bissett-Johnson, 'Financial Provision on Divorce in Scots Law: Does it Need Reform?' 2000 *Juridical Review* 265; A Bissett-Johnson and B Dempsey, '*McFarlane v McFarlane; Miller v Miller*: Time for a Review?' 2007 *Juridical Review* 65.
[114] Family Law (Scotland) Act 2006.
[115] *Miller v Miller; McFarlane v McFarlane* [2006] UKHL 24; [2006] 2 AC 618.
[116] See E Clive, 'Financial Provision on Divorce' (2006) 10 *Edinburgh Law Review* 413; K Norrie, 'Clean Break Under Attack' (2006) *Journal of the Law Society of Scotland* 16.

however, on a surprisingly narrow reading of the 1985 Act. His worry focused on the fact that in a case where a wealthy spouse has few capital assets, Scots law, with its emphasis on capital payment, would be unable to make an award of sufficient worth to achieve what the circumstances of the case required. Commentators responded that the payment of a capital sum can be postponed, and made in instalments.[117] The Scottish Government has indicated that it is not minded to act upon Lord Hope's call for reform.[118] This is sensible. Amending the law to deal with those rare cases (like both *Miller* and *McFarlane*) where there is a substantial surplus of assets over needs and the only unfairness lies in the economic disparity between the two does nothing for—and risks disrupting—the generality of cases where the underlying problem is that assets and income are insufficient to keep both ex-spouses/partners at the standard of living they enjoyed when together. The concentration in Scotland on assets acquired during the marriage/civil partnership obviates the need to make necessarily arbitrary distinctions between 'long' and 'short' marriages/civil partnerships and avoids the trap that, for example, English law seems to have fallen into in assuming that marriage/civil partnership involves an undertaking to share assets and income accruing even after divorce/dissolution. While it may well be true that Mrs McFarlane and Mrs Parlour[119] would have received less from a Scottish court than they received from the English court, this does not in itself make the Scottish system less 'fair'—because fairness is not an absolute concept and can be judged only in the light of underlying conceptions. The underlying understanding in Scotland is that marriage/ civil partnership necessarily involves a sharing of wealth generated during the marriage/civil partnership, but not during life. The English courts seem to see marriage/ civil partnership as involving an undertaking of life-long obligations.[120] Though socially the differences between Scotland and England may be slight in the structures of family life, the underlying understanding of what marriage/civil partnership means in the two countries must, it is suggested, have been affected by the fact that Scotland has had judicial divorce for 300 years longer than England.

Nor is there discontent at the enforceability of marital agreements, or at the parties' power to exercise autonomy by ousting the jurisdiction of the court to make orders for financial provision on divorce/dissolution. The court's limited power to set aside or vary such agreements is seen as striking an appropriate balance between party protection and contractual freedom. The only substantial amendment to the law on marital agreements in Scotland that is at all likely in the future is the extension of the protection granted to domestic contracts by section 16 of the 1985 Act to cohabiting couples. But even yet, such an extension is not within any existing governmental plans. Marriage/civil partnership remains at present the politically favoured form of family life.

---

[117] Ibid.

[118] Parliamentary Question S2W-28599, answered by the Deputy Minister of Justice 25 September 2006, reported in September 2006 *Journal of the Law Society of Scotland Online*.

[119] *Parlour v Parlour* [2005] Fam 171, conjoined in the Court of Appeal with *McFarlane v McFarlane*.

[120] Just as the (Episcopalian) Church of England continues, at least at a formal level, to see marriage as a life-long sacrament and is unwilling, unlike the (Presbyterian) Church of Scotland, to remarry divorced individuals. The Princess Royal was able to marry in a Scottish church notwithstanding that her ex-husband was still alive; her brother could obtain only a blessing from the English church when he (civilly) married a divorced woman with a living ex-husband.

Marital Agreements and Private Autonomy in Singapore

WAI KUM LEONG

CONTENTS

I. DEFAULT LAW ON THE FINANCIAL CONSEQUENCES OF DIVORCE: DIVISION OF MATRIMONIAL ASSETS AND MAINTENANCE OF FORMER WIFE

A. Division of Matrimonial Assets

Since 1980[1] the courts in Singapore have been empowered to make an order of division of matrimonial assets between the spouses upon the court awarding a judgment that terminates their marriage. The current version of the provision, the Women's Charter section 112, subsection (1) reads:

> The court shall have power, when granting or subsequent to the grant of a judgment of divorce, judicial separation or nullity of marriage, to order the division between the parties of any matrimonial asset or the sale of any such asset and the division between the parties of the proceeds of the sale of any such asset in such proportions as the court thinks just and equitable.

---

[1] By way of the Women's Charter (Amendment) Act 26 of 1980 that added the then s 106. S 106 has been replaced, in the current version of the Women's Charter (c 353, 2009 edn of Statutes of the Republic of Singapore), by the current s 112. For the imminent change that will avail the power even

This is the default law. On application the court can make an order that achieves the just and equitable division of the properties owned by either or both spouses that fall within 'matrimonial asset'. Although section 112(1) expressly mentions 'division ... of any ... asset or the sale of any such asset and the division ... of the proceeds of the sale', this should be understood together with subsection (3) that provides that 'the court may make all such other orders or give such directions as may be necessary or expedient to give effect to any order made under this section' and subsection (5) that, 'without limiting the generality of subsections (3) and (4)', lists several other kinds of orders the court may choose to make. Several observations of the way the courts have exercised this power are noteworthy.

i. Deferred Community of Property

There has been judicial acceptance of the author's depiction of the law in Singapore on the effect of marriage on a spouse's interest in property owned by the other as subscribing to the concept of deferred community of property.[2] While the concept of the 'deferred community of property', which originated in Scandinavia, is understood there to mean a right to half of the net value of the sum of both spouses' marital property, in the property division between the spouses undertaken upon their divorce,[3] the concept in Singapore does not mean anything quite as definitive as a right to half of the net value of the properties that are subject to the court's power under the Women's Charter section 112(1).

Upon granting a judgment that terminates marriage, section 112(1) empowers the court in Singapore to review the spouses' holding of properties and to make an order that, in the court's judgment, will achieve the 'just and equitable' division of the properties that are their matrimonial assets between them. The discretionary nature of the court's power, with the result that the order that the court will make is less predictable than it would be where, say, Swedish law applies (as Swedish law gives a spouse a 'right' to half), does not render the law in Singapore any less a 'deferred community of property' regime. In England, where the power in the court is equally laden with discretion, a noted family law academic has described a seminal decision of the House of Lords in 2001 as introducing 'community of property'.[4]

---

where the judgment that terminated the marriage was obtained outside Singapore, see the text below corresponding to nn 31 and 32. (All statutes in Singapore are accessible online at www.lawnet.com.sg.) The Women's Charter is the main family statute regulating all persons in Singapore other than persons who are married under Muslim marriage law. Its somewhat unusual title traces its original enactment in 1961 to the process of national reconstruction that the leading political party regarded as requiring the full participation of women in the workforce and the concomitant abolition of the then existing polygamous marriage regimes; see Leong Wai Kum, 'Fifty Years and More of the Women's Charter of Singapore' [2008] *Singapore Journal of Legal Studies* 1, 1–7.

[2] See Leong Wai Kum, 'Division of Matrimonial Assets: Recent Cases and Thoughts for Reform' [1993] *Singapore Journal of Legal Studies* 351, 353; and see Court of Appeal in *Lock Yeng Fun v Chua Hock Chye* [2007] 3 Singapore Law Reports (Reissue) 520 [40] (Andrew Phang JA) and *Lau Siew Kim v Yeo Guan Chye Terence* [2008] 2 Singapore Law Reports (Reissue) 108 [80] (VK Rajah JA). (The Singapore Law Reports from 1965 to 2009 have been reissued. Judgments of all courts in Singapore since 1991, whether or not reported, are available online at www.lawnet.com.sg.)

[3] See, eg, the understanding under Swedish law, as conveyed by Professor Maarit Jänterä-Jareborg's chapter in this volume.

[4] See Stephen Cretney in his comment on *White v White* [2001] 1 AC 596 entitled 'Community of Property Imposed by Judicial Decision' (2003) 119 *Law Quarterly Review* 349–52.

ii. Definition of Matrimonial Assets

Section 112(10) provides a definition of matrimonial assets that seeks to find a rational connection between the property and the marriage, in particular, the personal efforts of either spouse expended during the subsistence of the marriage towards the acquisition or improvement of the property. The courts have long striven to achieve an interpretation of the definition that promotes the objectives of the power.[5] 'Matrimonial assets' include all properties acquired during the marriage (whether of business, family or personal nature), all employee benefits (whether available now, compulsorily required to be saved for retirement or even of the nature of 'stock options', whether they have vested or simply may be anticipated for work performed during the course of the marriage), property acquired before marriage that had become used and associated with the family, as well as gifts and inheritances where these became the family's matrimonial home or were substantially improved by personal effort during the marriage.[6] There are hardly any pension rights in Singapore. For a long time now a compulsory savings for retirement scheme (called the Central Provident Fund, or 'CPF' for short) has replaced pension rights. Every employee must save a proportion of his or her salary in an account maintained by the CPF Board, to which the employer must also contribute a designated amount. The courts have long included the balance of CPF monies or properties bought with this money as a matrimonial asset available for division with the employee's spouse.[7] The inclusive approach to interpreting 'matrimonial assets' was set by the first important decision under the predecessor of section 112 and has continued since.[8]

iii. Objective of section 112 Power: Fairest Possible Division

The courts have established that the objective to be pursued in the exercise of the power under the Women's Charter, section 112 is fairness between the spouses. In 1999 the Court of Appeal, which continues to be the highest court in Singapore, observed: 'we are of the opinion that [s 112(1)] gives the court a very wide power to order the division of matrimonial assets in the fairest possible way'.[9] While it might be thought that fairness is malleable, the courts have been exceptionally clear about the context in which the fairness of the order must be judged.

---

[5] See the High Court in Singapore in *Koo Shirley v Mok Kong Chua Kenneth* [1989] 1 Singapore Law Reports (Reissue) 72, the first significant judicial discussion of the power introduced in 1980 (see above, n 1), working without the benefit of a statutory definition, to decide 'all [the husband's] assets were acquired during the marriage and came within the [power]'. This inclusive approach survived the enactment of the statutory definition, the current Women's Charter, above n 1, s 112(10), in 1996.

[6] See, eg, *Chan Teck Hock David v Leong Mei Chuan* [2002] 1 Singapore Law Reports (Reissue) 76, *Ng Sylvia v Oon Choon Huat Peter and another* [2002] 1 Singapore Law Reports (Reissue) 246 and *Chen Siew Hwee v Low Kee Guan (Wong Yong Yee, co-respondent)* [2006] 4 Singapore Law Reports (Reissue) 605.

[7] See *Lam Chih Kian v Ong Chin Ngoh* [1993] 2 Singapore Law Reports (Reissue) 460.

[8] *Koo Shirley v Mok Kong Chua Kenneth*, above n 5, remains good law and continues to be cited today.

[9] *Yeong Swan Ann v Lim Fei Yen* [1999] 1 Singapore Law Reports (Reissue) 49 [23] (Yong Pung How former CJ).

In a fairly recent judgment, the Court of Appeal elaborated upon its earlier observation thus:

> [U]ltimately the division of matrimonial assets is not simply a numbers game. The social policy underscored by the division of matrimonial assets, the joint product of a marital partnership, is just as important as the final award. The language of a power to 'divide' says to the whole society that the law acknowledges the equally important contributions of the homemaker to the partnership of marriage and its acquisition of wealth. It would be unfortunate if the process of division perpetuated an impression of simply 'dividing the spoils' of the economically more advantaged party. The entire process must involve a mutual respect for spousal contributions, whether in the economic or homemaking spheres, as both are equally fundamental to the well-being of the marital partnership.[10]

Judge of Appeal Andrew Phang made explicit the goal of giving value to all spousal contributions during marriage as the court affirmed the exhortation to the spouses to mutually respect each other's contributions whether this is in the economic sphere or in the homemaking sphere. The power given to the court to order the just and equitable division of matrimonial assets should be exercised in pursuit of this understanding of fairness between the former equal marital partners who have been exhorted to cooperate in expending different efforts for their mutual benefit during the subsistence of their marriage.

iv. Context: Marriage as Equal Co-operative Partnership of Different Efforts

The author has always urged for the power to order the just and equitable division of matrimonial assets to be set within the context of another remarkable provision in the Women's Charter that predated the enactment of the power over matrimonial assets. From its enactment, the Women's Charter has in the current section 46(1) provided thus:

> Upon the solemnization of marriage, the husband and the wife shall be mutually bound to co-operate with each other in safeguarding the interests of the union and in caring and providing for the children.

The provision is of imperfect obligation in not providing sanction for breach. Despite this, however, the author regards it to perform the laudable role of characterising marriage as the spouses' equal co-operative partnership of different efforts.[11] In so

---

[10] *NK v NL* [2007] 3 Singapore Law Reports (Reissue) 743 [41] (Andrew Phang JA). The author humbly suggests that the learned Judge of Appeal's words recall her own: 'the language of a power to "divide" says to the whole society that the law acknowledges the different but equal contribution of the homemaker to the partnership of marriage and its acquisition of wealth. The law ... tells us [that] both roles must be performed equally well if the partnership of marriage is to flourish'; see Leong Wai Kum, 'Division of Matrimonial Assets', above n 2, 355.

[11] See Leong Wai Kum, 'Supporting Marriage through Description as an Equal Partnership of Efforts', *The International Survey of Family Law* 2002 edn (Bristol, Jordan Publishing, 2002) 379; and see generally, Leong Wai Kum, *Elements of Family Law in Singapore* (Singapore, LexisNexis, 2007) 85–95. The author first started relating the power with the spouses' partnership efforts back in 1989; see Leong Wai Kum, 'Division of Matrimonial Property upon Termination of Marriage' (1989) 1 *Malayan Law Journal* xiii. The Women's Charter, s 46(1) performs a second laudable role, in its closing words, in characterising the parent-child relationship as one where the parents owe responsibility to care and provide for their child. The discussion of this, however, is beyond the interest of this chapter but see Leong Wai Kum, *Elements of Family Law in Singapore*, 246–59.

characterising marriage, the provision exhorts this moral attitude of both spouses to regard one another as equal partners working for their common good.

Section 46(1) was enacted within the original Women's Charter in 1961, apparently following the model of the Swiss Civil Code.[12] It provides the ideal context to understand how the power to divide matrimonial assets ought to be exercised. As matrimonial assets are properties acquired by the equal co-operative partnership of different efforts that is marriage, it makes simple good sense that, upon the termination of this partnership, the court should help achieve a just and equitable division of whatever matrimonial assets remain unused and thus available for division. This is done not so much to assist the spouse who may have become economically disadvantaged by the role he or she discharged during the partnership, even though this provides an equally persuasive justification for the power, but simply to return the just and equitable proportions of property to the two spouses who co-operated in their acquisition. The courts exercise their power, in other words, to give due credit to both financial and non-financial contributions to the partnership of marriage, which contributions the spouses made through the different roles each discharged.

v. Court-Ordered Division of Matrimonial Assets

The orders made by the courts in Singapore under the Women's Charter, section 112 have been nothing short of spectacular. In her latest survey, the author suggests:

> The majority of decisions resulted in a simple equal division ordered or an insignificant difference from 50 per cent ... The next most common proportions were where one spouse received 10 per cent more than the other ... With these two categories forming the vast majority of decisions given in recent years, it may be suggested that an order of division of matrimonial assets is likely to be of equal division or within a narrow range from equal division.[13]

The judges in Singapore were found to have exercised their power in a way that clearly conveyed their view of the financial and non-financial contributions spouses make during marriage. The judicial view was that both contributions bear close to equal value so that, whichever role(s) a spouse discharged during the marriage, he or she should obtain close to a half share of such property still available for division. The author is hopeful that this pattern of orders will continue. If the courts focus upon achieving results that convey 'mutual respect for spousal contributions, whether in the economic or homemaking spheres',[14] there is every reason for optimism.

B. Matrimonial Home

There is no special regime regulating the matrimonial home. It readily comes within the definition of matrimonial asset[15] even where its acquisition was originally through a gift to one spouse or as the inheritance of one spouse. There has only been one

---

[12] See Leong Wai Kum, 'Fifty years and more of the Women's Charter of Singapore' above n 1, 11–16.
[13] See Leong Wai Kum, *Elements of Family Law in Singapore*, n 11 above, 697–98.
[14] *NK v NL*, above n 10 (Andrew Phang JA).
[15] See the Women's Charter, above n 1, s 112(10).

decision where, exceptionally, the spouses' matrimonial home was never owned by either of them and they were only allowed to occupy it by the grace of the husband's wealthy father, the court decided it did not fall within the definition of matrimonial asset and was thus not subject to the power to divide.[16]

The matrimonial home may be said to be almost always subject to the power to divide. Indeed, the courts almost always divide the spouses' interest(s) in the matrimonial home equally between them. Most spouses in Singapore use the money in their compulsory savings for retirement (account within the Central Provident Fund) to help acquire their matrimonial home. There are stringent rules on how the proceeds of the sale of such properties should be refunded into their compulsory savings account(s). The Central Provident Fund Board developed rules in 2007 that permit the better enforcement of court orders of division of matrimonial assets, where one or more such assets were acquired, whether fully or partially, with money from a spouse's Central Provident Fund account. The principle, thus, is that the matrimonial home is handled no differently from any other kind of property, as far as the court's power to divide matrimonial assets is concerned, except that, being the cradle of the family, it is even more likely to be equally divided than other matrimonial assets.

If there is anything unique about the matrimonial home it has to do rather with the courts attempting to preserve its use for the children of the marriage and, by necessity, the spouse who will continue to be their care-giver after divorce. Like most other common law jurisdictions, courts in Singapore try to shield dependent children, as far as this is practicable, from the undesirable effects of their parents' divorce. It has become accepted that, where this is possible, the matrimonial home ought to be retained for occupation by the children so that their lives and environment are as little changed as possible.[17] This is effected, not at the stage of the decision as to what is the just and equitable division of this property as one of the matrimonial assets of the spouses, but subsequently. After the decision on what is the just and equitable division has been made, the court then makes incidental orders so that the order of division is executed.[18] At this last stage in the resolution of the application for an order of division of matrimonial assets, the practicability of keeping the matrimonial home for the use of the children and their care-giver is assessed. Where this is possible, the courts will so order.

C. Relating an Order of Division of Matrimonial Assets with an Order to the Husband to Continue to Maintain his Wife after their Divorce

Compared with the law of division of matrimonial assets, which only came into existence in 1980 and, from its inception, has always been gender-neutral, the law of maintenance in Singapore traces its origins to the common law and remains, unfortunately, a unilateral obligation. Within the common law, maintenance was a

---

[16] See the decision of the Family Court in Singapore in *Kng Poey Choo (mw) v Ong Chong Ken Kenneth* [2003] SGDC 83.

[17] See, eg, *Tham Khai Meng (mw) v Nam Wen Jet Bernadette* [1997] 1 Singapore Law Reports (Reissue) 336.

[18] See the Women's Charter, above n 1, s 112(5).

unilateral obligation—a husband owed the obligation to make reasonable provision for a dependent wife unless he was incapable of making such provision, although the obligation was enforced indirectly through the 'agency of necessity' whereby merchants could extend credit for the necessaries of life to a wife, in the confidence that she was her husband's agent. This obligation at the common law was rightly one-sided, as it 'compensated' for another common law rule that a wife lost her capacity to hold property immediately upon marriage and throughout its duration, so that any property she owned then was automatically transferred to her husband. He received all of his wife's property and was under an obligation to support her financially. The husband's obligation later became directly enforceable though a court order of maintenance. When, in time, the legislature created judicial divorce, it seemed a natural progression that the post-divorce maintenance obligation should similarly be one-sided.

Singapore received the common law as her basic law by an instrument emanating from the Colonial Office in London, called the Second Charter of Justice, in 1826. Developments in England on judicial enforcement of the husband's obligation, the creation of judicial divorce and the similarly unilateral obligation of post-divorce maintenance between the spouses were adopted. While England has, since then, made the maintenance obligation mutual between the spouses, Singapore unfortunately has not. The Women's Charter in section 113 continues to provide:

> The court may order a man to pay maintenance to his wife or former wife … (b) when granting or subsequent to the grant of a judgment of divorce, judicial separation or nullity of marriage.

This is not for the lack of calls by the author to remove this anomaly that flies in the face of the exhortation in the Women's Charter, section 46(1) to the spouses to co-operate to safeguard their union.[19] The court's power to order maintenance, it has been decided, should be exercised to achieve a fair and reasonable order.[20]

The author has observed that, between the far older power to order the husband to continue to maintain his wife, and the power to order the just and equitable division of matrimonial assets, it is the latter that has become far more significant. Indeed, it is suggested that the power to divide matrimonial assets 'has become the primary power leaving the power to order maintenance in a complementary or supplementary role.'[21] The Court of Appeal has agreed, observing: 'The order

---

[19] See Leong Wai Kum, 'The Duty to Maintain Spouse and Children During Marriage' (1987) 29 *Malaya Law Review* 56, 78 and her private representation to the Select Committee of Parliament of Singapore recorded in *Report of the Select Committee on the Women's Charter (Amendment) Bill [Bill No 5/96]* (Singapore, Government Printers, 1996) B37 and again in the joint paper she submitted with her colleagues, Associate Professors Debbie Ong and Chan Wing Cheong in October 2010 during the public consultation on proposed changes to the Women's Charter as contained in the Women's Charter (Amendment) Bill of 2010, www.reach.gov.sg.

[20] See the High Court's decision in *Quek Lee Tiam (mw) v Ho Kim Swee (alias Ho Kian Guan* [1995] SGHC) 23. The Court, by purposeful interpretation of a statutory direction, decided that it should aim for the 'financial preservation of the former wife' within the capability of the former husband to the extent that this is fair upon considering all the facts and circumstances of the parties. This interpretation has been endorsed many times since.

[21] See Leong Wai Kum, *Elements of Family Law in Singapore*, above n 11, 806.

for maintenance of a former wife thus plays a complementary role to the order for division of matrimonial assets.'[22]

It follows from this relationship between the powers that, where the order of division of matrimonial assets is adjudged to have equalised the financial situations of the former spouses, the court may make no order of maintenance or may make a mere nominal or extremely modest order.[23] Where the order of division of matrimonial assets has not managed to achieve this (usually because there was very little property that met the statutory definition of matrimonial asset to become subject to the power to divide, or the couple have gathered precious little property during their marriage), then an order of maintenance may be the only way to allow the wife to continue to share in the future income of the former husband which is, to an extent, attributable to the parties' efforts during marriage.[24] There may, lastly, be instances where it is appropriate to make substantial orders both of division of matrimonial assets and of maintenance of the former wife to be fair to both of them.[25]

Financial provision after divorce must largely be made by way of an order of division of matrimonial assets and/or of maintenance of the former wife, since the level of public assistance payments in Singapore is relatively low. It has become accepted that, upon the termination of marriage by the court, available matrimonial assets will be divided equitably between the former spouses and, where necessary, this may be supplemented by an order of maintenance of the former wife.

One of the reasons for the attraction of an order of division of matrimonial assets over maintenance is that, once executed, it achieves a clean break in the financial relationship of the former spouses. Where a substantial order is not practicable, however, the courts have shown that they are not averse to ordering the husband to continue to provide periodical maintenance to his former wife where this is the only way by which she may be given due credit for the non-financial contributions she made towards the marriage which had, to some extent, assisted the husband in developing his career.

D. Duty of Full and Frank Disclosure

The law in Singapore demands the full and frank disclosure by both parties in an application for an ancillary order upon termination of marriage by court judgment, whether it be for a financial order (of division of matrimonial assets, maintenance of former wife by husband or maintenance by a parent of a dependent child) or for a non-financial order (of custody, care and control or access to a child). The Women's Charter (Matrimonial Proceedings) Rules[26] contain detailed provisions for discovery that mirror the same rules in any other civil proceedings. The courts repeatedly

---

[22] *BG v GF* [2007] 3 Singapore Law Reports (Reissue) 233 [75] (Andrew Ang J).

[23] See, eg, *Ryan Neil John v Berger Rosaline* [2000] 3 Singapore Law Reports (Reissue) 647 and *NI v NJ* [2007] 1 Singapore Law Reports (Reissue) 75.

[24] See, eg, *Quek Lee Tiam (mw) v Ho Kim Swee (alias Ho Kian Guan)*, above n 20, and *Lee Yong Chuan Edwin v Tan Soan Lian* [2000] 3 Singapore Law Reports (Reissue) 867.

[25] See, eg, *BG v BF*, above n 22.

[26] Women's Charter (Matrimonial Proceedings) Rules, subsidiary legislation to c 353, 2009 edn *Statutes of the Republic of Singapore*, www.lawnet.com.sg.

remind parties of their responsibility to make full and frank disclosure and that, if there is any credible evidence that suggests their failing to discharge their duty, the court will readily draw an appropriate adverse inference against the non-disclosing party.

In *BG v BF*,[27] an appeal before the Court of Appeal in Singapore from an application for, inter alia, an order of division of matrimonial assets, Andrew Ang J reminded the Court that:

> [T]he general duty that every party to court proceedings owes to the court to make full and frank disclosure of all relevant information within his or her knowledge is particularly relevant in the context of the division of matrimonial assets. The position in law is that full and frank disclosure is important and in its absence the court is entitled to draw inferences adverse to the party who failed to do so.[28]

Upon a detailed examination, the judge observed: 'The implication from this is that there is at least one non-disclosure by the Husband … we should … draw an adverse inference against the Husband.'[29] There are many cases in similar vein.

E. Applications for Order of Division of Matrimonial Assets or Maintenance are Ancillary to Suits for Divorce Presented in Singapore

The Women's Charter requires parties seeking to marry to be 'respectively male and female'.[30] There is no provision in Singapore for homosexual couples to formalise their relationship, nor are there statistics on the prevalence of homosexual relationships. Inasmuch as the following discussion is largely about the consideration that a court hearing an application for an ancillary financial order made under the provisions of the Women's Charter may accord to a marital agreement, the law of ancillary financial orders is not available to a person who does not fall within the statute's understanding of 'husband' and 'wife'. An application for an order of division of matrimonial assets or for an order to the husband to continue to maintain his former wife can only be pursued by persons who have been married to one another. The marriage need not have been solemnised in Singapore. As long as the termination of marriage is pursued in Singapore, the ancillary powers become available upon the activation of the Singapore courts' matrimonial jurisdiction.

The ancillary character of the power in the court to order the division of matrimonial assets or of the former husband to continue to maintain his former wife, with the consequence that the courts in Singapore may only exercise either power upon an earlier application in Singapore for a judgment that terminates the marriage, however, looks set to change. When the change becomes implemented, the powers in the Women's Charter, sections 112(1) and 113 will extend beyond spouses who terminate their marriage in Singapore. The Law Reform Committee of the

---

[27] *BG v BF*, above n 22.
[28] Ibid [52].
[29] Ibid [66]–[67].
[30] The Women's Charter, above n 1, s 12(1), although subss (2) and (3) allow a post-surgery transsexual to be determined as having his or her post-surgery gender for the purpose of fulfilling this requirement.

Singapore Academy of Law in 2009 recommended a change in the law so that the powers in the court should be co-extensive, with some discretion, whether the termination of marriage by court judgment is achieved in Singapore or outside.[31] The government has accepted this proposal. It has proposed this change and others, not relevant to this discussion, and an amendment Bill has been presented for its first reading in the Parliament of Singapore.[32] The amendment Bill is expected to pass smoothly as it did not attract any major criticism during the period public consultation was sought. When the amendment comes into force, the Women's Charter, section 112(1) becomes more like an independent, rather than an ancillary, power and accessible whether spouses terminated their marriage by court judgment in Singapore or outside Singapore.

II. CONTRACTUAL PERSPECTIVES OF PRE-NUPTIAL AND POST-NUPTIAL MARITAL AGREEMENTS

A. Formation and Subsistence of Agreement

The courts in Singapore have consistently adopted the conservative approach that, before a pre-nuptial or post-nuptial marital agreement is given any consideration in court, it must be found to have complied fully with all the requirements of the law of contract as being validly formed and subsisting.

The case that settled that the whole of the law of contract on the formation of a valid agreement, as well as the part on whether it subsists, must be complied with is the High Court of Singapore decision in *Chia Hock Hua v Ching Choo Je*.[33] The husband had paid the wife S$30,000, which the wife admitted she received. Their disagreement was over the effect of this payment. The husband claimed that the agreement was in full and final settlement of their financial commitments. The wife opposed this. She claimed she had been tricked into signing the agreement. She, therefore, made an application to the Court for an order to her husband to continue to provide reasonable maintenance to her as his former wife. In her application she asked the Court to take the view that the agreement they had made was unenforceable, for a range of contractual reasons. The wife's claim was easily dismissed by the High Court, which had no difficulty in finding that the well-educated wife had not been tricked into entering the agreement. The High Court approved the agreement they had made, and dismissed the wife's application for an order of maintenance.

Chia Hock Hua v Ching Choo Je determines that for a marital agreement to have effect, it must pass muster from a purely contractual perspective. An agreement that fails the contractual requirements for validity has no place in a court of law.

---

[31] See Singapore Academy of Law's Law Reform Committee Report of July 2009, *Ancillary Orders after Foreign Divorce or Annulment*, www.sal.org.sg.

[32] See the Women's Charter (Amendment) Bill No 34 of 2010. See, now, the Women's Charter (Amendment) Act No 2 of 2011 wef 1 June 2011 add to Women's Charter, above n 1, Part X 'Chapter 4A – Financial Relief Consequential on Foreign Matrimonial Proceedings'.

[33] *Chia Hock Hua v Ching Choo Je* [1994] 3 Singapore Law Reports (Reissue) 159.

Amarjeet Singh JC summarised some of the issues that could undermine any agreement under the law of contract itself thus:

> The court must be satisfied that the parties were ad idem and—
>
> — whether the question of the benefit of legal advice was necessary if the case was a complicated one: *Peacock v Peacock*[34]
> — whether there was extreme pressure applied by the husband resulting in the wife accepting an unsatisfactory financing agreement: *Camm v Camm*[35]
> — whether unforeseen circumstances had arisen which made it impossible for the wife to work or otherwise maintain herself: *Wright v Wright*[36]
> — whether the agreement had been reached at arm's length and the parties had been separately advised which facts if found would constitute prima facie evidence of the reasonableness of the terms: *Dean v Dean*[37]
> — whether poverty and ignorance (20th century euphemism for 'a member of the lower income group' and 'less highly educated') produced an unfair and unacceptable arrangement for one side: *Fry v Lane*[38] applied in *Backhouse v Backhouse*[39]
> — whether on the construction of the agreement there was a good and effective consent: *Carter v Carter*[40] at pp 274–275, applied in *Cook v Cook*[41]
> — whether there was mistake, duress or undue influence such as the husband being in a superior bargaining position and he took an unfair advantage by exploiting his position and the agreement was entered into without the wife having full knowledge of all of the relevant facts and or legal advice;
>
> the weight to be given to the conduct of the parties and circumstances of the case was considered by Ormrod LJ who summed up the above stated considerations in *Edgar v Edgar* (CA)[42] and added that it may well be that there may be other considerations which affect the justice of the case.[43]

The principle is that, for a marital agreement to be accorded any effect in court, it should not have breached any requirement of validity of agreement as imposed by the law of contract.

The Court of Appeal in Singapore in *TQ v TR and another appeal*[44] affirmed the conservative approach. Here, the marital agreement was pre-nuptial and foreign. It was executed in the Netherlands between a Dutch man and his Swedish fiancée, who intended to set up matrimonial home in England after marriage. The Court of Appeal applied Dutch law and found this agreement was validly formed and remained subsisting at the time it came before the Court in Singapore. The Court of Appeal observed that, had there not been foreign elements, so that the agreement was completely local, the requirements of valid formation under the law of contract

---

[34] *Peacock v Peacock* [1991] FCR 121. (Footnote numbering in the quotation differs from the original.)
[35] *Camm v Camm* (1983) 13 Fam Law 112.
[36] *Wright v Wright* [1970] 3 All ER 209.
[37] *Dean v Dean* [1978] 3 All ER 758.
[38] *Fry v Lane* (1888) 40 Ch D 312.
[39] *Backhouse v Backhouse* [1978] 1 WLR 243.
[40] *Carter v Carter* [1980] 1 All ER 827.
[41] *Cook v Cook* [1984] FLR 446.
[42] *Edgar v Edgar* [1980] 1 WLR 1410.
[43] *Chia Hock Hua v Ching Choo Je*, above n 33, [17].
[44] *TQ v TR and another appeal* [2009] 2 Singapore Law Reports (Reissue) 961.

in Singapore would have had to be fully complied with. The same would be true of a post-nuptial marital agreement.

There has, however, been a decision of the High Court in Singapore that is slightly more bold in this regard. In *Tan Siew Eng (alias Tan Siew Eng Irene) v Ng Meng Hin*[45] the spouses had made a post-nuptial marital agreement that was expressed as their full and final settlement of financial obligations. The husband claimed that they had mutually repudiated it, so that it ceased to be binding on them. The High Court agreed. On this finding there was no longer any agreement subsisting. Despite so finding, however, Woo Bih Li J decided that the substantive terms in the locally formed post-nuptial marital agreement provided for the 'just and equitable' division of their matrimonial assets. This being so, the judge was content to make his order of the division of the spouses' matrimonial assets following the substantive term in their agreement. The judge made clear, however, that if the substantive term were not 'just and equitable', he would have had no qualms ignoring this repudiated agreement altogether. Woo Bih Li J decided thus:

> In the circumstances, although I had concluded that the Settlement Agreement was no longer contractually binding on the parties, I was of the view that I could and should still take it into account. After all, the general guiding principle is a division that would be just and equitable in all the circumstances. Both parties had stressed that the Settlement Agreement had been reached after extensive negotiations. This was not a case where either party had claimed to be misled into entering into the Settlement Agreement, although the husband stressed that he had entered into it to escape from the mental distress caused by the wife and despite advice from his own solicitors. However, I was of the view that while the husband may have genuinely wanted to escape from the mental distress caused by the wife, he was and is a tough and shrewd businessman who would not have put himself in such a disadvantageous position of keeping only 5.6% of the matrimonial assets for himself and his other family in Indonesia. Furthermore, the advice of his solicitors then would have probably been on the assumption that he had disclosed all his assets.

> In the circumstances, I was of the view that the terms in the Settlement Agreement were just and equitable and I made an order following the terms of the Settlement Agreement, where they were still applicable, and taking into account any payment which the husband had already made thereunder before he terminated it.[46]

The Court of Appeal in *TQ v TR and another appeal*[47] did not disapprove of the decision reached by the High Court in *Tan Siew Eng (alias Tan Siew Eng Irene) v Ng Meng Hin*, but did observe that it will not be the norm. In *TQ v TR and another appeal*, Andrew Phang JA left room for a degree of variation from the norm thus:

> [H]aving regard to the fact that the court is not dealing with commercial contracts as such, we are of the view that the court does retain a residuary discretion, even in a situation where the prenuptial agreement concerned does not comply with one or more of the legal doctrines and requirements under the common law of contract, to give some weight to that agreement ... However, we envisage that the exercise of such residuary discretion will, by its very nature, occur only in very limited circumstances ... Looked at in this light ... the

---

[45] *Tan Siew Eng (alias Tan Siew Eng Irene) v Ng Meng Hin* [2003] 3 Singapore Law Reports (Reissue) 474.

[46] Ibid [42] and [43].

[47] *TQ v TR and another appeal*, above n 44.

decision in *Tan Siew Eng* can be viewed as a specific application of this residuary discretion in what was … a much less egregious situation.[48]

The norm, then, is that the agreement must comply fully in formation with the requirements of the law of contract and remain subsisting if any consideration is to be accorded to it. An agreement that fails any requirement of the law of contract will not receive consideration. The author suggests a new approach to this effect of the law of contract upon marital agreements, discussed below.[49]

In summary, as far as the requirements of formation of valid contract and its subsistence at the time the marital agreement comes before the court are concerned, there is no family law rule that tempers the law of contract. A court in Singapore is prepared to hear all arguments derived from the law of contract. Where the agreement has relevant foreign connections, it is Singapore's choice of law rules that determine which jurisdiction's law of contract applies. For wholly local agreements it is the law of contract in Singapore that governs. As a general requirement as well the agreement should be subsisting before the court in Singapore accords it any consideration, although there may be some room for residual discretion, as illustrated by the Court of Appeal in *TQ v TR and another appeal*'s qualified approval of the High Court decision in *Tan Siew Eng (alias Tan Siew Eng Irene) v Ng Meng Hin*.

B. No Presumption of Intention to Create Legal Relations

The old English decision of *Balfour v Balfour*[50] decided that, with 'domestic' agreements between spouses and family members, the common law does not presume that the parties intended, by the agreement, to create legal relations with one another. This continues to represent Singapore law. Singapore received the common law as its basic law in 1826 and, until a particular rule is abolished or substituted by statutory provision to the contrary, the rule remains in existence. The courts in Singapore have not decided that this absence of presumption of intention to create legal relations, such as exists with commercial agreements, is obsolete.

Having said that, however, it is not particularly difficult to find evidence from which the court may infer that the spouses or would-be spouses or family members intended to create legal relations. The intention may expressly be found from any of several facts. For example, that the spouses had specifically directed their minds to their entering such an agreement, that the spouses put their agreement into writing and thus formalised it, or that the spouses engaged a lawyer to help them reach agreement. Any one of these could form the basis for a finding by the court of the spouses' intention to create legal relations between themselves. Thus, although the intention will not be presumed, it can rather readily expressly be found where the tenor of the marital agreement is serious and the contents reasonably clear. While the issue of intention to create legal relations remains live, therefore, it is unlikely to give rise to too many problems. It is quite unlikely for a marital agreement to fail

---

[48] Ibid [100].
[49] See section IX.B. below.
[50] *Balfour v Balfour* [1919] 2 KB 571.

for lack of the necessary intent to create legal relations between the spouses. It may be noted that the absence of intention to create legal relations has not been raised in issue in any reported case in Singapore.

C. When Marital Agreement is Unlawful

By the law of contract the agreement must not fall foul of rules that render the agreement unlawful, illegal, or null and void. It is not necessary for present purposes to distinguish between these states as, ultimately, the effect of any such argument is that the agreement becomes unenforceable. An unenforceable agreement will generally not receive any consideration in court. What is critical is that an agreement made between spouses, simply as such, is not by any principle of the law in Singapore, unlawful.

The Court of Appeal in Singapore in *Kwong Sin Hwa v Lau Lee Yen*[51] decided on the general lawfulness of pre-nuptial marital agreements. The Court was faced with a pre-nuptial agreement by the parties not to consummate their marriage until they had performed the Chinese customary rites of marriage (including, perhaps, a tea ceremony to pay respects to the family elders, and the celebratory wedding dinner). The male party relied on the refusal of the female party to perform these rites as evidence of her wilful refusal to consummate their marriage. For the Court to take cognisance of the pre-nuptial agreement, it had to be lawful. The High Court decided it could not take cognisance, but in the Court of Appeal LP Thean J decided:

> It is clear to us that not every prenuptial agreement regulating or even restricting the marital relations of the husband and wife is void and against public policy. Needless to say, much depends on the relevant circumstances and in particular, the nature of the agreement, the intention of the parties and the objective the agreement was designed to achieve. In our opinion, the law does not forbid the parties to the marriage to regulate their married lives and also the incidents of the marriage, as long as such agreement does not seek to enable them to negate the marriage or resile from the marriage as the *Brodie* prenuptial agreement did.[52]

The Court of Appeal in *TQ v TR and another appeal* quoted this paragraph in full with complete agreement.[53] *Kwong Sin Hwa v Lau Lee Yen* establishes that 'an agreement made between spouses, or between intended spouses, is not "inherently wrong".'[54] It is not illegal or unlawful or against public policy and thus not necessarily void in itself. The only pre-nuptial agreement that the law in Singapore forbids, whether we regard this as due to the agreement being illegal, unlawful, against public policy or necessarily void, and thus not to be accorded any significance in court, is one that would 'negate the marriage or resile from the marriage'.[55]

The threshold test of 'negate the marriage or resile from the marriage' is intentionally set very high. It would be the rare exception rather than the rule for a marital

---

[51] *Kwong Sin Hwa v Lau Lee Yen* [1993] 1 Singapore Law Reports (Reissue) 90.
[52] Ibid [38].
[53] *TQ v TR and another appeal*, above n 44, [54].
[54] *Kwong Sin Hwa v Lau Lee Yen*, above n 51, [30].
[55] Ibid [38].

agreement to fall foul of this threshold. As an illustration of a marital agreement falling foul of this high threshold, to thus become an unlawful agreement, the Court of Appeal in *Kwong Sin Hwa v Lau Lee Yen* cited the old decision of the High Court in England in *Brodie v Brodie*[56] where the spouses entered an agreement before they married, which they affirmed after they married, that they would never commence marital cohabitation as man and wife, but rather continue to live separately as unmarried persons. It may be surmised that this kind of agreement is most exceptional. LP Thean J observed:

> The *Brodie* prenuptial agreement was intended to enable the husband to resile from the marriage and evade his marital obligations altogether. That agreement, if implemented and enforced, would make a mockery of the law regulating marriages.[57]

It is the extreme nature of the *Brodie* agreement that must be noted. In *Brodie v Brodie*, the man was pressured by the woman expecting his child to marry her. He agreed to do so, but only on condition that he would always live apart from her as if they were unmarried and she would never compel him to do otherwise. It appeared that the fact they went through the formality of marriage satisfied the woman's family members with whom she would continue to live with her child. After the marriage was solemnised, the wife petitioned for a decree of restitution of conjugal rights, which was an order, now defunct, whereby a spouse who has failed to carry out his or her obligations to live with the other can be ordered by court to do so. The husband cited the agreement. The High Court in England decided that the agreement was against public policy and no answer to the petition.

The *Brodie* agreement was one that would invite the comment that it made a mockery of the solemnisation of marriage, or that marriage between the parties was a complete farce. It is not expected that many such extreme agreements will be made. Having set this high a threshold before a pre-nuptial marital agreement is condemned, the Court of Appeal decision in *Kwong Sin Hwa v Lau Lee Yen* has settled the issue so that few marital agreements will be found unlawful in having totally negated the marital condition. Of marital agreements relating to property or maintenance that are the interest of this chapter, it is highly unlikely for any such agreement to be found to negate the marriage or to be an attempt by the parties to resile from their marital condition. Such agreement is most unlikely to make a mockery of the marriage law.

D. Disregard Clause that Attempts to Oust Jurisdiction of Court

It is clear that the spouses cannot, by private agreement between themselves, exclude the court's powers. The House of Lords in the old decision of *Hyman v Hyman*[58] had settled that no one, including spouses, may by private agreement oust the jurisdiction of the courts. In this case a husband agreed in a Deed of Separation to give his wife a fairly large capital sum as well as a weekly amount.

---

[56] *Brodie v Brodie* [1917] P 271; [1916–17] All ER 237.
[57] *Kwong Sin Hwa v Lau Lee Yen*, above n 51, [22].
[58] *Hyman v Hyman* [1929] AC 601.

In return he was to be left to continue in adultery and she was not to go to the courts, including to obtain an order of maintenance against him. He kept up his weekly payments to her. A couple of years later the law of divorce in England changed, so that the wife could apply for a judgment of divorce based simply on the husband having committed adultery. When the wife applied for divorce she would also become entitled to apply for an order of maintenance. The wife did apply and obtained a judgment of divorce. Then, despite agreeing never to do so, she applied for an order of maintenance. The House of Lords was unanimous in deciding that the clause in which she agreed never to apply to the courts for maintenance could not be upheld.

The High Court in Singapore in *Wong Kam Fong Anne v Ang Ann Liang*[59] has adopted this view. The marital agreement, clearly negotiated through solicitors, contained two clauses that Michael Hwang JC had to focus attention on, which read thus:

(12) Nothing herein contained shall be deemed to prevent either of the parties from maintaining a suit for dissolution of marriage against the other in any jurisdiction, or to bar the other from defending any such suit. In the event any such action is instituted, this deed shall be submitted to the court by either party and may be incorporated in the decree or judgment of the court; but notwithstanding such incorporation, this deed shall not be merged in such decree or judgment but shall in all respects survive such decree or judgment and be forever binding and conclusive upon the parties. Each and every paragraph and provision hereof shall survive any such decree or judgment notwithstanding that such judgment or decree may incorporate only a portion or part of this deed, and notwithstanding that the parties may subsequently in any such action enter into a stipulation embodying or incorporating only a part or portion of this deed.

(13) This deed shall not be invalidated or otherwise affected by a temporary reconciliation between the parties hereto or a resumption of marital relations between them unless said reconciliation or said resumption be accompanied by a written statement signed by the parties with respect to said reconciliation and resumption and, in addition, setting forth that they are cancelling this deed, and this deed shall not be invalidated or otherwise affected by any decree or judgment or separation, annulment, or divorce made by any court in any action which may hereafter be instituted by either party against the other for a separation, annulment or divorce.[60]

In determining whether either or both clauses bound the court's powers so that it could no longer resolve the application for a court order of division of matrimonial assets, the Judicial Commissioner had no difficulty deciding thus:

It was therefore clear that, notwithstanding the terms of clauses 12 and 13 of the deed of separation, I was able to exercise the powers of the court under s [112 of the Women's Charter to make an order for the division of matrimonial assets between them]. The question was whether I should do so in the circumstances of this case, since s [112] is not an imperative section.[61]

---

[59] *Wong Kam Fong Anne v Ang Ann Liang* [1992] 1 Singapore Law Reports (Reissue) 347.
[60] Ibid [20].
[61] Ibid [24].

The agreement between the spouses in *Chia Hock Hua v Ching Choo Je*[62] had also contained a clause that the capital sum paid by the husband to the wife was 'full settlement' of any claim by her for maintenance. The effect of this was not put in issue and the court did not comment on it. It is submitted that, if the court were to comment on it, it is likely that it would have held this clause to be invalid. It would not be upheld if it were in the nature of an attempt to oust the jurisdiction of the court. If necessary the court can strike out the offensive clause.

It is permissible under the law of contract for a court in Singapore, when faced with a marital agreement, to disregard any attempt to oust its power of control over the agreement and/or where necesssary to strike out any offending clause. This leaves the court with the substance of the agreement that the court may then take into consideration.

E. Form and Procedure

No particular form or procedure need be followed to create a valid marital agreement. Indeed, it would appear, as with any agreement that is valid and subsisting by the general law of contract in Singapore, a marital agreement may even be concluded orally. It is, however, far more likely that the agreement will at least be evidenced by some document or be fully written. The only problem with an oral agreement may be with the absence of presumption to intend to create legal relations in a 'domestic' agreement, although it is not impossible for a court, considering all the evidence before it, to find that by their oral agreement the spouses did intend to create legal relations between them. It follows that there is no consequence for failing to meet a particular form or procedure.

There is complete freedom of contract. Spouses are free to make any agreement between themselves as they wish. This is not to say that the marital agreement will be enforced. The marital agreement must be valid and, to be discussed below, will only form one factor in the consideration by the court as to the ultimate order it chooses to make.

As with any private agreement, the state is not involved in its formation. There is also no requirement that either spouse or both spouses should have received legal advice before entering the agreement. At the same time there is no disadvantage if legal advice has been sought. Indeed, if the parties had sought legal advice, this can only reflect well upon the parties, as it suggests that there is unlikely to have been undue pressure or duress imposed upon either. It may even be said to be increasingly common for spouses in Singapore, especially those contemplating divorce, to seek legal advice before forming some arrangements for their future financial obligations with each other.

F. Content and Enforceability: Critical Difference in Effect During Marriage and upon Divorce Compared with Effect upon Death

The law that regulates spouses' property during marriage and upon divorce (the subject of this volume) is not the same law that regulates them upon the natural

---

[62] *Chia Hock Hua v Ching Choo Je*, above n 33.

termination of their marriage by the death of one or both spouses. Upon death, it is the law of succession that regulates what is to happen to property the deceased left behind. The areas of family and contract law that are the subject of this volume only apply while the marriage subsists and both spouses are living.

The case that demonstrates the delineation of the family law (as it may be affected by contract law and the law of property) and the law of succession is the Court of Appeal in Singapore decision in *Sivakolunthu Kumarasamy v Shanmugam Nagaiah and another.*[63] An interim judgment of divorce was awarded to the wife, Sivakolunthu, in 1982. During the subsistence of their marriage the spouses had owned a property as joint tenants. Upon the grant of the interim judgment of divorce, Sivakolunthu applied for and obtained a court order that the property be sold and the proceeds divided equally. Before this order was executed, however, her husband committed suicide so their marriage became terminated by his death, rather than through the divorce that had yet to be made final. Upon his death his valid will came into operation and, through it, he had bequeathed all his property to a charity. His personal representatives sought execution of the court order of division of matrimonial assets so the charity would receive half of the proceeds of sale. Sivakolunthu found herself in the awkward position, having obtained the court order of an equal division of the matrimonial asset she sought, of now opposing it in this application. She claimed that the court order had no effect, or ceased to have effect on the death of her husband. In consequence she would become sole owner of the property she used to own jointly with her now deceased husband by operation of the rule of 'survivorship' within property law. Which consequence is the property subject to?

The Court of Appeal decided that: (1) the court order dividing the property was properly made on the grant of the interim judgment of divorce; (2) the court order had irrevocably severed their joint tenancy in the property; and (3) the husband's portion went to the charity by his valid will that came into effect upon his death. As the court order automatically severed the joint tenancy (by the operation of a rule of property law), the husband's half of the property fell into his estate upon his death. By the law of succession, which also came into play upon his death, the half of the property in his estate was bequeathed to the charity.

The author assumes that the reader is not much interested in the part of the decision regarding the law of succession in Singapore. Of greater interest, however, is the principle that the court order dividing the matrimonial asset had irrevocably severed the joint tenancy in it. It should be noted that, even if the spouses had contracted in a marital agreement for what they intended to happen to their property or money upon the death of one or both of them, this clause in their agreement is not likely to be accorded effect. Upon either spouse's death, it is the law of succession that regulates the proper distribution of property left in the deceased's estate. All non-Muslim Singaporeans have complete freedom of testation, but to make a valid bequest this must be achieved by provision in a valid will. There are formal requirements of the execution of a valid will. Any part of the estate that is not bequeathed by provision in a valid will is regulated by the law of intestate succession. No further

---

[63] *Sivakolunthu Kumarasamy v Shanmugam Nagaiah and another* [1987] Singapore Law Reports (Reissue) 702.

discussion is included here of the law in Singapore of testate or intestate succession. Suffice it to note that the laws of division of matrimonial assets and the maintenance of a former wife upon divorce operate only where the spouses remain living. Upon either spouse's death, it is the law of succession that determines what happens to property or money left behind by the deceased.

III. LATEST CONSOLIDATION: EVEN VALID MARITAL AGREEMENT SUBJECT TO COURT SCRUTINY

The Court of Appeal in Singapore recently affirmed and consolidated the principles relating to the enforceability of marital agreements, most of which had been decided in earlier cases. The case is briefly analysed before the specific questions under this part of the chapter are discussed *seriatim*.

A. *TQ v TR and another appeal*[64]

A Dutch man and Swedish woman met, and she moved to London where he worked. Upon their decision to get married they executed a pre-nuptial marital agreement on 26 August 1991, some 16 years before it came before the courts in Singapore. It was prepared by a Dutch civil law notary in the Netherlands and executed following the requirements of law in the Netherlands. The agreement was interpreted by the Court of Appeal to provide, inter alia, that there was to be no division of matrimonial assets. The couple married in the Netherlands on 13 September 1991, less than a month after execution of their pre-nuptial marital agreement. They lived in London from 1991 to 1997, during which time they had three children.

In late 1997 the family moved to Singapore when the husband obtained a job here. Unfortunately the marriage deteriorated. The wife left the matrimonial home and filed for divorce on 15 March 2004. Upon the award of the interim judgment of divorce the judge below was asked to decide the ancillary applications. In 2007 the High Court ordered:[65]

(a) Custody of the children (who were then about 12, 9 and 7 years old) to be jointly held, care and control to the wife with liberal access to the husband.
(b) Husband to pay S$1200 a month for maintenance of each child.
(c) Husband to pay a lump sum of S$150,000 for wife's maintenance.
(d) No order of division of matrimonial assets.

Both parties appealed. The Court of Appeal varied the orders to some extent while it approved of the lower court's decision not to make an order of division of

---

[64] *TQ v TR and another appeal*, above n 44; for a case comment see Leong Wai Kum, 'Prenuptial Agreement on Division of Matrimonial Assets Subject to Court Scrutiny' [2009] *Singapore Journal of Legal Studies* 211.

[65] See *TQ v TR* [2007] 3 Singapore Law Reports (Reissue) 719. Choo Han Teck J's decision has been fully commented upon by Debbie Ong Siew Ling in 'Prenuptial Agreements and Foreign Matrimonial Agreements: *TQ v TR*' (2007) 19 *Singapore Academy of Law Journal* 397–408.

matrimonial assets. The unanimous decision was delivered by Andrew Phang JA in the following terms:

(a) The husband was to make payment within a year of a lump sum of S$150,000 to the wife as her maintenance, with the reservation that she could apply for further maintenance subsequently if there had been any misrepresentation of the husband's assets or income or if a material change in their respective circumstances comes about.

(b) Custody of the children was to be jointly held but their care and control, although now awarded to the wife, could be subject to review. Care and control of the daughters was to remain with the wife but the husband could apply for care and control of the son to be reviewed after he had complied with a further order to set up a trust for the maintenance of the children.

(c) Husband to pay the wife S$1200 a month for maintenance of each child until the child reached the age of 18 years or was no longer under the wife's care and control, whichever is earlier.

(d) An account in a Singapore bank was to be opened in the name of the wife's solicitors. The husband was ordered to pay into this account the sum of S$380,000 within 21 days, and a penal notice to back up this order was attached. This sum was the equivalent of the monies in a trust fund in Mauritius, worth US$261,540, designated for the benefit of the children that the husband claimed he had set up after the interim judgment of divorce. The Court made this order so as not to intrude on the jurisdiction of the Mauritius courts but, at the same time, to recognize that the husband's act was a 'naked attempt to present the Wife and the courts [here] a *fait accompli* in respect of the issues of maintenance and the distribution of the matrimonial assets.'[66] Either husband or wife was at liberty to draw from this account to pay for all reasonable expenses necessary for the welfare and education of the children. Where any issue arose, an application for direction could be made to court.

The father was thus ordered to continue to support his children fully. He was to pay the mother S$1200 a month for the maintenance of each child until the child reached 18 years or the mother relinquished care and control. The father was to transfer the equivalent of the sum he claimed to have put into a trust in Mauritius (estimated as S$380,000) which sum was to go into a bank account here in Singapore set up in the name of the wife's solicitors. This money was available to both mother and father, but dedicated to the welfare and education of their three children.

It appeared the husband had earned a very high income of some S$44,416.67 a month when he first came to Singapore. He had left that employment and, at the time of the application for financial orders, ran a consultancy that was registered in Singapore and Indonesia with operating units in Singapore, Thailand and Hong Kong. What he earned was not revealed but the Court was convinced he could comfortably continue to fully maintain his children. The wife was now a single mother earning S$3,225 a month. The husband was ordered to give her a lump sum of S$150,000

---

[66] *TQ v TR and another appeal,* above n 44, [27].

before the year was up. This was to be the former spouses' final arrangement regarding their personal finances, unless after this was fully paid over the wife could show that the husband had misrepresented his assets or income, or if there was a material change in the circumstances of either party. It should be noted that the wife had applied to the High Court for this lump sum of S$150,000 for herself so the High Court had ordered as she sought and the Court of Appeal approved, adding only that, if there had been misrepresentation on the husband's part or a material change in their circumstances, she could come back to court for more.

The wife had also applied for an order of division of matrimonial assets but it should be noted that 'the Husband asserted that he had no assets, and the Wife was unable to adduce any substantive proof to the contrary.'[67] Taking a holistic view, it may well be that rough justice had been achieved between these former spouses. The now single and self-sufficient woman received S$150,000 from her former husband for her own use. If they were Singaporeans and the husband was not proven to own property at the time of divorce, although he appeared to have accumulated money from years of working during the course of marriage and could expect to continue to make good earnings after the divorce, this financial arrangement between them might be regarded as fair to both former spouses.[68]

It is helpful to summarise the holdings of this important Court of Appeal decision in being the latest consolidation of the law of marital agreements.

B. Summary of Holdings

i. Unitary

The Court of Appeal in *TQ v TR and another appeal* affirmed that the law in Singapore treats all marital agreements alike.[69] It does not matter when the agreement was made, that is, whether it is pre-nuptial or post-nuptial, and, if the latter, whether it was during the subsistence of a functioning marriage, upon the separation of the spouses, in contemplation of divorce or even during the course of divorce proceedings. It also does not matter when the agreement was meant to operate, that is, whether during the marriage or upon divorce. The law of marital agreements may be said to be unitary. The same legal view is taken of all marital agreements.

ii. No Agreement Inherently Unlawful

No marital agreement is inherently unlawful, void or against the public policy in Singapore that promotes the continuity of the spousal relationship where this is practicable.[70] An agreement is unlawful only where it negates the marital relationship or resiles from the marriage so as to make a mockery of the marriage law.

---

[67] Ibid [28].

[68] The author has suggested that the provision of post-divorce maintenance is on the basis of 'financial preservation of the former wife in so far as this is practicable and in all the circumstances fair and reasonable'; see Leong Wai Kum, *Elements of Family Law in Singapore*, above n 11, 839–52 and section I.C. above.

[69] See *TQ v TR and another appeal*, above n 44, [63], [70] and [73].

[70] Ibid [53]–[54].

iii. Subject to Law of Contract Regarding Formation of Valid Contract

A marital agreement must have been validly formed and remain subsisting if it is to receive consideration by the court, although there may be some room to consider the substance of an agreement even though it has been terminated by their mutual repudiation.[71]

iv. Subject to Scrutiny by Court

The core principle is that even a valid subsisting marital agreement remains subject to scrutiny by the court.[72] It may thus be said that, in the final analysis, it is the principles of family law that will decide the resolution of the spouses' dispute on how to divide matrimonial assets upon divorce or how to rearrange maintenance obligations although, it should be noted, family law in Singapore allows for the proper consideration by the court of the consensual provisions the spouses negotiated for in their marital agreement as one factor. The point to note is that the consensual provisions in the spouses' marital agreement never supplant the default law of division of matrimonial assets and maintenance. The court, upon any such application even if there were a valid and subsisting marital agreement, will continue to aim for a just and equitable division of their matrimonial assets to be supplemented, where necessary, by the provision of fair maintenance from the husband to his former wife.

v. How Well the Agreement Reflects Current Financial Situations of Spouses

While there is nothing that restricts the court's discretion in its due consideration of the consensual provisions in the spouses' marital agreement, it may be that the closer in time to the court's consideration of it the marital agreement had been made, the greater the degree of significance the court would accord them. An agreement made closer in time to the application either for an order for division of matrimonial assets or for an order to the husband to continue to maintain his former wife, is more reflective of the spouses' current financial situations. It is for this reason alone that the marital agreement is accorded greater consideration. The point is no more or less significant than this.[73]

The defining nature of the law in Singapore is that a marital agreement, even if valid and subsisting, does not supplant the default laws of division of matrimonial assets or maintenance of the former wife after divorce. The marital agreement forms only one more factor for the court's consideration. The court continues to be bound by the statutory direction to aim to reach a just and equitable division of their matrimonial assets and, where necessary, supplement this with an order to the husband to provide reasonable maintenance to his former wife. A marital agreement is subject to scrutiny by the court, so the dispute between the former spouses continues to be resolved by the default laws of division of matrimonial assets and maintenance.

---

[71] Ibid [31]–[37] and [94]–[97].
[72] Ibid [61], [63], [67], [70], [73]–[75] and [103]–[104].
[73] Ibid [92].

IV. COURT SCRUTINY OF MARITAL AGREEMENT
ON SPOUSES' PROPERTIES

A. Agreement is Factor for Consideration by Court

The law in Singapore, by way of the Women's Charter, section 112(1), empowers the court, upon awarding a judgment that terminates the marriage,[74] to 'order the division between the parties of any matrimonial asset ... in such proportions as the court thinks just and equitable'. Section 112(2) continues:

> It shall be the duty of the court in deciding whether to exercise its powers under subsection (1) and, if so, in what manner, to have regard to all the circumstances of the case, including the following matters:
>
> (a) the extent of the contributions made by each party in money, property or work towards acquiring, improving or maintaining the matrimonial assets;
>
> ...
>
> (d) the extent of the contributions made by each party to the welfare of the family, including looking after the home or caring for the family or any aged or infirm relative or dependent of either party;
> (e) any agreement between the parties with respect to the ownership and division of the matrimonial assets made in contemplation of divorce ... .

The Court of Appeal in *TQ v TR and another appeal* read the provision in the Women's Charter, section 112(2)(e) to apply equally to a pre-nuptial agreement. A valid pre-nuptial marital agreement relating to the division of matrimonial assets forms but one factor for consideration by the court in coming to its decision on what would be the just and equitable division of their matrimonial assets. Andrew Phang JA reiterated an important working principle thus:

> If, as we have concluded, s 112(2)(e) covers prenuptial agreements as well, then it is clear that the courts are to consider, as part of all the circumstances of the case, the prenuptial agreement in arriving at a just and equitable division of the matrimonial assets that are available for distribution between the parties. However, it is pertinent to note that it follows that the prenuptial agreement cannot be enforced, in and of itself. It bears repeating that its terms constitute one of the factors that the court should take into account in arriving at its decision as to the proportions in which the matrimonial assets concerned are to be distributed.[75]

The Judge of Appeal continued:

> [N]otwithstanding the fact that a prenuptial agreement cannot be enforced in and of itself, much will depend, in the final analysis, on the precise terms of that agreement as viewed

---

[74] Whether this is by judgment of divorce or nullity of marriage, or even by judgment of judicial separation that merely acknowledges the cessation of marital cohabitation. It remains true, in Singapore, that the vast majority of marriages terminate only on the death of a spouse. The crude divorce rate (the total number of divorces awarded, including to Muslim persons, per 1,000 resident population) has been a steady 2.0 from 2005 to 2009. The number of judgments of nullity or judicial separation is practically negligible. See *Statistics on Marriages and Divorces 2009*, accessible at www.mcys.gov.sg. As for the imminent change that will make the power available even where the marriage is terminated outside Singapore, see above section I.E. corresponding to nn 31 and 32.

[75] *TQ v TR and another appeal*, above n 44, [77].

in the context of all the relevant circumstances as a whole ... . To this end, it might well be the case that a prenuptial agreement is, given the circumstances as a whole, considered to be so crucial that it is, in effect, enforced in its entirety. However it is important to reiterate that everything will depend upon the precise circumstances before the court.[76]

The decision, then, is that the law in Singapore on the division of matrimonial assets will be applied to resolve the application for an order of division of matrimonial assets. That law allows the court to consider the proper weight to accord to a pre-nuptial marital agreement between the spouses. It is upon consideration of this, in view of the other relevant facts and circumstances, that the ultimate resolution of the application depends.

B. Pre-Nuptial Marital Agreement

As outlined above, in *TQ v TR and another appeal*[77] a Dutch man and his Swedish wife made an agreement in the Netherlands before they married that there would be no division of matrimonial assets between them upon their divorce. It should be noted that the Court of Appeal found that, although the wife made a claim before the courts in Singapore for a share of the matrimonial assets, she was unable to adduce proof that they had any. The decisions by both the High Court in Singapore and the Court of Appeal in Singapore that the husband should make full provision for the children and pay a lump sum as maintenance of his former wife, but that there should be no division of matrimonial assets, must be appreciated with this crucial lack of proof of available matrimonial assets in mind.

We do not yet have a case where a pre-nuptial marital agreement not to divide matrimonial assets exists, and the applicant can prove that there is property available against which an order of division of matrimonial assets can bite, to show us how such a case might be decided. It also bears noting that *TQ v TR and another appeal* involved a Dutch man and his Swedish wife, albeit both now living in Singapore, and their Dutch pre-nuptial marital agreement. We need to await a purely Singaporean case where the spouses are Singaporeans and the pre-nuptial marital agreement was formed in Singapore, to see how these principles apply in a completely local context.

C. Post-Nuptial Marital Agreement

There have been decisions from the courts in Singapore upon scrutinising marital agreements made in contemplation of divorce, which are specifically referred to in the Women's Charter, section 112(2)(e)' as providing a factor for consideration of what would be the just and equitable division of matrimonial assets.

---

[76] Ibid [80].
[77] Ibid; and see section III above.

The Court of Appeal in Singapore in *Wee Ah Lian v Teo Siak Weng*[78] dealt at some length with the process by which the sophisticated spouses, each legally represented, arrived at their comprehensive private settlement. The wife had commenced divorce proceedings and obtained an interim injunction to restrain the husband from disposing of some monies and a piece of property in Penang in the neighbouring country of Malaysia. The next step in their proceedings was an appeal by the husband from this interim injunction. The wife's solicitors telexed the husband, through his solicitors, offering terms of a comprehensive settlement of their financial affairs. This was not accepted by due date, but subsequently the husband's solicitors telexed the wife's solicitors offering settlement on most of the items she had earlier proposed. This was accepted by the wife. In the view of the Court of Appeal:

> We therefore conclude that the husband's offer, by repeating the terms of the settlement contained in the wife's solicitors' telex of 11 July 1986 except for items 1, 10 and 11 made by his solicitors on 31 July 1986 and accepted by the wife's solicitors on her behalf on 1 August 1986, constituted a firm settlement notwithstanding the reservation.[79]

At the hearing of the ancillary matters the husband argued that there was no concluded settlement and made a proposal for the division of what he conceded were their matrimonial assets. The court below agreed with him and made an order that differed from the substantive terms of their agreement. The wife appealed. She argued that there was a concluded settlement and that the matrimonial assets should be divided according to it. The wife succeeded before the Court of Appeal. Karthigesu J said:

> We must still decide whether in the exercise of our discretion under s [112] of the Women's Charter we ought to uphold the settlement ...

> In our view, it is incumbent on the court to see that these provisions of the section are not violated when ordering a division of matrimonial assets following the granting of a decree of divorce, and the same would apply where the court's intervention is sought notwithstanding that the parties may have reached an agreement before seeking the court's intervention ...

> [Upon finding that the marital agreement was consistent with the provisions of law] [a]ccordingly we uphold the settlement and give effect to item 13 thereof.[80]

Here then was the response of the Court of Appeal in Singapore faced with a comprehensive settlement meticulously formed with legal representation of each spouse at a time when the spouses were not only contemplating divorce but already in the midst of it. In this relatively early decision of 1992 the Court was content to give effect to the settlement.

The High Court in Singapore in *Wong Kam Fong Anne v Ang Ann Liang*, earlier referred to,[81] was faced with 'a comprehensive financial and property settlement ... made at a time when the parties had already been separated and divorce was viewed as a real possibility.' Despite this, however, the husband applied for an order for a

---

[78] *Wee Ah Lian v Teo Siak Weng* [1992] 1 Singapore Law Reports (Reissue) 347.
[79] Ibid [30].
[80] Ibid [39], [40] and [45].
[81] *Wong Kam Fong Anne v Ang Ann Liang*, above n 59, [36].

share of the matrimonial home that, in his agreement with his wife, he had declared was owned solely by her. Michael Hwang JC decided:

> Put in a nutshell, the position was that, eight years ago, the parties agreed on a division of assets and to go their own financial ways. The court was now being asked to reopen the issue on the ground that one of the parties had not honoured the terms of the settlement. There was some evidence that the wife had not adhered strictly to the terms of the deed. If that were true, the remedy should have been for the parties affected by the breach (whether the husband or the children) to take appropriate legal action in respect of their rights under the deed, and not for the husband to disclaim the settlement so many years after it had been entered into and acted upon. Whatever the husband's complaints in the past, he did not appear to have taken the position that the terms of the deed were no longer applicable until these proceedings began, and I felt that this was far too late. Accordingly, I declined to exercise my powers under s [112 of the Women's Charter] in respect of the matrimonial home.[82]

In this relatively early decision of 1992, the Court declined to exercise its power under the equivalent of the current section 112(1) on considering the spouses' comprehensive settlement of the division of their matrimonial assets.

By 2003, however, the High Court would no longer speak of whether to directly enforce the spouses' marital agreement, whether comprehensive or not. Instead, the Court would only consider what effect to accord the spouses' marital agreement when exercising its power under the Women's Charter, section 112(1) to order the division of the spouses' matrimonial assets. In *Tan Siew Eng (alias Tan Siew Eng Irene) v Ng Meng Hin*[83] the spouses had made an agreement after the wife had filed her answer to the divorce petition[84] filed by the husband. The agreement was expressed as their full and final settlement of financial obligations. The husband claimed that they had mutually repudiated it so that it ceased to be binding on them, and the High Court agreed with him. The agreement had technically ceased to exist. Woo Bih Li J, however, upon finding 'the terms in the Settlement Agreement were just and equitable' 'made an order [of division of matrimonial assets] following the terms of the Settlement Agreement'.[85] In other words, the judge's own assessment of what would be the just and equitable division of the spouses' matrimonial assets was fairly close to the provisions the spouses had negotiated in their marital agreement. Therefore, despite the marital agreement having been repudiated, the judge adopted its provisions as the order he made under the Women's Charter, section 112(1).

After the Court of Appeal decision in *TQ v TR and another appeal*, the High Court had opportunity to apply the principles to *AFS v AFU*[86] that also concerned spouses who were both foreigners.

A Canadian husband and Hungarian wife, both permanent residents of Singapore, married in 1993 in Hungary and had two sons. While working in Singapore, the husband at some point left the family to live with another woman. The estranged

---

[82] Ibid [41] and [42].
[83] *Tan Siew Eng (alias Tan Siew Eng Irene) v Ng Meng Hin*, above n 45.
[84] Since 2005 the court papers are known by the more common names of 'Defence' and 'Writ of summons', respectively.
[85] *Tan Siew Eng (alias Tan Siew Eng Irene) v Ng Meng Hin*, above n 45, [43].
[86] [2011] 3 SLR 275.

spouses entered a Deed of Separation in 2003. The marriage was terminated by a divorce judgment in 2006. The case centered around clause 11 of the Deed that read 'Both parties agree that the asset(s) acquired by either party from the date of this Deed will remain as asset(s) of the acquiring party.' A year or so after the Deed was signed, the husband came into a large quantity of shares (about S\$12 million worth) and S\$985,000 both as remuneration rewards. He, of course, sought refuge behind clause 11 while the wife argued that it should not bind them so that the remuneration rewards, as matrimonial assets within the understanding of the Women's Charter section 112(10), became available for division in 'just and equitable' proportions between them.

Andrew Ang J was faced with a good opportunity to apply the decision of the Court of Appeal in *TQ v TR and another appeal*. The judge held:

> While the court is to have regard to the executed Deed (amongst other circumstances) under s 112(2)(e) of the Act in deciding whether to exercise its powers under s 112(1) and if so how; it should be noted that the courts '[would] be especially vigilant and [would] be slow to enforce agreements that [were] apparently not in the best interests of the child or the children concerned' (see *TQ v TR*). Additionally, the decision in *TQ v TR* held that an agreement between parties 'cannot be enforced *in and of itself*' [emphasis in original]. The terms of an agreement would only constitute one of the factors that the court should take into account in arriving at its decision as to the proportions in which the matrimonial assets concerned are to be distributed. Even if *prima facie* the court would not lightly set aside an agreement between parties, the court has liberty to decide that an agreement ought not to apply if the court does not consider it just and equitable.[87]

Applying these considerations to the Deed of Separation before him, the Judge had little difficulty finding that the husband had not fulfilled the duty of full disclosure required by its Recitals 1.5 and 1.6 and to have repeatedly failed to make frank and full disclosure to court.[88] The husband's claims of not knowing that he would, so soon after the execution of the Deed, come into such huge remuneration rewards were readily dismissed as unlikely.[89]

In the result, the judge decided thus:

> I therefore drew an adverse inference that the husband's reluctance to disclose those assets, as well as his failure to disclose the relevant documents, more likely than not meant that if revealed the documents would have shown that at the time of execution of the Deed he knew or ought to have known that he would receive some form of benefit from the buy-out. ... The husband thus contravened Recital 1.5 of the Deed ... . It would therefore be unjust and inequitable to hold the wife to ... cl 11 of the Deed, when she had been unaware of the stock option or other benefit that the husband knew he would or was likely to receive. ...

> Under the Deed, the husband agreed to the wife having a 50% share of the matrimonial assets. I could have taken that division as being what both parties considered just and equitable, applied that percentage in dividing [the S\$12 million worth of shares] and the S\$985,000. However, I had regard to the fact that the marriage had lasted only ten years up to the time of execution of the Deed (13 years as at the date of the decree *nisi)*. Moreover I

---

[87] Ibid [18].
[88] Ibid [21] and [40].
[89] Ibid [30].

doubted that the husband would have been ready to share equally if he had fully disclosed what he would or was likely to obtain in the near future. I therefore awarded the wife a 25% share of [the S$12 million worth of shares] and the S$985,000, leaving undisturbed the earlier agreed division of the other matrimonial assets.[90]

This appears to be an excellent application of the law and a most judicious exercise of the judge's discretion.

Even where the terms of a marital agreement have been recorded in a consent order, the courts in Singapore have shown their readiness, where this is appropriate, subsequently to vary the terms of the court order on division of matrimonial assets. In the Family Court in Singapore in *CT v CU*[91] Lim Hui Min DJ observed:

The court will not, of course, lightly re-open orders made in the ancillary matters, particularly those made by consent, but it has the power to do so, in the appropriate circumstances. In *Chia Chew Gek v. Tan Boon Hiang*,[92] for example, the Court of Appeal varied a consent order for the division of assets on the grounds that it was no longer workable. In my view, the parties would be able to apply to the court for a variation of a court order under Section 112(4) [of the Women's Charter] at least in those situations where the order of court is unworkable, and/or did not provide for a particular situation or contingency, which has now arisen. There must surely be a way for the court to plug any gap or lacuna in the ancillary matters order.[93]

In the result the District Judge's decision was:

The husband has asserted that if the respective parties' CPF accounts were refunded first from the sale proceeds of the matrimonial flat, and then used to pay off the outstanding housing loan, he personally would not have the resources to pay off that portion of the outstanding housing loan which could not be covered by the sale proceeds. The wife has not produced any evidence to contradict the husband's claim. ...

It is not unreasonable not to want to be a bankrupt, especially if you are a working adult in a white-collar job. In my view, it would not be just and equitable to make an order of court the effect of which would be to doom one or both parties to bankruptcy. It is not reasonable for the wife to demand that the husband take a path which would inevitably lead him to bankruptcy proceedings when there is a way for them to clear a large proportion of that debt. It is their joint debt, after all, and ought, in good conscience, to be paid. If both parties had made their downpayments and paid their housing instalments entirely in cash, there would be no question of them being able to get any of this cash back, given the current low sale price of the matrimonial flat.[94]

Thus while a consent order is not as readily subject to variation as an ordinary court order, there are circumstances where the court will continue to exercise its powers of scrutiny over the court order and, by implication, scrutiny over the marital agreement that formed the basis of the consent order. The court's powers under the default law are not circumscribed.

---

[90] Ibid [44]–[45] and [53]–[54].
[91] *CT v CU* [2004] SGDC 164.
[92] *Chia Chew Gek v Tan Boon Hiang and another appeal* [1997] 1 Singapore Law Reports (Reissue) 383. (Footnote numbering differs from original.)
[93] *CT v CU*, above n 91, [12].
[94] Ibid [18] and [21].

The courts in Singapore have, thus, not drawn any distinction between a marital agreement made before marriage, during marriage, in contemplation of divorce or during the course of divorce proceedings. The courts treat them all like. Importantly, the courts purposefully exercise their power of control over the agreements in closely scrutinising all of them.

The courts' power is wide and there appear to be no established limits to it. The courts have not laid down specific factors regarding how they will judge the agreement, beyond the requirement in the Women's Charter, section 112(1) that the ultimate objective is to make an order of division of matrimonial assets that is just and equitable in view of all the facts and circumstances of the case.

V. COURT SCRUTINY OF MARITAL AGREEMENT ON SPOUSES' MAINTENANCE

A. Agreement is Factor for Consideration by Court

Upon the award of a judgment of divorce, the courts in Singapore 'may order a man to pay maintenance to his wife or former wife'.[95] 'In determining the amount of any maintenance to be paid ... the court shall have regard to all the circumstances of the case'.[96] With regard to the broad discretion of the court, at least, the power to order maintenance is similar to the power to order the division of matrimonial assets, discussed above. It would follow that a marital agreement relating to maintenance of the former wife is a fact or circumstance the court should take into account in arriving at its order of maintenance, just as with the order of division of matrimonial assets discussed above.

B. Additional Statutory Regulation

There is, however, additional statutory regulation of marital agreements on maintenance. The Women's Charter, section 116 provides:

> An agreement for the payment, in money or other property, of a capital sum in settlement of all future claims to maintenance, shall not be effective until it has been approved, or approved subject to conditions, by the court, but when so approved shall be a good defence to any claim for maintenance.

Section 119 continues:

> Subject to section 116, the court may at any time and from time to time vary the terms of any agreement as to maintenance made between husband and wife, whether made before or after 1st June 1981, where it is satisfied that there has been any material change in the circumstances and notwithstanding any provision to the contrary in any such agreement.

---

[95] The Women's Charter, above n 1, s 113.
[96] Ibid s 114.

Sections 116 and 119 were first enacted in the Women's Charter (Amendment) Act 1980.[97] It is not clear which jurisdiction's statutory provisions they were modelled upon.[98] While there are also statutory provisions that empower an English court to vary terms relating to the provision of maintenance within marital agreements,[99] these English provisions are more clearly drafted to include only post-nuptial agreements.[100] Sections 116 and 119 refer, without providing a definition, to 'an agreement' and 'any agreement' respectively, albeit the latter continues: 'made between husband and wife'. They have not been discussed in depth by any court.

C. Pre-Nuptial Marital Agreement

In the Court of Appeal in Singapore in *TQ v TR and another appeal*[101] Andrew Phang JA was content to read both provisions as referring to 'postnuptial agreements' relating to the provision of maintenance, generally, and to allow the courts to scrutinise all such agreements:

> It is clear [from these provisions] that all postnuptial agreements with respect to maintenance are subject to the scrutiny of the court and may, in fact, even be varied if there has been any material change in circumstances. In other words, the courts have the statutory power to override any postnuptial agreement entered into between the spouses with regard to maintenance.[102]

The Judge of Appeal had little difficulty extending this statutory control to prenuptial marital agreements relating to maintenance: 'It is clear, in our view, that there is no reason in logic or principle why the aforementioned legislative policy which governs postnuptial agreements ought not to apply equally to prenuptial agreements.'[103] The Judge of Appeal noted the House of Lords decision in *Hyman v Hyman*,[104] discussed above, that a wife cannot decide by agreement never to make an application for maintenance as this amounts to an attempt to oust the jurisdiction of the court. The Judge of Appeal also noted that the principle has

---

[97] Women's Charter (Amendment) Act 1980, Act No 26 of 1980. The provisions were retained in the current Women's Charter as c 353, above n 1, first in the Reprint of the Women's Charter c 47, 1981, then c 353, 1985 Rev Edn, the 1996 Rev Edn and then in its current edition.

[98] Reading the debates in Parliament during the three readings of the Bill that lead to the Women's Charter (Amendment) Act of 1980, ibid, and the *Report of the Select Committee on the Women's Charter (Amendment) Bill* [Bill No. 23/79] (Government of Singapore National Printers, 1980) does not reveal the source of inspiration.

[99] See the (English) Matrimonial Causes Act 1973 that has contained, ever since the enactment of the (English) Matrimonial Proceedings and Property Act 1970, the current ss 34 on 'Validity of maintenance agreements', 35 on 'Alteration of agreements by court during lives of parties' and 36 'Alteration of agreements by court after death of one party'.

[100] See the (English) Matrimonial Causes Act 1973, s 34 which defines 'maintenance agreement' for the purpose of this provision and s 35 as 'any agreement in writing made, whether before or after the commencement of this Act, between the parties to a marriage, being—(a) an agreement containing financial arrangements, whether made during the continuance or after the dissolution or annulment of the marriage; or (b) a separation agreement which contains no financial arrangements in a case where no other agreement in writing between the same parties contains such arrangements'.

[101] *TQ v TR and another appeal,* above n 44.

[102] Ibid [57].

[103] Ibid [63].

[104] *Hyman v Hyman,* above n 58.

been accepted locally by the High Court in *Wong Kam Fong v Ang Ann Liang*[105] as well as *Chia Hock Hua v Chong Choo Je*,[106] both also discussed above. Once the Court of Appeal in Singapore in *Kwong Sin Hwa v Lee Lau Yen*[107] decided that there was nothing inherently wrong with spouses, including soon-to-be spouses, making agreements between themselves, unless the agreement attempts to completely undermine their marital relationship to an extreme degree, it follows that the statutory provisions relating to agreements between spouses would apply equally to agreements made during the marriage or in contemplation of divorce, as well as to pre-nuptial agreements.

Before a marital agreement becomes a factor for consideration by the court hearing an application for an order of maintenance for the former wife, the agreement, where it attempts to be the spouses' final settlement, should be approved by court and its terms may be varied. At the end of the day, however, it is within the power of the court to scrutinise and take only as much as it sees fit from the marital agreement relating to maintenance that is the common tenet and, thereby, the most significant principle in the law in Singapore regulating marital agreements.

D. Post-Nuptial Marital Agreement

The High Court in Singapore in *Chia Hock Hua v Ching Choo Je*[108] was faced with a post-nuptial marital agreement relating to maintenance. On finding the agreement made fair provision for maintenance for the now divorced wife, who was 'an intelligent and highly educated person' holding a good job in Australia and who 'could look after herself', Amarjeet Singh JC decided:

> I was satisfied on the evidence that the wife entered the agreement or arrangement voluntarily and there was nothing that reasonably suggested on the facts that the husband had acted in a manner that suggested undue pressure was used on her to reach such an agreement or arrangement. I was further satisfied on the evidence before me and the inference therefrom that the wife's version of events is all an afterthought. The burden of proof being on her, the wife in my opinion had not shown on any of the grounds or considerations I addressed myself to by reference to the many cases I discussed or on any other substantial ground that the husband had acted unjustly or unjustifiably or that the capital sum in settlement was unreasonable having regard to the husband's income then and the wife's earning capacity or now. I therefore give effect to the agreement and approve the same and dismiss the wife's claim for maintenance.[109]

In this relatively early decision of 1994, the High Court was content to decline to exercise its power to make a maintenance order, in view of the spouses' consensual provisions in their marital agreement.

---

[105] *Wong Kam Fong v Ang Ann Liang*, above n 59.
[106] *Chia Hock Hua v Chong Choo Je*, above n 33.
[107] *Kwong Sin Hwa v Lee Lau Yen*, above n 51.
[108] *Chia Hock Hua v Ching Choo Je*, above n 33.
[109] Ibid [22] and [23].

VI. COURT SCRUTINY OF MARITAL AGREEMENT RELATING TO CHILD OF MARRIAGE

For completeness of the discussion, although this is not the main interest of this chapter, it should further be noted that the Court of Appeal in *TQ v TR and another appeal* also discussed the law in Singapore on a marital agreement that contains provisions relating to a child or children of the marriage. It would not be surprising, given the discussion above, that Andrew Phang JA had no difficulty deciding that the court will scrutinise the provisions and uphold them only where they are consistent with the general law in Singapore regarding the responsibility parents and other adults owe a child where all legal issues are resolved by the first and paramount concern for what serves the welfare of the child.[110] The Judge of Appeal decided:

> There ought, in our view, to be a presumption that such agreements are unenforceable unless it is clearly demonstrated by the party relying on the agreement that that agreement is in the best interests of the child or children concerned. This is because such agreements focus on the will of the parents rather than on the welfare of the child which has (and always will be) the paramount consideration of the court in relation to such issues [see the Women's Charter, s 125(2)].[111]

By 2009, the Court of Appeal would no longer speak of directly enforcing any provision in a marital agreement. Instead, a court should only give consideration to relevant provisions in any marital agreement when exercising its powers to order the just and equitable division of the spouses' matrimonial assets or reasonable maintenance or make on order relating to a child.

VII. SEPARATION AGREEMENT

As has been pointed out above, the law in Singapore does not treat agreements upon the separation of the spouses differently from those made during the subsistence of marriage, before the solemnisation of marriage, when the spouses contemplate divorce or during the course of court proceedings for divorce. Such agreements are lawful (as they are most unlikely to be found to negate or resile from the marriage), and, if valid and subsisting, clauses relating to property ownership and use or the provision of maintenance for the wife will be considered as one factor in the court's assessment of what is a 'just and equitable' order of division of matrimonial assets or the provision of reasonable maintenance for the former wife. As was also noted above, since separation agreements will generally be made not too long before the court hears the application for an order either for division of matrimonial assets or for maintenance, it may be thought that the agreement merits closer consideration, as it was negotiated within the context of the spouses' current financial situations. The point cannot be put any higher than this.

---

[110] See, eg, Leong Wai Kum, *Elements of Family Law in Singapore*, above n 11, 246–59.

[111] *TQ v TR and another appeal*, above n 44, [70]. Of the law in Singapore relating to children and the centrality of the consideration of the best interests of the child concerned, see the author's *Elements of Family Law in Singapore*, above n 11, 246–59.

VIII. CONFLICT OF LAWS

Where a marital agreement has relevant foreign connections the courts in Singapore, by the rules of conflict of laws in Singapore, should take into consideration these connections. The main choice of law rule in this context is that the proper law of the foreign contract regulates its formation and how its content should be understood.

A. Proper Law of Contract: Validity and Interpretation of Agreement

The Court of Appeal in Singapore in *TQ v TR and another appeal*[112] was faced with a foreign marital agreement. The pre-nuptial agreement was executed in the Netherlands between a Dutch man and his Swedish fiancée who intended to set up matrimonial home after marriage in England. There was not one iota of connection with Singapore at its formation. Sixteen years later, though, the agreement was raised in argument before a court in Singapore. The wife applied for an order of division of matrimonial assets. The husband denied he had any but, in any case, also put the agreement before the court. These connections with foreign legal systems raised consideration of conflict of laws and how to choose the law to apply to the agreement.

It suffices to note that the Court of Appeal found Dutch law to be the proper law of the contract and that, by the substantive requirements of Dutch law, this agreement was validly formed and remained subsisting at the time it came before the courts in Singapore. Andrew Phang JA decided: '[t]he validity, interpretation and effect of the Agreement are thus governed by that law.'[113] In so deciding, the Judge of Appeal followed the established view of conflict of laws' jurists of the reach of the proper law of an agreement.[114]

The proper determination of how this pre-nuptial agreement might be interpreted under Dutch law was, however, rather hampered by the lack of evidence of Dutch law. The original agreement was clearly written in Dutch. The Court of Appeal, in noting its principal terms, stated that the agreement was 'translated from the Dutch'[115] and made reference to a letter from a notary public that had been tendered in evidence by the husband where the official 'stated that he had explained the Agreement to the parties in English, and had ensured that the parties understood its contents and implications'[116] before they executed it. The Court of Appeal was content to observe:

> Dutch rules of construction were not placed in evidence before us, so we presume that those rules are similar to our own. The general effect of the Agreement was that the Dutch matrimonial property regime applied to the parties' proprietary relations with

---

[112] *TQ v TR and another appeal*, above n 44.

[113] Ibid [41].

[114] See Debbie Ong Siew Ling, 'Prenuptial Agreements and Foreign Matrimonial Agreements: *TQ v TR*', above n 65, 400, where she suggests: 'The proper law governs the contract's validity, interpretation, effect and discharge', citing as support Collins, Briggs, Hill, McClean, Morse (eds), *Dicey & Morris: The Conflict of Laws*, 13th edn (London, Sweet & Maxwell, 2000) para 32–007.

[115] *TQ v TR and another appeal*, above n 44, [29].

[116] Ibid [36].

each other in accordance with the provisions in the 'Final declarations', except in so far as the community of property doctrine did not apply, as stipulated by Art 1 of the Agreement.[117]

B. *Lex Fori* to Resolve Application

Even with the presence of a foreign marital agreement on the spouses' property ownership and use, however, the Court of Appeal in Singapore in *TQ v TR and another appeal*[118] decided that the conduct of the ancillary application for an order of division of matrimonial assets is strictly according to the *lex fori*. Parties cannot, by private contract, require the courts to apply any law other than the *lex fori*, although there was no suggestion the spouses attempted to do this. While Singapore's conflict of laws may refer some of the contractual issues to the proper law of the agreement, our same conflict of laws gives the forum far tighter control over the resolution of an ancillary application between spouses upon termination of their marriage. In this regard the Court of Appeal in Singapore cited the decision of the English High Court in *NG v KR (Pre-nuptial contract)* that decided to similar effect in England.[119]

IX. FURTHER THOUGHTS

The current state of the law in Singapore may be summarised as follows: (1) marital agreements are not inherently unlawful at whatever point in time in relation to the solemnisation of marriage or its termination by divorce the agreement was formed; (2) all valid subsisting agreements will receive consideration by the court; but (3) the court controls the resolution of the application before it and accords the marital agreement as much significance as it sees fit to do in view of the developed law on division of matrimonial assets or the provision of maintenance after divorce.

A. Would Less Discretionary Treatment of Marital Agreements be More Robust Law?

It may be suggested that the law in Singapore regulating marital agreements, as discussed above, is less than robust in leaving the courts with control over the fate of a marital agreement, since the marital agreement forms only one factor for consideration towards the order that the court decides to make. Such criticism follows from another that regards a more certain rule to lead to a more predictable outcome, and thus necessarily as more robust law.

---

[117] Ibid [41]. This part of the decision may be less robust than the rest: see Leong Wai Kum, 'Prenuptial Agreement on Division of Matrimonial Assets Subject to Court Scrutiny', above n 64, 213–14.

[118] *TQ v TR and another appeal*, above n 44.

[119] *NG v KR (Pre-nuptial contract)* [2008] EWHC 1532 (Fam) [87]; [2009] 1 FCR 35.

The author disagrees that a less discretionary legal treatment will lead to more predictable outcomes. Indeed she questions the value of efforts to try to arrive at rules that appear to be 'certain'. The reality is that, however certain a rule appears to be, a spouse who wishes and can afford to can always create a dispute. A rule that appears more certain, for example that each spouse has a right to half of the net value of available matrimonial assets at the time of divorce, simply shifts the dispute. The dispute then centres upon whether this rule applies to the parties, whether a piece of property is matrimonial asset, or what its value or net value is. Similarly, a rule that a marital agreement conforming to certain legal requirements supplants the default law will also only shift the dispute to whether those legal requirements are really satisfied.[120] There is no rule that can truly be completely certain in not permitting dispute between the parties. It may almost be a waste of time to try to devise such a fixed rule.

It is more rational, within the reality that no rule can stop all disputes between the former marital partners, to direct the dispute to discovering what is fair in their current financial circumstances. This dispute is, at least, more meaningful than an equally involved dispute over whether a fixed rule applies to the parties or whether the legal requirements sought before the marital agreement supplants the default law have been satisfied. If the court's effort is to be expended anyway it is more usefully expended on assessing the current financial circumstances of the former marital partners and what would be the fair orders of division of matrimonial assets or maintenance between them at this time.

A discretionary rule that leaves the fate of a marital agreement to the court's assessment of what fairness demands at the time of divorce may further be thought to better encourage the spouses to aim for a marital agreement that will remain satisfactory to both of them at the time of divorce. An agreement to divide equally between the spouses any property acquired during marriage by either spouse's personal efforts that remains available at divorce may always be regarded as fair. Such agreement conveys 'a mutual respect for spousal contributions, whether in the economic or homemaking spheres'[121] and this must be fair since 'both [types of contributions] are equally fundamental to the well-being of the marital partnership'.[122] If a more specific agreement on which properties would go to which spouse were preferred, a fair agreement would allow for renegotiation between the spouses where circumstances have changed beyond what could be foreseen at the time the marital agreement was executed. Where provisions within the marital agreement remain satisfactory they will likely be performed voluntarily. It is inconceivable that either spouse will choose to engage in arguing over the agreement were it still largely fair under current circumstances. A rule is surely welcome if it encourages the spouses to try to make an agreement that remains satisfactory to both parties years down the road. Devising a law that encourages this may be the best assurance of amicable resolution between the former marital partners.

---

[120] See also Leong Wai Kum, 'The Law in Singapore on Rights and Responsibilities in Marital Agreements' [2010] *Singapore Journal of Legal Studies* 107, 124–27 and also in [2010] *The Sydney Law Review* 289, 306–09, where she briefly compares the law in Singapore with that in Australia.

[121] *NK v NL*, above n 10 (Andrew Phang JA).

[122] Ibid.

B. Academic Suggestion to Lessen Effect of Law of Contract on Marital Agreements

This is not to say that the legal regulation in Singapore of marital agreements cannot be improved. The author has suggested a new approach to marital agreements, basically to lessen the effect of the law of contract on marital agreements in recognition of the unique character of the legal relationship of the spouses that underpins the marital agreement.[123]

Two suggestions flow from this. The first is that not every option that the law of contract offers to a party to the contract should remain available to spouses of their marital agreement. It may be that no marital agreement should ever directly be enforced by court. Respect for the spouses' autonomy only requires that they be enabled to make agreements that satisfy both parties so that each spouse chooses to fulfil his or her obligation in the agreement. Where either party becomes dissatisfied with the agreement, it no longer serves the purpose of harmoniously regulating their relationship. A court should not proceed to consider whether to enforce its terms. The spouses should instead turn to the default law and apply for a court order.[124] In making an order, whether for division of matrimonial assets or for maintenance, the court may give consideration to the agreement the spouses made, but is not bound to enforce any of its terms.

The second suggestion would be that not every issue that the law of contract recognises to affect the validity of a contract should apply, or apply with the same force, to a marital agreement. The court considering the effect of a marital agreement may be spared the considerable effort of addressing all of the contractual issues either party chooses to raise. It is suggested that a court could be spared this effort since, whether or not the court finds in favour of the contractual issue raised, it may still take the substance of the marital agreement into consideration when making its financial order. The approach may be thought to be the most efficient compromise, respecting the spouses' autonomy to make agreements, to the extent this is exercised to craft a marital agreement that remains satisfactory to both spouses, and upholding principles of family law regarding what are fair financial orders between them should their marital agreement fail to satisfy either spouse.

As long as some aspects of the legal regulation of marital agreements remain in transition,[125] the best approach may well be to allow family law to play a guiding role. While spouses remain empowered to make agreements between themselves, these agreements must work without either party having to seek court enforcement. Where this becomes necessary, the court should be able to sidestep contractual enforcement in preference of the family law resolution of the dispute.

---

[123] See Leong Wai Kum, *Principles of Family Law in Singapore* (Singapore, Butterworths' Asia, 1997) 755–56.

[124] ie under the Women's Charter, above n 1, s 112(1) and see above section I.A., of division of matrimonial assets, and s 113, of post-divorce maintenance.

[125] For a general discussion of the issues, see Debbie Ong, 'When spouses agree' (2006) 18 *Singapore Academy of Law Journal* 96.

The Court of Appeal in *TQ v TR and another appeal*[126] acknowledged the suggestion but rejected it thus:

> The approach proffered by Prof Leong ... has much force. We are nevertheless of the view that the court ought still to have regard to the general principles of the common law of contract, if for no other reason than to place some legal parameters on what would otherwise be a wholly substantive exercise of discretion on the part of the court. Indeed, even if Prof Leong's approach is adopted, the court would still need to consider the various arguments centring on the validity of the prenuptial agreement in any event simply because, in many situations at least, these arguments would probably have an impact on the court's decision on the substantive issue before it. If, for example, a prenuptial agreement has been entered into as a result of fraud, duress, undue influence or unconscionability, its term(s) (based on the approach just mentioned) would be clearly unfair and probably be ignored by the court accordingly. However, this result would, in substance, be the same as the court finding that the prenuptial agreement is void or voidable and hence of no legal effect. There is also the need (fulfilled by the more traditional approach set out above ...) to also give effect to the general principles of the common law of contract ... .[127]

For the moment, therefore, the courts in Singapore will continue with the approach that may be said to be conservative in two respects: first, to get any consideration before a court in Singapore the marital agreement must be found to be valid by the law that governs the validity of the agreement and, second, once found to be valid and subsisting, it is still open to the court to enforce any term in the agreement directly just as it would any commercial agreement although this outcome is less likely than the court proceeding to make its own order of division of matrimonial assets or maintenance.

X. CONCLUSION

The current state of the law in Singapore is practicable. Legal practitioners in Singapore would appear to be fairly comfortable with the general principles that regulate marital agreements and welcome their affirmation and consolidation by the highest court of the land in *TQ v TR and another appeal*. The core principle is that no marital agreement will ever supplant the default powers in the court to order the just and equitable division of the spouses' matrimonial assets and, as supplement, to order the husband to provide reasonable maintenance to his former wife.

It is the author's belief that the state of the law, while perhaps still capable of improvement, is laudable in practicably permitting the courts to achieve the just and equitable division of matrimonial assets and/or to make a fair and reasonable maintenance order between former marital partners upon their termination of marriage. The law in Singapore chooses to prioritise the achievement of fairness in the difficult scenario where the choice is between this and giving full effect to an agreement between the former marital partners. We must remember that the former marital partners committed to an equal co-operative partnership of different efforts while married.

---

[126] *TQ v TR and another appeal*, above n 44.
[127] *TQ v TR and another appeal*, above n 44, [99] (Andrew Phang JA).

It follows that, upon the termination of their relationship, it is the achievement of fair financial orders that is more important than blindly giving effect to an agreement formed earlier, when their financial circumstances may have been quite different from those pertaining after years of co-operative partnership. While the state of the law leaves a fair measure of discretion in the hands of judges, a more fixed rule is not necessarily better law. An apparently fixed and more certain rule can be misleading, as it does not effectively limit dispute between the former marital partners. The state of the law in Singapore may well be about as good as law can be.

Marital Agreements and Private Autonomy in Spain

JOSEP FERRER-RIBA

CONTENTS

I. THE FINANCIAL CONSEQUENCES OF MARRIAGE AND DIVORCE

A. Family Law in Spain: A Realm of Diversity

Ahighly relevant feature of Spanish private law is its territorial diversity. Spain never completed the process of unifying its private law. In Spain, what is called *derecho común* (Spanish general law), whose basic private law text is the Spanish Civil Code (*Código civil*, hereafter CC), coexists with *derechos autonómicos* (territorial laws), also called in some regions *derechos forales*. The Spanish Constitution of 1978 acknowledged this diversity by awarding those regions which still had *derechos forales o especiales* the power to preserve, modify and develop their own private law (Art 149.1 No 8).[1]

Territorial laws, therefore, persist in several autonomous communities (Aragon, the Balearic Islands, the Basque Country, Catalonia, Galicia, Navarre and Valencia).[2] For the time being, some of these communities have limited themselves to preserving or updating branches or specific institutions of family or succession law, and their private law systems must be supplemented by the Spanish Civil Code. Catalonia, however, has developed an almost complete system of family law, the only exceptions being the requirements for marrying, for separating or divorcing, and for requesting annulment of the marriage, which are governed by Spanish general law.[3] The Catalan parliament brought traditional family law up to date by means of several particular regulations passed in the last decade of the twentieth century, which were merged into the 1998 Family Code (except for the Act 10/1998 concerning non-marital relationships, which remained outside the Code). This Code was recently replaced by Book 2 of the Catalan Civil Code (*Codi civil de Catalunya*, hereafter CCCat), dealing with personal and family law.[4] Book 2 came into force on 1 January 2011.

The diversity of civil legislation within Spain leads to an abundance of situations involving conflicts of law in family relationships. These conflicts are resolved by applying the norms of private international law (Art 13 CC). The determination

---

[1] On the history of Spanish private law, the constitutional framework and the diversity of legal systems, see A Vaquer, 'Introduction' in S van Erp and A Vaquer (eds), *Introduction to Spanish Patrimonial Law* (Granada, Comares, 2006) 1–17; T Rodríguez de las Heras Ballell, *Introduction to Spanish Private Law (Facing the Social and Economic Challenges)* (London and New York, Routledge-Cavendish, 2010) 1–11.

[2] Territorial legislation referring to matrimonial economic regimes and, where existing, to the consequences of family breakdown is mainly contained within the following laws: *Ley 2/2003 of 12 February 2003 de Régimen Económico Matrimonial y Viudedad* (Aragon); *Decreto legislativo 79/1990 of 6 September 1990 Compilación del Derecho Civil de las Islas Baleares* (Balearic Islands); *Ley 3/1992 of 1 July 1992 del Derecho Civil Foral del País Vasco* (Basque Country); *Ley 4/1995 of 24 May 1995 de Derecho Civil de Galicia* (Galicia); *Ley 1/1973 of 1 March 1973 sobre Compilación del Derecho Civil Foral de Navarra* (Navarre); *Ley 10/2007 of 20 March 2007 de Régimen Económico Matrimonial Valenciano* (Valencia) and *Ley 25/2010 of 29 July 2010 del libro segundo del Código civil de Cataluña, relativo a la persona y la familia* (Catalonia).

[3] On the Catalan codification process see E Arroyo Amayuelas, *The Plurality of Civil Codes in Spain (Spanish Decodification versus Catalan Codification)* (Rome, Aracne, 2006); A Vaquer, 'El proceso de la codificación civil catalana' (2009) *Blogs de la UAB* (blogs.uab.cat/dretcatala).

[4] Act 25/2010, 29 July (BOE No 203, 21 August). See also J Egea Fernández and J Ferrer Riba, *Codi civil de Catalunya i legislació complementària (amb notes de concordança i jurisprudència)* (Barcelona, EUB, 2011).

of which law to apply depends on the personal law of one or all the individuals involved in a relationship, and the Spanish Civil Code resorts to the concept of *vecindad civil* (Art 14.1 CC). *Vecindad civil*, a sort of civil status for the purposes of applying general or territorial laws, is usually passed on from parents to children via *ius sanguinis*, but may also be acquired by the free decision of the person if certain prerequisites are met, or by having been domiciled within a territory for an unbroken period of 10 years, provided the person does not file a contrary declaration during this time period (Art 14.5 CC).

B. Financial Consequences of Marriage: Systems of Community and Systems of Separation of Assets

Both general Spanish law and territorial laws allow spouses to arrange autonomously the financial consequences of their marriage. Spouses may decide in advance how to allocate economic surpluses generated during their marital life, and may lay down rules regarding the administration of all types of assets, and the division or redistribution of property upon dissolution of the marriage. These goals can be achieved by choosing a matrimonial property regime, or by modulating or modifying the regime that spouses have opted for or the default regime that applies in the absence of a contrary agreement.

The only restrictions on spousal autonomy are the rules making up what is known as the 'primary matrimonial regime', which are considered to be mandatory. Such provisions concern the duty of both spouses to contribute to the costs and expenses of the family household (Art 1318 CC, Art 231-6 CCCat), the conditions for one spouse acting as agent for the other and the liability for household debts (Art 1319 CC, Arts 231-4 and 231-8 CCCat), and the protection of the family home and household assets, disposal of which requires the consent of both spouses or court approval (Art 1320 CC, Art 231-9 CCCat).

Legal matrimonial property regimes—that is, those that apply in Spain as default regimes in the absence of an agreement—may be grouped, in broad terms, around two primary models: community of property and separation of property.

i. Community of Property

Community of property applies as a default regime, in the form of *sociedad de gananciales* (community of acquisitions), in those regions where the Spanish Civil Code is directly applicable, and in other forms in several territories with their own laws (Aragon, Biscay, the Basque Country, Galicia and Navarre).[5]

Under the *gananciales* regime, acquisitions made or income obtained by both spouses during the marriage, whether they are earnings from work or income from capital, are considered to be jointly owned (Arts 1344 and 1347 CC). These

---

[5] On the matrimonial property regimes in Aragon, Galicia, Navarre and Biscay see JL Gimeno y Gómez Lafuente and E Rajoy Brey (eds), *Regímenes económico-matrimoniales y sucesiones (Derecho común, foral y especial)*, vol I: *Matrimonial* (Cizur Menor—Navarra, Thomson Civitas, 2008) 135–64, 253–76, 322–55, 479–514.

common assets form what is known as the *patrimonio ganancial*. As a general rule, this common fund is administered jointly by both spouses. The law, nevertheless, permits each spouse to individually dispose of the common goods and money to attend to the family's daily needs, as well as for emergencies and the expenses connected with the practice of their profession (Art 1382 CC). Spouses also have the freedom to agree on specific rules, different to those provided by the law, to administer and dispose of their goods.

Besides the community assets, spouses retain their separate personal assets over which they maintain exclusive ownership. Personal assets comprise all assets which belonged to the owner before entering into the community property regime, as well as those acquired through gift or succession and those acquired in exchange for other personal assets (Art 1346 CC). The law contains special provisions regulating acquisitions made in exchange for money or other assets which were partly common and partly personal (Art 1354 CC), for goods acquired before the start of the regime but for which payment is completed afterwards (Art 1357 CC), and for improvements and accrual in value of professional or business assets (Arts 1359 and 1360 CC), among other situations. Spouses may agree to assign the condition of common property to assets acquired for value during the marriage, irrespective of the source of the funds expended in acquiring such assets (Art 1355 CC).[6]

ii. Separation of Property

Separation of property applies as a default regime in the autonomous communities of Catalonia, the Balearic Islands, and, since 2008, Valencia.[7] In Catalonia and Valencia, should spouses separate or divorce, this regime includes a right to compensation for household work or for unremunerated work carried out for the benefit of the other spouse, if this has brought about a significant inequality in the property acquired by both spouses during the marriage (Arts 232-5–232-12 CCCat, Arts 12–15 *Ley* 10/2007 in Valencia). Both systems, therefore, result in some sort of equitable distribution by the courts in the case of marriage breakdown. As a matter of principle, the compensation consists of a personal right against the spouse who benefited from the work. In Catalonia, as a general rule, the amount may be up to a quarter of the difference between either spouse's earnings (Art 232-5.4 CCCat). In Valencia, on the other hand, the law sets down certain guidelines for assessing the value of housework, such as the cost of domestic services in the labour market, the revenues forgone by the homemaker, or the revenues saved by the other spouse on account of not having to perform domestic tasks (Art 13 Act 10/2007), but

---

[6] For a thorough description of the regime of *sociedad de gananciales*, see the report on Spain by C González Beilfuss in K Boele-Woelki, B Braat and I Curry-Sumner (eds), *European Family Law in Action*, vol IV: *Property Relations between Spouses* (Antwerp/Oxford/Portland, Intersentia, 2009). In the Spanish legal literature see extensively L Díez-Picazo and A Gullón, *Sistema de Derecho civil*, vol IV: *Derecho de familia. Derecho de sucesiones*, 10th edn (Madrid, Tecnos, 2006) 157–207; JL Lacruz Berdejo et al, *Elementos de Derecho civil*, vol IV: *Familia*, 3rd edn (Madrid, Dykinson, 2008) 153–254; FJ Gardeazábal del Río and JC Sánchez González, 'La sociedad de gananciales' in JF Delgado de Miguel (ed), *Instituciones de Derecho privado*, vol IV-2: *Familia* (Madrid, Civitas, 2002) 19–275.

[7] See generally Gimeno and Rajoy, *Regímenes económico-matrimoniales*, above n 5, 178–91, 450f, 468f. Concerning the Catalan regime, see the report on Catalonia by M Martín-Casals and J Ribot in Boele-Woelki et al, *European Family Law: Property Relations*, above n 6.

ultimately the courts set the amount on an equitable basis, taking all circumstances into account.

iii. *Optional Regimes*

Apart from these legal regimes, both the Spanish Civil Code, as well as the territorial laws, offer spouses and future spouses the possibility of voluntarily opting for other systems of matrimonial property. The most important of these optional systems is the regime of participation in accrued gains, which was incorporated into Spanish general law in 1981 and into Catalan law in 1993, but has been used very little in practice.

C. Financial Consequences of Divorce

i. *Main Principles*

Spain introduced an unrestricted right of divorce in 2005.[8] Once three months from the marriage ceremony have elapsed, either of the spouses may unilaterally file for divorce without any allegation of specific grounds (Arts 81 No 2 and 86 CC). The system is based on the idea that a petition for divorce, even unilateral, is itself sufficient to show that the marriage has irretrievably broken down. In addition, the economic consequences of divorce are independent from the parties' behaviour and from the reasons leading to the divorce petition. In order to determine the amount of financial compensation that the spouse who is most prejudiced by the break-up is legally allowed to claim, the law sets out a list of criteria which ends with 'any other relevant circumstance' (Art 97 II (9) CC). Although this open clause could lead to an assessment of the spouses' behaviour (particularly, blameworthy behaviour on the part of the spouse claiming compensation) in order to deny or reduce the amount of compensation, courts never explicitly take the conduct of the spouses into consideration.

Broadly speaking, spousal separation or divorce in Spain may bring about four different types of financial consequence: the dissolution of the matrimonial property regime and subsequent distribution of assets; the allocation of the use of the family dwelling; the awarding of child maintenance; and the awarding of pension rights or a compensatory lump sum to the spouse who has been most prejudiced by the separation or divorce.[9]

---

[8] Act 15/2005, 8 July (BOE No 163, 9 July). See also J Ferrer-Riba, 'Same-sex Marriage, Express Divorce and Related Developments in Spanish Marriage Law' [2006] *International Family Law* 139; M Martín-Casals and J Ribot, 'The Postmodern Family and the Agenda for Radical Legal Change' in B Atkin (ed), *The International Survey of Family Law 2008 Edition* (Bristol, Jordan Publishing, 2008) 411–36; V Guilarte Gutiérrez (ed), *Comentarios a la reforma de la separación y el divorcio* (Valladolid, Lex Nova, 2005); P Ortuño Muñoz, *El nuevo régimen jurídico de la crisis matrimonial* (Cizur Menor—Navarra, Thomson Civitas, 2006).

[9] For an overview of the regulation of ancillary matters pertaining to separation and divorce, see L Flaquer and A Garriga, 'Marital Disruption in Spain: Class Selectivity and Deterioration of Economic Conditions' in H-J Andress and D Hummelsheim (eds), *When Marriage Ends (Economic and Social Consequences of Partnership Dissolution)* (Northampton, Edward Elgar Publishing, 2009) 187–89.

ii. Dissolution of the Matrimonial Property Regime and Distribution of Assets

The judicial decree of separation or divorce determines the dissolution of the matrimonial property regime and enables the set of measures aimed at the distribution of assets to be opened up. If the spouses have been subject to a community of property regime, this involves dividing joint assets and allocating half of them to each spouse, while respecting some preferential rights laid down by the law (Art 1406 CC).[10]

If spouses were married under a separation of property system, the main consequence of the separation or divorce is the possible emergence of a right to financial compensation for housework or work undertaken for the benefit of the other spouse without remuneration or with insufficient remuneration (Art 1438 CC, Art 232-5 CCCat). In Catalan law, where this compensation is particularly important, the payment has to be made in cash but may be delayed for up to three years if the judge deems it appropriate (Art 232-8 CCCat). The courts set the amount taking into account the length of time the couple lived together and the extent and intensity of the work, attaching particular importance to whether the work included bringing up children or the personal care of other members of the family who lived with the married couple (Art 232-5.3 CCCat). Under the Family Code 1998 the courts could establish the amount of compensation on a fair and equitable basis, the only limit being that it could not exceed 50 per cent of the other spouse's earnings.[11] Book 2 of the Catalan Civil Code substantially reduced this margin of discretion and brought the Catalan regime closer to a regime of participation in accrued gains. The law now lays down precisely what types of capital gains the other spouse may participate in and regulates how they must be calculated (Art 232-6). Compensation is still decided on an equitable basis, but is limited to a quarter of the difference between the spouses' earnings. This upper limit may only be exceeded if the creditor proves that the value of his or her contribution to the work done in the home or for the other spouse is notably greater than this 25 per cent (Art 232-5.4).

iii. Allocation of the Use of the Family Dwelling

In the absence of an agreement between the spouses, occupation of the family home and use of household goods has to be awarded with priority to the custodial parent for the benefit of minor children (Art 96 I CC, Art 233-20.2 CCCat). This measure is applied irrespective of the home occupancy regime; it is irrelevant whether the house is owned by the spouses (or by one of them) or whether it is held in tenancy. In the second case, the spouse to whom occupancy is assigned needs only to inform the landlord of his or her wish to continue the contract (Art 15 Act 29/1994 on Urban Leases).

This is a measure of enormous practical importance, especially when the spouses, or one of them, own the dwelling, bearing in mind its high use value. The award of a right of occupation is not an interim measure: it may last until the children come of age or, even longer, until they finish higher education and become financially independent. If there are no children, or they are grown up and living independently,

---

[10] On the distribution of the community assets upon dissolution and the preferential rights of the spouses, see the Spanish report by González Beilfuss in Boele-Woelki et al, above n 6, 501f, 564, 579.

[11] On the rules governing this compensation, see extensively the Catalan report by Martín-Casals and Ribot in Boele-Woelki et al, above n 6, 993–1000.

the judge may also order the use of the home to be assigned to the spouse who is not the owner, if it is his or her interests which are most in need of protection (Art 96 III CC, Art 233-20.3 CCCat). Naturally, the measure regarding allocation of the occupation of the family home has an influence on the amount of child maintenance and the spousal compensatory award, although the courts are usually reluctant to quantify this influence precisely.

iv. Child Maintenance

If there are minor or dependent older children, each parent's contribution needs to be set so that they both fulfil their duty of child support (Art 93 I CC, Art 233-4.1 CCCat). The duty to make maintenance payments normally falls on the spouse who does not have custody of the children, but it may fall on both if they alternate physical custody. If the spouses fail to reach an agreement, the amount of the maintenance payments is set at the court's discretion, taking into account each parent's assets and income (Art 146 CC, Art 237-9 CCCat). Spanish law does not contemplate resorting to obligatory or guiding tables stipulating minimum amounts in connection with family income to set these payments.

v. Spousal Compensatory Award

The law recognises a right to financial compensation of the spouse who endures an economic imbalance in relation to the other's position because of the marital breakdown (Art 97 I CC, Art 233-14.1 CCCat).[12] The imbalance has to involve a worsening of the creditor's previous financial situation during the marriage. In order to set the amount, the court has to take into account various circumstances enumerated by the law. In the Spanish Civil Code these circumstances, which are laid down in a non-exhaustive list, include age; state of health; professional qualification; past, present and future dedication to the family; duration of the marriage; potential loss of pension rights; and both spouses' financial means and needs (Art 97 II CC).

Compensation was traditionally awarded in the form of a periodic allowance for an indefinite time-period, ceasing only if the debtor or creditor's economic circumstances changed substantially, or if the creditor remarried or began cohabiting with another person. The Catalan Family Code 1998 made some significant adjustments to this compensation model, and introduced the possibility of restricting the duration of the allowance at the court's discretion, or its substitution, at the debtor's request, by payment of a lump sum or the transfer of property (Art 85.2 and Art 86.1). In 2005, Spanish general law, following a path set out by a previous decision of the Supreme Court,[13] moved in the same direction, allowing the courts to set compensation either as a temporary or indefinite allowance or as a single payment. Book 2 of the Catalan Code has significantly reinforced this trend. In accordance

---

[12] See the answers to questions 55–105 in the report on Spain by M Martín-Casals, J Ribot and J Solé in K Boele-Woelki, B Braat and I Sumner (eds), *European Family Law in Action*, vol II: *Maintenance Between Former Spouses* (Antwerp/Oxford/New York, Intersentia, 2003).

[13] STS 10 February 2005 (RJ 2005/133). Subsequently other judgments reaffirmed the same criterion: STS 19 December 2005 (RJ 2005/7840), STS 3 October 2008 (RJ 2008/7123), STS 17 October 2008 (RJ 2008/5702).

with Art 233-17 CCCat compensation may be awarded in the form of capital, consisting either of assets or a lump sum, or in the form of a pension. If there is no agreement, the judge decides what form the compensation should take. If it takes the form of a pension, this has to be awarded for a limited period except where there are exceptional circumstances that justify fixing it as indefinite.

The law does not state precisely the rationale for compensation. Considering the diverse forms it may take, the compensation may fulfil different functions and is therefore markedly hybrid in nature. Legal practice confirms this approach, which correlates with the coexistence of different family models.[14] In long-lasting marriages with a sole earner, courts usually award an allowance for the rest of the spouse's life and the compensation fulfils a maintenance function, although the amount of the award is not strictly limited to the recipient's basic needs, but takes into account the standard of living enjoyed during the marriage. In shorter marriages, or when the spouses still have a reasonable opportunity to remain in or enter the labour market, there is a clear tendency to emphasise the rehabilitative purpose of compensation. For this reason, it has become common practice to set time limits on the award or tie it to the benefiting spouse's commitment to the care of minor children. Court decisions setting compensation as a lump sum or ordering the transfer of property, as permitted by the law since 2005, remain exceptional.

Given that determining whether to grant such compensation (and, this being the case, to set the amount) requires taking into account the spouses' financial situation after the divorce, the courts usually look first at the outcome of the dissolution of the matrimonial property regime (division of joint assets; redistribution of property on account of housekeeping), at the financial value of a possible allocation of rights to occupy the family home, and at the amount to be paid for child maintenance. The decision to award spousal compensation is taken after giving consideration to the three previous decisions, although the Spanish CC does not expressly state this. Catalan law, however, does require the amount of any possible compensation for work and for the right to use the family home to be taken into account before the amount of the compensatory award is fixed (Arts 232-10, 233-20.7 CCCat).

If the compensatory award takes the form of periodic payments it may be modified or even terminated if there are substantial alterations in the wealth of one or other of the spouses (Art 100 CC, Art 233-18 CCCat). It also ceases if the creditor remarries or cohabits. If the debtor dies, maintenance may continue to be drawn from the deceased person's estate if the freely disposable assets permit this (Art 101 CC, Art 233-19 CCCat).

II. PRE-NUPTIAL AND POST-NUPTIAL AGREEMENTS

A. The Diverse Categories of Private Autonomy in Family Relationships

Private autonomy in family matters is a recent development in Spain. Traditionally this autonomy was very limited and was confined to agreements over the matrimonial property regimes of spouses. Since the 1990s, however, a more intensive and

---

[14] Martín-Casals and Ribot, 'The Postmodern Family', above n 8, 430–33.

imaginative use of marital agreements has emerged. While the marriage rate has stabilised at a fairly low level over the last 20 years, the number of marital agreements formalised by notarial deed shows a clear pattern of increase: from 15,000 in 1982, we see a rise to almost 29,000 in 1992, to 64,000 in 2001, to 122,000 in 2004 and to 132,000 in 2007, with a drop to 96,000 in 2009.[15] To these, another type of contract must be added, namely, separation agreements made on the occasion of a marital breakdown, which the spouses produce and the judge may approve within marriage annulment, separation or divorce proceedings. These agreements increased from 14,000 in 1982 to over 31,000 in 1992, to almost 65,000 in 2002 and to 86,000 in 2007, then experienced a decline in 2009 and 2010 (with just over 68,000 and 74,000 agreements, respectively), as a result of the fall in the total number of separations and divorces.[16] Contracts regulating cohabitation between non-married partners or the consequences of its breakdown can be formalised by private document, but no statistics about them are available.

To take account of the different functions they fulfil and the fact of their different legal regulation, three types of agreement must be analysed separately: (i) pre-nuptial or post-nuptial agreements directed at regulating the marital property regime or other financial consequences of marriage; (ii) agreements directed at establishing the consequences of a marital breakdown which has already come about (separation agreements); and (iii) ex ante agreements aimed at providing for these same consequences in a prospective sense, that is, in anticipation of a future spousal breakdown. The particular form legally required to adopt provisions regulating the financial consequences of marriage is known as *capitulaciones matrimoniales* (Arts 1325–1335 CC, Arts 231-19–231-26 CCCat) which must be authorised by notarial deed to be valid. The same deed may contain type (i) and type (iii) agreements, but both types present different problems as to their validity and enforceability and need to be analysed separately.

B. The Classic Framework of Marital Agreements: Pre-Nuptial and Post-Nuptial Agreements Concerning the Matrimonial Property Regime

Pre-nuptial and post-nuptial agreements concerning the matrimonial property regime have to be formalised by notarial deed, called *capitulaciones matrimoniales* (Arts 1325 and 1327 CC, Art 231-19 CCCat). In addition to the provisions relating to the matrimonial property regime, the *capitulaciones* deed may also comprise other stipulations or transactions, such as gifts or inheritance provisions in favour of one or both of the spouses. For this reason, it was not unusual in traditional practice for other people, such as the parents of the bride or groom, or other relatives, to participate in the conclusion of the contract.

Marriage contracts are made before a notary. Notaries may provide advice to the contracting parties as regards the adequacy of the agreement to the aims pursued.

---

[15] On this trend, with comprehensive statistical data to 2001–02, see A Lamarca Marquès et al, 'Separate Property and Family Self-Determination in Catalonia: A Peaceful Model under a Change?' (2003) 4 *InDret* Working Paper No 164, www.indret.com.

[16] Statistics available at www.ine.es (INEbase/Sociedad/Seguridad y Justicia: Estadística de nulidades, separaciones y divorcios).

They perform a very important pre-emptive function in policing the legality of the contractual terms. The enforceability of the agreement does not depend on the effective provision of advice or the quality of the advice provided. Notaries may, notwithstanding this, incur liability in the event of negligent practice.[17]

The law allows spouses or future spouses broad autonomy to reach agreements concerning the matrimonial property regime. Agreements made in *capitulaciones* need to respect mandatory law, good morals and the equality of rights of both spouses (Art 1328 CC). As regards the binding effect of *capitulaciones*, agreements reached and modifications undertaken during the marriage may in no case prejudice rights previously acquired by third parties (Art 1317 CC, Art 231-24 CCCat).

Resorting to marital agreements has different rationales in those regions applying default regimes of community of property and those applying separation of property:

(i) In regions with community regimes as a default rule, marriage agreements are mainly aimed at introducing separation of property.[18] The substitution of the default regime is relatively common in second or subsequent marriages, in marriages where one spouse carries out business activities which generate a high level of financial risk to which he or she does not wish to expose his or her partner, or, simply, between spouses with a significant imbalance in human capital or economic wealth. If the contract substituting separation of property for community of property is made during the marriage, it usually includes the division of previously acquired community assets. The post-nuptial dissolution of the community regime and its replacement by a separate property regime are fairly common too in cases of de facto separation, if neither spouse wants to file for legal separation or divorce.

(ii) In regions with separation of property as a default rule, it is of course possible for spouses or future spouses to shift to a community regime or a regime of participation in accrued gains with the aim of allocating in a more egalitarian manner the economic surpluses which may be generated during marriage by only one of the spouses, if they foresee a significant degree of functional specialisation (for example, household work) in their relationship. However, statistics in Spain show that it is much more common to move from a community regime to one of separation than the other way round.[19] In Catalonia, where separation of property is most widespread, married couples prefer to correct the imbalances typically created by the economic regime through joint acquisitions (eg the family home, holiday dwellings, investment products, luxury goods), gifts to the homemaker spouse or other transactions between spouses, including what are known as *compres amb pacte de supervivència* (joint acquisitions made for the benefit of the surviving spouse),[20] without ever replacing the separation of property regime with another involving a higher degree of participation.

---

[17] R Verdera Server, *La responsabilidad civil del notario* (Cizur Menor—Navarra, Thomson Civitas, 2008) 203ff.

[18] Lamarca et al, 'Separate Property', above n 15, 8ff.

[19] Ibid 14.

[20] See Arts 231-15–231-18 CCCat. *Compres amb pacte de supervivència* are joint acquisitions made by spouses married under a system of separation of property or participation in accrued gains including a clause which assigns the surviving spouse sole ownership of the asset.

As stated above, spousal autonomy concerning marital agreements permits not only changes of regime, but also the readjustment of the typical effects of default legal regimes by means of ad hoc specific stipulations. However, the possibility of adapting legal norms to suit the parties' preferences is used very little: spouses tend to place great trust in the typical regimes, such as the law defines them.

C. Pre-Nuptial and Post-Nuptial Agreements in Anticipation of a Future Marital Breakdown

i. Requirements for Validity

The conclusion of agreements in contemplation of a family breakdown is a relatively recent development in Spain. They were unknown in traditional notarial practice and the Spanish Civil Code contains no provisions regulating them. However, over the last 15 years, the increasing incidence of divorce, the growing awareness of its consequences and the increase of step-parenting and 'mixed' families have given rise to a more favourable culture for private agreements on family issues, including the consequences of family breakdown. The refinement and diversification of the legal services market have also contributed to the spread of this type of agreement. Several *Audiencias Provinciales* (provincial courts serving as appellate courts) have been driven to issue opinions on them, and case law regarding their validity is gradually emerging. The Spanish Supreme Court, in a groundbreaking decision of 31 March 2011, has expressly upheld the validity and enforceability of such agreements.[21]

In the absence of specific norms, it is assumed that these agreements must comply with the general requirements of family contracts regarding contractual capacity and freedom of consent. They are not subject to additional safeguards directed at reinforcing the free giving of consent, such as those related to the fixing of suitable time frames for conclusion, to the real possibility of having obtained previous independent legal advice, or to the availability of relevant financial information about the other spouse.[22] Following general contract law, their avoidance based on vitiated consent has to be effected by means of a claim in court on the grounds of mistake (under a fairly restrictive doctrine), deceit or duress (Arts 1265–1270 CC).[23]

It is arguable whether agreements contemplating a future separation or divorce should necessarily be formalised in *capitulaciones matrimoniales* or whether they could also be drafted in ordinary public deeds or in private documents. These agreements are frequently inserted in a broader contract concluded for the purpose of substituting or adjusting the property regime (for example, dissolving a community of property regime and replacing it with separation of property). In such cases, the *capitulaciones* form must be adopted. If the contract does not include provisions

---

[21] RJ 2011/3137.

[22] See SAP Madrid 27 February 2007 (JUR 2007/151411), validating an agreement entered into four days before the wedding.

[23] See E Arroyo Amayuelas, 'Vices of Consent' in Van Erp and Vaquer, *Spanish Patrimonial Law*, above n 1, 113–22.

concerning the property regime, however, observing this formality is not essential and agreements made by private document must also be considered valid. [24]

As regards the scope and limits of private autonomy in this field, the relevant legal provision is Art 1325 CC, which, in addition to the matrimonial property regime, allows marital contracts to lay down 'any other provisions by reason of marriage'. This formula contains a principle of freedom on which rests the prevalent view in legal literature defending the legality of such agreements.[25] Spouses' autonomy is circumscribed, however, by Art 1328 CC, which refers to three grounds of invalidity: provisions in marital agreements are null and void whenever they are against the law, against good morals, or limit the equal rights pertaining to each spouse. The Code does not specify, however, which legal principles and rules have to be considered mandatory and cannot be displaced by a contrary agreement.

Most cases examined by provincial courts up to this point have dealt with agreements aimed at waiving the spousal compensatory award or the compensation for housework available in the systems of separation of property (Arts 97 and 1438 CC), or at setting the amount beforehand by means of a calculation formula or the transferring of specific assets.[26] If these types of agreement are entered into once the marriage has broken down, their validity cannot be disputed, notwithstanding the judge's power to withhold approval if they are seriously detrimental to the interests of either spouse.[27] When they are concluded in anticipation of a future breakdown, the question of their validity is more controversial. Most authors tend to confer validity on such waivers on the understanding that there is no reason to treat them differently depending on whether they were concluded before or after the break-up.[28] Provincial courts' case law tends to favour this position.[29] Some isolated decisions, however, reject their validity when they are made in anticipation of a future breakdown, with the argument that renouncing rights that do not yet exist is not permissible.[30] This reasoning, however, does not seem very convincing as the law permits entering into contracts involving future rights and assets and

---

[24] MP García Rubio, 'Los pactos prematrimoniales de renuncia a la pensión compensatoria en el Código civil' (2003) *Anuario de Derecho Civil* 1660; AL Rebolledo Varela, 'Pactos en previsión de una ruptura matrimonial' in FJ Gómez Gálligo (ed), *Homenaje al profesor Manuel Cuadrado Iglesias*, vol I (Cizur Menor—Navarra, Civitas, 2008) 740ff.

[25] J Egea Fernández, 'Pensión compensatoria y pactos en previsión de una ruptura matrimonial' in A Cabanillas et al (eds), *Estudios Jurídicos en homenaje al profesor Luis Díez-Picazo*, vol III (Cizur Menor—Navarra, Civitas, 2002) 4556ff; García Rubio, 'Los pactos prematrimoniales', above n 24, 1659ff; Rebolledo Varela, 'Pactos en previsión', above n 24, 747ff; L Zarraluqui Sánchez-Eznarriaga, 'Acuerdos prematrimoniales: hacia la validez de los pactos preventivos de la ruptura conyugal' (2008) 118 *Economist & Jurist* 18ff.

[26] See the judgments cited below in nn 29, 30, 32 and 33.

[27] On the validity of separation agreements waiving compensatory awards, see STS 2 December 1987 (RJ 1987/9174).

[28] See works cited above in n 24 and also FJ Pastor Vita, 'La renuncia anticipada a la pensión compensatoria en capitulaciones matrimoniales' (2003) 19 *Revista de Derecho de Familia* 36ff, and E Roca, 'Autonomía, crisis matrimonial y contratos con ocasión de la crisis' in JM Abril Campoy and ME Amat Llari (eds), *Homenaje al profesor Lluís Puig i Ferriol*, vol II (Valencia, Tirant lo blanch, 2006) 2137.

[29] See, eg, SAP Murcia 29 October 2002 (JUR 2003/71008); SAP Madrid 27 November 2002 (JUR 2003/92086); SAP A Coruña 4 April 2006 (JUR 2007/135060); SAP Pontevedra 12 July 2006 (JUR 2006/220179) and SAP Madrid 27 February 2007 (JUR 2007/151411).

[30] SAP Asturias 12 December 2000 (AC 2001/151) and SAP Girona 1 March 2004 (JUR 2004/18887).

also allows exclusion of the application of non-mandatory rules (Art 6.2 CC). A middle-ground position is held by those who support the view that the compensatory award sometimes fulfils a maintenance function and, in as much as this is the case, it may not be waived, as the right to alimony cannot be disposed of.[31] The courts, however, have not accepted this approach.

With regard to agreements that aim to quantify in advance the financial rights and duties of the parties subsequent to a separation or divorce, the appellate courts' position is very pragmatic. In general, they have upheld the validity of the agreement and have enforced it if the outcome reached did not differ substantially from that which would have resulted in the absence of an agreement.[32] On the other hand, the courts have been much more ambivalent in validating agreements which hinder the possibility of acceding to separation or divorce, for example, through the setting of financial compensation that is unconnected with the circumstances that justify financial redress according to the law. Thus, an agreement penalising the filing for separation or divorce with financial compensation which depends exclusively on the duration of the marital relationship has been declared null and void.[33] This type of agreement has been considered contrary to the rule permitting spouses to accede freely to separation or divorce (Art 81, 86 CC), a rule that contains a fundamental family law policy decision, which cannot be circumvented or disrupted by means of a private agreement.

However, a judgment issued by the Supreme Court in 31 March 2011 takes a more favourable stance towards the enforceability of such agreements. In this case the spouses had signed a contract after a marital reconciliation, by which the husband promised to pay a monthly pension of €1,200 and 'donate' an apartment to her wife in case of a future separation, regardless of the reasons for the filing. The wife filed for separation two years later and claimed payment of the rent and delivery of the apartment. The Court ordered the former husband to pay the pension, giving no credit to the provincial court argument that enforcement of such clause would run counter to Article 1256 CC, which prescribes that the validity and performance of contracts cannot be left to the discretion of one of the contracting parties. On the other hand, the Court refused to enforce the promise to deliver the apartment, with the rather formalistic and weak argument that promises to donate property in the future are not valid (Art 635 CC).

Catalan law, in contrast to Spanish law, adopted an explicit stance in favour of the validity of pre-marital and marital agreements regulating the consequences of a future separation or divorce. Article 15 of the Family Code 1998, concerning the contents of marriage contracts (*capítols matrimonials*), already established

---

[31] Egea Fernández, 'Pensión compensatoria', above n 25, 4564f.

[32] See SAP Álava 25 April 2002 (JUR 2003/231109), where compensation of €90,000 for housework had been agreed in the event of divorce.

[33] See SAP Almería 17 February 2003 (AC 2003/623), where it had been agreed that in the case of divorce the husband would compensate his wife with payments of €6,000 for the first year of marriage and an additional payment of €500 for every month after the first year. The court considered that this agreement constituted a penalty clause limiting the right to marital separation, which is held to be a fundamental right. But see SAP Santa Cruz de Tenerife 7 July 2008 (JUR 2009/108893), a case in which the court enforced an agreement under which the wife was awarded compensation of €6,000 for every year of marriage.

that spouses could not only set out their matrimonial property regime, but also adopt any other provisions that they deemed expedient, 'even in anticipation of a marital breakdown'. However, the rule did not pinpoint the actual extent of this autonomy and its limits, and, for this reason, similar queries were being raised to those described above with regard to Spanish law. Book 2 of the CCCat substantially clarifies the situation and deepens the recognition of the autonomy of spouses or future spouses (as well as cohabiting couples) to regulate the consequences of a family breakdown.[34] It starts from an acknowledgement of the validity of agreements, but lays down some safeguards to guarantee that the contracting parties give free and informed consent. Its Art 231-20, in particular, requires the following conditions to be fulfilled: (i) if the contract is pre-nuptial, it has to be concluded at least one month before the wedding; (ii) before authorising the deed, the notary must inform each party separately of the extent of the intended changes to be introduced in relation to the default rules, and warn them of the reciprocal duty to provide each other with relevant financial information; (iii) agreements excluding or limiting rights have to be reciprocal and must clearly specify the rights being waived or limited. In addition to these limitations on the validity of agreements, Art 231-20 makes the binding force of these agreements conditional on providing sufficient evidence of informed consent. Specifically, the new legal framework puts the burden of showing that, at the time of signing, the other party had sufficient information about the claimant's property, income and foreseeable financial expectations, provided that this information was relevant in respect of the contents of the agreement, on the spouse seeking to enforce an agreement. Alongside this general rule, several other provisions also specify the conditions under which certain rights might be waived: in particular, the right to compensation for housework under the regime of separation of property is considered entirely waivable (Art 232-7), but the rights to financial compensation and occupation of the family home are only waivable as long as the creditor's possibilities of attending to his or her basic needs at the time of enforcement are not compromised (Art 233-16 and Art 233-21.3).

ii. Limitations to Enforceability

The binding force of agreements in anticipation of marital breakdown must be examined not only from the perspective of their validity requirements. It is also necessary to take into account the existence of diverse factors that may specifically condition their enforceability. These factors belong to general contract law and to family law.

From the perspective of general contract law, mention has also to be made of the principle that the waiving of rights cannot be detrimental to third parties (Art 6.2 CC), to the court's discretionary power to reduce grossly excessive penalty clauses (Art 1154 CC), and to the hardship or *rebus sic stantibus* doctrines which allow putting an end to or adapting a contract in the event of an unexpected and

---

[34] On the contents of Book 2 CCCat insofar as it concerns marital agreements, see Rebolledo Varela, above n 24, 753–55.

unforeseeable change of circumstances. Courts have applied a version of this doctrine in a few cases in which strict application of the marital agreement led to manifestly unfair consequences for one spouse. In particular, if the agreement was made on the assumption of the parties' financial independence and one of them subsequently changed position, taking on most of the housework and care of the children, to the detriment of his or her professional advancement, or lost his or her job and source of income, the courts have understood this change of circumstances to be sufficient to exclude the application of a waiver agreement to the award of financial compensation.[35] Article 231-20.5 CCCat expressly incorporates this limit on the enforceability of marital agreements, but requires the circumstances which may have changed at the time that enforcement of the agreement is sought to be relevant and not to have been foreseen or reasonably foreseeable at the time the contract was made.

From the perspective of family law, it is worth recalling that the content of certain agreements is subject to ex post judicial control. As will be explained below (section III.B.), Spanish general law gives the judge the power to set aside spousal agreements that have been adopted to regulate the consequences of a marital breakdown if they are harmful to the children or seriously detrimental to one of the spouses. Although Art 90 CC regulates this judicial power in respect of marital agreements negotiated on the occasion of a joint application for separation or divorce, it seems that this monitoring function could be extended to agreements in anticipation of a future breakdown. If the law grants the courts the power to interfere in the exercise of the autonomy to reach agreements when the parties negotiate 'in the shadow of the law'[36] (that is, in view of everything that has happened during the marriage and with the possibility of having an approximate idea of what the outcome of litigation will be, if this has to be resorted to), it is reasonable to assume that they have this same power when one or both spouses seek to make enforceable an agreement negotiated in advance.

III. SEPARATION AGREEMENTS

A. Types of Agreement

The validity of separation agreements is not particularly problematic. Once spouses are no longer living together, the law allows and indeed encourages them to reach agreements in order to regulate the personal, family and financial consequences of their separation or divorce. If proceedings for separation or divorce have already begun and circumstances hinder communication between the spouses, the judge may refer the couple to family mediation services (eg Art 233-6.3 CCCat). As a matter of fact, most separation and divorce proceedings in Spain are decided

---

[35] SAP Granada 14 May 2001 (AC 2001/1599) and SAP Las Palmas 12 November 2003 (JUR 2004/27329).

[36] In accordance with the famous expression coined by RH Mnookin and L Kornhauser, 'Bargaining in the Shadow of the Law: the Case of Divorce' (1979) 88 *Yale Law Journal* 950.

on a non-contentious basis, which essentially requires presenting a proposal of separation agreement, called *convenio regulador*, to the judge (Art 81 (1) CC, Art 233-2 CCCat).[37]

Two main categories of separation agreement should be distinguished: (i) agreements filed with the court and formalised within the separation or divorce proceedings (*convenio regulador*), and (ii) agreements concluded out of court, which may be formalised in a public deed or a private document. This second type of agreement is common in situations of factual separation, if neither party wishes to take steps to commence separation or divorce proceedings. It is particularly useful if spouses who are subject to a common property regime decide, on the occasion of separation, to dissolve the community, distribute the assets and settle on a regime of separate property. These contracts may also contain other agreements in matters of child custody, maintenance, occupation of the family home, and financial compensation.

B. Agreements Incorporated into Court Proceedings

If the separation or divorce is initiated by joint application of the spouses or by one of them with the other's acceptance, the petition must be accompanied by what is called a proposal of regulatory agreement (*propuesta de convenio regulador*).[38] The proposal must include the decisions reached by the parties regarding custody, parental responsibility, access rights, occupation of the family home, child maintenance, division or redistribution of assets, and spousal compensatory payments (Art 90 I CC; Art 233-2 CCCat). Should the spouses disagree on any of these issues, the procedure is handled as a contested divorce. If complete agreement is reached during the proceedings, the divorce will be handled through the procedural rules of mutual agreement, according to Art 770 No 5 Civil Procedure Act (*Ley de Enjuiciamiento Civil*, hereafter LEC).

The *convenio regulador* filed with the matrimonial proceedings needs to be approved by the judge. The law stipulates that the judge is obliged to do so, unless the agreements are harmful to the children or seriously detrimental to one of the spouses (Art 90 II CC). In the event that the judge denies approval, the spouses must submit a new proposal, limited to the points which have not been approved. If they fail to do this, or if their new proposal is not accepted either, the judge makes the final decision (Art 777.7 LEC). The judge's power of interference in decisions that do not affect minor children, comprising a right to reject agreements on the grounds that they are seriously detrimental to one spouse, is controversial and does not sit well with the principles of contract law. In practice, agreements on the dissolution of the property regime and compensatory payments between spouses—including their

---

[37] In 2010, 102,933 divorces and 7,248 legal separations were decreed in Spain, of which 69,459 (67.48%) and 5,128 (70.75%) were by mutual agreement, and 33,474 (32.52%) and 2,120 (29.25%) were contested. Statistics available at www.ine.es (*Estadísticas judiciales*).

[38] See generally Díez-Picazo and Gullón, above n 6, 119–21; Lacruz Berdejo et al, above n 6, 96–98; I Cordero Cutillas, *El convenio regulador en las crisis matrimoniales: estudio jurisprudencial* (Cizur Menor—Navarra, Thomson Aranzadi, 2004).

waiving, should this be the case—are always respected, notwithstanding contract annulment mechanisms. Unlike Spanish law, Catalan law only allows the judge to reject agreements on the basis that they would be harmful to minor children (Art 233-3.1 CCCat), and not those which could merely be considered seriously detrimental to one spouse.[39]

Agreements formalised in a *convenio regulador*, once approved by the judge, are incorporated into the judicial decision and are directly enforceable. The law permits modifying them subsequently in case of a substantial change of circumstances, be it by means of a court decision or a renewed agreement (Art 90 III CC, Art 233-7 CCCat).

C. Separation Agreements Concluded Out of Court

The spouses may also reach total or partial agreements outside judicial proceedings. This is the case when the spouses separate in fact, but neither of them decides to file a legal separation or a divorce petition. This also happens when former spouses agree to a private modification of any of the orders included in the divorce decree (eg motivated by a change of circumstances) after the divorce proceedings. Out-of-court agreements may be formalised in a notarial deed, but may also be concluded in a private document, or even be tacit and inferred from conclusive behaviour. Resorting to a notarial *capitulaciones* deed is only mandatory if the aim is to modify or dissolve a matrimonial property regime.

The Spanish Supreme Court has repeatedly declared that private separation agreements are valid and binding like ordinary contracts.[40] However, if one of the parties tries to enforce an agreement of this kind in contentious separation or divorce proceedings, the court will subject it to the same scrutiny as the terms of a *convenio regulador*, and may deny approval if it is harmful to the children of the marriage or seriously detrimental to one spouse (Art 90 II CC).

Out-of-court separation agreements carry a substantial risk of unfair advantage-taking, especially when they are concluded shortly after the separation in circumstances of remarkable emotional or economic upset. In such situations, in which spouses sometimes adopt interim decisions to organise their separate lives, it may also happen that one spouse, lacking sufficient legal advice, is induced by the other to accept prejudicial agreements of a more permanent nature. In Catalonia, where the law does not allow courts to dismiss separation agreements on the grounds of their being seriously detrimental to one of the spouses, the Higher Regional Court rejected the validity of an out-of-court agreement waiving compensation for domestic work, with the rather strained reasoning that the waiver was not explicit enough.[41] The effectiveness of this type of remedy against abuses of private

---

[39] Confirming this position, see STSJC 19 July 2004 (RJ 2004/5534).

[40] See, eg, STS 22.4.1997 (RJ 1997/3251); STS 27 January 1998 (RJ 1998/110); STS 21 December 1998 (RJ 1998/9649); STS 15 February 2002 (RJ 2002/1619), STS 3 February 2006 (RJ 2006/622). On this case law and also on the decisions issued by lower courts, see Roca, 'Autonomía', above n 28, 2124ff.

[41] STSJC 19 July 2004 (RJ 2004/5534). However, in a later judgment (STSJC 10 July 2006) the same Court validated an overall waiver covering all type of compensation, probably because it was fair under the circumstances.

autonomy is, however, limited. Taking this into consideration, Art 233-5.2 CCCat now formulates a more general rule, according to which agreements entered into after the family breakdown without intervening independent legal assistance to each party can be unilaterally revoked during the three-month period from their conclusion or until the commencement of judicial proceedings, if these start before the three-month period.

IV. CONFLICT OF LAWS

The coexistence in Spain of the Spanish Civil Code and territorial laws, as well as the large number of mixed marriages, both between Spaniards with different *vecindad civil* and between Spaniards and foreigners, generates many conflicts of law cases concerning the effects of marriage. According to Art 9.2 CC, these effects are generally governed by the spouses' personal law (ie the law of their nationality or *vecindad civil*) at the time of the wedding. If they do not share the same personal law, the future spouses can opt for the personal law or the law of the habitual residence of either of them. If they do not exercise this option, the law of their common and habitual residence as determined immediately after the wedding will apply.[42] Once the law governing the effects of marriage is established, it remains unalterable, except for the possibility of making contracts concerning the matrimonial property regime subject to a different law.

Spanish law, in effect, facilitates the exercise of private autonomy by spouses or future spouses who find themselves in situations with international connections. In particular, the law allows spouses to enter into marital contracts aimed at establishing, modifying or replacing the matrimonial property regime in conformity not only with the law which governs the effects of their marriage, but also with the personal law or the law of the habitual residence of either of them (Art 9.3 CC). According to the same provision, marital agreements concluded under foreign law are upheld and can be enforced in Spain if they are in conformity either with the law regulating the effects of marriage or with the law of the nationality or the habitual residence of either of the contracting parties.

Nevertheless, contractual terms agreed on the basis of foreign law are not enforceable in Spain if they are contrary to public order (Art 12.3 CC). The public order exception has, however, very limited relevance in this field, because Spanish law, as has been seen, is substantially favourable towards the validity and enforceability of marital contracts. The exception could be raised with possibilities of success in any case where an agreement substantially restricts the right to separation or divorce, or is harmful to the welfare of children. In both cases, the agreement would come into conflict with essential values of the Spanish legal system and the courts could refuse enforcement.

---

[42] See generally MP Diago Diago, *Pactos o Capitulaciones Matrimoniales en Derecho Internacional Privado* (Zaragoza, El Justicia de Aragón, 1999); E Rodríguez Pineau, *Régimen económico matrimonial (Aspectos internacionales)* (Granada, Comares, 2002).

V. CONCLUSION

Spanish law takes a favourable approach towards the exercise of private autonomy in family relationships. The idea that spouses must be free to adapt the property and financial consequences of the marital relationship to their preferences is deeply rooted in Spanish legal culture. Statutory law, judicial decisions issued by the Supreme Court and the high regional courts, as well as notarial practice, confirm this principle.

This holds true in the first place for the property relations between spouses during marriage. The diversity of matrimonial property systems coexisting in Spain furthers a respect for different property arrangements and reinforces private ordering practices. Spouses, irrespective of whether they are subject to a system of community of property or to a system of separation of property, are allowed to conclude pre-marital or marital contracts with the aim of excluding the application of the default rules or making adjustments to them. Statistics suggest that these contracts are mostly entered into to substitute a regime of separation of property for a regime of community of property. This substitution is common when one of the spouses undertakes business activities and wants to protect the other spouse's share of the common assets. It also frequently occurs when spouses start living apart with the intention of separating. On the contrary, replacement of a default regime of separation of assets with a system of community of property is quite exceptional. In regions having a default system of separate property the spouses' decision to share the economic surplus generated during marriage is not usually implemented through a change of property regime, but through particular decisions (joint acquisitions, gifts, succession contracts).

The law dealing with separation agreements is not particularly problematic. The high number of consensual separations and divorces suggests that the legal frame for separation agreements is adequate. Separation agreements are usually negotiated before commencing divorce proceedings with a view to filing a joint application, but can also be concluded in the course of the proceedings. If the terms agreed upon are approved by the judge, they are issued together with the divorce decree and are part of it. The legal power conferred on judges to reject terms that are deemed seriously detrimental to one of the spouses has been called into question, but it is very rarely used. Some concerns have also been voiced with respect to the unrestricted validity of separation agreements concluded out of court, insofar as the remedies to avoid the contract on the grounds of vitiated consent are not always effective for policing unfair taking of advantage.

The recognition of the binding force of agreements made in anticipation of a future family breakdown has been welcomed by practitioners and scholars. There is also consensus on the need for the law to provide a higher degree of certainty. The law should set up the specific requirements for concluding these agreements and clarify the limits to their validity. Policing validity and enforceability through the general rules of contract law has proved insufficient. Experience shows that courts tend to enforce agreements if their application leads to an outcome that does not deviate excessively from the default rules which would have applied but for the agreement. When the outcome is considered to be unfair, they resort, without much technical accuracy, to piecemeal remedies in order to set aside the contract terms. This modus operandi is unsatisfactory. The reform of pre-marital and marital agreements undertaken in Catalan law in 2010 is a major attempt to tackle all these problems and deserves close attention. It is still too early to assess its results. Law practitioners have taken a positive view of the greater legal certainty provided by the new system, insofar as it regulates exactly the rights that can be negotiated or waived. Ultimately, however, the system's success or failure will essentially depend on how the courts apply the rules which allow the binding force of settlements to be modified or even excluded, and on whether they manage to create a stable and well-grounded body of case law. It is foreseeable, in any case, that Spanish legal systems as a whole will evolve in a similar direction in the not too distant future.

Marital Agreements and Private Autonomy in Sweden

MAARIT JÄNTERÄ-JAREBORG

CONTENTS

I. THE FINANCIAL CONSEQUENCES OF DIVORCE

A. General Information

To understand the role played by private autonomy and, in particular, matrimonial property agreements, certain basic elements of the Swedish system need to be understood in respect of the effect of marriage on spouses' property.[1]

One such element relates to the 'all-inclusive nature' of Sweden's default regime, which is commonly labelled a deferred community property regime. As a rule, all property owned by a spouse becomes part of this regime upon marriage and is called 'marital property'. Only that property which is excluded by a marital property agreement between the spouses falls outside this regime. This property is called 'separate property'. Property that a spouse has acquired from a third person through inheritance, will or a gift on condition that that property is to be the recipient's 'separate property' also falls outside the regime.

It follows that spouses—or spouses-to-be—who wish to exclude property owned by either one of them from the deferred community property regime must conclude a marital property agreement to such effect. Alternatively, parents who wish to give property to their children can stipulate that it shall be the recipients' separate property. The effect of the agreement or the stipulation is that in a future property division between the spouses (or in the child's future marriage), property identified

---

[1] In addition to the references in this contribution, the following publications in English deal, inter alia, with the effect of marriage on the spouses' property under Swedish law: M Bogdan (ed), *Swedish Law in the New Millenium* (Stockholm, Norstedts Juridik AB, 2000) 243–72; H Tiberg, F Sterzel, P Cronhult (eds), *Swedish Law—A Survey* (Stockholm, Juristförlaget, 1994) 359–95; A Agell, 'The Division of Property Upon Divorce From a European Perspective' in *Liber Amicorum Marie-Thérèse Meulders-Klein, Droit Comparé des Personnes et de la Famille* (Brussels, Bruyland, 1998) 1–20; C Hamilton and A Perry, (eds) *Family Law in Europe*, 2nd edn (London, Butterworths, 2002) 629–32, 637–41. The most recent contribution is M Jänterä-Jareborg, M Brattström and K Walleng, 'Swedish National Report' in K Boele-Woelki, B Braat and I Curry-Sumner (eds), *European Family Law in Action*, Vol IV: *Property Relations Between Spouses* (Antwerp, Intersentia, 2008).

as 'separate property' will not be included. To the extent that property belonging to a spouse or the spouses has not been made 'separate', it is 'marital property' falling under the default regime.

At the beginning of this millennium there were indications that marital property agreements, transforming property into 'separate property', and third party stipulations with the same effect, were becoming increasingly common in Sweden,[2] even outside 'rich man's circles'. This was interpreted as a reaction to the all-inclusive scope of the default regime, and the fact that in many marriages today the spouses have not only property, but also children, from previous relationships. Another, related factor is that, although marriage rates have recently gone up in Sweden, approximately one-third of all couples living together cohabit outside of marriage.[3] The legal effects of marriage-like cohabitation on a couple's property are, generally, much more limited. More recently, however, the numbers of new registrations of marital property agreements have gone down.

Since 1 May 2009, Swedish legislation on marriage has been gender-neutral, and same-sex marriages are permitted. Not only has Sweden's Marriage Code been reformed to this effect, but all provisions in Swedish law relating to marriage are to be interpreted in a gender-neutral manner. The previous legislation on registered partnerships, in force since 1995, has been repealed.[4]

B. Characteristics of Sweden's Default Regime

In Sweden, a deferred community property regime applies as the default system. When a marriage is entered into, each spouse's property becomes, automatically (ex lege), 'marital property' belonging to the deferred community property regime.[5] Unless otherwise agreed between the spouses or stipulated by a third person, all the spouses' property belongs to the deferred community property regime, irrespective of when (before the marriage or during the course of the marriage) and how (income of earnings, gift, will, inheritance, etc) the property was acquired.[6] This system originates from Nordic legal cooperation in the early 1900s and has been, basically, intact in Sweden since its introduction in the 1920 Marriage Code. The adoption of the new Marriage Code in Sweden in 1987 brought forth some amendments but without altering the system's basic principles.[7] The relevant

---

[2] See statistics below in section II.D.ii.

[3] See M Jänterä-Jareborg, 'Regulation of Cohabitation Out of Marriage in Sweden/Rechtsregeln für nichteheliches Zusammenleben, Länderbericht Schweden' (in English) in I Kroppenberg, D Schwab, D Henrich, P Gottwald and A Spickhoff (eds), *Rechtsregeln für nichteheliches Zusammenleben* (Bielefeld, Gieseking, 2009) 208.

[4] The Act (1994:1117) on Registered Partnership covered only same-sex relationships. Since 1 May 2009, any couple who has registered a partnership in Sweden may convert it into a marriage in Sweden by simply notifying the authority in charge of population records. Alternatively, the registered partners may choose to go through a formal marriage ceremony, ie, marry in an ordinary manner. See Act (2009:260) Repealing the Act (1994:1117) on Registered Partnership, s 3.2.

[5] Marriage Code c 7, s 1.

[6] Ibid, ss 1–2.

[7] See MA Glendon, *The Transformation of Family Law. State, Law, and Family in the United States and Western Europe* (Chicago, The University of Chicago Press, 1989) 224–25.

provisions are found in the Marriage Code (*Äktenskapsbalken*) of 1987, primarily in Chapter 7 and Chapters 9–13.[8]

Under this system, there is no community of co-ownership between the spouses. Throughout the marriage, each spouse individually continues to own all of his or her property[9] and, as a rule, to administer it alone, regardless of whether he or she brought the property into the marriage or has acquired it during the marriage. All debts remain a spouse's own debts.[10] The total separation of debts is illustrated by the fact that a spouse cannot be made liable for any debt incurred by the other spouse, even when the debt arose as a result of a transaction for the needs of the joint household. In other words, during marriage, a separation of ownership and administration, as well as a separation of debts, applies. Nevertheless, the system gives each spouse a special claim, called a 'right in deferred community property' (*giftorättsanspråk*), to the other spouse's 'marital property', to be exercised when the regime is dissolved. This right implies in principle a right to claim and receive half of the net value of the sum of both spouses' 'marital property' in any future property division between the spouses.[11] The most common ground for property division between spouses in Sweden is divorce. In addition to divorce, the death of a spouse and an agreement between the spouses to carry out a property division during a subsisting marriage,[12] constitute grounds for dissolution of the deferred community property regime. In case of death, however, the surviving spouse normally inherits the dead spouse's property, and no property division needs to be carried out.[13]

During the marriage, it is of limited importance whether the property owned by a spouse is classified as 'marital property' or as 'separate property'. The owner spouse is in both cases free to dispose of his or her property.[14] The effects of the property's classification become, on the other hand, of utmost relevance when a property division is to be carried out. It follows that, in particular, the effects of a marital property agreement become concrete only at this point.

C. The Matrimonial Home and Household Goods as an Exception

The owner spouse's above-mentioned right of disposition does not include the matrimonial home, which the Marriage Code refers to as 'the joint dwelling of

[8] Whereas c 7 defines the property of the spouses by introducing the categories of 'marital property' and 'separate property', the focus of cc 9–13 is on property division.

[9] The spouses may, naturally, under general rules of private law, also own property jointly. Property owned jointly by the spouses is either 'marital property' or 'separate property', according to the rules described above.

[10] Marriage Code c 1, s 3.

[11] As explained by the prominent Swedish family law scholar Anders Agell, the main purpose of the Nordic system 'was to combine an independent and equal position of the spouses during marriage, with a right to equally divide all property at the dissolution of a marriage'. Agell, 'The Division of Property', above n 1, 9–10.

[12] Marriage Code c 9, s 1. Spousal agreements to carry out a property division without divorce proceedings being in progress are still exceptional in Sweden. For further information, see the answer concerning Swedish law in Boele-Woelki, Braat and Curry-Sumner, *European Family Law*, above n 1, 836.

[13] This applies, nevertheless, only on condition that the deceased spouse is either childless or is survived by joint children to both spouses. See Swedish Inheritance Code c 3, s 1.

[14] Certain restrictions apply, nevertheless, in respect of the matrimonial home and household goods intended for the spouses' joint use: Marriage Code c 7, ss 5–9.

the spouses'. The owner spouse may not without the consent of the other spouse dispose of the joint dwelling by alienation, pledging as security, mortgaging, letting or granting in any other way the use of property constituting the spouses' joint dwelling.[15] If a spouse refuses to give his or her consent to the other spouse's disposal, the court can, upon application by the owner, permit the action. No such consent or permission is required if the joint dwelling is the owner spouse's 'separate property' due to a stipulation by a third party, who has given the spouse that property on the condition that it shall be the recipient's 'separate property'.[16]

In addition, in respect of joint household goods the owner spouse's right of disposal is also subject to restrictions.[17] The Marriage Code defines 'the joint household goods of spouses' as referring to furniture, domestic appliances and other corporeal chattels for indoor use intended for the joint home. The owner spouse may not without the consent of the other spouse dispose of the household goods in the form of alienation or pledging as security. If a spouse refuses to give his or her consent to the owner spouse, the court may, upon application by the owner spouse, permit the action. Nevertheless, no such consent or permission is required if the household goods are the owner spouse's 'separate property' due to a stipulation by a third party, who has given the spouse that property on the condition that it shall be the recipient's 'separate property'.[18]

The matrimonial home and household goods are also subject to special (protective) rules as regards the allocation of property in a property division due to divorce.[19]

D. Property Division Due to Divorce

i. The Critical Point in Time

A divorce leads to dissolution of the deferred community property regime, at which point a division of all the spouses' 'marital property' needs to be undertaken. The 'critical point in time' as regards what 'marital property' is to be included in the property division and what debts are to be taken into account, is the date when the divorce proceedings were legally initiated.[20] It follows that the value of a spouse's claim in the other spouse's 'marital property' is dependent on how much 'marital property' the owner spouse has at this date. The owner spouse may have increased his or her 'marital property' during the marriage, but it can likewise have reduced in value.[21]

---

[15] Ibid, s 5.
[16] Ibid, s 5.2.
[17] Ibid, ss 4–5,
[18] Ibid, s 9.1.
[19] See below, section I.D.ii.
[20] Marriage Code c 9, s 2.1.
[21] A rule of compensation may apply, as a result of certain transactions taken by the owner spouse during the three years immediately preceding the divorce, reducing the value of his or her 'marital property': Marriage Code c 11 s 4. For further information, see the answers concerning Swedish law in Boele-Woelki, Braat and Curry-Sumner, *European Family Law,* above n 1, 850–51 and 854–55.

ii. Allocation of Property

When division of property takes place, the spouses' shares in the 'marital property' must first be calculated.[22] In calculating these shares, a deduction must be made from each spouse's 'marital property' sufficient to cover the debts which that spouse had.[23] The combined balance (net value) of both spouses' 'marital property' is then divided equally between the spouses.[24]

On the basis of the shares calculated for the spouses, the spouses' 'marital property' is distributed in portions.[25] Each spouse has a preferential right to be allocated to his or her portion his or her own property or such part of it as that spouse wishes.[26] The spouse whose assets exceed one half of the total divisible mass can choose whether he or she wants to surrender property to the other spouse or to pay a corresponding sum in money instead.[27]

Special rules apply, however, concerning allocation of the spouses' joint dwelling and joint household goods in a property division following a divorce. The spouse who is in greatest need of such property has the right to be allocated this property.[28] Nevertheless, if this property is owned by the other spouse, such allocation can take place only on condition that it is reasonable for the owner spouse, having regard to the overall circumstances. The spouse in greatest need is usually considered to be the spouse who, following the divorce, will have custody of the children or, in the case of joint custody, the actual care of the children.[29] Other factors such as the spouses' age and health and prospects of acquiring a new home can also be taken into consideration.[30]

As a starting point, this preferential right of allocation also applies when the joint dwelling or household goods are the other spouse's 'separate property' by reason of a marital property agreement.[31] This is an exception to the general rule that 'separate property' falls outside any property division between spouses. In this case, however, regard will be had to circumstances, such as the period of time that has passed since the marital property agreement was concluded, the spouses' purpose when making the agreement and how the spouses' financial circumstances have developed thereafter.[32] On the other hand, if the joint dwelling or joint household goods are the owner spouse's 'separate property' by reason of a stipulation in a gift or a will by a third person, such property cannot be allocated to the other spouse.[33]

---

[22] Marriage Code c 11.
[23] Ibid, s 2.
[24] Ibid, s 3.
[25] Ibid, s 7.
[26] Ibid, s 7.
[27] Ibid, s 9.
[28] Ibid, s 8.
[29] This ground has, nevertheless, lost much of its previous relevance due to the increasing popularity in Sweden of children's alternate residence, with both parents, after divorce. See A Agell and M Brattström, *Äktenskap, Samboende, Partnerskap* 4th edn (Uppsala, Iustus Förlag, 2008) 158.
[30] Ibid, 207–08.
[31] Marriage Code c 11, s 8.
[32] Governmental Bill 1986/87:1 (Proposition, Äktenskapsbalk m.m.) 180. See also the answer concerning Swedish law in Boele-Woelki, Braat and Curry-Sumner, *European Family Law*, above n 1, 872–73.
[33] Marriage Code c 11, s 8.1.

It should be noted that the spouse to whom the joint dwelling or household goods are allocated has to count this property in his or her share of the property division.[34] Only if the value of this property is very limited, for example, as regards a rental apartment, a spouse may be entitled to receive it without a corresponding deduction from his or her portion. If the spouses' 'marital property' is not sufficient to give the other spouse the full share, a bank loan making it possible to 'buy that other spouse out' may be the solution.[35] If this is not an alternative, for example, because of the low earning capacity of the spouse wishing to have the matrimonial home in his or her portion, and unless the spouses agree otherwise, the joint dwelling or joint household goods will need to be sold so that both spouses can receive their shares upon the property division.

iii. Private Autonomy

The rules concerning equal division of the value of the 'marital property' are dispositive and may be set aside by an agreement between the spouses at the time of the property division.[36] The spouses can agree to take shares other than half of the value of the 'marital property'—for example, the wife 60 per cent and the husband 40 per cent. The spouses may even agree that 'separate property' is to be included in the property division.[37] This creates flexibility in the system. Each spouse must, nevertheless, take account of the interests of his or her creditors and may not, to the creditors' detriment, allow 'separate property' to be included in the property division or in any other manner forgo property that is to be included in the property division.[38]

The division of property is primarily a private transaction to be performed by the spouses without the involvement of any public authorities. In practice, the division is normally carried out by means of an agreement between the spouses, upon divorce. Swedish law does not require that the spouses take legal advice in respect of the property division, which most spouses manage to conduct on their own. However, in complex cases, as well as in cases of disagreement, lawyers are normally consulted. In addition, in cases of disagreement, a spouse may apply to the court for appointment of a so-called property division executor (*bodelningsförrättare*), usually a practising lawyer, who decides upon the distribution of property on behalf of the spouses.[39] This is the normal course in those cases where the spouses are unable or unwilling to jointly carry out the division of their property. The task of the court-appointed property division executor is to settle all disputed questions relating to the property division in accordance with the provisions of the Marriage Code.

---

[34] Ibid, s 8.1.

[35] Ibid, s 10. See also the answer concerning Swedish law in Boele-Woelki, Braat and Curry-Sumner, *European Family Law*, above n 1, 872–73.

[36] See the answers concerning Swedish law in Boele-Woelki, Braat and Curry-Sumner, *European Family Law*, above n 1, 864–66 and 886–87.

[37] Marriage Code c 10, s 4.

[38] Ibid c 13, s 1.

[39] Ibid c 17, s 1.

E. The Origin and Ideology Behind Sweden's Default Regime

The Swedish deferred community property regime system can be traced back to Nordic legislative cooperation in family law in the early 1900s. This cooperation resulted in an almost identical legislative 'Nordic model' on marital property relations, which still basically (but with certain important modifications) is applicable in the five Nordic countries (Sweden, Denmark, Finland, Iceland and Norway).[40] In Sweden, the new rules were inserted into the 1920 Marriage Code (*Giftermålsbalken*), which came into force in 1921. The basic principles of the system have survived, and were transferred into the new Swedish Marriage Code (*Äktenskapsbalken*) enacted in 1987 and in force since 1988.

Through the claim to the other spouse's 'marital property', both spouses share each other's wealth in the property division following a divorce. The original justification was to compensate the home-maker (ie, the wife) for her contributions by giving her an equal share in whatever property existed upon the dissolution of the marriage. Divorces formerly were very uncommon and marriages were generally dissolved only by the death of a spouse. Today, it is questionable whether the ideology of the early 1900s, motivating the inclusion of all property in the deferred community property regime, can still be justified in a society such as Sweden with a well-developed social welfare system, where women are, almost to the same extent as men, gainfully active in the labour market,[41] where the independence, equality and personal responsibility of each spouse is emphasised in all areas of law, where many spouses have children from earlier relationships, and where approximately half of (newly concluded) marriages are estimated to end in divorce. Should property which the spouses bring into the marriage, as well as property which a spouse during the marriage inherits or receives through a gift or will, not be excluded? Should it not be of relevance whether the marriage is dissolved by divorce or through the death of a spouse?

F. The Relationship between Matrimonial Property, Post-Divorce Maintenance and Pension Rights

The starting point in Swedish law is that a divorce terminates all economic ties between the spouses, ie, there is a clean break philosophy.[42] The equal division of the spouses' 'marital property', which in most cases covers all the spouses' property, 'protects and compensates' the spouse with less property. After divorce, each spouse is responsible for his or her own support.[43] If the spouse is in true need of support,

---

[40] See J Scherpe, 'Privatautonomie im Familienrecht der nordischen Länder' in S Hofer, D Schwab and D Henrich (eds), *From Status to Contract?—Die Bedeutung des Vertrages im europäischen Familienrecht* (Bielefeld, Gieseking, 2005) 212–19.

[41] It is, nevertheless, more common for women with small children to work part-time than men in the same situation. In 2008, the UN Committee on the Elimination of Discrimination against Women (CEDAW) urged Sweden to pay more attention in legislation to the financial consequences of divorce. See Interpellation at Parliament 2008/09:55.

[42] See Glendon, *The Transformation of Family Law*, above n 7, 224–27.

[43] Marriage Code c 6, s 7.1.

social welfare benefits are available to him or her. Only exceptionally—after a number of conditions have been fulfilled—will a court order be obtained, obliging a spouse to contribute to the other spouse's maintenance after divorce.[44] Even so, such maintenance will, as a rule, only be granted for a transitional period, in the form of periodical payments or, exceptionally, as a lump sum payment. [45] The relevant provisions are found in Chapter 6 of the Marriage Code.

In the assessment of a spouse's need for maintenance after divorce, the court may take into account, inter alia, the outcome of the property division between the spouses and the effect of a marital property agreement. If the requesting spouse, due to such an agreement, is prevented from claiming a share of the wealthier spouse's property, the court may order a lump sum maintenance payment as a corrective. In practice, post-divorce disputes that go to court are rare and it is unusual for maintenance to be granted by courts in such cases. In case law, claims of post-divorce maintenance have been refused also in long-term marriages with joint children, where one of the spouses has had little or no income. The function of post-divorce maintenance in Swedish law is not to ensure that both spouses maintain the same standard of living as they had during the marriage.[46]

The Supreme Court judgment NJA 1984 p 493 is representative of the strict Swedish outlook. In this case the Court refused a 51-year-old wife's claim for maintenance after a marriage that had lasted 28 years and where two children had been born. The wife's economic situation was considered to be sufficiently secure after the division of the spouses' 'marital property', also taking into account the small income from a part-time job she had been able to find.

In the Supreme Court judgment NJA 1983 p 826, on the other hand, the Court ordered the husband to support the wife after divorce without time restrictions, due to the special circumstances of the case, namely the duration of the marriage (22 years), the fact that the wife had been the home-maker making it possible for the husband to establish a career and to earn a high income, the wife's age (50), her illness and lack of education making it very difficult for her to support herself, and the husband's ability to pay.

Pension rights are, normally, 'marital property' and belong to the deferred community property regime unless otherwise agreed.[47] Still, they can be exempted from a property division, if according to law they are 'not transferable'. In Swedish law, state pension and normally also occupational pension rights are considered to be 'property of a special nature' which cannot be transferred to another person. The ideology is that these pension rights are aimed to safeguard the entitled person's future ability to provide for his or her own subsistence. On the other hand, private

---

[44] Ibid, s 7.

[45] Ibid, s 8.

[46] See the answer concerning Swedish law in K Boele-Woelki, B Braat and I Sumner (eds), *European Family Law in Action*, Vol II: *Maintenance Between Former Spouses* (Antwerp, Intersentia 2003) 183–84. See also M Jänterä-Jareborg, 'Marriage Dissolution and Maintenance to a Spouse Following Divorce: Sweden', in S Hofer, D Henrich, D Schwab (eds), *Scheidung und nachehelicher Unterhalt im europäischen Vergleich* (Bielefeld, Gieseking, 2003) 282–87.

[47] See the answer concerning Swedish law in Boele-Woelki, Braat and Curry-Sumner (eds), *European Family Law*, above n 1, 792–93.

pension rights, based on individual saving schemes, are not exempted from property division unless otherwise stipulated in a marital property agreement.

II. PRE-NUPTIAL AND POST-NUPTIAL AGREEMENTS

A. The Function of Marital Property Agreements

The Swedish Marriage Code, Chapter 7, contains specific provisions relating to marital property agreements (*äktenskapsförord*). Both future spouses—before marriage—and spouses—at any time during a marriage—may in the form of a marital property agreement set aside, in full or in part, the default property regime. The spouses' property (present or future) becomes, correspondingly, 'separate property'.[48] Property that has been agreed to be 'separate property' can always be converted back to 'marital property' through a new marital property agreement to that effect between the spouses.[49]

The function of a marital property agreement under Swedish law is not to affect ownership of property. Irrespective of whether the property is 'marital property' or 'separate property', the owner spouse remains the sole owner of that property. The agreement's legal effects focus on a future property division. The main effect for the spouses is that 'separate property' will not be included in the division. From a creditors' point of view, marital property agreements are of limited importance.[50]

A marital property agreement which meets the requirements of form and substance[51] is normally respected, even in situations where its effect is that one of the spouses may need to leave a wealthy home empty-handed. The special provision of the Marriage Code concerning adjustment of marital property agreements has been interpreted and applied in a very restrictive manner by the courts.[52]

B. Form and Procedure

i. Agreements Made Before or During the Marriage

To be valid, a marital property agreement must be drawn up in writing, and signed by both spouses or future spouses. In addition, the agreement must be registered with a competent authority.[53] Until 1 October 2011, this required registration at a district

---

[48] Marriage Code c 7, s 2.1 and s 3.

[49] Ibid, s 3.1.

[50] The agreement can, nevertheless, be relevant in determining what property is to be included in the property division. If a spouse surrenders more of the property owned by him or her to the other spouse, and then cannot pay debts incurred by him or her, his or her creditors can claim back the value of the 'excess property' from the other spouse.

[51] See below sections II.B.–II.E.

[52] See below section II.D.ii. This provision was inserted to the new Marriage Code in 1987, c 12, s 3. It has been modelled on Sweden's generally applicable provision on the adjustment of contracts, which it replaced in respect of adjustment of marital property agreements. Concerning the relationship between the provisions on adjustment, see Agell and Brattström, *Äktenskap, Samboende, Partnerskap,* above n 29, 151 and Ö Teleman, *Äktenskapsförord* 2nd edn (Stockholm, Norstedts Juridik AB, 2006) 77ff.

[53] Marriage Code c 7, s 3 and c 16, s 2.

court in Sweden. Since that date, court registration is no longer required. Instead, a marital property agreement, to be valid, must be registered with Sweden's National Taxation Agency (*Skatteverket*).[54] This reform is a result of the government's policy to remove all primarily administrative matters from the courts' jurisdiction. The National Taxation Agency is, from this date, also in charge of the Central Marriage Registry of Sweden where all previously (at court) registered marital property agreements are documented. If the Taxation Agency refuses to grant registration, its decision may be appealed to court.[55]

In practice, it is not uncommon that Swedish citizens who are habitually resident abroad register their marital property agreements in Sweden. For example, many Swedish citizens who are long-term residents in England do so. In these cases, the parties have normally agreed on the application of Swedish law to their marital property relations and have made a marital property agreement along the lines of the Swedish Marriage Code.

A marital property agreement entered into by future spouses becomes valid from the date the marriage is entered into, on condition that it is given to the competent authority for registration within one month of the marriage.[56] If the (pre-nuptial) agreement is registered later, it becomes binding from the day the application for registration is made to the competent authority. A marital property agreement entered into during the course of the marriage becomes binding as of the day it is given to the competent authority.[57]

By signing the agreement, each spouse is considered to have consented to its registration. Once the agreement has been signed by the spouses, either of them can apply for its registration. The Marriage Code contains no time limits for registration, which may be applied for years after the agreement was concluded.[58]

In the Supreme Court decision NJA 1989 p 199 a marital property contract had been concluded in Poland between a Swedish citizen and a Polish citizen in accordance with the form requirements of Swedish law but not of Polish law. Six months later, when the spouses had already separated but not yet applied for a divorce and the wife (after two months' residence in Sweden) had returned to Poland, the husband applied for registration of the agreement at a Swedish court. The registration was granted.

In another Supreme Court decision, NJA 1983 p 775,[59] the husband applied for registration five years after the conclusion of the marital property agreement. Again, registration was granted.

This approach may appear surprising to a foreign lawyer, but it is firmly established in Swedish law. In fact, there is a Supreme Court decision from the 1940s, NJA 1946 B 1019, where registration of a marital property agreement was applied for—and granted—20 years after the agreement's conclusion. Nevertheless, if a long time passes after a marital property agreement is concluded without registration,

---

[54] In the wording of the relevant sections, ibid, 'court' has been changed to 'National Taxation Agency' (Skatteverket). See Government Bill 2010/11:119.
[55] Marriage Code c 16 s 5.
[56] Marriage Code c 7, s 3.3.
[57] Ibid, s 3.3.
[58] See Teleman, *Äktenskapsförord*, above n 52, 24f.
[59] See below section II.E.ii.

this delay may be seen as an indication of a subsequent agreement between the spouses not to register it.[60] On the other hand, a spouse's failure to register the agreement, contrary to an undertaking towards the other spouse to do so, can result in an adjustment of the property division, or in a duty to pay damages to the other spouse.[61]

There is reason to emphasise that it is the registration with the competent authority that makes the marital property agreement binding. Unless registration takes place, the agreement is not valid.[62] It should also be noted that although a marital property agreement can be made by future spouses, it can be registered only after the marriage has taken place.[63]

Contrary to earlier Swedish law, the present Marriage Code of 1987 does not require that a marital property agreement between spouses or future spouses be witnessed. This requirement was abolished because signatures by witnesses were considered often to come about hastily and without adding to the solemnity of the agreement, as well as because this kind of a requirement was considered to increase the risk for future disputes concerning the invalidity of an agreement, on the basis of alleged defects in form.[64]

ii. Agreements Replacing or Annulling a Previous Agreement

The above-mentioned form requirements also apply if the spouses subsequently wish to alter or annul their marital property agreement. In such cases, both spouses must sign the new agreement and have it registered.[65] It is not unusual for several marital property agreements to exist between spouses, each of them registered. In such cases, the agreements either supplement each other, or replace previous ones.[66]

iii. Registered Marital Property Agreements are Publicly Available

Upon granting registration, the court entered the agreement into its record and sent an attested copy of it to Sweden's Central Marriage Registry (*Äktenskapsregister*), kept by Statistics Sweden. A registered marital property agreement is available for anybody interested in its contents, after contact with the court where it was registered or with the Central Marriage Registry of Sweden. From the point of view of the spouses, the Registry also functions as a depository of their agreement. Since 1 October 2011, the National Taxation Agency is in charge of both registration of marital property agreements and of the Central Marriage Registry.

---

[60] See Teleman, *Äktenskapsförord*, above n 52, 26.
[61] Ibid, 25.
[62] See Agell and Brattström, *Äktenskap, Samboende, Partnerskap*, above n 29, 135.
[63] See Teleman, *Äktenskapsförord*, above n 52, 23.
[64] Agell and Brattström, *Äktenskap, Samboende, Partnerskap*, above n 29, 136.
[65] Marriage Code c 7, s 3.
[66] See, eg, the case in NJA 1997 p 37, described below in section II.C, where the spouses had registered several marital property agreements during the course of their marriage.

iv. The 'Cut-off Point' for Registration

After divorce proceedings have been initiated between the spouses, they can no longer register a marital property agreement.[67] An explanation for this 'cut-off point' is that the so-called 'critical time' concerning what property and debts are to be included in a property division is the day the application for divorce was made.[68] In this situation, the spouses can instead make use either of a so-called 'pre-agreement' (separation agreement, *föravtal*) or a property division agreement.[69] Since separation as such has no legal effect under Swedish law, not even when the spouses live apart without applying for divorce,[70] the spouses can apply for registration during a factual separation.

C. The Function and Effects of Registration

i. The Control Remains Formal

Although registration is necessary to make a marital property agreement binding, registration is still no guarantee that the agreement will, in full, be respected by a court in a future dispute following a divorce between the spouses.[71] The competent authority is under no duty to inspect the agreement's tangible content—for example, whether property specified in the agreement and claimed to belong to one of the spouses also in reality is owned by that spouse, or to assess its legal consequences. Basically, the competent authority upon registration of a marital property agreement only checks that the formal requirements (see above, section II.B.) are fulfilled before registration can be granted.

This position, after some speculation in the legal literature, was confirmed by the Swedish Supreme Court decision NJA 1997 p 37. In its judgment the Supreme Court stated that it is not up to the court, where registration of a marital property agreement is applied for, to assess its legal effects. In this case, the lower courts had refused the registration of the spouses' agreement on the basis that it, in addition to annulling the parties' previous two marital property agreements, contained a choice of law clause (in favour of application of the law of Germany, where the spouses were habitually resident). In the lower courts' opinion, the latter term went beyond what according to the Marriage Code could be agreed upon in a marital property agreement. The clarification made by the Supreme Court is in line with earlier case law from courts of appeal, according to which a court upon registration

---

[67] See A Agell, *Nordisk äktenskapsrätt, En jämförande studie av dansk, finsk, isländsk, norsk och svensk rätt med diskussion av reformbehov och harmoniseringsmöjligheter* (Copenhagen, Nord, 2003) 171.

[68] See Marriage Code c 9, s 2.1 and above section I.D.i.

[69] Ibid, s 13.

[70] Since a law reform in 1973, Swedish law does not provide the institution of legal separation (or marriage annulment). Only divorce is available in Sweden, during the lifetime of both spouses. See the answer concerning Swedish law in K Boele-Woelki, B Braat and I Sumner (eds), *European Family Law in Action*, Vol I: *Grounds for Divorce* (Antwerp, Intersentia, 2003) 52–53.

[71] See Agell and Brattström, *Äktenskap, Samboende, Partnerskap*, above n 29, 137.

should only focus on essentials. It has, for example, not been considered a sufficient reason to refuse registration because the content of the agreement is difficult to interpret.[72] This by now well-established position can be expected to be followed by the National Taxation Authority, which, since 1 October 2011 decides whether registration can be granted or not. Of relevance is that a decision by this authority regarding registration can be appealed to court.

The Supreme Court decision NJA 1997 p 37, mentioned above, was also a private international law case. During the course of their marriage the spouses, who had remained Swedish citizens, became German residents. In this new situation the spouses wished to annul their two previous marital property agreements, supplementing each other, and their contents following what is provided for under the Swedish Marriage Code, and to be subject to German law in their marital property relations. For this purpose they had made a new marital property agreement, which they wished to register with a Swedish court. Although Swedish private international law legislation—the Act (1990:272) on International Questions Concerning Spouses' and Cohabitees' Property Relations—permits parties a choice of law in favour of application of the law of the state of the habitual residence or nationality of a spouse, the Act only stipulates that such a choice must be made in writing.[73] In other words, under Swedish law a party choice of law is not required to be in the form of a registered marital property agreement to be legally valid.[74] The provisions of the Marriage Code concerning marital property agreements do not refer to terms on choice of law, or take into account situations where the marital property agreement has been drafted in accordance with a foreign law.

The Supreme Court emphasised the parties' need in this case to register their agreement, annulling the previous marital property agreements. That their new agreement also included a choice of law clause was, in the Court's opinion, not sufficient as to prevent registration.[75]

The procedure upon registration is based upon written documentation, and no oral hearing takes place.

ii. A Certain Basic Control Concerning the Substance is Included

Nevertheless, Swedish case law—in particular the Supreme Court judgment NJA 1970 p 320—provides that registration is to be refused if the agreement has contents

---

[72] See the appellate court decisions (second instance) RH 1985:95 and RH 1992:49.

[73] See s 3 of the 1990 Act.

[74] In 2006, the Nordic states (Denmark, Finland, Iceland, Norway and Sweden) agreed to introduce provisions on party choice of law regarding the law applicable to matrimonial property relations into the Nordic Convention on Rules of Private International Law Concerning Marriage, Adoption and Guardianship, originally of 1931. The new rules came into force on 1 December 2008. As regards Sweden, it was agreed that a formally valid party choice of law needs only to be in writing. See Regulation (1931:429) on Certain International Questions Concerning Marriage, Adoption and Guardianship, ss 3–4.

[75] From the point of view of private international law and the needs of the parties in cross-border cases, the reasoning of the Supreme Court gives very limited guidance. See M Jänterä-Jareborg, 'Utlandsanknytning, äktenskapsförord och lagvalsavtal—Självklarheter och oklarheter' in A Agell and M Jänterä-Jareborg (eds), *Familjerättsliga studier, Vänbok till Åke Saldeen, De lege, Juridiska fakulteten i Uppsala Årsbok 2003* (Uppsala, Iustus Förlag, 2004) 125–27.

which clearly go beyond the scope provided by the law concerning what the spouses (and future spouses) may agree in the form of a marital property agreement.

In NJA 1970 p 320 the spouses had agreed that each spouse's property would be the owner spouse's 'separate property', but that all property would gradually, during the first 10 years of the marriage, become 'marital property'. Registration of this marital property agreement was refused,[76] as it was not possible to register an agreement stipulating the successive transformation of property from 'separate' to 'marital' during the course of the marriage. As has already been pointed out, in Swedish law, marital property agreements serve only the purpose of directly classifying property as 'separate' or as 'marital', with a focus on future property division.[77]

According to prevailing opinion, Swedish law also does not permit marital property contracts where spouses (or future spouses) stipulate that the classification of the property in a future property division shall depend upon the ground of dissolution of the marriage, for example that property shall be 'marital property' when property division is occasioned by the death of a spouse, but 'separate property' in case of divorce.[78] In this respect, the Swedish position is more restrictive than that of the other Nordic countries where, today, such terms are permitted.[79] Swedish law alone has maintained the original position of the Nordic deferred community property regime, designed in the early 1900s.

On the other hand, if a marriage is dissolved by the death of either spouse, the starting point in Sweden's Inheritance Code Chapter 3 section 1, is that the whole estate of the deceased spouse goes to the surviving spouse, irrespective of whether the spouses' property is 'marital property' or 'separate property'. No property division needs, therefore, to take place. The surviving spouse has an extensive right of disposal of the other spouse's property which he or she has inherited, even if that property had been made 'separate' through the spouses' marital property agreement. This is, generally, considered to be the justification for why spouses may not stipulate in a marital property agreement that property shall be 'marital property' only in case of a spouse's death.[80] The spouses' joint children only inherit once the surviving spouse has died.

If, however, the first deceased spouse leaves children who are not the spouses' joint children, or if the deceased spouse has left a will to contrary effect, the surviving spouse is not entitled to the whole estate. Instead, a property division shall be carried out in accordance with the Marriage Code.[81] Property that qualifies as 'separate property' falls outside the property division. Nevertheless, a special provision of the Marriage Code entitles the surviving spouse to request that no division of the spouses' 'marital property' should take place; alternatively, that only part of

---

[76] See Teleman, *Äktenskapsförord*, above n 52, 35. According to Agell, *Nordisk äktenskapsrätt*, above n 65, 179, the outcome in a case like this might be different today, considering the 1987 revision of the Marriage Code and the application of the 'five- year-rule'. See below, section II.F.

[77] See above, section I.B.

[78] See Agell, *Nordisk äktenskapsrätt*, above n 67, 183–84.

[79] Ibid, 169–89.

[80] Ibid, 183–84.

[81] Marriage Code c 9, s 5.

their 'marital property' should be divided.[82] The effects of this kind of a request, which must be respected, resemble those of a marital property agreement, in the sense that the surviving spouse will be able to keep all of his or her property as if it had been 'separate property'.[83]

D. What Spouses May Agree Upon

i. The Close Link with the Default Regime

What the spouses (or future spouses) may agree in the form of a marital property agreement is regulated in Chapter 7, section 3 of the Marriage Code:

> By means of a marital property agreement, spouses or prospective spouses may determine that property belonging or accruing to either of them is to be that person's separate property. By means of a new agreement, spouses may determine that such property is to be marital property.

It follows that spouses' (and future spouses') freedom of contract regarding their marital property relations is totally adjusted to Sweden's default property regime, namely the deferred community property regime.[84] According to the quoted provision, the applicability of this regime can be set aside in relation to certain (or all) property of one of the spouses or both spouses, through the spouses' (or future spouses') marital property agreement. The parties can set the default regime aside as a whole, by stipulating that all property—present and future—shall be the owner's 'separate property', including any income or gain of the property. In that case the marital property agreement, in fact, introduces full separation of property into the marriage. As a result, upon divorce, no property division needs to take place between the spouses.[85] The spouses can also choose to stipulate that certain property—present or future, of one or both spouses—shall be the owner spouse's 'separate property'. In that case, only the agreed property falls outside the scope of the deferred community property regime. In addition, unilateral terms limited to the property of only one spouse, are permitted. These options create a considerable degree of flexibility in the system, in spite of the permitted contractual freedom's close link to the default regime.

As has been pointed out earlier, a Swedish marital property agreement has no effect on the ownership of property during marriage. Irrespective of whether a spouse's property is agreed to be his or her 'separate property' or 'marital property', the owner spouse remains the sole owner of that property. A marital property agreement is, therefore, not the proper instrument to transfer property from one

---

[82] Ibid c 12, s 2. According to Act (1990:272) on International Questions Concerning the Property Relations of Spouses and Cohabitees, s 10, this option is available in Sweden also when the spouses' marital property relations are governed by foreign law.

[83] See Agell and Brattström, *Äktenskap, Samboende, Partnerskap*, above n 29, 235–38. See also Governmental Bill 1986/87:1, 88.

[84] See also Scherpe, 'Privatautonomie im Familienrecht der nordischen Länder', above n 40, 222.

[85] If, however, the other spouse wishes to take over the matrimonial home or household goods belonging to the other spouse as that spouse's 'separate property', a property division covering those goods needs to be carried out. See above, section I.D.ii.

spouse to the other spouse. If the spouses have agreed, for example, that property which in fact belongs to the husband shall be the wife's 'separate property', difficult questions of interpretation arise. Since gifts between spouses become legally valid once the gift has been registered at competent authority,[86] it has been suggested that such a stipulation should be respected as including a gift from the owner spouse to the other spouse.[87] In a recent appellate court judgment, the Court found that a previous family home was jointly owned by the former spouses, despite the fact that the wife was recorded as the sole owner in the land registry, and that according to the spouses' marital property agreement all property was 'separate property'. In the Court's opinion, the criteria for so-called caveat ('hidden') joint ownership were fulfilled.[88]

A typical contractual clause in a Swedish marital property agreement is a term that certain assets—or all property belonging to a spouse or expected to be accrued by a spouse in the future—shall be the owner spouse's 'separate property'. It is estimated that 90 per cent of registered agreements contain such terms.[89] It is not uncommon for such a clause to relate to property that a spouse has inherited or received through gift or will from a third person (for example, parents) or may in the future inherit or receive by gift or will.[90] It is also common to stipulate that, in addition, property that may replace a spouse's 'separate property' shall be 'separate property',[91] together with any income or gain of that property.

Once the spouses have registered a marital property agreement introducing separation of property, in whole or in part, they may always register a new agreement where they stipulate that that property (ie, the property made 'separate' in the previous marital property agreement) shall be 'marital property'.[92] This agreement reintroduces the deferred community property regime into the marriage in respect of the property concerned.

The spouses may *not* create a regime of their own; such agreements should not be granted registration. Their freedom is basically limited to the right, in the form of a marital property agreement, to classify their property as 'separate' or 'marital'.[93]

---

[86] Marriage Code c 8, s 1.

[87] Teleman, *Äktenskapsförord*, above n 52, 59–60. Gifts between spouses no longer (since the 1987 reform) require the form of a marital property agreement, but must still be registered to receive full legal effects.

[88] See Svea Hovrätt, case T 8713–09, judgment 29 December 2010. For further information on Swedish law concerning caveat joint ownership between spouses or cohabitees, see Jänterä-Jareborg, 'Regulation of Cohabitation', above n 3, 222–23.

[89] The rest of the registered agreements reintroduce the deferred community property regime to property made separate in an earlier marital property agreement. See Agell and Brattström, *Äktenskap, Samboende, Partnerskap*, above n 29, 137.

[90] Another way of achieving this result is that the third person from whom the property comes stipulates it as a condition for his or her gift or will that the property shall be the recipient's separate property. Such stipulations are common in Sweden, in particular when parents donate or leave property to their children.

[91] See also Marriage Code c 7, s 2.1 p 6, which gives the same result.

[92] See Marriage Code c 7, s 3.1, and above, section II.A.

[93] In addition, Swedish law permits the spouses to carry out a property division during a prevailing marriage which makes it possible for them to realise each other's marital property claim in the deferred community property. See *Governmental Bill* 1986/87:1, 53 and Agell and Brattström, *Äktenskap, Samboende, Partnerskap*, above n 29, 159.

The purpose of these restrictions is to safeguard transparency and predictability.[94] The terms should be clear and it should be possible to identify the property referred to. The Marriage Code contains no alternative marital property regimes for the parties to choose instead of the deferred community property regime. It is also not possible to limit in time the validity of a marital property contract.[95] On the other hand, nothing prevents the spouses from achieving this by frequently revising and registering a new marital property agreement, replacing the previous one. In long marriages of wealthy spouses, one can find a chain of registered marital property agreements.

> **Example:** Preceding their marriage the spouses agree that all their property—present and future—shall be the owner's 'separate property'. The agreement is registered upon marriage. Five years later the spouses register a new marital property agreement in which they stipulate that the matrimonial home (real estate), owned by the husband, shall be his 'marital property', along with a specified[96] amount of money belonging to the husband. After yet another five years, the spouses register a new agreement where they stipulate that all the property, which either one of them owns, shall be 'marital property'.

It is, likewise, possible for the spouses during the course of the marriage to successively reduce the scope of the default regime, transferring more and more property from 'marital' into 'separate property'.

One can understand the motives behind such successive agreements. Still, their drafting occasionally shows amazing defects, even when a lawyer has been in charge. It can, for example, remain unclear whether the new agreement aims to replace or to supplement a previous agreement.

> **Example:** The spouses register a marital property agreement according to which all property, present and future, as well as any income, profit or gain of the property, shall be the owner spouse's 'separate property', with exceptions specified in the agreement. The exceptions consist of the spouses' summer house and city apartment, owned by the husband, which are stipulated to be 'marital property'. A few years later the husband donates half of the summer house and the city apartment to the wife; the gift is registered according to the provisions of the Marriage Code concerning gifts between spouses. Yet, a few years later, the spouses register a marital property agreement where they first agree that the new agreement replaces the previous marital property agreement, after which the husband stipulates that all his property shall be 'marital property'. If the new agreement is to replace the previous one, one wonders what now applies regarding the property owned by the wife!

ii. Statistics

The following data concerning the five-year period 2003–07 shows that the number of registered marital property agreements was on average 25–35 per cent in relation to marriages concluded each year.[97] This does not, however, mean that that

---

[94] See further, Agell and Brattström, *Äktenskap, Samboende, Partnerskap*, above n 29, 95–96.

[95] See NJA 1970, 320, described above in section II.C.ii.

[96] The amount of money must be specified. It follows that it is not sufficient to merely refer to money deposited on a certain bank account.

[97] These statitistics have been gathered by K Walleng, as part of a research project. They have been published previously, as part of the Swedish national report, in Boele-Woelki, Braat and Curry-Sumner (eds) *European Family Law*, above n 1, 1188.

percentage of the new marriages included a marital property agreement. On the contrary, registrations of the marital property agreements concern, in many cases, marriages celebrated earlier. The newly registered contracts may also aim to supplement, replace or annul an earlier registered marital property agreement between the spouses. Nevertheless, even if the numbers go up or down from one year to another, there is an increasing trend in making marital property agreements compared to what applied some decades ago.[98]

Year	Couples entering into marriage	Registered property agreements	Prescription separate property	Prescription marital property
2003	39,041	13,590	12,483	1,107
2004	43,088	10,949	9,684	1,265
2005	44,381	9,738	8,858	880
2006	45,551	9,746	8,971	793
2007	47,898	10,464	9,573	891

E. No Requirements of Disclosure or Legal Advice

i. The Reasons for Non-Disclosure

Spouses and future spouses are not required to disclose their assets (and debts) before making a marital property agreement. One explanation for this is that marriage, as such, does not create any co-ownership of property between the spouses. The effects of a marital property agreement are, basically, limited to a future division of the spouses' property, for example due to divorce. How much a spouse on that occasion can claim to receive from the other spouse's 'marital property' depends on the value of the owner spouse's 'marital property' at the time of divorce.

It is, nevertheless, true that the Marriage Code contains a general provision obliging the spouses to supply each other with the information needed to enable the financial circumstances of the family to be assessed.[99] Failure to comply with these rules, however, has no legal consequences, but is regarded as a kind of a 'moral guideline' for the spouses.[100] Furthermore, it aims to make it clear that both spouses are expected to contribute to the well-being and maintenance of the family. The rule cannot be invoked in support of disclosure as a condition of the validity of a matrimonial property agreement in case of dispute.[101]

In cross-border cases, where the other concerned jurisdiction requests disclosure, a kind of a 'semi-disclosure' is occasionally chosen by the parties upon drafting a

---

[98] See Agell and Brattström, *Äktenskap, Samboende, Partnerskap*, above n 29, 137.

[99] Marriage Code c 1, s 4. Upon property division due to divorce, each spouse has the duty to account for his or her property, ibid c 9, s 3.

[100] See Agell and Brattström, *Äktenskap, Samboende, Partnerskap*, above n 29, 149.

[101] According to Teleman, false information given by one party to the other could give rise to an adjustment of the marital property agreement; see Teleman, *Äktenskapsförord*, above n 52, 91.

marital property agreement in accordance with Swedish law. The owner (or a future owner) of property may, for example, wish to exclude his or her property from property division, while at the same time it may be important to secure the validity of the marital property agreement in the other jurisdiction. Such a party gives an indication to the other party of the approximate nature or amount of his or her wealth, without specifying it precisely. The parties then agree not to request a more specific disclosure from each other, but to follow the Swedish practice in this respect.

The lack of disclosure has not been considered to be a problem under the Swedish system. On the contrary, it seems to be a common opinion that 'nobody should marry for money', meaning that it should be irrelevant what one's future spouse owns. A not unusual opinion, not least among the wealthier, is that it would be 'embarrassing' to account for one's property upon marriage. Non-disclosure is also not considered problematic when a marital property agreement is entered during the marriage, since a marital property contract cannot be used to change ownership of property. In short, the kind of 'emotionality' that is reported to surround, in particular, the conclusion of pre-nuptial agreements in England, is absent in Sweden.

There would seem to be wide acceptance in Sweden, irrespective of the amount of property at stake, that it is fair to exclude, through a marital property agreement, property brought by a spouse into the marriage, as well as property that a spouse inherits or receives as gift during the marriage, from a future property division.[102] Likewise, it appears to be more controversial to exclude in this manner property acquired during the marriage. It is another story how the parties feel about the effects of a marital property agreement upon divorce. In that situation, both may wish to strive for the most favourable outcome from their personal perspective.

ii. Legal Advice is not Obligatory

Swedish law does not require the parties to have had any legal advice before concluding a marital property agreement, individually or jointly, although many spouses (and future spouses) consult legal experts with regard to such agreements. Nor does Swedish law require the assistance of a notary. In fact, in Sweden there exists no notary institution in the continental European sense. The spouses are instead free to draft the agreement themselves and to apply for registration on their own. Often spouses are content with using standard forms, available from well-stocked bookshops and on the internet. These kinds of agreements become binding once they are signed and registered.

This state of affairs under Swedish law finds an explanation in the requirement of registration as the condition for the agreement's binding nature.[103] As has been explained earlier, upon registration the competent authority carries out a certain basic control. Furthermore, the permitted terms regarding the marital property relations are, at least formally, generally the same, since they are restricted to categorising the concerned property as 'separate' or 'marital'. In this sense, a certain kind of a 'compulsory model' exists. It should also be emphasised that it has been a deliberate

---

[102] See Agell, *Nordisk äktenskapsrätt*, above n 67, 170.
[103] See Agell and Brattström, *Äktenskap, Samboende, Partnerskap*, above n 29, 137.

policy in Sweden to have a family law regulation which the parties can manage on their own, without engaging experts.[104]

The strict form requirements relating to marital property agreements are to ensure that an agreement will only be concluded after a careful and comprehensive consideration of the need for it and its effects. Case law contains examples where the fulfilment of such requirements appears to have been doubtful. An example is a case decided by the Supreme Court, NJA 1983 p 775. A man of Swedish nationality and a woman of Spanish nationality were married in Spain in 1967 after only a short acquaintance. The couple established their habitual residence in Sweden. In 1970, upon the initiative of the husband, the spouses made a marital property agreement stipulating that all the husband's property was to be his 'separate property'. The agreement was registered with the court in 1975. The marriage was dissolved by divorce in 1980. The ex-wife initiated court proceedings alleging that the agreement should be declared invalid, inter alia, because it would be contrary to good faith and honour to recognise it since she had not understood its contents or legal effects.

The Supreme Court found that the wife—some 16 years after the celebration of the marriage—had very poor knowledge of the Swedish language and that she, evidently, had not been able to understand the terms of the agreement. On the other hand, it was not in the Court's opinion evident that the husband had realised at the time of concluding the agreement that the circumstances were such that it would be against good faith and honour to give effect to the agreement. Special importance was given to the fact that the husband, before the marriage, through other Spanish-speaking tourists in Spain had explained to the wife (to-be) that she would not get a share of his property through the planned marriage.

On the other hand, it could be claimed that even marital property agreements entered into with the assistance of a lawyer often follow a standard model, without reflecting the particular circumstances of the marriage and the reason to conclude a matrimonial property agreement. Since it is difficult—or even impossible—to foresee what the property situation of the spouses will be in a future property division, taking place years or even decades after the agreement was concluded, adjustment of the agreement could provide a way out of an unreasonable outcome. The Supreme Court precedent on this issue, NJA 1993 p 583, shows, however, that Swedish courts are reluctant to interfere with or adjust agreements.[105]

F. Situations of Adjustment by Competent Authority

i. When the Default Regime Applies

The effects of the deferred community property system can be far-reaching and questionable, in particular when a short marriage ends in divorce and one spouse owns a lot of property and the other spouse much less. A special provision in the Marriage Code, added in 1987, deals with situations like this. In so far as it would be unreasonable, in view especially of the duration of the marriage and the spouses' financial situation and overall circumstances, for one spouse to surrender property

---

[104] See Governmental Bill 1986/87:1, 44.
[105] See below, section II.F.ii.

to the other spouse, to the extent specified under the general rules, the property shall instead be divided in such a way as to enable the first-mentioned spouse to retain more of his or her marital property.[106]

This provision operates as a corrective to the main rule of equal division of the value of the 'marital property', in favour of the spouse to whom most of this property belongs, in order to enable him or her to keep more of it. It has been drafted with the purpose of preventing a spouse from 'divorcing for money' after a short marriage and to protect the wealthier spouse.[107] As regards the relevant length of the marriage, according to a statement in the Governmental Bill to the Marriage Code, the provision should apply until somewhere around five years of marriage (including cohabitation preceding the marriage) after which time all 'marital property' should normally be divided equally.[108] This recommendation has been respected in case law. The Governmental Bill, nevertheless, emphasises that the spouses' joint dwelling and household goods should normally be divided equally, if they are 'marital property', irrespective of the length of the marriage.

In the Supreme Court decision NJA 1998 p 487, the Court permitted the wife to exempt half of her 'marital property' from the property division by reference to the fact that the spouses' marriage had been short—it had lasted for three years, after two years of marriage-like cohabitation—and that all the spouses' 'marital property' was owned by the wife, who had inherited it from her father and brother. Three children had been born during the couples' relationship. The 'marital property' consisted mainly of the spouses' joint dwelling, which was real estate inherited by the wife from her father. Interestingly enough, the Supreme Court did not follow the above-mentioned recommendation of equal division of the spouses' joint dwelling. The circumstances of a case like this were, in other words, not such as to justify it.

ii. When there is a Marital Property Agreement

Often the legal effects of a marital property agreement become apparent only when property division is to be carried out, years or maybe even decades after the agreement was made. Hardly surprisingly, in a divorce, the core of the problem is that property, which otherwise would have been included in the property division, has been made 'separate' by the marital property agreement. The spouses may, for example, have determined that all property shall be 'separate property', but when the marriage is dissolved it turns out that one spouse has considerable property acquired during the marriage whereas the other spouse has not increased his or her property during the marriage. If the marital property agreement is respected as it is, the spouse with less property will receive nothing from the other spouse. Another situation which, depending on the circumstances, can be problematic is when the spouses have stipulated that the property of one of the spouses shall be his or her 'separate property', whereas the property of the other spouse remains 'marital property'. On divorce, the spouse with 'marital property' may find it unreasonable to

---

[106] Marriage Code c 12, s 1.
[107] See Agell and Brattström, *Äktenskap, Samboende, Partnerskap*, above n 29, 187–96.
[108] Governmental Bill 1986/87:1, 187.

share in the property division the net value of all his or her property equally with the other spouse when that other spouse's property is not included in the division.[109]

In principle, if the result would otherwise be unreasonable, the Marriage Code permits adjustment of the marital property contract:

> If a term of a marital property agreement is unreasonable in view of the subject-matter of the agreement, the circumstances when it was drawn up, circumstances subsequently arising and the overall circumstances, it may be adjusted or disregarded in the division of property.[110]

Such adjustment, which in an extreme case can result in setting the marital property agreement aside, can be made by a court-appointed property division executor or by the court itself, upon application by a spouse.[111] To the extent that terms in the marital property agreement are set aside, the default regime becomes applicable.

The cited provision focuses on whether the agreement is unreasonable due to (a) its content, (b) the circumstances at the time of its conclusion, (c) subsequent circumstances, and (d) overall circumstances. According to the Governmental Bill preceding the 1987 Marriage Code, this provision aims at protecting the financially weaker spouse from receiving no property at all, in particular in the case of a long marriage, while the other spouse ends up with a considerable amount of property.[112] Nevertheless, the Bill also emphasises the need for restrictive application. The starting point is that a marital property agreement expresses the parties' joint will and should be respected, even when it is concluded to the disadvantage of one of the parties. This recommendation has been followed in subsequent case law.

The Supreme Court judgment NJA 1993 p 583 has set an important precedent in this respect.[113] In this case, the spouses, who had had two children and been married for 11 years, instead of a divorce which they had considered, decided to draw up a marital property agreement introducing full separation of property into the marriage. The initiative was taken by the husband, who at that time was facing considerable economic difficulties in his business enterprise. The wife agreed after certain hesitation, but after having consulted a lawyer. The spouses eventually divorced after a further 12 years, the marriage having lasted altogether 23 years. At the time of the marital property agreement the spouses' assets were of limited value, but at the time of the divorce the husband's property was of considerable value. The wife requested that the court declare the marital agreement void or adjust it. The Court (vote 3-2) maintained the agreement, finding that its terms were not unreasonable at the time of the agreement or with regard to later developments.

---

[109] Marriage Code c 12, s 1 (see above, section II.F.i.) may also be applicable and, in that case, takes priority. See the answers concerning Swedish law in Boele-Woelki, Braat and Curry-Sumner, *European Family Law*, above n 1, 886–87 and 1240–41.

[110] Marriage Code c 12, s 3.

[111] The spouses themselves may also *agree* to do so, Marriage Code c 10, s 4.

[112] Governmental Bill 1986/87:1, 193–94. See also L Tottie, *Äktenskapsbalken och promulgationslag m.m.* (Stockholm, Norstedts Juridik AB, 1990) 447.

[113] The previously mentioned case NJA 1983 p 775 dates back to the old Marriage Code. At that time, any adjustment of a marital property agreement could take place according to general contractual principles, by analogy.

This decision has been criticised in legal literature, but later Swedish case law also demonstrates a limited willingness to adjust or set aside terms of marital property agreements, in cases that also might be claimed to 'deserve' an adjustment.

A recent appellate court judgment (2008) serves as an example.[114] A marital property agreement had been drawn up prior to the marriage, stipulating that all the spouses' (to-be) property—present and future—shall be the owner's 'separate property', including any income, profit or gain of the property. When the agreement was concluded the husband (to-be) owned considerable property, whereas the wife (to-be) had very little property. The agreement was registered at court. After 14 years of marriage the couple divorced. By then, the husband's property had increased in value whereas the wife owned almost nothing. In its judgment the Court of Appeal pointed out that a marital property agreement can only exceptionally be adjusted. In this case, the economic imbalance between the spouses was essentially unchanged upon divorce, compared to what it had been upon the marriage and the conclusion of the agreement. Since it was not proven that the husband's property had increased in value at the expense of the wife, the wife's request of adjustment of the agreement was refused.

In Swedish case law it is difficult to find examples where adjustment of a marital property agreement has been requested and granted for grounds such as the wife's pregnancy, the existence of young joint children, the wife's lack of income due to the spouses' agreement that she should be the home-maker, etc. These kinds of factors may, on the other hand, be of relevance for the normally exceptional post-divorce maintenance to be granted by court order to a former spouse.[115] A marital property agreement concluded as a condition for the marriage or, during marriage as a condition for the continuation of the marriage, would, most likely, be respected.[116]

An exception to the well-established mainstream position is an appellate court judgment of 2002, concerning adjustment of a marital property agreement after the death of the husband.[117] The husband in this case was an extremely well-known Swedish actor who died after 21 years of marriage, leaving his wife (an actress), the couple's two joint children and two children of a previous marriage. Upon marriage the spouses had concluded a marital property agreement stipulating that all property, present and future, as well as any income or gain of the property, was to be the owner spouse's 'separate property'. The surviving spouse requested adjustment, claiming that the agreement was unreasonable to her. The deceased husband's children of the previous marriage denied her request as unfounded, also taking into account that the wife inherited half of her husband's estate (there being no will to

---

[114] Hovrätten för Nedre Norrland, case T 331–8, judgment 19 September 2008.

[115] See above, section I.F.

[116] See Teleman, *Äktenskapsförord*, above n 52, 73–75, with reference to Norwegian case law confirming this position. In these cases, a marital property agreement, favouring the wife, was made in order to 'save the marriage', in the one case because of the husband's abuse of alcohol, and in the other case, because of the husband's extra-marital affair. Upon divorce later on, the husband claimed that the agreement was to be set aside as void, due to its having been concluded under inappropriate pressure on him. The marital property agreements were, nevertheless, respected by the courts who found that the wife had had a sincere wish to save the marriage and that she had not at the time of the conclusion of the agreement planned divorce.

[117] Svea hovrätt, case T 1594–01, judgment 30 May 2002.

contrary effect) before the couple's joint children.[118] In support of her claim the wife referred to the following circumstances:

— Neither of the spouses had understood the legal implications and effects of the agreement, as they were artists.
— When the agreement was concluded the wife was at the beginning of her career. The husband wished her to give up her career, and to take care of the joint home and children.
— The wife had contributed to the value of the property owned by the husband, and the spouses had pooled their resources.
— It had never been the husband's intention to leave the wife without property. He had also spoken of the need to revoke the agreement.

Two witnesses supported the wife's claims. The Court of Appeal set the agreement aside as unreasonable towards the surviving spouse, with regard to the overall circumstances of the case.[119] The Court was not unanimous in its judgment. The Supreme Court decided not to review the case. The outcome in this case has remained an exception, and also in subsequent case law the previous strict line regarding adjustment of marital property agreements has been followed.[120]

G. Spousal Agreements on Post-Divorce Maintenance

As has been pointed out, it is unusual in Sweden for a court to order a spouse to maintain the other spouse after divorce.[121] This position does not, however, prevent spouses from agreeing on post-divorce maintenance. Such agreements are in practice normally limited to the payment of maintenance during a transitional period following the divorce, but may also establish a life-long undertaking by one of the spouses to maintain the other spouse.[122] If the agreement is made during the course of the divorce proceedings, it is often, at the request of the spouses, included in the divorce judgment. The spouses may also agree on maintenance after the divorce judgment is final. To be enforceable, an agreement on maintenance must be made in writing and witnessed by two persons.[123] There is no system for registration of such agreements.

The spouses' agreement is not ex officio controlled by any competent authority. However, upon the application of a spouse, the court may adjust the agreement if it

---

[118] See above, section II.C.ii. concerning the inheritance rights of a surviving spouse.

[119] The Court referred, in particular, to the husband's reported wish to annul the marital property agreement, in addition to the length of the marriage, the wife's contributions as a homemaker, the inbalance in the spouses' ownership of property and the fact that the wife, due to her age and the time that had passed since she had last been gainfully employed, could be presumed to have difficulty in supporting herself independently.

[120] See, eg, Hovrätten för Nedre Norrland, case T 331-8, judgment 19 September 2008, described above.

[121] See above, section I.F.

[122] For further information, see the answers concerning Swedish law in Boele-Woelki, Braat and Sumner (eds) *European Family Law in Action*, above n 46, 474, 484, 490. See also Agell and Brattstrom, *Äktenskap, Samboende, Partnerskap*, above n 29, 54–55.

[123] Code of Execution c 3, s 19.

is found unreasonable in view of the circumstances which existed at the time of the agreement, the overall circumstances or due to changed circumstances.[124]

In the Supreme Court decision NJA 1961 p 124 an agreement between the spouses whereby the wife renounced her right to claim maintenance after the divorce was declared void by the Court. The husband had failed to produce relevant information on his ability to pay maintenance.

III. SEPARATION AGREEMENTS IN ANTICIPATION OF DIVORCE

Under Swedish law spouses may, prior to an impending divorce, enter into an agreement on the subsequent division of property or on other matters relating thereto, a so-called 'pre-agreement' *(föravtal)*.[125] A 'pre-agreement' is an agreement made in anticipation of divorce and it is available for the spouses only if a divorce is immediately approaching. A 'pre-agreement' can be described as an agreement to make an agreement in the near future with certain content, due to the divorce. In their pre-agreement the spouses can, for example, agree that certain assets shall be allocated to one of them at the future division of property, how a deduction of a debt shall then be made or how the assets should be valued.[126] If a spouse, after the divorce proceedings have been commenced, refuses to confirm this agreement, the other spouse can request the court to appoint a property division executor. The property division executor is required to follow the 'pre-agreement', on condition that it is found to be valid and reasonable, or adjust it if on an overall assessment the terms appear unreasonable.

The right to enter into a 'pre-agreement' exists even after the proceedings for divorce have commenced, but before the marriage is dissolved, in spite of the fact that the spouses under Swedish law from that moment on also have the choice of entering into a final agreement on property division. In the Supreme Court decision NJA 2004 p 317 this extension in time was justified with reference to the need to promote agreement between spouses. If the spouses in a 'pre-agreement' have stipulated that certain assets shall be transferred from one spouse to the other, this does not have any effect against third parties, such as the spouses' creditors, until the pre-agreement has been confirmed by the spouses in a formal application for divorce.[127] The agreement must be drafted in writing and signed by both spouses. No requirements of registration apply.

IV. CONFLICT OF LAWS

A. Validity of Foreign Marital Property Agreements

As regards the validity of foreign marital property agreements, a distinction needs to be made between the formal validity of the agreement and its validity in substance, ie, what the parties may validly agree upon. The relevant provisions

---

[124] Marriage Code c 6, s 11.
[125] Ibid c 9, s 13.
[126] Tottie, *Äktenskapsbalken* above n 112, 282–86.
[127] See Supreme Court decisions NJA 1974 p 684 and NJA 1985 p 432.

in Swedish law[128] are found in s 5 of the Act (1990:272) on International Questions Concerning the Property Relations of Spouses and Cohabitees (the 1990 Act).[129]

The form requirements are subject to alternative solutions. To be formally valid, the marital property agreement must fulfil the form requirements of either (a) the law that applied to the spouses' marital property relations at the time of the agreement, or (b) those applicable in the jurisdiction where the agreement was made, or (c) those applicable in the jurisdiction where both spouses at the time of the agreement were habitually resident.[130] The validity as regards substance, on the other hand, is assessed in accordance with the law that at the time of the agreement governed the spouses' marital property relations. This law may be the law chosen by the parties (see below). In the absence of a party choice of law, so-called secondary choice of law rules apply.[131] If the agreement is concluded before the marriage, it is valid if it is regarded so according to the law that upon marriage becomes applicable to the couple's marital property relations. Nevertheless, if the marital property agreement is entered into between the spouses who at the time of the agreement are habitually resident in Sweden, it is regarded as valid in Sweden only if it is registered in Sweden in accordance with the provisions of the Swedish Marriage Code.[132]

A marital property agreement which has either been concluded abroad or concluded in Sweden but in accordance with foreign law, is valid and enforceable in Sweden if it fulfils the above-mentioned requirements of form and substance. If the property division later on takes place in Sweden, the marital property agreement may be adjusted in accordance with provisions of the Swedish Marriage Code.[133]

B. Party Choice of Law

The basic choice of law rule of the 1990 Act confirms party autonomy.[134] The parties may choose the law of a country with which at least one of them is connected, at

---

[128] The special Nordic conflict of laws regime will not be discussed in this contribution; see above n 74. The inter-Nordic rules concerning matrimonial property relations apply only on condition that (i) both spouses are citizens of Nordic states and (ii) that this applied also at the time of the marriage and (iii) that the spouses at the time of the marriage took residence in one of the Nordic states and are still residents of these states. For further information, see E Meurling, 'Less Surprises for Spouses Moving Within the Nordic Countries? Amendments to the 1931 Nordic Convention on Marriage' (2009) XI *Yearbook of Private International Law* 385–94.

[129] This Act was originally restricted to spouses. The Act's original 1990 version is described by M Jänterä-Jareborg, 'Rights of Property upon Divorce in Swedish Conflict of Laws' in N Lowe and G Douglas (eds), *Families Across Frontiers* (The Hague/Boston/London, Martinus Nijhoff Publishers, 1996) 793–805. See also M Jänterä-Jareborg, 'Egendomsförhållanden i internationella äktenskap. Om frihet att avtala om tillämplig lag samt om lagvalsfrihetens risker för make och borgenär' (1994) 79 *Svensk Juristtidning* 433–63. The Act was revised in 2001 (SFS 2001:1141), to cover also property relations of cohabitees. In addition, it was supplemented then by rules on recognition and enforcement of foreign decisions.

[130] 1990 Act, s 5.1–5.2.

[131] In the absence of a (valid) party choice of law (or a marital property agreement which includes an implicit party choice of law), matrimonial property relations are governed by the law of the country in which both spouses established their first joint habitual residence. If both of them, during the course of their marriage, change their habitual residence to another country, the law of that country replaces the previously applicable law in full after two years' residence. See s 4 of the 1990 Act.

[132] 1990 Act, s 5.3. Since 1 October 2011, registration in Sweden takes place at the National Taxation Agency (*Skatteverket*).

[133] This is explicitly provided by s 10 of the 1990 Act.

[134] 1990 Act, s 3.

the time of the designation, either by habitual residence or by nationality. Applicable law may be chosen (a) before the marriage, (b) during the marriage, and (c) after the marriage until the property division has taken place.[135] Only one country's law may be chosen and this law must then cover the matrimonial property relations as a whole.[136] It follows that a choice of law agreement between the spouses, made during the course of the marriage, also covers all previously acquired property. The parties' designation of the applicable law retains its validity irrespective of later changes in the spouses' habitual residence or nationality, until the spouses by mutual agreement revoke it or replace it by a new agreement.[137] The party choice of law must be made in writing.[138] Although an explicit designation of the applicable law is to be preferred for reasons of clarity, an implicit choice is also acceptable.[139] Such is the case, for example, when on the basis of the terms of a marital property agreement, it is evident that the spouses intended a certain country's law to be applicable. [140]

It is not uncommon that Swedish nationals who are resident abroad prefer to make a marital property agreement in accordance with the Swedish Marriage Code. To achieve this, they first agree in writing on the applicability of Swedish law to their marital property relations. This agreement is then followed by a marital property agreement where the spouses (or spouses-to-be), in whole or in part, stipulate that property owned by them shall be the owner spouse's 'separate property', in accordance with the terminology of the Swedish Marriage Code. To make this agreement binding, the spouses must register it in Sweden. Similar agreements are also popular among Swedish citizens, resident abroad, who marry foreign citizens.

Although there are no statistics on the issue, these kinds of agreements seem to be common among wealthy Swedish nationals residing and marrying in England. It appears to be common (good) practice that both parties, before entering into the agreement, acquire independent legal advice on the position of the law regarding pre- and post-nuptial agreements in both jurisdictions. If a future dispute is to take place in Sweden, for example, in connection with divorce proceedings in Sweden, a Swedish court can be expected to recognise the agreement, on condition that it complies with the provisions of the 1990 Act. The court's judgment can be enforced at least in relation to all property situated in Sweden. Often the parties also stipulate that Swedish courts, to the extent permitted by law, shall have exclusive competence to examine any future disputes between them arising out of their marital property agreement.

According to the 1990 Act a party choice of law is formally valid when concluded in writing and signed by both spouses. If the spouses have validly agreed on the application of Swedish law to their marital property relations and, then, made a marital property agreement in accordance with Swedish law, Swedish law can be expected to govern the effect of the marriage on the spouses' property even if the

---

[135] See M Jänterä-Jareborg, 'Utlandsanknytning, äktenskapsförord och lagvalsavtal', above n 75, 113 and M Bogdan, *Svensk internationell privat- och processrätt*, 7th edn (Stockholm, Norstedts, 2008) 204.

[136] Governmental Bill 1989/90:87, 42.

[137] Ibid, 41.

[138] 1990 Act s 3.

[139] Governmental Bill 1989/90:87 at 41.

[140] See M Jänterä-Jareborg, 'Utlandsanknytning, äktenskapsförord och lagvalsavtal', above n 75, 119–20.

marital property agreement is declared void in a future dispute, for example, due to a formal defect.

> **Example:** A Swedish man marries a German woman in Spain. On the day of their wedding the spouses in Spain, upon the husband's initiative, conclude a marital property agreement where they (a) stipulate that Swedish law is applicable to their marital property relations and (b) that all property will be the owner spouse's 'separate property'. Upon marriage the couple settle in Belgium. Divorce proceedings are initiated few years later in Sweden where the husband is now habitually resident. The question arises whether the marital property agreement is valid. Since it does not meet the form requirements of Swedish law—no registration had taken place in Sweden[141]—or of the laws of either Spain (where the agreement was concluded) or Belgium (where the spouses upon marriage took residence)—no notary had contributed to the drafting of the agreement—the agreement is found to be invalid. It should follow, due to the spouses' valid choice of Swedish law as the governing law, that Sweden's deferred community property system is then applicable, meaning equal division of all the spouses' property at the date of the divorce proceedings, contrary to the intention of the husband to exclude all property from division. Evidently, spouses should also take requirements of form most seriously in cross-border cases.

C. Marital Property Agreements with Additional Terms

In cross-border cases spouses (or future spouses) sometimes wish to conclude an agreement which, in addition to terms on marital property relations in accordance with the private autonomy granted by the Swedish Marriage Code, also contains terms relating to post-divorce maintenance, rights to the marital home upon divorce, or the welfare of the couple's children. In these cases, the inspiration comes from corresponding agreements in the jurisdiction where the parties reside. As a rule, one of the parties is a Swedish citizen and the parties wish to register the agreement in Sweden. These kinds of 'additional terms' are regarded as dubious by many Swedish lawyers, partly because they concern issues which are mandatorily regulated in Swedish domestic law and partly because such terms do not form a natural part of a marital property agreement under Swedish law. Ordinary Swedish lawyers also find it difficult to understand the point behind such terms and ask, in discussions on the topic, questions such as 'Is the purpose of these terms to buy him a wife/her a husband?' As a result of all these concerns, many lawyers doubt whether a marital property agreement including such terms can be granted registration in Sweden.

 This example illustrates how difficult it is for national lawyers with limited international experience to assess anything that deviates from the dominant 'domestic model'. Still, it should not be a surprise for anybody that cross-border cases unavoidably will carry with them elements that are unknown in one's own jurisdiction. Since the agreement also contains terms on marital property relations, in accordance with the Swedish Marriage Code, registration should in my opinion be

---

[141] An application for registration must be made before the divorce proceedings are initiated; see above, section II.B.iv.

granted,[142] and I do not know of any cases where registration has been refused on a ground like this. On the contrary, there appears to be plenty of cases where such agreements have passed the courts' registration test. [143] At the same time, it should be emphasised that the inclusion of these additional terms in a registered marital property contract is by no means any guarantee of their validity or binding nature. Questions of post-divorce maintenance, rights to the family home and the welfare of the child are governed in Swedish law by other sets of rules, including rules of private international law for cross-border cases.[144]

The point of departure is that non-permitted terms, or terms which do not belong to a *Swedish* marital property agreement, do not as such make the whole marital property agreement invalid. Normally, only the non-permitted terms will be considered to be without legal effect, while the agreement otherwise can be recognised as valid and enforceable, achieving the agreed legal effects upon the property division.[145]

All in all, however, there is a striking need for judgments by the appellate courts and the Supreme Court openly addressing the challenges brought about by cross-border cases, and for an active legal debate on these issues.[146]

V. CONCLUSION

A. Issues under Debate in Sweden

Apart from the recent reform of transferring registration of marital property agreements from courts to an administrative authority (Swedish National Taxation Agency, Skatteverket), Swedish law in this field seems to be well established. No other initiatives for a law reform have been taken by the Swedish Government or are pending in Parliament. Nevertheless, in the legal literature, criticism has been raised in particular with regard to the following issues.[147]

---

[142] The Supreme Court precedent NJA 1997 p 37, described above in section II.C.i., also supports such an interpretation. In its decision the Court emphasised the spouses' legitimate interest in registering a marital property agreement, although it also contained a stipulation not included within the parties' autonomy as regards the terms of a marital property agreement under the Marriage Code.

[143] Such agreements have been registered, for example, at Stockholm City Court (Stockholms tingsrätt).

[144] It follows that the court may be obliged to apply foreign law to these issues. In that case, the content of the foreign law becomes decisive for the agreement's validity.

[145] See Agell and Brattström, *Äktenskap, Samboende, Partnerskap*, above n 29, 151 and Teleman, *Äktenskapsförord*, above n 52, 65.

[146] In my opinion, the Supreme Court in its judgment in NJA 1997, p 37 missed an opportunity to address such issues. As a result, the judgment is commented on in the legal literature often as if the case was purely domestic. The spouses' interest in annulling their previous Swedish marital property agreements in favour of a choice of law clause to German law was not analysed. See M Jänterä-Jareborg, 'Utlandsanknytning, äktenskapsförord och lagvalsavtal', above n 75, 125–27.

[147] A similar discussion is at present taking place in Finland and is, in part, of direct relevance regarding the Swedish regulation. See, eg, P Välimäki, 'Är den oinskränkta giftorätten föräldrad?' (2007) 143 *Tidskrift utgiven av Juridiska Föreningen i Finland* 1–17, and M Helin, 'Onko aviovarallisuusjärjestelmämme vanhentunut?' (2010) 108 *Lakimies* 1310–25.

i. The Excessiveness of the Deferred Community Property Regime

The 'all-inclusive' scope of the deferred community property regime under Swedish law has been questioned.[148] For example, one may well ask whether the ideology of the early 1900s justifying the inclusion of all property, irrespective of when and how it has been acquired, can still be justified in a society where almost all women are gainfully employed and where the independence and individual responsibility of each spouse is, as a rule, emphasised in all areas of law. In Sweden most spouses today have economic wealth of a quality that was earlier reserved for only the wealthier classes of society (houses, cars, capital). It follows that upon a divorce there will be property to share. Today, spouses also often have children from previous relationships. It is estimated that approximately half of the marriages that are now celebrated in Sweden will be terminated by divorce. Should property which the spouses bring into the marriage, along with property which a spouse inherits or receives through a gift or a will, not be excluded?

Alternatively, one could ask if the right to claim a share of the other spouse's marital property should be acquired only successively during the marriage, as the years of marriage pass by, and not, as at present, immediately upon marriage.[149] If so, legislation should be reformed to achieve this.

Still, the prevailing system has its merits and may in many cases also be claimed to be superior to any other alternatives.[150] According to this outlook, the necessary correctives are built into the system, such as the right to set the regime aside through a marital property agreement or through adjustment of the outcome of the property division.[151]

ii. The Parties' Contractual Freedom should be Broadened

Another debated issue relates to the contractual freedom of the parties in the form of a marital property contract. With reference to the high divorce rates in Sweden, it has been asked if the law should not be reformed so as to make it possible for spouses to agree that the deferred community property regime shall apply if the marriage is dissolved through the death of a spouse, but not if the marriage is dissolved through divorce.[152] In the latter case the property would in whole or in part be separate property.

iii. Control should be Increased upon Registration

One could furthermore ask whether, upon registration, the competent authority's control of the terms in each marital property agreement should become more

---

[148] See Agell, *Nordisk äktenskapsrätt*, above n 67, 404–12.
[149] See Agell and Brattström, *Äktenskap, Samboende, Partnerskap*, above n 29, 96–97.
[150] See Välimäki, 'Är den oinskränkta giftorätten föråldrad?', above n 147, 15.
[151] See Governmental Bill 1986/87:1, 42–44. Helin, 'Onko aviovarallisuusjärjestelmämme vanhentunut?', above n 147, 1321, points out that it is unrealistic to believe that any matrimonial property regime could meet all needs in all marriages, considering not least the increasing variety of family formations. Marital property agreements remain a necessary tool.
[152] See Agell and Brattström, *Äktenskap, Samboende, Partnerskap*, above n 29, 95–96.

comprehensive. The competent authority could, for example, ascertain that the spouse who, according to the agreement owns certain assets, is the true owner of that property. In other words, registration of a marital property agreement should be developed so that it becomes a guarantee for the agreement's validity, save for situations where, in a later dispute between the spouses, an adjustment of the agreement is justified. Under prevailing law, this is not the case.

The present system is, as a result, criticised for creating a false impression on the parties that any marital property agreement, whatever its terms, becomes binding upon registration. Although registration is necessary for the legal validity of a marital property agreement, it is not a sufficient guarantee that the agreement in full will stand in a future dispute between the spouses on the matter. Upon divorce, either one of the spouses can initiate court proceedings against the other spouse claiming that the agreement, due to its content, is to be set aside as invalid or to be adjusted.

The recent (2011) law reform whereby registration of marital property agreements is transferred from courts to an administrative authority is not in line with this criticism. This reform regarded registration of marital property agreements as a largely formal and administrative function.

iv. There should be a Greater Willingness to Adjust Marital Property Agreements

In Sweden, a registered marital property agreement is normally respected in a property division between the spouses, irrespective of what the parties have stipulated. A spouse who takes a dispute to court wishing to set aside a marital property contract or to have its terms adjusted is according to Swedish case law very seldom successful against the other spouse. The principle of *pacta sunt servanda* applies. On the other hand, it is relatively uncommon for a spouse, after divorce, to initiate legal proceedings contesting a registered agreement's validity due to the terms of the agreement, the circumstances surrounding the agreement or later developments.

The prevailing restrictive case law should in my opinion be reconsidered in favour of increased adjustment. A change in this respect would, most likely, lead to most spouses consulting legal expertise before concluding any agreement, without this being a requirement of law.

B. Cross-Border Cases Require More Attention—an Obstacle to the Free Movement of Persons

Marital property agreements are becoming increasingly common in cross-border situations in Sweden and elsewhere. In Sweden, conclusion of such agreements is facilitated through modern legislation of private international law in the field, ie, the 1990 Act.[153] Nevertheless, this legislation has remained 'an expert's instrument' and general knowledge of it is poor. Case law in Sweden is as yet far too limited to have resulted in increased clarity regarding how the law works in practice. And

---

[153] See above section IV.A–B.

even if the legislation's position is clear on a certain issue, it may still be difficult for Swedish lawyers to foresee how the same issue will be addressed in a foreign jurisdiction, perhaps many years later.

Those spouses—or spouses-to-be—who take steps to conclude a marital property agreement in cross-border cases, at present risk their agreement becoming a 'limping document': although validly concluded and binding under the law of one of the concerned jurisdictions, there is the risk that the agreement will not be recognised or given full legal effect in another jurisdiction. This state of affairs is far from satisfactory. In fact, it prevents the free movement of persons within the European Union, or at least creates a hindrance to free movement. As such, it could be considered to be contrary to EU law, even without any specific union rules on marital property relations.[154] This conclusion is natural and consequent, not least with regard to the EU Court's recent preliminary rulings concerning respect to surnames, validly established under the law of one Member State, in another Member State with which the parties had a close connection (through nationality or habitual residence) with completely different rules on surnames.[155] Not to respect a validly established surname constitutes, depending on the circumstances, either direct or reverse discrimination of the person in question, preventing free movement. The same must be considered to apply in respect of spouses who have validly concluded a marital property agreement, when their agreement is not recognised or given full legal effect in another Member State because of that State's domestic outlook on marital property agreements.[156]

---

[154] In March 2011, the EU Commission presented its 'Proposal for a Council Regulation on jurisdiction, applicable law and the recognition and enforcement of decisions in matters of matrimonial property regimes.'

[155] See in particular the Court's rulings in the cases of C-148/02 *Garcia Avello* [2003] ECR I-11613, and C-353/06 *Grunkin-Paul*, [2006] ECR I-3561.

[156] Recognition of a marital property agreement as valid and binding does not exclude adjustment of the agreement if it was to be found to be unreasonable. These are two different aspects to be kept separate.

Marital Agreements and Private Autonomy in the United States[*]

IRA MARK ELLMAN

CONTENTS

---

[*] This draft was submitted on August 14, 2009 and is current to that date. Since then the Commissioners on Uniform State Laws have undertaken a project to revise or replace the Uniform Premarital Agreement Act. The first public draft of the revised act was presented to the Conference in the summer of 2011, and the final draft is expected to be presented for approval in the summer of 2012. The 2011 draft includes new procedural protections that bring it closer to the American Law Institute recommendations described in this article. It also has an optional provision that would allow, in states choosing to adopt it, a challenge to the substance of the agreement as 'unconscionable' at the time enforcement is sought. This chapter's discussion of Uniform Premarital Agreement Act provisions are therefore likely to become inaccurate after the new act's final approval. It is of course not possible to predict now whether or to what extent states will adopt the newly revised act. The Uniform Law Commission maintains a website that provides the text of their acts and a list of adopting states. See http://www.nccusl.org/.

I. DEFAULT RULES THAT APPLY WHEN THERE IS NO AGREEMENT

There are no public programmes in America designed specifically to provide financial assistance to divorced families. Divorced families may of course seek, along with never-married families and everyone else, assistance from any of the hodge-podge of state and federal public welfare programmes for which they may be eligible. In general, of course, the American social safety net is less comprehensive and less generous than European social security systems. The financial welfare of divorced families is thus largely a matter for private law.

The rules that govern financial claims between divorcing Americans are a challenge to summarise because there are in principle 51 sets of them. One must therefore rely more than one might prefer on generalisations about groups of states.[1]

A. Division of Property

At one time there was a sharp division between most American states, which followed traditional common-law principles in the allocation of property at divorce, and the eight states that followed community property principles. The common law treated property owned by the spouses during their marriage as the individual property of one of them unless, as to a particular piece of property, they had acted to create joint ownership. The title in which property was held was critical. The effect was to vest ownership in the spouse who earned the money with which the property was purchased, although that owner could make a gift to the other spouse by shifting property to joint title, or sole title in the other spouse's name. At divorce each spouse was allocated his or her property. The result in most cases was to allocate the bulk of the property to the husband. Alimony was therefore often the only financial remedy available to meet claims the divorced wife might have on her own behalf, as contrasted with claims of child support she might make on behalf of her children.

Community property law begins with the contrary presumption: all earnings from spousal labour during the marriage are the property of the marital 'community' in which each spouse has an undivided one-half interest. Property acquired with spousal earnings is therefore also owned equally by the spouses, regardless of whether purchased with funds earned by the husband, the wife, or both, unless the parties change the character of the property by agreement or gift. In California and two other community property states, all community property is divided at divorce into spousal shares equal in value, although not necessarily identical in kind. Alimony

---

[1] This section on default rules relies on the overview I prepared for the American Law Institute's *Principles of the Law of Family Dissolution*, (Newark, NJ, LexisNexis, 2002) with some updating to take account of later developments.

(renamed 'spousal support' or 'maintenance' in most jurisdictions) may also be allowed, as determined on a case-by-case basis.

This sharp dichotomy between common law and community property traditions no longer prevails in the United States. All the common-law states now allow the divorce court to distribute the spouses' property between them on a basis other than common-law principles of ownership, under a doctrine known generally as 'equitable distribution'. Five of the eight community property states also instruct their divorce courts to divide the community property between the spouses 'equitably' (rather than 'equally'). Equitable distribution is therefore the dominant rule today, followed everywhere but in the three 'equal division' community property states.[2]

The consensus, however, has not been as great as this description suggests. Different starting points in their underlying concepts of ownership can yield differences in the way judicial discretion is exercised under equitable distribution rules that are similar on their face. The concept of joint ownership is pervasive in community property states, applicable not only at dissolution but also at death (a spouse has testamentary power over only half the value of assets acquired through his or her labour during marriage, as the other half belongs to his or her spouse) and during marriage (with management control over community assets allocated under gender-neutral rules).[3] There is thus no doubt that in every sense, spouses in community property states own equal shares of all property that either spouse acquires through labour during their marriage. That means that the equal ownership principle is fully embedded in the legal culture of community property states, and an unequal division of equally owned property requires some special justification. In consequence, even the five community property states that do not have a formal rule requiring equal division nonetheless order it in almost every case.[4] At the same time, nearly all the community property states follow a rule requiring that 'separate property'—property the spouses earned before the marriage, or received by inheritance at any time—be confirmed at divorce as that spouse's sole property. In sum, property law is the primary basis on which the community property states allocate property at divorce.

The role of property law is more confused in the common-law states, all of which retain traditional common law separate ownership principles at both death and during marriage. They thus superimpose equitable distribution at divorce on top of these property rules. So equitable distribution reform did not change their marital property law, but displaced it: equity rather than property law would now govern the allocation of property at divorce. In its purer form this idea throws all property the spouses own into the pot, rather than only the property acquired during the marriage, because the point was to give courts roving authority to reassign any assets the parties had, without limit, as needed to achieve a fair result. This attitude can

---

[2] These three are California, Louisiana and New Mexico.

[3] For example, the will of a spouse in a community property state applies only to that spouse's half-share of the community property. The surviving spouse's ownership of the other half is not dependent upon the will and cannot be defeated by it.

[4] '[A]ll marital joint property should be divided substantially equally unless sound reason exists to divide the property otherwise. That approach simply reflects the principle that community property implies equal ownership. In most cases, therefore, an equal distribution of joint property will be the most equitable.' *Toth v Toth*, 940 P 2d 900, 903 (Arizona 1997).

be seen in the history of the Uniform Marriage and Divorce Act, the 1970s model that played a large role in these reforms. In its original form, § 307 of the Act distinguished marital from separate property, along lines that mimicked the community and separate property distinction.[5] Family law attorneys from common-law states raised sufficient objection to this formulation to put the Act's endorsement by the American Bar Association in jeopardy.[6] The result was a 1973 amendment that offered two alternative versions of the property section. Alternative A followed an 'all property' rule, and was designated as the preferred alternative, while Alternative B, meant for community property states, distinguished community from separate property. But in fact, it was the original version, with its distinction between marital and separate property, that in the end most states adopted. Indeed, in the years since, the minority of common-law states that chose the 'all property' version has shrunk further. There are today only a few left.[7] Moreover, the distinction between marital and separate property that most common-law states follow has been drawn more systematically in recent years. Today some common-law states even engage in the careful tracing of assets held at divorce, back to their original sources, to make the crucial classification between marital and separate property—something routinely done in the community property states.[8]

Of course, the strength of this trend toward a more property-oriented approach to equitable division varies among the states. Some have not moved in that direction at all, while others have gone quite far, their courts increasingly comfortable making fine property classification decisions that rely on authority in community property states for guidance.[9] The difference is important, because the more well-defined and narrow the class of property subject to equitable reallocation, the more certain the allocation rules that apply to it. An equal allocation rule makes no sense to most people if the pot to which it is applied includes property the spouses inherited, or owned before the marriage, and it would make little sense in New York, which continues to insist, alone among American states, that a portion of a spouse's expected future earnings be treated as if they were property, to be valued and then divided

---

[5] This original 1970 version is set out in the annotations to § 307 in Uniform Laws Annotated.

[6] 'During the American Bar Association meeting (I believe in 1970 after the Commissioners had given final approval to the Act as it came out of Committee) a group in the Family Law Section, led by Henry Foster, refused to approve the Act (preventing ABA approval) without a change in Section 307 to provide only for the "all property of either spouse" ("Hotchpot") alternative.' Email to Ira Ellman from Robert Levy, Reporter for the Uniform Marriage and Divorce Act, 5 August 2009.

[7] One recent review claims 14 'all property' states: Connecticut, Hawaii, Indiana, Kansas, Massachusetts, Michigan, Mississippi, Montana, New Hampshire, North Dakota, Oregon, South Dakota, Vermont, and Wyoming. J Thomas Oldham, *Divorce, Separation, and the Distribution of Property* (New York, Law Journal Press, 1987 & Supp 2008). However, the case law in many of these states creates presumptions that recreate the distinction between marital and separate property through allocation principles that take the method of acquisition into account in deciding on equity of any allocation. See Ellman, Kurtz, Scott, Weithorn and Bix, *Family Law: Cases, Text, Problems* 4th edn (Newark, NJ, LexisNexis, 2004) 299.

[8] Examples of common law courts engaging in such tracing include: *Merriken v Merriken*, 590 A 2d 565 (Md Spec App 1991) (allowing wife to claim an interest in the appreciation of husband's separate property where that appreciation resulted from the husband's labour during marriage); *Thomas v Thomas*, 377 SE 2d 666 (Ga 1989) (dividing the proceeds from the sale of the marital home between the spouses according to the marital and separate property sources of the funds used to acquire it).

[9] For an example of a common law state relying on community property principles, see *Niroo v Niroo*, 545 A 2d 35 (Md 1988) (issue is whether to treat as marital property renewal commissions earned by husband on insurance policies he sold during the marriage, but which are renewed after the divorce).

at divorce. So clear rules for distinguishing marital and separate property go hand in hand with clear rules for the division of property. This insight of the community property system has now made considerable inroads in the common-law states, even in parts of the country traditionally most attached to the common-law system.[10]

One issue on which the community property rule has been adopted by virtually all the common-law states is the treatment of pensions.[11] Allocation is made between the portion of any pension entitlement earned during the marriage, and the portion earned before or after the marriage. In the increasing proportion of pension plans that are *defined-contribution* rather than *defined-benefit*, the allocation is often straightforward: contributions made to the pension fund on the employee's behalf, whether by the employer or the employee himself, are marital or community property if earned (or made from earnings) during the marriage. Investment returns from these contributions are of course also marital. For defined-benefit plans, allocation is most often made by a relative time rule: the marital years contributing to the pension entitlement are divided by the total years over which the pension was earned to establish the fraction of the pension benefit that is marital or community property. In either case, the marital portion is always divided equally in the community property states and now, more often than not, also in the common-law states. In shorter marriages the retirement plan accumulation is often small enough that it is feasible to settle a spouse's claim in a lump sum at divorce, perhaps by way of trade-off against another asset on which the employee-spouse forgoes his or her share.

In longer marriages where the spouses are closer to retirement and the value of the accumulated retirement benefit is greater, it is usually more practical to allocate shares of the annuity, as this is paid each month. Federal legislation, the Employee Retirement Income Security Act (ERISA),[12] that applies to most private pension plans makes this much easier. It requires the administrator of any pension plan to send the employee's spouse that spouse's share of the monthly benefit directly, eliminating any need to rely on the employee spouse to make monthly payments to his or her former spouse of his or her share. ERISA also provides a convenient solution to the otherwise difficult problem that arises when the employee spouse, although eligible to retire, chooses instead to continue working and defer receipt of the pension, while the other spouse needs or want to begin receiving his or her share of the pension immediately. The court simply directs the pension administrator to bifurcate the benefits, starting payments to the other spouse immediately, in an amount equal to his or her share of the benefit the employee spouse would have received had he or she chosen to retire then. The employee receives no benefits until he or she actually retires, and his or her benefits are adjusted to take account of the earlier payments to the other spouse.

In about one-third of the states, marital misconduct may, in principle, be considered by courts in setting an equitable allocation, but in many of these states its

---

[10] Eg, Arkansas and North Carolina now have statutory presumptions that marital property should be divided equally. Arkansas Code Ann § 9-12-315(a)(1)(A)(2009) ('All marital property shall be distributed one-half to each party unless the court finds such a division to be inequitable.'); North Carolina Gen Stat Ann § 50-20(c)(2009) ('There shall be an equal division by using net value of marital property and net value of divisible property unless the court determines that an equal division is not equitable.').

[11] For a fuller description of the typical state pension rules and the federal law (ERISA), see Ellman et al, *Family Law*, above n 7, 316–21.

[12] Pub L 93-406, 88 Stat 829, enacted 2 September 1974.

consideration is limited by formal rules or local practice so that there are few cases in which it has an important impact. Financial misconduct, such as the destruction or concealment of marital assets, is more widely thought relevant, even in strict equal division states that leave nothing else for a judge to consider, because such conduct might otherwise deprive the victim of the true half-share to which they are entitled.

In sum, then, one can group together the American community property states, and an increasing share of the common-law states, as sharing an approach that distinguishes clearly between property acquired through labour during marriage, and property acquired through inheritance and gift, or before marriage. This group of states generally divide the former property equally, while confirming a spouse's separate ownership of the latter. The community property states in this group are in general more precise about the classification of property, and more faithful to the equal division principle, than are the common-law states, because they see the primary purpose of the property allocation at divorce as recognising the spouses' equal ownership, which is itself thought, in the great majority of cases, to vindicate any claims of equity. This difference is perhaps most likely to be seen in the occasional case involving a spouse who had a very high income during marriage that accounts for most of the spouses' considerable property accumulation. While the common-law states may depart from equal division in such cases, allowing a larger share to the spouse who earned the property (and who is still its owner under common law rules), the community property states will generally adhere to equal division in such cases with little hesitation.

B. Alimony (Spousal Support, Maintenance)

The American law of alimony (now often called spousal support or maintenance, but all three labels are in use among the various states) can be summarised at only the highest level of generality: alimony awards are governed by relatively vague statutory standards that leave much to the trial judge. The absence of more certain rules reflects the lack of consensus about alimony's rationale. It has always been difficult to explain why the duty to provide support continues past the end of the marriage on which it is based, but the collapse of gender role norms and the demise of fault-based divorce made the problem worse. So, early in the no-fault era some courts concluded that alimony was a remedy whose time had passed, hard to justify and now no longer needed because in the new world of gender equality, women, who had been homemakers in long-term marriages, could now obtain good jobs. Some policymakers in the common-law states also thought that the financially dependent spouse's newly acquired rights to share in the property accumulated during the marriage (the marital property reforms had just occurred) would eliminate the need for alimony.[13] The new goal was the 'clean break' and, many thought,

---

[13] This was the argument made, for example, as recently as the mid-1980s when Loretta O'Brien's lawyer argued to the highest New York court that it must treat her husband's medical degree as property, rather than accept the lower court's alternative remedy of an alimony award, because in adopting New York's new equitable distribution law the legislature also intended to limit alimony awards to short-term

these new developments would make it possible.[14] Perhaps transitional assistance—'rehabilitative alimony' was the phrase often used—would sometimes be necessary, but certainly nothing more than that. But, after a while, a new phrase—'displaced homemakers'—gained currency, as these expectations of alimony's fading relevance were frustrated. To the surprise of some policymakers, it turned out that newly divorced 45-year old homemakers who had been out of the labour market for 20 years could not easily transition to well-paid jobs after all; that most families did not have a lot of property to divide at divorce (certainly not enough to generate a middle class income from the share of it received by underemployed former wives); and that if there were minor children of the marriage, a clean break was not possible anyway, at least not if one meant to collect child support and encourage divorced fathers to continue to play a positive role in their children's lives. Once these lessons were learned it became clear that alimony could not be abolished after all.

Nonetheless, surveys suggest that alimony is requested in only a small minority of divorces, and granted in only some of those. It is certainly rare at the dissolution of short-term childless marriages, but undoubtedly more common in longer marriages and marriages with children. At the same time, appellate cases continue to affirm long-term alimony awards that trial courts grant to financially dependent spouses at the dissolution of their long-term marriages. So it seems that most courts still believe the law should intervene to reduce significant disparities in the post-dissolution incomes of those who have been married to one another for 15 or 20 years or more, even at the cost of maintaining financial ties between the former spouses.[15] Alimony may also be allowed in marriages of shorter duration where there are children of the marriage who are still young and the primary custodian's income is considerably less than the support obligor's. But if there is agreement on such propositions, it is not unanimous, and exists at only a very general level. Judgments of how great an income disparity to tolerate, how much of any disparity to close through an alimony award, and how long to continue the award for, will vary. The American Law Institute recommended that alimony guidelines be adopted, analogous to the guideline employed for child support, and some jurisdictions have tried this approach,[16] but it has not as yet been widely employed.

---

assistance. See the account of the *O'Brien* case in I Ellman, '*O'Brien v. O'Brien*: A Failed Reform: Unlikely Reformers', which appears in both C Sanger (ed), *Family Law Stories* (New York, Foundation Press, 2008) 269–94, and (2007) 27 *Pace Law Review* 949.

[14] An early case that proved influential in reversing this trend toward allowing only fixed-term rehabilitative alimony awards was *Marriage of Morrison*, 573 P 2d 41 (Cal 1978), which held that in longer marriages the courts should not assume the financially dependent spouse could successfully re-enter the job market and become able to support herself at an appropriate living standard.

[15] Examples include *Clapp v Clapp*, 653 A 2d 72 (Vt 1994) (middle-aged wife of 20 years with stable employment as public school guidance counsellor entitled to substantial long-term alimony award from higher-earning husband); *Rainwater v Rainwater*, 869 P 2d 176 (Ariz App 1993) (41-year old wife employed as secretary entitled to substantial alimony award of indefinite duration at dissolution of her 22-year marriage to higher-earning husband).

[16] For discussion of recent use of alimony 'guidelines' see T Larkin, 'Guidelines for Alimony: The New Mexico Experiment' (2004) 38 *Family Law Quarterly* 29, 38–49. A Commission of the American Academy of Matrimonial Lawyers developed its own guidelines in 2007, listed and discussed in MK Kisthardt, 'Rethinking Alimony: The AAML's Considerations for Calculating Alimony, Spousal Support or Maintenance' (2008) 21 *Journal of the American Academy of Matrimonial Lawyers* 61. The family courts in Maricopa County (Phoenix) Arizona adopted alimony guidelines by court rule, and their

C. The Relationship Between Alimony Awards and Property Allocations

Income flows and capital assets can be substituted for one another, and can be valued on a common scale. For this reason, an enhanced share of marital property may in principle always substitute for a fixed-term alimony award. However, few divorcing couples have capital assets sufficiently large to provide an adequate substitute for any but the most modest of alimony awards. While that means that alimony is often the only possible remedy for the spouse put at financial disadvantage from the divorce, its unreliability and unpredictability make it unsatisfactory. Lawyers have therefore sought to transform claims on a spouse's future earnings from alimony to property. Their technique has been to reduce expected future earnings to a present value that is then treated as a 'thing' acquired during the marriage, and is therefore marital property in which both spouses have an interest. Judicial reactions to such claims have depended largely on the extent to which they could be framed in familiar terms. All American states but New York have now rejected claims that professional degrees or licences are 'property' with a value measured by the earnings increment that the holders of such credentials typically realise.[17] On the other hand, some time ago most courts began accepting claims that professional goodwill is earning capacity, and a fair number accepted methods for measuring that goodwill that effectively include the professional spouse's earning capacity. More recently, however, more courts have favoured market price measures of goodwill that do not include earning capacity, although the states remain divided on this question.[18]

The American view contrasts with the English system, which does not make the same distinction between claims one spouse may make at divorce on property the other spouse owns, and claims one spouse may make on the other's post-divorce income. The English perspective appears similar to that taken at first by some American common-law states after the American reforms. As noted earlier, some American states initially concluded that if equity replaces property law as the source of principle for deciding on property claims between spouses, then there was no reason to distinguish between marital and separate property. That same perspective can be taken further to conclude there is also no reason to distinguish between claims on property and claims on post-divorce income: as equity provides the ultimate touchstone for both, they are simply two alternative tools to the same end, tools that may be used separately or jointly. New York's treatment of earning capacity as property can be understood as a way of implementing this perspective, different from the British approach on the surface, but not in fundamental principle. However, the rejection of this New York rule in the rest of the United States illustrates that in most of the country, income claims remain fundamentally distinct from property claims. Spouses are regarded as having some claim of right, akin to a property interest if not precisely that outside the community property states, to

---

use was approved by the Arizona Court of Appeals in *Cullum v Cullum*, 160 P 3d 231 (Ariz App Div 1 2007). There has also been movement towards alimony guidelines in Canada: see Department of Justice (Canada), 'Spousal Support Advisory Guidelines: A Draft Proposal' (2005) (prepared by C Rogerson and R Thompson), canada.justice.gc.ca/eng/dept-min/pub/ss-pae/proj/ssag-idpa.pdf.

[17] See the treatment of these questions in Ellman et al, *Family Law*, above n 7, 324–45.
[18] Ibid, 345–62.

assets acquired during the marriage. In contrast, claims on the post-divorce income of one's former spouse are regarded as claims of equity. It is this difference in the American understanding of these two kinds of claim that allows many, if not most, states to adopt at least a presumption that marital property is divided equally, while clinging tenaciously to the rule that alimony claims are matters of judicial discretion which cannot even be subject to presumptive guidelines. This same conception must also be part of the explanation for the difference we will see in the American law's treatment of terms in premarital agreements that fix property claims and terms that limit alimony claims. Contractual reallocation of property owned by the contracting parties is familiar and accepted, while contractual limits on the power of a court to make an equitable judgment are unfamiliar and suspect.

II. AGREEMENTS MADE BEFORE MARRIAGE

A. General Overview

i. Decline of Traditional Rules Barring Agreements Altogether

The traditional rule allowed agreements concerning the distribution of property at the death of a spouse, but barred agreements that 'contemplated divorce'. It was consistent with the prevailing law of the fault-divorce era: given that the law barred divorce by mutual consent, one would expect it to also look sceptically on premarital agreements setting forth divorce terms. As no-fault divorce was widely adopted during the 1970s and 1980s, this limitation on premarital agreements gradually disappeared as well. An early case adopting the modern view explained that '[p]ublic policy is not violated by permitting ... persons ... to anticipate the possibility of divorce and to establish their rights by contract in such an event as long as the contract is entered with full knowledge and without fraud, duress or coercion.'[19] This is now the dominant view.[20]

As a general matter, premarital agreements fall within the provision of the Statute of Frauds applying to promises made in consideration of marriage, and the cases require a writing whenever marriage is even part of the contract's consideration. Section 2 of the Uniform Premarital Agreement Act (UPAA) requires a writing, as does the American Law Institute's Principles of the Law of Family Dissolution, § 7.04(1). An oral agreement otherwise barred by the Statute of Frauds may be enforceable if one of the parties has performed in reliance upon it. That general rule has been applied in the context of marital or premarital agreements.[21]

[19] *Volid v Volid*, 286 NE 2d 42, 46–47 (Ill App 1972).
[20] For a general overview of the history of premarital agreements in the United States, see B Bix, 'Bargaining in the Shadow of Love: The Enforcement of Premarital Agreements and How We Think About Marriage' (1998) 40 *William and Mary Law Review* 145, 148–58.
[21] This was the holding of *Marriage of Benson*, 7 Cal Rptr 3d 905 (App 2003) (enforcing parties' oral agreement that husband's retirement account would remain his separate property in exchange for husband abandoning any community property interest in the marital residence, because the deed transferring the residence to a trust of which the wife was sole beneficiary had already been executed). In that case, however, the California Supreme Court later reversed, finding that a specific California statute displaced

Modern courts still occasionally say they will not enforce agreements 'encouraging' divorce, but no one appears to know precisely what this means. *Marriage of Noghrey*[22] relied on this principle in refusing to enforce a provision in a *ketuba*, the traditional Jewish marriage contract. The disputed provision required the husband to pay the wife $500,000 if they divorced, unlike the typical modern *ketuba* in which this traditional provision calls for only a symbolic payment. The parties were Iranian, and the wife claimed the payment was meant to compensate her for the difficulty she would have in finding a new Iranian husband when she was no longer a virgin. The court held the provision void because it created an incentive for the wife to seek divorce and was not meant to adjust property rights arising from the marriage.

More recently, in *Bellio v Bellio*[23] the court considered an agreement keeping the parties' earnings separate but giving the wife a lump sum of $100,000 if the marriage ended by either divorce or the husband's death. The husband had sought the earnings provision, which the wife accepted only after he added the provision giving her the lump sum. The wife had depended upon alimony payments from her first husband, which would terminate with this second marriage, and she wanted to protect herself in case the second marriage also ended in divorce. Citing *Noghrey*, the trial court held the provision invalid, but the appeals court reversed this decision, distinguishing *Noghrey* on the grounds that the payment was merely a reasonable financial plan to protect the wife from becoming worse off than before the marriage. If her waiver of community property rights in the husband's earnings was to be held to be valid, the court could hardly refuse enforcement of this modest substitute for the waived rights. Perhaps the lump sum provision could be seen as encouraging her to divorce, but then the earnings provision might be seen as encouraging the husband to marry.

The fact is that any agreement that does not track prevailing law will leave one spouse or the other better off than without it, which means that *any* meaningful agreement will make one spouse or the other more likely to seek divorce than if there were no agreement.[24] So if agreements are to be allowed at all, a rule casting doubt on those that 'encourage divorce' makes little sense, and few courts now rely upon such a rule to refuse enforcement. We may wish the law to refuse enforcement

the normal statute of frauds rule and did not allow the part performance claim: *Marriage of Benson*, 116 P 3d 1152, 32 Cal Rptr 3d 471 (Cal 2005).

[22] *Marriage of Noghrey*, 215 Cal Rptr 153 (App 1985).
[23] *Bellio v Bellio* 129 Cal Rptr 2d 556 (App 2003).
[24] Consider the agreement made by one-time spouses Donald Trump and Marla Maples, who announced in May of 1997 that they would divorce 'as friends' after a 'long relationship and a three-and-a-half year marriage.' An inside source reported that the parties' premarital agreement promised Ms Maples '$1 million to $5 million in the event of divorce' but would expire within 11 months, leaving her then entitled to a settlement based on Mr Trump's net worth, then estimated at $2.5 billion. The source claimed there was no third party involved in the divorce, which occurred because Mr Trump was 'forced economically to act. ... Unless you're married to someone you have 1000 percent surety in, you just can't do [otherwise].' 'Donald and Marla Headed for Divestiture' *New York Times* (3 May 1997) 20. Here, then, a provision promising Ms Maples a very large lump sum was said to have encouraged Mr Trump to seek divorce, since the provision protected him from the even larger claims she might make after it expired—just the opposite of the assumption of the *Noghrey* court that under the facts of that case, it was the wife who was promised the lump sum payment who would thereby be encouraged to seek divorce.

of some kinds of marital agreements, but our grounds for that refusal need be something else.

Most American states in fact apply procedural and substantive rules to premarital agreements that they do not apply to contracts generally. These are addressed below.

ii. Rules Limiting Agreements as to Particular Subjects

a. Provisions Concerning Children

The traditional rule that a contract between prospective spouses cannot bind a court in deciding child support or child custody matters seems largely preserved by both the UPAA and the American Law Institute (ALI). Both authorities state that 'the right of a child to support cannot be affected adversely' by an agreement.[25] Perhaps this rule leaves open the possibility of enforcing an agreement enlarging support, as, for example, by obliging a parent to support a child in college where the governing state law would not otherwise impose that duty. Such provisions are typically enforced when contained in separation agreements. As to custody, the UPAA is silent; it is omitted from the list of specific items that the agreement may address, but neither is it specifically barred by any provision analogous to the provision concerning child support. The American Law Institute reflects prevailing law in giving premarital agreements about custodial allocations a largely advisory role:[26] courts should 'take into account any prior agreement' of the parties 'that would be appropriate to consider in light of the circumstances as a whole'.[27] Separation agreement provisions on custody are given more weight by the ALI, as they typically are by the courts, although they also are not binding.[28] The Institute explains the lesser weight given to premarital agreements in largely the same terms that it explains more generally the limitations it places on the enforcement of pre-marital agreements; the Institute's views are explained further below.[29] On the other hand, a number of states accept, at least to a limited degree, separation agreement

---

[25] UPAA § 3(b); American Law Institute, *Family Law Principles*, above n 1, § 7.06.

[26] For an example of a court's refusal to apply a premarital agreement on custody see *Combs v Combs*, 865 P 2d 50 (Wyo 1993) (finding unenforceable a provision in a premarital agreement providing that 'any progeny resulting from this union, should this contract be terminated, shall remain in the custody of the parent of that progeny's sex', because state law forbids basing custody determinations solely on the gender of the parent).

[27] American Law Institute, *Family Law Principles*, above n 1, § 2.08(1)(e).

[28] The court is instructed to follow, in its custody order, a parenting plan agreed upon by the parents unless the agreement 'is not knowing or voluntary' or 'would be harmful to the child'. ibid, § 2.06 (1).

[29] Ibid § 2.08, Comment *i*, which explains: 'Prenuptial agreements are typically made in contexts, and with respect to matters, as to which individuals are unable to predict and assess realistically either the events that will happen in the future, or the significance of the interests they are bargaining away. The difficulty of enforcing agreements made when the family's future, and even its composition, are unknown, is particularly acute when it comes to the allocation of responsibility for children. Prenuptial agreements typically are made before the needs of a particular child are known—indeed, often before the child is born, or before it is known whether there will be any children. Along with the customary lack of realism most couples share about the likelihood of a separation or divorce, adults on the brink of marriage can be expected to be limited in their ability to evaluate their child's needs, judge the other parent's ability to meet the child's needs, or gauge their own interests. Such limitations exist as well, to be sure, with respect to agreements negotiated in the context of a separation. These Principles assume, however, that parties tend to be significantly less realistic before or during marriage than when separation is contemplated.'

provisions requiring arbitration of post-decree custody disputes, and similar provisions in premarital agreements might receive similar treatment. However, courts usually retain authority to override the arbitrator's decision, which is not how arbitrations are treated in commercial contexts.[30]

b. Provisions Concerning Fault or the Termination of the Marriage

Although the matter has not often arisen, American courts have in general declined to honour provisions in premarital agreements that attempt to alter state law concerning the circumstances under which a marriage may be dissolved, or which would penalise a spouse, in the financial arrangements at divorce, for marital misconduct that state law would not otherwise consider.[31] The UPAA is silent on this question, but the refusal to enforce such provisions is in agreement with the rule adopted on this matter by the American Law Institute.[32]

c. Provisions Limiting Alimony at Divorce

American courts and legislatures have historically been more resistant to enforcing waivers of alimony than waivers of marital property rights. This is in part motivated by the state's desire to look to a former spouse for support of an individual who would otherwise receive public assistance, as can be seen by the UPAA provision that expressly provides for overriding a contractual waiver of alimony in that situation.[33] The suspicion of alimony waivers goes beyond that concern, however. Many states that have otherwise adopted the UPAA have modified its language to limit provisions on alimony even further. Two allow courts to order spousal maintenance, despite contract terms to the contrary, when a spouse would otherwise suffer 'extreme hardship under circumstances not reasonably foreseeable at the time of the execution of the agreement.'[34] Two provide expressly that the right to spousal support may not be adversely affected by a premarital agreement.[35] Two other states changed the UPAA text to delete spousal maintenance from the list of subjects that a valid agreement may address. In one (South Dakota) the state supreme court later held the effect of this omission was to disallow provisions waiving alimony, but

---

[30] Cases like *Kelm v Kelm*, 623 NE 2d 39 (Ohio 1993), favour arbitration agreements, but still reserve ultimate judicial authority to override arbitrators' awards. For more on this topic see EG Spitko, 'Reclaiming the "Creatures of the State": Contracting for Child Custody Decisionmaking in the Best Interests of the Family', (2000) 57 *Washington & Lee Law Review* 1139; EA Jenkins, 'Validity and Construction of Provisions for Arbitration of Disputes as to Alimony or Support Payments or Child Visitation or Custody Matters' (1993) 38 *American Law Reports 5th* 69.

[31] *Diosdado v Diosdado*, 118 Cal Rptr 2d 494 (App 2002) (court refuses to enforce agreement providing various penalties, including 'liquidated damages' of $50,000, against a spouse who kisses 'on the mouth' or touches 'in any sexual manner' any third party); *Marriage of Dargan*, 13 Cal Rptr 3d 522 (App 2004) (follows *Diosdado* with respect to husband's agreement to grant wife his interest in specified items of community property if he used drugs).

[32] American Law Institute, *Family Law Principles*, above n 1, § 7.08.

[33] Delaware (Del Code Ann tit 13, § 326 (2009)) and Virginia (Va Code Ann § 20-151 (2009)).

[34] These are Indiana and Illinois. See *Rider v Rider*, 669 NE 2d 160, 163–64 (Ind 1996). Ill Comp Stat 10/7-§ 7(b) (2009).

[35] They are Iowa and New Mexico. See NM Stat Ann § 40-3A-4 (2009); Iowa Code Ann § 596.5 (2009).

in the other (California) the court held that it did not have this effect.[36] The California legislature then amended the statute to bar enforcement of agreements waiving spousal support if they are 'unconscionable at the time of enforcement' or if the waiving party was not represented by independent counsel at the time of the waiver.[37] In states that have not adopted the UPAA, traditional resistance to alimony waivers continues to be seen.[38]

B. Special Rules Policing Premarital Agreements: Overview

Premarital agreements may be treated differently from ordinary contracts by the imposition of special procedural requirements or special tests of substantive fairness. One traditional thread of American law, represented here by *Button v Button*,[39] does both. It enforces premarital agreements concerning the division of property at divorce only if: 1) the parties had knowledge of each other's assets, either independently or through disclosure; and 2) the agreement was 'voluntary'; and 3) its terms were fair at the time of execution; and 4) it is fair to apply it at the time of divorce. The first is a procedural fairness requirement, and it turns out, on examination, that the second is, as well. The third and fourth are requirements of substantive fairness. None are applied to ordinary commercial contracts. *Button* exemplifies the regulatory approach followed by some American states.[40] The other end of the American spectrum is exemplified by *Simeone v Simeone*,[41] which insists that premarital agreements should be treated like any other contract (with the one exception that it also requires a disclosure of financial assets).

Simeone is a new development that few if any other states have followed; *Button* is a traditional rule that many states have now abandoned. Most American states today fall somewhere between these bookends. The Uniform Premarital Agreement Act, adopted in about half the states,[42] is closer to *Simeone* than to *Button*, and this orientation has motivated considerable criticism by many commentators, as well as the American Law Institute. Many adopting states have modified the UPAA's recommended text to allow challenges that move back towards *Button*, as we will see

---

[36] The South Dakota decisions holding that alimony waivers are not allowed are *Walker v Walker*, 765 NW 2d 747 (SD 2009) and *Sanford v Sanford*, 694 NW 2d 283 (SD 2005); the California decision holding that the deletion of alimony from the list did not show the legislature's intention to bar provisions on alimony is *Pendleton v Fireman*, 5 P 3d 839 (Cal 2000).

[37] Cal Fam Code § 1612(c) (2009).

[38] Eg, *Lane v Lane*, 202 SW 3d 577 (Ky 2006) (agreement to waive spousal support unconscionable at time of enforcement, where husband became a millionaire, in part because he devoted himself entirely to his career while wife devoted herself to being a homemaker).

[39] *Button v Button*, 388 NW 2d 546 (Wis 1986).

[40] A more recent decision consistent with *Button* is *Blige v Blige*, 656 SE 2d 822 (Ga 2008) ('the party seeking enforcement bears the burden of proof to demonstrate that: (1) the antenuptial agreement was not the result of fraud, duress, mistake, misrepresentation, or nondisclosure of material facts; (2) the agreement is not unconscionable; and (3) taking into account all relevant facts and circumstances, including changes beyond the parties' contemplation when the agreement was executed, enforcement of the antenuptial agreement would be neither unfair nor unreasonable.').

[41] *Simeone v Simeone*, 581 A 2d 162 (Pa 1990).

[42] Uniform Laws Annotated lists 26 adopting states, plus the District of Columbia, although many of these have made substantive changes in the Act.

below in addressing particular provisions, although one state (Rhode Island) changed the language to move in the opposite direction, toward *Simeone*.[43] One criticism of the original UPAA test is that its provisions would in fact work an important policy change in many states, but that the change is effectively concealed in the guise of a technical improvement intended only to achieve interstate consistency.[44] Many critics believe the UPAA's orientation is simply wrong as a matter of policy.[45]

C. Special Rules Policing Premarital Agreements: Procedural Protections

i. The Voluntariness Requirement: a Form of Procedural Fairness

The UPAA would deny an agreement's enforcement if the spouse challenging it proves that he or she 'did not execute the agreement voluntarily'. Most other American authorities agree that an agreement must be 'voluntary' to be enforceable. But what does this mean? The UPAA itself offers no further explanation, and the cases that address the meaning of the voluntariness requirement, whether under the UPAA or pre-existing case law, are often unhelpful and certainly inconsistent with one another.

The debate among the Uniform Law Commissioners sheds some light on what they intended the voluntariness requirement to mean.[46] These debates took place in the context of the drafting committee's defence of their draft's severe limits on unconscionability challenges to agreements, limits considered further below. The narrow majority that ultimately approved the draft's language defended elimination of the unconscionability defence with assurances that the requirement of voluntariness would prevent enforcement of the questionable contracts that opponents were concerned about. They said, for example, that spouses could rely on the voluntariness requirement to resist enforcement of agreements whose effect they did not

---

[43] Rhode Island eliminates voluntariness as a separate basis for finding an agreement unenforceable. The party challenging the agreement in Rhode Island must show it was involuntary, *and* unconscionable, *and* that the other spouse's assets were not disclosed, *and* that there was no waiver of disclosure, *and* that the challenging party had no knowledge of the other party's assets. The failure to prove *any* of these facts by *clear and convincing* evidence—a heightened standard of proof rarely applicable in ordinary contract cases—is fatal to a challenge of a premarital agreement: RI Gen Laws 1956, § 15-17-6 (2009). These rules make it far more difficult to challenge the validity of a premarital agreement than of any commercial contract, and produce highly questionable results. See, eg, *Marsocci v Marsocci*, 911 A 2d 690 (RI 2006) (premarital agreement signed by unrepresented wife four days before wedding, in which the value of husband's assets was not disclosed, held enforceable because the party challenging enforcement must prove by clear and convincing evidence both unconscionability and failure of adequate disclosure.)

[44] B Atwood, 'Ten Years Later: Lingering Concerns about the Uniform Premarital Agreement Act' (1993) 19 *Journal of Legislation* 127, 128 ('Despite the representations of N.C.C.U.S.L., the U.P.A.A. departs, sometimes dramatically, from the common law of many states').

[45] K Silbaugh, 'Marriage Contracts and the Family Economy' (1998) 93 *Northwestern University Law Review* 65 (critical of the trend toward enforcement of agreements, noting that accepted arguments against enforcement of some nonmonetary terms may apply to monetary terms as well); GF Brod, 'Premarital Agreements and Gender Justice' (1994) 6 *Yale Journal of Law and Feminism* 229, 295 (arguing that the UPAA fails to give adequate weight to policies other than freedom of contract and personal autonomy, such as the 'attainment of economic justice for the economically vulnerable spouse at the end of marriage'). The American Law Institute's views are described more fully in the text.

[46] For a discussion of these Uniform Commissioner debates, see the Reporter's Notes to Comments *b* and *g* of §7.04 of American Law Institute, *Family Law Principles*, above n 1.

understand, and that it would also prevent enforcement of a one-sided agreement signed by a young pregnant girl told by her child's father that he would not otherwise marry her. These debates on the meaning of voluntariness, the discussion of the term in the case law, and the logic of statutory construction (why include the term unless it is meant to add something to the normal requirements for enforcing any contract?) combine to support the view that the voluntariness requirement imposes a test for premarital agreements that goes beyond what is required by standard doctrines, such as duress, that apply to all contracts. And so this view is widely accepted by the authorities (the principal exception being the Pennsylvania decision in *Simeone*).

One can compare the limited reach of the traditional duress doctrine to the kinds of facts that have caused an agreement to fail the voluntariness requirement. For example, in *Hamilton v Hamilton*,[47] the wife was 18, unemployed, and three months pregnant when she married the father. He had demanded, as a condition of the marriage, her agreement to waive all alimony claims. She signed such an agreement even though her counsel had advised her against it. The court enforced the waiver, concluding that '[w]here a party has been free to consult counsel before signing an agreement, the courts have uniformly rejected duress as a defense'.[48] *Hamilton* is not alone in this view of duress doctrine,[49] but the opposite result has been reached when the claim is analysed under a voluntariness rubric, in which courts have held that a 'coercive atmosphere' in securing the agreement casts doubt on its validity.[50]

The California Supreme Court's decision in the case of the baseball player Barry Bonds[51] is perhaps the most thorough judicial examination of the meaning of this requirement under the UPAA. Examining the cases cited in the Uniform Commissioners' debates, *Bonds* concludes 'that the voluntariness of a premarital agreement may turn in part upon whether the agreement was entered into knowingly, in the sense that the parties understood the terms or basic effect of the agreement.'[52] Because it is difficult to know what someone really understood, this requirement tends to be redefined as procedural safeguards ensuring the party had every chance to understand it: for example, was the party advised by independent counsel, were assets disclosed, and was an adequate explanation of the agreement's significance provided? A second thread that *Bonds* finds in the voluntariness cases reflects the view of some drafting Commissioners that the voluntariness requirement deals with cases of oppression, of which the young pregnant bride is just one example. Some

---

[47] *Hamilton v Hamilton*, 591 A 2d 720, 722 (Pa Super 1991).

[48] Ibid.

[49] Eg, *Lebeck v Lebeck*, 881 P 2d 727 (NM App 1994) (duress not shown by wife with independent counsel, who signed agreement demanded by her attorney-husband because she wished to legitimate their daughter; 'a threat to do that which the demanding party has the right to demand is not sufficient to support a claim of duress').

[50] *Williams v Williams*, 617 So 2d 1032 (Ala 1992), held that a rule requiring 'that the agreement was entered into freely and voluntarily' requires the lower court to decide whether, as a question of fact, 'the father's conditioning the marriage on the pregnant mother's signing the antenuptial agreement, joined with the mother's moral objection to abortion and the importance of legitimacy in a small town, created a coercive atmosphere in which the mother had no viable alternative to accepting the father's condition for marriage.'

[51] *Marriage of Bonds*, 24 Cal 4th 1, 5 P 3d 815, 99 Cal Rptr 2d 252 (Cal 2000).

[52] Ibid, 5 P 3d, 825 and 99 Cal Rptr 2d, 263.

courts have described this aspect of the rule as requiring that the parties have 'a meaningful choice',[53] but this does not provide much help. The victim of the armed robber makes a very meaningful choice when told 'your money or your life', and he probably would rather have that choice, than not. Nor can we expect a court to look into the soul of the signing party to determine whether his or her free will was then intact.

The American Law Institute concluded that the real meaning of the voluntariness requirement, as it is actually applied in practice, is to refuse enforcement of agreements obtained through improper bargaining tactics.[54] We say the robber's victim acted *involuntarily* in handing over his money because we condemn the robber's threat, not because we doubt the victim's cognitive capacity at the time he yielded to it. Similarly, we say assent to an agreement is involuntary when we condemn the bargaining tactics used to obtain it. This insight explains why the voluntariness requirement sets a different standard for premarital agreements than the duress defence sets for commercial contracts: hard tactics acceptable between business persons might be unacceptable in negotiations with one's intended spouse.

Assessing whether a bargaining tactic is improper in the marital context does require some subtle distinctions. On one hand, for example, the cases all find that one party's insistence on an agreement as a condition of marriage does not make the other party's assent to it involuntary. Such insistence is not inherently improper, for one is always entitled to decline to marry if one's terms for marriage are not met.[55] On the other hand, such insistence may be regarded as improper if first expressed on the eve of the wedding,[56] or in other circumstances in which it appears coercive.[57] Similarly, conditioning marriage on an agreement may be thought an improper bargaining tactic in pregnant bride cases like *Williams*,[58] if the groom is seen as exploiting the bride's vulnerability to gain an unfair advantage.[59] This understanding of the voluntariness requirement can in fact protect some vulnerable parties in situations in

---

[53]   See, eg, *Button v Button*, 388 NW 2d 546 (Wisc 1986).

[54]   American Law Institute, *Family Law Principles*, above n 1, § 7.04.

[55]   *Marriage of Shanks*, 758 NW 2d 506 (Iowa 2008); *Liebelt v Liebelt*, 801 P 2d 52, 55 (Idaho App 1990); *Gardner v Gardner*, 527 NW 2d 701, 706 (Wis App 1994); *Howell v Landry*, 386 SE 2d 610, 617–18 (NC App 1989); *Taylor v Taylor*, 832 P 2d 429, 431 (Okla App 1992).

[56]   'The presentation of an agreement a very short time before the wedding ceremony will create a presumption of overreaching or coercion if ... the postponement of the wedding would cause significant hardship, embarrassment or emotional stress ... The meaningfulness of the opportunity of the nonproponent party to seek counsel before executing an antenuptial agreement is ... [significant in determining] whether coercion or overreaching': *Fletcher v Fletcher*, 628 NE 2d 1343 (Ohio 1994) (but upholding the particular agreement before it because in this particular case the wedding's postponement would not have caused hardship or embarrassment). See also Cal Fam Code § 1615(c)(2009) which provides that an agreement is not voluntary if 'the party against whom enforcement is sought had not less than seven calendar days between the time that party was first presented with the agreement and advised to seek independent legal counsel and the time the agreement was signed.' This provision was adopted by the legislature after the *Bonds* decision, as an amendment to that state's version of the UPAA. It is modelled on ALI provisions.

[57]   Eg, *Peters-Riemers v Riemers*, 644 NW 2d 197 (ND 2002) wife's consent held involuntary where she read the agreement for first time in front of husband and his attorney, without her own counsel, creating a 'coercive environment', and where husband had only disclosed 50 per cent of his assets.

[58]   *Williams*, above n 50.

[59]   See also *Marriage of Shirilla*, 89 P 3d 1, 319 Mont 385 (Mont 2004), which found that a Russian national's consent was involuntary, rendering the agreement unenforceable, where she came to the United States in reliance on the husband's promise that if she married him she would 'be an equal partner for life',

which courts might otherwise rely upon the unconscionability doctrine to reach the same result, although it cannot deal with all the cases to which unconscionability claims might apply, as discussed further below.

ii. The American Law Institute's Approach to Voluntariness[60]

The ALI Principles avoid any use of the term *voluntary*. Concluding that 'the best understanding of the frequently stated voluntariness requirement is that it expresses the law's heightened sensitivity to duress and coercion concerns in the context of premarital agreements', the ALI chooses to meet this concern with special procedural requirements, rather than with reliance upon a requirement of voluntariness it regarded as too vague. It requires the party seeking to enforce the agreement to show that the other party's consent was informed and not obtained under duress. Section 7.04(3) then gives the agreement's proponent the benefit of a presumption (rebuttable) that this burden has been met, if the proponent shows that:

(a) [the agreement] was executed at least 30 days before the parties' marriage;
(b) both parties were advised to obtain independent legal counsel, and had reasonable opportunity to do so, before the agreement's execution; and,
(c) in the case of agreements concluded without the assistance of independent legal counsel for each party, the agreement states, in language easily understandable by an adult of ordinary intelligence with no legal training,
  (i) the nature of any rights or claims otherwise arising at dissolution that are altered by the contract, and the nature of that alteration, and
  (ii) that the interests of the spouses with respect to the agreement may be adverse.

Section 7.05 is thus an attempt to deal directly with concerns that the voluntariness requirement addresses only by implication: that the parties had a fair opportunity to understand the agreement's terms and their significance, and a reasonable opportunity to consult independent counsel. The agreement's proponent may prevail even if these requirements are not met, but only by carrying the burden of proving that 'the other party's consent was informed and not obtained under duress.' The Institute explained that a contract first presented on the eve of the wedding:[61]

> ... resembles new terms that one party insists upon adding to an agreement to marry that had already been reached and partially executed ... Premarital agreements are rarely proposed on impulse. They are usually planned. The party who wants the agreement typically hires a lawyer to draft it. There is usually no reason why this process cannot begin early enough to be completed a month before the wedding.

American law had not generally required any minimum time period between the agreement's execution and the wedding, so the ALI proposal, to require the proponent

---

only to have him present her with the agreement, once here, as a condition of the marriage. While she was provided an attorney, he did not speak Russian and she did not have the benefit of a translator.

[60] American Law Institute, *Family Law Principles*, above n 1, § 7.04. For commentary on the ALI Principles by an informed outsider who inventories its differences from current doctrine, see BH Bix, 'The ALI Principles and Agreements: Seeking a Balance Between Status and Contract' in Robin Fretwell Wilson (ed), *Reconceiving the Family: Critical Reflections on the American Law Institute's Principles of the Law of Family Dissolution* (Cambridge, Cambridge University Press, 2006) 272–91.

[61] American Law Institute, *Family Law Principles*, above n 1, § 7.05.

of a late-presented agreement to show the other spouse's consent was informed and obtained without duress, required new law and, perhaps, new legislation. *Bonds*, the California Supreme Court decision described earlier, interpreted for the first time that state's enactment of the UPAA, and involved a factual dispute on the voluntariness question which was resolved in favour of enforcing an agreement. The enforced agreement denied any share of the community property to the wife of a highly successful baseball player, who had married him at the beginning of his major league career, had little income of her own, and had borne two children during their marriage. After the *Bonds* decision, the California legislature amended its statute to adopt the ALI's approach. The new provision, Calif Fam Code § 1615(c), provides that an agreement is not voluntary (and thus not enforceable) unless two conditions are met:

(1) The party against whom enforcement is sought was represented by independent legal counsel at the time of signing the agreement or, after being advised to seek independent legal counsel, expressly waived, in a separate writing, representation by independent legal counsel.
(2) The party against whom enforcement is sought had not less than seven calendar days between the time that party was first presented with the agreement and advised to seek independent legal counsel and the time the agreement was signed.

One should note that neither the ALI's formulation, nor this California provision, would necessarily reach the case in which one party exploits the other's weakness to gain their consent to a one-sided agreement. The ALI, unlike the UPAA, preserves the defence of unconscionability, which may address such cases, and also contains another provision, addressed below, that deals more directly with agreements the enforcement of which would yield a substantial injustice.

iii. The Requirement of Disclosure of Assets

Disclosure has probably been the most universal of the heightened procedural requirements applied to premarital agreements, required under both pre-UPAA law as well as the ALI Principles. Even *Simeone*, the 'freedom of contract' bookend, says that absent a 'full and fair disclosure of the financial positions of the parties ... material misrepresentation in the inducement for entering a prenuptial agreement may be asserted.'[62] Disclosure helps to show that consent to the agreement was 'knowledgeable', one important part of the 'voluntariness' rubric, and concealment of one's assets in an effort to mislead the other spouse about them might be thought to be the kind of bargaining tactic that the rule was meant to bar. Section 7.04(5) of the ALI Principles requires the person seeking to enforce an agreement limiting the other party's financial claims at divorce to prove that prior to the agreement's execution, he or she had disclosed his or her assets and income to the other party, or that disclosure was not necessary because the other party already knew what they were, at least approximately.

The Uniform Premarital Agreement Act's treatment of the disclosure requirement is therefore a puzzling shift in the law, and one reason for criticism of the Act. The

---

[62] *Simeone*, above n 41, 167.

UPAA allows the parties to waive their right to disclosure. It also requires the spouse objecting to an agreement on non-disclosure grounds to prove a negative: that he or she 'did not have, or reasonably could not have had, an adequate knowledge of the property or financial obligations of the other party.'[63] Most importantly, the UPAA has a unique provision that ties the non-disclosure to unconscionability: an objecting spouse must prove *both* to resist enforcement of an agreement; neither non-disclosure nor unconscionability alone will affect the agreement's validity. Indeed, the waiver provision in § 6(a)(2)(ii) of the UPAA creates the stunning possibility that an unconscionably unfair agreement could be enforced against a party who was uninformed because he or she *waived* disclosure, because having lost the non-disclosure objection to the agreement, he or she necessarily also loses the unconscionability objection. For most adopting states, this provision would constitute a significant change in their law, perhaps a change a legislature might not notice unless its significance was called to the legislature's attention.[64]

Indeed, there may be reason to wonder whether the Commissioners themselves understood this result. The official UPAA commentary to § 6 cites with approval a well-known case that is entirely inconsistent with these UPAA provisions: it requires disclosure, disallows its waiver, and does not treat disclosure as redeeming an otherwise unconscionable agreement so as to allow its enforcement.[65] At least three states that otherwise adopted the UPAA changed its language to avoid the implication that disclosure can be waived, and to preserve disclosure and unconscionability as separate requirements, so that failing either one alone makes an agreement unenforceable.[66] A fourth state that does allow waivers nonetheless changed the UPAA language to provide that unconscionability and failure to disclose assets are each an adequate basis alone for refusing enforcement of an agreement,[67] while another state that retains the UPAA's connection between disclosure and unconscionability disallows waivers of disclosure by a party who did not have legal counsel.[68]

The UPAA rule seems to confuse the concepts of voluntariness and conscionability. An agreement might not be so one-sided so as to raise a question of its unconscionability, yet still have terms that were unfavourable to a party, who would not have signed it had they known key facts—such as the other party's income and assets. To limit the relevance of non-disclosure to cases of unconscionability is thus to limit considerably the reach of the voluntariness doctrine. It allows enforcement of an unfair agreement which the disadvantaged party would not have signed if disclosure had been made, unless it is so unfair as to be unconscionable. In any event,

---

[63] UPAA, above n 23, § 6.

[64] Another indicator of the extent to which the UPAA falls outside the legal mainstream in the limits it places on claims of unconscionability is the guarded support offered for the unconscionability doctrine by Richard Espstein, who is otherwise well-known for his libertarian opposition to paternalistic intervention in contract matters. He believes the doctrine might be necessary to afford protection against parties victimised by duress, undue influence, or misrepresentation that could not be proven. RA Epstein, 'Unconscionability: A Critical Reappraisal' (1975) 18 *Journal of Law and Economics* 293–315.

[65] *Del Vecchio v Del Vecchio*, 143 So 2d 17 (Fla 1962).

[66] The three are Connecticut, New Jersey, and Iowa. See Conn Gen Stat Ann § 46b-36g (2009); Iowa Code Ann § 596.7 (2009); NJ Stat Ann § 37: 2-38 (2009).

[67] Nevada Revised Statutes § 123A.080 (2009).

[68] Arkansas allows waiver only after a consultation with counsel, Ark Code Ann § 9-11-402 (2009).

the consequence of the UPAA is to leave voluntariness as the only basis upon which to challenge an agreement in which disclosure was made or waived.

iv. Independent Counsel

Some state courts do not allow enforcement of an agreement against a party who did not have independent counsel, unless the agreement is itself reasonably understandable to a layman.[69] In most states, however, independent counsel for each contracting party is not required, but its presence or absence, or some alternative source of explanation of the agreement's terms and significance, is often said to be an important fact to consider in deciding whether an agreement was entered into voluntarily. This is the position, for example, taken by the *Bonds* case, after noting that the UPAA itself imposed no separate counsel requirement. I earlier noted that the American Law Institute's recommended rule would deny the party seeking to enforce an agreement the benefit of a presumption that the other party's assent was informed, and not given under duress, if the agreement is executed less than 30 days before the wedding. An additional and separate requirement for applying the presumption, however, is that 'both parties were advised to obtain independent legal counsel, and had reasonable opportunity to do so, before the agreement's execution'.[70] In commentary, the Institute explains that a party does not have a 'reasonable opportunity' to consult independent counsel if that party does not have the funds with which to hire counsel.[71] That means that a party who wants an enforceable agreement must pay for the other party's counsel, if the other party cannot, in order to have the benefit of a presumption that the other party was informed and not under duress at the time of the agreement's execution.

Following the *Bonds* decision, the California legislature added two sections to that state's version of the UPAA, imposing a stronger requirement of independent counsel than *Bonds* had held applicable under the original UPAA text. The first, mentioned above because it also required seven days' time between execution of the agreement and the wedding, provides that an agreement is not voluntary unless 'the party against whom enforcement is sought was represented by independent legal counsel at the time of signing the agreement or, after being advised to seek independent legal counsel, expressly waived, in a separate writing, representation by independent legal counsel.'[72] If this section had applied to the *Bonds* agreement itself, that agreement would not have passed the voluntariness test. In a separate section, the legislature also provided that any provision in an agreement waiving alimony was not enforceable if the waiving party was not represented by independent counsel at the time of the waiver.[73]

---

[69] *Gant v Gant*, 329 SE 2d 106 (W Va 1985). Connecticut provides by statute that an agreement is not enforceable against a party who 'was not afforded a reasonable opportunity to consult with independent counsel.' Conn Gen Stat Ann § 46b-36g (2009).

[70] American Law Institute, *Family Law Principles*, above n 1, § 7.04(3)(b).

[71] Ibid, § 7.04, Comment *e*.

[72] Cal Fam Code §1615(c) (2009).

[73] Cal Fam Code § 1612(c) (2009).

D. Special Rules Policing Premarital Agreements: Substantive Protections

i. Unconscionability and Its Alternatives: the Problem of Foreseeability

Section 208 of the *Restatement Second, Contracts* states the classic American rule of unconscionability:

> If a contract or term thereof is unconscionable at the time the contract is made a court may refuse to enforce the contract, or may enforce the remainder of the contract without the unconscionable term, or may so limit the application of any unconscionable term as to avoid any unconscionable result.

The Restatement attempts no further definition of unconscionability. It is not inadvertent, however, that § 208 specifies that the question is whether an agreement is unconscionable 'at the time the contract is made' and not at some later time when its enforcement is sought. This feature of the unconscionability principle is inherent in its rationale. As explained in Comment *d* of § 7.01 of the ALI Principles:

> The doctrine goes primarily to defects in the bargaining process, including unfairness in the negotiating tactics used to obtain agreement. Along with procedural defects, however, the law has also recognized substantive unconscionability, or a gross one-sidedness in terms. The two often go hand in hand, for one may tend to prove the other. A grossly one-sided agreement may corroborate unconscionable bargaining tactics, while unfair bargaining tactics may most often be employed to obtain a one-sided agreement.

In other words, one would not usually expect a competent adult to agree to contract terms that are oppressive—substantively unconscionable—at the time of the agreement, unless there was a defect in the bargaining process. That process defect might be of the sort contemplated by other contract doctrines, such as misrepresentation or duress, but it might not, and then the unconscionability doctrine is important. An example is the unfair exploitation by one party of the other's special vulnerability.[74] Substantive unconscionability thus suggests the likelihood of procedural unconscionability, and can be said to depend upon that likelihood as part of its rationale for denying enforcement of an unconscionable agreement. But if an agreement's terms would have seemed fair at the time of execution, then there is no reason to suspect procedural unconscionability in securing either party's consent to it. Nor is any doubt created about procedural regularity in execution by substantive terms that seem unfair at enforcement only because of facts that neither party anticipated at the time of execution. We still may wish, of course, to deny enforcement of terms that may have seemed reasonable at execution but which, as things turn out, become enormously one-sided later. But doing so requires the development of a different doctrine than unconscionability, for while substantive unconscionability exists as a legal concept, it is not entirely independent from concerns with procedural unconscionability.

That need for a different doctrine is obscured by courts and statutes which, by their terms, deny enforcement of an agreement if it is unconscionable at the time

---

[74] See Eisenberg, 'The Bargain Principle and Its Limits' (1982) 95 *Harvard Law Review* 741 (explaining how the unconscionability doctrine is necessary to deny enforcement of the stranded desert traveller's promise to pay a million dollars for a jug of water).

of enforcement. Some states that adopted the UPAA have modified it to add such language.[75] It may seem that this approach has the advantage of applying an established doctrine to a new situation, but the temporal shift robs the unconscionability doctrine of much of its rationale. Some courts that apply a 'second look' at an agreement's fairness (a look at the time of enforcement, in addition to the time of execution) do not use the word 'unconscionable' but simply hold that an agreement can be reviewed for 'fairness' as of the time of enforcement. This may not be entirely satisfactory either, for it seems inconsistent with basic ideas of contract law to allow courts to reject any agreement they find 'unfair.' Indeed, concern with just such freewheeling judicial scrutiny is what appears to have motivated the Uniform Commissioners to circumscribe the unconscionability doctrine in the UPAA. The challenge, then, is to develop a doctrine dealing with agreements that seem wrong to enforce because of circumstances prevailing at the time of enforcement, while doing so in a way that is more limited than just allowing courts to refuse enforcement of any contract they believe unfair.

The American Law Institute, borrowing an analysis found in some of the cases,[76] concludes that the real concern in most 'second look' cases is the difficulty of foreseeing, at the time of the agreement's execution, the circumstances under which enforcement will be sought years later. This is not a problem of unconscionability in the classic sense, because it is not a case in which one party has necessarily imposed unfairly on the other. It may be that neither party really foresaw, at the time of execution, the impact of enforcing its terms later. In adopting this general approach, the ALI Principles necessarily fill in some details. Its language, and some of the supporting commentary, is worth quoting, as an example of how such an approach might work.

American Law Institute, Principles of the Law of Family Dissolution, § 7.05

§ 7.05 When Enforcement Would Work a Substantial Injustice

(1) A court should not enforce a term in an agreement if, pursuant to Paragraphs (2) and (3) of this section,
   (a) the circumstances require it to consider if enforcement would work a substantial injustice; and
   (b) the court finds that enforcement would work a substantial injustice.

---

[75] Eg, Conn Gen Stat Ann § 46b-36g(a)(2) (2009) (agreement is not enforceable if 'unconscionable when it was executed or when enforcement is sought'); ND Cent Code §14-03.1-06(1)(2009) (similar, see *Lutz v Schneider*, 563 NW 2d 90 (ND 1997)); NJ Stat Ann 37:2-38(b)(2009) (defining as unconscionable any agreement that 'would provide a standard of living far below that which was enjoyed before the marriage'); Cal Fam Code §1612(c) (2009) (with respect to spousal support terms only).

[76] See, in particular, *Gant v Gant*, 329 SE 2d 106 (W Va 1985), described above, and *McKee-Johnson v Johnson*, 444 NW 2d 259, 267 (Minn 1989) (enforcement may be denied to a premarital agreement fair at its inception 'if the premises upon which [the contract was] originally based have so drastically changed that enforcement would not comport with the [original] reasonable expectations of the parties … to such an extent that … enforcement would be unconscionable.') *McKee-Johnson* was overruled as to a different issue in *Estate of Kinney*, 733 NW 2d 118, 125 (2007) ('the opportunity to consult with independent counsel [is] relevant when assessing whether the agreement was fair and equitable, [but it] is not a *sine qua non* under common law. To the extent that *McKee-Johnson* could be read to indicate otherwise, [it is] overruled on that issue.')

(2) A court should consider whether enforcement of an agreement would work a substantial injustice if, and only if, the party resisting its enforcement shows that one or more of the following have occurred since the time of the agreement's execution:

  (a) more than a fixed number of years have passed, that number being set in a rule of statewide application;

  (b) a child was born to, or adopted by, the parties, who at the time of execution had no children in common;

  (c) there has been a change in circumstances that has a substantial impact on the parties or their children, but when they executed the agreement the parties probably did not anticipate either the change, or its impact.

(3) The party claiming that enforcement of an agreement would work a substantial injustice has the burden of proof on that question. In deciding whether the agreement's application to the parties' circumstances at dissolution would work a substantial injustice, a court should consider all of the following:

  (a) the magnitude of the disparity between the outcome under the agreement and the outcome under otherwise prevailing legal principles;

  (b) for those marriages of limited duration in which it is practical to ascertain, the difference between the circumstances of the objecting party if the agreement is enforced, and that party's likely circumstances had the marriage never taken place;

  (c) whether the purpose of the agreement was to benefit or protect the interests of third parties (such as children from a prior relationship), whether that purpose is still relevant, and whether the agreement's terms were reasonably designed to serve it;

  (d) the impact of the agreement's enforcement upon the children of the parties.

Comment:. ...

b. ... [N]early all premarital agreements involve special difficulties arising from unrealistic optimism about marital success, the human tendency to treat low probabilities as zero probabilities, the excessive discounting of future benefits, and the inclination to overweigh the importance of the immediate and certain consequences of agreement—the marriage—as against its contingent and future consequences. Paragraph (2), however, does not call for the court's examination at divorce of all premarital agreements, but only a subset in which these difficulties are particularly likely. Paragraph (2)(a) identifies contracts made more than a fixed period of years before enforcement is sought, that period having been set in a uniform rule of statewide application. A period of about 10 years would ensure scrutiny of agreements whose enforcement is particularly likely to be problematic, while leaving a clear majority of divorces unaffected (because most divorces occur after fewer years of marriage). Paragraph (2)(b) identifies for scrutiny those cases in which the parties had no children in common at the time of the agreement, but do so at the time that its enforcement is sought. Even childless parties who anticipate having children are often unable to anticipate the impact that children will have on their values and life plans. Once they are parents, the effect of the terms they earlier agreed upon are therefore likely to seem quite different than they expected when childless. Note that, when the parties have children, there are policy issues as well. See Comment c.

c. Most of the fact patterns justifying a substantial-injustice inquiry when enforcement is sought will be captured by Paragraphs (2)(a) and (2)(b), but not all. There are additional cases in which the cognitive difficulties are particularly severe, but which are not easily identified by the simple objective indicators employed in Paragraphs (2)(a) and (2)(b). Paragraph (2)(c) states a more general standard under which at least some of these problem cases may be reached ... .

Illustrations:

1. Prior to their marriage, Susan and George enter into an agreement that keeps most of their property separate rather than marital, and that limits claims for compensatory payments. At the time of the contract, they are childless, have no plans to have children, and work at jobs yielding similar, comfortable incomes. Two years after their marriage, Susan's sister dies unexpectedly, and Susan becomes the legal guardian of her two nieces, then four and seven. Susan changes to part-time work so that she can spend more time with the children. She eventually reduces her employment even further, with George's acquiescence, to devote more time to her nieces.

In the eighth year of their marriage, George and Susan divorce. Susan will remain the children's primary caretaker. Their state has set 10 years as the applicable period under Paragraph (2)(a). Paragraph (2)(a) therefore does not apply because 10 years have not passed since the agreement was executed. Paragraph (2)(b) does not apply, because Susan and George have no children in common. (The conclusion would be different had they adopted Susan's nieces.) However, under Paragraph (2)(c), the court should consider whether the enforcement of this agreement would work a substantial injustice. There has been a change in the parties' circumstances since the agreement was executed that significantly alters the impact of the agreement's enforcement on the parties. Susan has not worked full time for some years. It is unlikely that contracting parties would anticipate the events that brought about this change. Moreover, the changes in the marriage are similar to those that might have occurred if the parties had their own children, in which case Paragraph (2)(b) would have applied. Paragraph (2)(c) requires the same result here, and therefore the court should consider whether enforcement would work a substantial injustice.

The ALI thus offers an approach that is more limited than the traditional cases that seemed to invite a freewheeling judicial review of the agreement's fairness. It permits the inquiry in only a subset of premarital agreement cases, and lists the considerations that bear upon whether an agreement works a substantial injustice.

ii. Foreseeability and Amendment by Conduct

While the law is generally clear that a writing is required to establish a premarital agreement, courts have occasionally held that the parties' conduct during their marriage negated an earlier written agreement. For example, in *Baxter v Baxter*,[77] the parties had kept their finances separate during the first half of their 13-year marriage, but during the second half the wife left her own employment and worked without pay as manager of the husband's golf course, and applied some of her separate assets to the business's debts. The court found that this conduct 'demonstrated mutual intent to rescind' their agreement to retain separate ownership of their assets.[78] New Mexico has put such a principle in its statute, providing that 'a premarital agreement may be amended or revoked ... by a consistent and mutual course of conduct, which evidences an amendment to or revocation of the premarital

---

[77] *Baxter v Baxter* 911 P 2d 343 (Ore App 1996).

[78] For a compilation of such cases, see Annotation by JM Zitter, 'Antenuptial Contracts: Parties' Behavior During Marriage as Abandonment, Estoppel, or Waiver Regarding Contractual Rights' (1987) 56 *American Law Reports 4th* 999. The UPAA has been criticised for appearing to bar such modifications of agreements by later conduct: B Atwood, 'Ten Years Later: Lingering Concerns about the Uniform Premarital Agreement Act' (1993) 19 *Journal of Legislation* 127, 147.

agreement.'[79] Doctrinally, it is possible to understand this rule as merely a particular application of the principle that partial performance takes a contract out of the Statute of Frauds, so that the partially performed oral agreement may permissibly modify the terms of the original writing. But more broadly, these cases and the New Mexico statute illustrate a recognition that the law invites difficulties if it does not take account of the inevitable fact that many parties will end up conducting their lives differently than they contemplated at the time of an agreement made years earlier—thus justifying a second look. Jurisdictions that permit their courts broad equitable authority to decline to enforce premarital agreements may employ equitable doctrines such as estoppel to provide relief in such cases.[80]

iii. The Rationale for a Second Look Review

Why impose special process requirements on premarital agreements, and why allow courts ever to inquire into the fairness of enforcing them? The ALI Principles summarises the arguments it relies upon, in Comment *c* of § 7.02:

> While there are good reasons to respect contracts relating to the consequences of family dissolution, the family context requires some departure from the rules that govern the commercial arena. First, the relationship between contracting parties who are married, or about to marry, is different than the usual commercial relationship in ways that matter to the law's treatment of their agreements. Persons planning to marry usually assume that they share with their intended spouse a mutual and deep concern for one another's welfare. Business people negotiating a commercial agreement do not usually have that expectation of one another ... These distinctive expectations that persons planning to marry usually have about one another can disarm their capacity for self-protective judgment, or their inclination to exercise it, as compared to parties negotiating commercial agreements. This difference justifies legal rules designed to strengthen the parties' ability and inclination to consider how a proposed agreement affects their own interest, such as rules that require transparency in the agreement's language and that encourage parties to seek independent legal counsel.

> Second, even though the terms of agreements made before, or during, an ongoing family relationship address the consequences of its dissolution, the parties ordinarily do not expect the family unit to dissolve. Even if the possibility of dissolution is considered, it is necessarily imagined as arising at some indefinite time in the future. The remoteness of dissolution in both likelihood and timing, as well as the difficulty of anticipating other life changes that might occur during the course of the marriage, further impedes the ability of persons to evaluate the impact that the contract terms will have on them in the future when its enforcement is sought. ...

---

[79] NM Stat Ann § 40-3A-6 (2009).

[80] See, eg, *Krejci v Krejci*, 667 NW 2d 780 (Wisc App 2003), which finds it inequitable to enforce an agreement that excluded the appreciated value of a resort hotel from the marital property division where, during their 18-year marriage, the parties combined their resources, including inheritances, savings, and incomes, operated the resort as a partnership, and generally ignored the agreement, which no longer comported with their expectations. One must distinguish the claims in these cases, which are based on the parties' conduct during marriage with respect to their assets, from claims that one party's marital misconduct should allow the other to avoid an agreement about their property. This latter claim is not ordinarily allowed: see, eg, *Perkinson v Perkinson*, 802 SW 2d 600 (Tenn 1990), rejecting the claim of a wealthy widow to avoid her agreement to provide her new husband with $150,000 in full satisfaction of any claim he might have on her separate property, on the basis of her allegation of his cruel and inhumane treatment.

The two concerns just identified describe distinctive limits on the cognitive capacity with which persons may enter family contracts, as contrasted with commercial agreements. There is, in addition, the point that the rights and obligations that parties might seek to waive through private agreements are designed to protect the interests of persons who enter into family relationships, and the interests of their children. Enforcement of agreements about the consequences of family dissolution therefore present a different policy question than enforcement of commercial agreements between persons who otherwise have no claims on one another's property or income. Family contracts set aside otherwise applicable public policies while commercial agreements do not. Two implications of this difference are noted here. First, when a contract departs from otherwise applicable public policies that are designed to protect parties, the law can reasonably require greater assurance that the parties understand and appreciate what they are doing, than when the contract does not. Second, vindication of the public policies may require rules that limit the enforcement of private agreements that significantly infringe upon them. These policy concerns thus suggest a rationale for special rules for family contracts that is additional to the rationale based upon the cognitive limitations that are likely to impinge upon persons entering into family contracts ... Indeed, the cases in which the parties are most likely to make errors of cognition overlap considerably with those in which significant public policies are most likely implicated: long marriages and marriages producing children.

The Institute thus offers two complementary explanations for treating premarital agreements differently than ordinary commercial contracts: a cognitive rationale, and a policy rationale. The cognitive rationale, as the Institute later explains, arises from the fact that '[c]ontract law is ... based not only upon a philosophical commitment to individual autonomy, but also upon a factual assumption about the abilities of contracting parties.'[81] In this respect, the Institute relies on modern studies from behavioural economics which suggest that the cognitive capacities necessary for the kind of assessment of self-interest assumed by contract doctrine are more likely to be deficient in the premarital agreement context than in the commercial context, and particularly so in the case of long marriages and marriages with after-born children. The policy rationale notes that as the legal obligations arising from family relationships were not based upon contract in the first place, they are not necessarily waivable by contract, either. This point seems obvious with respect to the obligations of parents to their children, but applies as well, the Institute argues, to duties arising between spouses in a long-term relationship. Of course, the law may well allow parties to waive obligations to one another that the law imposes, fully or partially, or only under specified conditions. Permitting such partial or limited waiver is the approach taken by the ALI.

The competing view is stated is *Simeone*, which stands largely alone in its unrestrained commitment to contractual freedom in marital relations. In enforcing the agreement before it, *Simeone* observed that 'the possibilities of illness, birth of children, reliance upon a spouse, numerous other events that can occur in the course of a marriage cannot be regarded as unforeseeable. If parties choose not to address such matters in their prenuptial agreements, they must be regarded as having contracted to bear the risk of events that alter the value of their bargains.'[82] Of course, the real question is not, for example, whether the parties may anticipate having

---

[81] American Law Institute, *Family Law Principles,* above n 1, § 7.05, Comment *b.*
[82] *Simeone,* above n 41, 166.

children, but rather whether they can anticipate all the changes in their life that the presence of children—and all other future developments in their marriage—may bring. As one leading American scholar of contract law has observed,

> It is almost impossible to predict the impact that a prenuptial agreement will have if it does come into play. Personal income may increase or decrease; job skills may be acquired or lost; family obligations may vary in regard to both the other spouse and children; personal expectations may change. Change in the course of marriage is foreseeable, but the specifics of the change are not. The limits of cognition therefore provide a strong justification for a second-look approach to prenuptial agreements.[83]

III. AGREEMENTS MADE DURING MARRIAGE: FIDUCIARY RELATIONSHIPS AND UNCONSCIONABILITY

Nearly all American states treat spouses as having a 'confidential' or 'fiduciary' relationship with one another that gives rise to heightened duties in their mutual dealings—akin to the obligations, for example, of trustees with respect to the beneficiaries of the assets to which they hold legal title. This is clearly the case, for example, in a community property state when either spouse exercises management authority during the marriage over their jointly owned property.[84] In exercising that authority, the spouses have fiduciary obligations to another. Such obligations affect the rules that might govern any contract into which they enter.

Many American states have also treated parties intending to marry as in a 'confidential' or fiduciary relationship. An older opinion of the Washington Supreme Court is typical and often quoted on this point:

> [A]n engagement to marry creates a confidential relationship. Parties to a pre-nuptial agreement do not deal with each other at arm's length. Their relationship is one of mutual confidence and trust which calls for the exercise of good faith, candor and sincerity in all matters bearing upon the proposed agreement.[85]

Contracts between persons in a confidential relationship to one another are subject to heightened judicial scrutiny to prevent either party from exploiting their position of trust to gain a contractual advantage over the other. It appears that a majority of states treat prospective spouses as being in a confidential relationship, and traditional rules imposing special requirements on premarital agreements can be understood as grounded on this difference between their legal relationship as compared to the legal relationship between commercial actors.[86] Just for that reason, in effect, the California Supreme Court in *Bonds* reaffirmed that state's rule that while spouses are in a confidential relationship, those still planning their marriage to one another are not. *Bonds* explains that one common consequence of a fiduciary relationship is

---

[83] MA Eisenberg, 'The Limits of Cognition and the Limits of Contract' (1995) 47 *Stanford Law Review* 211, 254–58.

[84] See, eg, *Bonds*, above n 51.

[85] *Friedlander v Friedlander*, 494 P 2d 208 (Wash 1972).

[86] For more recent cases so holding, see *Friezo v Friezo*, 914 A 2d 533 (Conn 2007) (follows majority rule that parties to premarital agreement in confidential relationship); *Cannon v Cannon*, 865 A 2d 563 (Md 2005) (prospective spouses in a confidential relationship as a matter of law; also, agreement must meet test of substantive unfairness at time of execution).

that the fiduciary will have the burden of justifying any contract between the parties which confers any benefit or advantage upon the fiduciary, and that burden might include showing that no 'undue influence' was applied.[87] Requiring the spouse, seeking to enforce a premarital agreement that advantages him, to make that showing would be inconsistent, *Bonds* observes, with the UPAA. Some other states have taken the same position.[88]

The preceding discussion suggests that as a matter of logic, a state's position on whether prospective spouses have the same confidential relationship as actual spouses should decide whether premarital agreements and agreements made during marriage (marital agreements) receive the same legal treatment. Despite this logic, it is not clear that the states divide along precisely these lines on the question of whether marital agreements are governed by stricter rules than premarital agreements. But they do divide. The statutes of many states seem to indicate clearly that there is no difference in the legal treatment of marital and premarital agreements.[89] On the other hand, a 1994 Minnesota enactment imposes a series of special requirements on marital agreements that the state does not impose on premarital agreements: each party must be represented by separate legal counsel, and the agreement is not enforceable if either spouse commences an action for legal separation or divorce within two years of its execution unless the spouse seeking to enforce it proves it is fair and equitable.[90] Louisiana, in an apparently unique provision, requires marital agreements, but not premarital agreements, to be judicially approved, the judge being required to find that the agreement serves both parties' 'best interests' and that both understood 'the governing rules and principles'.[91] A recent compilation concludes that 17 American states impose requirements on agreements concluded during a marriage that they do not impose on premarital agreements, while 11 states make no distinction between them, with the remaining states having not yet had occasion to address the issue.[92] A few states have never overruled older authorities that find marital agreements invalid as contracts because they lack consideration; these authorities hold that agreeing to remain married, in contrast to agreeing to marry, does not constitute lawful consideration.[93] Both the American Law Institute

---

[87] *Bonds,* above n 51, 831.

[88] Eg, *Mallen v Mallen,* 622 S.E.2d 2d 812 (Ga. 2005) (prospective spouses not in a confidential relationship as a matter of law).

[89] Statutes that apply the same rule without regard to whether the agreement was executed before or during the marriage include Wis Stat § 767.61(3) (2009), which was the basis of the Wisconsin Supreme Court's opinion in the *Button* case (in which the spouses had made both kinds of contract) and North Carolina GS § 52-10(a) ('Contracts between husband and wife not inconsistent with public policy are valid, and any persons about to be married and married persons may release rights which they might respectively acquire or may have acquired'). A case that takes the same position is *Reese v Reese,* 984 P 2d 987 (Utah 1999) ('spouses or prospective spouses may make binding contracts with each other and arrange their affairs as they see fit, insofar as the negotiations are conducted in good faith and do not unreasonably constrain the court's equitable and statutory duties').

[90] Minn Stat Ann §519.11(1a)(2)(c) and § 519.11(1a)(2)(d) (2009).

[91] LA Civ Code Ann art 2329 (2009).

[92] SH Williams, 'Postnuptial Agreements' (2007) *Wisconsin Law Review* 827, 881.

[93] See, eg, *Bratton v Bratton,* 136 SW 3d 595 (Tenn 2004), holding the husband's agreement to give his wife half the property in the event of divorce failed for lack of consideration. The dissent argued that 'the consideration Dr. Bratton bargained for and received was the benefit of domestic tranquility … [and] Ms. Bratton's promise that she would stay in the marriage.' The majority disagreed: 'While life may have been "much better" for Dr. Bratton after he signed the agreement, this "domestic tranquility" does not

and the Commissioners on Uniform State Laws reject this position, adopting instead the rule that consideration is not required for an enforceable agreement, whether premarital or concluded during marriage.[94]

The American Law Institute takes the position that the same principles should apply to agreements made before or during marriage, but observes that those principles are likely to have different application in these two settings. The Institute notes, in particular, that while prospective spouses may have difficulty foreseeing the eventual impact of their agreement, problematic marital agreements are more likely to fail under the traditional unconscionability rule that asks whether the agreement was unconscionable at the time it was executed:

> [O]pportunities for hard dealing may be greater in the context of marital agreements, making claims of unconscionability more likely, than in the premarital context. When one spouse has changed position in reliance upon the marriage, such that divorce will place a particular burden on that spouse, the other spouse's threat to divorce, as a tactic to extract one-sided marital terms, is suspect. In addition, the presence of children, more likely in the developed relationship that is usually the subject of a marital agreement, may create additional opportunities for problematic hard dealing.[95]

The Institute offers several examples. Here is one:

> When Eugene and Dolores marry, they are both employed with comparable incomes, and have no children. Thirteen years later, they have two children, ages seven and 11. Dolores has been the primary caretaker of the children since their birth, and has not been regularly employed since that time. The younger child has learning disabilities, and Dolores has borne the primary responsibility for closely monitoring the child's school performance, and for making sure that the child's school provides the child with appropriate services.

> Eugene, who has been employed as a software engineer, has devoted evenings and weekends to developing a new software product, BugFree. He believes he may soon be ready to license BugFree to a major software company, and hopes to realize significant profits. From a friend who was recently divorced, Eugene learned that under the law of his state his wife would have an equal property interest with him in BugFree, were they to divorce.

---

constitute consideration adequate to support the contract ... This was not a situation in which the parties were already arguing about other issues, after which time a post-nuptial agreement was drafted and entered into. Under the dissent's theory, consideration could be found in many instances which would otherwise amount to or border on coercion. For example, if spouse A wanted to get spouse B to enter into a post-nuptial agreement that was essentially for the sole benefit of A, A could simply create such a hostile environment at home by badgering B until B signed the agreement.'

See also *Simmons v Simmons*, 249 SW 3d 843 (Ark App 2007) (husband's agreement to treat real property held in trust for him as marital property not enforceable for lack of consideration; their marriage is 'past consideration' that cannot support the agreement) and *Whitmore v Whitmore*, 778 NYS 2d 73 (wife's waiver of claims on husband's property in agreement signed three months after marriage unenforceable for lack of consideration: 'Although the wife released her claims on the husband's business property, he did not relinquish any rights to any of her property or give the wife anything in return. The husband claims that his continuing to remain married to the wife provided adequate consideration. We disagree.') The American Law Institute notes, American Law Institute, Family Law Principles, above n 1, § 7.01, Comment c, that cases declining to enforce during-marriage agreements on consideration grounds often present facts that suggest the agreement is problematic on other grounds as well, such as coercive tactics. Bratton would seem to be an example of that point.

[94] American Law Institute, *Family Law Principles*, above n 1, § 7.01(4); Uniform Premarital Agreement Act § 2; Uniform Marital Property Act §§ 10(a) and 10(d).

[95] American Law Institute, *Family Law Principles*, above n 1, § 7.01, Comment *e*.

In recent years, he has had doubts about their marriage. Eugene therefore presents Dolores with a marital agreement, drafted by an attorney he has hired, under which Dolores gives up any marital-property claims she otherwise would have to BugFree. Eugene tells Dolores that, if she does not sign this agreement, he will seek an immediate divorce, because he does not feel he can go forward with BugFree's development and marketing if he does not retain sole ownership of it.

Dolores is stunned to learn that Eugene is considering divorce and at a loss to imagine how she would live and care properly for the children if divorce were to occur. She strongly believes her children's welfare would be seriously compromised were she to return full time to work, yet does not see how she and the children could maintain their accustomed life on compensatory payments and child support alone. As the manager of the couple's household finances, she knows that their current assets are modest. She is also fearful of the impact that divorce and the accompanying disruption would have on the children. She is not certain whether Eugene's threat is serious but feels she cannot take the risk. Unhappily and reluctantly, she signs the agreement.

Five years later, Eugene files for divorce. In the meantime, BugFree has been a success, and Eugene's interest in it worth several million dollars, which would be marital property but for the agreement. The couple's other marital property is worth less than $ 100,000. Eugene seeks enforcement of the marital agreement, and thus allocation of the entire value of BugFree to him as his separate property, with the parties' other property divided equally between Eugene and Dolores.

Because the parties' circumstances at divorce are not different than was contemplated at the time they made their agreement, § 7.05 [dealing with the legal treatment necessitated by the difficulty of foreseeing future developments] is unlikely to present any bar to its enforcement. The contract doctrine of unconscionability, however, is applicable. Dolores, in reliance upon the marriage, had left her employment and made herself financially dependent upon Eugene, so that their potential divorce was a much greater threat to her welfare than to his. In addition, Eugene's threat was effective in part because it exploited Dolores's responsible concern for the welfare of their children. Under the circumstances present here, Eugene's threat to divorce Dolores if she did not sign, as a tactic to obtain her consent to a very one-sided agreement that denied Dolores any claim at all on the fruits of Eugene's marital labor in BugFree, renders the agreement unconscionable, and thus unenforceable.[96]

IV. CHOICE OF LAW RULES: WHICH STATE'S LAW APPLIES

People in the United States move, and they are especially likely to move at the time they divorce. Consider then the Smiths, who meet at college in Massachusetts, marry at the bride's family home in New York, and set up their marital home in California, where they live for the next 10 years while Mr Smith acquires considerable

---

[96] The conclusion of this illustration, that the agreement is not enforceable, is consistent with the result in *Pacelli v Pacelli*, 725 A 2d 56 (NJ App Div 1999), but that case argues that different principles should apply to marital agreements than premarital agreements because 'the dynamics and pressures' are different. For a thoughtful discussion of the difficulties with contracts between persons already married, see M Trebilcock and S Elliott, 'The Scope and Limits of Legal Paternalism: Altruism and Coercion in Family Financial Arrangements' in Peter Benson (ed), *The Theory of Contract Law* (Cambridge, Cambridge University Press, 2001).

stock options in the Silicon Valley company for which he works. Their marriage then runs aground and Mrs Smith moves with their children to Arizona, to where her parents have retired and her sister now lives. Mr Smith moves to Washington state for a new job with Microsoft. Which state's court will hear and decide the matters relevant to their divorce, and whose law will it apply?

American courts generally apply the forum's law in divorce cases, although there are occasional exceptions. For the unexceptional cases, the question of whose law applies is thus transformed into the jurisdictional question of whose courts will hear the case. This brief overview focuses on the jurisdictional and choice of law questions that arise with respect to questions of divorce status, alimony, property, and agreements. This simplified overview does not pretend to provide a complete description of the relevant rules and how they work. Nor does it address at all the special rules for jurisdiction and choice of law that apply to child support and child custody disputes.

Section A below considers the rules that would apply if there were no premarital agreement. The possible impact of the premarital agreement, including the question of which state's law governs its enforceability and interpretation, is treated in Section B. Background principles of American constitutional law that could in theory deny a forum the right to apply its own law to a dispute in which its interest is limited are discussed in Section B. They could in principle be relevant to the analogous choice of law issue addressed in Section A, although the matter seems not to have arisen.

A. Divorce Status, Property, and Alimony

American jurisdictional law has two sources. Federal constitutional principles determine the circumstances under which a state *may* assert jurisdiction; each state's law then determines whether in any particular situation it does. Constitutional principles allow states to dissolve a marriage if one of the spouses is domiciled in that state, no matter where the other spouse lives, and all states entertain divorce petitions filed by their own domiciliaries.[97] Many will also entertain a divorce petition by a non-domiciliary if the respondent spouse is domiciled in the state. So once Mr Smith is settled in Washington, or Mrs Smith in Arizona, either can petition the courts in his or her new home state to dissolve their marriage, and may also be able to petition the court in the other spouse's new home state. Whichever valid petition is filed first will normally govern.

Although the matter is not often addressed, constitutional principles almost certainly also allow a state to adjudicate a divorce petition filed by a non-domiciliary if the state has personal jurisdiction over the other spouse, as it can for any other civil law suit.[98] A state court has personal jurisdiction not only over its domiciliaries, but also over persons served with process while physically present in the state, or persons served outside the state whose contacts with it are sufficient, in both quantity and

---

[97] I Ellman et al (eds), *Family Law: Cases, Text, Problems*, 5th edn (New Providence NJ, LexisNexis, 2010) 759–60.
[98] Ibid, 760–61.

relationship to the dispute in question, to justify the state's exercise of jurisdiction over that particular matter. So, for example, a state that served as the marital domicile for many years could constitutionally exercise jurisdiction over a spouse who no longer lives there, as to a matter involving that marriage. With limited exceptions, however, states do not usually assert divorce-status jurisdiction when neither spouse is currently domiciled in the state.[99] But in any event, the court that hears the divorce petition will almost certainly apply its own law governing the process for dissolving a marriage and the findings necessary for dissolving it. In our example, Arizona would apply Arizona law to that question, and Washington would apply Washington law. This is the principle under which, in the era of fault divorce, individuals whose marital home was in a state with restrictive divorce laws could obtain a 'migratory' divorce, by moving to and establishing domicile in a state with more liberal rules.

Jurisdiction over divorce status does not itself confer jurisdiction over the ancillary issues of spousal support and property allocation. To decide on a petition for alimony, a court must have personal jurisdiction over the respondent spouse. So, for example, if Mr Smith visited his children in Arizona, where Mrs Smith now lives, and she had him served with process for an Arizona proceeding, the Arizona court would have personal jurisdiction over him to adjudicate her alimony claim. A court in a state which was the recent marital home, such as California in our example, may also have personal jurisdiction for this purpose, because the alimony obligation arises from the marriage. If neither spouse lives there, however, and jurisdiction is available in another state which appears to be a more convenient forum, a state in California's position might decline to exercise the jurisdiction it could in theory claim. Once again, whichever court ends up adjudicating the alimony claim will do so under its own law.

The rules governing property claims are somewhat more complex. Jurisdiction to determine a party's claim to personal property (movables) arises in any state with personal jurisdiction over that party, but in theory the rule is different for real property, the ownership of which can only be adjudicated in the state in which the real property is located (the 'situs state'). In the divorce context this standard situs-state rule is often entirely impractical. Consider, for example, the divorcing California couple who have lived there their entire marriage, but who own a vacation home in Colorado. It is obvious that only the California court can decide how to allocate ownership of the Colorado property, as that determination cannot be made in isolation but must take account of the court's allocation of the remaining property as well. The normal solution is for the California court to decide the matter as if it had jurisdiction. While it cannot implement its decision by directly ordering a change in the title to the Colorado property, it can normally expect Colorado courts to honour its decision and effectuate the change in title if need be, even though they are not bound to do so, upon presentation of the California judgment. Alternatively, the California court can order one spouse to convey his or her interest in the property to the

---

[99] The one common exception is for individuals in the military forces who have been assigned to a military base within a state that is not their home state. Nearly all states will hear divorce petitions in marriages in which one of the spouses is a soldier stationed in that state, even if the soldier is not domiciled there. (Military personnel are often not domiciled in the state in which they are based because they usually have no intention to remain there indefinitely or to treat that state as their home.)

other, an order it can enforce through its contempt powers so long as it has personal jurisdiction over the spouse subject to it. Finally, in deciding on the allocation of the Colorado vacation home, the California court will apply its community property law, and not the marital property law of Colorado. That means, for example, that if the Colorado home was purchased with earnings during the marriage, it will be considered community property owned in equal shares by the spouses and divided between them accordingly, regardless of the title in which it is held in Colorado.

Under the more complicated facts of our opening hypothetical, the matter may seem more difficult. Let us assume the principal property question is the allocation of valuable stock options Mr Smith earned while working in California. Assume as well that Mrs Smith filed for divorce in Arizona, and served Mr Smith while he was there visiting their children, so that the Arizona courts have personal jurisdiction over him and can thus decide how to allocate the stock options. Should they apply the law of the forum (Arizona), the state in which the parties lived during the marriage in which they acquired the property (California), the state in which Mr Smith, who earned the property, now lives (Washington), or the state in which the marriage took place (New York)?[100]

Neither Washington nor New York deserve much consideration as the state whose law governs the matter, and they will not get it. Washington has no connection with either the marriage or Mrs Smith. Nor does New York, after conclusion of the original wedding ceremony years ago. California seems a more plausible candidate. Tom Oldham tells us the most common European approach to this question, often called 'total immutability', determines the relevant law at the time of marriage, usually 'either the law of the first marital domicile or the common nationality of the spouses'.[101] 'Common nationality' is not a helpful concept in choosing among the American states, but a rule establishing the first marital domicile would in our case enshrine California law permanently as the source of law for deciding questions about the Smiths' property. Oldham observes that the 'obvious benefit' of this rule is that it 'is clear and the law applicable to the parties' rights is known from the beginning of the marriage.'[102]

In the American context, however, the apparent advantages of 'total immutability' may be illusory. That point is illustrated by considering a second hypothetical couple, the Johnsons, who marry in New York in 1978 and divorce there in 1986 without having ever stepped outside its borders. Between the time of their marriage and divorce, the governing New York law changed dramatically, as the state shifted from a traditional common law system to a unique equitable distribution rule that, alone among American states, treats Mrs Johnson's medical degree as property in which Mr Johnson has an interest. Like every other American state, New York will deal with the Johnsons' property according to the law in place at the time of their divorce, not the law at the time of their marriage. If one conceived of the marriage as a contract in the normal sense, this result would be wrong. Why should the Johnsons'

---

[100] For a helpful review of the varying approaches employed for deciding this question, see T Oldham, 'Marital Property Rights of Mobile Spouses When They Divorce in the United States' (2008) 42 *Family Law Quarterly* 263.
[101] Ibid.
[102] Ibid 265.

property rights be determined by a relatively extreme form of equitable distribution that they could never have anticipated, when they signed up for the common law system? The answer is that American law does not treat marriage as a contract at all, even though the word 'contract' is often used metaphorically to describe it. The fact is that the rules of marriage are not determined by agreement of the parties but by the state, which is entitled to change them along the way.[103] And as we have seen, while the state may allow the parties to set their own rules via marital contracts, it is not bound to honour their choice, and often does not. If this set of rules seems somehow insufficiently deferential to the spouses' wishes, consider whether, as a factual matter, many couples choose their marital domicile on the basis of its marital property rules. A small handful of the very wealthy may, but they are surely an exception. Normal people consult their families, not their lawyers, when deciding where to hold their marriage ceremony.

If 'total immutability' does not make sense, what of a second alternative, 'partial mutability', under which each item of property is governed by the law of the state in which the spouses lived when they acquired it. In the American context in which people frequently move across state lines, the practical advantages of American courts applying their own marital property law at the parties' divorce overwhelms any arguments for partial mutability. It is not just the inherent difficulty of one state mastering another's marital property rules, because in other contexts courts are often asked to perform analogous tasks. It can be done. But a rule of partial mutability that requires the court to decide part of the case by the law of one state and another part by the law of a different state might make it impossible to produce coherent results that implement either state's policies. Suppose, for example, that the forum state's rules require equal division, while some of the property before the court was acquired while the spouse lived in a state that has a rule of equitable division under which departures from strict equality are common. To vindicate the other state's rules, the forum state would have to take into account its equal division of forum-acquired property, because the proper allocation of this other property might be affected by the fact that the forum-state property was divided equally. But should it, for example, let its equal division of forum-acquired property justify a less then equal share of the other property to the financially dependent spouse, when that violates its own policies? Or should it consider the other property as if it were the only property, perhaps justifying a more generous award to the financially dependent spouse under the other state's rules, but only through the device of ignoring facts the other state would want to consider? Multiply these complications by the reality that many married couples will have lived in three or more states by the time of their divorce, and the difficulties become apparent.[104]

---

[103] The estranged wife of the entertainer Jackie Gleason learned this lesson to her detriment after she agreed to a legal separation from Jackie. When New York later changed its law to allow Jackie to obtain a no-fault divorce from her on the basis of that agreement—something he could not have done before the law's change—she resisted his divorce petition on the grounds that application of the new law to her old agreement constituted an impairment of her contractual rights in their marriage, in violation of the Constitution. Rejecting her claim, the court held, among other things, that marriage is not a contract within the meaning of the Contracts Clause of the Constitution. *Gleason v Gleason*, 256 NE 2d 513, 308 NYS 2d 347 (NY 1970).

[104] While the Restatement of Conflicts 2d, § 258, appears to endorse the partial mutability rule criticised here, courts and commentators have not. *Ismail v Ismail*, 702 SW 2d 216, 222 (Tex App 1985) (restatement rule is 'anachronistic' and 'unworkable in modern mobile America'); *Marriage of Martin*, 752

In sum, American courts will generally apply one state's rules to all the property before them in a divorce cases, and that will usually be the forum state's rules. So, for example, a California or Arizona court adjudicating a divorce between spouses who are its current domiciliaries will apply community property law in allocating their property, even if the property in question was acquired by the marital partners while they were domiciled in a common-law state.[105] Tom Oldham has suggested that, in at least some cases, states should apply the marital property law of the spouses' last common residence, rather than the law of forum state.[106] This rule could be a workable alternative, although Oldham recognises that it would have to provide an exception to allow forums to refuse to apply a law that violates an important forum policy. The need for this exception might undermine the advantages the rule is said to offer. In any event, the dominant American rule is in fact that divorce courts apply their own law in deciding on the allocation of the spouses' property at divorce.

B. Whose Law Determines the Validity and Enforceability of an Agreement?

If a premarital agreement is a contract, then it would seem that the choice of law that governs its validity and interpretation ought to be determined by the same rules that determine the law governing any other contract. That could mean, depending upon the forum's choice of law rule, that one would apply the law where the contract was made, or was intended to be performed, or the law chosen by the parties themselves in the contract, if they made a choice and the chosen jurisdiction has some colourable connection to the contract. Yet on the other hand, premarital agreements are also instruments of family law. States need not honour them at all, and most once did not. And, as we have seen, most states still impose both procedural and substantive limitations on them. It would be thus consistent with the approach courts take to adjudicating other divorce issues for the forum to apply its own policies as to the agreement's validity and effect, at least in cases in which the parties have some connection with the forum.

Background constitutional principles can limit a forum's choice of the law to apply in determining a contract's enforceability. In *Home Insurance v Dick*,[107] a Texas domiciliary brought suit in Texas on a fire insurance contract issued to him

---

P 2d 1026 (Ariz App 1986) (same); JJ Sampson, 'Interstate Spouses, Interstate Property, and Divorce' (1982) 13 *Texas Tech Law Review* 1285, 1344.

[105] Under the governing rubric, this is called 'quasi-community property', which means that at divorce, assets acquired by the spouses through labour during the marriage will be treated as if they were community property even though the labour was performed while the spouses lived in a common law state. See *Addison v Addison*, 399 P 2d 897 (Cal 1965) (sustaining the constitutionality of the quasi-community property statute). California has expressed some reluctance in extending the quasi-community property regime to cases in which only one spouse moved there, *Marriage of Roesch*, 147 Cal Rptr 586 (App 1978) (statute not applicable to divorce of California husband from wife who remained in common law marital domicile where they had lived 26 years), but Arizona has rejected this limitation, *Marriage of Martin*, 752 P 2d 1026 (Ariz App 1986) (Arizona and not the conflicting California law applies in determining, for purpose of the parties' divorce, whether assets earned by husband in California, after wife had moved to Arizona, are community or separate property; California had been the marital domicile and husband had never lived in Arizona).

[106] Oldham, 'Marital Property Rights of Mobile Spouses', above n 100, 290–91.

[107] *Home Insurance v Dick* 281 US 397 (1930).

in Mexico, by a Mexican insurance company, protecting him from loss of his tugboat in Mexican waters. The contract itself barred claims brought more than a year after the loss. Mexican law would have enforced this bar, but Texas law disallowed provisions imposing time limits of less than two years. So if the Texas law applied, the suit was allowed; if Mexican law applied, it was barred. When the Texas courts applied Texas law, the defendants appealed. The Supreme Court reversed the Texas courts, holding that application of the Texas statute violated the Due Process Clause of the American Constitution. The Court conceded that a state may ordinarily 'declare invalid the making of certain contracts within its borders' and may prohibit within its borders the performance of contracts made elsewhere if the performance would violate its laws. But this case was different because 'nothing in any way relating to the [insurance] policy sued on ... was ever done or required to be done in Texas.'[108]

> All acts relating to the making of the policy were done in Mexico. [A]ll things in regard to performance were to be done outside of Texas. Neither the Texas laws nor the Texas courts were invoked for any purpose, except ... the bringing of this suit. The fact that [the plaintiff's] permanent residence was in Texas is without significance. At all times here material, he was physically present and acting in Mexico. Texas was, therefore, without power to affect the terms of contracts so made. Its attempt to [to do so] violates the guaranty against deprivation of property without due process of law ...

> ... It is true that ... in the absence of a contractual provision, the local statute of limitation may be applied to [allow a claim of] a right created in another jurisdiction even where the remedy in the latter is barred....When, however, the parties have expressly agreed upon a time limit on their obligation, a statute which invalidates the agreement and directs enforcement of the contract after the time has expired increases their obligation and imposes a burden not contracted for.[109]

This general approach was reaffirmed a few years ago when the Supreme Court sustained Nevada's application of its own law allowing a suit brought by its domiciliary against a California agency (rather than applying the California law that would have barred the suit).[110] The Court quoted with approval from an earlier case observing that '[f]or a State's substantive law to be selected in a constitutionally permissible manner, that State must have a significant contact or significant aggregation of contacts, creating state interests, such that choice of its law is neither arbitrary nor fundamentally unfair.'[111] Nevada's application of its own law was upheld in this case because when such contacts exist, 'a State need not "substitute the statutes of other states for its own statutes dealing with a subject matter concerning which it is competent to legislate".'[112]

What these cases seem to teach is that an American court can constitutionally apply its own law in deciding whether to enforce a premarital agreement, so long as it has a 'significant contact or aggregation of contacts creating state interests' with the marriage. The usual jurisdictional rules keep American states from dissolving marriages unless at least one of the spouses is their domiciliary, and do not permit

---

[108] Ibid 408.
[109] Ibid.
[110] *Franchise Tax Board v Hyatt*, 538 US 488 (2003).
[111] Ibid 494-495.
[112] Ibid.

them to bind a respondent spouse to decisions on alimony or property allocation unless they have personal jurisdiction over that spouse. Although exceptions are possible, a court that meets both these jurisdictional tests is also likely to have sufficient contacts to justify, as a constitutional matter, applying its own law to the question of whether a premarital agreement should be enforced as written. But the question of whether a state can apply its own law is perhaps put most starkly when the parties' agreement itself specifies that another state's law should govern.

If one focuses on party autonomy, one reference point sometimes used in choice of law questions, the refusal to honour the parties' own choice of law provision would seem especially problematic. On the other hand, recall that forums can change the law they apply to their own domiciliaries over time. When they change their requirements for dissolving the marriage, or their rules for allocating property, they can and generally do apply their new rules to marriages commenced under their old ones.[113] While the American constitution does not allow states to impair the obligation of contracts, marriage is not regarded as a contract for the purpose of this rule.[114] The rules of marriage and divorce are instead understood as expressions of fundamental public policies, policies the state may reconsider and revise without the constraint that would be imposed by allowing individual citizens a vested right to have their divorce governed by the law in force when they married—a law the state has now determined to change. The same kind of reasoning explains how a state may conclude that it must apply its own law in deciding whether to enforce a premarital agreement that could alter its otherwise applicable divorce rules. A state's rules may express important policy choices the state is not inclined to allow the parties to override by specifying the law of another state which would so allow. When courts take this approach to premarital agreements they effectively emphasise their family law as opposed to their contractual nature. *Marriage of Bonds*,[115] the lengthy, thorough, and important decision of the California Supreme Court construing the Uniform Premarital Agreement Act (UPAA), is an example. Its analysis of California law was discussed above. But was it clear that California law should apply?

Barry and Sun Bonds met in Montreal, Canada, where Sun was then living. She moved to Arizona in 1987, when they became engaged and commenced living together. Their premarital agreement was drafted by an Arizona attorney with whom they met and in whose office it was executed. They were married in Las Vegas, Nevada, in 1988, after which Barry began the season as a professional baseball player for the Pittsburgh, Pennsylvania Pirates. Barry continued to play for Pittsburgh until the 1993 season, when he moved to the San Francisco Giants. When Barry and Sun filed for divorce in 1994 in California, the court noted that they were then California residents. So whose law should determine the validity of this agreement: Arizona's, Pennsylvania's, Nevada's, or California's? Barry and Sun disagreed on this point: Barry argued California law should apply, while Sun argued for Arizona law. Our discussion of the *Bonds* case in a prior section of this chapter has already revealed the punch line of this story: California law was applied, and the contract was enforced. But it is instructive to review how this conclusion was reached.

---

[113] See the *Gleason* case, described above n 103.
[114] Ibid.
[115] *Marriage of Bonds* above n 51.

As one might surmise from the spouses' conflicting positions, California and Arizona law differed in ways that mattered. Even though states routinely apply new family law rules to marriages entered into before they were adopted, the UPAA itself, interestingly enough, and perhaps consistently with its more general contractual orientation, took the opposite tack: it provides that it shall not apply to premarital agreements entered into before its adoption. California had already adopted the UPAA by the time Barry and Sun executed their agreement, but Arizona had not. Arizona law would thus test the validity of the Bonds' agreement by its pre-UPAA law, which would have required Barry, in seeking to enforce the agreement, to prove by 'clear and convincing' evidence that Sun had 'acted with full knowledge of the property involved and [her] rights therein,' and that the agreement was 'fair and equitable'[116]—rules far more favourable to Sun than the UPAA rules under which the agreement was eventually upheld.

Although the Bonds' agreement contained what seemed to be a choice of law provision, it was, like the rest of the agreement, somewhat sloppily put together.[117] An 'obscure provision entitled "Situs" … stated the following: "This Agreement shall be subject to and governed by the laws of the state set forth as the effective place of this Agreement."'[118] Unfortunately, no other provision in the agreement identified its 'effective place'. The trial court, observing that at the time of the agreement the parties could not have anticipated that they would eventually live in California, decided that Arizona law should apply because that was where the agreement was drafted and executed, and where the spouses lived at that time. The intermediate court of appeals disagreed. It first applied the UPAA's own choice of law rule to reject the agreement's deficient choice of law provision. While that rule allows the parties to specify 'the choice of law governing the construction of the agreement', the court, quoting a commissioner's comment during the Uniform Act debates, emphasised that 'construction' was different from 'validity and enforcement'.[119] 'A forum', this commissioner said, 'will not enforce a contract and provide a remedy which is contrary to its local public policy'.[120] Whether or not this principle is really different from that applied to other contracts may be subject to debate.[121] But in any event, the result was that the sloppiness of the agreement's choice of law provision didn't much matter, because the court found the parties could not choose the law applicable to the main issue in the case (whether the agreement was enforceable) even if it were drafted clearly and meticulously. Note that the implicit assumption of the UPAA commissioner on whose statement the appeals court relied was that on

---

[116] *Marriage of Bonds* 83 Cal Rptr 2d 783, 791 (1999) (quoting Arizona authorities).

[117] This description of the agreement is taken from the opinion of the intermediate court of appeals, ibid, 789, which, unlike the California Supreme Court, did address the choice of law question.

[118] Ibid, 789–90.

[119] Ibid, 791–92.

[120] Ibid.

[121] For example, in the case of employment contracts, one scholar in the area concludes that 'The ability of employers to bind mobile employees to the law of a particular state through a choice-of-law clause depends in large part on which state's courts decide the question. This is because, as indicated by cases reported in the Surveys of previous years, choice-of-law clauses fare significantly better in the courts of the state whose law is chosen by the clause than in other states.' SC Symeonides, 'Choice of Law in the American Courts in 2007: Twenty-First Annual Survey' (2008) 56 *American. Journal of Comparative Law* 243, 287.

this question of enforceability, the forum would apply *its* law, and properly so. This position was implicitly adopted by the appeals court when it rejected Arizona law on the grounds that Arizona's pre-UPAA policies on enforceability conflicted with the UPAA policy that California had adopted. The California Supreme Court never addressed this choice of law question, saying only: 'We ... do not review the determination of the Court of Appeal that California law, rather than Arizona law, governs the enforceability of this agreement, and we express no opinion on this point.'[122] But if it had addressed the question, one guesses it would have agreed that California law should apply. It is not so much that American courts *never* apply the law of another state in deciding the enforceability of a premarital agreement. In *Bradley v Bradley*, for example, the Wyoming Supreme Court agreed to honour a choice of law provision in the parties' premarital agreement specifying that Minnesota law would govern its 'validity, execution, enforcement, and construction'. The spouses executed a post-nuptial amendment to the agreement that did not comply with Minnesota law because they did not have separate counsel and they failed to sign the amendment in the presence of two witnesses or a notary. Although no similar requirements were imposed by Wyoming law, the court followed Minnesota law and found the amendment (but not the original agreement) invalid.[123] On the other hand, the court also found that these Minnesota requirements were not 'contrary to Wyoming law, public policy, or the general interests of our citizens',[124] and cautioned that if they were, they would not be followed. The court thus made clear that the parties' choice of another state's law would not govern if that would mean violating a local policy the court believed important—even where, as here, the parties' contacts with that other state made their choice of its law reasonable.

The difference, then, between *Bonds* and *Bradley* seems to be the forum's different views of the centrality of the public policy as to which the competing laws differ. It is a subtle difference, because in both cases the validity of the disputed contract provisions lay in the balance. It is not that differences in the competing laws matter to the outcome in one case but not the other, but rather the importance to the forum state of the policy choice that produces that different outcome. In *Bonds,* Arizona but not California required that the agreement be fair, and that its proponent carry the burden of so showing, under a heightened standard of proof—a rule the adoption of which would indeed seem of some import. One could argue that in *Bradley*, by contrast, the differences between the Minnesota rules and the Wyoming rules were more procedural and less substantive. Even if crucial to the outcome in this

---

[122] *Marriage of Bonds* 99 Cal Rpr 2d 252, 263 (2000). One should note that neither Sun nor Barry had raised the choice of law question in the intermediate court of appeals, which addressed it (and requested their briefs on the matter) *sua sponte*. From the public record is it not possible to tell whether either party raised the question with the California Supreme Court. And often other American courts do not even acknowledge there is a choice of law question to address. For example, in *Stawski v Stawski*, 43 AD 3d 776, 843 NYS 2d 544 (2007), the wife, an American citizen who married a German citizen in 1975, sought to set aside a prenuptial agreement drafted by a German lawyer in German and executed by the parties in Germany before a German notary the year before they wed. Because the parties has spent their married life in New York, it was reasonable to apply New York law to the agreement. Nonetheless, the court not only analysed the agreement's validity under New York law, it never even considered the choice of law question.

[123] *Bradley v Bradley*, 164 P 3d 537 (Wyo 2007).

[124] Ibid 544.

particular case, this argument would go, they were mere details of execution as to which California as well as Wyoming might have less concern. Perhaps one could, in this way, reconcile the two cases. But one could plausibly argue the opposite as well, that the difference between the Minnesota and Wyoming laws were also important.[125] In that case, one is left with the impression that the real distinction between *Bonds* and *Bradley* is the greater inclination of the California court to insist on its law. If that is the case, then given the absence of any good basis upon which to say whether California's or Wyoming's inclinations are more typical, one is left with little more guidance than the observation contained in some standard texts that forums do tend to apply their own law.[126] Indeed, one guesses that an important reason that forums usually apply their own law is that the parties do not often even raise with the court the possibility of doing anything else.

V. CONCLUSION

American law recognises premarital agreements but remains somewhat ambivalent about them. The dominant understanding is that the law must limit them, but both the appropriate extent of the limits, and the details of their implementation, vary between the states and between the two leading models offered to guide them, the UPAA and the ALI Principles. Fifteen or 20 years ago the clear trend was toward fewer limitations on the subject matter of agreements and less stringent review of their terms and the circumstances under which they are executed and enforced. That trend was propelled by the UPAA and reached its zenith in the Pennsylvania case of *Simeone*. More recently that trend has halted, and in some cases reversed, as exemplified by California's revisions of statutory provisions based on the UPAA. This more recent trend was encouraged by the ALI Principles. While the law is thus somewhat unsettled at present, states seem, for the most part, inclined to view their own rules on premarital agreements as part of their larger set of marriage and divorce policies, as to which they are reluctant, in adjudicating divorces, to yield to conflicting rules that may have been adopted by another state in which an agreement was executed or where the spouses once lived.

---

[125] Certainly, the requirement that each party have his or her own counsel might reasonably be thought important. Moreover, the Minnesota law appears to contain other uncommon provisions that would have barred enforcement of this amendment, not mentioned or focused on by the Wyoming court, but which seem quite significant. For example, it disallows the enforcement of a post-nuptial agreement when either party files for dissolution within two years of its execution—which was in fact the case in *Bradley*, measuring from the time of the disputed amendment.

[126] An American text that observes that the choice of law governing a premarital agreement 'is subject to the same tests concerning governing law as are other contracts', but then goes on to concede that 'several factors tend to weigh in favor of forum law, which the court often views as more equitable'. L McDougal, R Felix, and R Whitten, *American Conflicts Law*, 5th edn (Ardsley NY, Transnational Publishers, 2001) 775.

Marital Agreements and Private Autonomy in Comparative Perspective

JENS M SCHERPE

CONTENTS

I. INTRODUCTION

In an ongoing marriage, the financial relations of the spouses are often of little importance; it does not matter very much which of the spouses owns which asset, who earns more etc. But when one of the spouses dies or the marriage ends in divorce, these issues matter greatly.

This book focuses on the financial relief available upon divorce, in England generally referred to as 'ancillary relief', and, in particular, on the question of whether and to what extent the spouses themselves can agree on what their financial relations are going to be—in other words, how much autonomy the spouses have to regulate their own financial affairs. As a marriage (at least in most legal systems, and certainly in all those considered in this book) requires the consent of both parties involved, it is not unreasonable to assume that the spouses should, in principle, also be free to come to an agreement regarding the financial consequences of the marriage—but the matter is, of course, much more complicated than that, as the comparative view taken in this chapter shows.

Historically, contracts *about* persons to be married were much more relevant than contracts *between* them, not least because, for a long time, women in many jurisdictions did not have the full legal capacity to conclude contracts at all. For example, in early Rome, the *pater familias* had a position of considerable authority and legal power in the family. The wife through marriage became part of the husband's family and subject to his authority (*conventio in manum*). The *manus*-free marriage only became common much later. In the Germanic *munt* marriage, which was the typical form of marriage for freemen (and -women), a contract was concluded between clans. The person having the *muntwalt* over the bride or the clan in the marriage contract pledged to transfer the *munt* (literally: protection, authority) to the groom. In the so-called *Friedel* marriage, on the other hand, the marriage was concluded by the consent of the spouses and the husband did not acquire the *munt* over the wife.

The underlying policies and the nature of marriage as understood by the respective jurisdictions continue to have an enormous impact on the legal rules concerning marital agreements to the present day. In European laws a strong Christian influence can still be seen, and this has had (and to a certain extent still has) an impact on marital agreements. By contrast, in Jewish or Islamic law, marriage itself is considered a contract.[1] In Islam, marriage always includes the payment of a dower (*mahr*) by the husband to the wife, either at the time of marriage or in the event of the dissolution of the marriage. The spouses may negotiate the terms of the dower with regard to content, amount and time of payment, but may not exclude the dower. The Jewish *ketubah* is payable should the marriage end in divorce. Both *mahr* and *ketubah* have a protective function for the wife. These agreements are not only generally accepted, but a (traditional religious) marriage cannot be concluded without them.

In contrast, as the Christian understanding of marriage comprises its principal indissolubility, agreements contemplating the dissolution of a marriage (other than by death) were virtually unheard of before the introduction of divorce and, in any event, were not considered to have any legal effect. However, agreements concluded to regulate the formal separation (separation *a mensa et thoro*) of the couple gradually became accepted.

Even after the introduction of divorce, agreeing on or planning the consequences of the end of the marriage was generally seen as contrary to public policy,[2] as the couple apparently were 'planning to fail'. Today we can see a shift towards a different attitude to marital agreements, namely that in this day and age, with a high number of marriages ending in divorce, not having at least considered the consequences of that happening is seen as 'failing to plan'.[3] In a way, therefore, marital agreements can be seen as something akin to car insurance: one does not plan to have an accident, but is aware of the risk and therefore is taking precautions and insuring oneself against that risk so that financial consequences become manageable and predictable. But marital agreements can have a function that extends well beyond 'insurance', and may be based on other considerations, such as wanting to ring-fence property owned before the marriage, making sure children from a previous marriage receive a fair share of one's property, tax reasons, protecting the

---

[1] See, eg N Yassari, 'The Islamic *Mahr* in German Courts: Characterisation in Private International Law and Accommodation in German National Family Law' in R Mehdi and J Nielsen (eds), *Embedding Mahr in the European Legal System* (Copenhagen, DJØF Publishing, 2011) 193–217, esp 194–99 and the other contributions in that volume; R Arshad, *Islamic Family Law* (London, Sweet & Maxwell, 2010) 4 et seq; D Davidovitch, *The Ketuba: Jewish Marriage Contracts Through The Ages* (Tel Aviv, Lewin-Epstein, 1968); EE Scheftelowitz, *Das religiöse Eherecht im Staat* (Cologne, Carl Heymanns Verlag, 1970) 37 et seq; EE Scheftelowitz, *The Jewish Law of Family and Inheritance and its Application* (Tel Aviv, Edition Olympia, 1947) 92 et seq; M Elon (ed), *The Principles of Jewish Law* (Jerusalem, Keter Publishing, 1975) 387 et seq.

[2] See generally B Lehmann, *Ehevereinbarungen im 19. und 20. Jahrhundert* (Frankfurt am Main, Lang, 1990) and for England and Wales *Hyman v Hyman* [1929] AC 601 (HL) esp 608 and 629.

[3] On the arguments concerning 'planning to fail', see section III.A.ii below. I would like to thank my former student Sarah Hitchins for allowing me to use the phrase 'planning to fail—failing to plan', which was the title of her 2008 dissertation in the 'Family in Society' Seminar.

other spouse from one's creditors etc—and, of course, generally seeking one's own financial advantage.

As already explained in the introductory chapter of this book, none of the legal rules regarding marital agreements can be understood without the legal and social context in which they apply. In the case of a comparative study, this means looking at a great number of different contexts, although a full exploration of these contexts for all the jurisdictions involved in this comparative project is virtually impossible and this chapter does not claim to undertake a 'complete' comparison. The focus will be on identifying the underlying structures, rather than on the details of the legal rules in the respective jurisdictions, but in order to have at least a basic understanding of the function and purpose of marital agreements, it is essential to know what the rules are that apply in the absences of such an agreement; the 'default system'. It must be assumed that the agreement was concluded because the couple wanted rules other than the default ones to apply to their relationship, otherwise the marital agreement would be rather pointless. This comparative chapter will, therefore, begin by describing in brief the default regimes that apply to the financial relations of the spouses in case of divorce and then undertake a comparison of these regimes (see section II below),[4] before pre- and postnuptial agreements (see section III below) and separation agreements (see section IV below) are looked at in the same way. The chapter ends with a comparative analysis and some conclusions regarding marital agreements (see section V below).

II. FINANCIAL RELIEF ON DIVORCE—THE DEFAULT SYSTEMS

A. Overview

As a starting point, it can be observed that in the jurisdictions considered in this book there are two basic approaches to the default matrimonial property regime: either some form of community of property is formed through the act of marriage[5] or the marriage as such does not change the ownership of the assets of the spouses, so during marriage there is a separation of property.[6] In the former case the communal property will be divided at divorce. In the latter case there are a variety of different approaches taken in case of divorce in order to allow a spouse to gain a share of the other's property, to 'participate' in the other's property.

In addition, there are two different ways in which the division of/participation in the property is achieved: the division/participation is either primarily based on rules by providing a matrimonial property regime[7] or, in principle, left to the discretion of the court, so there is no matrimonial property regime as such.[8] That said, in some of the jurisdictions where the division of property is primarily rule-based, there is an element of discretion, just like in some of the jurisdictions where the division of property

---

[4] For this, some jurisdictions will be included for which there are no national reports in this book.
[5] On this see section II.B below.
[6] On this see sections II.C and D below.
[7] On this see sections II.B and C below.
[8] On this see section II.D below.

is left to the discretion of the court, rules are provided in statute or case law to guide the exercise of that discretion. Nevertheless, the fundamental distinction remains.

Looking at the jurisdictions where the division/participation is primarily rule-based, we can group the jurisdictions based on the first observation above.

In the first group we find jurisdictions where there is some form of community of property from the day of marriage (see section II.B below).

In the second group are jurisdictions where the marriage as such does not affect the ownership of the assets (whether acquired before or during the marriage) of the spouses, so during marriage there is a separation of property, but upon divorce the spouses partake in the assets of the other in some form; Pintens[9] has referred to these as 'participation systems', and this term shall be used in this chapter (see section II.C below).

Then looking at the jurisdictions where the division of property in case of divorce is based on the discretion of the court, we can distinguish between those where the discretion is still largely unfettered (third group, see section II.D.i below) and those where the guidance (or even presumptions) provided by statute and/or case law has solidified to such a degree that they now have what can be called a 'rule-based discretionary approach' and the respective jurisdiction can almost be said to have a matrimonial property regime (fourth group, see section II.D.ii below).

Because the division of property is central to financial relief upon divorce and the approaches to this division in each of the groups are so distinctive, this chapter will follow the grouping just set out for the comparison of financial relief upon divorce in general, despite the fact that, of course, financial relief upon divorce comprises much more than just a division of property.

Without wanting to pre-empt the comparative analysis, the key difference between the primarily rule-based approach and the discretion-based approach to the division of property in case of divorce is the primary aim of that division. In the former the aim is to provide certainty as to who owns what (as is generally the aim of property law) or at least who can claim what, whereas in the latter the overarching aim is to achieve 'fairness' (as in England and Wales), or 'proper provision' for the spouses and the children (as in Ireland), or a 'just result' (as in Australia). That said, of course the jurisdictions where the division of property is primarily rule-based also generally aim to achieve an overall 'fair' result for the parties and 'proper provision' upon divorce, but they go about this in a rather different way—by separating the various issues (and remedies) arising. This approach has fittingly been called a multi-pillar approach by Dutta,[10] and this term will be used in this chapter to describe this separation of issues. In these jurisdictions matrimonial property, maintenance and sometimes pensions and allocation of the use of the matrimonial home and

---

[9] W Pintens, 'Ehegüterstände in Europa', *Zeitschrift für Europäisches Privatrecht (ZEuP)* 2009, 268 et seq. W Pintens, 'Ehegüterrecht' in J Basedow, KJ Hopt and R Zimmermann (eds), *Handwörterbuch des Europäischen* Privatrechts (Tübingen, Mohr Siebeck, 2009) vol I, 350 et seq; W Pintens, 'Matrimonial Property Law in Europe', in K Boele-Woelki, J Miles and JM Scherpe (eds), *The Future of Family Property in Europe* (Antwerp, Intersentia, 2011) 19 et seq; see also in the same volume K Boele-Woelki and M Jänterä-Jareborg, 'Initial Results of the Work of the CEFL in the Field of Property Relations Between Spouses', 47 et seq.

[10] See Dutta, Germany, this volume 161; see also JM Scherpe and A Dutta, 'Cross-border enforcement of English ancillary relief orders—Fog in the channel, Europe cut off?' [2010] *Family Law* 385.

household goods are considered separately and, in principle, independently of each other.[11] Hence the financial relief upon divorce rests on several independent 'pillars' which, nevertheless, jointly seek to achieve the overall policy aims. But the policies behind the various pillars may (and do) differ—and, as noted, the primary aim for the matrimonial property pillar is certainty. By contrast, the systems primarily based on discretion do not separate these matters, but generally aim for a 'package solution'—one in which all available remedies are considered at the same time and the court strives to come up with an overall solution that is fair to both parties.

While comparative studies of financial relief upon divorce (including this one) generally put the division of property at the centre, it should therefore be borne in mind when reading this chapter that the property division is only part of the financial relief and that the 'fairness' (or unfairness) of the outcome of the property division needs to be seen and judged in conjunction with the other remedies available upon divorce.

B. Community of Property

In the first group of jurisdictions where the division of property upon divorce is primarily rule-based, the matrimonial property regimes are based on a community of property. In the Netherlands the community of property is a universal one (see section II.B.i below) whereas in the other jurisdictions the community property is generally limited to the marital acquest (see section II.B.ii below).

i. Universal Community of Property

The Netherlands is the only jurisdiction in Europe where the default matrimonial property regime remains[12] the universal community of property: in principle, everything owned (and owed[13]) before the marriage becomes joint property on the day of the marriage, and (with very few exceptions) so does everything acquired during the marriage—even gifts and inheritances, unless the donor/the deceased specifically stipulated that the property should become personal property.[14] Upon divorce, the joint property is to be divided equally and the courts can only depart from the equal division in exceptional cases.[15] While pension rights are nominally to be considered separate from matrimonial property (and thus are a different 'pillar') those accrued during the marriage are also to be shared equally.[16] Thus, despite the broadness of the default matrimonial property (and pension) regime, there is almost no room for discretion.

---

[11] See eg Ferrari, Austria, this volume 51 et seq; Dutta, Germany, this volume 158 et seq; Ferrer-Riba, Spain, this volume 350 et seq.

[12] Eg Portugal abolished the universal community of property as the default matrimonial property regime in 1967; *cf* G de Oliveira, R Martins and P Vítor, 'Portugal' in K Boele-Woelki, B Braat and I Curry-Sumner (eds), *European Family Law in Action IV: Property Relations between Spouses* (Antwerp, Intersentia, 2009) answer to Question 16.

[13] Boele-Woelki and Braat, The Netherlands, this volume 237.

[14] Ibid, 233 et seq.

[15] Ibid, 239 et seq.

[16] Ibid, 242.

This is very different for maintenance (the third 'pillar'), where the courts are awarded wide discretion and can be said to be guided by 'fairness' generally, and two principles ('lack of means' and 'ability to pay') specifically.[17] It is interesting to note that there is a statutory limit for maintenance obligations (with exceptions in cases of hardship) of 12 years and of five years for short, childless marriages.[18]

On the face of it, the universal community of property makes the Netherlands sound like a 'gold-digger's paradise', and, unsurprisingly, marital agreements concerning property are very common.[19]

ii. Community of Acquests

The matrimonial property regime of a community of acquests[20] is, in effect, nothing but a limited community of property: the community property is generally limited to that which was gained non-gratuitously during the marriage (the acquest), and the matrimonial property regime therefore usually excludes inheritances and gifts from the community property. These remain the personal property (sometimes also called 'separate property') of the spouses, as does everything that was owned before the marriage.

The community of acquests is prevalent in the Romanic jurisdictions and, for example, is the default matrimonial property regime in Belgium,[21] France,[22] Luxembourg[23] and Portugal,[24] but it is worth noting that Italian law takes a somewhat different approach.[25] It is also the default matrimonial property regime in Spanish general law (*derecho común*), Aragon, Galicia, Navarre and the Basque Country.[26] Most jurisdictions in Middle and Eastern Europe also have a community of acquests regime as the default matrimonial property system.[27] Several states in the United States, referred to as community of property states in the US report, also functionally operate as community of acquest systems as assets owned before the marriage and gifts and inheritances do not become part of the communal property.[28]

---

[17] Ibid, 242 et seq.

[18] Ibid, 243 et seq.

[19] Ibid, 254.

[20] Sometimes also referred to as 'community of acquisitions', see eg Boele-Woelki and Jänterä-Jareborg, above n 9, 47 et seq.

[21] See the report by Pintens, France and Belgium, this volume 68 et seq.

[22] Ibid.

[23] Pintens, 'Matrimonial Property Law in Europe', above n 9, 22.

[24] de Oliveira, Martins and Vítor, above n 12.

[25] Italian law distinguishes between the personal property of the spouses, the communal property and the communal property *de residuo* (Art 177–79 *Codice civile*). See Pintens, 'Matrimonial Property Law in Europe', above n 9, 270 and Pintens, 'Ehegüterstände', above n 9, 270 and the answers by S Patti et al for Italy in Boele-Woelki, Braat and Curry-Sumner, above n 12.

[26] In Spain family law is not unified and several regions have their own territorial laws (*derechos autonómicos* or *derechos forales*) in family law. See Ferrer-Riba, Spain, this volume 350 et seq; Pintens, 'Matrimonial Property Law in Europe', above n 9, 22 and Pintens, 'Ehegüterstände', above n 9, 269.

[27] See the national reports, especially the answers to Questions 16 and 18a in Boele-Woelki, Braat and Curry-Sumner, above n 12; Pintens, 'Matrimonial Property Law in Europe', above n 9, 23 and Pintens, 'Ehegüterstände', above n 9, 269 et seq.

[28] Ellman, United States, this volume 404 et seq, 408.

a. Basic Structure

The basic structure of the community of acquests is deceptively simple—in principle there are three groups of assets: the communal (or joint) property and each spouse's personal property.[29]

The division into these three groups of assets generally follows the same patterns in all jurisdictions, but there are some very important differences in the detail. In principle, the personal property of the spouses comprises everything they owned before marriage as well as assets they gained during the marriage gratuitously, ie through inheritance or gift. Assets very closely connected to a person are also part of the personal property, namely clothes and personal items, but also, at least in some jurisdictions, damages received for personal injury and for pain and suffering. Assets received or acquired as a replacement for personal property also become personal property. The communal property thus comprises everything that was otherwise gained during the marriage, ie income through work, pensions etc. In most community of property jurisdictions (for example, Belgium, France, Spain and Portugal), income derived from assets that are personal assets also becomes communal property.[30] This could be, for example, rents received from a house or flat that is part of the personal property, dividends from shares, or interest paid from bonds. However, in other community of property jurisdictions, income derived from the personal property remains personal property as it is not seen as 'fruits of the marriage' and is thus independent from it in the same way as gifts and inheritances.[31]

As for debts (including liability for the other spouse's debts), it is difficult to generalise, as the rules vary greatly from jurisdiction to jurisdiction. One can say, however, that there are usually specific rules for debts incurred for the upbringing of the children and for debts incurred for the household. As long as the money spent reflects the normal standard of living of the couple, these are considered joint debts and both are fully liable. For most external debts the other spouse is not liable, but creditors can go after the communal property. This is where the need for a marital agreement may arise. So, for example, where one spouse incurs great risk in his or her business, the couple might agree to a separation of property regime as their matrimonial property regime, so that the income by the other spouse remains his or her personal property; this way it does not become part of the communal property and thus is safe from the other spouse's creditors.

b. Division of Property

When the community of acquests comes to an end (by divorce, judicial separation, death or agreement), in principle the communal property is divided equally and the

---

[29] See Pintens, France and Belgium, this volume 71 et seq, Ferrer-Riba, Spain, this volume 352 et seq, Ellman, United States, this volume 404 et seq and the references in n 27.

[30] For Belgium (Art 1405 Civil Code) and France (Art 1401 Civil Code) see Pintens, France and Belgium, this volume 72; for Spain (Art 1347 Civil Code) see Ferrer-Riba, Spain, this volume 352; for Portugal (Art 1728 Civil Code) see the answers to the questionnaire provides de Oliveira, Martins and Vítor, above n 12; see generally Pintens, 'Matrimonial Property Law in Europe', above n 9, 23.

[31] Eg Slovenia, Serbia and Croatia; see the answers to the questions for those jurisdictions in Boele-Woelki, Braat and Curry-Sumner, above n 12 and Pintens, 'Matrimonial Property Law in Europe', above n 9, 23 et seq.

spouses keep their personal property. However, it is not quite that simple. Because if one of the assets groups has 'benefited' financially from one of the other asset groups, the benefit has to be compensated before the division of the acquest takes place. A typical example is where a spouse has paid for the extension or renovation of a house that is communal property from his or her personal property; in this case, the communal property owes the personal property the relevant sum. Likewise, if one of the spouses uses his or her salary to renovate a house that is personal property, a compensation payment has to be made. The same applies where debts of one spouse were paid off from the communal property, or vice versa. These compensation payments are, therefore, part of the overall balance for the division of the assets.

The 'benefit' one group of assets derived from the payment of another is calculated nominally in most jurisdictions. So if the husband paid 50,000 for an extension of the jointly owned home from his personal property, his claim is 50,000. However, some jurisdictions (for example, Belgium and France) take a different position if the payment was made to buy, maintain or improve property;[32] in that case, the 'benefit' is calculated to include a later increase in value. For example: the couple buy a house for 500,000. This is paid for by the communal property, except for 50,000 which the wife pays from her personal property. At the time of the divorce the house is worth 600,000. The wife's claim against the communal property is then 60,000: the original 50,000 plus the 20 per cent increase in value for her 'share'.

Once all the compensation calculations are done, the parties each have a claim to half the remaining communal property. Importantly, the claim is a claim in rem, i.e. they actually already both own half of the assets.[33]

Crucially, the division of property in almost all[34] of the European community of acquest jurisdictions is static: there is no room for judicial discretion. The judge cannot do anything but determine the shares and then divide them equally. In five of the eight community property states of the US there is nominally to be an 'equitable' (rather than equal, as in the other three) distribution, although equal division seems to be the rule. The judge, however, retains the discretion to divide the assets differently.[35]

Finally, most community of acquest systems allow the court to allocate specific assets to one spouse if there is a good reason for it. Most often this will be the matrimonial home which is allocated to the spouse who continues to take care of the children, but also household goods or assets needed for the exercise of a profession. However, this does not mean that anything other than an equal division of the communal property takes place; the beneficiary of such an allocation has to compensate the other for the full amount and does not receive a larger share than half of the community property. An alternative to the preferential allocation of the property itself is the allocation of the *use* of the property.[36]

---

[32] See Pintens, France and Belgium, this volume 74 et seq.

[33] It is important to keep in mind here that the civil law jurisdictions do not distinguish between legal and equitable ownership.

[34] Poland and Serbia allow for a limited discretion, but apparently, in practice, the courts do not very often depart from equal sharing; cf Pintens, 'Matrimonial Property Law in Europe', above n 9, 26.

[35] Ellman, United States, this volume 405.

[36] See, eg Ferrer-Riba, Spain, this volume 355 et seq; Pintens, France and Belgium, this volume 76 et seq.

c. Maintenance (and Compensation)

In addition to—and, in principle, independently of—the division of property, payments can be claimed in case of divorce in all community of acquest jurisdictions. These payments can take the form of periodical payments or a lump sum payment. Despite the fact that these payments are referred to in some systems as compensatory payments (*prestation compensatoire* in France,[37] *pension compensatoria* in Spain[38]), the function of these payments extends beyond (but certainly includes) mere compensation for marriage-generated disadvantages, and has a clear maintenance function as well. The maintenance component is not limited to the basic needs of the spouse, but can take into account the marital standard of living.[39]

In determining the additional payments, the courts in general have a wide discretion and are to take into account all the circumstances of the case.[40] As the determination takes place after the division of property and allocation of the use of certain property, the courts will take into account those outcomes when assessing the (further) need and compensation of the claimant spouse. Thus, although technically they are separate matters, the courts to a certain extent consider what the claimant will receive or has received under one of the other 'pillars'.[41]

d. Pension Rights

The treatment of pensions differs significantly in the community of acquest jurisdictions, but in all jurisdictions pension rights play an important role. For example, in Spain and France they can be taken into account and compensated for in the *pension compensatoria/prestation compensatoire* as just described[42] and in some of the US states they are considered—and divided—separately.[43]

iii. Summary

The common feature of the community of property jurisdictions, unsurprisingly, is that either a universal or partial community of property is created by the act of marriage; from the day of the marriage the couple own some property jointly (and increasingly so during the marriage). Marriage thus has an immediate property law effect. This is seen as an expression of marital solidarity, of the marriage as a partnership and a community of sharing.

There virtually is no room for discretion by the court when it comes to the division of the communal property in case of divorce, and the communal property is generally shared equally. As such, community of property systems, despite potential disputes

---

[37] See Pintens, France and Belgium, this volume 76 et seq.

[38] Ferrer-Riba, Spain, this volume 356 et seq.

[39] Ibid, 357; Pintens, France and Belgium, this volume 76.

[40] Pintens, France and Belgium, this volume 76; Ferrer-Riba, Spain, this volume 356; Ellman, United States, this volume 410 et seq.

[41] Ferrer-Riba, Spain, this volume 357; Ellman, United States, this volume 410; Pintens, France and Belgium, this volume 76 et seq.

[42] Ferrer-Riba, Spain, this volume 356 et seq; Pintens, France and Belgium, this volume 77.

[43] Ellman, United States, this volume 410 et seq.

about valuation of some assets and compensation payments between the different groups of assets in the community of acquest jurisdictions, offer a significant degree of certainty as to who owns the property and/or what the property entitlements are. As discussed below,[44] the property consequences can generally be contracted out of by the spouses. However, property division is only part of the picture.

Another central expression of marital solidarity in the community of property systems is the availability of further claims in case of divorce, particularly for maintenance in one form or another. These, in principle, are to be seen as distinct from property; here the courts have a very wide discretion and are to take into account all the circumstances of the individual case. It can be said that the policy aims of family law to a certain extent depend on the claims other than those for matrimonial property. As is discussed later,[45] contracting out of these further consequences of divorce is much more difficult and restricted, if not impossible, in many of the community of property jurisdictions.

C. Participation Systems

In the second group of jurisdictions where the division of property upon divorce is primarily rule-based, the matrimonial property regimes are based on a separation of property during marriage. What they have in common is that the marriage as such does not alter the proprietary relations of the spouses: during marriage both spouses retain their personal property, including everything acquired during the marriage. Once the marriage has ended, however, the spouses participate in each other's property. Two different approaches to matrimonial property in this group can be distinguished: jurisdictions with a deferred community of property (see section II.C.i below) and jurisdictions with 'statutory compensation clauses'[46] (see section II.C.ii below).

i. Deferred Community of Property

a. Division of Property in Case of Divorce

The default matrimonial property regime in the Nordic countries (Denmark, Finland, Iceland, Norway and Sweden)[47] is a deferred (universal) community of property regime: the marriage as such does not alter the proprietary relations of the

---

[44] See section III below.

[45] Ibid.

[46] As they are called by Pintens, 'Matrimonial Property Law in Europe', above n 9, 29. See also Pintens, 'Ehegüterstände', above n 9, 271 et seq.

[47] While the matrimonial property regimes in the Nordic countries are quite similar and go back to the Nordic cooperation around 1910, there are some differences. The family laws of the Nordic countries can be grouped into two subgroups with greater similarities, namely the east Nordic countries (Sweden, Finland) and the west Nordic countries (Denmark, Iceland, Norway). However, the basic underlying principles are very much the same. For a full comparison see A Agell, *Nordisk äktenskapsrätt* (Copenhagen, Nordiska Ministerrådet, 2003). See also Jänterä-Jareborg, Sweden, this volume 377; JM Scherpe, 'Privatautonomie im Familienrecht der nordischen Länder' in S Hofer, D Schwab and D Henrich (eds), *From Status to Contract?—Die Bedeutung des Vertrages im europäischen Familienrecht* (Bielefeld, Gieseking, 2005) 212–19; JM Scherpe, 'Matrimonial Causes for Concern?—A Comparative Analysis of *Miller v Miller; McFarlane v McFarlane*' (2007) 18 *King's Law Journal* 348 et seq.

spouses and, in principle, each spouse can deal with his or her property as they see fit, including contracting with each other. Some safeguards are in place, especially restrictions as to the disposal of the family home etc.[48] However, in the event of a divorce, all the assets (including pension rights) of both spouses become communal property, except where these assets were acquired by gift or inheritance with the express stipulation that they should become personal property.[49] So the community of property is deferred until the divorce, when the communal property is in principle divided equally.[50]

While this deferred community of property regime and the principle of equal division might have been appropriate for the traditional family situation in the 1900s, social circumstances have changed considerably since then and a rigid system of equal division could now lead to manifestly unfair results in some cases.[51] All Nordic countries, therefore, now have statutory provisions that allow for a departure from the principle of equal division, unsurprisingly called 'unequal division'.[52]

In short, a departure from equal division is generally possible at the discretion of the court when an equal division would be inequitable. In Denmark this is deemed to be the case when the marriage was short (which is generally assumed to be a marriage of less than five years), did not involve an economic community *and* where there was a considerable asset disparity between the parties at the beginning of the marriage or one arose during the marriage through an inheritance of gifts received by one of the spouses.[53] In this case some assets can be 'taken out' of the matrimonial property pool by the court and do not have to be shared. In Sweden[54] and Finland[55] the criteria are more general and allow for an unequal division if, considering the economic situation of the spouses, it would be inequitable to come to an equal division. Finland even has an additional provision that there should not be an equal division if this would result in an improper economic advantage for one of the spouses. In Iceland the general clause for unequal division is even wider[56] and allows for a departure from equal division if dividing the assets equally would be

---

[48] Jänterä-Jareborg, Sweden, this volume 373 et seq.

[49] Ibid, 371.

[50] Ibid, 375.

[51] Denmark is now considering a reform of its matrimonial property regime and established a commission to that effect (*Retsvirkningsudvalget*), see Justitsministeriet, *Kommissorium for Retsvirkningslovsudvalget*, 3 September 2009, sagsnr 2009-793-0052, dok LVM40539. The first meeting of the commission took place on 5 January 2010; the commission expects to complete its review of the law and recommendations in 2013.

[52] On the 'unequal division' see Agell, above n 47, 373 et seq and the answers to Question 127 for Denmark (I Lund-Andersen and I Magnussen), Finland (K Kurki-Suonio), Norway (T Sverdrup) and Sweden (M Jänterä-Jareborg, M Brattström and K Walleng) in K Boele-Woelki, B Braat and I Curry-Sumner (eds), *European Family Law in Action IV: Property Relations between Spouses* (Antwerp, Intersentia, 2009); see also Scherpe, 'Matrimonial Causes for Concern', above n 47, 214 et seq; JM Scherpe, 'A Comparative View of Pre-Nuptial Agreements' [2007] *International Family Law* 18 et seq and Scherpe, 'Privatautonomie', above n 47, 214 et seq.

[53] Fællesboskiftelov, s 69a; see the answer to Question 127 for Denmark by Lund-Andersen and Magnussen, above n 52; Scherpe, 'Privatautonomie', above n 47, 215; Agell, above n 47, 376 et seq.

[54] Äktenskapsbalk, ch 12, s 1; see the answer to Question 127 for Sweden by Jänterä-Jareborg, Brattström and Walleng, above n 52; Scherpe, 'Privatautonomie', above n 47, 215 et seq; Agell, above n 47, 377 et seq.

[55] Äktenskapslag, s 103b; see the answer to Question 127 for Finland by Kurki-Suonio, above n 52; Scherpe, 'Privatautonomie', above n 47, 216 et seq; Agell, above n 47, 380 et seq.

[56] Ægteskabslov, s 104; Scherpe, 'Privatautonomie', above n 47, 217; Agell, above n 47, 382.

unreasonable. In Sweden, Finland and Iceland, as in Denmark, unequal division is supposed to be an exception and mainly applicable in cases of short marriages or, to a more limited extent, if the assets were acquired before the marriage or by gift or inheritance.[57] So the systems remain rule-based, but have an element of discretion which can be applied if and when appropriate.

Norway has gone a step further, and in 1991[58] introduced a provision that gives a spouse the right in divorce proceedings to apply to the court to have property he or she owned before the marriage (as well as gifts and inherited assets during the marriage) excluded from the matrimonial property pool. This right, however, may be set aside if it would be inequitable to make use of it. The section of the relevant act expressly mentions that in making that decision, the court not only has to take into account the duration of the marriage, but also the contribution to the family made by the spouses. But, in principle, all it takes in Norwegian law to exclude property from the equal division is an application supported by proof that the property was owned before the marriage or was an inheritance or gift during the marriage, as long as excluding it is equitable. This brings the Norwegian system very close to being a deferred community of acquests or a deferred community of accrued gains[59] rather than a deferred community of property jurisdiction.

b. Maintenance

Periodical payments to cover maintenance are of limited importance in the Nordic countries. It is a general policy aim to achieve a clean break, to totally sever the ties between the former spouses and periodical payments are seen as upholding those ties.[60] Maintenance, if granted at all, will only be awarded for a short period, and is only granted for an unlimited period in exceptional cases. The function of maintenance, where it is awarded, is not to ensure that the spouse maintains a certain standard of living, but rather to enable the receiving spouse to have a 'fresh start'; a lump sum payment can be awarded for this, but this is very rarely done.[61] The basic position is that each spouse is responsible for his or her own maintenance after divorce, and if the spouse cannot meet his or her maintenance needs, then social welfare benefits should be available.[62] Hence 'need' as a matter of principle

---

[57] Agell above n 47, 376 et seq; for Sweden see A Agell and M Brattström, *Äktenskap, Samboende, Partnerskap* 4th edn (Uppsala, Iustus Förlag, 2008) 186 et seq; A Erkisson, *Den nya familjerätten* 8th edn (Stockholm, Norstedts Juridik, 2006) 40 et seq; A Wickström and U Komujärvi, *Familherätten— En introduktion* 2nd edn (Stockholm, Norstedts Juridik, 2005) 38 et seq.

[58] Ekteskapslov, s 59. See the answer to Question 127 for Norway by Sverdrup, above n 52; Scherpe, 'Privatautonomie', above n 47, 217 et seq; Scherpe, 'Matrimonial Causes for Concern', above n 47, 352; Agell, above n 47, 383 et seq.

[59] See section II.C.ii.a below for the community of accrued gains.

[60] Jänterä-Jareborg, Sweden, this volume, 377; Scherpe, 'Privatautonomie', above n 47, 233 et seq; JM Scherpe, 'Eigenverantwortung von Frauen und Männern nach einer Ehe in Schweden und England' in Bundesministerium für Familien, Senioren, Frauen und Jugend (eds), *Rollenleitbilder und -realitäten in Europa: Rechtliche, ökonomische und kulturelle Dimensionen*, Forschungsreihe Band 8 (Baden-Baden, Nomos, 2009) 201 et seq.

[61] Jänterä-Jareborg, Sweden, this volume, 378.

[62] Ibid, 377 et seq; M Jänterä-Jareborg, 'Marriage Dissolution and Maintenance to a Spouse Following Divorce: Sweden' in S Hofer, D Schwab and D Henrich (eds), *Scheidung und nachehelicher Unterhalt im europäischen Vergleich* (Bielefeld, Gieseking, 2003) 277 et seq, esp 282 et seq; Scherpe, 'Privatautonomie',

is to be covered by the State rather than the ex-spouse—which presents a stark contrast to the position in other jurisdictions.[63]

The following Swedish case illustrates the general approach quite well.[64] The couple were married for 28 years and had several children, when the wife became incapable of working due to an illness; a divorce followed. Her inability to work was not considered a reason to award her maintenance, despite the fact that she still took care of one of the children. The argument simply was that her need was not generated by the marriage and the husband was therefore not responsible for her needs arising from the illness, so no maintenance payments for her personally were awarded. While this may at first sound rather harsh, this result of course has to be understood first in the context of the community of property system (in principle entitling her to an equal share of the matrimonial property, as explained above) and secondly (and perhaps more importantly) the state welfare systems in the Nordic countries with their high social security benefits; the woman in the case, for example, presumably received a state pension because of her illness which, together with other benefits (for example, for housing, childcare facilities etc), covered her needs.

c. Summary

In the Nordic countries the default matrimonial property regime is the deferred community of property: a separation of property during the marriage which becomes a universal community of property in case of divorce.[65] In principle, all assets (including pension rights) are then to be shared equally, but exceptions from equal sharing can be made at the court's discretion, particularly in cases of short marriages, property acquired before the marriage or during the marriage by gift or inheritance.[66] So in a way, this system could be called a 'discretion-based rule system' (meaning a system primarily based on rules with discretion in some circumstances).[67] In practice, however, the courts are reluctant to deviate from equal sharing and rarely exercise their discretion except in the case of short marriages.

Maintenance is considered separately from the matrimonial property regime, but is rarely awarded for long periods as the provision for needs is seen as a duty of the state rather than of the ex-spouses. Maintenance does not, therefore, play a great role in financial relief upon divorce.

---

above n 47, 233 et seq; Scherpe, 'Eigenverantwortung', above n 60; Scherpe, 'Matrimonial Causes for Concern', above n 47, 353; On maintenance obligations in Sweden generally see M Jäntera-Jareborg, 'Answers for Sweden', in K Boele-Woelki, B Braat and I Sumner (eds), *European Family Law in Action II: Maintenance Between Former Spouses* (Antwerp, Intersentia, 2003).

[63] On this see section II.E.v below.

[64] Högsta Domstolen, Nytt Juridisk Arkiv (NJA) 1998, 238ff. See also Jäntera-Jareborg, Sweden, this volume, 378 and S Schwarz and JM Scherpe, 'Nachehelicher Unterhalt im internationalen Privatrecht' *FamRZ* 2004, 665, esp 667 et seq.

[65] Only assets that are personal property because of a marital agreement or because they were specifically designated as such in a case of gifts or inheritance are not part of this communal property.

[66] But note the different approach in Norway, described above.

[67] As the starting point is the rule rather than the discretion. See section II.D.ii below on 'rule-based discretion' jurisdictions.

ii. Statutory Compensation Systems

In the other sub-group of the jurisdictions in which marriage does not alter the property relations of the couple are the jurisdictions in which there is never any form of community of property. However, at the time of divorce, statutory rules apply (called 'statutory compensation clauses' by Pintens)[68] which allow one spouse to make monetary claims against the other. The main legal systems in which this can be found are the so-called 'Germanic' legal systems: the community of accrued gains (*Zugewinngemeinschaft*) is the default matrimonial property regime in Germany,[69] and in Switzerland and Greece the regime is one of participation in acquests (*Errungenschaftsbeteiligung*).[70] Some other jurisdictions, like Catalonia and Valencia also operate a separation of property regime with a (much more limited) statutory compensation clause, but both cannot be discussed here.[71]

a. Community of Accrued Gains

The community of accrued gains (*Zugewinngemeinschaft*) is the default matrimonial property system in Germany. Its name is somewhat misleading, as at no point in time is there actually any form of community of property: the property of the spouses stays personal property not only during marriage, but also upon divorce. However, upon divorce a spouse may claim his or her participation in the other's gains accrued during the marriage (so-called *Zugewinnausgleich*).

The community of accrued gains, in principle, offers mathematical precision as to the division of property upon divorce, and—issues of valuation not withstanding—determines with certainty the amount of the monetary claims of the spouses.[72]

In Germany this is achieved by looking at the assets (and debts) of each of the spouses at two points in time: at the time of marriage (called initial assets, *Anfangsvermögen*) and at the time of divorce (called final assets, *Endvermögen*). Gifts and inheritances received during marriage count as initial assets. The burden of proof lies on the respective spouse, and if it cannot be proved that an asset was an initial one, it will be considered as a final asset, and there are mutual duties of disclosure.[73] Following recent reforms, debts are included in this calculation; so, for example, a reduction in debts will also constitute a gain.[74]

In order to determine the accrued gain of each of the spouses, the initial assets are subtracted from final assets. If one spouse has a greater gain than the other, then the

---

[68] Pintens, 'Matrimonial Property Law in Europe', above n 9, 29.

[69] See section II.C.ii.a below.

[70] See section II.C.ii.b below.

[71] But see Ferrer-Riba, Spain, this volume, 353 et seq and Pintens, 'Matrimonial Property Law in Europe', above n 9, 32.

[72] See Dutta, Germany, this volume, 161 et seq. See also the answers for Germany to Questions 57 et seq by N Dethloff and D Martiny, in Boele-Woelki, Braat and Curry-Sumner, above n 12.

[73] ss 1377, 1379 BGB, see Dutta, Germany, this volume, 162.

[74] *Gesetz zur Änderung des Zugewinnausgleichs- und Vormundschaftsrechts* of 6 July 2009, BGBl 2009 I 1696, see Dutta, Germany, this volume, 162. See also R Hoppenz, 'Reformbedarf und Reformbestrebungen im Zugewinnausgleich' *FamRZ* 2008, 1889 et seq; E Koch, 'Die geplanten Neuregelungen des Zugewinnausgleichs' *FamRZ* 2008, 1124 et seq.

difference in gain has to be shared equally and the spouse with the lower gain then has a claim against the other accordingly.[75]

There is virtually no room for discretion in this system, and the hardship clause in German law is only applied in extraordinary circumstances, for example, if one spouse has tried to kill the other.[76]

In Germany the system is purely mathematical and is based solely on the value of the assets and not on their origin or source. While this provides a significant degree of certainty, this may lead to outcomes that are perceived as unfair, for example, when damages for pain and suffering are effectively shared.[77] Another criticism of this matrimonial property system is that if the initial assets increase or decrease in value[78] this all becomes part of the calculation, despite the fact that the marriage had absolutely nothing to do with this change in value. For example: a house owned at the time of marriage was worth 500,000, at time of divorce it is worth 1.2 million—that means that there is a gain of 700,000 which now has to be shared (which often leads to the house being sold). Likewise, income derived from initial assets becomes part of the accrued gain and is to be shared. It is, therefore, not uncommon in cases where such a situation might arise to have matrimonial property agreements that expressly exclude specific assets so that neither the income nor the value increase are to be shared.

Pension rights are considered a different 'pillar' and are dealt with separately and independently of the property division. Pension rights acquired during marriage are subject to (equal) pension sharing for which there are strict (and complicated) rules.[79]

Even after the recent reforms in Germany[80] maintenance still plays a central role in financial relief on divorce and, in principle, is awarded at the court's discretion if one of the circumstances defined in the statute is met (for example, inability to maintain oneself because of ongoing childcare, old age, illness, unemployment etc).[81] It is worth noting that the duty to maintain extends beyond needs generated by the marriage.

b. Participation in Acquests

The Swiss participation in acquests regime (*Errungenschaftsbeteiligung*) follows a somewhat different pattern and distinguishes four different groups of assets, namely

---

[75] Dutta, Germany, this volume, 161 et seq. See also Dethloff and Martiny, above n 72 answers to Questions 80 et seq.

[76] s 1381 BGB. See BGH 18.3.1992, *FamRZ* 1992, 787.

[77] *Cf* BGH 27.5.1981, *BGHZ* 80, 384 and BGH 29.10.1981, *BGHZ* 82, 145.

[78] Other than by inflation, as the value of the initial property is indexed for the purposes of the calculation of the gains, *cf* Pintens, 'Matrimonial Property Law in Europe', above n 9, 30; BGH 14.11.1973, *FamRZ* 1974, 83; BGH 14.3.1990, *FamRZ* 1990, 603.

[79] See Dutta, Germany, this volume, 162; Dethloff and Martiny, above n 72 answers to Question 88; J Hauß and R Eulering, *Versorgungsausgleich und Verfahren in der Praxis* (Bielefeld, Gieseking, 2009); P Friederici, *Praxis des Versorgungsausgleiches* (Cologne, Luchterhand, 2010); F Ruland, *Versorgungsausgleich: Ausgleich, steuerliche Folgen und Verfahren* (Munich, Beck, 2011).

[80] On which see K Kroll, 'The Reform of German Maintenance Law' in B Atkin (ed), *The International Survey of Family Law 2007* (Bristol, Jordan Publishing, 2007) 85 et seq.

[81] See Dutta, Germany, this volume, 164 et seq.

the personal assets of each spouse and the acquest of each spouse.[82] The personal assets comprise personal items and assets owned before the marriage, as well as gifts and inheritances and damages for pain and suffering, the acquests comprise all other assets, and debts are allocated accordingly.[83] If it cannot be proved that an asset is personal, it is presumed to be part of the acquest.[84]

Unsurprisingly, the spouses retain their personal assets in case of divorce, but can claim half of the value of the acquest of the other. However, just as in the community of acquest jurisdictions, before such a claim can be made compensation payments between the four asset groups need to be made/calculated.[85] So for every financial 'benefit' one of the assets groups derived through investment etc., this benefit has to be compensated for before the division of the acquest takes place.

Maintenance and pensions are considered a different 'pillar' and are dealt with separately and independently of the property division. While there are rules on how pensions are to be shared,[86] maintenance is to be awarded at the court's discretion.[87]

While Greek law follows the same principles as the German community of accrued gains, it takes a different approach as it does not operate with initial and final assets but rather excludes certain assets from the calculation altogether, namely assets owned before the marriage and those acquired during the marriage by gift or inheritance.[88] This has the advantage that, unlike in Germany, the increase or decrease in value of these assets does not enter into the calculation of the acquest, and neither does income derived from these assets. Therefore, the Greek matrimonial property regime is better characterised as a participation in acquests system.

However, in Greek law the marital acquest is not shared equally, but is to be shared according to the contribution of the spouses. There is statutory a presumption that each spouse has only contributed one-third to the gain of the other and therefore can only claim one-third of the gain (rather than half). Importantly, though, this presumption is rebuttable. So if a spouse can prove that he or she contributed more (or the other spouse can prove there was a lower contribution) then this will increase or decrease the claim accordingly.

In Greece the dissolution of the matrimonial property regime through divorce apparently does not have an effect on pension rights and related claims.[89] Maintenance can

---

[82] See the answers to Questions 57 et seq for Switzerland by I Schwenzer and A Bock, in Boele-Woelki, Braat and Curry-Sumner, above n 12. See also Pintens, 'Ehegüterstände', above n 9, 275.

[83] Ibid, answer to Question 59.

[84] Art 200(3) Swiss Civil Code.

[85] See section II.B.ii.b.

[86] For the division of pensions see H Hausheer, 'Vertragsfreiheit im Familienrecht in der Schweiz', in S Hofer, D Schwab and D Henrich (eds), *From Status to Contract?—Die Bedeutung des Vertrages im europäischen Familienrecht* (Bielefeld, Gieseking, 2005) 73 et seq, but see Schwenzer and Bock, above n 82 answer to Question 88.

[87] Arts 125–32 ZGB. On this see the answer to Questions 55 et seq for Switzerland by H Hausheer and S Wolf in K Boele-Woelki, B Braat and I Sumner (eds), *European Family Law in Action*, Vol II: *Maintenance Between Former Spouses* (Antwerp, Intersentia, 2003) and Schwenzer and Bock, above n 82 answer to Question 87.

[88] See the answers to Questions 57 et seq for Greece by A Koutsouradis, S Kotronis and F Hatzantonis in Boele-Woelki, Braat and Curry-Sumner, above n 12; Pintens, 'Matrimonial Property Law in Europe', above n 9, 32 and Pintens, 'Ehegüterstände', above n 9, 275 et seq.

[89] Koutsouradis, Kotronis and Hatzantonis, above n 88, answer to Question 88.

be awarded at the court's discretion if the claiming spouse is not able to maintain him- or herself.[90]

c. Summary

In statutory compensation systems marriage does not have an immediate property law effect and no form of community of property is created through the marriage or through divorce. Only the 'fruits of joint labour' (either as accrued gains or as marital acquest) are shared in case of divorce, but not assets owned before the marriage or acquired through gift or inheritance during the marriage.[91] With the exception of Greece, the assets to be shared are shared equally, and there is, in practice, no discretion to divide the property otherwise. While the same is true for the sharing of pensions, in awarding maintenance the courts have greater discretion, and maintenance plays a key role in financial relief in these jurisdictions.

D. Jurisdictions with Primarily Discretionary Financial Relief Upon Divorce

The common law jurisdictions traditionally have had a very different approach to financial relief upon divorce. In these systems, marriage, as such, does not alter the proprietary relations of the spouses, and general property law thus applies. So, in a way, this could be categorised as a separation of property approach. However, on divorce the courts are given wide discretionary powers, allowing for a variety of orders concerning property adjustment (including ordering the sale of property), maintenance and pensions.

Leaving the full gamut of remedies in case of divorce to the discretion of the court makes predicting outcomes difficult (if not impossible) and thus there is little certainty. This is accepted, however, because of the overarching objective of achieving a 'fair' outcome in each individual case.

However, in some of the common law jurisdictions, statute or case law has led to the discretion 'solidifying' to such a degree that their approach to financial relief upon divorce can be called 'rule-based discretionary approach' and the respective jurisdictions, particularly New Zealand, Singapore, Scotland and several of the US jurisdictions, can be said to have come close to having a matrimonial property regime.[92] These jurisdictions, together with Austria, will be discussed in section II.D.ii below.

In other common law jurisdictions, particularly England and Wales, Ireland and Australia, the courts take what is often called a 'holistic' approach to financial relief upon divorce, meaning that property, maintenance and pensions are not seen as separate 'pillars' and considered separately as in the continental European jurisdictions.

---

[90] Art 1442 Greek Civil Code; *cf* Koutsouradis, Kotronis and Hatzantonis, above n 88, answer to Question 87 and the answers concerning Greece provided by AG Koutsouradis in Boele-Woelki, Braat and Sumner, above n 87.

[91] Although the German community of accrued gains arguably includes gains in the equal sharing that are not really 'fruits of joint labour', namely the increase (or decrease, as the case may be) of the value of assets owned before the marriage; see section II.C.ii.a above and Dutta, Germany, this volume 161 et seq.

[92] See Briggs, New Zealand, this volume 256 et seq, Leong, Singapore, this volume 311 et seq, Norrie, Scotland, this volume 289 et seq and Ellman, United States, this volume 403 et seq; also see section II.D.ii.b.–d below.

Instead the court is to consider all of the issues together and come to a 'package solution' which is fair (or at least as fair as possible) to those involved. These 'full discretion jurisdictions' are looked at in section II.D.i below.

As Pintens has pointed out,[93] the latter approach has been very aptly described by Lord Denning (with regard to ancillary relief in England) as follows:

> The Family Court takes the rights and obligations of the parties all together and puts the pieces into a mixed bag. Such pieces are the right to occupy the matrimonial home or have a share in it, the obligation to maintain the wife and children, and so forth. The court then takes out the pieces and hands them to the two parties—some to one party and some to the other—so that each can provide for the future with the pieces allotted to him or to her. The court hands them out without paying any too nice a regard to their legal or equitable rights but simply according to what is the fairest provision for the future—for mother and father and the children.[94]

That said, there is, of course, guidance on the exercise of discretion in statutes and case law in the jurisdictions concerned. Unsurprisingly, these differ quite significantly from jurisdiction to jurisdiction and will, therefore, be looked at in turn.

i. Full Discretion Jurisdictions

a. England and Wales

In England and Wales the Matrimonial Causes Act 1973 offers some—limited—guidance as to how the discretion regarding financial relief upon divorce (usually referred to as 'ancillary relief') is to be exercised. First, consideration is to be given to the welfare of any child of the family.[95] All the circumstances of the case are to be taken into account, and the statute provides a non-exhaustive list of factors to guide the judge:[96]

(a) the income, earning capacity, property and other financial resources which each of the parties to the marriage has or is likely to have in the foreseeable future, including in the case of earning capacity any increase in that capacity which it would in the opinion of the court be reasonable to expect a party to the marriage to take steps to acquire;

(b) the financial needs, obligations and responsibilities which each of the parties to the marriage has or is likely to have in the foreseeable future;

(c) the standard of living enjoyed by the family before the breakdown of the marriage;

(d) the age of each party to the marriage and the duration of the marriage;

(e) any physical or mental disability of either of the parties to the marriage;

(f) the contributions which each of the parties has made or is likely in the foreseeable future to make to the welfare of the family, including any contribution by looking after the home or caring for the family;

(g) the conduct of each of the parties, if that conduct is such that it would in the opinion of the court be inequitable to disregard it.

---

[93] Pintens, 'Matrimonial Property Law in Europe', above n 9, 34; Pintens, 'Ehegüterstände', above n 9, 277.

[94] *Hanlon v Law Society* [1981] AC 124 (HL) 147.

[95] s 25(1) Matrimonial Causes Act 1973. Note that 'child of the family' includes children that have been treated by the couple as child of their family, s 52(1)(b) Matrimonial Causes Act 1973, and thus can include children that are not the joint children of the couple.

[96] s 25(2) Matrimonial Causes Act 1973.

The factors to be considered are not set out in any particular order of priority.[97] In addition to those factors, the court is under a duty to consider the possibility of a 'clean break', ie ending the financial ties between the spouses by avoiding ongoing payments.[98]

The overarching aim—and indeed the point of having a discretionary approach in the first place—is to produce a 'fair' outcome for the persons involved. But, as Lord Nicholls has pointed out:[99]

> Everyone would accept that the outcome on these matters, whether by agreement or court order, should be fair. More realistically, the outcome ought to be as fair as is possible in all the circumstances. But everyone's life is different. Features which are important when assessing fairness differ in each case. And, sometimes, different minds can reach different conclusions on what fairness requires. Then fairness, like beauty, lies in the eye of the beholder.

At the beginning of this century case law radically changed the general approach to financial relief upon divorce[100] and the courts have developed more substantial guidance as to how the discretion to achieve this is to be exercised.[101] In *Miller v Miller, McFarlane v McFarlane* the House of Lords identified three 'strands' or 'rationales' of fairness: needs, equal sharing and compensation (for relationship-generated disadvantages).[102] As Miles rightly points out, these 'strands' are difficult to reconcile, as each of them represents a different view of the function of marriage; also it is unclear how these 'strands' are to work together in practice as there seems to be considerable overlap.[103] Be that as it may, certain tendencies seem to be developing in case law.

First, it appears to be clear that where the assets of the parties do not exceed their needs, it is the needs that dominate the allocation of the assets and there will generally be no consideration of compensation or equal sharing. As the welfare of the children is the first consideration, this usually means that the needs of the children, and thus of the primary carer, will take precedence. The needs do not, unlike for example in the Nordic countries,[104] have to be relationship-generated.[105] Hence it could be said that covering the needs is not only the dominant 'strand', but

---

[97] A Barlow, 'England' in Boele-Woelki, Braat and Curry-Sumner, above n 12, answer to Question 161.

[98] s 25A Matrimonial Causes Act 1973.

[99] *White v White* [2001] 1 AC 596, 599.

[100] See especially *White v White* [2001] 1 AC 596; *Miller v Miller, McFarlane v McFarlane* [2006] UKHL 24; *Charman v Charman (No 4)* [2007] EWCA Civ 503.

[101] Cf Miles, England and Wales, this volume 90 et seq; Barlow, 'England', above n 97; J Miles, '*Charman v Charman (No 4)*—Making Sense of Need, Compensation and Equal Sharing after *Miller/McFarlane*' (2008) 20 *Child and Family Law Quarterly* 378.

[102] *Miller v Miller, McFarlane v McFarlane* [2006] UKHL 24 [11]–[16] (Lord Nicholls) and [138]–[141] (Baroness Hale).

[103] Miles, England and Wales, this volume, 93; Miles, '*Charman*', above n 101. See also J Miles, 'Principle or Pragmatism in Ancillary Relief: The Virtues of Flirting with Academic Theories and Other Jurisdictions' [2005] *International Journal of Law, Policy and the Family* 242 et seq.

[104] See section II.C.i.b above.

[105] *Miller v Miller and McFarlane v McFarlane* [2006] UKHL 24 [11] (Lord Nicholls). See also ibid [137] and [138] (Baroness Hale), who while principally focusing on relationship-generated needs apparently also includes disability (as she distinguishes disability arising after the marriage has ended); for her the link to the relationship is either causal or temporal, [137].

also reflects the general view in England and Wales on fairness: fairness first and foremost means that the needs of the children and the spouses should be covered in the event of divorce—this can also be seen from the way the English courts have dealt with marital agreements.[106]

Second, in *Miller v Miller, McFarlane v McFarlane* the two lead speeches by Baroness Hale and Lord Nicholls both addressed the matter of which assets are to be considered for equal sharing, and in both speeches the assets were grouped into what can be called matrimonial and non-matrimonial property (although Baroness Hale used different terms). Likewise there seems to be agreement that the longer the marriage the less important the distinction between the groups of property should become. The approach taken to the categorisation of property in the speeches differs somewhat and it is therefore unclear where the exact boundaries lie, but the speeches have in common that gifts and inheritances generally belong to the non-matrimonial property pool. Lord Nicholls also wanted to include property owned before the marriage in the non-matrimonial property, whereas Baroness Hale would count such property as matrimonial if it was used for the family. Assets acquired during the marriage as 'fruits of the partnership' or as the product of 'joint endeavour' are to be considered as matrimonial property in any event.[107] Both agreed that the matrimonial home was always to be considered matrimonial property, irrespective of by whom and when it was acquired.[108] While equal sharing in principle applies to all property, it seems that the courts are more likely to depart from equal sharing if the property is non-matrimonial. Other reasons accepted for departure from equal sharing include the short duration of the marriage or one party's 'stellar' contribution to the marriage.[109] However, it needs to be repeated that the source of the assets, and indeed the 'strand' of equal sharing, are irrelevant when the needs of the spouses require resorting to any of the spouses' property.

Third, there seems to be a growing tendency to subsume the 'strand' of compensation into needs, as 'needs generously assessed', or consider that compensation is achieved through equal sharing (which resembles the view taken in some continental European jurisdictions).[110] It certainly appears that of the three 'strands', compensation is not only the most difficult one, but also the one least utilised to achieve a fair outcome.

---

[106] See Miles, England and Wales, this volume 96 et seq; *Radmacher v Granatino* [2010] UKSC 42; and generally section III below.

[107] Barlow, above n 97. Cf *Miller v Miller, McFarlane v McFarlane* [2006] UKHL 24, [91], [141]–[143], [149], [154]. In *S v AG (Financial Remedy: Lottery Prize)* [2011] EWHC 2637 (Fam) a recent lottery win was held to be non-matrimonial property rather than a joint endeavour.

[108] Given property prices and the tradition of house ownership in England, the matrimonial home often is the most valuable asset of the spouses, and excluding it from the matrimonial pool (and from equal sharing) would often lead to needs not being covered.

[109] Miles, England and Wales, this volume, 94; Barlow, above n 97. It should be noted that for 'stellar' contributions to be considered, they must be exceptional; cf *Lambert v Lambert* [2002] EWCA Civ 1685.

[110] See, eg *Lauder v Lauder* [2007] EWHC 1227; *VB v JP* [2008] EWHC 112; *McFarlane v McFarlane (No 2)* [2009] EWHC 891. See Miles, England and Wales, this volume, 94.

In any event, the courts so far seem to have resisted developing what could be termed 'rules' or presumptions[111] and have emphasised the discretionary nature of financial relief in England and Wales.[112]

b. Ireland

Ireland only introduced divorce in 1996, and much of the current law is explained by the social, historical and constitutional background.[113] The discretion to award financial relief upon divorce in Irish law is structured by a list of factors set out in statute which must be taken into account when exercising the discretion:

(a) the income, earning capacity, property and other financial resources which each of the spouses concerned has or is likely to have in the foreseeable future,

(b) the financial needs, obligations and responsibilities which each of the spouses has or is likely to have in the foreseeable future (whether in the case of the remarriage of the spouse or otherwise),

(c) the standard of living enjoyed by the family concerned before the proceedings were instituted or before the spouses commenced to live apart from one another, as the case may be,

(d) the age of each of the spouses, the duration of their marriage and the length of time during which the spouses lived with one another,

(e) any physical or mental disability of either of the spouses,

(f) the contributions which each of the spouses has made or is likely in the foreseeable future to make to the welfare of the family, including any contribution made by each of them to the income, earning capacity, property and financial resources of the other spouse and any contribution made by either of them by looking after the home or caring for the family,

(g) the effect on the earning capacity of each of the spouses of the marital responsibilities assumed by each during the period when they lived with one another and, in particular, the degree to which the future earning capacity of a spouse is impaired by reason of that spouse having relinquished or foregone the opportunity of remunerative activity in order to look after the home or care for the family,

(h) any income or benefits to which either of the spouses is entitled by or under statute,

(i) the conduct of each of the spouses, if that conduct is such that in the opinion of the court it would in all the circumstances of the case be unjust to disregard it,

(j) the accommodation needs of either of the spouses,

(k) the value to each of the spouses of any benefit (for example, a benefit under a pension scheme) which by reason of the decree of divorce concerned, that spouse will forfeit the opportunity or possibility of acquiring,

(l) the rights of any person other than the spouses but including a person to whom either spouse is remarried.[114]

---

[111] But see *Charman v Charman (No 4)* [2007] EWCA Civ 503 where a more structured approach was taken.

[112] See, eg *B v B* [2008] EWCA Civ 543, which takes a rather different approach than the earlier decision of *Charman v Charman (No 4)* [2007] EWCA Civ 503. See Miles, England and Wales, this volume, 95; Miles, '*Charman*', above n 101.

[113] Crowley, Ireland, this volume, 200 et seq.

[114] s 20(2) Irish Family Law (Divorce) Act 1996.

There is no hierarchy amongst the listed criteria, but it has been held that taking them into consideration is mandatory.[115]

The overarching objective of financial relief upon divorce is not fairness, as in England and Wales, but rather 'proper provision' for the spouses and dependent children.[116] It was held in the seminal case of *T v T*[117] that the discretionary exercise is not focused on *division* (of property) but on *provision*;[118] any notion that financial relief in case of divorce required a 'rule of equality' or a sharing of the assets was rejected.[119] In the same case it was also said that developing principles and guidelines should be avoided and that each case should be considered on its own particular circumstances.[120] Essentially, the approach, therefore, appears much more strictly needs-based than the English one.

On the face of it this seems to rule out a participation in any marital acquest and/or compensation and is thus rather disadvantageous to the financially weaker spouse, particularly if the financial disadvantages were incurred because of family work. Indeed, to some degree this would almost seem contrary to the constitutional protection of the family and the constitutional recognition of value of 'life in the home'.[121] However, it has also been held that 'proper provision' is not restricted to basic needs but should 'reflect the equal partnership of the spouses' and:

> should seek, so far as the circumstances of the case permit, to ensure that the spouse is not only in a position to meet her financial liabilities and obligations and continue with a standard of living commensurate with her standard of living during marriage but to enjoy what may reasonably be regarded as the fruits of the marriage so that she can live an independent life and have security in the control of her own affairs, with a personal dignity that such autonomy confers, without necessarily being dependent on receiving periodic payments for the rest of her life from her former husband.[122]

'Proper provision', understood this way—an interpretation presumably supported by the constitution—would include an equal share of the acquest, the 'fruits of the marriage' and, to a certain extent, compensation for marriage-related disadvantages.

However, a more structured approach such as that developed in England and Wales in *Miller v Miller; McFarlane v McFarlane*[123] has expressly been rejected and so far no distinction between different groups of property has been suggested.

c. Australia

Similarly to Ireland, no express distinction is made in Australia with regard to the source of the assets.[124] In principle it does not matter whether they are

---

[115] *MK v JPK* [2003] 1 IR 326.
[116] Crowley, Ireland, this volume, 206 et seq, 210; G Shannon, 'Ireland' in Boele-Woelki, Braat and Curry-Sumner, above n 12 answer to Question 161.
[117] *T v T* [2002] 3 IR 321.
[118] Ibid, 383 (Denham J), and 398 (Murphy J).
[119] Ibid, 398 (Murphy J), 417 (Fenelly J), and 407 (Murray J).
[120] Ibid, 418 (Fenelly J), and 409 (Murphy J); see Crowley, Ireland, this volume, 210.
[121] Art 41, Irish Constitution. See Crowley, Ireland, this volume, 201.
[122] *T v T* [2002] 3 IR 321, 408 (Murray J). See Crowley, Ireland, this volume 208.
[123] *Miller v Miller, McFarlane v McFarlane* [2006] UKHL 24; see section II.D.i.a above.
[124] Jessep, Australia, this volume, 19.

'matrimonial' or not, part of what could be considered as 'marital acquest' or not (although these matter of course can be taken into account when the court exercises its discretion). The overarching objective, however, resembles the 'fairness' approach of England and Wales, namely that a 'just and equitable' result is to be achieved.[125] The discretion to award financial relief, like in the other discretion-based jurisdictions, is to be guided by a list of statutory factors.[126]

Of those, two have been seen as fundamental by the courts when deciding on an equitable distribution of assets and financial relief in general; namely the contribution to the family made by each of the spouses during the course of the marriage[127] and the economic circumstances of the spouses now and in the future. The latter expressly includes future family work such as childcare etc, and within this factor relationship-generated advantages and disadvantages are to be taken into account.

For maintenance, the principal criteria are the reasonable needs of one spouse and the reasonable capacity to pay of the other.[128] Long-term maintenance is uncommon, the political objective being to encourage spouses to be self-supporting.[129] That said, there is an express provision prohibiting the consideration of the availability of public support, so, like in England and Wales and Ireland, the primary resource for maintenance, where financial support is needed, is the former spouse.[130]

In Australia there is little certainty as to what the outcome of proceedings regarding financial relief are going to be, which of course is the price to pay for a largely discretion-based system.[131] However, the current framework of 'just and equitable result' certainly could accommodate considerations as to the source of the assets and, perhaps, even a more principled distinction between matrimonial and non-matrimonial assets or notions of a 'marital acquest'. As the system stands, the discretion of the judge is largely unfettered, but of course subject to the list of factors set out in the relevant legislation.

d. Summary

In the jurisdictions discussed in this section the financial relief, including property adjustment, maintenance and pensions, is based on the court's largely unfettered discretion, and all remedies upon divorce are part of a 'package solution'. While in Ireland the overarching aim is 'proper provision' and in the Australia and England and Wales the financial relief needs to be 'fair', 'just' or 'equitable', the notion of sharing is embedded in all of them, albeit to varying degrees.

It seems that Australia and Ireland have not (yet?) drawn a line between marital and non-marital property in the same way that England and Wales appears to be beginning to do. In light of the developments in England and Wales, one could argue

---

[125] Family Law Act 1975 (Cth), s 79(2) for property. For maintenance 'the court may make such order as it considers proper for the provision of maintenance' according to s 74(1).

[126] Family Law Act 1975 (Cth), s 79(4) for property orders and s 75(2) for maintenance orders.

[127] Jessep, Australia, this volume, 20, esp n 11.

[128] Ibid, 20 et seq; Family Law Act 1975 (Cth) s 75(2).

[129] Jessep, Australia, this volume, 20 et seq.

[130] See Family Law Act 1975 (Cth) ss 75(2)(f), 75(3) as amended by the Family Law Amendment Act 1987 (Cth). See Jessep, Australia, this volume 20 et seq.

[131] Jessep, Australia, this volume, 20.

that the exercise of the discretion is developing from a largely unfettered one to what could be called 'rule-based discretion'.

ii. 'Rule-Based Discretion' Jurisdictions

Austria, New Zealand, Scotland, Singapore and the 'common law jurisdictions' of the United States have in common that their approach to the division of the matrimonial property is, in principle, discretionary. However, unlike the jurisdictions discussed in the previous section, this discretion is either guided by express statutory provisions[132] or by case law that has firmly established that the matrimonial property is to be divided equally, although the discretion to decide otherwise is retained. Irrespective of whether the rule for the division of property is established by statute or case law, a deviation from equal sharing in these jurisdictions requires specific justification. In a way, therefore, they are 'hybrid systems', combining rule-based and discretion-based approaches which could be called 'rule-based discretion'.

It could also very well be argued that the Nordic countries (see section II.C.i above) belong in this 'rule-based discretion' group, as equal sharing is also the statutory rule with the courts retaining the discretion to order differently. However, the statutory rule establishing equal sharing is much stronger than a mere (rebuttable) presumption and is generally not departed from to achieve 'fairness' or to compensate for marriage-related disadvantages. Therefore perhaps the approach in the Nordic countries is better described as a 'discretion-based rule' approach (ie primarily based on a rule with discretion in some circumstances), although admittedly, in practice, the distinction might merely be semantic.

a. Austria

Finding Austria in this group is somewhat surprising, given that it is surrounded in continental Europe by jurisdictions with strictly rule-based matrimonial property regimes. But in Austria the matrimonial assets (and debts) and matrimonial savings are to be shared in the event of divorce at the discretion of the court, and not according to a rule laid down in a statute.

The matrimonial assets comprise all assets that have been at the disposal of the couple during their marriage, including the household goods and the matrimonial home, but also, as the case may be, assets like holiday homes and even horses.[133] Matrimonial savings are monies and investments accrued during the marriage.[134] All these, in principle, are to be shared at divorce, but if these assets and savings were received as a gift or inheritance or were owned by one spouse at the time of the marriage, they are exempt from sharing.[135] However, the matrimonial home and the household goods are nevertheless to be included if the other spouse is dependent

---

[132] See, eg the statutory presumptions in Arkansas and North Carolina (see Ellman, United States, this volume, 406 et seq esp n 10) and Scotland (see Norrie, Scotland, this volume 293) and the statutory rule on equal sharing in New Zealand (see Briggs, New Zealand, this volume 259 et seq).

[133] s 81(2) EheG; Ferrari, Austria, this volume, 53.

[134] s 81(3) EheG.

[135] s 82 EheG; Ferrari, Austria, this volume, 52 et seq; also some other exceptions apply, see ibid.

on their continued use, for example, if he or she is the primary carer for the children and requires these assets. Still, apart from this exception, the assets to be shared are effectively limited to the marital acquest.

The distribution of the assets in the event of divorce is to be effected in kind, and compensatory payments as in Germany are the exception.[136]

Interestingly, unlike in most continental European jurisdictions, there is no statutory rule that the assets are to be shared equally; instead the courts are given wide discretion on the matter, the central criteria being the contribution to the acquisition of the assets and the contribution to the welfare of the family.[137] That said, equal sharing is the most common outcome in practice.[138] Still, one Supreme Court case deserves special mention. In this case the woman had been in full employment and at the same time had been solely responsible for the housekeeping and the children's education to which the husband, who was in full-time employment as well, did not contribute. The Supreme Court decided that the wife should receive two-thirds of the assets and the husband only one-third, having contributed twice as much as the husband.[139] This case—which on its facts does not appear very exceptional—shows that the courts in Austria will exercise their discretion in appropriate cases and deviate from equal sharing.

Maintenance in Austria is considered entirely independently from the division of the assets, and, unlike in most jurisdictions, the question of who is solely or predominantly at fault for the marital breakdown still plays an important role, as only the 'innocent' spouse can claim maintenance, unless he or she continues to be the primary carer of the children.[140] Again, the award is at the discretion of the court, but the judiciary have developed percentage rates as guidelines, with a cap at 33 per cent of the other spouse's income. In addition, maintenance is generally only awarded for a limited period of time.[141] Unlike in Germany, for example, there is no specific system for the sharing of pensions in Austria.[142]

b. New Zealand

In New Zealand the default regime not only applies to marriages (and civil unions) but also to de facto relationships, provided that the relevant criteria are fulfilled.[143] As such, the terminology used is different, and the property of spouses etc is quite correctly referred to as 'relationship' rather than 'matrimonial' property. However, because the focus of this comparative study is on marriage, in the following references

---

[136] M Roth, 'Austria', in Boele-Woelki, Braat and Curry-Sumner, above n 12 answer to Question 150.
[137] s 82 EheG; Ferrari, Austria, this volume, 53 et seq.
[138] Ibid, 54.
[139] Ibid.
[140] Ibid, 54 et seq.
[141] Ibid.
[142] Ibid, 53.
[143] Briggs, New Zealand, this volume, 257, 260 et seq; O Jessep, 'Legal Status of Cohabitants in Australia and New Zealand', in JM Scherpe and N Yassari (eds), *Rechtsstellung nichtehelicher Lebensgemeinschaften—The Legal Status of Cohabitants* (Tübingen, Mohr Siebeck, 2005) 529 et seq; A Maak, 'Neuseeland', in A Bergmann, M Ferid, D Henrich (eds), *Internationales Ehe- und Kindschaftsrecht mit Staatsangehörig-keitsrecht* (Frankfurt, Verlag für Standesamtswesen, 2011) esp 28 et seq.

will be made to 'marriage', 'divorce', 'spouses', 'matrimonial property' etc, only, despite the rules evidently having broader application.

The default rule with regard to property is that all matrimonial property, but not the parties' personal property, is to be shared equally upon divorce. Matrimonial property comprises what can be called the marital acquest (including pension rights acquired during the marriage), but also all assets that were acquired before the marriage for the benefit of the family, and the matrimonial home and the household goods irrespective of when they were acquired. Other property acquired before the marriage, or acquired during the marriage through gift or inheritance but not intermingled with the matrimonial property, remains the personal property of the spouses.[144] Thus sharing is limited to the matrimonial property and the default regime is not really comparable to the (full) deferred community of property in the Nordic countries.

Upon divorce the matrimonial property is to be shared equally unless one of the very narrow exceptions applies; these are, for example, certain marriages of short duration or where equal sharing would be repugnant to justice under the given circumstances.[145]

In addition, the courts have the discretionary power to make a further award based on notions of compensation if, after the division of property, the income and living standards of one partner are likely to be significantly higher than those of the other partner because of the division of functions within the relationship,[146] for example, if one of the spouses gave up his or her career to take care of the children. However, it appears that the courts in New Zealand have been rather cautious in using this discretionary power, and one of the reasons for this may be the additional power the courts have to award post-marital maintenance to meet the 'reasonable needs' of the other spouse.[147] The relationship between the compensatory and maintenance awards is as yet unclear.[148] What is clear, though, is that maintenance is not meant to compensate for different earning capacities of the (former) spouses and is generally seen as a short-term measure to help the receiving spouse become self-supporting, although the age of the parties and the duration of the marriage may lead to maintenance being awarded for longer periods.[149]

c. Singapore

In Singapore the courts are granted a wide discretion to deal with the assets of the couple on divorce, namely to deal with them as is 'just and equitable', and there is statutory guidance on which factors are to be considered.[150] This, at first glance,

---

[144] Briggs, New Zealand, this volume, 259 et seq; Maak, 'Neuseeland', above n 143, 30 et seq. For an (English) comparative view see Miles, 'Principle or Pragmatism', above n 103.

[145] Briggs, New Zealand, this volume, 262, esp n 45; ss 13, 14 Property (Relationships) Act 1976.

[146] Briggs, New Zealand, this volume, 262 et seq; Maak, 'Neuseeland', above n 143, 30 et seq; s 15 Property (Relationships) Act 1976.

[147] Under the Family Proceedings Act 1980. See Briggs, New Zealand, this volume, 262 et seq; Maak, above n 143, 32.

[148] Briggs, New Zealand, this volume, 263.

[149] Ibid, 263 et seq.

[150] s 112(1) Women's Charter.

resembles the English or Australian system of discretionary relief, but the statute expressly limits the pool of assets to be shared to 'matrimonial assets'.[151] These matrimonial assets comprise in the first instance what can be described as the marital acquest (which includes the compulsory savings for retirement). In addition, assets that were owned before the marriage or were acquired during the marriage are also considered matrimonial assets, provided that they were used for or associated with the family.[152] Thus assets that are not in any way associated with the family, no matter how significant and substantial, will not be shared. Hence, unlike in the deferred community of property systems of the Nordic countries, the sharing is limited to the matrimonial property and is not 'universal'.[153]

The division is to be done in the 'fairest possible way', which includes seeing the homemaker and the breadwinner, in principle, as making equal contributions to the family welfare. In the majority of cases this appears to lead to equal sharing, or a percentage very close to this.[154]

Under the current law, the approach to maintenance is still a gendered one, and post-divorce maintenance can only be claimed by a wife and not by a husband. Maintenance is to be awarded to the wife at the discretion of the court[155] and only appears to play a complementary or supplementary role.[156]

d. Scotland

While marriage as such has no proprietary effect on spouses in Scotland and the couple can be said to live under a separation of property regime during marriage, at divorce the courts have the to make a variety of orders regarding the property of the spouses, maintenance etc; in this respect the system resembles that of England and Wales. However, financial relief in Scotland is fundamentally different from that south of its border, and it has been said that the matrimonial property system is functionally a deferred community of acquests.[157]

While the financial relief is discretionary, there is clear statutory guidance in the form of five principles for the exercise of this discretion. The first and most important of these principles states that upon divorce the matrimonial property is to be shared 'fairly',[158] and there is a statutory presumption that 'fairly' means equal sharing unless different proportions are justified by special circumstances.[159] Such circumstances are further defined in the statute to include agreements between the

---

[151] s 112(10) Women's Charter.

[152] Leong, Singapore, this volume, 314. There are some similarities to the approach in Austria and New Zealand in that respect, see 467 et seq above. This also resembles—to a certain extent—the approach taken by the House of Lords in the English case of *Miller v Miller; McFarlane v McFarlane* [2006] UKHL 24; see section II.D.i.a above.

[153] See also Leong, Singapore, this volume, 314 and WK Leong, 'Division of matrimonial assets: Recent cases and thoughts for reform' [1993] *Singapore Journal of Legal Studies* 351, 353.

[154] Leong, Singapore, this volume, 315 et seq.

[155] See the factors listed in s 114 Women's Charter.

[156] Leong, Singapore, this volume, 317 et seq.

[157] Norrie, Scotland, this volume, 293; J Mair, 'Scotland' in Boele-Woelki, Braat and Curry-Sumner, above n 12 answer to Question 1e.

[158] s 9(1)(a) Family Law (Scotland) Act 1985; Norrie, Scotland, this volume, 293 et seq.

[159] s 10(1) Family Law (Scotland) Act 1985; Norrie, Scotland, this volume, 294.

parties, the sources of the assets, the nature of the property and the way the property was used.[160] Hence the statutory rule is clearly equal sharing, and any deviation from it requires justification.

Furthermore, only 'matrimonial property' is to be shared this way, and the nature and scope of such matrimonial property is also defined in the statute.[161] It comprises what can be described as the marital acquest (thus excluding property owned before the marriage or acquired during the marriage by gift or inheritance, but including pension rights[162]) plus any property acquired before the marriage 'as a family home or as furniture or plenishings for such a home'.[163] Thus the pool of property to be shared is limited, but can be wider than the mere acquest.

In addition to this sharing rule, the courts also have discretionary power under the second principle to make compensatory awards to take 'fair account' of 'any economic advantage derived by either party from contributions, whether financial or otherwise, of the other, and of any economic disadvantages suffered by either party in the interests of the other party or of the family'.[164] These compensatory orders are limited to 'property orders', namely payment of a lump sum, transfer of property or pension splitting.[165]

The further principles, which can justify property orders as well as periodical payments, concern the sharing of the economic burden of bringing up the children, allowing the other (dependent) spouse time to adjust and alleviating serious financial hardship.[166] Thus there is no general duty to maintain one's former spouse after divorce, but any maintenance award needs to be based on the principles just mentioned, is generally granted for limited periods only (except in hardship cases), and is considered supplementary to the property orders.[167]

e. 'Common Law Jurisdictions' of the United States

The US jurisdictions that take what has been called the 'common law-approach' to the allocation of property on divorce[168] follow a somewhat different approach to financial relief upon divorce to the European common law jurisdictions or Australia. Crucially, maintenance (in the United States, usually referred to as alimony) and pensions appear to be considered separately from property division, and, for the latter, the source of the assets is a relevant factor in many of the US jurisdictions.

The starting point for the division of the assets, however, is one of 'equitable distribution' (rather than equal distribution).[169] That said, in many states a principled distinction is made between marital and personal property. The latter comprises

---

[160] Norrie, Scotland, this volume, 295; s 10(6) Family Law (Scotland) Act 1985.
[161] s 10(4) Family Law (Scotland) Act 1985.
[162] Norrie, Scotland, this volume, 298; ss 8(1)(ba) and 12A Family Law (Scotland) Act 1985; pension sharing is also possible, s 8(1)(baa) Family Law (Scotland) Act 1985 and can be justified by any of the principles in s 9(1) and not merely s 9(1)(a) Family Law (Scotland) Act 1985.
[163] s 10(4)(a) Family Law (Scotland) Act 1985.
[164] s 9(1)(b) Family Law (Scotland) Act 1985.
[165] Norrie, Scotland, this volume, 295 et seq.
[166] s 9(1)(c)–(e) Family Law (Scotland) Act 1985; Norrie, Scotland, this volume, 296 et seq.
[167] Norrie, Scotland, this volume, 299 et seq; Mair, above n 157 answer to Question 1e.
[168] Ellman, United States, this volume, 404 et seq.
[169] Ibid, 405.

assets owned before the marriage and/or received by inheritance during the marriage and is not necessarily to be shared at divorce.[170] For example, in Arkansas and North Carolina there are statutory presumptions that marital property should be divided equally.[171] In other US jurisdictions the source of the assets is taken into account in the discretionary division of the assets.[172] Hence treating assets differently because of their source is perceived to be 'fair' under the equitable distribution, and there is a clear trend towards accepting that (only) the marital property should be divided equally.[173] In that sense, it could be said that these jurisdictions have moved very far towards being rule-based in their approach to the division of matrimonial property, while of course retaining discretion, which justifies including them in this part.

Pensions are considered separately and more often than not are divided equally.[174] Maintenance is to be granted at the discretion of the judge, but, unlike in England and Wales, is considered to be separate from the property division.[175] One could, therefore, almost say that in the US states discussed here, there is a 'pillar' approach akin to that in the European civil law jurisdictions.

f. Summary

Austria, New Zealand, Scotland, Singapore and the 'common law jurisdictions' of the United States are often categorised as belonging to one of the other groups discussed above. Austria, for example, is often grouped together with the countries that have a statutory compensation clause or named as a deferred community of property jurisdiction. Scotland, the US 'common law jurisdictions', Singapore and New Zealand are often categorised as jurisdictions where the distribution of assets is primarily based on the discretion of the judge—or also as deferred community of property jurisdictions.

These labels do not really capture the nature of the approach to the division of property for two basic reasons: (1) the property pool essentially is limited to what can be called 'matrimonial property' and is not universal as in the Nordic countries[176] and thus is not a full deferred community of property; and (2) the systems, in principle, remain discretionary ones.

As for the first reason, admittedly there are some similarities to the deferred community of property systems: there is a separation of property during marriage and a form of community of property upon divorce, but crucially the community property is limited to the 'matrimonial' property pool as defined in the respective jurisdiction. In the jurisdictions considered in this part, the matrimonial property always comprises what can be called the marital acquest,[177] ie all assets gained during the marriage except those acquired through gift and inheritance. But, in addition, the matrimonial property in all jurisdictions grouped together here (albeit to varying

---

[170] Ibid, 405 et seq.
[171] Ibid, 407 esp n 10.
[172] Ibid, 406 esp n 7.
[173] Ibid, 406, 410.
[174] Ibid, 407.
[175] Ibid, 408 et seq.
[176] See 453 et seq above.
[177] See section II.B.ii above.

degrees) also includes assets that were used by or intended for the family such as the matrimonial home and the household goods; in other words, assets that have a special connection to the family. So the property considered to be matrimonial property can (and often will) comprise *more* than merely the acquest. Thus the property to be shared is wider than in what could be called a 'deferred community of acquests',[178] but narrower than in the deferred community of property of the Nordic countries. Therefore 'deferred community of matrimonial property' might be the more precise term—albeit one that does not reflect the remaining discretion of the court.[179]

The impression that in these jurisdictions a 'real' matrimonial property regime is developing (and Austria certainly always was considered to have one) is supported by the fact that maintenance in these jurisdictions in principle is considered separately, as a distinct 'pillar' of financial relief upon divorce. This indeed makes them more like the continental European approach described above (see section II.B and C above), but a distinctive feature remains, which is the second reason for grouping these jurisdictions in a different category: the courts retain their discretion. One could of course argue that this leaves these jurisdictions with 'the worst of both worlds' regarding the division of matrimonial property: a system that is based on a rule of equal sharing to provide certainty at the expense of flexibility, but with the residual discretion of the court essentially nullifying this certainty. Whether the latter actually is the case depends on how frequently and for what reasons the courts depart from equal division, and also how the interplay with maintenance is utilised. In the Nordic countries, where the courts also retain discretion within a rule-based equal-sharing framework (see section II.C.i above) there does not seem to be the feeling that outcomes generally are uncertain in the way they are, for example, in England and Wales or Australia. Perhaps therefore, it could be said that the 'rule-based discretion' jurisdictions described in this part have 'the best of both worlds': an approach that generally provides certainty but allows for a discretionary correction of the rule-based outcome in exceptional cases when the (also discretionary) maintenance payments are insufficient or inadequate to achieve the relevant policy aims.

E. Brief Comparison

As pointed out in the overview at the beginning of this chapter, two key distinctions can be found when looking at financial relief on divorce.

The first, and narrower, one relates to the approach to the property relations of the spouses only: whether at the point of marriage some form of community of property is created or whether the spouses during marriage (and in many jurisdictions also at divorce and after) retain their personal property. This is explored in section II.E i below.

The second distinction relates to the general approach to financial relief, namely whether the relief should be primarily rule-based or discretion-based.

---

[178] See Ferrari, Austria, this volume, 52 et seq; Norrie, Scotland, this volume, 294 et seq. Norway, as pointed out above (section II.C.i.a) after the 1991 reforms is in fact quite close to this approach as well.

[179] But neither does the term 'deferred community of property' for the matrimonial property regimes of the Nordic countries, which, as explained, also retain a discretionary element.

This appears to be based on whether in the respective jurisdictions certainty or individual fairness are considered to be the primary aim of financial relief. This theme is examined in section II.E.ii below.

What is generally seen as the biggest divide between the continental European jurisdictions and their 'pillar' approach and those common law jurisdictions that take a 'holistic' view by not separating the issues of property and maintenance is addressed in section II.E.iii below.

In England and Wales three 'strands' of fairness were identified in *Miller v Miller; McFarlane v McFarlane*[180] which are to guide the exercise of discretion in financial relief upon divorce, namely sharing, needs and compensation. In section II.E.iv and v below it is shown that very similar policy considerations underpin financial relief in all the jurisdictions considered in this study, despite the apparently fundamentally different approaches to financial relief.

This part of the chapter ends with an excursus that suggests how the law on ancillary relief in England and Wales might develop in the future in the light of the comparative findings (section II.E.vi below).

i. Community vs Separation

The crucial difference between the community of property jurisdictions[181] and those jurisdictions where marriage as such does not change the spouses' ownership of the assets[182] is, of course, the immediate proprietary effect of the community of property regime: in community of property jurisdictions the couple from the day of the marriage own some assets jointly. This is said to be an expression of the solidarity the spouses owe each other, as in this system the spouses immediately participate in the 'fruits of joint labour',[183] usually the marital acquest.[184] No distinction is made based on the roles of the spouses in the marriage, and thus marriage is treated as a partnership of equals. By contrast, where there is a separation of property during marriage the solidarity of spouses with regard to the sharing of assets is deferred until divorce when adjustments one way or the other can be made.[185] However, this is not to say that in these systems marriage is not perceived as a partnership of equals—one could even argue that the latter approach is the more egalitarian one.

By creating an immediate joint pool of property, community of property systems, to a certain extent, ensure equality at the beginning and throughout the marriage by allowing immediate participation in the accrued wealth.[186] It can be said that this system is particularly well-suited for more 'traditional' marriages in which there is

---

[180] *Miller v Miller; McFarlane v McFarlane* [2006] UKHL 24.

[181] See section II.B above.

[182] See section II.C and D above.

[183] Pintens, 'Matrimonial Property Law in Europe', above n 9, 42; Pintens, 'Ehegüterstände', above n 9, 279 et seq.

[184] In the Netherlands this 'solidarity' of course is taken to its extreme as all assets of the spouses immediately become joint property through the marriage.

[185] See section II.C and D.

[186] A Röthel, 'Die Zugewinngemeinschaft als europäisches Modell?' in V Lipp, E Schumann and B Veit (eds), *Die Zugewinngemeinschaft als europäisches Modell?* (Göttingen, Göttinger Juristische Reihe, 2009) 66; Pintens, 'Matrimonial Property Law in Europe', above n 9, 42; Pintens, 'Ehegüterstände', above n 9, 279 et seq.

financial dependency of one spouse on the other, as it secures immediate ownership of the assets and hence affords a dependent spouse greater autonomy—of course, at the expense of the autonomy of the other spouse.[187]

The separation of property during marriage on the other hand seems to assume or presuppose equality at the beginning and throughout the marriage. Both spouses remain (largely) financially independent during the marriage, and the autonomy of the spouses seems to be the basis of the system rather than its objective. This system can be seen to be better suited to financially independent (or not so dependent) spouses or 'modern' relationships.[188] But if there is a dependency of one spouse on the other, this is perpetuated through the separation of property approach.

Which system better supports the idea of a partnership of equals depends on one's view of equality. If equality primarily means that no distinction should be made between breadwinner and homemaker and that this should manifest itself during marriage through property ownership, then the community of property systems would be the better choice. If equality is seen as full autonomy of the spouses, and the partnership is seen as one of independents, the separation of property system seems appropriate where the objective of non-discrimination between breadwinner and homemaker is realised at divorce.

It appears, therefore, that the policy message sent by the two systems is a very different one: the separation of property promotes a model of financially independent spouses with a safety net in case of divorce; the community of property system, it could be argued, promotes a model that better enables the spouses to choose to forgo financial independence to focus on the family, should they so wish.

That said, it is to be assumed that the relevance of this distinction in most cases is a purely theoretical one. In an ongoing (and functioning) marriage there will hardly be any difference and the couple will usually share their assets during the marriage anyway. Only in the event of crisis will the distinction become relevant, but irrespective of what the system is, the financial consequences will usually have to be settled through legal mechanisms and, where the parties cannot agree, through the courts anyway. Whether in a community or a separation system, if one of the spouses refuses to hand over (or disclose) certain assets legal action will need to be taken. Both approaches ensure that the spouses partake in the 'fruits of joint labour'. So perhaps the differences in practice are not as great as they seem at first. Still, having a claim in rem as in the community of property systems might make the realisation of this claim for the assets easier in practice.

ii. Rules vs Discretion—Does This Actually Mean Certainty vs Fairness?

The more general distinction between the various approaches is whether financial relief should primarily be based on rules or left to the discretion of the judge. When analysing—and judging—the distinction it should be kept in mind that the rule-based approach is largely restricted to the matrimonial property regimes (and

---

[187] Pintens, 'Matrimonial Property Law in Europe', above n 9, 43; Pintens, 'Ehegüterstände', above n 9, 279 et seq.
[188] Pintens, 'Matrimonial Property Law in Europe', above n 9, 43; Pintens, 'Ehegüterstände', above n 9, 279 et seq.

pensions, where applicable) and that maintenance, as a separate 'pillar', is usually still discretion-based even where the division of matrimonial property is (solely) rule-based. The relevance of the latter cannot be underestimated, as one of the functions of maintenance is to alleviate hardship that might arise from the rule-based division of property and, to lesser extent, to compensate for marriage-related disadvantages.

So when one perceives the difference between the rule-based approach and the discretion-based approach as one giving priority to either fairness or certainty, this can really only apply to matrimonial property. As noted in the overview at the beginning of this chapter, the systems that rely on a rule-based division of property also aim to achieve an overall fair outcome for financial relief, but they do so on the basis of a certain (or at least relatively certain) outcome with regard to the property division.

Particularly in 'hybrid' systems which in this chapter have been grouped under the heading 'rule-based discretion jurisdictions'[189] and also in the deferred community of property jurisdictions in the Nordic countries (which could be called 'discretion-based rule jurisdictions'[190]) the different approaches seem to have been reconciled to a certain degree. Whether primarily rule-based or primarily discretion-based, these systems build on the same foundation (although with a different emphasis): namely that the sharing of property is based on a rule and that any departure from the rule needs justification. This, of course, has an effect on how cases need to be presented and argued. Where no rule is in place and the remedies are entirely at the discretion of the court, the burden falls on those who are arguing for sharing (or a greater share), compensation for marriage-related disadvantages, and even needs. However, if one assumes that the rule essentially is fair in the majority of cases, a rule-based approach has a lot to commend it, particularly if combined with a residual discretion for the court in appropriate cases.

iii. Of 'Pillars' and 'Packages'

The primarily discretion-based jurisdictions with 'full' discretion (England and Wales, Ireland and Australia, see section II.D.i above) take a 'holistic' approach to financial relief by not making a clear distinction between division of property, maintenance and other financial remedies upon divorce. The remedies are not determined individually, but seen as a coherent whole, so the outcome is a 'package solution' aiming at the overall objective of a 'fair' (England) or 'just and equitable' (Australia) outcome, or 'proper provision' (Ireland). The dominant consideration for this is whether the 'needs' (as perceived in the respective jurisdiction)[191] of the children and the weaker party are met. For this, though, the courts will generally also consider the division of property first, particularly the allocation of the matri-monial home, before turning to maintenance and other issues.

---

[189] Above section II.D.ii.
[190] Above section II.C.i.
[191] Scherpe and Dutta, above n 10.

In the community of property jurisdictions and the participation jurisdictions,[192] the financial consequences of divorce are, in principle, determined independently of each other and are considered different 'pillars' of financial relief.[193] In the 'rule-based discretion' jurisdictions there seems to be a similar trend to separate issues of property and maintenance.[194] For the 'pillar' of maintenance, the courts generally have a wide discretion. As already pointed out in the overview at the beginning of this chapter and in the previous section, in the 'pillar' jurisdictions the courts also try to achieve a 'fair' outcome, but do so not holistically, but rather through the combination of the remedies for each separate pillar. While the needs (as defined in the respective jurisdiction) of the spouses (and the children) generally do not play a role under the property 'pillar', making sure that these needs are covered is a central consideration for the award of maintenance. As the outcome of the division of property and pensions will have an effect on the maintenance needs of the spouses, the courts tend to take this outcome into account when exercising their discretion in awarding maintenance. In addition, many jurisdictions also include compensatory elements in the other 'pillars'.

Therefore the 'package' and the 'pillar' approaches, at least on a theoretical level, do not necessarily lead to different outcomes with regard to the policy aims— 'fairness' is to be achieved and 'needs' covered. But in the 'package' jurisdictions, 'need' is the dominant consideration in achieving 'fairness' and, for policy reasons, will trump all other considerations. In practice this means that in cases where the available assets do not exceed what is required to cover 'needs', the outcome in 'package' and 'pillar' jurisdictions can be rather different because in the 'pillar' jurisdictions the covering of 'needs' remaining after the division of property will be dealt with only by the other 'pillars', most often maintenance payments (see section II.E.v below for needs and compensation).

All in all, financial relief upon divorce seems to be more influenced by the general policy aims and the culture and tradition of the respective jurisdiction than the technical approach. The determining factor appears to be the role and function of marriage in a society and, consequentially, what is seen as a 'fair' outcome of financial relief on divorce.

That said, the differences in the 'package' and 'pillar' approaches do matter greatly with regard to the European private international law instruments. These generally follow the 'pillar' approach, so that, for example, different European regulations apply to the division of property and maintenance.[195] Because of the absence of such a clear-cut division, jurisdictions following a 'holistic' or 'package' approach such as England and Wales and Ireland find it very difficult to opt into or apply these regulations.[196] Likewise, the enforcement of judgments from England and Wales and Ireland can cause difficulties, because the orders made in these

---

[192] See section II.B and C above.

[193] *Cf* section II.A above.

[194] See section II.D.ii above.

[195] See, eg Council Regulation (EC) 4/2009 on jurisdiction, applicable law, recognition and enforcement of decisions and cooperation in matters relating to maintenance obligations [2009] OJ L7/1.

[196] As evidenced by the Council Decision of 30 November 2009 on the conclusion by the European Community of the Hague Protocol of 23 November 2007 on the Law Applicable to Maintenance Obligations (2009/941/EC) [2009] OJ L331/17.

jurisdictions will not necessarily reflect a clear distinction between the 'pillars' of property division and maintenance.[197]

iv. A Common View on Sharing?

Despite the differences in detail there seems to be considerable common ground among the jurisdictions included in this book on the sharing of assets, particularly on three points.

First, there is a broad consensus on a principal equal sharing of assets. This is based on the underlying idea that in a marriage, one should not distinguish between the roles of homemaker and breadwinner. Both spouses and their contributions to the family welfare are considered to be equal, in principle, irrespective of whether they work inside or outside of the home. Marriage is seen as a partnership of equals and the assets should, therefore, be shared equally.[198]

Second, there appears to be a growing consensus that certain assets are not under all circumstances to be shared, namely assets owned before the marriage and gifts and inheritances received during the marriage. The view seems to be that as these are not 'fruits of the marriage' or the result of a 'common endeavour'.[199] Thus they are not necessarily connected to the marriage, and most legal systems do not see them as part of the asset pool that should be shared when the marriage ends.[200] However, some jurisdictions extend the asset pool to be shared beyond the 'fruits of the marriage' to include assets closely connected to the marriage. This means that in those jurisdictions a specific justification is required for those assets to be included; for example, that the asset was the matrimonial home or was used in the joint household (Austria), or that the assets were in another way 'intermingled' (New Zealand) or 'associated' (Singapore) with the family.

In England and Wales the approach just described is less pronounced and certainly not 'cast in stone', but there is a growing body of case law accepting and using distinctions between the property groups as just described when exercising the discretion to share the assets of the couple.[201] Australia and Ireland so far seem to be exceptions to the general approach of distinguishing between marital and

---

[197] See eg Bundesgerichtshof (XII ZB 12/05, FamRZ 2009, 1659; MDR 2009, 1225, NJW-RR 2010, 1); ECJ, *de Cavel (N. 2)* Case 120/1979 [1980] ECR 731. See also Scherpe and Dutta, above n 10.

[198] Except in Greece (section II.C.ii.B above), where a presumption needs to be rebutted to gain a share larger than one-third of the assets of the other, and some of the *derechos autonómicos* in Spain, especially Catalonia (Ferrer-Riba, Spain, this volume 355).

[199] However, different views seem to prevail when it comes to the question of the income derived from assets owned before the marriage (and potentially gifts and inheritances); some jurisdictions apparently see them as part of the 'joint endeavour' as they are included in the sharing. For example, in Germany the value increase (albeit indexed) of such property and the income derived from it is to be included in the sharing, and the Dutch universal community of property and the deferred community of property in the Nordic countries, in principle, include these as well. In the community of acquest jurisdictions the income derived from the personal assets are included in the acquest for example in Belgium, France, Spain and Portugal, but not in Slovenia, Serbia and Croatia; see section II.B.ii.a above.

[200] In the Netherlands and Sweden, for example, assets received during the marriage as inheritance or gifts can be excluded for the universal community of property and thus from the sharing, in the event of divorce through express stipulation by the testator of the person giving the gift; see Boele-Woelki and Braat, The Netherlands, this volume, 233 et seq; Jänterä-Jareborg, Sweden, this volume, 372 et seq.

[201] See for example *B v B (Ancillary Relief)* [2008] EWCA Civ 543; *Charman v Charman (No 4)* [2007] EWCA Civ 503; *McCartney v Mills McCartney* [2008] EWHC 401; *K v L* [2011] EWCA Civ 550;

non-marital assets for the sharing exercise, but the source of the assets could be (and presumably will be in appropriate cases) taken into account when the courts exercise their general discretion.

It is important to add that even in those jurisdictions where pre-marital assets and those acquired through gift or inheritance during the marriage are excluded from the sharing of property, there are other provisions offering protection to the non-owning spouse. Rather than relying on sharing of the property, this is dealt with through the possibility of allocating the use of the property to the non-owning spouse. It should also be noted that, generally, the housing market and/or the social welfare systems in many jurisdictions make it possible for the spouses to rehouse without too many problems, so that 'housing needs' as such do not arise in the same way as, for example, in England and Wales. So in one way or another, the housing needs of the spouses are considered and taken care of in all jurisdictions (see also section II.E.v below for needs and compensation).

A third similarity is that short marriages do not seem to be regarded as meriting equal sharing of assets; this, unsurprisingly, is particularly pronounced in the jurisdictions where all assets are included in the property division (for example, the Nordic countries, England and Wales). Yet, technically, the same applies in other systems where only the marital acquest (or something close to it) is to be divided, as in a short marriage there usually will only be a limited acquest.[202]

v. A Common View on Needs and Compensation?

Apart from sharing, two further policy considerations feature prominently in all jurisdictions looked at in this study: covering the 'needs' of both spouses and ensuring that marriage-related disadvantages are compensated for. These, of course, often overlap and a clear distinction may be impossible;[203] for example, if one of the spouses stops working for a long period of time to take care of the children, the fact that he or she did not acquire pension rights is a marriage-related disadvantage that also results in needs. Therefore, the two will be dealt with together in this section.

Views of what the 'needs' of the spouses comprise differ significantly from jurisdiction to jurisdiction.[204] Given the diversity of the social, cultural and economic backgrounds, this is hardly surprising. There seems to be a general consensus, though, that 'needs' (as perceived in the respective jurisdiction) should be covered. In most jurisdictions the view is that the obligation of the spouses to cover these needs continues after divorce even where those needs are not marriage-related

---

N v F [2011] EWHC 586(Fam); *Jones v Jones* [2011] EWCA Civ 41. See generally Miles, England and Wales, this volume, 94.

[202] Although there can be an extraordinary acquest, as for example the one earned by Mr Miller in *Miller v Miller; McFarlane v McFarlane* [2006] UKHL 24 shows. In such cases matrimonial regimes without a discretionary element are powerless and will have to divide the assets.

[203] Hence English courts usually do not expressly address compensation as a separate 'head', but absorb compensation into 'needs, generously assessed'. See The Law Commission, *Marital Property Agreements—A Consultation Paper* (Consultation Paper No 198, 2011) 32 et seq, www.justice.gov.uk/lawcommission/docs/cp198_Marital_Property_Agreements_Consultation.pdf.

[204] Scherpe and Dutta, above n 10.

(for example, where one of the spouses is incapable of working because of illness).[205] In that sense, marriage indeed remains a commitment for life. Another more or less openly pronounced reason for this is that the financial burdens of these needs should not be passed on to the state but should be borne by the other spouse where this is possible.[206] Only the Nordic countries expressly take a different view.[207]

The housing needs of the spouses (and the children) in jurisdictions like England and Wales and Ireland are central to the financial relief upon divorce and regularly dominate the outcome, often in combination with periodical payment to cover other needs. This is frequently seen as setting those jurisdictions apart particularly from the continental jurisdictions where the division of assets as such is not based on the housing needs.[208] However, on a policy level the distinction may not be as great as it seems at first glance. As explained in the previous section, as a matter of fact the housing needs in all jurisdictions are taken care of, but not necessarily through reallocation of property; instead the spouse in need of housing might be allocated the right to use the property. Also, renting adequate accommodation in most jurisdictions is not a problem, so the 'housing needs' issue as such does not arise but can be covered by periodical payments (and/or state support for rent). In addition, maintenance is generally seen as the tool to alleviate hardships and to cover ongoing needs (including rent).

Generally, the equal sharing of matrimonial property in combination with periodical payments is perceived to be sufficient to also cover compensation of relationship-generated disadvantages. In some jurisdictions, such as France and Spain, there is the possibility of making awards beyond the division of property which can have a compensatory nature as well as well as a maintenance function.[209]

In any event, while the approaches may differ and may rely on 'pillars' or 'packages', in all jurisdictions aspects of need and compensation are central to financial relief upon divorce. Indeed, it can be observed that in all jurisdictions examined in this book the remedies to address need and compensation are based on the discretion of the court, as having 'hard and fast' rules in this area is impossible. The difference is merely that in the 'pillar' jurisdictions this discretion is limited or non-existent with regard to property division/matrimonial property regimes and only applies to the other remedies, whereas in the 'package' jurisdictions the discretion comprises the whole 'package' and thus includes property.

---

[205] eg Dutta, Germany, this volume 164 et seq; Miles, England and Wales, this volume 95 et seq; *Radmacher v Granatino* [2010] UKSC 42, [190].

[206] For England and Wales see, eg *Hyman v Hyman* [1929] AC 601, 628–29: 'to prevent the wife from being thrown upon the public for support'; *Bennett v Bennett* [1952] 1 KB 249, 262 (Lord Denning): 'it is in the public interest that the wife and children of a divorced husband should not be left dependent on public assistance or on charity when he has the means to support them'; Jessep, Australia, this volume 21; Dutta, Germany, this volume 164 et seq. See also *Radmacher v Granatino* [2010] UKSC 42, [81] and [190] and *Miller v Miller and McFarlane v McFarlane* [2006] UKHL 24 [11] (Lord Nicholls), and [137] and [138] (Baroness Hale).

[207] See section II.C.i.b above and Scherpe, 'Eigenverantwortung', above n 60. See also Miles, 'Principle or Pragmatism', above n 103, 252 et seq.

[208] But after the nominal shares have been determined, a preferred allocation of specific assets is possible in community of property jurisdictions and also in Austria. Assets received that way of course count towards the share.

[209] Pintens, France and Belgium, this volume, 69, 76 et seq; Ferrer-Riba, Spain, this volume, 356 et seq.

vi. Excursus: Towards Rule-Based Discretion in Ancillary Relief in England and Wales?

The House of Lords decision in *White v White*[210] radically changed the approach to ancillary relief away from merely looking at the 'reasonable requirements' of the spouse towards a system of equal sharing.[211] Indeed, with regard to *White v White*, Cretney provocatively stated that the decision imposed a community of property regime on England and Wales.[212] This was expressly rejected first by Bennett J in *Sorrell v Sorrell*[213] and later by Baroness Hale in *Miller v Miller; McFarlane v McFarlane*,[214] the second House of Lords case which significantly changed the approach to ancillary relief. But in rejecting the suggestion of a deferred community of property, Baroness Hale stated that England and Wales 'do not yet have a system of community of property, whether full or deferred'.[215] It is the 'yet' which makes this statement remarkable and leaves much room for further thought.

In any event, ancillary relief continues to be one of the most controversial areas of family law in England and Wales, and there certainly is at least the beginning of a discussion on whether a matrimonial property regime should be adopted.[216] And, to give Cretney credit, there also is the general perception, at least among comparative family lawyers, that England is indeed moving towards some form of community of property.[217]

If one were to suggest—and there appears to be some support for this in case law, particularly in *Miller v Miller; McFarlane v McFarlane* and *Charman v Charman (No 4)*[218]—a more rule-based approach to financial relief in England and Wales, taking into account the comparison with continental European jurisdictions and Scotland as well as other common law jurisdictions such as Singapore and New Zealand, the future approach could be as follows:

— The overarching aim of ancillary relief is to achieve fairness for which the court in principle retains full discretion, guided by the factors set out in section 25 of the Matrimonial Causes Act 1973, with first consideration given to the welfare of any children of the family.
— Property division/sharing of the assets is the starting point for the discretionary exercise, which will require a 'computation stage' as in *Charman*[219] and classifying the assets as either matrimonial or non-matrimonial.

---

[210] *White v White* [2001] 1 AC 596.

[211] See eg Pintens, 'Matrimonial Property Law in Europe', above n 9, 35.

[212] S Cretney, 'Community of Property Imposed By Judicial Decision' (2003) 119 *LQR* 349.

[213] *Sorrell v Sorrell* [2005] EWHC 1717 [96].

[214] *Miller v Miller; McFarlane v McFarlane* [2006] UKHL 24 [151].

[215] Ibid.

[216] See eg E Cooke, A Barlow and T Callus, *Community of Property. A regime for England and Wales?* (London, Nuffield Foundation, 2006); E Cooke, 'The Future for Ancillary Relief' in G Douglas and N Lowe (eds), *The Continuing Evolution of Family Law* (Jordans, Bristol, 2009) 203 et seq.

[217] Ibid, 40 et seq; Pintens, 'Matrimonial Property Law in Europe', above n 9, 42; Scherpe, above n 47; W Pintens, 'Europeanisation of Family Law' in K Boele-Woelki (ed), *Perspectives for the Unification and Harmonisation of Family Law in Europe* (Antwerp, Intersentia, 2003) 12; Pintens, 'Ehegüterstände', above n 9, 276 et seq.

[218] *Charman v Charman (No 4)* [2007] EWCA Civ 503. See also *K v L* [2011] 2 FCR 597; *N v F* [2011] EWHC (Fam) 586 and *Jones v Jones* [2011] EWCA Civ 41.

[219] Ibid, [67].

— Matrimonial assets comprise all assets (including pension rights) gained during marriage except through gift or inheritance (ie the marital acquest) and the matrimonial home and the household goods. The matrimonial assets are to be shared equally upon divorce unless considerations of fairness demand otherwise. Such considerations can include the duration of the marriage and 'stellar' contributions.

— Non-matrimonial assets are all other assets, particularly those obtained before the marriage (except the matrimonial home) or through gift or inheritance, and any income derived from these assets. These are not to be shared equally unless considerations of fairness demand otherwise. Such considerations can include the duration of the marriage and the contributions made to the overall welfare of the family, particularly past and future child-care and related sacrifices, as well as other relationship-generated advantages and disadvantages and, more generally, the needs of the spouses.

— Maintenance and other orders can be made at the court's discretion.

The advantage of this approach, and of classifying the property this clearly, is that a deviation from equal sharing requires justification; at the same time such justification can easily be provided, for example, in case of apparent needs. There appears to be a growing consensus in England and Wales that property which is not 'fruit of the partnership' or the product of 'joint endeavour', such as pre-owned property, gifts and inheritances—as a starting point—should not be included in the sharing unless they are the matrimonial home and the household goods.[220] Such a development has taken place in the 'rule-based discretion' jurisdictions and the distinction between different groups of assets has long been the norm in the continental European jurisdictions.

Such an approach would make ancillary relief in England and Wales more rule-based and thus could provide greater certainty. Equal sharing of the matrimonial assets (and no sharing of non-matrimonial property) would be the starting point for the exercise of the discretion, but aspects of needs and compensation would allow for departures from the outcome under the starting point. This way the strand of needs would remain what it now is, namely the decisive element in the discretionary exercise where the funds available do not go beyond covering needs. That said, determining what needs and compensation mean in each individual case will, of course, remain an issue, and it is to be hoped that the courts or the legislature develop firmer guidelines so that these strands can be approached with greater certainty as well.

This approach would bring the jurisdiction much more in line with the general development in Europe (and indeed beyond), without sacrificing one of the great strengths and virtues of the English approach to financial relief upon divorce; the fact that it is discretion-based and thus able to achieve fairness in individual cases. A 'rule-based discretion' system, similar to that in some other common law jurisdictions (see section II.D.ii.b–e above), would not compromise the discretion of the courts in any way. It would merely require them to rationalise departures from the basic sharing rule for which the system expressly allows and indeed expects if fairness requires so. All assets, matrimonial and non-matrimonial, would still be available for the financial relief, although the burden of proof to justify including

---

[220] *Cf* Cooke, Barlow and Callus, *Community of Property*, above n 216.

them in the sharing would differ: the party who wants the sharing to deviate from the basic sharing rule would need to argue his or her case. However, needs would still be central to the discretionary exercise. Importantly, this approach would not necessarily require a reform of the statute or of financial relief in general, as it fits within the framework provided by *Miller v Miller; McFarlane v McFarlane.*

A final thought regarding private international law: the private international law instruments of the European Union that concern the financial consequences of divorce are principally based on the 'pillar' approach and this makes it difficult if not impossible for England and Wales to opt into or apply some of the respective instruments.[221] However, even when the instrument is not opted into, this does not mean that the existence of such an instrument can be ignored. Approaching ancillary relief as just described would make it easier for courts to set out clearly which parts of the orders are meant to address aspects of maintenance and property-sharing respectively, thus making enforcement of English orders in Europe easier. Of course this approach would also allow England and Wales to 'fit' more readily into the European private international law framework, just as Austria as a jurisdiction with 'rule-based discretion' already does today.

III. PRE-NUPTIAL AND POST-NUPTIAL AGREEMENTS

Having looked at default rules for financial relief on divorce, we can now return to the question asked in the introduction of the book:

> If the spouses do not want the default rules to apply to their financial relations, should they be free to conclude an agreement to 'contract out' of the default regime—and if so, to what extent?

Unsurprisingly, the answers to this question differ just as much as the default systems do.[222] An obvious thought would be that the freedom to contract out of the default regime would be greatest where the default system is the most rigid and therefore most likely not to fit every couple's situation.[223] On the other hand, another equally obvious thought would be the exact opposite: that the freedom to determine one's financial relations should be greatest where the default system provides for little or no certainty, and that the spouses could achieve such certainty through entering into an agreement.

At the same time one needs to consider what it is that the marital agreement actually does, namely derogate from the default system. The default systems were implemented with specific policy goals in mind and reflect the way the role of marriage is perceived in the respective jurisdictions: how much the state should interfere in private affairs, the influence of religion and the ideology behind marriage in general. The same then of course must be true for the extent of the freedom granted to the

---

[221] But see n 196 above. See also Cooke, 'The Future for Ancillary Relief' above n 216, esp 214 et seq.

[222] For a collection of nine national reports on international marital agreements written by practitioners see D Salter, C Butruille-Cardew, N Francis and S Grant, *International Pre-Nuptial and Post-Nuptial Agreements* (Bristol, Jordan Publishing, 2011).

[223] *Cf* N Dethloff, 'Contracting in Family Law: A European Perspective', in K Boele-Woelki, J Miles and JM Scherpe (eds), *The Future of Family Property in Europe* (Antwerp, Intersentia, 2011) 71.

spouses to depart from these default rules.[224] Indeed, the central question, as Dethloff has put it, is how a balance can be struck between private autonomy and ensuring 'fairness' for (or protection of) the economically vulnerable spouse upon divorce.[225] Complete autonomy could lead to one of the spouses in the event of divorce being left destitute, without any means to support him- or herself and, potentially, the children. This does not necessarily presuppose that one of the spouses sought to gain an (unfair) advantage over the other through the agreement; since both pre-nuptial and postnuptial agreements (but not separation agreements, on which see section IV below) are basically agreements about a more or less uncertain future, it could simply be a change of circumstance which led to this situation.

In any event, not one of the legal systems looked at allows for such complete freedom to contract out of the default systems. The comparison, therefore, will focus on the limits that each jurisdictions sets to the freedom; the safeguards that are in place to protect the economically vulnerable spouse (and indirectly the children).[226]

This theme of 'limits' and 'safeguards' will be explored in this part. It appears that all jurisdictions—more or less of necessity—have one thing in common, namely that the rules regarding the safeguards focus on two points in time: either the time when the marital agreement is concluded or the time when the agreements is invoked. This division will, therefore, be followed in this comparative part (see sections III.B and C below), but first a few general points need to be discussed.

A. Some General Points on Pre- and Post-Nuptial Agreements

i. Are They Marital Agreements or Divorce Agreements?

A crucial point when comparing marital agreements is the general function the agreement is supposed to fulfil, namely whether it should regulate the financial relations of the spouses during marriage or only in the case of divorce. This question has huge implications for the public policy considerations regarding marital agreements.

In jurisdictions where marriage has an immediate effect on the property relations of the spouses, namely the community of property jurisdictions,[227] the function of a marital agreement regarding the property is very different from that in other jurisdictions because it has immediate effect: the pre-nuptial agreement regulates the property relations of the spouses from the very beginning of their marriage; a post-nuptial agreement does so from the time it is stipulated to apply. Thus the agreement is not meant to regulate the case of divorce only; it is to regulate the property relations *during* marriage. The couple are choosing a matrimonial property regime *for* their marriage that applies immediately. Its application therefore does not require, or even premeditate, divorce.

---

[224] Ibid, 67.
[225] Ibid, 68.
[226] As explained in the introduction of this book, agreements regarding the children directly (eg, on custody/parental responsibility, maintenance etc) were not part of this study.
[227] See section II.B above.

In many jurisdictions marital agreements are perceived as an attempt by one spouse to secure a financial advantage over the other in case of divorce, but in the community of property jurisdictions it could be the exact opposite: not *taking* advantage but *giving* an advantage. So the underlying idea is not necessarily to exclude one spouse from the other's wealth but, for example, to protect one of the spouses from the financial risks incurred by the other in his or her professional capacity. The reason for the agreement could actually be to protect, rather than disadvantage, the spouse.[228] A further reason could be that the default regime is simply inappropriate for the specific circumstances of the couple, for example, because it is a second marriage and the couple want to ensure that property acquired before their marriage goes to their children from the previous marriage when they die.

Where the default matrimonial property regime is not one based on an immediate community of property but on a separation of property during marriage,[229] the same reasoning does not apply as the marital agreement is not meant to apply during marriage as such—although of course it will have an impact on a range of issues (particularly the administration of the assets, for example the right to dispose of certain assets without the consent of the other spouse etc). However, there may still be good reasons for such agreements that go beyond 'wanting to secure an advantage in case of divorce', particularly if there is a matrimonial property regime in place from the day of the marriage, such as in the continental European jurisdictions. This regime may have (and usually does have) significant consequences during the marriages as well (for example, accrued gains become part of the property to be shared as in Germany),[230] so there can be perfectly acceptable reasons for wanting to exclude some assets from the matrimonial property regime. Similar considerations apply in case of the death of one of the spouses where an existing matrimonial property regime can have a significant impact, so that a marital agreement may be concluded to put the spouse or the children (and especially children from previous relationships) in a better position with regard to their succession rights and inheritance tax.

It is, therefore, important to explore what the purpose and the function of the agreement was when judging 'foreign' marital agreements. This is of particular importance in those jurisdictions which apply the *lex fori* in financial relief upon divorce, for example, England and Wales. As pointed out elsewhere,[231] many 'foreign' matrimonial property agreements will have had a very real legal effect on the couple's property relations already (for example, if the couple is from a community of property jurisdiction), and third parties such as creditors and other family members may also have relied on that agreement. The same is true for the intended consequences in case of death. Ignoring the agreement and not even taking a 'sideways look'[232] may be fatal to what the agreement intended to achieve in the first

---

[228] Pintens, France and Belgium, this volume, 77 et seq; Ferrer-Riba, Spain, this volume, 357 et seq; JM Scherpe, 'Foreign Marital Agreements: the Approach of the English Courts' [2010] *Private Client Business* 184.

[229] See section II.C above.

[230] See section II.C.ii.a above.

[231] Scherpe, above n 228, 184 et seq.

[232] As the Supreme Court seems to suggest in *Radmacher v Granatino* [2010] UKSC 42, [74], where the 'foreign element' effectively is limited to determining whether the couple intended to be bound by the agreement.

place and might lead to manifest unfairness. Therefore the approach favoured by Thorpe LJ in the Court of Appeal decision in *Radmacher v Granatino* clearly is to be preferred:

> in future cases broadly in line with the present case on the facts, the judge should give due weight to the marital property regime into which the parties freely entered. This is not to apply foreign law, nor is it to give effect to a contract foreign to English tradition. It is, in my judgment, a legitimate exercise of the very wide discretion that is conferred on the judges to achieve fairness between the parties to the ancillary relief proceedings.[233]

As noted, in order to determine the 'due weight' that marital agreements should be given, it is crucial to understand the function they have in the relevant jurisdiction in each individual case.

ii. Public Policy Objections—'Planning to Fail'?

If the agreement is meant to apply during marriage, the term 'marital agreement' seems more appropriate than if the agreement is only to apply in case of divorce— the agreement is then perceived to be a 'divorce agreement'. This, of course, is an explanation for the resistance of many jurisdictions against the latter type of agreement, for example, in England and Wales,[234] but also in continental European jurisdictions.[235] Since marriage was seen as indissoluble and a union for life, an agreement regulating the consequences of a potential dissolution of the marriage could be perceived to be against that public policy—the couple would be 'planning to fail'.[236]

Additionally, where divorce was based on fault, and as such many of the consequences were dependent on fault as well, it seemed patently absurd to allow the couple to 'plan' this event in advance, thereby violating the spirit and sanctity of the marital union.

While these concerns might have been appropriate in their time, the law has moved on. In no jurisdiction in Europe (and indeed hardly any jurisdiction at all worldwide) where divorce is possible can it solely be obtained based on fault; the role of fault as a base for divorce has been losing ground internationally.[237] Even where fault plays a role, its impact on the financial consequences of divorce is not as great as it used to be—if there is any at all. At the same time, unfortunately, more and more marriages end in divorce in all jurisdictions. Family patterns have changed, and often spouses will have been married before and children from previous relationships will live with them. The nature of marriage has changed as well. Divorce is perhaps not the rule (and hopefully never will be), but it certainly is no longer a rare exception. With divorce being a reality of life, an agreement regulating

---

[233] *Radmacher v Granatino* [2009] EWCA 649, [53].

[234] Miles, England and Wales, this volume 90 et seq. See also N Francis, 'Pre-nuptial and Post-Nuptial Agreements in the UK (England and Wales)' in Salter et al, above n 222, 431 et seq.

[235] Cf Scherpe, 'Ehevertrag' in Basedow, Hopt and Zimmermann, above n 9, 354 et seq.

[236] See n 3 above.

[237] K Boele-Woelki, B Braat and I Curry-Sumner (ed), *European Family Law in Action. Vol I—Grounds for Divorce* (Antwerp, Intersentia, 2003); K Boele-Woelki, W Pintens, F Ferrand, C Gonzalez-Beilfuss, M Jänterä-Jareborg, N Lowe and D Martiny, *Principles of European Family Law Regarding Divorce and Maintenance Between Former Spouses* (Antwerp, Intersentia, 2004); M Antokolskaia, *Harmonisation of Family Law in Europe: A Historical perspective* (Antwerp, Intersentia, 2006).

the financial consequences of such an (undesired) event is no longer unthinkable, but by many seen as 'common sense'; not doing so could be seen as 'failing to plan' rather than 'planning to fail'.[238] The fundamental public policy objections against marital agreements, even if they are 'divorce agreements', no longer apply.[239]

iii. Are Pre-Nuptial Agreements Different from Post-Nuptial Agreements?

A further important point is the timing of the agreement, which in this section is meant to refer to whether the agreement was concluded before the wedding (pre-nuptial agreement) or after the wedding (post-nuptial agreement). Post-nuptial agreements concluded at a point in time when the couple have decided to separate and divorce and merely want to regulate the financial consequences of this (called separation agreements in this book) will be considered separately (see section IV below).

Given the differences in the default regimes, the necessity for a distinction between pre-nuptial and post-nuptial agreements for some jurisdictions should be apparent. In jurisdictions without an actual default matrimonial property regime, such as England and Wales, Ireland and Australia, the differences between the two types of marital agreement might be less important as both types of agreements only apply in case of divorce;[240] but in community of property systems a post-nuptial agreement essentially aims to change the already *existing* property structures rather than prospective ones. The same is true for participation systems where the other spouse can be said to have 'built up a claim' or to have an entitlement[241] to participate in the property of the other during the marriage already, thus the agreement while prospective can actually mean that the spouse signs away an existing claim (or at least a claim that could be made should the couple divorce at that point in time, for example, the German *Zugewinn*). This not only has an impact on the spouses themselves but potentially also on third parties, like creditors and family members, who have relied on these existing property rights or claims/entitlements. So for many jurisdictions it can, therefore, be said that the function and impact of post-nuptial agreements differ from the one of pre-nuptial agreements, as pre-nuptial agreements are solely *prospective* in the sense that they will regulate the financial (and especially property) relations of the future spouses from the very beginning of their marriage, whereas post-nuptial agreements can also alter the *existing* financial relations.

Against the background of existing property rights or claims and entitlements, it is understandable that post-nuptial agreements are (or were) subject to more intense scrutiny in some jurisdictions.[242] For example, in Belgium and France, where the default matrimonial property regime is the community of acquests, until the reforms

---

[238] See n 3 above.

[239] See eg the Privy Council decision in *MacLeod v MacLeod* [2008] UKPC 64, [38]–[39], and especially the subsequent Supreme Court decision in *Radmacher v Granatino* [2010] UKSC 42, [31 et seq].

[240] But see the Privy Council decision in *MacLeod v MacLeod* [2008] UKPC 64, [36], now essentially overruled by the Supreme Court decision in *Radmacher v Granatino* [2010] UKSC 42, [52 et seq].

[241] *Cf* Dethloff, above n 223, 89.

[242] Ibid, 76. For the position in the United States see Ellman, this volume, 429 et seq. On contracts between married persons generally, see M Trebilcock and S Elliott, 'The Scope and Limits of Legal Paternalism: Altruism and Coercion in Family Financial Arrangements' in Peter Benson (ed), *The Theory of Contract Law* (Cambridge, Cambridge University Press, 2001) 45 et seq.

of 2006 (France) and 2003 (Belgium) a post-nuptial agreement, either generally or at least in some cases, required a ratification (*homologation*) by the courts.[243] In Belgium one of the main reasons for the abolition of this requirement given in the parliamentary debates was the differential treatment of pre- and post-nuptial agreements which was felt to discriminate against already married couples.[244] While couples can now enter into post-nuptial agreements freely in Belgium following further reforms in 2008, there still are some exceptions in France: if the couple has under-age children, a *homologation* is mandatory, and adult children and the creditors may oppose a post-nuptial agreement, in which case a *homologation* is still required (although, in practice, is rarely refused).[245] In any event, a post-nuptial agreement changing or amending the matrimonial regime is only possible if the regime has been in operation for at least two years and is 'in the interest of the family'.[246] In the Netherlands, where the default matrimonial property regime is the universal community of property, the approval of the court is still required, the rationale for this principally being the protection of creditors; however, a Bill has been proposed that would abolish this requirement.[247] In Spain post-nuptial agreements are possible but not binding on third parties insofar as their rights were established before the agreement.[248] In Malta the couple is allowed to vary their 'marriage agreements'[249] without prejudice to the rights of children and third parties only 'with the authority of the court'.[250] In Portugal, also a community of acquest jurisdiction, post-nuptial agreements are not possible at all, as the 'old' principle of the immutability of the matrimonial property regime still applies; thus couples can choose their matrimonial property regime before but not after the wedding.[251]

The closer scrutiny of post-nuptial agreements contrasts starkly with the (now basically overruled) position taken by the Privy Council in *MacLeod v MacLeod*[252] where pre-nuptial agreements were seen as the 'price which one party may extract for his or her willingness to marry' and thus considered against public policy and subject to stricter scrutiny than post-nuptial agreements. In some Eastern European

---

[243] On this, see Pintens, France and Belgium, this volume, 79.

[244] Pintens, France and Belgium, this volume, 79.

[245] Arts 1396(3), 1397(1), (5) French Civil Code; Pintens, France and Belgium, this volume, 79; Dethloff, above n 223, 76; F Ferrand and B Braat, 'France' in K Boele-Woelki, B Braat and I Curry-Sumner (eds), *European Family Law in Action IV: Property Relations between Spouses* (Antwerp, Intersentia, 2009) answer to Question 192.

[246] Art 1397(1) French Civil Code; Dethloff, above n 223, 76.

[247] Art 1:119 (1) New Dutch Civil Code; Boele-Woelki and Braat, The Netherlands, this volume, 248; K Boele-Woelki and F Schonewille and W Schrama, 'The Netherlands' in K Boele-Woelki, B Braat and I Curry-Sumner (eds), *European Family Law in Action IV: Property Relations between Spouses* (Antwerp, Intersentia, 2009) answer to Question 192.

[248] Art 1317 Spanish Civil Code; C González Beilfuss, 'Spain' in K Boele-Woelki, B Braat and I Curry-Sumner (eds), *European Family Law in Action IV: Property Relations between Spouses* (Antwerp, Intersentia, 2009) answer to Question 192.

[249] At the time of writing, divorce still was not available in Malta, although in a referendum held on 28 May 2011 52.56 per cent of voters had voted in favour of introducing divorce.

[250] Art 1244 Maltese Civil Code; R Farrugia, 'Malta' in K Boele-Woelki, B Braat and I Curry-Sumner (eds), *European Family Law in Action IV: Property Relations between Spouses* (Antwerp, Intersentia, 2009) answer to Question 192. See generally ch 16, Title V 'Of Marriage Contracts' on pre- and post-nuptial agreements in Malta.

[251] Art 1714 Portuguese Civil Code; de Oliveira, Martins and Vítor, above n 12, answer to Question 192.

[252] See, above n 240.

jurisdictions[253] pre-nuptial agreements are still subject to more restrictions for different public policy reasons, namely that they contemplated a failure of the marriage before it was even entered into (the 'planning to fail' argument, see section III.A.ii above).

But apart from these exceptions[254] it can be said that pre- and post-nuptial agreements (but not separation agreements, on which see section IV below) are more or less subject to the same legal rules, and they will therefore be discussed together.

iv. Binding Effect of a Pre- or Post-Nuptial Agreement

Another issue is the seemingly fundamental distinction between the jurisdictions where post- or pre-nuptial agreements are 'binding and enforceable' (provided certain requirements are fulfilled) and those where they are not. As has been explained above (section III.A.i), in many jurisdictions marital agreements have the function of choosing a matrimonial property regime. In that sense they are 'binding and enforceable'. This does not mean, however, that the courts in the relevant jurisdictions do not—to varying degrees—retain the power to review the substance of the marital agreements, as do the courts in all other jurisdictions examined here. In Australia there seems to have been an—arguably rather unsuccessful—attempt to oust the jurisdiction of the court to review to substance of an agreement completely as long as certain formalities are fulfilled, but now essentially a review of the substance of the agreement is possible.[255]

Particularly in England and Wales the perception of marital agreements is that once they are validly concluded, the courts would no longer retain the jurisdiction to review the substance of an agreement. Indeed, such 'cast-iron' agreements (for all assets or only parts) are one of the options the Law Commission of England and Wales discusses in its Consultation paper, but without much enthusiasm.[256]

'Cast-iron' agreements do not really exist in any of the jurisdictions examined for this project, as at least some safeguards operate to protect the (prospective) spouses' autonomy—and, to a certain extent, to protect them from their autonomy.

B. Safeguards Applying at the Time of the Conclusion of the Pre- or Post-Nuptial Agreement

The first scrutiny undertaken in all jurisdictions is an examination of the circumstances at the time of the conclusion of the agreement. As is to be expected, in all jurisdictions the general rules of contract apply to marital agreements, ie doctrines of fraud, mistake, deceit, duress, undue influence etc. These rules are generally in

---

[253] Eg Slovakia and the Ukraine, see Dethloff, above n 223, 76.

[254] But see also Ellman, United States, this volume, 429 et seq.

[255] Jessep, Australia, this volume 33 et seq.

[256] The Law Commission, *Marital Property Agreements—A Consultation Paper* (Consultation Paper No 198, 2011), www.justice.gov.uk/lawcommission/docs/cp198_Marital_Property_Agreements_Consultation.pdf 7.20 et seq. See also Cooke, The Law Commission's Consultation on Marital Property Agreements, this volume 144 et seq, and E Cooke, 'The Law Commission's Consultation on Marital Property Agreements' [2011] *Family Law* 145 et seq.

place to ensure that the contract was concluded based on an unimpeded, free and autonomous decision of the parties. However, in virtually all jurisdictions additional, special rules apply to marital agreements; rules that go beyond the standard doctrines of contract law and thus lower the threshold for intervention and offer greater protection to 'weaker' parties.[257] The existence of those rules can be explained by the subject matter the agreements are dealing with and the social situation in which they apply.

First, special protection is generally deemed necessary because a marital agreement differs significantly from other contracts due to the subject matter. The financial relations of the spouses are regulated specifically with (more or less clearly) defined policy goals in mind, and a 'default system' in place. So, in the absence of a marital agreement the default rules apply—whereas normally in the absence of a contract in other areas of law no mutual obligations arise.[258] These rules are in place because this area of law was not meant to be dealt with by the 'general rules' of property law (which would amount to a full separation of property), and specific rules for the financial relations of married couples are meant to support certain policy goals. Hence the state has a specific interest in regulating the financial relations of spouses, and it is not surprising that there are also special rules regulating whether and to what extent the spouses can opt out of the default system provided.

Second, the social situation is also a completely different one which justifies special legal rules. The American Law Institute has succinctly summarised the rationale for these rules:

> While there are good reasons to respect contracts relating to the consequences of family dissolution, the family context requires some departure from the rules that govern the commercial arena. First, the relationship between contracting parties who are married, or about to marry, is different than the usual commercial relationship in ways that matter to the law's treatment of their agreements. Persons planning to marry usually assume that they share with their intended spouse a mutual and deep concern for one another's welfare. Business people negotiating a commercial agreement do not usually have that expectation of one another … These distinctive expectations that persons planning to marry usually have about one another can disarm their capacity for self-protective judgment, or their inclination to exercise it, as compared to parties negotiating commercial agreements. This difference justifies legal rules designed to strengthen the parties' ability and inclination to consider how a proposed agreement affects their own interest.[259]

---

[257] Pennsylvania seems to be the sole exception for some aspects—see *Simeone v Simeone*, 581 A 2d 162 (Pa 1990) and Ellman, United States, this volume, 415.

[258] Compare for example the legal situation of cohabitants where many jurisdictions do not offer a 'default system'. On this see (for England and Wales) Law Commission, *Cohabitation: The Financial Consequences of Relationship Breakdown* (Consultation Paper No 179, 2006) and Report Law Com No 307 (2007), both available, www.justice.gov.uk/lawcommission/areas/cohabitation.htm and the national reports in J Scherpe and N Yassari (eds), *Rechtsstellung nichtehelicher Lebensgemeinschaften—The Legal Status of Cohabitants* (Tübingen, Mohr Siebeck, 2005) and I Kroppenberg, D Schwab, D Henrich, P Gottwald and A Spickhoff (eds), *Rechtsregeln für nichteheliches Zusammenleben* (Bielefeld, Gieseking, 2009).

[259] American Law Institute, *Principles of the Law of Family Dissolution—Analysis and Recommendations* (St Paul MN, American Law Institute Publishers, 2002), comment c on § 7.02, 1063 et seq. See also Ellman, United States, this volume, 427.

The existence of special rules where there is a danger that the contracts concluded are one-sided because of a potentially unequal bargaining position are not unusual—they can be found in many areas of law, such as consumer law and labour law. While in purely commercial relationships an asymmetry of information, superior knowledge or a superior bargaining position in many situations (but by no means all) may be acceptable and one may 'use' the superior position to one's advantage, in other relationships (for example, employer—employee; landlord—tenant; spouses) legislators generally have taken a different position and implemented rules to prevent an abuse of such superiority. The rationale behind these rules is generally that while there may be *nominal* autonomy in such situations, the social realities the parties find themselves in mean that there is no *actual* autonomy to make a free and informed choice. The rules are to ensure that there is an actually equal bargaining position rather than a merely nominal one; in other words: their role is to protect the autonomy of the parties.

i. Form and Legal Advice

In many—but not all—of the jurisdictions examined, specific requirements as to the form of the marital agreement exist. As they usually are closely connected to requirements of legal advice, these two aspects will be dealt with together.

There is a surprising divergence when it comes to the formal requirements of marital agreements. While some jurisdictions require the strict form of notarial deeds (Germany,[260] Netherlands,[261] Belgium and France,[262] Spain[263]) others do not seem to require a specific form and rely solely on general contract law (Singapore,[264] Scotland,[265] England,[266] Ireland,[267] Austria[268]). In other jurisdictions it generally suffices that the agreements are in writing and signed by the parties (Australia,[269]

---

[260] Dutta, Germany, this volume 172 et seq.

[261] Art 1:115 (1) Dutch Civil Code. But for post-nuptial agreements an 'approval' by the district court is required. Boele-Woelki and Braat, The Netherlands, this volume, 248 et seq and above section III.A.iii.

[262] But for some post-nuptial in France a *homologation* is still required, see 487 et seq above and Pintens, France and Belgium, this volume, 79. See also generally C Butruille-Cardew, 'A French Perspective on International Pre-nuptial and Post-nuptial agreements' in Salter et al above n 222, 131 and 144.

[263] Ferrer-Riba, Spain, this volume, 360 et seq.

[264] Leong, Singapore, this volume, 321 et seq.

[265] Norrie, Scotland, this volume, 301.

[266] Miles, England and Wales, this volume, 99 et seq; but maintenance agreements need to be in writing, s 34 Matrimonial Causes Act 1973, ibid 102. See also Francis, above n 234, 461.

[267] Crowley, Ireland, this volume, 215 et seq; but recommendations by Study Group suggest written form, see ibid 219 and Study Group on Pre-Nuptial Agreements, *Report of the Study Group on Pre-Nuptial Agreements*, presented to the Tánaiste and Minster for Justice Equality and Law Reform, April 2007, 81 et seq.

[268] Ferrari, Austria, this volume, 58; but for agreements on specific matters a notarial deed is required. See also A Kriegler, 'Pre-nuptial Agreements in Austria' in Salter et al, above n 222, 77 and 88.

[269] s 90G Family Law Act 1975 (Cth); Jessep, Australia, this volume, 26 et seq; O Jessep, 'Section 90G and Pt VIIIA of the Family Law Act 1975 (Cth)' (2010) 24 *Australian Journal of Family Law* 104; Wilson above n 351, 38.

New Zealand,[270] US jurisdictions[271]). In Sweden the written and signed agreement also has to be registered at a court.[272]

These differences can—at least in part—be explained, however, if seen in conjunction with two further points, namely the role and form legal advice plays in the various jurisdictions and the level of scrutiny the substance of an agreement is subject to when it is invoked (on this see section III.C. below). On the latter it can be said that, as a general rule, where there are low formal requirements the substance of the agreement can be reviewed anyway and thus it is deemed unnecessary (if not futile) to have specific formal requirements.[273]

An issue that seems to divide the civil law jurisdictions and the common law jurisdictions is the role of legal advice in the conclusion of marital agreements. As just explained, in most of the continental European jurisdictions a marital agreement requires a notarial deed. Common lawyers especially seem to find it puzzling that no further independent legal advice is required and that in those jurisdictions no one seems to be particularly worried about potential duress or unfairness.[274] Perhaps this puzzlement is the result of the role and function of the notary being not fully understood.[275] In brief, notaries in continental European jurisdictions are duty-bound to be neutral, independent advisers and owe duties to both parties. In many jurisdictions they are even considered organs or representatives of the state and the powers vested in them are essentially public rather than private—in many jurisdictions they are accorded the status of a public official.[276] Their role in the

---

[270] s 21F Property (Relationships) Act 1976; Briggs, New Zealand, this volume, 269 et seq.

[271] Ellman, United States, this volume, 411 et seq; specifically for New York see PE Bronstein, 'Pre-Nuptial Agreements in the United States of America' in Salter et al, above n 221 at 473 et seq.

[272] The registration is a formality and does not involve an actual scrutiny of the agreement; Jänterä-Jareborg, Sweden, this volume, 379 et seq.

[273] See, eg Leong, Singapore, this volume, 328, Norrie, Scotland, this volume, 303 et seq; Jänterä-Jareborg, Sweden, this volume, 381; Miles, England and Wales, this volume, 99 et seq; Crowley, Ireland, this volume, 215.

[274] See, eg D Hodson, 'English Marital Agreements for International Families after *Radmacher*' [2011] *International Family Law* 31.

[275] On the role and function of the notary see generally Center of Legal Competence, *Notaries in Europe—Growing Fields of Competence* (Antwerp, Intersentia, 2007) and particularly S Matyk, 'The European Union—A Driving Force for a European Notarial Profile' in the same volume, 15 et seq. See also Ferrer-Riba, Spain, this volume, 358 et seq; Dutta, Germany, this volume, 172 et seq; Pintens, France and Belgium, this volume, 78 et seq; Dethloff, above n 222, 74 et seq; G Brambring, 'Die Ehevertragsfreiheit und ihre Grenzen', in S Hofer, D Schwab and D Henrich (eds), *From Status to Contract?—Die Bedeutung des Vertrages im europäischen Familienrecht* (Bielefeld, Gieseking, 2005) 17 et seq.

[276] Cf the description of the notary's role on the webpage of the Council of the Notariats of the European Union, www.cnue.be, and the European Notarial Code of Conduct (ibid), where it is stated:
'2.4. Public service
The notary exercises his or her functions with integrity, availability and diligence.
The notary has a duty to inform the parties of the content and effects of the instruments concerning them, and to advise them fully. He or she shall research the most relevant ways to achieve the result desired by the parties, in accordance with the applicable law.
The notary shall verify the identity, the capacity and the quality of all parties' consent, and shall verify the legality of their agreements. He or she is personally involved in issuing the instrument.
2.5. Impartiality and independence
A notary shall advise and operate fully impartially and independently. He or she shall play the role of trusted third party neutral between parties.'
Cf also Council of the Notariats of the European Union (eds), *Comparative Study on Authentic Instruments*, www.cnue-nouvelles.be/en/000/actualites/aae-etude-acte-authentiquefinal-25-11-2008-en.pdf.

conclusion of marital agreements goes well beyond mere formalities: they have to advise both parties and explain the consequences of the agreement. It is a central part of the duty of the notary to ensure that both spouses, but particularly the spouse who potentially is 'signing away' any existing or prospective rights and claims, fully understand what he or she is doing and thus to ensure that the 'weaker' spouse is protected. Failure to fulfil this duty will expose the notary to liability. That said, it can of course not be ruled out that the notary in question is an 'old family friend' of one of the spouses or has regular business with one of them, which might lead to a certain lack of neutrality (and essentially to the notary neglecting his or her duties).

Still, the system of protection through the notary has been in place for a long time (and indeed is applied in many other contexts as well), and there is no serious concern in any of the jurisdictions that this protection might be inadequate. Puzzling as that may be to common lawyers, the system appears to be functioning very well. There certainly is no indication that more 'unfair' agreements are concluded in systems relying on notarial deeds rather than those requiring independent legal advice.

That said, even in those jurisdictions where no notarial deed or any other form of legal advice is prescribed spouses will often seek independent advice, particularly in 'big money' cases. Whether or not the parties have been independently advised then also carries weight as one of the factors to be considered when judging the agreement (see section III.C below)

However, the requirement of independent legal advice seems to be perceived as essential the common law jurisdictions of England,[277] Ireland,[278] New Zealand,[279] many (but not all) of the US jurisdictions[280] and Australia.[281]

In Australia, particular importance was (and still is) attached to the legal advice in the statute, and indeed form and content of the advice to be given were very strictly circumscribed—to such an extent that practitioners not only found it too burdensome, but simply too risky to offer advice because of potential liability.[282] This, of course, has to be seen against the background of the effect of marital agreements which were meant to be 'cast iron' and thus to oust the jurisdiction of the court for financial relief on divorce. The relevant Australian statute was subject to several amendments, and the most recent amendment actually allows agreements to be binding even if the required legal advice was not received, provided that the court is satisfied that it would be unjust and inequitable under the circumstances if the agreement were not binding on the spouses.[283]

---

[277] The Law Commission, *Marital Property Agreements*, above n 203, 103 et seq; Cooke, The Law Commission's Consultation on Marital Property Agreements, this volume 144 et seq; Miles, England and Wales, this volume 89 et seq; Harper and Frankle, An English Practitioner's View, this volume, 128 et seq; Home Office, *Supporting Families: a Consultation Document* (HMSO 1998) 4.23.

[278] Study Group on Pre-Nuptial Agreements, above n 267, 84; Crowley, Ireland, this volume, 220 et seq.

[279] See Briggs, New Zealand, this volume, 269 et seq.

[280] Ellman, United States, this volume, 422 et seq.

[281] Jessep, Australia, this volume, 26 et seq; Jessep, 'Section 90G', above n 269; B Fehlberg and B Smyth, 'Binding Pre-Nuptial Agreements in Australia: The First Year', (2002) 16 *International Journal of Law, Policy and the Family* 127.

[282] See references in previous footnote.

[283] Jessep, Australia, this volume, 36 et seq, esp 30; Jessep, 'Section 90G', above n 269.

This appears somewhat similar to the approach of the Supreme Court of the United Kingdom in *Radmacher v Granatino,* where only *material* lack of advice was held to be relevant:

> Sound legal advice is obviously desirable, for this will ensure that a party understands the implications of the agreement, and full disclosure of any assets owned by the other party may be necessary to ensure this. But if it is clear that a party is fully aware of the implications of an ante-nuptial agreement and indifferent to detailed particulars of the other party's assets, there is no need to accord the agreement reduced weight because he or she is unaware of those particulars.[284]

In that sense, both in Australia and in England and Wales independent legal advice is not a necessary requirement for a marital agreement to be binding/followed by the court.[285] Likewise in the American Law Institute's Principles of the Law of Family Dissolution in § 7.04(3) independent legal advice is merely one of the requirements to establish a *presumption* that party gave fully informed consent, but not more.[286] This means that independent legal advice is a factor—and certainly an important factor—to be considered, but it leaves open the possibility for marital agreements to be concluded without independent legal advice. Interestingly, that has always been the position in Singapore.[287]

Indeed, one may wonder whether legal advice in the end can be more than a factor when determining whether the decision to sign the marital agreement actually was a fully informed and free one. As the American Law Institute quite rightly pointed out with reference to pre-marital agreements (although the reasoning principally applies to all post-nuptial agreements as well):

> [N]early all premarital agreements involve special difficulties arising from unrealistic optimism about marital success, the human tendency to treat low probabilities as zero probabilities, the excessive discounting of future benefits, and the inclination to overweigh the importance of the immediate and certain consequences of agreement—the marriage—as against its contingent and future consequences.[288]

And:

> even though the terms of agreements made before, or during, an ongoing family relationship address the consequences of its dissolution, the parties ordinarily do not expect the family unit to dissolve. Even if the possibility of dissolution is considered, it is necessarily imagined as arising at some indefinite time in the future. The remoteness of dissolution in both likelihood and timing, as well as the difficulty of anticipating other life changes that might occur during the course of the marriage, further impedes the ability of persons to evaluate the impact that the contract terms will have on them in the future when its enforcement is sought.[289]

---

[284] *Radmacher v Granatino* [2010] UKSC 42, [69].

[285] See also See Harper and Frankle, An English Practitioner's View, this volume, 128 et seq.

[286] See Ellman, United States, this volume, 419 et seq; American Law Institute, above n 259, 1067 et seq. See also Harper and Frankle, An English Practitioner's View, this volume, 137.

[287] Leong, Singapore, this volume, 328.

[288] Ellman, United States, this volume, 423 et seq; American Law Institute, above n 259 comment b) on § 7.05, 1098.

[289] Ellman, United States, this volume, 427 et seq; American Law Institute, above n 259 comment c) on § 7.02, 1064.

While legal advice may go a long way in helping each spouse to understand the consequences of the marital agreement and therefore, as the Supreme Court of the United Kingdom has put it in *Radmacher v Granatino*, 'obviously is desirable'[290] it is by no means a guarantee and complete safeguard against a party signing an agreement that is severely disadvantageous to them and where for any objective bystander it is utterly clear that they will come to regret it. As Hardie Boys J put it in a decision of the New Zealand Court of Appeal, the provisions on legal advice do 'not protect one who ignores the advice'.[291]

Even negotiating or renegotiating the terms of the agreement for many would seem a breach of trust and therefore might lead to the (future) spouse accepting terms that he or she otherwise would not have accepted.[292] In the special circumstances of marital agreements, particularly pre-nuptial agreements, what might be 'unrealistic optimism' about the marriage can never be 'advised away' fully. Even the best legal advice cannot be more than *a* safeguard, but never *the* safeguard.

ii. Disclosure

The duty to disclose seems to divide the jurisdictions almost as much as the requirement for legal advice. In the continental European jurisdictions there is generally no duty to disclose assets for pre-nuptial agreements,[293] whereas in many common law jurisdictions disclosure plays an important role or is even a requirement for the marital agreement.[294]

The absence of requirements to disclose assets may strike many common lawyers as odd, but when looking at what the substance is that the agreement covers more closely it actually becomes apparent why such a duty would make little sense: in the jurisdictions where no disclosure in case of pre-nuptial agreements is required, assets owned before the marriage generally are not part of the (matrimonial) property that is to be shared under the default regime.[295] This means that disclosure (which might be burdensome and expensive) would not 'reveal' any assets which the other spouse could potentially claim in case of divorce even without a pre-nuptial agreement. This, of course, is different where—like in England and Wales, Australia and Ireland—all assets (at least in principle) are subject to the discretionary financial

---

[290] *Radmacher v Granatino* [2010] UKSC 42, [69].

[291] *Coxhead v Coxhead* [1993] 2 NZLR 397 (CA), 404; Briggs, New Zealand, this volume, 270.

[292] *Cf* Dethloff, above n 223, 87.

[293] Eg Ferrari, Austria, this volume, 58; Jänterä-Jareborg, Sweden, this volume, 388 et seq; Ferrer-Riba, Spain, this volume, 360 et seq; Pintens, France and Belgium, this volume, 79; Boele-Woelki and Braat, The Netherlands, this volume, 248. However, post-nuptial agreements in Belgium and the Netherlands require disclosure (and in the Netherlands even a *homologation*); see below and section III. A.ii above.

[294] The Law Commission, above n 203, 97 et seq; Home Office, *Supporting Families: a Consultation Document* (HMSO 1998) 4.23; Miles, England and Wales, this volume, 99 et seq; Harper and Frankle, An English Practitioner's View, this volume, 135; Study Group on Pre-Nuptial Agreements, above n 267, 84 and Crowley, Ireland, this volume, 220; Jessep, Australia, this volume, 26 et seq; Ellman, United States, this volume, 420 et seq. In New Zealand the level of disclosure required is lower for pre- and post-nuptial agreements than for separation agreements; Briggs, New Zealand, this volume, 270, 277 et seq.

[295] Likewise inheritances and gifts received during the marriage, see sections II.B.ii.a and b, C.i and ii above.

relief upon divorce. Here the spouse could potentially 'sign away' assets he or she could potentially rely on in the event of divorce.[296]

Likewise this explains why in jurisdictions where there is no duty to disclose for *pre*-nuptial agreements there often is one for *post*-nuptial agreements. In community of property jurisdictions the act of marriage itself creates communal property of which the spouses own a share;[297] without disclosure a spouse might unknowingly give up that share in a post-nuptial agreement.[298] It is interesting to note, however, that not all community of property jurisdictions seem to require disclosure for the validity of a post-nuptial agreement. However, the other spouse is protected either through the requirement of *homologation*[299] or by a general duty to disclose assets during the marriage.[300] Legal advisors (including the notary) have a duty to advise accordingly. Thus if the spouse has the opportunity (and right) to ask for disclosure but decides not to do so, this then—in principle—has no effect on the validity of the post-nuptial agreement.

While in the deferred community of property systems there is no joint property during the marriage so that there are no existing property claims or rights arising from the marriage, one could say that because these claims would arise in case of divorce some form of 'entitlement' already exists. The same is basically true for participation systems like the German *Zugewinngemeinschaft* and other systems based on a separation of property where even at the end no community of property is created: while there will not be a claim *in rem* at the end of the marriage, the spouse can claim a share in the accrued gains. While here, like in some community of property states, there is no duty to disclose and thus the uninformed spouse could be left in a vulnerable position as he or she might unknowingly sign away a claim he or she might have had in case of divorce, this is compensated for by general duties of the spouses to disclose assets to each other.[301] In all systems requiring notarial deeds for marital agreements, the notary would, in case of post-nuptial agreements, have to explain this to the spouses and thus ensure disclosure or, at least, an express or implied waiver of disclosure and thus an informed decision.

In any event, what the jurisdictions have in common is that in some situations disclosure is either required or there is a right to ask for disclosure, namely where existing claims or claims regarding assets which would be subject of future entitlements would be 'signed away'. It is apparent that in such situations disclosure can be a very important factor in ensuring that the decision concerning the marital agreement is a fully informed one. However, while at first glance the views on the extent of required disclosure differ, there seems to be a broad consensus: in no jurisdictions requiring disclosure will the failure to disclose some assets necessarily lead to the agreement failing as a whole.

---

[296] Dethloff, above n 223, 89.

[297] Either the acquest or in the Netherlands a share of the universal community of property; see section II.B above.

[298] Ibid; see eg Pintens, France and Belgium, this volume, 79.

[299] See section III.A.iii above.

[300] Answers to Question 39 in K Boele-Woelki, B Braat and I Curry-Sumner (eds), *European Family Law in Action IV: Property Relations between Spouses* (Antwerp, Intersentia, 2009).

[301] Answers to Questions 74 and 110 in K Boele-Woelki, B Braat and I Curry-Sumner (eds), *European Family Law in Action IV: Property Relations between Spouses* (Antwerp, Intersentia, 2009).

For example, in *Radmacher v Granatino* (as quoted above) the United Kingdom Supreme Court decided that only *material* lack of disclosure should be held to have that effect.[302] Similarly, the Study Group on Pre-Nuptial Agreements in Ireland recommended that all *relevant* information must be disclosed.[303] In Australia rather strict rules on the advice that needs to be given ensure disclosure, [304] and, in addition, non-disclosure of *material* matters are regarded as fraud and invalidate the agreement.[305] Somewhat comparable to Australia, it is through the required legal advice that disclosure is supposed to be ensured in New Zealand.[306] In the United States, § 7.04(5) of the American Law Institute Principles requires disclosure or that disclosure was not necessary because the party 'knew, at least approximately' the income and assets of the other party.[307] The US Uniform Premarital Agreements Act in section 6 allows a waiver of disclosure, and (as has been explained above) in many jurisdictions there is a right to ask for disclosure, and not making use of that right could be interpreted as an (implied) waiver of disclosure.

So, to sum up: where being informed about the assets etc. of the other spouse makes a difference,[308] disclosure is generally either required or there is a right to demand disclosure. This is generally supported by duties of legal advisors[309] (or, in case of *homologation*, the court) to explain the consequences of a marital agreement which often will require disclosure. This is very much in line with the general thrust of wanting to protect autonomy of the spouses—a decision that is not only nominally, but actually, autonomous requires sufficient information. At the same time, the jurisdictions examined generally avoid overly burdensome duties to disclose, as only material or relevant lack of disclosure will invalidate an agreement. It is difficult to see, for example, why a marital agreement should be invalid if a spouse disclosed there were assets of 100 million but it later turns out that there actually were 110 million worth of assets—unless, of course, the other spouse can prove that those extra 10 million would have been relevant/material to their decision to sign the agreement in that form. Likewise, if it is very clear that one spouse is 'very rich' and the couple agree on a separation of property in their marital agreement (as in *Radmacher v Granatino*), it is difficult to see why knowing exactly (or even approximately) how much the assets of the other spouse are worth would normally make a difference. Should the policy behind the law seriously allow an argument such as 'I thought he/she was worth 10 million and therefore agreed to the separation of property—had I know he/she was worth 125 million, I would never have done so'? If special circumstances apply this could, of course, be different, but it seems right to assume that in the ordinary course of events (if such circumstances can be called ordinary) disclosure would not have changed the decision to sign the agreement.

---

[302] *Radmacher v Granatino* [2010] UKSC 42, [69]. See also Miles, England and Wales, this volume.

[303] Study Group on Pre-Nuptial Agreements, above n 267, 84; Crowley, Ireland, this volume, 220.

[304] Jessep, Australia, this volume, 26 et seq.

[305] Ibid; s 90K(1)(a) Family Law Act 1975 (Cth).

[306] Briggs, New Zealand, this volume, 278 et seq.

[307] See Ellman, United States, this volume, 420 et seq; American Law Institute, above n 259 comment g to § 7.04, 1090 et seq.

[308] ie, not where the assets to be disclosed would not be available for the financial relief anyway, see above.

[309] Either in the form of requiring independent legal advice or by the notary being duty-bound to advise both parties.

Where the right to obtain disclosure is not exercised or waived, there of course is the risk that the decision really is an uninformed one, for example, if one spouse is unaware that the other spouse is actually very wealthy. In that case through the requirements of legal advice/notarisation at least it is ensured that not knowing about the other spouse's assets is wilful ignorance and that there was the opportunity to receive the relevant information. In that sense, the absence of disclosure was not material to the decision to enter into that agreement.

As with all formal requirements, hardships and special circumstances, these generally can be dealt with by the other, particularly the substantive, safeguards (on this see section III.C below).

iii. Time Factors

Several common law jurisdictions have either considered or implemented rules that stipulated that pre-nuptial agreements concluded within a certain time-frame before the wedding should not be binding.[310] Examples for this for England and Wales are the proposals by the Home Office (21 days),[311] and the Centre for Social Justice (28 days);[312] Resolution (the family solicitors' organisation) recommended 42 days as a 'minimum "buffer"' between the date of the agreement and the date of the marriage.[313] The Irish Study Group on Pre-Nuptial Agreements proposed a period of 28 days.[314]

The American Law Institute's Principles take a slightly more nuanced approach and state that if the agreement was executed at least 30 days before the parties' marriage then there is a rebuttable presumption that the other party's consent to the agreement was informed and not obtained under duress.[315] Hence an agreement can be concluded within that time-frame, but the presumption does not apply then, so the Principles set an incentive to discuss and enter into pre-nuptial agreements at an earlier stage.[316] Still, such a presumption then faces the same principled problems as a general bar introduced by a time limit.

As one of the very few civil law jurisdictions operating with a time limit, under Catalan law a pre-nuptial agreement must be concluded at least one month before the wedding.[317]

The underlying idea of a time limit is that 'this would prevent a pre-nuptial agreement being forced on people shortly before their wedding day, when they may not

---

[310] In civil law jurisdictions (and the other common law jurisdictions without such rules) strict time limits do not exist, but are taken into account under the general rules regarding marital agreements.

[311] Home Office, *Supporting Families: a Consultation Document* (HMSO 1998) 4.23; Miles, England and Wales, this volume, 99; Harper and Frankle, An English Practitioner's View, this volume, 127.

[312] Centre for Social Justice, *Every Family Matters* (2009, www.centreforsocialjustice.org.uk/client/downloads/WEB%20CSJ%20Every%20Family%20Matters_smallres.pdf) 192, 223.

[313] Resolution, Family Agreements—*Seeking Certainty to Reduce Disputes: the Recognition and Enforcement of pre-nuptial and post-nuptial agreements in England and Wales* (2009, www.resolution.org.uk/site_content_files/files/family_agreements.pdf) 5.11–5.12.

[314] Study Group on Pre-Nuptial Agreements, above n 267, 84

[315] American Law Institute, above n 259, § 7.04(3)(a), esp 1073 et seq.

[316] Ibid, comment d, 1074.

[317] Ferrer-Riba, Spain, this volume, 363.

feel able to resist'[318] and allow them sufficient time to seek legal advice.[319] This seems to assume that pre-nuptial agreements are (or at least can be) what the Privy Council in *MacLeod v MacLeod* called 'the price which one party may extract for his or her willingness to marry'[320] and thus offer great potential for putting pressure on the other spouse. While this assumption—at least in this generality—seems questionable in itself, the effectiveness of the mentioned time-frames seems rather dubious. Not only do the number of days proposed seem somewhat arbitrary but, as the Law Commission of England and Wales has rightly pointed out, the idea of having a fixed number of days faces additional problems:

> The first is a practical problem: with ceremonies commonly arranged—and deposits paid, for example, on reception venues—many months in advance, it would be hard to find an acceptable legal time limit that really addressed the issue of pressure. The second is a logical problem: any deadline for the making of prenuptial agreements simply diverts the pressure to another day. Rather than it being argued that one of the parties was compelled to sign on the day before the wedding, it could be argued with equal force that they felt compelled to sign the day before the deadline.[321]

The Law Commission is right in saying that a time limit cannot really fulfil the function that its proponents hope that it will and offer useful protection.[322] Indeed, a time limit can fail the parties concerned in two ways: first, even agreements concluded shortly before the wedding can be the result of careful and considerate negotiations which took place over a long period of time and even without such negotiations the content of the agreement might be completely unobjectionable; second, the time limit just moves the pressure but does not neutralise it. No time limit can prevent one of the spouses from using 'sign this now or else there is no wedding' tactics. Therefore, the more appropriate way of dealing with potential pressure at the time of signing appears to be not to single out a specific cause of pressure, but to deal with all forms of pressure in a coherent way (on this see sections III.C and V below). If the concern that led to the proposal of a time limit is related to not being able to obtain legal advice,[323] then the matter really should be dealt with under the requirements of legal advice rather than a time limit (on this see section III.B.i above).

---

[318] Home Office, *Supporting Families: a consultation document* (HMSO 1998) 4.23. See also American Law Institute, above n 259, § 7.04(3)(a), comment d, 1073 et seq.

[319] Yet the requirement of independent legal advice is also seen as an *additional* requirement for the validity anyway, *cf* Home Office, *Supporting Families: a consultation document* (HMSO 1998) 4.23; Study Group on Pre-Nuptial Agreements, above n 267, 84; and section III.B.i above.

[320] *MacLeod v MacLeod* [2008] UKPC 64, [36].

[321] Law Commission, above n 203, 109. See also the criticism of the 21-day deadline proposed by the Home Office, above n 318, by B Hooker, 'Prenuptial Contracts and Safeguards' [2001] *Family Law* 56 (57), who calls the deadline a 'mistake'.

[322] Law Commission, above n 203, 110 et seq. But see Harper and Frankle, An English Practitioner's View, this volume, 143.

[323] It is interesting to note here that the Californian Family Code in § 1615(c)(2) requires a period of seven days between the time a 'party was presented with the agreement and advised to seek independent legal counsel and the time the agreement was signed', thus tying the time limit not to the wedding but using it to ensure that there is, least the opportunity to seek legal advice. See Ellman, United States, this volume, 420.

iv. Consequences of Failing to Comply with Formal/Procedural Requirements

In all jurisdictions the question arises as to how failure to comply with the formal and/or procedural requirements is to be dealt with. In the continental European jurisdictions the answer is generally that the agreement is considered void/voidable and, therefore, the default rules will apply if the failure is invoked by one party.[324] Particularly for agreements regarding matrimonial property, which are essentially an opt-out of the otherwise applicable default property regime, this seems to be an obvious position to take. However, there is the possibility that the agreement is only partially void and that the remaining clauses will be upheld, provided that the void clauses are severable.[325]

By contrast, in some common law jurisdictions even marital agreements that do not comply with the formal and procedural requirements can still have an effect. The most marked examples for this are the new Australian section 90 (1A) Family Law Act 1975 (Cth) and the New Zealand section 21H Property (Relationships) Act 1976, where the courts can declare a marital agreement to be binding despite it not meeting the formal requirements. In Australia the proviso is that the court is satisfied that it would be unjust and inequitable under the circumstances if the agreement were not binding on the spouses, and in New Zealand the court needs to be satisfied that the non-compliance did not materially prejudice the interests of any party to the agreement.[326]

One of the options the Law Commission of England and Wales suggests in its consultation paper is that agreements that do not meet the standards of a 'qualifying' marital agreement (by complying with certain formal and procedural rules) should still be considered under the rules now established by the *Radmacher* decision.[327]

That even agreements not meeting the required formal standards can still have an impact and will be considered by the court can be explained with the general discretion to award financial relief upon divorce. Nevertheless, at first this might appear to create a position where a spouse gets another bite at the cherry if the agreement in the first instance is held to be invalid because of non-compliance. This could be seen as encouraging tactics which are on the borderline (or beyond) what is acceptable, because as a fall-back option the content of the agreement could/would still be taken into account. However, the converse may also be true, namely that too strict an adherence to the formal rules may lead to unfairness or injustice, and it is precisely this that the Australian and New Zealand provisions are aiming at and, presumably, what the intention behind the Law Commission of England and Wales' suggestion is—and not the second bite. In a system where financial relief upon divorce is based on discretion, it is therefore advisable to also give the courts discretion to consider

---

[324] See, eg Dutta, Germany, this volume, 172; Boele-Woelki and Braat, The Netherlands, this volume, 248; Jänterä-Jareborg, Sweden, this volume, 379 et seq; Pintens, France and Belgium, this volume, 82.

[325] See, eg the German § 139 BGB; Pintens, France and Belgium, this volume, 82.

[326] Jessep, Australia, this volume, 35 et seq, esp 37; Briggs, New Zealand, this volume, 276 et seq.

[327] See Cooke, The Law Commission's Consultation on Marital Property Agreements, this volume, 153 et seq; Law Commission, above n 203, 114 et seq. Of course one could say that England has a long 'tradition' of giving some effect to marital agreements that were until recently considered to be against public policy and therefore not binding; see Miles, England and Wales, this volume, 96 et seq.

the agreement in part or in full to 'rescue' certain cases of non-compliance where this is appropriate.

C. Safeguards Applying at the Time the Pre- or Post-Nuptial Agreement is Invoked

i. *Distinctions Based on the Substance or Function of the Financial Claim*

In order to understand and evaluate marital agreements it is crucial to look at the substance they intend to regulate and what policy aims are pursued. As pointed out above (sections II.A.–C), many jurisdictions take a 'pillar' approach to financial remedies upon divorce, and the decisions regarding property, maintenance, pensions and allocation of the use of certain property are independent. The function of each of those 'pillars' is also perceived differently in those jurisdictions, but the overall policy aims are to be achieved through all 'pillars' together and not by each individual 'pillar'. By contrast, jurisdictions such as England and Wales, Ireland and Australia take a 'holistic' approach and the outcome is a 'package solution' to achieve 'fairness', 'proper provision' or a 'just result' respectively.[328]

This difference in approach has consequences for the way marital agreements are operating in the particular jurisdiction. Agreements solely regarding matrimonial property are less problematic where the other 'pillars' can ensure that the overall policy aims for financial relief upon divorce are met. In the 'pillar' jurisdictions much of the 'work' done to achieve the policy aims is not achieved through the property 'pillar', but rather through maintenance and other mechanisms.[329] This explains why these jurisdictions generally hold agreements regarding the matrimonial property to be binding and enforceable, but are very restrictive regarding maintenance agreements and other matters. Take, for example, the German core theory doctrine (*Kernbereichslehre*) developed by the Federal Court of Justice.[330] The default provisions of financial relief are put on a scale with regard to their 'closeness to the core of the protective scope of divorce law'. The closer to the core, the less likely it is that the default provisions can be derogated from by contract; closest to the core are maintenance needs because of ongoing child care duties or old age or infirmity, the default matrimonial property regime is furthest away from the core and thus can generally be contracted out of.[331] Hardship is generally to be dealt with through maintenance payments. The situation in Austria, Sweden and the Netherlands is quite similar, and in France and Belgium compensation for marriage-related disadvantages cannot be the subject of pre- or post-nuptial agreements at all, while the spouses have considerable freedom to regulate their property relations.[332]

---

[328] See the respective national reports in this book and sections II.D and E above.

[329] See section III.C.iii below.

[330] See Dutta, Germany, this volume, 176 et seq; Scherpe, 'A Comparative View of Pre-Nuptial Agreements', above n 52.

[331] Dutta, Germany, this volume 179 et seq; B Dauner-Lieb, 'Gütertrennung zwischen Privatautonomie und Inhaltskontrolle' 210 (2010) *Archiv für die civilistische Praxis (AcP)* 580 et seq, esp 586 et seq.

[332] Pintens, France and Belgium, this volume, 82; Butruille-Cardew, above n 262, 130.

By contrast, in jurisdictions with a 'holistic' approach to financial relief upon divorce there is no such distinction between property, maintenance and other remedies. Thus a binding agreement regarding property would exclude assets from the discretionary exercise and consequently directly interfere with the ability of the judge to create the package that provides for an outcome in pursuance of the respective policy objectives. Hence fully binding matrimonial property agreements would quite significantly limit the scope for the court's discretion. This explains why in the jurisdictions with a 'holistic' approach to financial relief (with the exception of Australia) marital agreements generally have not been accepted as binding in the sense that they oust the jurisdiction of the courts, even if they are restricted to property matters—because the property is part of the 'package'.

One, therefore, needs to take great care when comparing or judging marital agreements in the different jurisdictions; the substance they regulate, based on the underlying default regimes, aims at achieving the policy aims of family law in different ways. Indeed, the 'pillar' approach taken by the default regimes equally applies to marital agreements, and the 'pillars' of the agreements are also looked at independently in the respective jurisdictions.

ii. A General Yardstick of Fairness?

While all the jurisdictions examined have in common that there is some form of review of the substance of the marital agreement, the criteria for this at first glance appear to vary significantly. When examined more closely, however, they all seem to have at their core that agreements will either be set aside or adjusted should the outcome be 'unfair' (or 'unjust').[333] However, 'fairness' or 'unfairness' not only inevitably are vague concepts (if they can be considered concepts at all), but what is perceived to be 'fair' will of course vary from jurisdiction to jurisdiction, based on the relevant legal, historical and social background. In addition, as Lord Nicholls quite rightly pointed out in the oft-quoted passage from his speech in *White v White*,[334] fairness is an inherently subjective concept. Nevertheless, a closer examination of how the different jurisdictions have sought to define fairness, or at least guide the judges when making their decision, can be helpful. For this, the jurisdictions can be groups into those that have a 'simple' fairness test and those that apply a 'qualified' fairness test.

a. 'Simple Fairness' Test Jurisdictions
In England and Wales, following *Radmacher v Granatino*, the standard to be applied is as follows:

> The court should give effect to a nuptial agreement that is freely entered into by each party with a full appreciation of its implications unless in the circumstances prevailing it would not be fair to hold the parties to their agreement.[335]

---

[333] See also Dethloff, above n 223, 82 et seq and J Miles and JM Scherpe, 'The Future of Family Property in Europe' in Boele-Woelki, Miles and Scherpe, above n 9, 427 et seq.

[334] See, n 99 above.

[335] *Radmacher v Granatino* [2010] UKSC 42, [75].

The Supreme Court then offered some further guidance, namely that the reasonable requirements of the children of the family must not be prejudiced, but that the autonomy of the parties and particularly their desire to protect non-matrimonial property should generally be respected.[336] The Court further held that it is two strands of fairness—needs and compensation—that are most likely to lead to a departure from the agreements, and that the third strand, sharing, is the one most susceptible to being excluded or limited by an agreement of the parties.[337]

In Singapore a marital agreement is merely one of the factors to consider in the discretionary decision-making process,[338] which of course means that the substance of the agreement is subject to review by the courts. This review then follows the same rules as the financial relief in general, namely that the distribution of assets etc should be 'just and equitable' and be done in the 'fairest possible way'.[339]

The proposals by the Irish Study Group on Pre-Nuptial Agreements likewise suggest expressly making pre-nuptial agreements another factor that the courts should have regard to when exercising the discretion in respect of financial relief upon divorce by inserting a provision into the Family Law (Divorce) Act;[340] the ultimate aim of the discretionary power of the courts to award financial relief is to achieve 'proper provision'.[341]

While in Scotland marital agreements, in principle, are binding and enforceable, the courts retain the power to make 'incidental orders' to vary or set aside these agreements, and this follows the same principles as financial relief generally, namely that the property is to be shared fairly etc.[342] However, these orders are apparently not applied for very often.[343]

In Austria, marital agreements can be departed from by the court if the outcome would be inequitable.[344] In Sweden the same is achieved via an express statutory provision which reads as follows:

> If a term of a marital property agreement is unreasonable in view of the subject-matter of the agreement, the circumstances when it was drawn up, circumstances subsequently arising and the overall circumstances, it may be adjusted or disregarded in the division of property.[345]

---

[336] Ibid, [77]–[79].

[337] Ibid, [81]–[82].

[338] s 112(2)(e) Women's Charter list among the criteria to be considered 'any agreement between the parties with respect to the ownership of the matrimonial assets made in contemplation of divorce', which according to the Court of Appeal decision in *TQ v TR and another appeal* [2009] 2 Singapore Law Reports (Reissue) 961 (at [77]) applies equally to pre-nuptial (and thus all) marital agreements. See Leong, Singapore, this volume 330 et seq and D Ong, 'Prenuptial Agreements: a Singaporean Perspective in *TQ v TR*' [2009] *Child and Family Law Quarterly* 536.

[339] s 112(1) Women's Charter and *Yeong Swan Ann v Lim Fei Yen* [1999] 1 Singapore Law Reports (Reissue) 49 [23] (Yong Pung How CJ). See Leong, Singapore, this volume, 333.

[340] Study Group on Pre-Nuptial Agreements, above n 267, 73 et seq.

[341] s 20(1) Family Law (Divorce) Act 1996; see Crowley, Ireland, this volume, 206 et seq and 220 et seq.

[342] ss 14(2)(h), 8(2), 9 Family Law (Scotland) Act 1985; see Norrie, Scotland, this volume, 303 et seq.

[343] Ibid.

[344] Also, while post-marital maintenance can be waived by marital agreement, this is subject to certain limitations which effectively mean that the needs of the spouse are to be covered; see Ferrari, Austria, this volume, 61 et seq. See also Kriegler, above n 268, 82 and 93.

[345] Swedish Marriage Code c 12 s 3, see Jänterä-Jareborg, Sweden, this volume, 391 et seq.

Despite the potential for a very broad application, the Swedish courts apply this provision very restrictively, and hardship is usually dealt with via maintenance payments.[346]

In Spain marital agreements can be set aside or adapted if there are unforeseen events or circumstances, or if they would be harmful to the children or 'seriously detrimental' to the spouses;[347] this essentially amounts to a general 'fairness' test.[348]

In the Netherlands marital agreements can be set aside as contrary to 'good faith' if they would lead to unacceptable results in exceptional cases.[349] Similarly, Germany also relies, inter alia, on the good faith provision in the German Civil Code[350] to determine whether an agreement should be upheld.[351]

In Australia marital agreements can be set aside according to section 90K Family Law Act 1976 (Cth) if the court is satisfied that:

> (c) in the circumstances that have arisen since the agreement was made it is impracticable for the agreement or a part of the agreement to be carried out; or

> (d) since the making of the agreement, a material change in circumstances has occurred (being circumstances relating to the care, welfare and development of a child of the marriage) and, as a result of the change, the child or, if the applicant has caring responsibility for the child (as defined in subsection (2)), a party to the agreement will suffer hardship if the court does not set the agreement aside;

Therefore, apart from cases of 'impracticality', not only is a 'material' change of circumstance required, but the child or the caring spouse also needs to suffer hardship because of the outcome under the agreement because of the changed circumstances. However, it needs to be borne in mind that the courts, according to s 90F Family Law Act 1976 (Cth), retain the power to make maintenance orders if it was shown that at the time when the agreement came into effect the relevant party was unable to support himself or herself without the assistance of a means-tested social security pension.[352] Still, the threshold for setting aside the agreement is rather high, as intended by the legislature, and indeed appears to be the highest among the jurisdictions examined in this study.

Finally, in France and Belgium there is no 'fairness' test for agreements regarding matrimonial property, but maintenance and, to a lesser extent, compensatory claims against the spouse in case of divorce cannot be waived by agreement.[353] This in itself can be seen as an expression of fairness.

---

[346] Jänterä-Jareborg, Sweden, this volume, 393.

[347] Ferrer-Riba, Spain, this volume, 361.

[348] Whether maintenance and the *pension compensatoria* can be the subject of a pre- or post-nuptial marital agreement is disputed; see Ferrer-Riba, Spain, this volume, 361 et seq.

[349] Boele-Woelki and Braat, The Netherlands, this volume, 250.

[350] § 242 BGB.

[351] See generally Dutta, Germany, this volume, 174 et seq and 183 et seq.

[352] Jessep, Australia, this volume, 28; see also G Wilson, 'An Australian Perspective on International Pre-Nuptial Agreements' in Salter et al, above n 221, 5 et seq and esp 19 et seq and C Luhn, *Privatautonomie und Inhaltskontrolle von Eheverträgen* (Frankurt, Peter Lang, 2008).

[353] Pintens, France and Belgium, this volume, 80 et seq; Butruille-Cardew, above n 262, 137.

b. 'Qualified Fairness' Test Jurisdictions

In New Zealand a 'qualified' standard of fairness is embodied in section 21J Property (Relationships) Act 1975 which requires 'serious injustice':

> (1) Even though an agreement satisfies the requirements of section 21F, the Court may set the agreement aside if, having regard to all the circumstances, it is satisfied that giving effect to the agreement would cause serious injustice.
>
> (...)
>
> (4) In deciding, under this section, whether giving effect to an agreement made under section 21 or section 21A or section 21B would cause serious injustice, the Court must have regard to—
> (a) the provisions of the agreement:
> (b) the length of time since the agreement was made:
> (c) whether the agreement was unfair or unreasonable in the light of all the circumstances at the time it was made:
> (d) whether the agreement has become unfair or unreasonable in the light of any changes in circumstances since it was made (whether or not those changes were foreseen by the parties):
> (e) the fact that the parties wished to achieve certainty as to the status, ownership, and division of property by entering into the agreement:
> (f) any other matters that the Court considers relevant.

This provision replaced the previous one which only required 'injustice', and the intention by the legislator was very clearly to raise the threshold.[354] That said, the criteria listed by themselves to not carry a heightened standard of 'seriousness', and actually are rather similar to those applied in the 'simple' fairness jurisdictions. In the Court of Appeal decision *Harrison v Harrison*[355] it was held that substantial economic disparity between what a spouse would have received under default regime and what would be received according to the agreement is not sufficient in itself to set aside a marital agreement;[356] likewise, pressure to vary or end the relationship as such were not sufficient.[357] The focus, it seems, is on an inequality of process rather than mere outcome.[358] Nevertheless, as Briggs observes, an order is likely to be set aside if there is no sharing even if a substantial contribution to the assets was made;[359] essentially this would mean that contracting out of compensation would be restricted to a certain extent. In addition, agreements regarding maintenance can generally be varied by the courts,[360] and children (and thus indirectly their carer) can also apply for additional orders under section 26 Property (Relationships) Act 1975.[361]

The American Law Institute's Principles of the Law of Family Dissolution in § 7.05(1) state that a term of an agreement should not be enforced if (a) the circumstances require the court to consider whether enforcement would work a

---

[354] Briggs, New Zealand, this volume, 271. See also Law Commission, above n 203, 121.
[355] *Harrison v Harrison* [2005] 2 NZLR 349 (CA).
[356] See also Harper and Frankle, An English Practitioner's View, this volume, 137.
[357] *Harrison v Harrison*, n 355 above, [116].
[358] Briggs, New Zealand, this volume, 271.
[359] Ibid, 272 et seq.
[360] Ibid, 267.
[361] Ibid, 274 et seq.

substantial injustice, and (b) the court then finds that enforcement would work a substantial injustice.[362] This approach therefore requires the court to look at the matter in two stages, with the burden of proof resting on the spouse wanting to resile from the agreement. In the first stage it needs to be determined that 'the circumstances require' the court to consider the matter, and the Principles limited this to three circumstances, namely that a number of years has passed since the agreement was made (the exact number to be specified by state legislation); that a child was born to or adopted by the parties; or that there was a change of circumstances which has a substantial impact on the parties or their children, and that neither the change nor the impact was 'probably' not anticipated by the parties when making the agreement. Once that threshold is passed, the Principles offer further criteria that should be considered, namely the magnitude of the disparity between the outcome under the agreement and under the default system; provided this is practical to ascertain, the difference between the circumstances of the spouse wanting to resile from the agreement if the agreement were to be followed compared to what that spouse's position would have had the marriage not taken place; whether the purpose of the agreement was to benefit or protect the interests of third parties (such as children from a previous relationship); and the impact of the agreement's enforcement on the children. The first stage effectively works as a filter and reduces the number of cases where 'substantial injustice' can be invoked; that said, the filter covers the main reasons why an agreement might lead to unfairness, namely passage of time, arrival of children or change of circumstances. The criteria listed for the second stage are not exhaustive but give an indication on what might constitute a 'substantial' injustice. Interestingly, comparisons to the outcome under the default regime are made; considering that the whole point of the agreement is to derogate from the 'default' outcome, this is remarkable. It is to be presumed that this is to be understood very much along the lines of the New Zealand approach taken in *Harrison v Harrison* where, as just explained above, it was held that a substantial difference between the outcomes as such cannot be sufficient by itself to amount to 'substantial injustice'.

c. Qualifying the 'Qualified Fairness Tests'

Whether much is to be gained by having a 'qualified fairness test' is debatable. As Law Commissioner Professor Cooke has pointed out, tests that include 'substantial injustice' or 'serious injustice' seem to imply that 'normal injustice' is acceptable,[363] and it could very well be argued that the law should not promote or allow any form of injustice. On the other hand, it is arguable that if the threshold is not passed, there actually is no injustice in the eyes of the law—which then begs the question why the terms 'serious' or 'substantial' etc were used in the first place.

That said, both in New Zealand and the American Law Institute's Principles of the Law of Family Dissolution it is clear that the intention behind using the qualifications was to 'raise the bar', and, in New Zealand's case, to make quite clear the contrast to the previous legislation. Nevertheless, the same presumably could have

---

[362] *Cf* American Law Institute, above n 259, 1093 et seq; Ellman, United States, this volume, 424 et seq.

[363] In a public lecture, King's College London on 31 March 2011 entitled 'The end of romance? The Law Commission's consultation on marital property agreements'.

been achieved by including criteria for (or defining) simple 'injustice' or 'unfairness' in the specific context of marital agreements to make clear that the threshold is to be a high one. As, for example, the Swedish, Scottish and German approaches show, a 'high threshold' can be achieved by 'simple' fairness tests, as long as they are interpreted restrictively. Therefore, it seems that little is gained by 'qualifying' the fairness test in the first place,[364] and the focus should rather be on giving firmer guidance as to what fairness itself actually means.

iii. Common Criteria for Fairness

Despite the differences in the default systems, and consequently the way marital agreements are dealt with by the law in the jurisdictions examined in this study, some common themes can be identified in the determination of what is regarded as 'fair'.

a. Passage of Time, Children and Change of Circumstances

Unlike separation agreements (on which see section IV below), pre-nuptial and post-nuptial agreements aim at regulating a more or less unknown future. It is therefore hardly surprising that in all jurisdictions a change of circumstances is one of the central criteria that is considered when determining whether an agreement is 'fair'.

In some jurisdictions the criterion of change of circumstance is dealt with expressly. For example, in Sweden the relevant statutory provision refers to 'circumstances subsequently arising',[365] and the United Kingdom Supreme Court in *Radmacher v Granatino* stated that a marital agreement should be given effect 'unless in the circumstances prevailing it would not be fair' to do so.[366] Other jurisdictions 'qualify' the change of circumstance, namely that it needs to be 'material' (Australia)[367] or 'substantial' (Spain)[368] or have a 'substantial impact' (American Law Institute's Principles of the Law of Family Dissolution, § 7.05(2)(c)).[369]

Some jurisdictions also expressly refer to certain 'events' like the birth of children,[370] but the arrival of (and care for) children is, of course, covered by the 'general' change of circumstance in the other provisions, as these are the reasons most likely leading to a change in the spouses' lives. The same applies to provisions which require the 'the length of time since the agreement was made' (New Zealand)[371] or that stipulate a minimum number of years since the making of the agreement for it to qualify as reviewable (American Law Institute's Principles of the Law of Family Dissolution, § 7.05(2)(a)).[372]

---

[364] See also Law Commission, above n 203, 123 et seq.

[365] Swedish Marriage Code c 12 s 3, see Jänterä-Jareborg, Sweden, this volume 392.

[366] *Radmacher v Granatino* [2010] UKSC 42, [75].

[367] s 90K(1)(d) Family Law Act 1976 (Cth).

[368] While Art 90 III CC nominally only applies to separation agreements, it is to be presumed that it a fortiori will also be applied to other marital agreements, *cf* Ferrer-Riba, Spain, this volume, 363 et seq.

[369] American Law Institute, above n 259, 1093 et seq; Ellman, United States, this volume, 424 et seq.

[370] Eg Jessep, Australia, this volume, 38 et seq; see American Law Institute, above n 259, § 7.05(2)(b), 1093 et seq; Ellman, United States, this volume, 424 et seq.

[371] s 21J(4)(b) Property (Relationships) Act 1975.

[372] American Law Institute, above n 259, 1093 et seq; Ellman, United States, this volume, 424 et seq.

Another 'qualification' that it is required in some jurisdictions is that the change of circumstance must not have been foreseeable (Spain)[373] or 'probably not antici-pated' when the agreement was signed (American Law Institute's Principles of the Law of Family Dissolution § 7.05(2)(c)).[374] By contrast, New Zealand law expressly excludes foreseeability and merely asks 'whether the agreement has become unfair or unreasonable in the light of any changes in circumstances since it was made (whether or not those changes were foreseen by the parties)'.[375]

What can be seen from the comparison is that criteria that go beyond the 'general' change of circumstance merely seem to have a—more or less—explanatory function and are supposed to provide some guidance. As noted out, children are a very obvi-ous reason why the circumstances might be different from what the couple antici-pated when signing the agreement, and the longer ago the agreement was made, the more likely it is that a relevant change of circumstance has occurred. Adding quali-fications like 'material' likewise really only have an explanatory function, namely to signal that the change of circumstance must have reached a certain 'intensity' in order for the agreement to be set aside—which could be (and in most jurisdictions is) achieved by the equivalent interpretation an application of the requirement of a 'general' change of circumstance.

The one criterion that can make a real difference is that of foreseeability. An obvi-ous argument for this criterion is that if the spouses knew (or at least could have known) about the change of circumstances, then it would be 'fair' to hold them to the agreement, and indeed protect and respect their autonomous decision. On the other hand, for most jurisdictions it is clear that there are limits to what the spouses can agree to; which parts of the protection offered by the default system the spouses can actually contract out of. Where such limitations exist, it would be absurd to include foreseeability as a criterion to allow a circumvention of the protective func-tion of these limitations. These substantive limits or pre- and post-nuptial agree-ments were mentioned briefly in section III.C.i above and will now be explored further in the following section.

b. Contracting Out of Sharing, Needs and Compensation?

As already set out above, contracting out of sharing the matrimonial property, as regulated in the default matrimonial property regimes in most 'pillar' jurisdictions seems to be relatively unproblematic.[376] In many legal systems this is even seen as an essential requirement because of the existence of a matrimonial property regime in the first place: such regimes are presumed to be 'fair' for most couples, but at the same time the legislature is aware that for some couples this might not be so. Allowing the contracting out is therefore a logical consequence and, indeed, nec-essary to prevent an overly paternalistic, 'one size fits all' approach. Generally it appears that in those jurisdictions that operate with matrimonial property regimes,

---

[373] Ferrer-Riba, Spain, this volume, 363 et seq.

[374] American American Law Institute, above n 259, 1093 et seq; Ellman, United States, this volume, 424 et seq.

[375] s 21J(4)(d) Property (Relationships) Act 1975.

[376] Dutta, Germany, this volume 181; Jänterä-Jareborg, Sweden, this volume 382 et seq, Boele-Woelki and Braat, The Netherlands, this volume 249.

the issues and remedies surrounding the matrimonial property have more of a property law than a family law character, and that certainty is therefore the dominant policy consideration. Of course, this might leave one of the spouses without any resources, and particularly where that spouse has made significant sacrifices for the marriage and/or the family, this is deemed inappropriate. However, in the 'pillar' jurisdictions the mechanism to rectify this is generally not the matrimonial property pillar, but—in different forms, depending on the jurisdiction—the other pillars, and particularly maintenance. In those jurisdictions contracting out of the default rules concerning the other 'pillars' is, therefore, generally much more restricted, and sometime not possible at all. So the other pillars will alleviate hardship created by pre- and post-nuptial agreements, and indeed those created by the default system should there not be an agreement in the first place.

Nevertheless, a comparable approach can be observed in the jurisdictions that are primarily based on discretion. In Australia, which of those jurisdictions is the one with the greatest opportunities to conclude marital agreements regarding property, the courts retain the power to order maintenance in certain cases. In other jurisdictions, the courts retain the power to vary or set aside agreements (such as Austria and Scotland) or agreements are generally only considered as one of the factors to be taken into account, and in this exercise the courts generally will a order departure from (equal) sharing, as long as the other spouse and the children are reasonably provided for (for example, Singapore, Ireland if the proposals by the study group are implemented, England and Wales and, to a certain extent, also New Zealand).

So it appears that there is a common view among the jurisdictions of this study that—provided certain requirements are met—contracting out of sharing property is permissible and thus generally seen as 'fair'.

The House of Lords for English law in *Miller v Miller; McFarlane v McFarlane* identified two 'strands' of fairness in addition to 'sharing', namely 'needs' and 'compensation'.[377] 'Compensation' and particularly 'needs' are very difficult to define in the abstract and in any event are highly dependent on the legal and social context of each jurisdiction,[378] but as explained above (section II.E.iv and v) this categorisation is nevertheless quite helpful for the comparative analysis as well. For marital agreements it seems that when the other elements or 'pillars' of the financial consequences of divorce (ie not those related to sharing/the matrimonial property regimes) touch upon what can be seen as needs or compensation for marriage-related disadvantages, the laws of the respective jurisdictions seem to be much more restrictive. Of the jurisdictions looked at, this is most apparent in France and Belgium where pre- and post-nuptial agreements regarding maintenance are not permissible at all (except as part of divorce proceedings), and agreements regarding the *prestation compensatoire* in France are restricted as well.[379] Indeed, in *Radmacher v Granatino*

---

[377] *Miller v Miller, McFarlane v McFarlane* [2006] UKHL 24.

[378] See, eg the ECJ Cases 143/78, *de Cavel (No 1)* [1979] ECR 1055; Case 120/1979 *de Cavel (No 2)* [1980] ECR 731; Case C-220/95 *van den Boogaard* [1997] ECR I-1147; see also *Moore v Moore* [2007] EWCA Civ 361; Bundesgerichtshof (XII ZB 12/05), FamRZ 2009, 1659; on the latter, see Scherpe and Dutta, above n 10.

[379] Pintens, France and Belgium, this volume, 80 et seq; Butruille-Cardew, above n 262, 137; Dethloff, above n 223, 83.

the United Kingdom Supreme Court expressly drew a distinction between sharing, needs and compensation for marital agreements with regard to fairness:

> Of the three strands identified in *White v White* and *Miller v Miller*, it is the first two, needs and compensation, which can most readily render it unfair to hold the parties to an ante-nuptial agreement. The parties are unlikely to have intended that their ante-nuptial agreement should result, in the event of the marriage breaking up, in one partner being left in a predicament of real need, while the other enjoys a sufficiency or more, and such a result is likely to render it unfair to hold the parties to their agreement. Equally if the devotion of one partner to looking after the family and the home has left the other free to accumulate wealth, it is likely to be unfair to hold the parties to an agreement that entitles the latter to retain all that he or she has earned.

> Where, however, these considerations do not apply and each party is in a position to meet his or her needs, fairness may well not require a departure from their agreement as to the regulation of their financial affairs in the circumstances that have come to pass. Thus it is in relation to the third strand, sharing, that the court will be most likely to make an order in the terms of the nuptial agreement in place of the order that it would otherwise have made.[380]

While the wording, particularly the use of the term 'real needs', has created room for debate in England and Wales,[381] the distinction drawn by the Supreme Court with regard to the fairness of contracting out of sharing, needs and compensation nevertheless seems to encapsulate the general policy approach in the jurisdictions examined in this book: it is generally fair to contract out of property sharing, but contracting out of need or compensation is generally not considered fair.[382]

That said, there is a significant criticism of this 'clear cut' division.[383] As Dauner-Lieb and Dethloff have pointed out, quite correctly, the function and nature of marriage as a partnership of equals entails a recognition that not only needs, but also compensation, are an essential element of that union, which the spouses should not be able to contract out of.[384] This might be more of a problem for jurisdictions with matrimonial property regimes which generally can be contracted out of. When the compensatory element of the matrimonial property regime is excluded because of a marital agreement (and in the absence of other legal mechanisms to award property such as through the French *prestation compensatoire* of the Spanish *pension compensatoria*) this essentially only leaves maintenance payments to deal with the compensatory aspects of financial relief. But leaving the compensation of marriage-related disadvantages to maintenance is problematic in a number of ways; maintenance is not necessarily a reliable form of compensation, as there might be

---

[380] *Radmacher v Granatino* [2010] UKSC 42 [81]–[82].

[381] See Miles, England and Wales, this volume 105, esp n 121; Joanna Miles, 'Marriage and Divorce in the Supreme Court: for Love of Money?' (2011) 74 *Modern Law Review* 431 et seq, esp 443 et seq; The Law Commission, *Marital Property Agreements*, above n 203, 125 et seq.

[382] See also Miles and Scherpe, above n 333, 428 et seq.

[383] See, eg for Germany Dauner-Lieb, above n 331, esp, 607 et seq; E Wiemer, *Inhaltskontrolle von Eheverträgen* (Bielefeld, Gieseking, 2008) 53 et seq; A Sanders, *Statischer Vertrag und dynamische Vertragsbeziehung* (Bielefeld, Gieseking, 2008) 354 et seq. See also the see also the seminal article by B Dauner-Lieb, 'Reichweite und Grenzen der Privatautonomie im Ehevertragsrecht' 201 (2001) *AcP* 295 et seq. For criticism from a comparative perspective see Dethloff, above n 222, 90 et seq.

[384] See Dauner-Lieb above n 331, 584 et seq; Dethloff, above n 222, 91 et seq.

difficulties with enforcement—or the debtor simply not having an income anymore. Also, there is generally a tendency in many jurisdictions towards wanting to achieve a 'clean break' after divorce, which involves time-limiting, or even excluding, maintenance payments (see, for example, Sweden or the recent maintenance reforms in Germany).[385] While in some jurisdictions some of the 'pillars' other than the matrimonial property regime are expressly set up to cover compensation as well (again, for example, the French *prestation compensatoire* and the Spanish *pension compensatoria*) and thus property transfers are possible under another 'pillar' to reflect the contributions and/or sacrifices of the other spouse,[386] this is not necessarily the case in other jurisdictions, for example, Germany. Therefore, often other legal remedies, which are referred to as 'secondary matrimonial property regimes' (*Nebengüterrecht* in German), have been utilised to compensate for the lack of a compensatory element, for example, by resorting to implied contracts, partnership law and unjust enrichment.[387] It would be preferable to have the compensatory element reflected in 'real' family law remedies. This would entail not allowing the spouses to contract out (completely) of compensation, and marital agreements regarding the property division generally would need to be scrutinised in this regard, as they are now in many jurisdictions, and not almost automatically accepted as 'fair'.[388]

iv. Consequences of Failing to Meet Substantive Requirements

Unlike cases of non-compliance with regard to form and procedure, where certain substantive criteria are not met, the agreement as such is, in principle, valid (and binding/enforceable in jurisdictions where these agreements generally are). The most common consequence of failing to meet substantive requirements is that the agreement (or the part of the agreement in question) will not be applied, but rather adapted to the situation at hand (which of course can also mean that the default rules are applied)—in order to achieve a 'fair' outcome under the circumstances.[389] The same obviously applies where the effect of the marital agreement is subject to the discretion of the court in the first place.[390]

IV. SEPARATION AGREEMENTS

Separation agreements are a different form of post-nuptial agreement (according to the definition used for this project) insofar as they are agreements concluded at a point in time when the couple have decided to separate and eventually divorce, and the agreement is the result of trying to deal with the financial (and other, as the case may be) consequences. Thus they are not, as pre-nuptial and other post-nuptial

---

[385] Jänterä-Jareborg, Sweden, this volume 377; Dutta, Germany, this volume 164 et seq; Dauner-Lieb, above n 331, 603 et seq.

[386] Ferrer-Riba, Spain, this volume 356 et seq, Pintens, France and Belgium, this volume 76 et seq.

[387] See Dauner-Lieb above n 331, 589 et seq, esp fn 55.

[388] Dauner-Lieb above n 331, 602 et seq; Dethloff, above n 223, 91 et seq.

[389] See eg Jänterä-Jareborg, Sweden, this volume, 391 et seq; Dutta, Germany, this volume, 184, and esp the cases cited nn 224 and 225.

[390] Eg Singapore, England and Wales, Ireland, Australia and New Zealand, but also Scotland (see Norrie, Scotland, this volume 303 et seq).

agreements, meant to apply in an uncertain future; on the contrary, they are meant to regulate what both spouses perceive to be a certain future. While, of course, these agreements are dealing with an unfortunate turn of events for the spouses, they are generally seen in a more positive light and actively encouraged in most jurisdictions, because amicable settlements not only mean that the courts do not have to deal with the matters, but also generally increase the chances of the couple having a better relationship in the future—which is particularly important where they have children. Therefore in many jurisdictions the law actually encourages separation agreements, often by subjecting them to less scrutiny by the court, or making them mandatory if the divorce is based on consent and then basing the court orders on that agreement, thereby offering greater certainty.

That said, in several jurisdictions, no express distinction is made between separation and other marital agreements.[391] Even where there are nominally different rules, the substance of the separation agreement is often reviewable by the courts in part or in full. In France, agreements regarding the *prestation compensatoire* are compulsory in cases of divorce based on mutual consent, and permitted if divorce is based on other grounds. The court must scrutinise and approve the substance of the agreement and will reject it if the interests of one spouse are infringed.[392] In Sweden, agreements concluded when divorce proceedings have commenced will be followed by the courts if they are valid and reasonable; the substance of the agreement therefore remains reviewable.[393] In Scots law these agreements are subject only to general contract law, but can be varied and set aside if they are considered not to be fair and reasonable at the time they were entered into.[394]

While separation agreements in England and Wales never have been and still are not binding,[395] they have been given significant weight for a long time, and often determine the outcome of the discretionary exercise with regard to ancillary relief.[396] In *Edgar v Edgar* Ormrod LJ held that:

> formal agreements, properly and fairly arrived at with competent legal advice, should not be displaced unless there are good and substantial grounds for concluding that an injustice will be done by holding the parties to the terms of their agreement.[397]

In practical terms this presumably means that after *Radmacher v Granatino*, where this passage from *Edgar v Edgar* was cited with approval, all marital agreements are in many respects now subject to the same considerations,[398] although for

---

[391] Eg Dutta, Germany, this volume, 159; Leong, Singapore, this volume, 343; Jessep, Australia, this volume, 27; Crowley, Ireland, this volume, 223; Study Group on Pre-Nuptial Agreements, above n 267, 68 et seq.

[392] Pintens, France and Belgium, this volume, 82 et seq.

[393] Jänterä-Jareborg, Sweden, this volume, 395.

[394] s 16(1)(b) Family Law (Scotland) Act 1985; see Norrie, Scotland, this volume, 304 et seq.

[395] Because the jurisdiction of the court cannot be ousted, *Hyman v Hyman* [1929] AC 601, as recently confirmed in *Radmacher v Granatino* [2010] UKSC 42.

[396] ss 34 and 35 Matrimonial Causes Act deal with so-called 'maintenance agreements', but never carried much weight in practice (despite the weight accorded to them by the Privy Council *Macleod v MacLeod* [2008] UKPC 64, as matters can still be taken to court). Indeed the provisions have been called 'dead letters' by Wilson LJ (as he then was) in *Radmacher v Granatino* [2009] EWCA Civ 649, [134]; see generally Miles, England and Wales, this volume, 108.

[397] *Edgar v Edgar* [1980] 1 WLR 1410.

[398] Miles, England and Wales, this volume, 109 et seq; Miles, 'Marriage and Divorce', above n 381, 437.

separation agreements the 'fairness' threshold will be somewhat higher, given that (and of course only if) the agreement was concluded in full knowledge of the relevant facts and not about an uncertain future. If embodied in a consent order the agreements can only be varied or appealed in extraordinary circumstances,[399] although periodical payments can generally be adapted if there is a change of circumstance.

In other jurisdictions the threshold to overcome to review separation agreements is expressly somewhat higher than the one for other marital agreements, reflecting the different factual situation compared to other agreements and the desire to encourage couples to regulate the financial consequences of their divorce themselves. For example, in the Netherlands, agreements concluded to regulate the finances in an impending divorce (called 'divorce covenants') can be reviewed by the court, particularly if a radical change of circumstance has rendered the agreement unfair.[400] In Spain, agreements reached outside of the court, whether later filed with the court (as *convenio regulador*) or not, also remain reviewable. A court will not approve a *convenio regulador* if it is harmful to the children or seriously detrimental to one of the spouses;[401] a later review is possible if there was a substantial change of circumstances.[402] In Austria and Belgium separation agreements with regard to property cannot be reviewed by the courts at all as regards the substance of the agreement, although agreements regarding maintenance are restricted: in Austria a total waiver of maintenance is not possible if this would leave one spouse destitute,[403] and in Belgium agreements regarding maintenance are not permissible at all (in the sense that they do not bind the courts when concluded).[404]

From a comparative perspective, the position taken New Zealand is somewhat of an oddity. While separation agreements (in New Zealand, referred to either as 'compromise agreements' or 'settlement agreements') are subject to the same statutory rules as other marital agreements, they appear to be treated rather differently by the judiciary.[405] The New Zealand Court of Appeal in *Harrison v Harrison* held:

> [T]he parties will presumably set out to provide for a division of property which accords, at least broadly, to what would be ordered under the statutory regime. So where there is a significant discrepancy between what the agreement provides and the way in which the relevant statutory regime would have operated, this in itself may well suggest that the agreement is unfair or unreasonable and, as well, may well require explanation.[406]

The Court then contrasted separation agreements with other marital agreements, and stated that only for the latter the 'very purpose' of the agreement was to contract out of the default regime, which—with all respect—is a rather questionable assumption. Still, the Court in *Harrison v Harrison* clearly established a general

---

[399] *Barder v Calouri* [1988] AC 20; *Livesey v Jenkins* [1985] AC 424; *Myerson v Myerson* [2009] EWCA Civ 282; *Walkden v Walkden* [2009] EWCA Civ 627. See generally Miles, England and Wales, this volume, 112 et seq.

[400] Art 1:159 para 3 Dutch Civil Code; see Boele-Woelki and Braat, The Netherlands, this volume, 252.

[401] In Catalonia only if harmful to the children, Art 233-3.1 CCCat; see Ferrer-Riba, Spain, this volume, 366.

[402] Art 90 III CC; Ferrer-Riba, Spain, this volume, 364 et seq.

[403] Ferrari, Austria, this volume, 64 et seq.

[404] See Pintens, France and Belgium, this volume, 83.

[405] Briggs, New Zealand, this volume, 278 et seq.

[406] *Harrison v Harrison* [2005] 2 NZLR 349 (CA), [81].

presumption that the outcome under the default regime is what is 'fair', and that deviations from it will need special justification. This contrasts very starkly with the position taken in the other jurisdictions which give the parties greater freedom (and certainty) to decide on their financial relations at time when they have decided to divorce and know what the facts are; if they then choose an outcome that is different from the one that would have been reached under the default regime, the courts assume that they did so knowingly and willingly and respect that autonomous choice. The New Zealand position is much more paternalistic and assumes the exact opposite, namely that the parties must have wanted (more or less) what the default position would have been, thereby severely restricting the autonomy of the spouses. It seems rather peculiar to limit the freedom of the spouses more in a situation where they are agreeing on the basis of known facts rather than in a situation where they are making an agreement about an uncertain future.

To summarise, in many jurisdictions separation agreements are subject to rather similar rules like those applying to other marital agreements with regard to the 'fairness' and reviewability of the agreement, and the same issues arise with regard to need and compensation (as discussed in section III.C.iii above); just as for other marital agreements, contracting out of the remedies dealing with needs and compensation is much more difficult or even impossible. Still, in some form in all jurisdictions the specific situation of separation agreements (that the couple now know or at least can know what the financial consequences will be) is taken into account when determining what is 'fair'.

This specific factual element of separation agreements is expressly given greater weight in some jurisdictions by requiring a 'radical' change of circumstance, 'serious detriment' or requiring 'good and substantial grounds for concluding that an injustice will be done by holding the parties to the agreement'. While this is meant to raise the threshold for reviewability and, at first, appears as a 'qualification' of fairness, it also is an *expression* of fairness, namely that it is perceived to be fair to hold the parties to the agreements if they entered into it in full knowledge of the circumstances and consequences, while at the same time leaving open the possibility to mitigate hardship that can arise later, either by varying the order if the 'qualified' circumstances are met or through maintenance payments.

Of all the jurisdictions looked at, New Zealand is the only one where separation agreements appear to be subject to a stricter scrutiny by the courts than other marital agreements, and where the couple are actually given less freedom to decide on their financial relations, which, at least from a doctrinal point of view, is difficult to explain.

V. CONCLUSION

Professor Kevin Gray, in a different context, has distinguished between 'unconscionability of dealings' and 'unconscionability of outcomes'.[407] This distinction is also very pertinent for marital agreements, as it makes clear that at the stage of

---

[407] K Gray, 'Property in Common Law Systems' in GE van Maanen and AJ van der Walt (eds), *Property Law on the Threshold of the 21st Century* (Antwerp, Maklu, 1996) 259. See also K Gray and

unconscionability of dealings it is merely the conduct at the time and not the substantive outcome of the marital agreement as such that is scrutinised. The latter then is to be done at a later, separate stage, where of course the circumstances of the conclusion of the agreement will continue to play a role. But the task at the stage of 'unconscionability of dealings' is to deal with conduct or circumstances that are disapproved of per se and should therefore lead to the agreement being disregarded irrespective of the outcome. The objective is to secure procedural fairness and thus protection of autonomy. Protection of autonomy very clearly is not the objective of the stage of 'unconscionability of outcomes', where the substantive fairness of the agreement will be looked at and agreements that were entered into freely, knowingly and autonomously at the time might be overridden.

i. Protection of Autonomy and Procedural Fairness: Unconscionability of Dealings

In all jurisdictions examined for this project the circumstances under which the marital agreements was entered into are subject to scrutiny. The safeguards in place, be they purely formal or procedural, appear to have in common that they want to ensure that the decision is an informed and conscious one—in short: the aim is the protection of autonomy. The mechanisms employed for this of course differ from jurisdiction to jurisdiction, but in all jurisdictions they appear to go beyond the 'normal' requirements of contract law, for the reasons set out (above, section III.B). While there will always be some form of pressure when such agreements are negotiated or signed, it is where the pressure goes beyond what is seen as acceptable in the respective jurisdiction, where the bargaining positions of the spouses can no longer be seen as equal,[408] that the safeguards come into play.

The conduct that is deemed to be inappropriate in connection with marital agreements, therefore, in all jurisdictions does not have to reach the intensity of duress or fraud etc, it suffices that it is unconscionable under the special circumstances of concluding a marital agreement. 'Unconscionable' indeed is the term expressly used in Australia, where an otherwise binding marital agreement can bet set aside if 'a party engaged in unconscionable conduct in relation to the making of the agreement'.[409] Generally the legal systems at this stage want to protect the autonomy of the spouses, the 'voluntariness' and 'procedural fairness' of the agreement[410]—and penalise what following Gray can be called 'unconscionability of dealings'.[411]

The way issues of unconscionability of dealings are addressed vary from jurisdiction to jurisdiction, but often include specific formal requirements, legal advice and duties to disclose assets. As explained above (section III.B), the effectiveness of these safeguards seems to be somewhat limited and in some cases complying with them

---

S Francis Gray, *Elements of Land Law* 5th edn (Oxford, OUP, 2009) 1234 and B Sloan, *Informal Carers and Private Law* (Oxford, Hart Publishing, forthcoming in 2012).

[408] See esp the decision of the German Federal Constitutional Court of 6 February 2001, FamRZ 2001, 343, 346 and Dutta, Germany, this volume, 175.

[409] s 90K(1)(e) Family Law Act 1975 (Cth); see Jessep, Australia, this volume, 28 et seq.

[410] *Cf* Ellman, United States, this volume, 416 et seq.

[411] See the references in n 407 above.

is overly onerous and/or even just 'repositions' the underlying problem. As Leong quite rightly observes:

> [a] rule that a marital agreement conforming to certain legal requirements supplants the default law will also only shift the dispute to whether those legal requirements are really satisfied.[412]

This certainly seems to adequately reflect the development and problems with Part VIIIA of the Family Law Act 1975 (Cth) in Australia.[413] Here the law on marital agreements originally made it possible to very significantly limit any further scrutiny of the substance of the agreement provided that the—very demanding—formal and procedural requirements were fulfilled.[414] The idea underlying this approach was to provide the necessary protection at the outset through legal advice, sufficient information etc. However, as pointed out above, even the best legal advice and full disclosure cannot guarantee a 'fair' or 'just' agreement, particularly since the agreements are meant to apply in as yet unknown future circumstances. This makes it difficult, if not impossible, to comprehensively evaluate the substance of an agreement at the time of its conclusion. Therefore the review of the substance of the agreement can only undertaken in a meaningful way when one of the spouses seeks to rely on the agreement—only then can it really be determined whether there would be an unconscionability of outcome should the agreement be applied or followed. This is, therefore, where the emphasis of the enquiry on marital agreements should lie, and where the outcome as such, taking into account the circumstances of the conclusion of the agreement, will be examined.

When a more extensive scrutiny with regard to an unconscionability of outcome will be undertaken in any event, this also allows for a more relaxed approach to the form and procedure for marital agreements. A good example of this is the view taken by the United Kingdom Supreme Court in *Radmacher v Granatino* on legal advice and disclosure: only where the lack of such advice and disclosure was *material* to the outcome should it be relevant.[415] The same 'spirit' is reflected in the new Australian section 90G(1A) Family Law Act 1975 (Cth) and the New Zealand section 21H Property (Relationships) Act 1976 where a marital agreement will be followed/declared binding even in cases of non-compliance with formal and procedural rules provided that not holding the spouses to the agreement would be unjust (Australia) or the non-compliance did not materially prejudice the interests of any party to the agreement (New Zealand).[416] Likewise, in Sweden one of the formal requirements (witnessing the agreement) was abolished because it was found that such a requirement would only lead to future disputes based on alleged defects of form, and that generally issues arising from this could be dealt with when the substance of the agreement was reviewed anyway.[417] In Singapore the position is

---

[412] Leong, Singapore, this volume 345 et seq; See also Leong Wai Kum 'The Law in Singapore on Rights and Responsibilities in Marital Agreements' [2010] *Singapore Journal of Legal Studies* 107, 124–27; Jessep, 'Section 90G', above n 269; Fehlberg and Smyth, 'Binding Pre-Nuptial Agreements', above n 281.

[413] See the comparison made by Leong Wai Kum, 'The Law in Singapore on Rights and Responsibilities in Marital Agreements' [2010] *The Sydney Law Review* 289, esp 306–09.

[414] Which lead to many practitioners refusing to be involved in the drafting of marital agreements; on this see Jessep, Australia, this volume, 29 and the other references in n 281 above.

[415] *Radmacher v Granatino* [2010] UKSC 42, [69].

[416] See section III.C.iv above and Jessep, Australia, this volume, 35 et seq, esp 37; Wilson, above n 352, 13; Briggs, New Zealand, this volume, 276.

[417] Jänterä-Jareborg, Sweden, this volume, 381; Agell and Brattström above n 57, 136.

the most extreme one, where there are no actual formal or procedural requirements that need to be followed, so that the scrutiny focuses almost solely on the substance of the agreement.[418]

Thus it can be concluded that many jurisdictions have not only decided to follow what in this section has been called a division between 'unconscionability of dealings' and 'unconscionability of outcomes', but also as a consequence of this many jurisdictions also set relatively low thresholds for the procedural and formal requirements—meaning that only the 'worst' kind of conduct or circumstance should disqualify the agreement from the outset—because they amount to unconscionability of dealings and call for the autonomy of the respective spouse to be protected.

Instead of singling out individual issues as determinative to indicate whether the agreement or its conclusion is 'procedurally fair', such as full and frank disclosure, making individual legal advice mandatory, time factors etc, these issues should merely seen be as factors or indicators for a potential procedural unfairness. Non-compliance with any, or even all, of these requirements by itself should not necessarily determine that the agreement should 'fail'. After all, even a marital agreement concluded on the evening before the wedding, without legal advice or full disclosure might nevertheless be perfectly fair and acceptable, notwithstanding this might seem unlikely on the facts.

The circumstances at the time of the conclusion of the agreement might also need to be considered together with the substance when the agreement is invoked and it is determined whether there is an unconscionability of outcomes. Hence many of the jurisdictions looked at allow for a more extensive review of the substance of the agreement and focus on the protection *from* autonomy with regards to the outcomes rather than restrict the ability of spouses to enter into agreements in the first place (or make agreements to particularly burdensome procedural requirements), which is a very sensible approach.

ii. Protection from *Autonomy and Substantive Fairness: Unconscionability of Outcomes*

Once the threshold criteria applied to the circumstances of the conclusion of the marital agreements have been matched, the analysis in all jurisdictions then focuses on the substance of the agreement—whether the outcome is unconscionable or unfair. Of course the circumstances at the time of the conclusion might have a bearing on the finding whether there is an unconscionability of outcome, as this cannot be decided in a vacuum and not necessarily by just looking at the end-result in financial terms; still, the actual outcome of course is the most important criterion to be looked at to determine whether the agreement is deemed to be is unconscionable or unfair and should therefore be set aside or disregarded.

An unconscionability of outcomes could either be inherent in the stipulations of the agreements from the time it was drafted or the agreement can have *become unconscionable* after it was concluded through a change of circumstances or simply because of the way the lives of the spouses developed. In both situations, even if the circumstances of the conclusion are perfectly acceptable, the law may for policy

---

[418] Leong, Singapore, this volume, 328.

reasons override the autonomous decision of the couple and disapply or avoid the marital agreement—to protect the weaker spouse and the children. In other words, the law then protects the spouses *from* their autonomous decision.

Thus the idea of having 'cast-iron' pre-nuptial and post-nuptial agreements that regulate all the financial relations of the spouses in case of divorce (and during marriage, as the case may be) no matter what happens in the future if certain procedural safeguards are fulfilled, seems to defy the polices underlying family law in general and the law of marriage in particular. However, this does not mean that certain elements of these agreements cannot be 'cast-iron', and from the comparison it transpires that contracting out of the general sharing principle/the matrimonial property regime appears to be acceptable in the jurisdictions looked at, and more or less cast-iron in many jurisdictions.

Because opting out of the general provisions regarding sharing of property/matrimonial property regimes in the jurisdictions examined in this study is usually deemed to be 'fair', it appears a comparison with what the spouses would have received under the default regime[419] can only be of limited usefulness; after all,—as the New Zealand Court of Appeal put it in *Harrison v Harrison*—'the very purpose of the parties is to make provision which differs from the statutory regime'.[420] So the analysis of what is 'fair'—and hence permissible to opt out of in the jurisdictions looked at—generally focuses on what the House of Lords in *Miller v Miller, McFarlane v McFarlane* the House of Lords[421] has identified as the two other 'strands of fairness', namely 'needs' and 'compensation'. One matter for concern is that in many jurisdictions the compensatory element of property is not recognised,[422] and matters of need and compensation are sometimes left to be dealt with by maintenance payments.[423]

While it undoubtedly is difficult to define what exactly the two concepts of needs and compensation embody, and this certainly varies from jurisdiction to jurisdiction, from the comparison it is apparent that agreements concerning these elements of financial relief upon divorce are much more restricted by the laws in the jurisdictions examined in this book and often are not possible at all. So summing up, from a comparative perspective the substance of a marital agreement appears to be deemed unfair or unconscionable and will not be upheld if the needs of the spouses (and the children) are not met and where there is insufficient compensation for disadvantages suffered by one spouse and related to the marriage and, particularly, the division of labour in the relationship.

---

[419] As, eg, suggested as one the criteria American Law Institute's *Principles of The Law of Family Dissolution* in § 7.05(3)(a), see American Law Institute, above n 259, 1093 et seq.

[420] *Harrison v Harrison* [2005] 2 NZLR 349 (CA), [81]. As already mentioned above (section IV), the Court at the same time somewhat surprisingly did not see this as a rationale of separation agreements. See also Harper and Frankle, An English Practitioner's View, this volume, 137.

[421] *Miller v Miller, McFarlane v McFarlane* [2006] UKHL 24 [11]–[16] (Lord Nicholls), and [138]–[141] (Baroness Hale). See also section III.C.iii above.

[422] Whereas one could argue for England and Wales, for example, that all a marital agreement regarding property does is to move the property to the 'non-matrimonial property pool' which is not to be shared—unless fairness (ie, aspects of needs and compensation) demand otherwise. See section II.E.vi above.

[423] *Cf* section III.C.iii.b above; Dethloff, above n 223, 90 et seq; Dauner-Lieb above n 331, 602 et seq.